Advances in Motivation in Sport and Exercise

Glyn C. Roberts, PhD
Norwegian University of Sport Science
Editor

Human Kinetics

Library of Congress Cataloging-in-Publication Data

Advances in motivation in sport and exercise / [edited by] Glyn C. Roberts.
    p. cm.
  Includes bibliographical references and index.
  ISBN 0-88011-849-0
   1. Sports--Psychological aspects. 2. Exercise--Psychological aspects. 3. Social
perception. I. Roberts, Glyn C.

  GV706.4 .A36 2001
  796'.01--dc21

                                      00-053523
  ISBN: 0-88011-849-0

Copyright © 2001 by Human Kinetics Publishers, Inc.

Acquisitions Editors: Linda Bump and Amy Pickering; **Developmental Editor:** Melissa Feld; **Assistant Editors:** Susan C. Hagan, Derek Campbell, Lee Alexander, and Laurie Stokoe; **Copyeditor:** Joyce Sexton; **Proofreader:** Erin T. Cler; **Indexer:** Craig Brown; **Permission Managers:** Courtney Astle and Dalene Reeder; **Graphic Designer:** Nancy Rasmus; **Graphic Artist:** Dawn Sills; **Photo Manager:** Clark Brooks; **Cover Designer:** Jack W. Davis; **Photographer (interior):** Tom Roberts; **Art Manager:** Craig Newsom; **Illustrator:** Tom Roberts; **Printer:** Edwards Brothers

Printed in the United States of America   10 9 8 7 6 5 4 3 2 1

Human Kinetics
Web site: www.humankinetics.com

United States: Human Kinetics, P.O. Box 5076, Champaign, IL 61825-5076
800-747-4457
e-mail: humank@hkusa.com

Canada: Human Kinetics, 475 Devonshire Road Unit 100, Windsor, ON N8Y 2L5
800-465-7301 (in Canada only)
e-mail: orders@hkcanada.com

Europe: Human Kinetics, Units C2/C3 Wira Business Park West Park Ring Road
Leeds LS16 6EB, United Kingdom
+44 (0) 113 278 1708
e-mail: hk@hkeurope.com

Australia: Human Kinetics, 57A Price Avenue, Lower Mitcham, South Australia 5062
08 8277 1555
e-mail: liahka@senet.com.au

New Zealand: Human Kinetics, P.O. Box 105-231, Auckland Central
09-523-3462
e-mail: hkp@ihug.co.nz

In memory of John G. Nicholls (1940-1994): A respected mentor, a collegial colleague, and most important, a good friend.

CONTENTS

PREFACE

As was its predecessor in 1992, this book is firmly placed within the current zeitgeist of social cognitive perspectives of motivation. Achievement behavior occurs within a dynamic social context; and as this book amply documents, it is the thoughts and beliefs about what is needed to achieve within that context that drive achievement behavior. Social cognitive perspectives on motivation are now dominant in psychology, even though the thought processes that determine achievement behavior may differ from one investigator to another. The contributors to this book are all firmly entrenched in the social cognitive approach, but they examine a variety of thought processes as determinants of motivated behavior in exercise, physical education, and sport, or, more generically, physical activity.

The social cognitive approach to motivation has given motivation research an impetus and over the past 30 years has yielded some valuable insights into the motivational equation. It was Weiner in 1972 who signaled the beginning of the new era by arguing that individuals who were high in motivation and those who were low in motivation were likely to *think* differently about why success and failure occurred. The notion that thoughts were the critical variables transformed the study of motivation and has led to a lively interest in how these thoughts determine motivation.

This book reviews and integrates important contemporary contributions to the study of motivation. The authors are distinguished contributors to the conceptual understanding of motivation, as well as to the application of these thought processes to enhance motivation in applied contexts. Each chapter represents an important avenue of research in the physical activity area. In this volume, as well as inviting distinguished veterans of the motivation research community in exercise and sport psychology, I invited some younger, dynamic contributors to illustrate the richness and the depth of our research endeavors.

The themes of this volume center on the understanding and enhancement of achievement behavior in physical activity. Each contributor sheds some light on the dynamics of the process of motivation and on the variables and constructs that help our understanding of why we are motivated or are not motivated. Each contributor also examines how motivation may be enhanced within the framework he or she professes. Each contributor has a perspective that differs a little, or a lot, from those of the other contributors. These differences include ideas about what the determinants of the motivated state are (personal goals, personal agency beliefs, and/or values), how the context contributes to the motivated state, and how we can change the motivated state and can further the practical side of our work—the enhancement of motivation. However, there is agreement that thoughts, or a constellation of cognitions, are the major determinants of the investigation of the energization, direction, and regulation of achievement behavior.

If there is one way we can illustrate the advancement during the nine years between the 1992 book and this one, it is in the insights we now have about applying our knowledge in exercise, sport, and physical education contexts. As befits a field that is applied in character, our understanding of how to enhance motivation in physical activities has progressed a great deal. Each of the contributors to this book addresses this aspect. But are our findings being implemented where they can make a difference—in the gym, on the sport field, or in the exercise group? That is a different question. There is always a time lag between research and practice. It takes several years for research findings to enter textbooks and become general knowledge, and then eventually to become part of the lore of teaching. Many of the suggestions contained in this book will remain the exclusive knowledge of the professionals in universities. But slowly—too slowly for those of us who do the research—the suggestions will be accepted and will become part of what is taught to teachers, coaches, and even parents.

I thank and acknowledge the efforts of my fellow contributors. Thank you for agreeing to my demands and responding to my continual harping for you to do this and that. I especially thank the contributors who were timely in their submissions and who were patient as we waited and harassed the "tardy trio" to get their chapters in to me. Frankly, this book is a year late because we had to wait for some to submit, but those chapters were crucial and it was worth the wait. Thank you all. And I thank the people at Human Kinetics (and Melissa Feld in particular) for their patience and understanding.

Best of all, the winter is just beginning; I now have some time to get some skiing in!

ACKNOWLEDGMENTS

I would like to acknowledge the contributions of my present and former colleagues and students (most of whom are now my colleagues) to my modest achievements in sport psychology and to the understanding of motivation in physical activity. Without these people, I never would have come so far, and whatever strengths I have I attribute to their mentoring. Whatever weaknesses I have remain my own. And at this stage of my career, my weaknesses no doubt will continue!

As John Nicholls stated in 1989, "To take someone's ideas seriously enough to question them is a significant form of respect." Given that, I have certainly enjoyed the respect of my colleagues over the years! To my colleagues at the University of Illinois Children's Research Center (Carole Ames, Carole Dweck, Ken Hill, Doug Kleiber, Marty Maehr, and John Nicholls) and the Department of Kinesiology (Dan Gould, Rainer Martens, Eddie McAuley, Karl Newell, Steve Petruzzello, and Steve Silverman), thanks for taking me seriously enough to argue with me. It helped shape my thoughts. A special thanks to my former PhD students (Kevin Spink, Marti Ewing, Joan Duda, Debbie Pascuzzi, John Evans, Cindy Pemberton, Gloria Balague, Jay Kimiciek, Barid Bhattachurya, Howard Hall, Billy Strean, Darren Treasure, Vance Tammen, Maria Kavussanu, Anne-Marte Pensgaard, Jessie Daw, and Brent Walker). I learned something from each of you, and working and discussing issues with you helped me grow and think better both professionally and personally. Having such gifted colleagues and students has been a privilege.

To my present colleagues in psychology here in Norway (Yngvar Ommundsen, Odd Kjormo, and Marit Sorensen), thank you for your tolerance, for giving me a new impetus to my professional career, and for showing respect for my ideas by arguing with me! Thanks to those who gave me feedback on my chapter for this book

(Darren, Howard, Joan, and Sakis). My wish is that each chapter of this book will promote more discussion and more dialogue among colleagues. In so doing, it will only serve to sharpen our thoughts and enlighten our understanding and enhancement of motivation in physical activity.

Understanding the Dynamics of Motivation in Physical Activity: The Influence of Achievement Goals on Motivational Processes

Glyn C. Roberts

Understanding and enhancing motivation constitutes one of the most central concerns of human affairs. Research on motivation varies greatly and crosses many disciplines. In everyday life, we hear of politicians discussing the will of societies to change, voters incredulous about politicians' lack of motivation to make just decisions, business leaders concerned about the effectiveness of the workforce, parents discussing the displayed effort of their children, teachers bemoaning the study habits of pupils, coaches complaining about the commitment of sport participants, and exercise leaders lamenting the lack of persistence of exercisers. All are addressing motivation at one level of abstraction or another, and research in the various disciplines, from economics to physiology, is very active. Research in psychology, however, has addressed the role of motivation primarily in individual lives, especially in achievement contexts. Research aimed at understanding the motivational equation is among the most prolific in the psychological sciences. Indeed, one-third of all studies in psychology deal with motivation in one form or another (Roberts, 1992a). Motivation in the lives of individuals has been considered when the context is tasks that are self-regulated or tasks that require us to interact with others, as in sport teams. Motivation in psychology has usually referred to managing the motivation of others, which is often the concern of the parent, the teacher, or the coach, or to managing one's own motivation. This chapter (and this book) assumes this approach, and all the authors in this volume focus on the *process* of motivation in the lives of individuals in sport, physical education, exercise, or more than one of these. The generic term for the contexts of sport, physical education, exercise, and other contexts such as dance or gross motor leisure activities is *physical activities.*

At the outset, one must confess that despite its obvious importance to physical activities, exemplified by the newspaper column inches and television air time devoted to motivational issues in sport, motivation is a poorly understood concept in the "trenches" (the gymnasium, the exercise setting, the playing field, the dance studio, and so on). Motivation is often assumed to be synonymous with arousal (witness locker room pregame pep talks), and coaches and teachers often use questionable arousal tactics in the quest of motivation. The coach of the Mississippi State University football team, Jackie Sherrill, had a longhorn bull castrated in front of his players in order to "motivate" them before they took the field against the University of Texas Longhorns (Sherman, 1992). And the football coach of Libertyville High School in Illinois, Dale Christensen, staged a fake shooting in the school to "motivate" his players to be "combat ready" for an upcoming game (Sakamoto & Parsons, 1993). Fortunately, most coaches do not go to such extremes. Coaching folklore to the contrary, motivation and arousal are separate constructs.

Most coaches and teachers assume also that positive thinking (often described as "confidence," "a winning attitude," or "being competitive") has immense motivational attributes. The belief is that if you are confident and can "see" yourself winning or achieving success you will be more motivated to realize the dream. But to have motivational properties, expectations have to be realistic; otherwise they can be demotivating (see

Locke & Latham, 1985; Hall & Kerr, this volume). Finally, many coaches and teachers believe that motivation is genetically endowed. Thus if coaches believe that an athlete is "motivated," they consider the motivation a desirable, stable entity and expect the athlete to display it all the time. But if they judge an athlete to be low in motivation, the same coaches do not believe that this can change and often cut such players from the team or display their disapproval so that the athlete feels uncomfortable and eventually drops out. Although all these beliefs are grounded in certain research evidence, such simplistic assumptions do not begin to capture the complexity and richness of the process of motivation.

One must admit, however, that the term *motivation* is overused and vague. It is defined so broadly by some that it incorporates the whole field of psychology, so narrowly by others that it is almost useless as an organizing construct. At least 32 theories of motivation have their own definitions of the construct (see Ford, 1992). There are almost as many definitions as there are theorists (Pinder, 1984). The solution for many has been to abandon the term and use descriptions of cognitive processes such as self-regulation or self-systems (e.g., Bandura, 1988, 1989b; Harter, 1985; McAuley, Pena, & Jerome, this volume), or to discuss processes such as personal goals or goal setting (e.g., Locke & Latham, 1985; Nicholls, 1989) or emotional processes (e.g., Weiner, 1986). However, to understand motivation, we must attempt to understand the theories that purport to explain it, as well as the concepts that undergird the term.

Understanding Motivation and Achievement Behavior

The history of motivation theory has been the search for the "right" theory; and we have assumed that when that theory evolved, not only would we better understand a whole range of achievement behaviors, but intervention opportunities would also present themselves (Roberts, 1992a). Despite the efforts of many and the proclamations of some (e.g., Bandura, 1986), this Holy Grail remains elusive. But the search continues. The chapters in this book reflect the excellent efforts that are in progress to find theoretical concepts and processes through which we can understand and enhance achievement behaviors within physical activity.

The study of motivation and its effect on achievement behavior is the investigation of the *energization, direction,* and *regulation* of behavior. Theories are not true motivation theories unless they address all aspects of achievement behavior. Thus some avenues of research that describe the direction and/or the regulation of behavior without specifying why the behavior was energized are not true motivational theories, even though they may depict achievement behavior very well. Goal setting in sport is an example. Goal setting specifies the direction and regulation of achievement behavior, but to date it has offered no sufficient psychological explanation for why behavior from a goal-setting perspective may be initiated (see Hall & Kerr, this volume, for a discussion of goal setting). Motivation theories are predicated on a set of assumptions about individuals and about the factors that give impetus to achievement behavior (Roberts, 1992a, 1992b). Motivation theories ask *why*.

When motivation matters, various theoretical models have been proposed as governing motivation and achievement behavior. There is no shortage of theories! As already mentioned, there are at last count 32 clearly distinguished theories of motivation. But only the most important ones for sport and exercise behavior are included in this book. Whether we have included all of the most important theories could be debated, but I would argue that we have included the major theories pertinent to motivation in sport, physical education, and exercise and most of their principal advocates.

One could say that motivation theories lie on a continuum from mechanistic to cognitive, or organismic (for a more extensive treatment of motivation theories, see Ford, 1992; Weiner, 1972). According to mechanistic theories, humans are passive and are impelled by psychological drives; according to cognitive theories, humans are active and initiate action through subjective interpretation of the achievement context. In the early part of this century, mechanistic psychoanalytic drive theories dominated the field, and terms such as equilibrium and hedonism were in use. But motivation is more than striving for equilibrium or maximizing hedonism. Theorists gave credence to behaviorism during the 1940s and 1950s, but the attraction of the attempt to understand humans as input/output connectors waned as the cognitive revolution had its impact on psychology (Roberts, 1992a).

Theories of motivation have been based on divergent assumptions about humans. Some have considered humans as robots, their motivation determined by biological or situational forces (e.g., Skinner, 1953). Others have viewed humans as driven by needs for self-improvement or self-actualization (e.g., Maslow, 1968). According to still another view, humans are naive scientists who rationally plan their own behaviors (e.g., Atkinson, 1957; Weiner, 1972). For a brief historical overview of motivation theory in sport and exercise, see Roberts, 1992a. More recently, theories tend to be based on more sophisticated conceptions assuming that the human is an active participant in making decisions and planning achievement behavior (e.g., Bandura, 1986; Deci & Ryan, 1985b; Dweck & Leggett, 1988; Kuhl, 1986; Maehr & Nicholls, 1980; Nicholls, 1989). Contemporary theoretical arguments are based on the relative influence of situation and personal sources of motivation and their interaction in decision making and the planning of achievement behavior (e.g., Roberts, Treasure, & Kavussanu, 1997).

Although motivation scholars in physical activity have begun to recognize the capability of humans to be intentional, self-directed organisms, too many contemporary writers of textbooks in the physical activity area still use concepts such as motives, needs, drives, reinforcers, and so on to describe the determinants of motivation. These outdated concepts are perpetuated in sport psychology textbooks, written by colleagues who should know better, that use the old concepts of biological and situational determinism to explain motivation. In addition, books for practitioners of sport psychology often use simplistic and mechanistic conceptions of motivation to describe how to motivate people in sport and exercise. Many of these sport psychology textbooks and "how-to" books fail to recognize the capability of physical activity participants for self-direction, autonomous decision making, and personal responsibility.

This conceptual confounding distracts many students of motivation and does not serve our field well. Thus motivation as a term becomes vague, ambiguous, and less than useful. As an example (certainly not the only one), the aim in a motivation chapter in one of our major sport psychology textbooks is to look at several theories of motivation and then bring them all together in a comprehensive model. But many of the theories rest on different assumptions about the psyche and about the energization of achievement behavior; these create conceptual constraints that the final model does not consider. The chapter serves only to create an amorphous concept that is not very useful either as an organizing theory or as a base for practical application. In contrast to attempts to conceptualize motivation in broad terms with multiple variables, some contemporary motivational theorizing has become more precise and microanalytical but thus more restricted in scope. An example is self-efficacy theory. Self-efficacy is defined very narrowly and as such becomes very useful within very specific contexts, such as the way it is operationalized within the exercise context. However, the usefulness of the concept for physical activity apart from exercise remains quite limited despite the attempt by Bandura (1986) to broaden it into a theory of social cognition. This trend to conceptual narrowness is considered healthy by some (e.g., Pintrich & Schunk, 1995), and there is little question that within context the concepts become powerful (e.g., self-efficacy within exercise settings; see McAuley, Pena, & Jerome, this volume). However, most contemporary theorizing attempts to achieve precision along with a broader understanding of achievement behavior. And that is the aim of most of the chapters in this volume. But all this begs the question: What is motivation? That is what the next section addresses.

What Is Motivation?

Typically in the research literature on motivation in physical activity, motivation refers to dispositions, social variables, and/or cognitions that come into play when a person undertakes a task at which he or she is evaluated, or enters into competition with others, or attempts to attain some standard of excellence (e.g., see Roberts, 1992a). It is assumed that at such times the individual is responsible for the outcome of the task and that some level of challenge is inherent in the task. Moreover, such circumstances are assumed to facilitate various motivational dispositions and/or cognitive assessments that influence human behavior in achievement situations. Specifically, it has been hypothesized that the determinants of achievement behavior are approach and/or avoidance dispositions, expectancies, incentive values of success and failure, and/or cognitive assessments of success and failure, including the possibility of succeeding or failing.

The research in physical activity contexts focusing on motivation has, over the past 30 years, adopted a social cognitive approach (e.g., see Duda, 1992, 1993; Duda & Whitehead, 1998; Roberts, 1982, 1984a, 1984b, 1992a, 1992b; Roberts et al., 1997). Motivation is considered a social cognitive *process* in which the individual becomes motivated, or demotivated, through assessments of his or her competencies within the achievement context and of the meaning of the context to the person. Thereby, from a social cognitive point of view, motivation may be defined as the organized patterning of at least one of three psychological constructs that energize, direct, and regulate achievement behavior in physical activity: personal goals, emotional arousal, and personal agency beliefs (Ford, 1992). I shall address each construct in more detail later. In one way or another, the writers of the chapters in this volume use the social cognitive approach to understand the concept of motivation.

In the literature, achievement behavior, which motivation theories purport to explain, has typically been defined as behavioral intensity (trying hard), persistence (continuing to try hard), choice of action possibilities, and performance (outcomes). In physical activity settings, achievement behaviors are those behaviors witnessed when participants try harder, concentrate more, persist longer, pay greater attention, perform better, choose to practice longer, and/or join or drop out of physical activities. The behavioral patterns just identified are not all-inclusive; they refer only to typical behaviors in physical activities. Further, they represent assessments of behavior from which we infer motivation or the lack of motivation. But they do describe the behaviors we refer to when we state that an individual is or is not motivated in a physical activity setting.

Individuals are assumed to be motivated to achieve when they exhibit these achievement behaviors. But what do they want to achieve? This is a critical question, and it is at this point that many motivational theories differ. For the purposes of this chapter, and of this book dealing with achievement motivation in primarily sport, physical education, and exercise settings, we take a social cognitive perspective whereby achievement may be defined as *the attainment of a personally or socially valued goal in a physical activity context*. The goal may differ for each individual; but whether it is to lose weight, to improve a skill, or to beat an opponent, the attainment of that goal is perceived to be either personally or socially valued. Hence, achievement is subjectively defined, and success or failure in obtaining the goal is a subjective state based on assessment of the outcome of the achievement behavior by the participant (Maehr & Nicholls, 1980; Spink & Roberts, 1980). Thus motivation is a dynamic and complex cognitive process based on subjective assessments of the outcome by the participant depending on the goal of action and the meaning of the context to the participant. Let us look at these processes in more detail.

Defining Motivational Processes

There is no consensus in the literature on how to define motivation so that it is a useful concept from many perspectives. However, as is clear already, there is consensus in contemporary theorizing that we need to understand the psychological processes that undergird motivation. What are those processes? First, motivation processes are qualities of the person. We want to know how a person thinks. That is the central issue for an understanding of motivation in physical activities. Although motivation may be partially understood in terms of the context (see Biddle, Treasure, this volume), it is the impact of the environment on personal assessments that is important. The environment has no motivational qualities unless the participant perceives it to have them. Thus motivation is a process that resides in the person. Second, motivation processes are future oriented rather than past or present oriented. Motivation processes help people anticipate and predict future events and consequences that are meaningful to them. These processes form the basis for decisions about the amount of personal resources (time, talent, and effort) people are prepared to invest in the activity in order to reach the personal or socially valued goal. Motivation prepares the individual to move forward to reach desired goals or to produce desired outcomes. Third, motivation processes are evaluative. These evaluations may be self-referenced or may involve pertinent others as criteria of reference. Motivation involves the person's assessing whether to increase or decrease behavioral striving to affect the desired outcome or goal. However, the outcome or goal is subjectively defined. What is success for one may not be success for another (Maehr & Nicholls, 1980; Spink & Roberts,

1980). Thus to understand achievement behavior, we must take the function and meaning of behavior into account and must recognize that the processes determining the amount of striving (the motivation factor) are within the person, future oriented, and evaluative.

The components crucial to the social cognitive process approach to understanding motivation are threefold: The psychological constructs that energize, direct, and regulate achievement striving are personal or socially valued goals, personal agency beliefs, and emotional arousal (Ford, 1992). The individual develops personal goals within any achievement context, and it is these personal goals that give meaning to achievement striving and energize subsequent action. Personal goals reside in the person, but they may be derived from context cues (e.g., Ames, 1992b) or through instructions given by significant others (e.g., Locke & Latham, 1990). The personal goals may also be culturally or socially defined (e.g., Maehr & Nicholls, 1980) but will be useful as a part of a motivational process only if the person adopts them. Clearly, it is these personal and/or socially valued goals that often energize achievement striving, and we will discuss these goals in more detail later in the chapter.

The second component involves personal agency beliefs. These direct and regulate the ongoing stream of achievement behavior. Personal agency beliefs may be based on one's beliefs in one's capability to attain the goal or on evaluation of the context to support one's goal striving. Thus social cognitive theories entail some evaluative criteria pertaining to one's capability and/or capacity to attain the personal achievement goal. The various theories may use differing nomenclature to refer to these beliefs, but whether they are labeled self-efficacy, control, perceived ability, or perceived competence, these theories focus on the understanding that the person believes he/she is able to attain the goal or has the conviction or confidence that he/she is able to execute the behaviors necessary to achieve the goal. It is these beliefs that serve to initiate, maintain, increase, or inhibit achievement striving.

The third component, often labeled emotional arousal, may serve as a source of energy or evaluation to affect achievement striving (Ford, 1992). In the motivation theories discussed in the present text, emotional arousal is not an important component; but for the sake of completeness its potential in the overall motivational equation must be recognized (e.g., Ntoumanis & Biddle, 1999a). Whether emotional arousal is a consequence of assessments of the results of achievement striving or is a determinant of motivation is an issue to be resolved. As the various theories ebb and flow in influence over time and as they increase in sophistication with the fitting together of more of the motivational puzzle, emotional arousal may become more, or less, important.

, All the motivation theories included in the present text use the constructs I have introduced, either singly or in combination, to describe and explain achievement striving in physical activity. As defined earlier, motivation is the organized patterning of one or more of the constructs to energize, regulate, and direct achievement behavior (see Ford, 1992). Thus motivation is an integrative construct that represents the energy with which the goal will be pursued and the perception whether the person can or will reach his or her goal.

The Social Cognitive Approach to Motivation

As is clear from the foregoing, the social cognitive approach draws on past theories to portray a dynamic process incorporating sets of cognitive, affective, and value-related variables that are assumed to mediate and/or moderate the choice and attainment of achievement goals. But within the social cognitive approach are embedded several theories that purport to describe and/or explain motivated behavior. Some are more relevant than others to various physical activity contexts. The three theories, and one empirical approach, that have begun to dominate motivation research in physical activities are achievement goal theory (e.g., Biddle; Duda; Fry; & Treasure, this volume), self-efficacy theory (e.g., McAuley, Pena, & Jerome, this volume), self-determination theory (e.g., Vallerand, this volume), and the goal setting empirical approach (e.g., Hall & Kerr, this volume). Achievement goal theory, self-determination theory, and the goal setting approach are very pertinent to understanding motivation in sport. Self-efficacy theory has demonstrated its efficacy in exercise. Although I will not repeat the statements I made in 1992, I offer the following observations. In the earlier volume (Roberts, 1992b), I stated that I thought the relationship of self-efficacy to sport performance modest and its usefulness in sport contexts limited. Feltz (1992) disagreed, but it is a fact that research work in self-efficacy in sport has come almost to a standstill. Other theories to explain achievement behavior in sport are more powerful and appropriate, especially achievement goal theory. I argued that self-efficacy within exercise, on the other hand, was conceptually consistent and empirically reliable. It is true that in the meantime, research work with self-efficacy in exercise has expanded remarkably (see McAuley, Pena, & Jerome, this volume). There are two new social cognitive approaches in this volume: one on the perception of control by Brawley and colleagues (Dawson, Gyurcsik, Culos-Reed, & Brawley, this volume) that pertains to exercise, the other an expansion of self-determination theory within the sport context by Vallerand and colleagues (this volume). I leave it to my colleagues to argue for the efficacy of these approaches to sport and exercise.

Clearly, no one motivation theory has emerged as "the theory" in physical activity. Each has its band of supporters and its band of detractors. But we now have a great deal of data on the process of motivation; and as this book demonstrates, we do have theories that give meaning to the data. At present, although it is useful and desirable to continue within our own frameworks to further our respective understandings of the motivational equation, it must be confessed that we still need to attempt to move toward integration and a synthesis of theory and data (Roberts, 1992a). However, there is a danger in seeking universal applicability: the effort may blind us to the very real cultural and social dynamics that affect the ongoing stream of achievement striving. In our quest for understanding, we must tolerate some ambiguities and apparent inconsistencies. But we must continue to attempt to move forward to a more general set of concepts to integrate our respective efforts.

Since 1992, the motivation theory that has emerged as the most popular in sport and physical education is achievement goal theory. In 1998, Duda and Whitehead identified 135 research studies reported in the 1990s; just two years later, Brunel (2000) identified 160 studies. In sport psychology research meetings, it is clear that achievement goal theory is the one used most frequently to give meaning to motivation data. To this theory I now turn my attention.

Achievement Goal Theory in Sport and Physical Education

The achievement goal approach has become the most important conceptual avenue to address motivation in sport and physical education. It has evolved from the collaborative and independent classroom work of Ames (e.g., Ames, 1984b, 1984c, 1992a, 1992b, 1992c), Dweck (e.g., Dweck, 1986; Dweck & Leggett, 1988), Maehr (e.g., Maehr & Braskamp, 1986; Maehr & Nicholls, 1980), and Nicholls (e.g., Nicholls, 1980a, 1984b, 1989). This framework assumes that the individual is an intentional, goal-directed organism that operates in a rational manner and that achievement goals govern achievement beliefs and guide subsequent decision making and behavior in achievement contexts. It is argued that to understand the motivation of individuals, we must take into account the function and meaning of the achievement behavior to the individual and must understand the goal of action. By so recognizing the meaning of behavior, we see that there may be multiple goals of action, not just one (Maehr & Braskamp, 1986). Thus variation of behavior may not be a manifestation of high or low motivation per se but an expression of differing perceptions of appropriate goals. An individual's investment of personal resources such as effort, talent, and time in an activity is dependent on the achievement goal of the individual in that activity.

Maehr and Nicholls (1980) argued that the first step toward understanding achievement behavior is to recognize that success and failure are psychological states based on the person's interpretation of the effectiveness of his/her achievement striving. If the outcome of the evaluation is seen to reflect desirable attributes of the self, such as high effort and/or ability, then the outcome is seen as a success. Conversely, if the outcome is seen as reflecting undesirable attributes of the self, such as low ability, laziness, and/or low effort, then the outcome is seen as a failure. Success, failure, and achievement can be recognized only in terms of the goal of behavior. As stated earlier, what is success for one may not be success for another. Even in sport competition, where winning and losing are considered paramount, participants do not always consider winning and losing synonymous with success and failure (Spink & Roberts, 1980).

While many achievement goals are possible, the ones that emerge consistently across studies in physical activity generally support the hypotheses of Maehr and Nicholls (1980). Even though today the major researchers in achievement goal theory advocate somewhat varying approaches, the original goal orientations are the ones most studied and the ones most relevant to physical activity contexts.[1]

Conceptions of Ability

The goal of action—the energizing force—in achievement goal theory is assumed to be the demonstration of competence. But competence (or ability; see Fry, this volume) has more than one meaning; thus the *conception of ability* becomes the central variable. Nicholls's (1984b) unique contribution was to argue that more than one conception of ability exists and that we can understand achievement behavior in terms of the conception of ability adopted. Nicholls argued that two conceptions of ability appear in achievement contexts: an *undifferentiated concept of ability*, within which the individual does not or chooses not to differentiate ability and effort, and a *differentiated concept of ability*, within which ability and effort are differentiated (Nicholls, 1984b, 1989).

Further, Nicholls (1976, 1978, 1980b, Nicholls & Miller, 1983) argued that children originally possess an undifferentiated conception of ability—that is, that they are not able to distinguish luck, task difficulty, and effort from ability. From this undifferentiated perspective, children begin to associate ability with learning through effort and thereby see that the more effort one puts forth, the more learning (and ability) one achieves. Following a series of experiments, Nicholls (1978; Nicholls & Miller, 1984b) determined that by 12 years of age, children are able to differentiate luck, task difficulty, and effort from ability so that a differentiated perspective becomes possible. When utilizing this differentiated perspective, children begin to see ability as capacity and see that competence involves outperforming others. In terms of effort, one infers high ability when outperforming others but expending equal or less effort, or performing as well as others but expending less effort. Reaching this developmental stage, however, does not mean that individuals will automatically invoke a differentiated conception of ability even though they are clearly able to do so. Rather, people approach a task with certain goals of action reflecting their personal perceptions and beliefs about the particular achievement activity they are engaged in (Dennett, 1978; McArthur & Baron, 1983; Nicholls, 1984a, 1984b, 1989). The conception of ability they employ and the ways that they interpret their performance can be understood in terms of these perceptions and beliefs. These perceptions and beliefs form a *personal theory of achievement* at the activity (Nicholls, 1989; Roberts et al., 1997). The personal theory of achievement one adopts affects one's beliefs about how to succeed at the activity. Therefore, according to their personal theory of achievement, people differ in their conceptions of ability and criteria of success and in the ways they use these conceptions.

The two conceptions of ability become the source of the criteria by which individuals assess success. The goals of action are to meet the criteria by which success is assessed. Nicholls identifies achievement behavior that utilizes the undifferentiated conception of ability as *task involvement* and achievement behavior that utilizes the differentiated conception of ability as *ego involvement*. When one is task involved, the goal of action is to develop mastery, improvement, or learning, and the demonstration of ability is self-referenced. Success is realized when mastery or improvement has been attained. The goal of action for an ego-involved individual, on the other hand, is to demonstrate ability relative to others, or to outperform others, so ability is other-referenced. One realizes success after having exceeded the performance of others, especially after having expended less effort than others (Nicholls, 1984b, 1989).

At this point, it is appropriate to react briefly to some recent criticisms of achievement goal theory and research made by Harwood, Hardy, and Swain (2000). In a provocative paper, they propose that the differentiation of ability does not activate task and ego involvement. They argue that when individuals have reached the age at which they can differentiate, they will, and that it is not possible to not differentiate in sport: "One cannot have a tendency to both differentiate and not differentiate" (p. 241). They proceed to argue that in sport, this leads to the possibility of a third state of goal involvement termed self-referenced ego involvement. Second, they argue that the definitions of task and ego involvement have been incorporated into sport from the classroom and that there is not a natural transfer. Last, they criticize the current procedures we have for measuring task and ego orientation.

As we go to press, several colleagues and myself (Darren Treasure, Marty Maehr, Joan Duda, Howard Hall, and Carole Ames) are preparing a fuller reaction to these criticisms that will appear in an issue of the *Journal of Sport and Exercise Psychology* in 2000, but I want to respond briefly here because it is crucial to avoid misinterpretations. However, I first want to state that I believe it is important to have debates such as the one Harwood et al. (2000) have begun. By throwing down the gauntlet as they have, they force each of us to re-evaluate our own statements and positions. This is healthy and worthwhile. And as we state in the reaction, having respected colleagues criticize our work is the highest form of flattery.

One of their major issues is that they question whether we can be undifferentiated in our conception of ability once we are able to differentiate. I believe we can. As I have already argued here and elsewhere, we can be involved in an achievement activity in sport and "choose not to differentiate" (Roberts et al., 1997, p. 415) even though we are capable of doing so. The important aspect to realize is that the conception of ability one holds forms the foundation of one's personal theory of achievement for that task, which becomes the source of the criteria of success one adopts. We can hold a differentiated conception at one task (e.g., tennis) and be ego involved to do our best to beat someone at that activity but hold an undifferentiated conception at another task (e.g., golf), be totally task involved, and be totally concerned with improving our ability to play the game. Indeed, we can even shift our conception of ability during a game. We may begin a game with the intent of winning but later realize that we will not win, then one avenue is to become more task involved and more concerned with improving our ability (another avenue is to "give up" and withdraw effort. In sport lore, we tank the game). The fact that we are able to differentiate does not force us to differentiate all the time.

According to Harwood et al. (2000), to interpret Nicholls (1989) literally is to say that if we are undifferentiated in our conception of ability, we equate effort with ability. Once we are able to differentiate, Harwood et al. argue, it is unreasonable to think that we would continue to equate effort with ability. My argument is that it is not that we are equating effort and ability; rather we are choosing not to differentiate, and this impacts the criteria of success we use in a given context. Simply put, we choose to focus on effort and improvement and ignore the demonstration of ability as capacity. While I argue that we can hold an undifferentiated conception of ability and still focus on effort and improvement, I think one of the arguments of Harwood et al. is fair comment—that it may be better to use the term *conception of achievement* rather than conception of ability. Indeed, it may help with clarification if we refer to conceptions of ability as conceptions of achievement. This is consistent with the notion that we hold personal theories of achievement (Nicholls, 1989; Roberts et al., 1997). What underpins the personal theories is the understanding of the meaning of achievement in a given context, whether to demonstrate self-referenced (undifferentiated) or normative-referenced (differentiated) ability. The essential element is the meaning of achievement for the person, which, I would argue, is understanding the meaning of the demonstration of ability in terms of the criteria of success one adopts.

Addressing a second issue, Harwood et al. (2000) argue that when one is able to differentiate and one can evaluate one's own capacity relative to oneself, and one chooses to focus on self-referenced criteria of success, then a new state of involvement exists. This state the authors label *self-referenced ego involvement*. One simply competes with oneself. This is an interesting point, but I disagree. When you evaluate your own performance relative to your own previous performance, you are not engaging in normative evaluations with present others; therefore you are not invoking ego-involving comparisons. This argument harks back to our discussions in the 1970s about defining competition. Sherif (1976) maintained that you could compete with yourself—that competition did not need the presence of others. Martens (1975) disagreed, stating that a competitive context "excludes the comparison of a person's performance with his [sic] previous performance in the absence of an evaluative other" (p. 71). I would invoke a similar argument here—that ego involvement necessitates the presence of others who are capable of evaluating one's performance. Otherwise, the context is not normative, even when a standard of excellence is known and the person is trying to achieve that standard. This is a task-involving context, however invested the person is in the activity.

Also according to Harwood et al. (2000), we have borrowed heavily from education in our theorizing in achievement goal research, and this has contaminated our research. Have we blindly converted educational theory into sport contexts? As indicated in my first footnote, I argue that sport psychology has been at the forefront of research in achievement goals. The first-ever empirical data in achievement goals were collected by a sport psychologist (Ewing, 1981). And shortly thereafter, studies by Duda (1981) and Pascuzzi (1981) were completed. Sport psychologists have been at the forefront of research in achievement goals, both then and now. And sport psychologists have clearly focused on physical activity settings, therefore the data has been generated within context. As an example, the Perception of Success Questionnaire (see Roberts, Treasure, & Balague, 1998) was developed by sport psychologists within the context of sport psychology for use by sport psychologists. I believe the evidence speaks for itself.

The last point of Harwood et al. (2000) is that if their arguments hold, we must rethink our measurement technology when studying achievement goals. I contend that this is so even when the arguments of Harwood et al. do not ring true. Yes, we should always be open to upgrading our measurement technology, especially with respect to states of involvement (see also Duda, this volume). However, I refer the reader to our reaction for a more complete discussion of this issue and others in light of the criticisms of Harwood et al. In the meantime, let us return to the implications of assessing ability as task or ego involving.

States of Involvement

Whether a person is in a state of ego or task involvement depends on the dispositional orientation of the individual as well as situational factors (Nicholls, 1989). Let us consider the dispositional aspect first. It is assumed that individuals are predisposed to act in an ego- or task-involved manner. These predispositions are called achievement goal orientations. In this chapter, the two goal orientations are termed *task* and *ego* (Nicholls, 1980a, 1984b, 1989).[2] An individual who is task oriented is assumed to become task involved in the activity and utilizes an undifferentiated conception of ability (or uses a task-involving conception of achievement), or chooses to be task involved, to assess demonstrated competence in the achievement task. The individual evaluates personal performance to determine whether effort is expended and mastery achieved; thus the demonstration of ability is self-referenced, and success is realized when mastery or improvement has been demonstrated. In contrast, an individual who is ego oriented is assumed to become ego involved in the activity and utilizes a differentiated conception of ability (or uses an ego-involving conception of achievement) to assess competence (cf. Roberts, 1984a, where I discussed the complex steps that individuals go through to assess competence in sport contexts). The individual evaluates personal performance with reference to the performance of others; thus the demonstration of ability is other referenced and success is realized when the performance of others is exceeded, especially if little effort is expended (Dweck & Elliott, 1983; Maehr & Braskamp, 1986; Nicholls, 1984b, 1989; Roberts, 1984a).

Each major theory of achievement goal motivation (e.g., Ames, 1984b, 1992b, 1992c; Dweck, 1986; Dweck & Leggett, 1988; Maehr & Braskamp, 1986; Maehr & Nicholls, 1980; Nicholls, 1984b, 1989) holds that important relationships exist among the states of goal involvement, the perception of ability, and achievement striving. Briefly, if the person is task involved, then the conception of ability is undifferentiated and perceived ability is not relevant, as the individual is trying to demonstrate mastery or improvement at the task rather than normative ability. The achievement behaviors will be adaptive in that the person is more likely to persist in the face of failure, to exert effort, to select challenging tasks, and to be interested in the task (Duda, 1992; Dweck, 1986; Nicholls, 1984b, 1989; Roberts, 1984a, 1992a; Roberts et al., 1997). On the other hand, if the individual is ego involved, then the conception of ability is differentiated and perceived ability is relevant: the individual is trying to demonstrate normative ability, and how his/her ability compares to that of others becomes important. If the individual is ego involved and perceives him- or herself to be high in ability, then he or she is likely to engage in adaptive achievement behaviors. In this context it is likely that high normative ability will be demonstrated; therefore the individual is motivated to persist and to demonstrate that competence to pertinent others. Demonstrating ability with little effort, however, is evidence of even higher ability. Thus the ego-involved person is inclined to use the least amount of effort to realize the goal of action (Nicholls, 1984b, 1992; Roberts, 1984a; Roberts et al., 1997). If the perception of ability is low, on the other hand, then the individual realizes that ability is not likely to be demonstrated, and he/she is likely to manifest maladaptive achievement behaviors (Nicholls, 1989). Maladaptive behaviors are avoidance of challenge; reduced persistence in the face of difficulty; not exerting effort; and, in sport, dropping out if achievement of desired goals appears difficult. While the participant may view these behaviors as adaptive because they disguise a lack of ability, they are considered maladaptive in terms of achievement.

In 1992, I outlined a dynamic conceptual framework (Roberts, 1992a, p. 16) to help us understand the concepts just presented. Then I argued that the variables presented in the framework (achievement goals, perception of ability, and motivational climate) were important for understanding the ongoing stream of achievement behavior. I further stated that ignoring any of these variables meant ignoring important elements of the dynamic process. That statement is still true, but in the meantime we have progressed in our understanding of the process of motivation. I believe we have sharpened our understanding of the motivational equation. We now have research that allows us to better appreciate the role of the motivational climate and its interaction with achievement goals to affect the state of involvement (e.g., Roberts et al., 1997; Treasure, this volume; Treasure & Roberts, 1998). Our understanding of the role of perceived ability in the motivational equation is also being sharpened, as I document later in the chapter (see also Duda, this volume; Sarrazin, Cury, Roberts, Biddle, & Famose, 1999).

I would like to make a clarification here about achievement goal theory. Several times I have been asked at research meetings whether I believe that achievement goal theory is *the* theory of motivation. Although I may become somewhat missionary in discussing achievement goal theory (a theory I introduced into sport and exercise psychology, both through my students and through publications; e.g., Roberts, 1984a) and preach the gospel according to Glyn on occasion, I have discussed the constraints of the theory too (e.g., Roberts 1992a). Achievement goal theory applies only to people who are trying to achieve a desired personal or socially constructed goal in an achievement context. Achievement goal theory concerns *why* you are in the context and argues that the major reason you strive to achieve is to demonstrate a valued competence. Self-efficacy, in contrast, does not concern why you enter the task, only whether you value the task for any reason, and whether you have thoughts about being able to execute the behaviors necessary for the completion of the task (see McAuley, Pena, & Jerome, this volume). Thus you can enter an exercise task with one or more goals (weight control, heart rehabilitation, social contact, etc.) that are not pertinent to achievement, and self-efficacy will still be a useful theory. However, when you enter a context with a goal other than an achievement goal, then the predictions of achievement goal theory simply do not apply. But, again, if you enter an exercise task for an achievement reason (e.g., if you attempt to achieve a certain weight in a certain time), then achievement goal theory applies. This is one of the reasons that achievement goal theory applies so well to sport contexts. Not only are the goals clearly achievement goals most of the time, but success and failure, and personal competence tend to be unambiguous to all participants, players, and spectators. Thus sport is an important arena for the study and development of achievement goal theory.

Now we will return to the work in the physical activity arena that uses achievement goal theory.

Dispositional Goals in Physical Activity

Individual differences in the disposition to be ego or task oriented may result from socialization through task- or ego-involving contexts in either the home or the classroom, or through the previous physical activity experiences of the individual (Ames, 1984b, 1992b; Duda, 1992, 1993; Nicholls, 1984b, 1989, 1992; Roberts, 1984a, 1992a; Roberts et al., 1997). The individual is assumed to be predisposed to be task and/or ego goal involved and to exhibit the behaviors associated with the held orientation. The goal orientations are not to be viewed as "traits." Rather they are considered cognitive schemas that are subject to change as one processes information pertaining to one's performance on the task. But the orientations do have some stability over time too (Duda & Whitehead, 1998; Roberts, Treasure, & Balague, 1998). Thus being task or ego oriented refers to the inclination of the individual to be task or ego involved in the achievement task. It is important to note here that the cognitive schema assumed are specific to the task. While we do assume some degree of generality, we learn to be task or ego involved in a particular task. Thus, as mentioned earlier, we can be task involved at one task and ego involved at another. What changes is the meaning for the individual of achievement in that task.

One of the assumptions of the Nicholls (1984b, 1989) approach to achievement goal theory is that goal orientations are orthogonal; thus a person can be high or low in either or both at the same time. Since this was first theorized to be the case in physical activity contexts too (e.g., Roberts, 1984a), ample empirical supporting evidence has accumulated, as this book demonstrates. The implications are discussed later in the chapter (see also Duda, this volume).

To study goal orientations in sport, one must have a reliable and valid means of measurement. To measure the goal orientations, researchers have typically created questionnaires that are assumed to assess ego and task goal orientations (e.g., Nicholls, Patashnick, & Nolen, 1985). Although Dweck and her colleagues (e.g., Dweck & Leggett, 1988) conceptualize and measure the achievement goals as dichotomous, researchers have more often assumed that the two goals are conceptually orthogonal and have measured them accordingly (Duda & Whitehead, 1998; Nicholls et al., 1985; Roberts et al., 1998).

Nicholls (1989) has argued that to assess personal achievement goals, researchers should ask individuals about the criteria that make them feel successful in a given situation. In line with this suggestion, Duda (1989) and colleagues (Duda & Nicholls, 1992; Duda & Whitehead, 1998) and Roberts and colleagues (Roberts & Balague, 1989, 1991; Roberts et al., 1998; Treasure & Roberts, 1994b) have developed scales to measure task and ego goal orientations in sport. Both scales have shown acceptable reliability and construct validity (Duda & Whitehead, 1998; Marsh, 1994; Roberts et al., 1998). While other scales exist, the Perception of Success Questionnaire (POSQ) and the Task and Ego Orientation in Sport Questionnaire (TEOSQ) are the scales that best meet the conceptual criteria of measuring achievement goals in sport (Duda & Whitehead, 1998).

Both POSQ and TEOSQ have their detractors, too. Even though POSQ emerges a little less scathed than TEOSQ (Harwood, 2000) primarily because POSQ was empirically derived in sport contexts, Harwood et al. (2000) have criticized both scales for not assessing reality in a valid manner in the context of sport. Earlier in this chapter I responded to some of the conceptual criticisms on which Harwood et al. base their arguments. However, the detailed arguments among us must take place in another forum. I now turn to the research that has investigated achievement goals in physical activity contexts.

Motivational Concomitants of Goal Orientations

Nicholls (1989) contends that one of the basic differences between task- and ego-oriented individuals is the way they define and judge competence. A task orientation should foster perceptions of ability, as the goal of action is improvement or mastery of a task, and perceptions of one's own ability are self-referenced (Nicholls, 1989; Roberts, 1992a). An ego orientation, on the other hand, may either lower or increase one's perceived ability.

Perceived Ability

Various terms have been used to describe the construct of perceived ability, but as I have argued (1992a), the function of this construct as described in the various theories is quite similar. The terms self-efficacy (Bandura, 1977, 1986), perceived ability (Dweck, 1986; Nicholls, 1984b, 1989), perceived competence (Harter, 1978, 1981a), and sense of competence (Maehr & Braskamp, 1986) have been used in the literature to embrace the various definitions of competence: the individual's assessment of his or her own competencies to complete the task, his or her capacity to meet the environmental demands, or his or her capacity in relation to relevant others. Whichever theory is used, the construct has important implications for maladaptive or adaptive achievement striving.

The development of perceived competence and its importance in achievement contexts have received particular emphasis in achievement goal theory (Duda, 1992; Dweck, 1986; Nicholls, 1984b, 1989; Roberts, 1992a). A fundamental difference between task- and ego-oriented athletes is the way they define and judge competence (Nicholls, 1989). Task-oriented individuals focus on self-referenced criteria such as personal improvement and learning in order to determine their competence, whereas ego-oriented athletes tend to use normative criteria such as how their own ability compares to that of others. Because task-oriented individuals tend to construe competence based on self-referenced criteria and are primarily concerned with mastery of the task, they are more likely than ego-oriented persons to develop perceived competence over time (Elliott & Dweck, 1988). In contrast, the ego-oriented individual is concerned with the adequacy of his or her current ability level. Because the person feels competent when he or she compares favorably with others, self-confidence is less likely to be maintained in ego orientation, especially for those participants who already question their ability (see Dweck, 1986).

Research examining the impact of different conceptions of ability on self-efficacy, the situation-specific form of self-confidence, has yielded interesting findings. Wood and Bandura (1989) found that individuals who were told that performance in a cognitive task reflected their aptitude experienced high self-doubts regarding their personal efficacy when they faced difficulty, whereas participants who performed the task under the conception of ability as an acquirable skill showed a more flexible sense of self-efficacy. In a second study (Jourden, Bandura, & Banfield, 1991), performing the pursuit rotor tracking task under the conception of ability as an inherent aptitude conferred no self-efficacy benefits across the trials and produced negative self-reactions and low interest in the activity. Performing the same task under the conception that ability is an acquirable skill resulted in a progressive growth of self-efficacy, increased interest in the activity, and high performance. Finally, in a well-controlled experiment, Hall (1990) showed that participants with preexisting low levels of perceived ability who performed the stabilometer task in an ego-involving condition (i.e., under the conception that ability is capacity) expressed lower expectations for performance than low-perceived-ability individuals who performed the task in the task-involving condition (i.e., under the conception that ability is an acquirable skill).

Other work in the physical activity domain has produced similar results. Chi (1993), for example, found that high-task-/low-ego-oriented college students reported higher perceived competence before two cycling races than those high in ego and low in task orientation. Among college students participating in beginning tennis classes, task orientation corresponded to high self-efficacy for performing selected tennis strokes (Kavussanu & Roberts, 1996a). No appreciable association was revealed between ego orientation and self-efficacy when we statistically controlled for perceived normative ability.

Cury, Sarrazin, and Famose (1997) have confirmed that task- and ego-oriented participants use different information to judge their competence. While performing a motor task, task-oriented participants used less-objective information to evaluate their performance, allowing them to evaluate the extent of their progress. Ego-oriented participants used normative information to estimate the value of a performance, as long as it did not include information about their weaknesses. Thus, ego-oriented participants were not concerned with learning but instead with gaining an understanding of their position relative to others. Task-oriented participants, on the other hand, searched for information about their progress that would help them learn.

Research has also supported the predicted relationships between goal orientations and perceived ability. Studies have revealed that a task orientation is positively related to perceived ability (Chi, 1993; Vlachopoulos, Biddle, & Fox, 1997). These findings were obtained with collegiate students prior to cycling races (Chi, 1993) and in 11- to 14-year-old participants in a track and field event or a shuttle run physical fitness test (Vlachopoulos et al., 1997).

Similarly, Vlachopoulos and Biddle (1997) found that a task orientation was positively associated with perceptions of success for physical education students and that this relationship was not moderated by perceived ability. Thus even task-oriented individuals who initially did not believe in their ability experienced perceptions of success. Further, Cury, Biddle, Sarrazin, and Famose (1997) found that ego-involved individuals (a high ego orientation coupled with an ego-involving situation) with low perceived ability had lower success expectations on a basketball task than ego-involved individuals with high perceived ability or than task-involved individuals regardless of perceived ability. Viewing oneself as successful is likely to aid one's perception of competence.

Sarrazin, Cury, Roberts, Biddle, and Famose (1999), using a climbing task of differing levels of difficulty, found that perceived ability interacted with goal orientation. Task-involved boys exerted most effort at the levels of difficulty they thought "challenging" for their perceived ability. Boys with low perceived ability exerted effort on the moderately difficult course, and boys with high perceived ability exerted the most effort on the very difficult course. In contrast, the ego-involved boys with high perceived ability exerted the most effort in the average and difficult courses. The boys with low perceived ability exerted the most effort on the easiest courses and little effort on the average and very difficult courses. This work demonstrated that the boys with high ego involvement were concerned about exhibiting low ability, exerting effort only on those tasks they thought would allow them to demonstrate competence.

Thus several lines of research suggest that using the undifferentiated conception of ability (task-involving conception of achievement) to judge demonstrated competence enhances resiliency of perceived competence. The implications of these findings are particularly important in learning contexts. For example, for individuals beginning to learn a new physical skill, holding a task orientation may be instrumental in their perceptions of competence, their effort and persistence, and consequently their success in the activity. It is not surprising that VanYperen and Duda (1999), in their study with Dutch male soccer players, found that athletes high in task orientation were judged by their coaches to possess greater soccer skills from pre- to postseason. A task orientation fosters perceptions of competence and success for individuals who are either high or low in perceived competence and encourages the exertion of effort. An ego orientation, on the other hand, may decrease perceptions of success, perceived competence, and thus effort, especially for those individuals who already are unsure of their ability.

Beliefs About the Cause of Success

Nicholls (1989, 1992) suggests that one's goal, in conjunction with one's beliefs about the causes of success in a situation, constitutes an individual's personal theory of how things work in achievement situations. In research across various age groups and contexts, a task orientation has been linked to the belief that effort and cooperation with others are antecedents of success, whereas an ego orientation has been linked with the notion that ability, trying to beat others, and even deceptive (sometimes illegal) means are precursors to success. Findings in the physical activity domain using a wide variety of samples resemble those in academe. Research on young athletes (e.g., Hom, Duda, & Miller, 1993; Newton & Duda, 1993a; Nyheim, Kavussanu, Roberts, & Treasure, 1996), high school students (Duda & Nicholls, 1992; Lochbaum & Roberts, 1993), British youth (Duda, Fox, Biddle, & Armstrong, 1992; Treasure & Roberts, 1994a), young athletes with disabilities participating in wheelchair basketball (White & Duda, 1993), participants in physical activity (Kavussanu & Roberts, 1996b), and elite adult athletes (Duda & White, 1992; Guivernau & Duda, 1995; Roberts & Ommundsen, 1996) has consistently demonstrated an association between a task goal orientation and the belief that hard work and cooperation lead to success in sport. In general, ego orientation has been associated with the view that success is achieved through having high ability, as well as through using deception strategies such as cheating and trying to impress the coach. A similar pattern of results has emerged in the physical education context (Walling & Duda, 1995), as well as in research with college students participating in a variety of physical activity classes (Guivernau, Thorne, & Duda, 1994a; Kavussanu & Roberts, 1996b; Roberts, Treasure, & Kavussanu, 1996).

The belief that ability is an antecedent of success may be detrimental for physical activity and sport participants of all ability levels. For the low-perceived-ability individual, this belief will most likely lead to frustration, a lack of confidence, and even to dropping out. In the physical activity domain, where practice and hard work are so essential for improvement especially at the early stages of learning, the belief that effort leads to success is the most adaptive for sustaining persistence. Seeing ability as the precursor of success is important for those who aspire to participate at high levels of competition but does not tend to foster adaptive achievement patterns in physical activity. Individuals have little control over inherited athletic abilities. A belief that ability leads to success will not be of much help to youngsters who are not naturally gifted. In contrast, believing that success in physical activity comes through hard work and cooperation can lead even the least-gifted individuals to experience success and is crucial for talented youngsters. For the high-perceived-ability individual, a reliance on the belief that ability causes success may lead to complacency. This is especially true for young children, where maturation levels often predict success. A belief that ability causes success may lead to a lack of development since a child who relies on ability for success may not be as likely to put forth the effort required to develop ability.

Not only has research demonstrated that belief systems are differentially linked to goal orientations, studies (Duda & Nicholls, 1992; Fry, this volume; Guivernau et al., 1994a; Guivernau & Duda, 1995) also suggest that belief systems may be consistent across contexts (i.e., classroom and sport). Therefore, underlying belief systems are an important indicator of personal theories of achievement held by the individual.

Beliefs About the Purposes of Sport

Goal orientations are also meaningfully related to the individual's beliefs concerning the wider purposes of the achievement activity (Duda, 1993, this volume; Nicholls, 1989). In classroom-based research, ego orientation has been associated with the belief that the purpose of education is to provide one with wealth and social status, which is evidence of superior ability. Task orientation, on the other hand, has been linked to the view that an important purpose of education is to enhance learning and understanding of the world and to foster commitment to society (Nicholls et al., 1985; Thorkildsen, 1988). Similar findings have been reported in the athletic arena (e.g., Duda, 1989; Duda & Nicholls, 1992; Roberts & Ommundsen, 1996; Roberts et al., 1996, 1997; Treasure & Roberts, 1994b; White, Duda, & Keller, 1998), indicating that world views cut across educational and sport contexts. Task orientation has been associated with the belief that the purpose of sport is to enhance self-esteem, advance good citizenship, foster mastery and cooperation (Duda, 1989), and encourage a physically active lifestyle (White et al., 1998), whereas ego orientation has been linked to the view that sport should enhance one's popularity (Duda, 1989; McCarthy, Kavussanu, & White, 1996) and career mobility, build a competitive spirit (Duda, 1989), enhance status, and teach superiority and deceptive tactics (McCarthy et al., 1996).

Roberts and colleagues (Roberts, Hall, Jackson, Kimiecik, & Tonymon, 1995; Roberts & Ommundsen, 1996) have provided additional evidence regarding the differential link between achievement goals and beliefs about the important functions of sport. Among Norwegian elite athletes involved in team sport (Roberts & Ommundsen, 1996), task-oriented individuals endorsed involvement as fostering prosocial values such as social responsibility, cooperation, and the willingness to follow rules, as well as lifetime skills. In contrast, ego-oriented athletes believed that sport should provide one with social status. Roberts and colleagues have reported similar findings with college students (Roberts et al., 1995).

Congruent with classroom-based research, this work clearly suggests that personal motivational goals correspond to different world views. Individuals holding predominantly task-oriented goals are more likely to focus on mastery and learning as an end in itself and to emphasize the socializing value of sport, for example the development of lifelong physical activities and interests, cooperation, and prosocial attitudes and behavior. In contrast to task-oriented individuals, ego-oriented athletes tend to perceive as salient the outcomes of sport participation, such as social status, career mobility, and popularity among peers. These individuals seem to take a "what is in it for me" approach to sport participation (Duda, 1996).

A similar pattern of results has emerged in the physical education context (Walling & Duda, 1995). Ego-oriented students endorsed the view that the physical education lesson should provide students with an easy class and teach them to be more competitive, whereas those high in task orientation viewed improvement, hard work, and collaboration with peers as important purposes of physical education. Papaioannou and McDonald (1993) reported similar results with Greek physical education students.

Thus young athletes' views regarding the socializing value of sport and physical education vary as a function of their goal orientation. Investigations in both sport and physical education settings have revealed interdependencies between goals and beliefs about sport and physical education that are conceptually consistent with research findings in the academic domain. This work has provided valuable insight into the meaning young people find in participation in sport activities.

Achievement Strategies

Achievement goal theory and research in educational and sport settings suggest that personal theories of achievement comprise different beliefs about what leads to success (Nicholls, 1989). Such beliefs are reflected in the achievement strategies employed in competition as well as in practice. For example, a belief that success comes through hard work would lead people to a greater commitment to practice. In contrast, a view that success comes through demonstration of superiority over others should lead one to downplay the importance of practice and to focus on competition, as this allows demonstration of competence in the normative sense. Recent research in the athletic domain has provided some insight into the interrelationships between goal orientations and achievement strategies.

Research (Lochbaum & Roberts, 1993; Roberts et al., 1995; Roberts & Ommundsen, 1996) has demonstrated that task orientation is associated with adaptive achievement strategies, such as being committed to practice, learning, and effort. Typically in these investigations, ego orientation corresponds to a tendency to avoid practice and a focus on winning during competition. Goals also differentiate athletes in terms of the perceived benefits of practice. Thus, ego-oriented athletes consider practice a means of demonstrating competence relative to other athletes, whereas their task-oriented counterparts view practice as a means to foster team cohesion and skill development (Lochbaum & Roberts, 1993). In the Roberts and Ommundsen (1996) study with elite athletes, task-oriented athletes tended to endorse practice as a means to enhance improvement and learning and to obtain coach approval. Interestingly, ego orientation in this study corresponded to practice avoidance as well as seeking practice.

Investigators have also looked at the cognitive processing strategies of task- and ego-oriented participants. Thill and Brunel (1995b) found that soccer players differed in their processing strategies according to their goal orientations. Task-oriented participants engaged in deeper processing strategies than ego-oriented participants when faced with competence or incompetence feedback. This difference was reversed when competence or incompetence feedback was not present. Thus by allocating mental resources on social comparison strategies, normative-referenced behavior limits the capacities of working memory and results in shallow processing that requires little cognitive effort (Kuhl, 1986; Kuhl & Koch, 1984).

Studies have produced preliminary evidence that an ego orientation is related to other unacceptable achievement strategies such as the use of aggression. Rascle, Coulomb, and Pfister (1998) found a positive correlation between an ego orientation and aggression in handball. Players high in an ego orientation displayed more instrumental aggression than participants low in an ego orientation. These findings suggest that participants high in an ego orientation may adopt the philosophy of "win at all costs." Further, the demonstration of aggression should not be surprising considering that participants high in an ego orientation believe that deception and illegal means are the cause of success.

These studies show that the achievement strategies endorsed by physical activity participants are meaningfully related to their goal orientations. Across the studies, task orientation was coupled with adaptive learning strategies. In particular, task-oriented athletes seemed to emphasize the value of practice for learning new skills and improving. Clearly, task orientation has positive motivational implications for involvement in sport. In contrast, ego-oriented athletes endorsed avoiding practice as an achievement strategy. Ego-oriented athletes apparently prefer to compete, as this allows them to demonstrate superiority to others (Roberts & Ommundsen, 1996).

Affective Correlates of Goal Orientations

Affect is an important determinant of motivation in some theories (e.g., Weiner, 1986), but affect and emotion have been considered as consequences of achievement striving in achievement goal research. The variables most used in achievement goal research have been satisfaction, enjoyment, interest, and anxiety.

Enjoyment and Interest

One of the most consistent findings in this literature is the link between task orientation and experienced enjoyment, satisfaction, and interest during participation in physical activity. This finding has emerged in investigations using high school students (Duda, Chi, Newton, Walling, & Catley, 1995; Duda & Nicholls, 1992), summer sport camp participants (Nyheim et al., 1996), and college students in a variety of physical activity classes (Duda et al., 1995; Kavussanu & Roberts, 1996a, 1996b). A positive relationship has also been reported between task orientation and flow, an intrinsically enjoyable experience (Csikszentmihalyi, 1975), in college athletes (Jackson & Roberts, 1992). Findings for ego-oriented athletes have been similar but only for those who were convinced of their high ability. College athletes with low perceptions of ability experienced flow less frequently when competing (Jackson & Roberts, 1992). In these studies, ego orientation was either inversely related or unrelated to intrinsic interest, satisfaction, or enjoyment.

The relationship between an ego orientation and enjoyment varies, and often depends on one's level of perceived ability as well as one's task orientation. Participants with a high task orientation, in combination with either a high or a low ego orientation, experience greater enjoyment than those high in ego orientation and low in task orientation (Biddle, Akande, Vlachopoulos, & Fox, 1996; Goudas, Biddle, & Fox, 1994a). Further, Cury et al. (1996) found that a task orientation predicted intrinsic interest in physical education classes; and Vlachopoulos and Biddle (1997) found that a task orientation had direct effects on positive emotion. An ego orientation, on the other hand, was not associated with intrinsic interest (Cury et al., 1996) and slightly augmented negative affect and minimized positive affect for individuals with low perceived ability (Vlachopoulos & Biddle, 1997). A task orientation seems to be especially important for continued participation in physical activity as it is associated with enjoyment, and this is the case regardless of one's perceived success (Goudas, Biddle, & Fox 1994b) or perceived ability (Vlachopoulos & Biddle, 1997). An ego orientation, on the other hand, when not accompanied by a high task orientation, appears to detract from enjoyment during participating in physical activity; and this appears to be so especially for the low-perceived-ability individual.

There is little doubt that enjoyable and satisfying activities are more meaningful to the individual than others. Therefore promoting intrinsic interest in the activity is important. Maintaining high levels of intrinsic interest during participation in an activity is also instrumental for further participation. Goudas, Underwood, and Biddle (1993), for example, found that intrinsic interest predicts students' intentions to maintain their participation in physical education classes.

The research reviewed in this section indicates an interdependence between the individual's goal orientation and the enjoyment he or she experiences while participating in physical activity. Such work also highlights the significance of task orientation in maintaining participation in physical activity. In contrast, a focus on social comparison, competition, and outperforming others has the potential to diminish intrinsic motivation (Deci & Ryan, 1980; Ryan, 1980). When holding an ego goal, the individual views achievement striving as a means to an end, that end being the demonstration of superior ability. This focus is incompatible with the most fundamental element of intrinsic motivation—participating in the task for its own sake.

Another interesting research finding relates to the different sources of satisfaction that are associated with different goal perspectives. Three studies investigating this issue using children and adolescents (Nyheim et al., 1996; Treasure & Roberts, 1994a), and elite athletes (Roberts & Ommundsen, 1996) have revealed a consistent pattern. Ego-oriented athletes gain satisfaction when they demonstrate success in the normative sense and please the coach and their friends, whereas task-oriented individuals feel satisfied when they have mastery experiences and perceive a sense of accomplishment during their sport participation. Thus determinants of satisfaction in sport seem to vary depending on the individual's goal orientation. For task-oriented athletes, learning, accomplishment, and mastery of the task are important sources of satisfaction. For ego-oriented athletes, however, it is unlikely that mastery experiences will suffice to engender satisfaction in sport, as the demonstration of ability in the normative sense necessitates outperforming others (Treasure & Roberts, 1994a). Thus, ego-oriented individuals may have developed a dependency on competitive outcomes for feelings of satisfaction. It is not surprising that they also exhibit a greater preference for competence information based on normative criteria (Williams, 1994).

Probably the most significant study to illustrate the association of goals with affect was conducted by Ntoumanis and Biddle (1999a). They performed a meta-analysis with 41 independent samples and found that task orientation and positive affect were moderately to highly correlated in a positive fashion, whereas the correlation to negative affect was negative and relatively small. The relationship between ego orientation and both positive and negative affect was small. Ntoumanis and Biddle concluded that the links between affect and goal orientations are slight, except for the relationship of positive affect to task orientation. In essence, being task involved fosters positive affect in physical activities.

Anxiety

Achievement goal theory suggests that athletes adopting an ego orientation experience anxiety as a function of whether or not they believe they can demonstrate ability in a situation. A task orientation, on the other hand, should not lead to stress to the same degree, as the athlete is focused on self-referenced mastery of an activity rather than on comparing performance with that of others. Anxiety should also be less likely with a task orientation because the individual's self-worth is not threatened (Roberts, 1986).

Research has generally supported the tenets of goal theory, as a task orientation has been negatively associated with precompetitive anxiety (Vealey & Campbell, 1988), cognitive anxiety in young athletes (Ommundsen & Pedersen, 1999), somatic and cognitive anxiety (Hall & Kerr, 1997), task-irrelevant worries and the tendency to think about withdrawing from an activity (Newton & Duda, 1995), and concerns about mistakes and parental criticisms (Hall & Kerr, 1997; Hall, Kerr, & Matthews, 1998). Further, a task orientation has been associated with maintaining concentration and feeling good about the game (Newton & Duda, 1995). An ego orientation, on the other hand, has been positively related to state and trait anxiety (Boyd, 1990; Boyd, Callaghan, & Yin, 1991; Newton & Duda, 1995; Vealey & Campbell, 1988; White & Zellner, 1996), cognitive anxiety in the form of worry (White & Zellner, 1996), getting upset in competition (Yin, Boyd, & Callaghan, 1991), and concentration disruption during competition (Newton & Duda, 1995; White & Zellner, 1996).

As Ommundsen and Pederson (1999) remind us, however, it is not necessarily sufficient simply to state that task involvement is beneficial in terms of anxiety. More research is needed, but these investigators found that being task involved did decrease cognitive trait anxiety, while low perceived competence increased somatic and cognitive anxiety. This suggests that although being task involved is beneficial, perceived competence is an important predictor of anxiety too. Being task oriented and perceiving one's competence to be high are both important antecedents to reduction of anxiety in sport.

Motivation for Participation

Goal orientations are also predictive of the reasons for participating in an activity. White and Duda (1994), for example, in their study of youth, intercollegiate, and recreational sport participants, found that task orientation was associated with the more intrinsic motives for involvement such as skill development and enhancing one's level of fitness. In contrast, ego orientation was linked to extrinsic motives for participation such as social recognition and increasing one's social status. In addition, high-ego-oriented athletes were less likely to cite team membership and affiliation as important reasons for sport participation. Papaioannou (1990) reported similar results in his study with Greek students participating in physical education classes.

In addition, Papaioannou (1998) has found that reasons for being disciplined in physical education relate to goal orientations. A task orientation was associated with intrinsic reasons, caring, responsibility, and introjected reasons for being disciplined during participation in physical education classes. An ego orientation was positively related to extrinsic reasons and to no reasons for being disciplined. Overall, high-task-oriented individuals perceived themselves as more disciplined than low-task-oriented students, and this was linked to their reasons for being disciplined. High-task-oriented students, compared to low-task-oriented students, considered that learning something important, caring for others, being a responsible person, and enjoying the learning process were more important reasons for behaving well. Utilizing more internal reasons for being disciplined increases the likelihood that individuals will behave appropriately in the classroom and makes learning more enjoyable and successful.

The reasons people participate in a specific activity constitute an important component of the meaning of the activity to a person (Maehr & Braskamp, 1986). The work described in this section suggests that goal orientations can provide insight into the reasons individuals engage in physical activity.

Perceptions of Appropriate Achievement Behavior

Among the most significant findings of recent research within the achievement goal framework are the relationships between goal perspectives and perceived achievement behaviors appropriate within various achievement settings in physical activity. Behaviors assumed to reflect motivation are task choice, exerted effort, persistence, and performance (Maehr, 1984; Maehr & Braskamp, 1986; Roberts, 1992a; Roberts et al., 1997). Adaptive behavioral patterns such as choosing moderately challenging tasks, exerting effort, and showing persistence in the face of obstacles are expected to result when one is task oriented or when one is ego oriented and has a high perception of ability (Dweck & Leggett, 1988; Roberts et al., 1997). Ego orientation coupled with low perception of ability is associated with maladaptive behavioral patterns such as choosing very easy or very difficult tasks, as well as the inability to sustain effort in the face of difficulty.

Research in physical activity contexts has provided empirical support for these predictions. Kavussanu and Roberts (1996a) examined the link between goal orientation and task choice among college students in a variety of physical activity classes. Students high in task orientation reported that they were more likely to choose challenging activities—that is, activities that would offer the opportunity for learning but would also be somewhat difficult to accomplish. Further, Spray and Biddle (1997) found that students who volunteered to participate in physical education were higher in a task orientation than those who did not participate.

Among the important indicators of motivated behavior are effort and persistence. When people invest their time in an activity, apply effort, and persist under difficult circumstances, they are clearly motivated. These behaviors are among the criteria we use to assess motivation. Variation in the amount of effort young people exert in physical activity contexts can be attributed, to a large extent, to individual differences in goal orientation. Research (Cury, Biddle et al., 1997; Duda et al., 1995; Kavussanu & Roberts, 1995, 1996b; Sarrazin, Cury, Roberts, Biddle, & Famose, 1999) has shown a strong relationship between a task orientation and reported exerted effort, and nonsignificant (Kavussanu & Roberts, 1995, 1996b) or negative (Duda et al., 1995; Sarrazin et al., 1999) relationships between an ego orientation and exerted effort. Other work revealed that intramural high-task-oriented participants practiced their sport more in their free time than their low-task-oriented counterparts (Duda, 1988). Cury, Biddle et al. (1997) found that ego-involved individuals with low perceived ability attributed less importance to, and invested less time preparing for, a basketball task than high-perceived-ability ego-involved individuals or task-involved participants regardless of perceived ability.

Further, children high in task orientation reported higher levels of involvement in physical activity (Weitzer, 1989). Most important, this relationship between task orientation and participation held regardless of the level of perceived competence. Children who were ego involved and who doubted their physical ability reported the lowest levels of physical activity. Only when perceptions of ability were high did ego-involved children report high levels of physical activity. Ego-oriented athletes are the most likely to drop out of sport (Ewing, 1981), while task-oriented intramural sport participants are the most likely to continue involvement in their sport for a longer time (Duda, 1988).

VanYperen and Duda (1999) found that task orientation was associated with beliefs that effort, team play, and parental support were important for success in sport, but also, importantly, that task orientation led young players to improve in their performance. Future research should focus on whether the increase in performance is because these players adopted more appropriate achievement strategies or whether it led to better use of achievement strategies in that they may have applied greater effort. Clearly, being task involved seems to lead to more appropriate achievement strategies.

Avoidance Goals

Researchers in education and sport psychology have begun to examine the goal of avoiding failure or a demonstration of incompetence (Elliot, 1997; Elliot & Church, 1997; Elliot & Harackiewicz, 1996; Elliot & Sheldon, 1997; Middleton & Midgley, 1997; Skaalvik, 1993, 1997; Skaalvik & Valas, 1994). The study of an avoidance goal harks back to an older and more mechanistic conceptualization of achievement motivation (e.g., Atkinson, 1957). However, the contemporary conceptualization is not inconsistent with a social cognitive approach to motivation or with the achievement goal approach (Roberts & Walker, in press). According to Nicholls (1984b), "achievement behavior is defined as that behavior in which the goal is to develop or demonstrate—to self or to others—high ability, or to avoid demonstrating low ability" (p. 328). Thus Nicholls delineated between goals aimed at a demonstration of ability and goals aimed at avoiding a demonstration of low ability. Despite including this approach-avoidance distinction in his early work, Nicholls subsequently argued for two orthogonal approach-oriented achievement goal states, task and ego involvement.

Although researchers examining the effects of avoiding failure have used different terms to describe the same concept (Skaalvik uses the terms *self-defeating* or *defensive goals*, whereas Elliot, and Middleton and Midgley, use the term *avoidance goals*), their conceptualizations of avoidance goals appear to converge. Elliot (1997), Middleton and Midgley (1997), and Skaalvik (1997) describe an avoidance orientation as one in which individuals are concerned with being negatively judged by others. In accordance with Nicholls (1984b), these authors have suggested that avoidance goals are most likely to be adopted by low-perceived-ability individuals because appearing incompetent is what these individuals wish to avoid.

Dispositional Avoidance Goals[3]

Elliot (Elliot & Church, 1997), Middleton and Midgley (1997), and Skaalvik (1997) have developed separate dispositional instruments to measure an avoidance orientation. Elliot has developed a six-item questionnaire, as have Middleton and Midgely; Skaalvik has developed a seven-item scale.

Factor analyses have demonstrated that an avoidance orientation is distinct from an ego approach orientation and a task orientation. Correlation analyses all demonstrated that ego approach and ego avoidance orientations are not orthogonal; the two scales are significantly correlated in all three instruments. However, this may not be too surprising because both orientations concern comparing oneself to others. At least the scales are a step forward from the original two questions Nicholls used to assess avoiding inferiority, which loaded onto an ego approach orientation (Nicholls, Cheung, Lauer, & Patashnick, 1989). Nicholls later combined the avoidance items with the ego approach items but eventually dropped the avoidance goal.

Initial research using avoidance goals has attempted to determine the antecedents as well as consequences of the adoption of avoidance goals. A consistent finding within this research has been the relationship between low perceptions of ability and adoption of the avoidance goal. Avoidance goal adoption has been related to lower success expectations (Elliot & Church, 1997) and lower perceived life skills (Elliot, Sheldon, & Church, 1997). Additionally, Middleton and Midgley (1997) found that students with low grade-point averages were more concerned with their performance relative to others (ego approach and ego avoidance) than participants with high grade-point averages. Finally, Skaalvik (1993) found that students with reading problems were very concerned with their ability relative to others and about looking "stupid" in the classroom. This led them to adopt a variety of self-protective strategies to avoid negative perceptions on the part of other students. The findings of these studies support the original notions of Nicholls (1984b) indicating that individuals who doubt their ability are more likely to adopt avoidance goals.

Besides seeking to understand the antecedents of avoidance goals, researchers have also attempted to ascertain the cognitive, behavioral, and affective consequences of pursuing avoidance goals. Elliot and Church (1997) found that pursuing avoidance goals proved to be deleterious to both intrinsic motivation and graded performance. The adoption of a task goal facilitated intrinsic motivation but had no appreciable effects on grades, whereas pursuing ego approach goals led to null effects on intrinsic motivation but resulted in high grades. Research by Elliot and Sheldon (1997) and Elliot et al. (1997) has also shown that pursuing avoidance goals leads to decreases in perceived success, which in turn lead to decreases in subjective well-being.

Middleton and Midgley (1997) evaluated the relationship among avoidance goals, perceived academic efficacy, test anxiety, and avoiding help seeking in math classes. Results indicated that an ego avoidance orientation negatively predicted academic efficacy and positively predicted avoiding help seeking and test anxiety in math. An ego approach goal did not significantly predict academic efficacy or self-regulated learning but was positively related to anxiety in math.

Skaalvik (1997) examined the relationship among goal orientations, academic self-concept (a general feeling of doing well or poorly in school), self-efficacy for schoolwork, self-esteem, anxiety, achievement, and intrinsic motivation in students participating in Norwegian and math classes. Avoidance (self-defeating) goals were negatively related to academic self-concept, self-efficacy for schoolwork, and self-esteem. Interestingly, an ego approach (self-enhancing) orientation was positively related to these variables. Additionally, an avoidance orientation predicted high anxiety in math and Norwegian classes, whereas a self-enhancing ego orientation and task orientation predicted low anxiety in math classes and did not relate significantly to anxiety in Norwegian classes.

Consistent across the studies in education is the fact that avoidance goals undermine the cognitive, behavioral, and affective responses of students in education. Students pursuing avoidance goals experience greater anxiety, lower task involvement, lower grades, lower perceived success, less enjoyment, and lower subjective well-being than individuals who adopt approach goals. Further, this research suggests that individuals who doubt their abilities may adopt avoidance goals in an attempt to avoid a demonstration of ability.

As Elliot and Harackiewicz (1996) have argued, there are a number of reasons why an avoidance goal is not an effective achievement strategy. First, an individual adopting an avoidance goal orients him-/herself toward avoiding failure as opposed to approaching success, resulting in self-protective processes (i.e., threat construal, sensitivity to failure information). These self-protective processes are likely to lead to a lower level of task involvement as the individual is forced to identify and block all potential negative outcomes rather than merely focusing on the task at hand. Thus inherent in an avoidance orientation is a certain amount of task distraction. Further, focusing on negative outcomes yields a perceptual-cognitive sensitivity to negative stimuli and heightens one's awareness of negative information (Derryberry & Reed, 1994; Higgins & Tykocinski, 1992; Wegner, 1994). This focus on negative information that accompanies an avoidance goal may lead to reduced levels of perceived competence and enjoyment. Thus the adoption of avoidance goals may be detrimental to individuals for multiple reasons (Roberts & Walker, in press).

Future research with avoidance goals should verify the relationship between an avoidance orientation and achievement responses found in education and in physical activity settings. Future research should also examine the situational and dispositional factors leading to states of avoidance involvement. We should attempt to determine what contexts elicit a concern with appearing incompetent (i.e., the effects of repeated failures).

Despite the consistent finding that low-perceived-ability individuals adopt avoidance goals, an avoidance orientation should not be viewed as an ego orientation for low-perceived-ability individuals. Especially in sport, where the underdogs often prevail, people who perceive their ability to be low may adopt approach goals (Roberts & Walker, in press). Individuals low in perceived ability are not always prone to a fear of failure, and individuals with high perceived ability are not immune to avoiding failure (Covington, 1992; Covington & Omelich, 1991).

Moral Functioning in Physical Activities

Before we consider the research on moral behavior and achievement goals, we should recognize the assumption that performance in physical activity is important in the socialization process of the child toward the development of appropriate moral behaviors. It is generally assumed that in play, games, and sport, children come into contact with the social order and the values inherent in society, and that within this context they develop desirable social and moral behaviors (Brustad, 1993; Evans & Roberts, 1987). This assumption has given rise to cultural expectations that in turn have led to steadily increasing levels of involvement of children in all aspects of physical activity, especially adult-organized competitive sport. Research has demonstrated that the domain of competitive sport is a particularly important context for psychosocial and moral development in that peer status, peer acceptance, and self-worth are established and developed, and moral behavior and perspective taking are enhanced (e.g., Evans & Roberts, 1987; Kavussanu, 1997; Kavussanu & Roberts, 1998; Roberts & Treasure, 1995). These social and moral attributes are based on many factors, but one way a child can gain acceptance and social visibility is to demonstrate competence in an activity valued by society and other children. Clearly, one area of competence highly valued by society and by children is sport ability (Roberts, 1993; Roberts & Treasure, 1992). Being good at sports is a strong social asset for a child, especially boys (Roberts, 1993; Roberts & Treasure, 1995). But is it true that sport fosters character development? And how do achievement goals feature in the equation?

Character is often defined in terms of prosocial behavior and appropriate moral functioning. The notion that sport builds character has been a fond belief of many adults. Many sport participation advocates still believe that sport provides an appropriate context for learning social skills such as cooperation and prosocial and moral behavior. Sport is assumed to provide a vehicle for learning to cooperate with teammates; negotiate and give solutions to moral conflicts; develop self-control; display courage; and learn virtues such as fairness, team loyalty, persistence, and teamwork (e.g., Shields & Bredemeier, 1995; Weiss & Bredemeier, 1990). While many maintain that sport builds character, others argue that it does the opposite (Shields & Bredemeier, 1995). It is easy to find stories of illegal recruitment, use of performance enhancing drugs, aggressive behaviors, and acts of cheating in the sport context at all levels of participation. Further, research suggests that an overemphasis on competitive outcomes generates moral problems (e.g., Orlick, 1978, 1990), that competition reduces prosocial behavior (e.g., Kleiber & Roberts, 1981), and even that it promotes antisocial behavior (Kohn, 1986).

Goal orientations may be differentially related to moral functioning and maturity. At lower stages of moral development, individuals focus on their own needs and desires; and when trying to reason about moral solutions to moral conflicts, they give priority to the needs of the self. It is only when a person has progressed to more advanced stages of moral development that he or she is able to take the perspective of others, give equal consideration to the needs of all parties involved in a moral conflict, and feel concern about fairness and justice. In achievement goal theory, ego-involved individuals are primarily focused on the self and on how they rank in comparison to others. It is argued that the preoccupation with normative success and social comparison may inhibit moral development of the ego-involved person. In contrast, task-involved individuals feel competent when they have achieved mastery and demonstrated learning of the task. Progress and improvement become compatible with achieving progress in the moral arena.

Duda and colleagues (Duda, Olson, & Templin, 1991) were the first to examine the role of goal orientations in sportspersonship attitudes and the perceived legitimacy of intentionally injurious sport acts. Ego orientation was positively related to the endorsement of unsportspersonship acts and cheating. Significant gender differences also emerged, with females being more task and less ego oriented than males and perceiving unsportspersonship play and cheating as less acceptable. More recently, Stephens and Bredemeier (1996) examined the role of goal orientation on aggression with young girls in soccer. The girls who viewed themselves as more likely to aggress against an opponent were also more likely to perceive their coach as emphasizing ego-involving criteria of success. However, reported likelihood to aggress against an opponent was not significantly related to players' goal orientations. Stephens and Bredemeier (1996) reasoned that for girls at this age (9-14 years), perceptions of coach's attitudes and values play a more significant role in the likelihood to aggress than does individual goal orientation. However, because age 12 seems to be a watershed for the development of ego involvement as documented by

Fry (this volume), it is likely that many of the participants in this study were not ego involved. In research with young children, it is important to establish the participants' level of task and ego orientation.

Stephens (1993) also assessed the temptation to violate moral norms by lying to an official, hurting an opponent, or breaking one of the rules. She found that players who reported higher temptation to play unfairly were more likely to be ego involved and perceived their coaches as more ego involved. Temptation to play unfairly was also associated with the belief that more teammates would play unfairly and with greater approval of behaviors designed to obtain an unfair advantage.

With colleagues, I (Treasure, Roberts, & Standage, 1998) investigated sportspersonship with elite young male soccer players. We found that low-ego-involved players who thought the team atmosphere to be ego involving had less respect for the rules, officials, and social conventions than players low in ego involvement who perceived a low-ego-involving atmosphere. In another study, Kavussanu (1997) and colleagues (Kavussanu & Roberts, 1998, in press) investigated moral functioning with elite college basketball players. When the coaching staff was perceived as encouraging moral transgressions in the quest to win, and when teammates were perceived as likely to engage in the acts, then these players reported more likelihood to cheat. Further, we found (Kavussanu & Roberts, 1998) that ego-oriented players had lower levels of moral functioning, more strongly approved of unsportspersonlike behaviors, and judged that intentionally injurious acts are legitimate. Dunn and Dunn (1999) obtained similar results with male elite hockey players. Task-involved athletes were higher in reported sportspersonship. We (Kavussanu & Roberts, in press) also found some gender differences: males reported higher ego orientation, lower task orientation, and lower levels of moral functioning than females.

Treasure and Roberts (2000) examined the contribution of dispositional goal orientations, perceptions of the motivational climate, and the interaction effect of these two variables in predicting sportspersonship orientations of elite male youth soccer players ($N = 431$; M age = 15.1 years; range 12-18 years). With age controlled for, results revealed separate main effects as well as significant interaction effects between goal orientations and perceptions of the motivational climate in predicting the sportspersonship of the players. With regard to respect for the social conventions of soccer and the rules and officials (as measured with the scale developed by Vallerand, Brière, Blanchard & Provencher, 1997), being in an ego-involving climate moderated the ego goal orientation of players. Specifically, perceptions of a high-performance-oriented climate led to a reduction in sportspersonship for low-ego-oriented individuals. In contrast, low-ego-oriented individuals who perceived a low-performance-oriented climate responded with higher levels of sportspersonship. For high-ego-oriented individuals, however, perceptions of the climate had little effect on either their respect for the rules and officials or their respect and concern for the opponent.

In studying values, attitudes, and goal orientations with young adolescents, Lee and Whitehead (1999) found that status values were positively related to negative attitudes and that moral values were negatively related to negative attitudes. However, disposition mediated this relationship; task orientation was predicted by competence values, and competence values predicted positive attitudes. Ego orientation, on the other hand, was predicted by status values, and status values predicted negative attitudes. Interestingly, Lee and Whitehead found that high-ego-, low-task-oriented participants with low perceived ability were more likely to endorse cheating in sport than high-ego- and low-task-oriented participants who were high in perceived ability. And high-task-oriented participants were less likely to endorse cheating than any other participant, regardless of perceived ability.

More recently, colleagues in Norway and I have been investigating the impact of achievement goals and motivational climate on sportspersonship in elite children's soccer. In one study we investigated moral reasoning of children aged between 12 and 14 years who played competitive football (Roberts & Ommundsen, 2000). When children were ego involved, they used lower levels of moral reasoning. Children high in task involvement reported less likelihood to engage in inappropriate behaviors. We (Lemyre, Ommundsen, & Roberts, 2000) also looked at dispositional goals and perceived ability in predicting moral functioning. A total of 511 Norwegian football players competing in the elite Norway Cup tournament, from age 13 to 16, participated in the study. The players with a high-ego-/low-perceived-ability profile were more likely to endorse poor sportspersonship behavior and to demonstrate lower moral functioning. Finally, we (Ommundsen, Roberts, & Lemyre, 2000) examined the relationship of perceived motivational climate to players' self-reported sportspersonship, moral reasoning levels, and morally inappropriate behaviors. The study comprised 280 players aged 12 to 14 years who were taking part in an elite soccer tournament. The findings supported the proposition that different situational goal structures elicit qualitatively different patterns of social functioning. In a performance-oriented motivational climate, the development of acceptable moral attitudes and behavior was inhibited, as was making use of advanced social-moral reasoning levels when participants faced soccer-specific moral dilemma situations.

As we can appreciate from the research described, being task or ego involved has implications for moral functioning in sport and physical education contexts. And being high or low in perceived competence moderates this relationship in some cases. As John Nicholls was fond of saying when explaining why ego-involved participants would engage in cheating and inappropriate behaviors during participation in achievement tasks, when winning is everything, you do anything to win! This is a productive line for future research. Now we can begin to empirically determine the impact of involvement in physical activity on the moral development of children and the moral functioning of participants in sport, rather than engaging in philosophical debates.

Orthogonality of Goal Orientations

At the conclusion of this section on goal orientations, it is important to discuss more fully a topic I alluded to earlier: the orthogonality of achievement goals. Nicholls, in all his writings (e.g., 1989), argued for the orthogonality of the goal orientations: he held that task and ego goal orientations are independent, meaning that one can be high or low in each or in both orientations at the same time. Indeed, Nicholls (1992) was at pains to emphasize this point. On the basis of developmental research with children, he concluded that by the age of 12, an individual can be high or low in both task and ego goal orientation, or high in one and low in the other. In the sport and exercise literature, this orthogonality has been supported, for the most part (e.g., Duda & Whitehead, 1998; Roberts et al., 1997, 1998).

In the education domain, Ames and Archer (1988) investigated how the salience of task and ego goals (or mastery and performance goals, respectively, as Ames and Archer termed them) in classroom settings relates to specific motivational processes. The authors (1988) divided students into four groups, based on a median split on each scale (so that they had high/high, high/low, low/high, and low/low groups), in order to examine differences among profiles of students. Students who perceived a task goal as salient in the classroom reported using more-effective learning strategies, had a stronger belief that success is the result of one's effort, and had a more positive attitude toward the class. In contrast, students who perceived that an ego goal was emphasized in the classroom tended to focus on their ability and attributed failure to a lack of ability.

Duda (1988) examined the relationship between achievement goal orientation and specific motivated behaviors such as persistence and behavioral intensity. Based on their orientations to both achievement goals, participants were also classified into four groups. A participant was classified as high or low on a given goal if the participant was at least a half standard deviation above or below the mean, respectively. Further analyses revealed significant differences among the four groups. Specifically, participants who were high on task orientation participated in intramural sport longer and devoted more time to practicing their intramural sport than those who were low in task orientation.

In the context of physical education, Walling and Duda (1995) found that students high in ego orientation were more likely than low-ego-oriented students to express the belief that success is achieved when one possesses high ability. In addition, high-task-oriented students were significantly more likely than low-task-oriented students to believe that success is achieved through intrinsic interest in the activity, cooperation, and high effort. Finally, high task/low ego students were the least likely to believe that success stems from learning to skillfully deceive the teacher.

Roberts et al. (1996) investigated the relative effect of task and ego goal orientations on beliefs about the causes of success and satisfaction in sport. Based on a median split of the task, participants were divided into four groups (high task, high ego; high task, low ego; low task, low ego; low task, high ego). Analyses revealed that the high task groups attributed success to effort more than low task groups did. In contrast, high ego groups attributed success to ability more than did low ego groups. Participants high in task orientation and low in ego orientation were more satisfied than those who were low in task orientation. In this study, task-oriented participants endorsed adaptive achievement beliefs and experienced the greater satisfaction. Steinberg (1996) found that those who were instructed to emphasize both task and ego involvement goals exhibited higher levels of enjoyment, persistence, and performance in a putting task than those instructed to adopt either a task- or an ego-involving goal.

Even with elite Olympic athletes—those we would expect to exhibit high ego involvement (Hardy, 1997) and to succeed with such a profile (Weinberg & Gould, 1999)—we find that elite athletes seem to function better when high ego orientation is tempered with high task orientation (Pensgaard & Roberts, in press). This was also true of young elite soccer players (Lemyre et al., 2000).

Findings such as these have led many sport psychologists to conclude that task involvement better enables participants to manage motivation in the sport experience, especially younger participants. Consequently, they have urged people engaged in pedagogy to promote task involvement as well as to develop mastery-oriented environments to facilitate effective motivational patterns for all participants, not just those who currently excel (e.g., Brunel, 2000; Duda, 1993; Hall & Kerr, 1997; Nicholls, 1989; Roberts, 1984a, 1992a, 1993; Roberts et al., 1997; Theeboom et al., 1995; Treasure & Roberts, 1995). However, some (Hardy, Jones, & Gould, 1996; Harwood et al., 2000; Steinberg, 1996; Swain & Harwood, 1996) have criticized the recommendation that we create task-involving contexts and foster task orientation to optimize motivation. These scholars argue that such recommendations fail to capture the true dynamics of sport, maintaining that for some people, ego involvement is essential for participation.

Hardy et al. (1996) have argued that ego involvement may be essential to successful long-term achievement for sport participants and that we may have to emphasize normative criteria for elite participants. Further, they suggest ego-involving competition provides a source of motivation during practice sessions. Indeed, we are continuing to debate whether we should endorse task-involving criteria or ego-involving criteria for participants in sport, especially elite athletes, if we wish to optimize their motivation (Duda, 1997b, this volume; Hardy, 1997, 1998; Harwood et al., 2000); and no doubt this debate will rage on. Harwood et al. have suggested that we in goal achievement research have simply transferred the research paradigm from education into sport without considering the unique dynamics of the sport experience and that achievement striving in sport is compounded differently than in the classroom. A major argument of Harwood et al. is that there may be an achievement goal important in sport that has not yet been considered. As stated previously, that goal is termed self-referenced ego involvement.

Some have suggested that being high in both task and ego orientation is valuable in the learning process because it provides multiple sources of competence information to the athlete. Swain and Harwood (1996) go so far as to state that an individual with both goal orientations cannot fail to be satisfied. They contend that when one goal is not attained, the second goal can be achieved. Duda (1988) has asserted a similar notion, stating that having both orientations may increase persistence because the person has two sources for determining success.

I agree that being both task and ego oriented toward an activity is intuitively plausible and conceptually consistent with achievement goal theory. I suggest that an experienced athlete can switch between ego and task involvement, more or less at will, and adopt the appropriate motivational strategy for the context—but that this capability is the product of experience. Thus an athlete may be very ego involved in a sport when competing but become very task involved when training in the same sport. Further, an athlete may be ego involved in a competition but then at a point when the outcome is certain, for example, become task involved. We must not forget that task and ego involvement are dynamic constructs, subject to ebb and flow as the athlete plays the game or continues with the activity (see the earlier discussion of conceptions of ability; Roberts, 1992a). I like to argue that the issue is not whether an individual should be task or ego involved but rather when it is more appropriate to be task or ego involved.

The foregoing makes an assumption that the reader should recognize: while you can be task oriented and ego oriented, at any one moment you can only be task involved or ego involved. Personally, I do not think it possible to be in both states of involvement at the same time. You choose to be task or ego involved—your choice determined by your goal orientation or your reading of the criteria of success in the context. Thus if you are both ego and task oriented, both states of involvement are possible, and likely. However, we have not yet addressed the major issue of Harwood et al. (2000), that being ego involved is motivationally compatible with sport competition.

I believe the research is now definitive (for reviews, see, e.g., Biddle, this volume; Duda, 1992, 1993, this volume; Roberts, 1984a, 1992a; Roberts et al., 1997; Treasure, 1993, this volume; Treasure & Roberts, 1995). Clearly, when one is learning physical skills, a mastery climate and being task involved are motivationally conducive to learning. For children, and for all learners in physical activity, task involvement optimizes motivation. However, for athletes who compete at the highest levels of their sport, being ego involved is probably unavoidable. And for an elite athlete, being ego involved may be motivationally appropriate. But being ego involved all the time has motivational implications, too, and is affected by two important dynamic variables: one's perception of relative competence and the perception of task-involving criteria.

If one is high in perceived relative ability, then being ego involved is consistent with demonstrating high motivation. If the feedback from the evaluative assessment of ability is favorable, then the athlete is comfortable with competing and strives to achieve in order to demonstrate superior ability. The athlete may exhibit all the adaptive achievement behaviors of the task-involved athlete. However, the ego-involved athlete is vulnerable to decreasing motivation when perceived ability deteriorates (Dweck & Leggett, 1988). For the ego-involved athlete who suddenly finds him or herself lower in perceived ability through changing competitive levels, for example, or following an injury, or because of the aging process, then motivation is likely to suffer. It is the athlete who is high in ego and low in task orientation, and who is also low in perceived ability, who is the most at risk motivationally (Duda, 1993; Roberts et al., 1997). This is when task involvement becomes desirable.

So where does this leave us? The research is clear: being task involved is beneficial, even for elite athletes high in ego orientation. Pensgaard and Roberts (in press) found that Olympic athletes with coaches who created a mastery climate and thereby fostered task involvement were less stressed and more motivated than athletes with coaches who created an ego-involving atmosphere. In addition, Roberts et al. (1996) found that high-ego-/high-task-oriented individuals exhibited the same achievement beliefs as the high-task-/low-ego-oriented individual. These findings suggest that rather than depressing a high state of ego involvement and replacing it with a high state of task involvement in competitive sport, we should concentrate on enhancing the task orientation of athletes and/or enhancing the task-involving criteria of success in the context to complement ego orientation. It has always been a "tough sell" to convince coaches to depress ego involvement. And for elite athletes, they may well be right. Although most coaches (and several colleagues as identified earlier) believe one *must* be ego involved to achieve competitive success, the research suggests that we should enhance task involvement to moderate the potentially debilitating effects of high ego orientation. Certainly, in the Roberts et al. (1996) study, those most at risk motivationally were the high-ego-/low-task-oriented athletes. Coaches would be well advised to advocate task-involved criteria of success for athletes, whether the athletes are currently high or low in ego orientation.

I think it important here to state the obvious: being task involved is the state that most researchers in physical activity advocate for motivational purposes (e.g., Duda, 1992, 1993; Roberts, 1984a, 1992a, 1993); and this advice is based on research on achievement goals in physical activity, especially sport, that has clearly shown task involvement to be better for optimizing motivation. If in doubt, foster task involvement! Advocating ego involvement alone, under any guise, is not conducive to long-term motivation, even for elite athletes who are secure in their perception of holding high ability. If your beliefs are such that you wish to encourage ego involvement, despite the research evidence, then advocate task involvement too.

Summary

The preceding section has addressed the research in physical activity dealing with achievement goals from a dispositional, or individual-difference, perspective. And the research supports meaningful relationships between personal goals of achievement and cognitive and affective beliefs about involvement in physical activity, leading to a better understanding of motivation in physical activity. Whether one is in a state of task or ego involvement affects one's perceptions concerning competence, the cause of success, the purposes of sport, appropriate achievement strategies, enjoyment and interest, anxiety within the achievement context, motives for participation, adoption of an approach or avoidance ego goal, sportspersonship, and the choice to endorse cheating or not. We also discussed the implications of the orthogonality of achievement goals.

As demonstrated by this avenue of research on achievement goals in the context of physical activity, individual differences in goal orientation are associated with different motivational processes and different achievement behaviors. However, another avenue concerns situational influences (e.g., Biddle, this volume; Goudas & Biddle, 1994b; Papaioannou, 1994, 1995a, 1995b; Roberts et al., 1997; Treasure, this volume; Walling, Duda, & Chi, 1993). This research has examined how the structure of the environment put in place by the coach, teacher, or parent—referred to as the motivational climate (Ames, 1992a, 1992b)—is more or less likely to induce an ego or task state of involvement in the individuals in the context.

Situational Aspects of Achievement Goals

The premise of the research from a situational perspective is that the nature of an individual's experiences and the way he/she interprets these experiences influence the degree to which he/she perceives a mastery and/ or performance climate as salient (Roberts et al., 1997; Treasure, this volume). This is assumed to affect an individual's interpretation of the criteria of success and failure that exist in the context and to affect achievement behavior. People will employ adaptive achievement strategies (namely, to work hard, seek challenging tasks, persist in the face of difficulty) in a climate in which they feel comfortable. For most people, and especially children, this occurs in climates that emphasize mastery (see Biddle, this volume; Roberts et al., 1997; Treasure, this volume).

It is not my task to review this research here; rather I refer you to the thorough reviews for physical education settings (Biddle, this volume) and sport and other physical activity settings (Treasure, this volume). The results reviewed in those chapters demonstrate that perceptions of the motivational climate—whether it has been created by teachers, coaches, or parents—greatly influence motivation and achievement striving by participants, both young and old.

Achievement goal theory states that dispositional goal orientations and perceptions of the climate are two independent dimensions of motivation that interact to affect behavior (Nicholls, 1989), but research to date primarily deals with these as separate constructs. An interactionist approach that looks to combine the two variables promises to provide a more complete understanding of achievement behaviors in sport and physical education (e.g., Duda et al., 1995; Roberts, 1992a; Roberts & Treasure, 1992; Roberts et al., 1997; Treasure, this volume).

As we (Roberts et al., 1997) noted in an earlier review, an interactionist approach integrates dispositions and the motivational climate, and states that dispositional goal orientation is an individual-difference variable that determines the probability of adopting a certain goal of action and displaying a particular behavior pattern—while "situational factors are seen as potentially altering these probabilities" (Dweck & Leggett, 1988, p. 269).

This area of investigation is in its infancy, and we need more research to fully understand the interaction of situational variables and achievement goals on achievement striving. To reiterate a point I made earlier, the climate is conceptually important only because it has a critical impact on personal assessments. Motivation is a process that resides in the person. We need the research to determine the influence of the environment on that process.

Concluding Remarks

In the final analysis, a theory of motivation is good only insofar as it allows us to inform practice to enhance motivation. Research from an achievement goal perspective in physical activity contexts has clearly demonstrated that dispositional achievement goals and perceptions of the criteria of success and failure within the motivational climate pertain to the understanding of motivational processes and have relevance for the ongoing stream of achievement behavior. The chapters by Biddle and Treasure in this book, as well as other sources (e.g., Roberts et al., 1997), provide ample evidence of the usefulness of achievement goal theory to enhance motivation in physical education and sport contexts. Thus achievement goal theory is a powerful, useful, and practical theory. But much remains to be done, and there are important issues to address (see also Duda, this volume).

Is There Conceptual Convergence?

In 1992, I called for research to determine whether we could achieve conceptual convergence in the theories within the social cognitive framework (Roberts, 1992a). I articulated some tasks we needed to do to accomplish this. These tasks have not yet been performed. All of us who work in motivation have continued with research within our own conceptual frameworks. But meanwhile in the research shakedown, two motivation theories have become dominant within the physical activity area. Self-efficacy has become dominant in exercise psychology (see McAuley, Pena, & Jerome, this volume), and achievement goal theory has become dominant in sport psychology. But we may still be moving toward a synthesis of theory and data (Duda, this volume), and may be moving toward more general and comprehensive theories of motivation in physical activity. Certainly achievement goal theory is becoming broader in scope and is being applied successfully to new arenas as documented in this chapter and by other researchers (e.g., Duda, this volume). As this volume illustrates, there are researchers who are very thoughtful about what we need to do to understand motivation and expand our intervention possibilities to enhance motivation. Vallerand (this volume), in particular, has articulated a model of motivation that is comprehensive and multilayered; only with time to test the theory with data in sport will we know how far this theory will influence our understanding. But we still do not seem to be making any serious attempt within sport and exercise psychology to integrate theories and enhance conceptual convergence. As stated earlier, when writers simply put constructs from various theories together without regard to the conceptual constraints inherent in the constructs and create rather thoughtless hypothetical flow diagrams, this is not integrating theories and enhancing conceptual convergence.

All the authors in this book present thoughtful attempts to articulate new avenues of conceptual concern. We also have a broader theory of motivation and amotivation articulated from the viewpoint of self-determination theory (Vallerand, this volume), and Dawson and colleagues (this volume) too attempt to integrate theories in the exercise domain. What we have, then, are researchers endeavoring to expand our conceptual boundaries, which will allow us to move closer to a comprehensive understanding of motivation and achievement behavior. Clearly, much more research is needed, both on the constructs important for understanding motivation and on the association between different constructs, that will allow us to grasp the total dynamic process. Other constructs and other processes may emerge in our ongoing research. Within my own area of concern, the achievement goal framework is not meant to be definitive; it applies only to achievement tasks. However, the variables within the framework are critical ones to study at the present time. Only further research will reveal the true dynamics of the process of motivation, regardless of our starting point.

Measurement of Goal Orientations and the Motivational Climate

Since the last book was published in 1992, we have sharpened our measurement tools to study individual and situational determinants of motivation. Recent research has demonstrated that the POSQ (Roberts & Balague, 1989, 1991; Roberts et al., 1998) and the TEOSQ (Duda & Nicholls, 1992; Duda & Whitehead, 1998) adequately assess task and ego goal orientations in physical education and sport (e.g., Chi & Duda, 1995; Goudas & Biddle, 1994b; Papaioannou, 1994; Treasure & Roberts, 1995; Walling & Duda, 1995; Roberts et al., 1998). But there are criticisms of both the achievement goal approach and the POSQ and the TEOSQ (e.g., Harwood et al., 2000), and only the clash of theory and data within sport will determine whether we need to rethink our approach and measurement technology.

The perception of the motivational climate in sport has been measured by the Perceived Motivational Climate in Sport Questionnaire (PMCSQ; see Duda & Whitehead, 1998), which has been used successfully in sport. However, Duda and colleagues (e.g., Duda & Whitehead, 1998; Newton & Duda, 1993b; Newton, Duda, & Yin, 2000) are developing a second version of the measure that takes into consideration three issues. First, they assume that the climates of mastery and performance are probably composites of a number of dimensions that must be assessed for a fuller understanding of the dynamics of the motivational climate. Second, they are adding a subscale structure to help account for unexplained variance in the original scale. Third, they are assessing various components of the motivational climate to add to our conceptual understanding of the way the goal structure impacts the motivation of athletes (Duda, this volume; Duda & Whitehead, 1998; Newton et al., 2000). Such concern can only help reveal the dynamics of the process of motivation and enhance our understanding of how the climate impacts the components of the goal structure of individuals. I would like to add one caveat here though. If, as a researcher, you are interested in investigating the dynamics of the climate and how various situational aspects might influence the motivational equation, then use the latest version of PMCSQ (e.g., Newton et al., 2000). But if you want to investigate the impact of a mastery versus a performance motivational climate on various indices of achievement, then use the original scale (Seifriz, Duda, & Chi, 1992). It is valid and reliable, simply measures the perception of the individual of the criteria of success and failure inherent in the context, and serves the purpose of the investigator well. We must never forget that parsimony and elegance are important attributes in science.

The Relationship of Goal Orientations to Motivational Climate

We have already discussed this aspect, but there is a need to extend our knowledge of the relationship between perceptions of the motivational climate and dispositional goals. Nicholls (1989) argued that dispositional goal orientations and perceptions of the climate are two dimensions of motivation that interact to affect achievement behavior. However, research to date has dealt with dispositional goal orientations and perceptions of the motivational climate primarily as separate constructs. Dweck and Leggett (1988) suggested how these two dimensions of motivation might interact, but very little empirical research has addressed this critical issue. Is it that achievement goal orientations color the perception of the motivational climate, or does the motivational climate moderate the effect of achievement goal orientations and subsequently affect whether one becomes task or ego involved? To date, the latter has been assumed (e.g., Swain & Harwood, 1996; Treasure & Roberts, 1995; Treasure & Roberts, in press), but it could well be that one's goal orientation predisposes one to attend to certain cues in the environment and to interpret the context in a way that is consistent with this orientation. Only research utilizing an interactionist approach can further our understanding of this dynamic process (see Treasure, this volume).

Should We Always Foster Task Involvement?

As discussed previously, an important assumption of achievement goal theory is that the goals are orthogonal—that task and ego involvement are independent. We also considered how individuals who are high in one orientation and low in the other differ from individuals who are high or low in both. An impressive array of research has now clearly demonstrated that a state of task involvement is conducive to optimizing motivation, for most participants most of the time. Being task involved has been consistently associated with desirable cognitive and affective responses (see earlier discussion). The research shows clearly that if we wish to optimize motivation in physical activity we ought to promote task involvement. It does not matter whether we do it through enhancing socialization experiences so that the individual has a task goal orientation and is naturally task involved (Nicholls, 1989) or through structuring the physical activity context so that it is more task involving (Ames, 1992b; Roberts & Treasure, 1995).

Some have argued that always fostering task-involving criteria may not satisfy all individuals in sport, especially elite athletes (Hardy, 1997; Harwood et al., 2000). It may well be that athletes would benefit from being ego involved. Thus, although encouraging task involvement in achievement tasks optimizes motivation, even with elite athletes, we need not ignore the fact that some athletes do favor and are motivated by ego-involving criteria. The task for the investigator and the practitioner is to determine when task- or ego-involving criteria of success are motivational. In this chapter I suggested, as have others (e.g., Duda, 1993), that the criterion determining whether or not ego involvement is motivational is the perception of ability held by the individual. Ego-involved people with a high perception of ability may well be the ones who seek out ego-involving tasks and are motivated by ego-involving criteria. And these may well be elite athletes whose experience convinces them that they are superior, and they enjoy demonstrating the fact! Only further research will verify this hypothesis. However, the hypothesis raises further questions.

The implications of this hypothesis lead us to speculate about the moderating or mediating role of perceived competence on achievement goals. It may well be that achievement behavior is affected by the interaction of perceived competence and achievement goals. Is it the ego-involved athlete with high perceived ability who demonstrates approach behaviors (e.g., Elliot & Church, 1997; Skaalvik, 1997) to achievement tasks? However, approach behavior may also be exhibited by athletes high in both task and ego orientation (see earlier), or those high in task orientation and low in ego orientation, regardless of perceived ability at the task (Roberts, 1992a). The athlete who exhibits avoidance behavior may be the one who is high in ego involvement and low in perceived ability. Last, the athlete low in both task and ego orientation may be the one who has low motivation in general and exhibits learned helplessness (Dweck, 1999) or be the person who is amotivated (Vallerand, this volume). Future research must determine the veracity of these speculations.

States of Involvement

One of the important tasks for future research and measurement development is to determine ways to measure the states of involvement (see Duda, this volume; Duda & Whitehead, 1998). We use POSQ (Roberts et al., 1998) and TEOSQ (Duda & Whitehead, 1998) to measure whether people are prone to be task or ego involved in achievement tasks in sport. We assume that the scores reflect whether athletes are task or ego involved in the context. Most of us do not measure states of involvement separately. Some have done this (e.g., Hall & Kerr, 1997; Swain & Harwood, 1996; Williams, 1998), but we need to develop specific scales to measure these states (see Duda, this volume).

As Vallerand (this volume) has demonstrated, scales that measure states of involvement allow us to determine, rather than infer, the criteria athletes are using within the context. This has proved useful to Vallerand and colleagues in investigating intrinsic and extrinsic motivation from a self-determined theoretical point of view. Brunel (2000) has used the Vallerand scales to measure the states of involvement of task- and ego-oriented athletes, finding that task-oriented athletes were intrinsically motivated and ego athletes were extrinsically oriented in their achievement behaviors. The results were interesting, and we need more research of this type. However, we also need to develop state-of-involvement scales that are conceptually consistent with achievement goal theory (Duda, this volume).

Summary

In this chapter I have discussed motivation processes and the role of the achievement goal framework in understanding those processes. I also discussed arenas in which the achievement goal approach seems particularly pertinent. It is important to understand the process of motivation and to have a clear notion of what motivation is in order to understand the motivational equation in physical activity. I have also considered some of the constraints to our understanding. Clearly, there is much to do. But the measurement technology is now in place, or is being put in place, to enhance our research on motivational issues and processes in the physical activity realm. The next few years can only add to our knowledge of the dynamics of motivation and achievement behavior in physical activity. Let's get on with it, and be task involved in our quest!

Endnotes

[1] At this juncture, I insert a personal note, mostly to "keep the record straight" about the development of achievement goal theory. I think it important to give recognition for its development to the right people. This note was prompted by my recent reading of a book on achievement goal theory (Dweck, 1999). The book documents the excellent research record of Dweck over the past 20 years. But what irritated me was that the only two references to Nicholls in the book were to two of his empirical studies. His contribution to the development of the theory was not recognized. For those of us who were at Illinois (John Nicholls, Marty Maehr, Carole Dweck, Carol Ames, Russ Ames, Ken Hill, Carol Farmer, and myself) during the fledgling years of achievement goal theory, we know that the story was different; and not giving John Nicholls the recognition he deserves is simply not just.

In 1977, those of us (identified above) in the Institute for Child Behavior and Development at the Children's Research Center of the University of Illinois decided to have a seminar series in the fall to talk about motivation. It was John Nicholls's idea not to have our graduate students present so that we could say "silly things without worrying about what our students will think." Each of us chatted about our research data and ideas and where we were going in the future. It was John Nicholls who introduced us to the concepts that we now recognize as integral to achievement goal theory—ego and task involvement. John presented his ideas about equality of motivation through task involvement and how equality of motivation would optimize the achievement of everyone. The ideas eventually became a publication in *American Psychologist* (Nicholls, 1979). We all had our input and gave our ideas. It was the most stimulating and exciting academic experience of my life. And that seminar series changed the research of all of us and directly led to the first article to introduce the concepts in the form that we would recognize today (Maehr & Nicholls, 1980). We all became achievement goal people in one form or another after that seminar series. All of us who were there have acknowledged the importance of the fall of 1977 in the development of achievement goal theory. We all contributed, but the intellectual leader was clearly John Nicholls.

My own research changed (from attribution work), and I became an achievement goal researcher from that point in time. I immediately set about convincing my own doctoral students to conduct research in the area. Indeed, the first-ever research study in achievement goal theory per se was done by a doctoral student of mine in sport psychology, Martha Ewing (1981). And another of my students at the time did a study using achievement goal concepts in a cultural context (Duda, 1981). Rather than following the pack in psychology, as is usually the case in sport psychology research, sport psychologists were in the forefront in conducting research on achievement goals and still are today.

[2] In 1992 (Roberts, 1992a), I termed these orientations *competitive* and *mastery* orientations. My thinking at the time was to use terms that were sport pertinent and to get away from the term *ego* as it harked back to an older, more deterministic understanding of psychology. However, in my more recent work, I use the terms *task* and *ego* to refer to the two orientations. I agree with Duda (this volume): the use of "task" and "ego" not only conforms with what Nicholls did—there is less confusion if we all use the same terms to refer to the same concepts.

[3] I am grateful for conversations with Brent Walker (2000) for insight into avoidance goals and collaboration in a chapter (Roberts & Walker, in press).

The Development
of Motivation in Children

Mary D. Fry

In various writings, including the first edition of this book, Roberts (e.g., 1984b, 1992b; Roberts & Treasure, 1992) and Duda (1992, 1987) have emphasized the need for more developmental research in sport and exercise psychology, specifically with regard to goal perspective theory. They have made the case that researchers must better understand the cognitive changes in children during the first 13 years of life if they are to offer direction about how to foster an enjoyment of and interest in physical activity that will accompany individuals across the life span.

Understanding the cognitive capabilities youngsters acquire across childhood is critical for adults who are in a position to interact with and provide services for children. An incident in Memphis highlights the importance of this understanding (Bailey, 1994). After interviewing a two-year-old girl, firefighters determined that she was responsible for starting a fire that had burned her family home to the ground and killed her two younger brothers. A local newspaper reporter named Bailey also spoke with the child, and in this interview, the child again responded affirmatively that she had been playing with a cigarette lighter. But the reporter also asked a series of questions such as, "Can you drive a car?" and, "Have you ever climbed a mountain?" to which the child smiled and gave similar positive responses. When Bailey handed the child a cigarette lighter and encouraged her to make a flame, she was unable to. Even with instruction to help the child initiate a flame, she did not grasp the complexity of the device and failed to press the gas lever while simultaneously turning the striker wheel. It appeared to Bailey that this small girl lacked the hand strength and coordination to activate the lighter. In a newspaper column following the incident, Bailey wrote an open letter to the child telling her that someday when she was older it would be important for her to have this additional information to reflect on. Though Bailey concedes the possibility that the child could have started the fire through a chance circumstance, it remains disturbing that trained professional firefighters were willing to take a two-year-old's testimony at face value. This tragic incident illustrates how important it is for adults to understand the cognitive processes of children over time. Though misjudgment of a child's cognitive abilities is not typically associated with a life-and-death situation, the incident highlights the kinds of problems that can occur when adults have limited knowledge of child development but are in a position to interact with children.

In the physical domain, there is tremendous potential harm to children who are exposed to sport and physical education programs structured in a way that does not consider children's varied levels of cognitive development. For example, if teachers and coaches emphasize outcome and normative comparison among young participants, they may be creating a stressful situation that drives some children away from sport and physical activity. Teachers and coaches sometimes justify this approach by suggesting that children prefer highly competitive settings where outcome is emphasized, that winning is most important to children, and that children are bored in other kinds of environments. Considerable evidence argues against such notions (Biddle, this volume; Ewing & Seefeldt, 1989; Gould, Wilson, Tuffey, & Lochbaum, 1993; Smith, 1998; Smoll & Smith, 1998; Treasure, this volume).

The cognitive changes that occur throughout the childhood years are an important area of inquiry. The purpose of this chapter is to present the research in sport and exercise psychology that has utilized a developmental perspective. This research has shed light on the cognitive processes that children experience throughout their development. Researchers have drawn primarily from two developmental theories of motivation, specifically the work of Nicholls (1978, 1984b, 1989) and Harter (1978, 1981a, 1999). Both of these researchers' agendas have focused on the academic domain, but many of their theoretical tenets have recently been examined in relation to physical activity. This chapter includes a summary of Nicholls's and Harter's theories and supporting research but emphasizes research in the physical domain.

Nicholls's Developmental Framework

As a teacher, Nicholls became disillusioned with the educational system and came to feel that the competitive nature of the majority of American schools creates an environment in which a few children thrive and the majority grow discouraged and fail to reach their potential. He believed that each person is born with an innate desire to achieve or to seek challenge and master new tasks. In the introduction to his book, Nicholls (1989) included a picture of a little boy who has for the first time pulled himself up to a standing position. The child's face is lit up with a huge smile, as he is no doubt pleased with his accomplishment. Nicholls observed that this flame of natural desire to achieve in young children, sadly, has often been diminished or even extinguished by the time youngsters reach the adolescent years. Nicholls (1979, 1989) was frustrated with the maladaptive motivational behaviors (e.g., avoidance of challenge, disinterest in learning) that he observed among students, and he became devoted to developing a theory of motivation that would address the question, "How can the motivational levels of all students be maximized?" In essence, the answer he discovered was task involvement. The key to helping individuals reach their potential lies in helping them become task involved so that the focus is always on their own effort and improvement in achievement situations rather than on their normative standing. When individuals are ego involved, they are concerned with their normative ranking. In this volume, Roberts has described the major tenets of Nicholls's goal perspective theory and explained how dispositional tendencies, perceptions of the motivational climate, and cognitive developmental levels determine whether an individual is task or ego involved at a given moment in time. In particular, Roberts summarizes the research on task and ego orientation, while Biddle (this volume) and Treasure (this volume) address the research on motivational climate.

According to Nicholls (1978, 1989), numerous socialization experiences impact youngsters during childhood, and by the approximate age of 12 years they have developed dispositional goal orientations and display a tendency to be high and/or low in task and ego orientation. In this volume

Duda, Biddle, Roberts, and Treasure outline the multiple benefits for individuals who are high in task orientation (e.g., increased effort and enjoyment), as well as the potential risks that accompany a high ego orientation (e.g., higher competitive state anxiety; less favorable sportspersonship attitudes). In Nicholls's view, children are naturally task oriented until they develop a mature understanding of ability, which occurs for most children around the 12th or 13th year. Nicholls maintains that children are incapable of displaying ego involvement until they understand specific concepts that are necessary for an accurate assessment of normative ability. When children develop a mature conception of ability they are able to distinguish effort from ability and luck from ability, and are capable of judging task difficulty in normative terms (see figure 2.1). These three concepts represent the core of the developmental component of Nicholls's goal perspective theory. Nicholls worked extensively to identify the levels children progress through as they come to fully understand these concepts. As children gain this mature conception of ability they become capable of employing a more (i.e., ego orientation) or less differentiated (i.e., task orientation) conception of ability in achievement situations. Thus, children do not inevitably become ego involved as they reach adolescence. Rather, for the first time they are cognitively capable of displaying task or ego involvement.

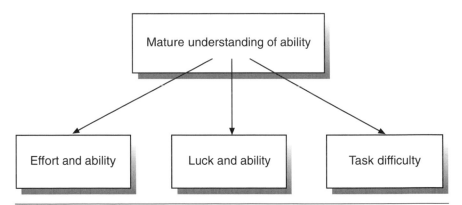

Figure 2.1   The developmental component of Nicholls's theory of achievement motivation.

Effort and Ability

In the case of effort and ability, Nicholls (1978) identified four stages that children progress through as they learn to distinguish the two terms. At Level 1, children do not differentiate effort and ability. The terms are tautological in that high effort is seen as reflecting high ability and vice versa. In other words, at Level 1 children believe that individuals who try hard also perform well and have high ability, and it would be inconsistent in their reasoning to consider an individual who has high ability or who performs well but does not try hard. At Level 2, children begin to recognize differences in ability, yet they still expect high effort to lead to the most favorable outcome regardless of skill level. Thus, they acknowledge that one individual may have more ability than another; but when presented with the scenario in which two individuals with contrasting ability levels exhibit their maximal effort on a task, Level 2 children predict an equal outcome or believe that the one who exerted the most effort initially will excel. Level 3 is a transitional period in which children are beginning to distinguish effort and ability. They show a glimpse of a complete understanding of the terms, yet something in their reasoning reverts back to the logic that characterizes Levels 1 and 2. Finally, at Level 4, children display a complete understanding of effort and ability, realizing that high ability is sometimes negatively correlated with effort; that is, high ability may be reflected when an individual can perform a task with less effort than a peer. At Level 4, children understand that in the present, effort helps maximize performance up to one's level of capacity but that effort cannot assist one in performing beyond one's present capacity.

Nicholls (1978) determined that in order to examine these levels, he must force children to consider a situation in which one child displays less effort but outperforms another child in an activity. He developed videotapes of pairs of children sitting side by side in a classroom working on math problems. One child is working diligently the entire time, while the other child is often distracted, staring into space, playing with an eraser, and so on. After children watched the films they answered a series of questions aimed at tapping into their understanding of effort and ability.

Nicholls used a Piagetian structural developmental analysis (see Nicholls, 1978 for a description of the procedure) to examine the children's responses to the interview questions. He found considerable variability in children's reasoning about effort and ability across age, although the four levels of reasoning were dominant at the following ages: Level 1: 6 to 7 years; Level 2: 7 to 9 years; Level 3: 10 to 11 years; and Level 4: 12 to 13 years.

Recently, Fry and Duda (1997) replicated Nicholls's work in the academic domain and extended it by examining children's understanding of effort and ability in the physical domain. Besides creating films that showed children working on math problems like the ones Nicholls had used, we developed a series of films showing two children throwing beanbags at a target. One child was taking careful aim and demonstrating obvious concentration with each throw, while the other child appeared to display low effort (e.g., did not take careful aim, threw a beanbag between his/her legs, played with a soccer ball, talked to friends). Children aged 5 to 13 years watched two films in each domain (i.e., physical and academic). In one film they were told that the actors had obtained the same score, and in the other film they were given scores indicating that the lazier child had outperformed the hardworking child. We followed Nicholls's interview guide and conducted a similar analysis of the children's responses in order to determine their levels of understanding of effort and ability across domains. The results provided support for our hypothesis that the levels Nicholls identified in the academic domain would appropriately describe children's cognitive development in the physical domain. Results revealed a significant relationship between age and children's levels of understanding of effort and ability in both the academic and physical domains.

In addition to examining within-domain differences, this research explored children's levels of reasoning about effort and ability across domains and yielded similar results, although there was considerable variability. Fifty-six percent of the students were rated at identical levels of understanding of effort and ability in the physical and academic domains. Twenty-seven percent were rated higher in the physical than in the academic domain, while 17% received a higher rating in the academic than in the physical domain. This discrepancy may be attributable to the fact that tasks in the physical domain focus children on process cues to a greater extent than do activities in the academic domain. For example, the films in our study had young actors throwing beanbags at a hula-hoop target and sitting quietly at a desk working on math problems. The viewers would undoubtedly have been privy to a number of performance cues in watching the physical tasks as they could formulate judgments about the actors' level of concentration, effort, throwing technique, and fluidity of the motion. When the actors worked on math problems, viewers were more limited in the performance cues they could observe; their primary source of information was the outcome score on the math assignment. Interestingly, the majority of children exhibited identical levels of reasoning about effort and ability across the physical and academic domains.

A final purpose of the Fry and Duda (1997) study was to examine potential gender differences among children in their ability to reason about effort and ability. Although in an early study Nicholls found that boys displayed Level 4 reasoning about effort and ability in greater proportion than did girls, work with American samples (including the Fry & Duda study) has not revealed gender differences in children's conceptions of effort and ability (Miller, 1986; Nicholls & Miller, 1984b; Nicholls, Patashnick, & Nolan, 1986).

A few other studies have explored the relationship between children's understanding of effort and ability in the physical domain. For example, Whitehead and Smith (1996) conducted a small-scale replication of Nicholls's procedure using films of two college students shooting basketball free throws. In general, results were similar to those of Fry and Duda (1997), providing further support for Nicholls's developmental levels with regard to children's understanding of effort and ability in the physical domain. A strength of the Whitehead and Smith study was that they utilized a sport task (i.e., basketball free-throw shooting) that is perhaps more relevant to older children than the beanbag task used by Fry and Duda (1997). A limitation of their procedure was the enormous differentiation in the number of shooting attempts made by the actors in the basketball scenarios; this imbalance led some participants to focus on the number of shots attempted rather than the real issues related to participants' effort and ability levels. Even though Whitehead and Smith (1996) had to exclude data from several participants because of this, their study provides nice support for Nicholls's developmental levels.

In a recent study including 4th, 8th, and 11th graders, Xiang and Lee (1998) linked the development of youngsters' conceptions of effort and ability to their formulation of goal orientations. As compared to participants who demonstrated an undifferentiated or partially differentiated view of effort and ability, the youngsters who demonstrated a mature conception of effort and ability were higher in ego orientation and indicated a preference for achieving success via high ability and low effort (i.e., rather than high effort and low ability). Xiang and Lee have been the first to experiment with measuring conceptions of effort and ability using written scenarios rather than visual aids (e.g., videos, pictures). Their study is unique, too, in that they included older participants (i.e., 11th graders) whereas the majority of research has been limited to youngsters aged 14 years and younger. Nicholls reported that most children demonstrate a mature conception of ability by the time they reach adolescence, so it is interesting to note that only 50% of the 11th graders in Xiang and Lee's study reflected a mature conception of effort and ability. The findings suggest that it may be important in future work to consider a broader range of ages among participants in order to examine the ongoing development of conceptions of ability.

Though not directly testing Nicholls's theory, Watkins and Montgomery (1989) utilized a qualitative approach to explore children's and adolescents' conceptions of athletic excellence. They interviewed youngsters in 3rd, 6th, 9th, and 12th grades to ascertain their views about the characteristics of elite athletes. It is not surprising that when participants were asked to identify sources of athletic excellence, high effort was the most frequent response put forward by 3rd through 9th graders. Twelfth graders were more likely to recognize the complex aspects of athletic ability, as their responses reflected more balanced frequency counts in the percentages that identified natural ability, social facilitation, and emotions/attitudes as important sources of information that help to identify excellent athletes. The results of this study support Nicholls's notion that as children mature they better understand the complicated relationship among effort, ability, and performance.

In summary, the developmental component of children's reasoning about effort and ability has begun to receive attention in the physical domain, but there is still much to learn about this cognitive process. Future research has much to offer in terms of describing the developmental processes children experience as they learn to distinguish these important concepts.

Luck and Ability

The second component of Nicholls's developmental framework concerns children's understanding of luck and ability. Nicholls and Miller (1985) found that youngsters do not fully comprehend the concept of luck until they reach adolescence. Piaget and Inhelder (1975) described the advanced reasoning required for an understanding of the concept of chance. They noted, for example, that an individual cannot comprehend the significance of a disaster such as a hurricane strike in a particular area without having an awareness of the low odds that such an event will happen. Because children have limited life experiences, it is not surprising that they may lack the capacity to fully comprehend the element of chance in the occurrence of such events.

Nicholls and Miller (1985) developed a research design for examining children's understanding of luck and ability. Specifically, they designed two versions of a task—one in which successful performance required skill and the other in which success required luck. The task involved a card game in which one card served as a standard and the objective was to correctly identify the card that matched the standard. After participants were familiarized with the tasks, they were told that two children had given incorrect responses, one on the luck task and the other on the skill task. Participants were then asked a series of questions.

Nicholls and Miller (1985) identified four levels of reasoning that children progress through as they develop a mature understanding of luck and ability. At Level 1, children made no distinction between the activities requiring luck and those requiring skill. Further, they expected effort to enhance performance equally on tasks that require luck and those requiring skill. At Level 2, children recognized that performing well in a game that involves luck is more difficult than it is in one that requires skill. However, they still believed that increasing effort would positively impact performance on both tasks, although more so on the skill activity. Level 3 is a transitional period in which children demonstrated an understanding of luck and ability, yet their reasoning lacked consistency throughout the interview. Though they showed a glimpse of Level 4 understanding, at some point in the interview they reverted to reasoning characteristic of Level 1 and/or Level 2. At Level 4, children clearly distinguished luck and ability and recognized that effort would not influence outcomes on tasks in which the outcome was determined by luck. Their reasoning at Level 4 was consistent throughout the interview.

On the basis of the children's responses, Nicholls and Miller (1985) found the following developmental trends by age for children's levels of understanding of luck and ability: Levels 1 and 2—kindergarten and second grade; Level 3—fourth and sixth grades; Level 4—eighth grade. The results provide support for the complexity of the concept of luck, as the majority of children did not grasp this concept until they reached the eighth grade.

The tasks Nicholls and Miller (1985) used were cleverly designed in that the students indicated the degree to which they felt that effort would influence the skill outcome but did not need to use the terms "luck" and "chance" to convey their understanding of the concept. This careful design of the tasks and the interview guide provided an important source of validity.

In addition to identifying the levels of children's understanding of luck and ability, Nicholls and Miller (1985) linked these levels to children's behavioral responses. For example, when participating in activities in which the outcome was based on either skill or luck, younger children spent more time on the luck tasks and older children spent a greater proportion of the time on the skill tasks. In addition, children were provided scenarios describing youngsters who were successful and unsuccessful on the tasks. Next, the children were asked to speculate on the reasons for these youngsters' outcomes. Further, when asked for attributions of children who performed well in either skill or luck tasks, younger children gave attributions of effort and ability on both types of tasks. In contrast, older children attributed outcomes on skill tasks to effort or ability while attributing luck outcomes to chance or guessing.

Interestingly, Nicholls (1989) noted that the differentiation of luck and ability has positive behavioral implications for children. That is, spending less time trying to accomplish tasks based on chance could protect a child's sense of competence. Exerting high effort on tasks that are not likely to result in success may lead to frustration for children.

Recently I replicated Nicholls and Miller's work (1985) in a study examining children's understanding of luck and ability in the physical domain

(Fry, 2000a). I developed a luck and a skill version of a beanbag tossing game. In the skill version of the game, a child would randomly select from a deck one of four types of cards that had neon-colored stars (i.e., either pink, orange, yellow, green) on them. A line of four black baskets, each bearing a colored star, stood in front of the child. After selecting the card, the child was to attempt to toss a beanbag into the basket that had the star corresponding in color to the one on the child's card. If the beanbag went into the correct basket, a point was scored. In the luck version of the game, a child tossed a beanbag into one of the baskets and then drew a card to see whether the color of the star on the basket matched the color of the star on the card. If so, the child would receive a point. After the format of the game was explained to study participants, they were told of two children who had played the respective games. Max (Beth for the female participants) had attempted to score a point on the luck game but had failed, and Dale (Peggy for the female participants) had tried to score a point on the skill game but was unsuccessful. I employed a slightly adapted version of the interview questions that Nicholls and Miller (1983) used and conducted a Piagetian structural analysis of the children's responses; the results provided further support for the levels of understanding of luck and ability that Nicholls and Miller identified (Piaget, 1952). A strong positive relationship between age and children's levels of understanding of luck and ability was revealed. Specifically, the following age trends emerged: Level 1—ages 5 to 6 years; Level 2—ages 7 to 11 years; Level 3—ages 9 to 11 years; and Level 4—ages 12 to 13 years. Interesting to note was the finding that only 69% of the 13-year-olds reflected a mature conception of luck and ability, which provides additional support for the views of Piaget and Inhelder (1975).

In addition to considering children's levels of understanding of luck and ability, we examined their responses to the luck and skill games. For example, participants were given the opportunity to play one or both games (i.e., their preference) for 5 min after they were interviewed, and the amount of time they spent on each game was secretly monitored. After playing the games, children were asked which game they thought was more fun and which game they would choose to play on another day if they were allowed to choose only one. Nicholls (1989) indicated that as children obtain a mature understanding of luck and ability, they will demonstrate a preference for skill, rather than luck, activities, as skill activities are perceived to be more interesting and challenging. Such was the case for the participants in the study. The majority of children who demonstrated a mature understanding of luck and ability (i.e., were rated at Level 4) spent more time on the skill game, indicated that the skill game was more fun (e.g., challenging), and reported that if they were to play one of the games on another day they would prefer the skill game. It appears that children's behaviors and attitudes are impacted by their level of understanding of luck and ability. To my knowledge, presently this is the only study in the physical domain that has examined Nicholls's developmental component focusing on children's reasoning about luck and ability.

Task Difficulty

The third aspect of the developmental component of Nicholls's theory of achievement motivation concerns children's gaining an understanding of normative task difficulty. Nicholls (1989) identified three levels that children progress through as they acquire this understanding. He refers to Level 1 as an egocentric period in which a child judges the difficulty of an activity based on his/her own subjective probability for successful performance. At Level 2, children are able to process objective information and can judge task difficulty on a spectrum from more to less difficult. For example, children at Level 2 comprehend that a puzzle with 500 pieces would be more difficult to complete than a puzzle with only 50 pieces. At Level 3, children are able to process normative difficulty cues and understand that tasks at which few people are successful represent a high level of difficulty. Further, children recognize that adequately judging the difficulty of a task requires some degree of normative information.

In several studies, Nicholls (1978, 1980b; Nicholls & Miller, 1983) documented the progression of these three levels of understanding of task difficulty with regard to academic tasks. Perhaps the most revealing of the three studies is the one in which Nicholls and Miller (1983) employed a cross-sectional and longitudinal design. Specifically, they tested two groups of children (i.e., aged approximately 6 and 7.5 years, respectively) to determine their understanding of task difficulty on two occasions separated by nine months. Children were shown a variety of arrays (e.g., pictures, puzzles) reflecting objective and normative information and were then interviewed about their understanding of the arrays.

On the basis of a structural developmental analysis of the interview responses, children's levels of understanding of task difficulty were determined. Specifically, children's responses to the question about which puzzle only very smart children could do provided the critical information for categorizing the responses. Children were identified at Level 1 (i.e., egocentric) if they were unable to identify the puzzle with the most pieces as the most difficult. In contrast, youngsters were categorized at Level 2 (i.e., objective information) if they indicated that the puzzle with the most pieces was the most difficult and would require the greatest ability to successfully complete. Finally, participants were rated at Level 3 (i.e., normative) if they identified the puzzle that the fewest children could complete as the most difficult. In each case the children explained their reasoning, thus providing support for their responses.

In terms of the cross-sectional analyses, Nicholls and Miller (1983) found strong support for the developmental progression of the levels. That is, children who were rated at Level 2 demonstrated an understanding of objective information but failed to process the normative cues. However, children who were able to interpret the normative cues were also able to process the objective information. Thus, it was unusual to find a child who understood the normative array but did not comprehend the objective arrays.

Of interest was the greater variation identified in the longitudinal data. Although not prevalent, there were a few cases of children who demonstrated a lower level of understanding of task difficulty at Time 2 than they had demonstrated at Time 1 nine months previously. This finding suggests that there may be a transitional period in which children display some variability in their cognitive processes as they begin to grasp the concepts related to ability and achievement. Thus it may not be unusual for a child to demonstrate understanding at a particular level of reasoning that is not maintained over a period of time. With previous cross-sectional work, Nicholls (1978) had noted the transitional nature of some children's responses within or across interviews conducted over short periods. However, his and Miller's (1983) longitudinal examination of children's understanding of task difficulty probably best reflects the true transitional nature of these developmental processes.

Nicholls and Miller (1983) also predicted that children's preferences for difficulty levels would be associated with their levels of understanding of task difficulty. Specifically, there was support for the prediction that children rated at Level 2 would indicate a preference for objectively difficult puzzles because they understood that the more difficult the puzzle was, the greater would be the challenge to succeed. However, since these children did not comprehend the normative array, their preference for a normatively based puzzle was not hypothesized to be associated with their Level 2 understanding of task difficulty, and no significant relationship emerged.

For children rated at Level 3 in their understanding of task difficulty, their preferences for both normative and objective tasks were highly correlated with their developmental levels, as Nicholls and Miller (1983) had predicted. This link is to be expected because children at Level 3 are aware of the value placed on successful completion of tasks that are more difficult (i.e., either objectively or normatively). In summary, across these studies Nicholls (1978, 1980b; Nicholls & Miller, 1983) was able to identify the link between children's understanding of normative task difficulty and their recognition that greater value derives from successful completion of difficult tasks.

I (Fry, 2000b) recently examined children's understanding of task difficulty in the physical domain by utilizing Nicholls's approach in previous studies. Children ranging in age from 5 to 13 years were shown a variety of arrays (e.g., objective and normative) that highlighted physical activities (e.g., throwing beanbags at targets; sports). After the children viewed and demonstrated an understanding of each array, they answered the following questions: "Which one (i.e., target, game) could only the children who are very skilled at games and sports hit/play?"; "Which one would you have to be very skilled to hit/play?"; "If you could choose one, which one would you want to aim for/play?"

A structural developmental analysis was employed to determine children's levels of understanding of task difficulty. The analysis revealed that the levels Nicholls identified in the academic domain were equally descriptive of and relevant to understanding children's cognitive conceptions in the physical domain. There was a strong significant and positive relationship between age and children's levels of understanding of task difficulty.

Further analysis of the responses of the children (i.e., those rated at Level 3) to the two items on the normative array provided interesting results. The questions tapped into the students' perceptions of the game they felt they would have to be very skilled to play and the game they would attempt to play if given the opportunity. Based on their responses to the two questions, children were assigned to one of three groups. Group 1 (29%) consisted of those children who indicated a preference for an easier task than what they believed they were capable of performing. Children in Group 2 (35%) indicated their preference for a moderately challenging task, one that adequately matched their perceptions of the game they could successfully play. Group 3 (36%) included children who responded that they believed they could play a particular game but if given the opportunity would prefer to tackle an even more challenging game. The results suggest that children in Group 1 may be displaying a maladaptive motivational response in that they indicate a preference for easy tasks that would not challenge their current capabilities. The responses of these children suggested that some of them were very conscious of the ramifications of performing poorly, as they mentioned the embarrassment they would experience with an unsuccessful attempt to play the game. Nicholls suggested that as children develop a mature understanding of ability they may be at risk of engaging in such maladaptive behaviors. This finding is of concern because children are not likely to maximize their potential if they avoid challenge when possible.

This study (Fry, 2000b) was a first attempt to investigate the task difficulty component of Nicholls's developmental framework in the physical domain. It demonstrates that continued probing and description of this component should be a valuable and relevant area for future research.

Future Research Directions

A number of future directions seem apparent with regard to further examination of the developmental aspect of Nicholls's theory of achievement motivation. First, research should continue to explore children's development of a mature conception of ability and the link to a display of subsequent maladaptive motivational responses. Miller (1986), for example, observed that only children who displayed a mature understanding of effort and ability were prone to reduce effort and persistence at a task after experiencing repeated failure. Other research has suggested that as children obtain a mature understanding of ability they are less inclined to ask the teacher for help, as they realize they may give the appearance of being less intelligent than others (Ames, 1983). In addition, such children report lower intrinsic interest in their schoolwork, are more likely to choose easier tasks when provided the opportunity, and show a greater interest in social comparison (Boggiano & Ruble, 1986; Butler, 1987; Nicholls, 1980b). According to Nicholls (1989), such relationships are to be expected:

> And if we doubt our ability we will—when we construe ability as capacity—have less faith in the power of effort to raise our performance relative to that of others. All of this adds up to the conclusion that if we feel we lack ability, even though we might be able to learn, we will see our best as not good enough and this deficiency will be experienced as more fundamental than it was before we construed ability as capacity. This feeling would make for our devaluing activities that might reveal our incompetence and lead to attempts to avoid such activities. (p. 60)

Though Nicholls presents a compelling argument for the association between a mature conception of ability and maladaptive responses, the supporting evidence for this relationship could be much stronger, particularly in the physical domain. Thus, in addition to the individual components of Nicholls's developmental framework, an important task for the future will be to explore the ramifications for children as they develop a mature conception of ability.

Another beneficial avenue for further inquiry involves a complete replication of Nicholls's 1978 study, in which he examined two of the three developmental components (i.e., effort and ability; task difficulty) with the same children in one large project. He also assessed children's ability to accurately judge their competence. This comprehensive project allowed him to compare and contrast the time periods at which children, both individually and as a group, displayed varying levels of reasoning about ability. The time commitment for that data collection is rather remarkable, as it involved multiple sessions with each of the nearly 150 participants. However, the project represents a landmark study that has provided a meaningful and significant contribution to the literature in achievement motivation.

As in the majority of research areas in sport and exercise psychology, there is much to learn from studies that utilize a longitudinal design, and this is particularly true in the case of children's cognitive development in the physical domain. Though there has been minimal longitudinal research up to now, interesting findings emerged when Nicholls and Miller (1983) employed a longitudinal design in examining children's understanding of task difficulty. Their results suggest that the predominant use of cross-sectional designs may limit the contribution of developmental research to investigators' understanding of the cognitive processes youngsters experience throughout the childhood years.

A final important avenue for future research in the physical domain involves employing a qualitative approach to examine how teachers structure and create a particular motivational atmosphere in their classrooms. Several years before his death, Nicholls became convinced that a meaningful extension of his research required him to spend time in the public schools to observe, learn from, and assist teachers in implementing the tenets of his theoretical framework in schools. He describes the experiences of spending a year in the classroom with an elementary teacher (Sue Hazzard) and her class in *Education as an adventure: Lessons from the second grade* (Nicholls & Hazzard, 1993). The relationship between Nicholls and Hazzard was collaborative: their aim was to create a motivational climate within the classroom that empowered students by giving them a voice, focusing them on their effort and improvement as a gauge of success, and building relationships within the classroom that emphasized mutual respect and understanding. This qualitative account of Nicholls and Hazzard's experiences throughout the year is a rich source of information for both teachers and researchers interested in maximizing children's interest in and commitment to learning.

A collection of narratives of other teachers who have attempted collaborative efforts with their students was presented by Nicholls and Thorkildsen (1995). In this edited volume, a group of teachers describe their frustrations and continuous challenges in trying to establish a classroom atmosphere in which students felt comfortable, respected, and optimally motivated to learn.

Though their stories are ongoing and do not imply easy answers to difficult situations, the narratives are refreshing in that the teachers are genuinely striving to draw from research, as well as their own experiences in the classroom, to better understand how to maximize the potential of their students.

In the physical domain, such a qualitative approach offers an important avenue for future research that has not yet been employed. A description of collaborative efforts among researchers in sport psychology, coaches and physical education teachers, and athletes and students would make a tremendous contribution to the literature. Though it was not qualitative, Taylor's (1997) study may provide a starting point for subsequent qualitative work in the physical domain. Taylor surveyed physical education teachers and researchers in sport and exercise psychology to determine their views about the effectiveness of a number of strategies that are sometimes employed to foster motivation among students who demonstrate low interest in achievement. He found that in general, teachers and researchers had very similar views about the effectiveness and ineffectiveness of particular strategies, but also a few significant differences. For example, researchers rated getting to know students and giving them choices as significantly more effective strategies for optimizing motivation than did the physical education teachers. Research designs such as this can help bridge the gap between theory and practice and set the stage for meaningful discussion among researchers and teachers about motivation.

Challenges of Employing Nicholls's Developmental Framework in the Physical Domain

The number of studies in the physical domain that have employed Nicholls's developmental framework is relatively small. This is unfortunate because Nicholls's theory appears to be highly relevant for an understanding of the cognitive processes that impact children's motivational responses in physical activity settings. There may be several reasons why the developmental component of Nicholls's theory has received so little attention in the physical domain. To begin with, the nature of Nicholls's research questions requires study designs that are very time intensive to conduct. In addition, with use of a developmental approach it is typically preferable to include children from the age of five years to the ages of those approaching or in early adolescence. The qualitative nature of the research requires that each participant be interviewed individually. Such a data collection can easily require three to six weeks (and often longer) of full-time work on the part of the interviewer, followed by rigorous data analyses that may include transcription of interviews. Though the time-intensive nature of such research should not deter interest, the reality may be that it does prevent some individuals from pursuing the area.

Another challenge of employing Nicholls's developmental theory is the difficulty of recruiting a random sample of children in the schools. Twenty years ago Nicholls was not under the same stringent human subjects requirements that are in place today. For example, the schools allowed him to include all students in his studies, and Nicholls did not need to obtain parental consent. While the new regulations are understandable, they do make it challenging to obtain random samples of youngsters.

The complexity of Nicholls's developmental framework may also explain why few researchers have pursued work in this area. Nicholls's theory is elaborate and comprehensive, and some people have difficulty reading and absorbing his work (Duda, 1997b). This may be a deterrent to some, who may in turn pursue other areas within sport psychology. For those researchers who do take an interest in his work, the challenge is in designing carefully thought-out studies that explore the issues relevant to Nicholls's theory. As has become clear in the literature in recent years, there have been some misunderstandings/misconceptions when it comes to interpreting Nicholls's theoretical tenets (e.g., Duda, 1997b, this volume; Duda & Whitehead, 1998; Roberts, this volume).

Whatever the reasons for the minimal attention that has been afforded Nicholls's developmental component, it is clear that Nicholls laid the groundwork for a rich area of inquiry, the results of which have tremendous potential to add to the sport psychology literature base with regard to maximizing children's experiences in physical activity settings.

Harter's Developmental Model

Another developmental theory that has received significant attention in the physical domain is that of Susan Harter (1978, 1981a, 1999). This section deals with Harter's theory and the supporting research.

Harter and her colleagues have devoted considerable effort to examining the antecedents and correlates of children's motivational orientations (see Harter, 1999, for a review). Early on, Harter was intrigued by White's notion of an internal motive that compels individuals to strive for competence (White, 1959, 1963), but she felt that his global approach to motivation was problematic in that it was difficult to examine theoretically and did not consider constructs (e.g., perceptions of control and competence) that might be specific to a particular domain (e.g., physical, academic). In an early paper, Harter (1978) commended White for bringing the topic of motivation to the forefront of psychology and for challenging scholars and researchers to think critically about it. She proceeded to propose refinements and extensions to White's model of effectance motivation that addressed her major concerns. In addition to proposing that effectance motivation be considered via potential domain-specific components rather than as a global construct, she suggested that extrinsic, not just intrinsic, motivational patterns should be examined; that individuals' responses to failure and not only success experiences should be considered; and that cognitive constructs such as perceived competence (i.e., self-esteem) and perceptions of control should receive thoughtful attention in future research. Harter's personal research agenda has addressed these concerns over the past 20 years.

Perceptions of Competence and Control

In a landmark study, Harter and Connell (1984) gathered data on third- to eighth-grade students in order to test a number of models to determine which model best described the relationship between children's motivational orientation (i.e., intrinsic vs. extrinsic) and perceptions of competence and control, and achievement in the academic domain. The study included seven variables that the investigators speculated were of primary importance: achievement (i.e., standardized test scores), unknown control (i.e., children's perceptions that they could not identify the causes of their successes/failures), internal control (i.e., children's perceptions that they determined the cause of their achievement outcomes), autonomous judgment (i.e., children's perceptions that they could adequately judge their performance and the appropriateness of actions without feedback from the teacher), intrinsic motivation (children's levels of curiosity and preference for challenge and mastery), competence evaluation (children's judgments of their competence), and competence affect (children's feelings about their perceived competence).

Of four models tested, one emerged as the strongest for both elementary and junior high students. On the basis of structural equation modeling analyses, the model focusing on cognitive processes showed the strongest fit to the data. Harter and Connell's (1984) results revealed both similarities and differences among the elementary and junior high students. For children at the elementary age, perceptions that they had little understanding about the causes of success and failure (i.e., unknown control) were negatively related to achievement. In turn, achievement was a positive predictor of children's perceptions of competence, which were positively correlated with their affective responses to their perceptions of competence. These feelings were then positively and significantly associated with their autonomous judgment (children employ internal criteria for judging success and feel comfortable choosing appropriate tasks in the classroom without the aid of the teacher) and intrinsic motivational orientation (children display curiosity and a desire for challenge and mastery).

The findings suggest that for children, perceptions of control are a critical factor in determining their achievement patterns. Thus, children are not likely to display high achievement if they perceive that they have little control over their success/failure outcomes in the academic domain. In contrast, children who reflected high levels of achievement displayed high perceptions of competence and positive feelings about their competence levels, which had strong links to intrinsic motivation. Thus, perceptions of competence and affective responses to one's competence appear to be important factors impacting children's motivational responses.

The junior high students revealed a model similar to that derived from the elementary students, yet it was more complex in that it showed a number of additional significant paths. Specifically, unknown control was linked to low achievement and low perceptions of internal control, but it was also negatively associated with perceptions of competence, competence affect, and autonomous judgment. As the authors (Harter & Connell, 1984) indicated, the results showed that "the child who is in the know thinks he/she is competent, feels good about this competence, and is inclined to make independent judgments in the classroom" (p. 239). Harter's work has served to highlight the importance of considering children's perceptions of control over achievement outcomes. In addition, perceptions of competence have proved to be a critical factor in her model.

Harter and Connell's (1984) results reveal a chain of events whereby children's perceptions that they have control over their successes and failures are positively associated with normative achievement, which is positively correlated with their perceptions of competence—which are thus positively linked to their levels of intrinsic motivation. While the results appear to offer an accurate description of achievement settings, such a model is problematic in practical terms because it provides less insight to coaches and teachers who are striving to maximize the motivational levels of all youngsters (i.e., those with high and low perceptions of ability). Specifically, when perceptions of competence are considered in normative terms, it is inevitable that 50% of children will fall below the median score. In other words, it is impossible for all children to have high perceptions of normative ability.

Causes of Self-Esteem

From a theoretical viewpoint, Harter's (1978, 1981a) contributions to understanding the development of competence motivation among children have been significant, but perhaps her more recent research avenues represent an even more interesting and notable area of inquiry. In the last few years Harter and her colleagues (1987, 1990, 1993, 1999; Harter & Marold, 1991; Harter, Marold, Whitesell, & Cobbs, 1996; Harter, Waters, & Whitesell, 1998; Harter, Waters, Whitesell, & Kastelic, 1998; Harter, Whitesell, & Junkin, 1998) have branched out to examine the causes and consequences of self-esteem among children and adolescents. She (Harter, 1993) defines self-esteem, or self-worth, as "the level of global regard that one has for the self as a person . . ." (p. 88). She has drawn primarily from two theorists, James (1892) and Cooley (1902), in developing her research questions. According to James, self-esteem is determined by the combination of a person's perceptions of competence in a particular domain and the importance to the individual of competence in that domain. Thus, if a person excels in the sport arena and he/she places high value on such competence, then it is predicted that the individual will display high self-esteem. In contrast, if the individual desires to excel in athletics but falls short of that aspiration, it is predicted that he/she will experience low self-esteem. Cooley, on the other hand, saw self-esteem as a social construct that developed as an individual sought and assessed the opinions of others with regard to the self. Harter (1999) has presented evidence for both of these approaches to understanding self-esteem. When examining James's (1892) views, she found that the greater the discrepancy between a youngster's perceptions of competence in a domain and the importance the youngster places on competence in that domain, the lower the youngster's self-worth.

It is interesting to note along these lines that a discrepancy model is not predictive for younger children. According to Harter (1993), "Competence does not appear to be as critical to young children's self-esteem, nor are young children cognitively able to compare two concepts such as importance ratings and self-evaluations simultaneously" (p. 92). This proposal is in line with Nicholls's findings that children are incapable of understanding the concept of ability until they reach adolescence (Nicholls, 1989).

In addition to providing support for James's model (i.e., the relationship between perceptions of competence and self-esteem), Harter's (1993) results also revealed support for Cooley's (1902) model of self-esteem. In fact, across a number of studies Harter has found correlations of .50 to .65 for the relationship between adolescents' levels of self-esteem and their perceptions of support from significant others (i.e., parents, teachers, classmates, and close friends). Nicholls's (1989) theory supports Harter's findings in that he holds that the motivational climate established by significant others is important in fostering motivation. Interestingly, the combination of James's formulation (importance of a specific domain) and Cooley's (perceptions of support from significant others) results in the most powerful prediction of self-esteem as reported by adolescents.

Research on Harter's Developmental Model in the Physical Domain

Horn and her colleagues have led the way in exploring Harter's developmental competence motivation framework in the physical domain (Horn, Glen, & Wentzell, 1993; Horn & Hasbrook, 1986, 1987; Horn & Weiss, 1991; Weiss, Ebbeck, & Horn, 1997; Weiss & Horn, 1990). They have examined children's accuracy in assessing their physical competence as well as the sources of information children use to judge their ability.

Horn and Hasbrook (1986) initiated a line of research by developing the Sport Competence Information Scale to tap into the sources of information children use to judge their physical competence. Children in three age groups (i.e., 8-9, 10-11, and 12-14 years) participating in a soccer camp completed the measure. Twelve information sources included in the survey were reduced to six through factor analysis and consisted of the following: social comparison, social evaluation I (i.e., coaches, peers), social evaluation II (i.e., parents, spectators), internal information, game outcome, and affect (e.g., enjoyment of the sport). Results of MANOVA revealed that younger children relied more heavily on parent/spectator evaluation and game outcome in judging their success than did the older athletes. Further, the older athletes rated social comparison as a more important source of information than did the younger groups. These results are consistent with the developmental psychology literature suggesting that as children mature they rely more heavily on their peers for information about their competence than do young children. Along these lines, recent investigators have explored the meaning that friendship has for children in the physical domain (Weiss & Smith, 1999; Weiss, Smith, & Theeboom, 1997). The role that peers play in the sport socialization process will likely be an important area for future inquiry.

In a follow-up to their 1986 study, Horn and Hasbrook (1987) again sampled young soccer players to determine whether particular psychological characteristics (e.g., perceived competence, perceived performance control) were linked to the sources of information they used to judge their competence. Results revealed that children who reported external perceptions of control with regard to the causes of their successes and failures indicated a preference for external sources of information. In contrast, children who displayed internal perceptions of control and high perceptions of competence indicated a preference for internal sources of information in judging their physical ability. This study supports Harter's findings that perceptions of competence and locus of control are important factors impacting children's motivational responses.

Horn and Weiss (1991) continued this line of research by evaluating the degree to which children are able to accurately assess their physical ability in normative terms. Using youngsters' responses to Harter's Perceived Competence Scale for Children (PCSC) and teachers' ratings of their students' physical competence, the authors found a significant relationship between children's age and their accuracy in judging their normative ability. In addition, the study provided further support for the idea that younger children rely on feedback from significant adults as an important source of information in judging their ability, while older children value peer comparison as a more important source of information than their younger counterparts. Further, on the basis of the youngsters' responses and the teacher's rankings, the children were classified as underestimators, accurate estimators, or overestimators of their normative ability. Results revealed that children's accuracy levels in judging their physical competence were associated with their preferences for information sources used to judge their ability. Overestimators rated self-comparison as a more important source of information for judging their ability than did the underestimators. In contrast, under- and accurate estimators rated peer comparison/evaluation as a more important source of information.

Two studies have extended Horn and Weiss's (1991) results with older adolescents. McKiddie and Maynard (1997) surveyed British 7th- and 10th-grade physical education students and found that 10th graders were more accurate in judging their physical ability than were 7th graders. Further, regardless of age, students who more accurately judged their physical competence indicated that they used peer comparison and evaluation as important sources of information. Horn, Glenn, and Wentzell (1993) reported that the sources of information used by 14- to 18-year-old male and female high school athletes to judge their competence varied by age and gender. Specifically, older athletes (11th-12th graders) were more likely to judge their sport ability based on self-comparison/internal and enjoyment information, while the younger athletes (9th-10th graders) depended more on feedback from peers. In terms of gender, males relied more heavily than females on competitive outcome and information about ease of learning to judge their physical ability, and females utilized more self-comparison/internal information and evaluation from peers to judge their ability than did males.

Weiss and Horn (1990) extended their research agenda by examining the relationship between children's accuracy estimates of their physical competence and their achievement-related characteristics. Children 8 to 13 years of age who were attending a summer sport camp completed Harter's PCSC, while the camp instructors rated each child's normative standing among peers in terms of his/her physical competence. Results revealed that children who underestimated their physical competence showed a less adaptive pattern of motivational responses, which was more severe for females (e.g., preferred less-challenging tasks) than males (e.g., perceived that they did not know the causes of their success/failure outcomes).

Most recently, Weiss, Ebbeck, and Horn (1997) examined the relationship between age, personal characteristics (children's perceptions of physical competence), general self-esteem, competitive trait anxiety, and the sources of information children use to judge their physical competency. Using a cluster analysis technique, they found that the children showed four distinct profiles. The third cluster represented 45% of the children and reflected perhaps the most adaptive profile, in that the children had higher scores on physical competence and self-esteem, had moderate scores on competitive trait anxiety, and indicated a preference for self-referenced and parental evaluation criteria. Children in the other three clusters all reported lower physical competence, which was accompanied by less-desirable characteristics such as high competitive trait anxiety, low self-esteem, and a preference for social comparison/evaluation criteria in judging their competence.

In summary, Horn, Weiss, and their colleagues have made a significant contribution to the developmental literature in sport and exercise psychology. In fact, without their work, the body of developmental sport psychology literature would be meager. Their research has highlighted the developmental processes children experience as they develop perceptions of ability and gain the cognitive capacity necessary to interpret information from a variety of sources to evaluate their abilities. This research has direct implications for professionals working with children and adolescents: coaches and teachers need to be cognizant that children become increasingly more sophisticated in their ability to interpret information, not only from their parents, but also from peers, teachers, and coaches, that will affect their motivational responses in physical activity settings. In addition, this research should serve to remind professionals that children who perceive that they are low skilled and have little control over their sport performances are at risk of demonstrating maladaptive responses, including a preference for low challenges, and higher anxiety.

Future Research Directions

Harter's research (1999) over the last decade suggests a number of valuable avenues for future inquiry in sport and exercise psychology, and I will note three of these areas. First, Harter has published interesting work on youngsters' global self-worth as it relates to relationships they have with significant others (e.g., parents, peers). Second, Harter has taken a close look at how youngsters develop the emotions of shame and pride in particular situations; and third, she has thoughtfully examined gender differences in youngsters' global and domain-specific self-worth.

In terms of relational self-worth, Harter, Waters, and Whitesell (1998) found that youngsters' global self-worth varied depending on which of four contexts they considered (e.g., parents, teachers, female students, male students). For example, some children reported experiencing high global self-worth around their friends but low global self-worth around their parents. Interestingly, the majority of adolescents reported that their self-worth did vary significantly depending on the relational context. In fact, adolescents' perceptions of global self-worth in particular contexts (e.g., with parents) were more highly associated with their perceptions of support from significant others in those respective relational contexts (e.g., with parents) than with their perceptions of self-worth in the other relational contexts (e.g., with teachers, male classmates, female classmates). Investigation of these relationships with regard to sport and physical education settings could prove insightful. For example, in the physical domain, an examination of the relationship between athletes' relational self-worth (i.e., with coaches) and their perceptions of support from their coaches could highlight the role that significant adults play in the psychological and emotional development of young athletes.

Another interesting research avenue that Harter (1999) has pursued is the examination of children's development of the emotions of pride and shame. An interview study (Harter & Whitesell, 1989) with children aged four to nine years revealed four distinct development stages. Specifically, four- to five-year-olds (i.e., Stage 1) made no mention of the terms "pride" and "shame," although they did indicate that they would be excited after success (e.g., performing a flip on the monkey bars) and scared if they engaged in a transgression (e.g., stole money from the family coin jar), while their parents would be happy and mad, respectively. Children at Stage 2 (i.e., 5- to 6-year-olds) used the terms pride and shame and reported the same feelings (i.e., excited and scared) as the younger children, explaining that their parents would feel pride in their success and shame for their transgressions. At Stage 3 (i.e., 6- to 7-year-olds) the youngsters described feeling pride in themselves after success and shame after transgressions but only if they had been observed by their parents. At Stage 4 (i.e., 7- to 8-year-olds) the children described their feelings of pride after success and shame after transgressions even if their parents were not aware of the acts. An understanding of this developmental sequence associated with the experience of pride and shame would be particularly poignant in the physical domain, as many adults recall experiencing shame as children because of their demonstration of low ability in physical activity settings. In particular, investigating the incidents that cause children to experience pride (e.g., winning vs. exerting high effort) and shame (e.g., making a critical mistake in a competition vs. exerting low effort) in the physical domain reveals how coaches, teachers, and parents could assist children in developing healthy emotional perspectives.

A final area for future inquiry that builds on Harter's work relates to her examination of gender differences in global self-worth as well as the domain-specific areas of competence. Harter has consistently found that males report higher perceptions of global self-worth, physical competence, and physical attractiveness than do females. Some might be surprised to learn that Harter has reported correlations of .52 to .80 across samples between students' perceptions of their global self-worth and of their physical attractiveness. The manifestation of these gender differences should be of great concern to researchers in sport psychology and professionals working with children and adolescents in physical activity settings, as they hint that the stage may not be set for females to optimize their potential to the same extent that males do. One suggestion for further work on these reported gender differences would be to examine the longitudinal effects that participation in high-quality, developmentally sound physical activity programs throughout childhood has on youngsters' self-worth and self-concept. One could speculate that engagement in seminal physical activity programs might decrease (and/or eliminate) some of the observed gender differences by enhancing children's global self-worth and their perceptions of physical attractiveness and physical competence.

Harter's contribution to the cognitive developmental literature has been rich and consistent. Her ideas and research findings offer numerous avenues for important and relevant study in the physical domain.

Comparing and Contrasting Harter's and Nicholls's Frameworks

As researchers, Nicholls and Harter share a number of similarities. Nicholls invested two decades in researching the cognitive processes that youngsters experience as they gain an understanding of their ability, develop perceptions about themselves, and formulate their personal views about the nature of the world, as Harter has done also. The impact of each researcher on the literature in educational psychology, as well as sport and exercise psychology, has been enormous. Both of their theoretical frameworks have helped to advance knowledge and practice about optimizing young people's experiences in achievement settings. Sadly, Nicholls's death occurred prematurely, before his research agenda reached full fruition.

Harter's research agenda continues to develop in relevant and meaningful ways (Harter, 1999).

While having similarities, the approaches of Harter and Nicholls differ in at least two important ways. First, both scholars acknowledge the significant role that normative perceptions of ability play in fostering motivation, but their outlooks on this variable are different. Second, this difference in outlook leads them to offer varying strategies for intervention to optimize youngsters' motivational responses. These two differences are at the core of their respective theoretical frameworks and need further elaboration.

Nicholls (1979) observed early in his career that helping all individuals develop normative perceptions of ability was not a realistic strategy for maximizing motivational responses. He believed that individuals must learn to define success (i.e., task orientation) in personal terms whereby they feel good when they try hard and display high effort, despite how their performance might be judged by normative standards (see Roberts, this volume, for a review). Nicholls maintained that perceptions of normative ability do not have to be a critical factor in optimizing individuals' motivational levels. He was clear in articulating that professionals who endeavor to focus children and adolescents on their own effort and improvement and who de-emphasize normative standings with regard to ability will likely aid in developing individuals who have positive self-concepts, thrive on challenge, and persist in the face of adversity even when they have low normative perceptions of ability (see Biddle, Treasure, this volume).

In contrast, Harter (1993) seems skeptical that a focus on effort and mastery will significantly impact youngsters, as she refers to "the cultural preoccupation with . . . who is the best" and the "punishing peer standards" that will serve as a reality check even for those children who strive and achieve a higher level of improvement (p. 94). In addition, she (Harter, 1993) paints a rather bleak picture of the potential to impact adolescents' levels of self-esteem. According to James (1892), the two routes to enhancing self-esteem for an individual are through increasing his/her perceptions of competence in a domain and through lowering his/her perceptions of the importance of competence in the domain. Harter (1993) questions the plausibility of either strategy for children in our society. She writes, "Beginning in middle childhood . . . one adopts the cultural preoccupation with how individuals are different from one another—with competition, with who is the 'best,' with who ascends to the top. Thus, how one measures up to one's peers, to societal standards, becomes the filter through which judgments about the self pass" (p. 94). In continuing, she describes how high achievement is attainable by only a few individuals, presenting a long shot for the many who have low perceptions of ability:

> Thus, even if an individual who is motivated to improve does demonstrate actual gains compared to his or her own past performance, he or she will likely fall short relative to the punishing peer standards that provide the metric for self-evaluation. As a result, it becomes difficult to greatly increase one's perceptions of competence, relative to others, as a potential route to reducing the discrepancy between importance and competence that contributes to low self-esteem. (p. 94)

Such a view is in line with Nicholls's description of ego orientation. However, Nicholls (1984b, 1989) differs from Harter in allowing that some individuals are not preoccupied with their normative standing and instead judge their success in personal terms relative to their own mastery of tasks and improvement over time. Harter's somewhat skeptical view may explain why she has offered less direction for avoiding the pitfalls that occur when youngsters develop low normative perceptions of ability and low self-concept. She (Harter, 1999) has focused on research to explore how children develop adaptive self-concepts, and her direct aim has not been to suggest specific strategies or intervention protocols for optimizing self-concept among children. At best, she makes general statements suggesting that intervention strategies need to be addressed individually for each youngster. Nicholls, on the other hand, believed that creating a task-involving climate would bring out the best in each child.

It is worth noting that Nicholls would reject some of Harter's general suggestions about intervention strategies. For example, in employing James's model of global self-esteem, Harter suggests that one way to address high discrepancies (which are associated with low global self-worth) between individuals' perceptions of ability in a particular domain and the importance they place on success in that domain is to convince youngsters that domains in which they have little normative success are not very important. Harter's idea is to emphasize the importance of domains in which individuals have experienced high success. She (Harter, 1999) writes:

> It is hoped that the importance of those arenas in which one is less talented can be appropriately discounted. The goal, therefore, is actively opting to spend more psychological time in those life niches where favorable self-appraisals are more common and avoiding arenas in which one feels inadequate. (pp. 316-317)

This strategy is in conflict with Nicholls's (1989) aim of optimizing the motivational responses of all youngsters. Nicholls believed that such a strategy would be a surefire way to quell the innate desire to learn and improve that each human being possesses. This strategy sends a strong message to children that they should not maintain interest in activities in which their normative ability is lacking. Nicholls's approach is to encourage children in all their interest areas and to stress that normative standings are unimportant in relationship to displaying high effort and gauging improvement. If children are encouraged to give up their interest in domains they believe are important, the stage is set for tremendous potential to be lost. Who is in a position to know that a child who starts with low ability in a domain might not excel over time, making significant contributions?

A second strategy that Harter suggests involves removing children who perceive low levels of peer support from ego-involving motivational climates. While Nicholls would not necessarily disagree with this strategy in some cases, he would maintain that it may not be addressing the issue (i.e., children are at risk for maladaptive motivational responses in ego-involving motivational climates) and that all effort should be made first to transform the atmosphere into a task-involving climate. This would be particularly important in the case of motivational climates in academic and physical education classes and on sport teams.

In summary, Nicholls and Harter share a deep commitment to understanding children's cognitive development in relation to the development of self-perceptions. Their contributions have been valuable, yet there are distinctions between their approaches.

Summary

This chapter reviewed the two developmental theories of motivation that have received the most attention in the sport psychology literature. Specifically, Nicholls's and Harter's frameworks were described, and the research supporting each was highlighted. Research utilizing a developmental perspective has not widely addressed the physical domain, even though results have much to offer coaches, teachers, and parents who are striving to maximize youngsters' motivation to engage in physical activity. The future holds much in store in terms of further exploration of children's development of motivation in the physical domain.

Acknowledgments

I would like to thank Maria Newton and Tammy Schilling for their thoughtful comments on earlier drafts of this paper.

Enhancing Young People's Motivation in Youth Sport: An Achievement Goal Approach

Darren C. Treasure

The number of children and adolescents who regularly engage in adult-organized sport outside of the school system make this activity one of the most popular achievement contexts among young people today. Understanding and enhancing motivation in this context therefore constitutes a very meaningful topic of research for those interested in child and adolescent development. Commensurate with the number of young people participating in sport, research on the social dynamics of this experience has accelerated in the past 20 years. Stimulating this upsurge has been the adoption of a social cognitive conceptual perspective by many researchers. Instead of focusing on how variables contribute to, and predict, performance and achievement, the current concern with social cognitive dynamics places emphasis on the cognitive and affective determinants and consequences of behavior. Both variables are presumed to exert considerable influence on the direction and persistence of achievement behavior, the quality of involvement in achievement endeavors, and commitment to learning (Ames, 1992c). Consequently, they are considered important outcomes in their own right, quite apart from their influence on performance and achievement. The assumption in this perspective is that an individual's perception of reality is a powerful predictor of the ongoing stream of behavior and has an important effect on his/her perception of the sport experience (Roberts & Treasure, 1992).

Although various theories have been proposed to account for the motivational determinants of behavior in youth sport (see Roberts, 1992a, this volume), recent research stemming from a social cognitive perspective has focused on an achievement goal analysis of children's behavior, cognition, and affective response patterns. The present chapter, therefore, focuses on the process of motivation as it relates to research conducted on youth sport from an achievement goal perspective. Although I do not deal with physical education specifically (see Biddle, this volume), I utilize research from this achievement context to illustrate my points. The chapter begins with a review of research on the effects of the motivational climate on children's and adolescents' cognitive, affective, and behavioral responses to the sport experience. I next review recent research that has demonstrated the efficacy of examining the interaction between goal orientations and perceptions of the motivational climate to better understand achievement behavior in youth sport settings. The chapter concludes with an assessment of the potential utility of adopting an achievement goal approach to enhance children's motivation in sport and with suggestions for future research.

Achievement Goal Theory

Achievement goal theory assumes that the individual is an intentional, goal-directed organism operating in a rational manner (Nicholls, 1984a) and that achievement goals govern achievement beliefs and guide subsequent decision making and behavior in achievement contexts (e.g., Ames & Archer, 1987, 1988; Dweck, 1986; Dweck & Elliott, 1983; Maehr & Nicholls, 1980; Nicholls, 1980a, 1984a, 1989; Roberts, this volume). The energizing construct in this framework is assumed to be the goal of demonstrating competence. Other goals are assumed to operate in nonachievement contexts; but in sport when achievement is desired, when a standard of excellence is implicated, and when the activity has value to the individual, research from an achievement goal perspective assumes that the goal of action is to demonstrate competence and that perceived ability is the distinguishing feature of achievement motivation (Dweck, 1986; Maehr, 1984; Nicholls, 1984a).

Nicholls (1984a, 1989) contends that two achievement goals, namely task and ego, exist in achievement settings and that these goals are determined by both dispositional and situational factors (see Roberts, this volume, for a description of the fundamental tenets of achievement goal theory). While one avenue of research related to achievement goals in sport has demonstrated that individual differences in goal orientation are associated with different motivational processes (see Biddle, Duda, this volume), another has focused on situational factors (e.g., Balaguer, Duda, & Crespo, 1999; Ommundsen & Roberts, 1999; Thill & Cury, 2000; Treasure & Roberts, 1998). Consistent with other motivation research that has emphasized situational determinants of behavior (e.g., deCharms, 1976, 1984; Grolnick & Ryan, 1987; Ryan & Grolnick, 1986), research from an achievement goal perspective has examined how the structure of the environment, referred to as the motivational climate (Ames, 1992a), can make it more or less likely that achievement behaviors associated with a particular achievement goal are adopted. The premise of research from a situational perspective is that the nature of an individual's experiences and the way he/she interprets these experiences influence the degree to which task and ego goals are perceived as salient within the context. This is assumed to affect the achievement behaviors of individuals through their perception of the behaviors necessary to achieve success (Roberts, Treasure, & Kavussanu, 1997).

Perceptions of the Motivational Climate

Treasure (1997) reported a strong positive relationship between elementary school children's perception of a mastery-oriented motivational climate in their physical education class and adaptive motivational processes. As shown by a canonical correlation analysis, students who perceived a high-mastery-/moderate-performance-oriented climate reported a positive attitude toward the class, high perceived ability, the belief that effort and ability cause success, and feelings of satisfaction. In contrast, students who perceived a high-performance-/low-mastery-oriented climate focused on ability as a cause of success, reported a negative attitude toward the class and feelings of boredom. Treasure also examined the interaction of mastery- and performance-oriented percepts by way of a two-factor (2×2) quadrant analysis. After dividing the students into four groups based on a median split on their mastery and performance scores, he found that the level of mastery orientation was the critical dimension. Consistent with research from the classroom setting (Ames & Archer, 1988), Treasure found that when students perceived the classroom as high in mastery orientation, they reported feelings of satisfaction, a favorable attitude to physical education, high perceptions of ability, and a stronger belief that success results from one's own effort irrespective of level of performance orientation.

Similar findings have been reported by Ommundsen and Roberts (1999), who examined the relationship between perceptions of the motivational climate and various indexes of motivation in a sample of Norwegian University team sport athletes. Specifically, athletes who were classified as perceiving the climate to be high in mastery orientation reported a more adaptive pattern of achievement strategies (i.e., were less likely to avoid practice), beliefs about the purposes of sport (i.e., the development of social skills), and conceptualization of perceived ability (i.e., endorsed an improvement-oriented conception of ability) than athletes designated as low in mastery orientation. Consistent with the findings of Treasure (1997), athletes in the Ommundsen and Roberts study who perceived the motivational climate as high in mastery and high in performance reported psychological responses that were more adaptive than athletes perceiving the climate as low in mastery and high in performance criteria. The findings also showed that those high in performance and low in mastery were the least likely of all the athletes to endorse the belief that the purpose of sport is to develop social responsibility and lifetime skills.

The positive relationship between perceptions of a mastery climate and various indexes of motivation reported by Treasure (1997) and Ommundsen and Roberts (1999) has also been shown in a number of other studies with various nationalities and populations in both sport and physical education. Examples are paralympic athletes (Pensgaard, Roberts, & Ursin, 1999), competitive Spanish tennis players (Balaguer et al., 1999), French university students (Brunel, 1999b), elite female soccer players (Pensgaard, 1999), English physical education students (Carpenter & Morgan, 1999), Greek physical education students (Papaioannou & Kouli, 1999), and children with movement difficulties (Dunn, 2000). In addition, the pattern has been confirmed in a recent meta-analysis consisting of statistically estimated effect sizes from 14 studies ($n = 4484$) that examined the impact of different motivational climates in sport and physical education on cognitive and affective responses (Ntoumanis & Biddle, 1999b). The evidence, therefore, strongly supports the position that perceptions of a mastery climate are associated with more adaptive motivational and affective response patterns than perceptions of a performance climate in the contexts of sport and physical education.

Other Situational Factors

Situational factors in the social context, in addition to the motivational climate of the achievement situation itself, however, need to be examined if researchers are not to take too narrow a view of the influences outside of the individual that may determine a child's behavior in sport. To this end, research has begun to examine the perceived situational goal structure initiated by parents and its impact on children's responses (e.g., Roberts, Treasure, & Hall, 1994; White & Duda, 1993; White, Duda, & Hart, 1992). In addition, the effects of situational variables such as competition value, perceived state goal preference of significant others (e.g., parents, coach, sport governing body), perceived readiness, and social/personal perceptions of ability have also recently been explored in the literature (Harwood & Swain, 1998; Swain & Harwood, 1996). As Harwood and Swain (1998) correctly argue, research from achievement goal theory in sport needs to "extend beyond a general perception of the environmental structure or motivational climate" (p. 359) if researchers are to enhance our understanding of motivation in this achievement context.

Although the results of this research on situational influences suggest that perceptions of the motivational climate (whether created by teachers, coaches, or parents) may be a critical variable in understanding motivation, achievement goal theory states that dispositional goal orientations and perceptions of the climate are two independent dimensions of motivation that interact to affect behavior (Nicholls, 1989; Roberts, this volume). Research to date, however, has dealt with dispositional goal orientations and perceptions of the motivational climate primarily in isolation. It has been suggested, therefore, that an interactionist approach seeking to combine the two variables promises to provide a more complete understanding of children's achievement behaviors and their perceptions of the sport and physical education experience (Duda, Chi, Newton, Walling, & Catley, 1995; Roberts, 1992a, this volume; Roberts & Treasure, 1992; Roberts et al., 1997).

An Interactionist Approach

In an interactionist approach that integrates these two variables, dispositional goal orientation may be viewed as an individual-difference variable that will determine the probability of adopting a certain goal of action and displaying a particular behavior pattern while "situational factors are seen as potentially altering these probabilities" (Dweck & Leggett, 1988, p. 269). Commenting on the possible interaction of these two dimensions of the motivation equation, Dweck and Leggett (1988) suggest that in an achievement context where the situational cues in favor of either a task or ego goal are vague or weak, an individual's dispositional goal orientation should be more predictive than situational criteria. If, on the other hand, the situational cues are strong in favor of either a performance- or mastery-oriented climate, dispositions should be less predictive, and greater homogeneity among responses of individuals within that context should result. The stronger the disposition, the less likely situational cues are to be predictive or the stronger will be the situational cues necessary to influence it. Alternatively, the weaker the disposition, the more easily it can be altered by situational cues. Dweck and Leggett contend that one should expect individuals to behave inconsistently across situations when the strength of the situational cues varies across these settings. It is also likely that children and young adolescents, who have yet to firm up their personal theories of achievement, may be more susceptible to the structure of the motivational climate than older adolescents and adults (Roberts & Treasure, 1992).

In the sport context, a study by Seifriz, Duda, and Chi (1992), with high school male basketball players, examined the degree to which intrinsic motivation and attributional beliefs were a function of perceptions of the motivational climate, dispositional goal orientation, or a combination of the two variables. The findings indicated that attributional beliefs were best predicted by an individual's goal orientation. Specifically, a task orientation predicted the belief that effort causes success, whereas an ego orientation predicted the belief that ability causes success. Both perceptions of the motivational climate and goal orientation were predictive of intrinsic motivation. While perceptions of the motivational climate and dispositional goal orientation emerged as predictors of enjoyment, dispositional goal orientation was the predominant predictor of reported effort exerted and perceived competence in basketball, whereas the motivational climate significantly predicted reported tension in basketball.

Measuring Interaction Effects

Although Seifriz et al. (1992) claimed to be testing the possible interactive effects of dispositional goal orientations and perceptions of the motivational climate in a youth sport setting, the statistical analyses utilized were not consistent with this statement. Specifically, Seifriz and colleagues assessed the unique variance in the respective dependent variables accounted for by dispositional goal orientations and perceptions of the motivational climate when controlling for the effect of the other variable. These are main effect analyses. In none of the statistical analyses conducted was the interactive effect included in the regression equations that were created.

The influence of achievement goal orientations and perceptions of the motivational climate has also been examined in a study by Cury and colleagues (1996; Biddle, this volume). Here the researchers utilized structural equation modeling (SEM) to examine the interest of adolescent girls in physical education. Cury and colleagues hypothesized that direct paths would emerge from mastery- and performance-oriented perceptions of the climate to the pupils' interest in physical education. They also expected the effects of the climate to be mediated by an individual's goal orientation and level of perceived ability. Specifically, mastery and performance perceptions were expected to positively influence the corresponding dispositional goal orientation, while mastery perceptions were hypothesized to be related to perceived ability, which in turn would affect pupil interest. The results showed an excellent fit of the data to the hypothesized model, with perceptions of the motivational climate in the physical education class emerging as more important predictors of pupil interest than achievement goal orientations. More accurately, perceiving a mastery-oriented motivational climate enhanced pupil interest and perceived ability in physical education. The researchers conclude by suggesting that their findings support the positive effects of a mastery-oriented motivational climate in physical education and offer evidence of a possible shaping effect of the climate on an individual's goal orientation.

It is interesting to note that SEM has been recently employed in the achievement goal literature (e.g., Goudas, Biddle, & Fox, 1994b; Ntoumanis & Biddle, 1998; Vlachopoulos, Biddle, & Fox, 1997) because it is a useful tool for the development and testing of complex social theories (Duncan & Stoolmiller, 1993). Structural equation modeling has an advantage over regression analytic techniques in that parameters of a model can be specified simultaneously. For example, the link between ego orientation and perceived ability is assessed in the presence, and under the potential influence, of all the other variables in the model—something that cannot be accomplished using regression analysis. Structural equation modeling statistical packages such as LISREL (Joreskog & Sorbom, 1993) and EQS (Bentler, 1995) also provide modification indexes that make suggestions about how the model could be improved. Although modification indexes are useful tools to use in improving the model, one must be aware of numerous issues prior to use (McCullum, 1995). Most significantly, it is important to recognize that the modification indexes are statistically, rather than theoretically, derived. Consequently, only those revisions that are theoretically defensible should be used in subsequent runs. This is not an insignificant issue. The use of statistical techniques such as SEM should always be driven by theory and the research question being addressed.

Discussing the merits and limitations of SEM is not part of the purpose of this chapter, but it is important to recognize that although SEM may be an appropriate technique for examining potential relationships among achievement goals and perceptions of the motivational climate, it is limited in that it does not allow for the testing of interactive effects. As Hardy (1998) has recently stated, the only way interactive effects can be assessed is via multiple-sample analyses or moderated hierarchical regression analysis (Jaccard, Turrisi, & Wan, 1990). To this end, researchers have begun to analyze data using moderated hierarchical regression analysis, contending that this approach will provide some interesting insights into how goal orientations and situational variables may interact in the context of youth sport (Newton & Duda, 1999; Harwood & Swain, 1998; Swain & Harwood, 1996; Treasure & Roberts, 1998).

In a study designed to examine the antecedents of state goals in age-group swimmers, Swain and Harwood (1996) looked at the main and interactive effects of a variety of individual and situational variables by means of moderated hierarchical regression analyses. Results revealed separate main effects as well as significant interactions between the individual and situational predictors of the different goal types. Specifically, there was a significant main effect for situational variables, in this case social perceptions and race-specific criteria, which were the major predictors of ego involvement. In contrast, the interaction of individual and situational variables predicted the intensity of task involvement, namely the product of a single trait task goal of the athlete and the perceived state goal preference of significant others. This interaction effect suggests that when significant others are perceived as task involved, these situational perceptions complement a task orientation in creating high levels of task involvement.

Treasure and Roberts (1998) have reported similar findings with a sample of female adolescent basketball players. Specifically, they found goal orientations to be fairly robust in the face of the perceived motivational climate, with the theoretically hypothesized goal orientation predicting the participants' cognitive and affective responses in a coherent fashion. The fact that perceptions of the motivational climate, as well as the interaction of goal orientations and perceptions of the climate, were also found to be significant predictors, however, suggests that a solely dispositional approach provides a less-than-complete picture of the sport experience. Accordingly, evidence emerged in support of Dweck and Leggett's (1988) contention that situational variables may moderate the influence of goal orientations. Treasure and Roberts (1998) found that task goal orientation interacted with perceptions of a mastery-oriented climate in the prediction of mastery experiences as a source of satisfaction. The interaction showed that when an individual is task oriented, perceptions of a mastery climate complement his/her focus on task involvement. Perhaps more significantly, when the athlete displayed low task orientation, perceptions of a strong mastery climate appeared to override the weaker goal orientation, serving to maintain the importance of task involvement. A similar relationship emerged for the belief that ability was a cause of success, as this was predicted by the interaction of ego goal orientation and perceptions of a performance climate. The interaction showed that when an individual perceives a high-performance-oriented climate and is highly ego oriented, this serves to attenuate the focus on ability as a cause of success. Interesting, however, was the finding that perceptions of the climate had no effect on the beliefs of the low-ego-oriented individual. If an individual did not enter the achievement context with a strong ego orientation, perceiving the climate as highly performance oriented did not moderate that belief. In this case, perhaps, the performance-oriented cues were not powerful enough to moderate the low-ego-oriented individual's level of ego involvement.

Not all research that has utilized moderated hierarchical regression analyses, however, has shown significant interaction effects. For example, when examining the antecedents of pre-competition states of task and ego involvement in elite junior tennis players, Harwood and Swain (1998) found no significant interactions between the dispositional and situational variables. Results of these analyses, however, did reveal significant main effects for the dispositional and situational factors on the athletes' different goal types. Specifically, perceptions of the state goal preference of significant others, the achievement value of the match, and perceptions of the athlete's ability were the significant predictors of task involvement. In contrast, pre-competition intensity of ego involvement was predicted by an athlete's ego orientation combined with perceptions of significant others and match value.

It must also be noted that although moderated hierarchical analysis does enable the researcher to examine the separate, as well as the interactive, effects of goal orientations and situational variables, this type of analysis is not particularly powerful. Thus, future research needs to examine whether the few interactions that emerged in'the studies just discussed are attributable to the sample size and/or the low statistical power of this type of analysis to detect moderators (Aguinis & Stone-Romero, 1997; Finney, Mitchell, Cronkite, & Moos, 1984). The fact that significant main effects emerged for both situational and individual variables in the respective studies appears to confirm the utility of investigating the independent effects of goal orientations and perceptions of the motivational climate as the majority of achievement goal research has done to date. Of more interest, perhaps, was the finding that the interaction of situational and individual variables added to our understanding of the motivation process in the youth sport context (Newton & Duda, 1999; Swain & Harwood, 1996; Treasure & Roberts, 1998). To date, the limited amount of research from an interactionist perspective has found support for Dweck and Leggett's (1988) contention that situational factors may moderate the effect of goal orientations in determining the probability of adopting a certain goal of action and displaying a particular behavior pattern. Further research, however, is clearly needed to explore the exact nature of the relationship between goal orientations and situational variables (see Biddle, this volume; Roberts et al., 1997).

Enhancing Motivation

Research from an achievement goal perspective in the context of youth has revealed that dispositional goals and perceptions of the motivational climate are relevant to the ongoing stream of achievement behavior, cognition, and affect. The issue remains, however, of how to enhance motivation in this context. Although it may be effective to focus on the individual to enhance the quality of motivation by affecting change in his/her dispositional goal orientation, this approach centers on the child as the motivational problem, which may not be the case. In addition, research from a situational perspective suggests that concentrating on individual change may not be the most effective strategy, as from a motivational standpoint the subjective meaning of the environment has been shown to be a critical factor in determining motivation (Maehr, 1983). A more practical solution, therefore, is suggested by research showing that individuals perceive the meaning and purpose of the achievement context in different ways (e.g., Balaguer et al., 1999; Brunel, 1999b; Dunn, 2000; Pensgaard et al., 1999; Treasure, 1997; Treasure & Roberts, in press) and indicating that these perceptions may moderate the effect of an individual's goal orientation, thereby influencing the quality of motivation (Newton & Duda, 1999; Swain & Harwood, 1996; Treasure & Roberts, 1998). Founded on the fundamental tenets of achievement goal theory, therefore, some have suggested that time and effort be spent in developing strategies and instructional practices to help the physical education teacher and youth sport coach create a mastery-oriented motivational climate (Ames, 1992a, 1992b, 1992c; Biddle, this volume; Duda, 1996, this volume; Roberts et al., 1997; Treasure & Roberts, 1995, in press).

Although research directly examining this suggestion is scant, there is some evidence supporting the adoption of an achievement goal approach to enhancing motivation. Contrasting the effects of competitive and cooperative aerobic programs on physical fitness and multidimensional self-concepts with adolescent females, Marsh and Peart (1988) found that when compared to results for a control group, physical fitness improved in both the competitive and cooperative programs, but no self-concept variables were affected except in the cooperative program. Specifically, participants assigned to the cooperative context reported higher levels of physical self-concept and physical appearance self-concept than those in the competitive context. Although the study was not framed within an achievement goal perspective per se, one can argue that the competitive program stressed a state of ego involvement in that students could achieve their own goals only when others failed. In contrast, the cooperative program appeared to emphasize a state of task involvement since students could achieve their goals only by working with others as they did so.

Lloyd and Fox (1992) more directly examined the utility of adopting achievement goal theory as a framework to enhance motivation in physical activity contexts. They studied the effect of two contrasting approaches to teaching an aerobics/fitness course on adolescent females' exercise motivation and enjoyment in a physical education setting. They created different motivational climates by manipulating certain verbal cues and teaching strategies. In the mastery-oriented condition, emphasis was on self-improvement through working at one's own level and on task mastery, while in the performance-oriented condition, emphasis was on demonstrating competence through peer-performance and normative comparisons. After the effectiveness of the context manipulations had been assessed, participants in the mastery condition reported higher motivation to continue participating in aerobics, as well as more enjoyment, than those who participated in the performance-oriented condition.

Epstein's TARGET Structures

Encouraging though the results from these studies are, more research is needed to develop our understanding of how teachers and youth sport coaches can go about structuring mastery-oriented achievement contexts. To this end, in the academic setting Epstein (1988, 1989) has argued that various structural features of the achievement context have been consistently identified as influencing a wide range of motivational processes. These structural features are interdependent variables, and when taken together they define the motivational climate of a context. Epstein coined the acronym TARGET to represent the Task, Authority, Recognition, Grouping, Evaluation, and Timing structures that she defined as the "basic building blocks" of the achievement setting (1988, p. 92). As Ames (1992c) correctly states, however, although achievement contexts have frequently been described in terms of the ways in which certain structural constraints relate to various cognitive and affective responses (e.g., Brophy, 1983; Grolnick & Ryan, 1987; Marshall & Weinstein, 1984; Rosenholtz & Simpson, 1984), there has been little systematic analysis of how certain structures within the context make different goals salient. Ames, therefore, took the important step of examining what it is about the design of tasks, distribution of authority or responsibility, use of rewards, the way groups are formed, evaluation practices, and the pace of instruction and time allotted for completing tasks that makes a performance and/or mastery motivational climate salient.

Task

A central element of sport and physical education contexts is the design of tasks, drills, exercises, and learning activities for children. According to Blumenfeld's (1992) summary, the salient task dimensions include variety, diversity, challenge, control, and meaningfulness. Embedded in tasks is information that children use to make judgments about their ability, their willingness to apply effort, and feelings of satisfaction (Ames, 1992a). Research has demonstrated that tasks entailing variety and diversity are more likely than others to facilitate an interest in learning and in task involvement (e.g., Marshall & Weinstein, 1984; Nicholls, 1989; Rosenholtz & Simpson, 1984). Rosenholtz and Simpson (1984) demonstrated that the design of tasks can influence students' perceptions of their own and others' ability. These authors defined uniformity of tasks as one factor contributing to what they called a unidimensional classroom structure. In classrooms of this type, students tended to use the same materials and had the same assignments at the same time. Although it is important not to confuse knowledge of one's ability relative to others with self-evaluation of oneself in terms of that ranking, as Rosenholtz and Simpson (1984) do, achievement contexts of this type are likely to translate performance differences into ability differences and consequently to evoke ego involvement. In contrast, in what Rosenholtz and Simpson (1984) characterized as multidimensional classrooms, students tended to work on different tasks, or had different assignments, that created less opportunity, or need, for students to compare their performance to that of others. Hence students developed a sense of their own ability that was not dependent on social comparison.

Authority

The locus of responsibility in the learning situation, often defined as the degree to which a teacher or coach involves children in decision making, is related to adaptive or positive motivation patterns (Ames, 1992a). Evidence suggests that children's feelings of perceived ability tend to be higher in contexts that are autonomous (self-determined) in orientation (e.g., Deci, 1992; Deci & Ryan, 1991; Ryan & Deci, 2000b; Vallerand, this volume). This autonomy-oriented climate is described as one in which teachers involve students in the learning process by giving them choices. It is important to note, however, that when children are given a choice, they must perceive the choice to be real. In some instances, telling children that they can choose any task they wish may result only in some children's choosing tasks that are too difficult and other children's choosing tasks that are too easy. This is especially likely to occur when the children anticipate normative evaluation of their performance and have low perceptions of ability (e.g., Nicholls, 1989). If children's choices are motivated by a fear of failure, feelings of personal control are unlikely to be enhanced. As Ames (1992a) states, for a mastery-oriented climate to be salient, choices must be perceived as equal choices, as would be the case if the choice was among a range of equally difficult tasks; this will ensure that choices are guided by a child's interest and not by efforts to protect perceptions of ability.

Recognition

The use of rewards and incentives is one of the more obvious aspects of sport during childhood and adolescence. It often seems that rewards and incentives are more important than the activity itself. Although often given with good intentions, that is, to motivate, rewards and incentives can have paradoxical and detrimental effects when applied to an entire group of children with varying abilities and levels of interest (Lepper & Hodell, 1989). Considerable research evidence from varied contexts demonstrates the undermining effects of rewards when they are perceived as bribes or as controlling (Ryan & Deci, 2000b). Perhaps most significantly, because rewards are often public and given on a differential basis, they invite social comparison. When recognition for accomplishment or progress is private, however, between the teacher or coach and the child, feelings of pride and satisfaction do not derive from doing better than others and are likely to foster a mastery-oriented perception of the motivational climate.

Grouping

The basis by which children are brought together or kept apart, and the ease with which they may change groups are particularly salient practices in determining the motivational consequences of the grouping structure (Ames, 1992a; Epstein, 1988). Research has shown that teachers and coaches treat groups differently, giving more instructional time, opportunities, encouragement, and attention to the brighter or more able groups (Martinek, 1989; Weinstein, 1989). This structure would appear to be most important in the youth sport and physical education setting where the coach or teacher must often accommodate children of widely differing levels of *current* ability. By placing children in homogeneous ability groups, the coach or teacher is inviting social comparison and, consequently, a state of ego involvement. In contrast, coaches and teachers who promote movement between groups and use heterogeneous and varied grouping arrangements are likely to reduce the opportunity and necessity for children to compare themselves to others in their group (Marshall & Weinstein, 1984).

Evaluation

How children are evaluated is one of the most salient features of any achievement context that can affect motivation. The issue is not merely whether or not children are evaluated but also how children perceive the meaning of the evaluative information. A great deal of research has accumulated to suggest that evaluation practices can have deleterious effects on motivation when they are normatively based, public, and linked to ability assessments (e.g., Butler, 1987, 1988; Covington & Omelich, 1984; Jagacinski & Nicholls, 1984; Nicholls, 1989). Evaluation systems that emphasize social comparison and normative standards of performance evoke a state of ego involvement that focuses children on evaluating their ability compared to their peers. As a consequence, children's self-worth (e.g., Covington, 1984), level of intrinsic interest (e.g., Butler, 1987, 1988), and perceived ability (e.g., Nicholls, 1989) are all impaired.

It must be emphasized, however, that the mere availability of social comparison information is not problematic. Rather, it is when this information is emphasized (Cury, Biddle, Sarrazin, & Famose, 1997; Hall, 1990; Jagacinski & Nicholls, 1987) that the linkages among effort, outcome, and affect are undermined. This would appear to be a very important point when one considers the pervasiveness of social-comparative information in the sport context. In contrast, when evaluation is self-referenced, based on personal improvement, progress toward individual goals, participation, and effort, children are more likely to be task involved (Ames, 1984b; Cury, Biddle, et al., 1997; Hall, 1990). Children tend to focus on their effort rather than on ability and to utilize specific task strategies that will contribute to improvement and skill mastery.

Timing

Research in education has indicated that the pace of instruction, as well as the time allotted for completing tasks, significantly influences children's motivation (Ames, 1992a; Epstein, 1988). As Ames (1992a) contends, the time dimension is closely related to the other areas, such as task design (e.g., how much children are asked to accomplish within a specific time), authority (e.g., whether children are allowed to schedule the rate, order, or time of completion of tasks), grouping (e.g., whether quality of instructional time is equitable across groups), and evaluation (e.g., time pressure on performance). Extrapolating from the education research, time would appear to be an important factor in the youth sport context. For example, some children need more time than others to develop the necessary skills to actively compete and participate in sports. It seems, however, that often the children who need the most practice and playing time are the ones who receive the least time.

Applications of TARGET in Sport and Physical Education

It is interesting to note that although achievement goal theory was developed in the context of education, very little research has applied and tested the contextual relevance of this theory to physical education, particularly in terms of developing intervention programs designed to enhance motivation. This may be a significant oversight if we are interested in affecting change in the physical activity behavior of the greatest number of children. As Sallis and colleagues state, "the setting with the most promise for having a public health impact is the schools because virtually all children can be reached in school" (Sallis, Simons-Morton, et al., 1992, p. S251). In congruence with this argument, Biddle and Goudas (Biddle, this volume; Goudas & Biddle, 1994b) maintain that an additional benefit of conducting research in the context of physical education is that it removes the biased samples one contends with in volunteer sport situations, as this context includes children with a wide range of interests and abilities in sport and physical activities. To this end, two recent studies provide some insight into the potential utility of adopting an achievement goal framework to guide motivation enhancement interventions in physical education (Solmon, 1996; Treasure, 1993).

Adapting an intervention model developed by Ames and Maehr (1989) in the academic setting, Treasure (1993) conducted a 10-session soccer intervention that began with identifying strategies consistent with promoting either a performance- or a mastery-oriented motivational climate and organizing these strategies into Epstein's six TARGET areas. Each strategy was then operationalized in terms of a wide range of specific instructional practices to facilitate the instructor's actual implementation of the strategies. The intervention model, therefore, afforded the comparison between a performance-oriented motivational climate that emphasized normative standards of performance and a mastery-oriented motivational climate that focused on learning and personal improvement. Although another study had successfully manipulated the motivational climate in a classroom setting (Ames & Maehr, 1989), Treasure's (1993) study was the first to attempt to manipulate the motivational climate of a physical education context utilizing Epstein's (1988, 1989) TARGET principles as a guideline. Consistent with research from classroom settings, the results of a series of manipulation checks suggest that situational factors and instructional demands can influence a child's perception of the physical education experience. Specifically, the findings demonstrate that the children who participated in the performance treatment condition perceived the motivational climate to be performance oriented, whereas those who participated in the mastery condition perceived a mastery-oriented motivational climate.

Treasure's (1993) study demonstrated that by manipulating the TARGET structures of the achievement context, a physical education teacher can affect the motivational climate of the achievement context to such an extent as to override the dispositional goal orientations of students. Specifically, results of hierarchical regression analyses revealed that perceptions of the motivational climate were the most important predictors of the children's cognitive and affective responses during the intervention. Congruent with the classroom-based work of Ames and Maehr (1989), the results of this study show that a teacher may be able to structure a motivational climate that will foster a particular achievement state of involvement and in so doing play an active role in the construction of a child's physical education experience. The results of this study also demonstrate that participants who perceive a motivational climate in which the demonstration of ability is based on personal improvement and effort manifest a significantly more adaptive pattern of achievement cognition and affective responses than those who perceive a climate in which the demonstration of ability is based on normative ability and outperforming others. Specifically, participants in the mastery treatment condition indicated that they preferred to engage in more challenging tasks, believed success was the result of motivation and effort, and experienced more satisfaction with the activity than participants in the performance treatment condition. Participants in the performance treatment condition, however, reported that deception was a key to success.

A study by Solmon (1996) provides support for the strategies outlined by Ames (1992a, 1992c) to create a mastery-oriented motivational climate in physical education. Seventh- and eighth-grade students participated in single-gender juggling classes in either a mastery or performance motivational condition. Instructors in the mastery condition stressed individual challenge, short-term goals, improvement, and self-referenced criteria for success. Effort, improvement, and persistence were rewarded in this condition; students were encouraged to work together, at their own pace, and to try to improve on performance in previous trials. In contrast, the emphasis in the performance-oriented climate was on other-referenced criteria for success. Solmon states that the focus in this condition was to win contests and to be the best juggler. The results show that the students perceived the treatment conditions differently and that participants in the mastery-oriented condition demonstrated a greater willingness to persist on a difficult task than those in the performance-oriented condition. In addition, participants in the performance condition were more likely to attribute success during the intervention to normative ability than were participants in the mastery condition. This finding replicates previous research and confirms Nicholls's (1989) contention that achievement goals and beliefs about the causes of success are linked in a conceptual fashion.

In the youth sport context, Theeboom, De Knop, and Weiss (1995) have provided additional support for the adaptive responses of children to a mastery climate. In a three-week intervention, they investigated the influence of a mastery and a traditional motivational climate program, created by manipulating Epstein's (1988, 1989) TARGET structures, on children's (aged 8 to 12 years) psychological responses and motor skill development during what the authors described as an organized sport program. Although the children's perceptions of the motivational climate were not assessed, and no significant differences emerged between the mastery and traditional coaching programs for perceived competence and intrinsic motivation, the authors argue that during in-depth interviews the children in the mastery condition reported high levels of perceived competence and intrinsic motivation, whereas those from the traditional condition showed less pronounced effects.

It has been suggested that fostering task involvement may be a particular challenge in the context of youth sport because ego involvement is inherent in the activity (Duda, 1992). The results of the intervention studies just discussed suggest, however, that in a relatively short time, a teacher or youth sport coach may be able to structure a physical activity context in such a way as to influence a child's recognition of a mastery motivational climate and in so doing significantly enhance her/his quality of motivation. It is important to note, however, that each study reviewed here took place in a far more controlled environment than is normally found in naturally occurring physical education and especially youth sport settings. From a motivational perspective, nevertheless, the findings from these studies suggest that it may be possible to create a mastery-oriented climate and that children thrive in such a context.

Although the classroom and physical activity research suggests that teachers and coaches may be effective in enhancing the motivation of children, Maehr and Midgley (1991) argue, with respect to school-based interventions, that efforts at the classroom level can be easily undermined by schoolwide policies and procedures. Thus, a given teacher can be working hard to create a mastery-oriented climate in the classroom only to have the principal announce the establishment of a schoolwide academic contest associated with external rewards. As Maehr and Midgley (1991) astutely observe, "the classroom is not an island, and it is difficult to develop and sustain changes in the classroom without dealing with the wider school environment" (p. 405). Extrapolating from this research, just as a classroom teacher alone cannot carry the burden of school change, neither can an individual physical education teacher or youth sport coach. For example, a coach's effort to reward athletes privately for effort and improvement will be subverted by a league-wide end-of-season award ceremony at which the winners and the most able athletes are publicly acknowledged. Similarly, the coach who decides to give equal playing time to all athletes will struggle in a league in which all other coaches allow only their best athletes to play.

The point made by Maehr and Midgley (1991) clearly demonstrates the interacting network of significant others that may influence what criteria a child uses to define success in any achievement activity. In sport, some suggest that motivational interventions designed to foster children's adaptive achievement striving will be enhanced or inhibited by the behavior of not only sport leaders but also parents (e.g., Roberts, Treasure, & Hall, 1994; White & Duda, 1993). For example, by making certain types of performance feedback and sporting behaviors salient, a parent can influence children's attitudes toward the activity and their perceptions of success. A child may return from a weekly soccer game to have a parent ask, "Did you win?"; the child receives a rather clear message about what the parent considers most important—a message that may entirely subvert the efforts of a coach to enhance task involvement. Just as educational researchers are beginning to recognize the importance of the home (e.g., Ames & Maehr, 1989; Epstein, 1989) as well as the general motivational climate of the school (e.g., Maehr, 1991) in influencing the quality of children's motivation, it is suggested that any intervention designed to promote task involvement in sport must recognize the role that parents and other significant adults may play in determining a child's physical education and competitive sport experience (Roberts et al., 1997).

Applied Implications

From an applied perspective, the research reviewed supports the utility of adopting an achievement goal approach to enhancing motivation in the context of youth sport. Specifically, the findings provide evidence in support of the contention that significant adults, that is, parents, coaches, and teachers, play an active role in the construction of a child's perception of the motivational climate in the contexts of physical education and sport—and consequently the quality of motivation. In congruence with the work of Ames (1992b), this research also demonstrates that mastery-oriented climates may be induced in a physical education and youth sport context. To this end, researchers have taken the important step of translating an organized and coherent set of strategies into guidelines for instruction and the organization of the achievement context (Solmon, 1996; Theeboom et al., 1995; Treasure & Roberts, in press). It is important to recognize, however, that as pertinent as it may be to provide a working taxonomy of actions that may influence the perceived performance- or mastery-oriented nature of the context, implementation of any future intervention programs will be greatly facilitated by operational detail guiding the teacher or coach in strategy choice and selection. Critically, in an achievement activity in which the overwhelming emphasis is on normative standards of performance (Duda, 1992), youth sport coaches need to have resources available that will guide them in their attempts to foster task involvement. Likewise, it is suggested that training programs need to be developed to assist physical education teachers and youth sport coaches in constructing mastery-oriented achievement contexts. Similar to the coaching effectiveness program established by Smith, Smoll, and their colleagues to enhance the communication behaviors of coaches (Smith, Smoll, & Curtis, 1979; Smith, Smoll, & Hunt, 1977; Smith & Smoll, 1990; Smoll & Smith, 1989), training programs need to be developed to help coaches construct mastery-oriented achievement contexts.

Future Directions

The findings of the research discussed in this chapter suggest that there is much to be gained, both conceptually and practically, from pursuing an understanding of children's motivation in youth sport and physical education settings from an achievement goal perspective. The research has given much insight into the process of motivation, but more work remains to be done and there are important issues to address. Given that perceptions of the motivational climate appear to be a key dimension of children's achievement motivation in physical education and youth sport, researchers must develop valid and reliable ways of assessing this construct. The development of valid and reliable measures, therefore, is extremely important if researchers are to be able to discriminate among contexts with differing climates and to facilitate the accurate assessment of the effects of intervention programs over time.

Although most research in the sport context to date has used the Perceived Motivational Climate in Sport Questionnaire (Seifriz et al., 1992), Newton, Duda, and Yin (2000) have recently published data suggesting that the motivational climate should be conceptualized in a hierarchical fashion, with several dimensions underlying the higher-order mastery- and performance-oriented climates (see Duda, this volume). Although concern with measuring the dimensions of the goal structure of the achievement contexts may be important (Biddle, this volume), researchers should determine whether the hierarchical approach suggested by Newton and her colleagues best captures the essence of the motivational climate. From a practical perspective, it is also important to determine whether the hierarchical model will add significantly to our understanding of motivated behavior in achievement settings over and above the higher-order perceptions of a performance- and mastery-oriented climate that have been studied to date.

The achievement contexts of both education and sport are characterized by greater evaluation and greater emphasis on performance outcomes as children progress through the system (i.e., from one grade to the next or one competitive sport level to the next) (Chaumeton & Duda, 1988; Eccles, Midgley, & Adler, 1984). Duda (1992) has stated, therefore, that this increase in the performance-oriented character of the sport context should relate to a corresponding increase in ego orientation among sport participants. Although no research has yet directly addressed this developmental process, if it is correct, it is interesting to speculate about the long-term effects of an intervention designed to enhance the mastery-oriented nature of the sport context on dispositional goal orientations across the same developmental time span. It must be noted here that goal orientations are not "traits." Rather, they should be viewed as cognitive schema that are subject to change as information pertaining to one's performance on the task is processed (Roberts et al., 1997). Thus individual differences in dispositional goal orientation may be the result of socialization through mastery or performance motivational climates in either the home, school, or previous physical activity experiences. A longitudinal study would provide some insight into how increased exposure of children to mastery-oriented situations might shape dispositional goal orientations (Nicholls, Cobb, Wood, Yackel, & Patashnick, 1990; Williams, 1998). For example, do children become less ego oriented and more task oriented following prolonged exposure to a mastery-oriented intervention program? Beyond goal orientations, longitudinal research would also afford researchers the opportunity to examine the effects of an intervention designed to foster a mastery-oriented motivational climate on other key motivational variables. For example, what happens when children are in a mastery-oriented sport context for one, two, or three years? Do these children differ from those participating in a context in which the situational cues are more ambiguous or in a performance-oriented climate?

Further research is also needed on the design of intervention programs utilized in youth sport and physical education settings. To date, interventions have been based on extrapolations from classroom-based research, as identification of instructional strategies and methods that may influence children's motivation in physical education and youth sport is at an initial and exploratory stage, awaiting more systematic analysis and study. Although the results of previous research (e.g., Solmon, 1996; Treasure & Roberts, in press) indicate the effectiveness of adopting and adapting successful classroom-based intervention programs, it is important to recognize that sport and education are different achievement domains (Nicholls, 1992). To date, Becker's (1995) is the only study in the context of youth sport to my knowledge that has examined this important issue. Specifically, Becker designed an investigation to examine the relationship between high school athletes' perceptions of the TARGET structures constructed by the coach, the perceived motivational climate in practice, and goal orientations. The results suggest that the TARGET structures may not be the most salient structures within the context of youth sport (see Biddle, this volume). In assessing and implementing interventions to enhance the quality of children's motivation in sport, therefore, researchers need to be sensitive to any possible significant differences between classroom and sport contexts. It is also suggested that researchers work with physical educators and sport practitioners to help define the key dimensions of these contexts, as well as to develop strategies that would enhance task involvement. In this way, a wide variety of policies, procedures, and strategies should emerge that can be implemented and evaluated.

When coining the acronym TARGET, Epstein (1988, 1989) conceptualized the task, authority, recognition, grouping, evaluation, and timing structures of the classroom as interdependent. They were conceptualized as such because they were thought to impact a common set of dependent variables related to children's focusing on either task or ego goals in achievement contexts. An issue emanating from intervention studies that have adopted the TARGET structures, however, concerns exactly how these structures relate to each other and the effects of their relationships on the effectiveness of intervention programs. Specifically, do the manipulations of the task, authority, recognition, grouping, evaluation, and timing structures operate in an additive or multiplicative fashion (Ames, 1992c; Krug, 1989)? If they are additive, the structures become complementary, and the inadequacies in one structure can be attenuated by strengths in another. If, however, the structures are multiplicative, they cannot compensate for each other. For example, if a teacher or coach set different sport tasks for children taking into account different levels of skill development or physical maturity and then evaluated the children on some normatively based skills test, he/she would not be able to foster perceptions of a mastery-oriented motivational climate. Clearly this is a vital question from an applied perspective, as in sport it is highly unlikely that all aspects of the achievement context will be mastery oriented. It is suggested that this question would be best addressed through laboratory-based experimental research in which the differing structures of an intervention program can be manipulated and their exact relationship to each other determined.

Conclusion

A recent criticism of achievement goal researchers has been that they are overly optimistic in suggesting that a teacher or coach may positively affect a child's motivation in physical education and youth sport (Pringle, 2000). But, I would argue, the research evidence clearly shows that if the objective of adult-organized youth sport is to offer an achievement experience that allows *all* children to succeed, then a state of task involvement should be the goal. Adults responsible for the development of children in achievement activities such as sport, therefore, should look to foster task involvement, as it ensures equality of motivational opportunity for all (Nicholls, 1989). In addition, in an activity in which performance during childhood is so closely linked to physiological, motor skill, cognitive, and other psychosocial developmental issues (see Bar-Or, 1996), it seems sensible—even for those interested solely in developing elite-level adult performers—to promote task involvement during childhood. Through an emphasis on ego involvement, less mature children are likely to make inappropriate perceived ability assessments when the demonstration of high ability is restricted to those children who are *currently* the top performers.

In addition, task involvement should be fostered with those children who are *currently* the top age-group performers. As in education, children participate in different sport contexts with different peer groups. For example, children move from one sport team to another, from one competitive level to another, and from one age group to another. When this occurs it is unlikely that the hierarchy of ability within the respective contexts will remain constant. In such instances, if the demonstration of ability is continually based on the comparison of ability to that of relative others, an individual's perception of high ability may weaken; and this may lead to maladaptive behaviors including, potentially, withdrawal from the activity. By emphasizing task involvement, therefore, through the construction of a mastery-oriented motivational climate, the teacher or coach may be able to provide the young athlete with sources of competence information other than the outcome of the contest. In this way, it may be possible to cultivate a high task goal orientation to complement a high ego goal orientation—which recent research has suggested may be the most adaptive achievement goal profile at the elite adult level (Hardy, 1998).

Enhancing Motivation in Physical Education

Stuart J.H. Biddle

Physical education (PE) is an environment in which motivational concerns can be clearly observed. Some children are highly motivated toward PE and see it as the highlight of their school day. Indeed, research has long shown that sporting prowess is a major source of social status for children, especially boys (Coleman, 1961). Motivation to succeed in the PE or sport environment, therefore, is expected to be high for some, if not many, children and youth. However, PE has also been identified as a source of stress for some children and can be a major reason for truancy. Clearly, such children are "amotivated" with respect to PE. One could suggest that few areas of achievement generate such contrasting motivational orientations, hence PE becomes an important area for the study of motivation.

In PE classes, children are involved in a relatively public arena where effort and ability are salient. Effort is often required more overtly than elsewhere in the school curriculum, given the physical nature of the tasks. Ability is also salient as teachers in PE emphasize skill learning as a major objective. Many skills require a degree of "competence," however perceived or defined. The salience of effort and ability means that the achievement goals approach, currently so popular in exercise and sport psychology and covered in depth elsewhere in this text (see Roberts, this volume), has been studied extensively in recent years. In contrast to youth sport research, studies in PE contexts allow for the investigation of motivation in samples diverse in their actual and perceived competence, and varying greatly in their motivation. This is important if we are to fully understand motivational processes.

The study of achievement goal orientations has usually involved investigating people's beliefs about defining success in self-referenced (task) terms and normative-comparative (ego) terms (see also Roberts, this volume). Because other chapters in this book deal with these constructs, rather than repeat basic theoretical principles of achievement goal orientations, I present results from a set of studies conducted mainly in European school PE settings, with the aim of discussing the enhancement of motivation in the PE context. I draw extensively on the studies from our own research group for the sake of coherence but present supporting evidence from elsewhere.

Most work has been conducted on achievement goal *orientations*—orientation referring to a *generalized* tendency to define success in sport/PE in task and/or ego terms. I will not deal much with the role of goal involvement *states* in specific situations, as we have less information on this. Nevertheless, the study of goal involvement is important and is likely to be increasingly so, as we seek more situation-specific predictors of motivation (see Harwood & Swain, 1998; Roberts, this volume; Vallerand, 1997, this volume).

Correlates of Achievement Goal Orientations

The study of achievement goals in PE has followed several themes, and these form the basis of this chapter. They include the correlates of goals, in terms of both beliefs about sport success and beliefs concerning the nature of sport ability, as well as motivational, affective, and behavioral correlates of goals. Whereas achievement goals research has addressed individual goals, the situational "climate" has also received attention. Intervention studies are less common, but I discuss them briefly. I also consider related motivational constructs, including attributions and perceived autonomy, in the context of seeking possible mechanisms of motivated behavior.

Beliefs About Success

A fundamental psychological need identified by Deci and Ryan (1985b) is that of competence. We are unlikely to freely choose behaviors in which we will demonstrate incompetence. Similarly, other theoretical perspectives, such as self-efficacy (Bandura, 1997b), suggest that beliefs in personal agency are central motivational constructs. The goal orientations approach recognizes that achievement motivation is based on personal definitions of success and views of the causes of success, some reflecting beliefs in greater personal agency or perceived competence than others. The study of the links between goal orientations and beliefs about the causes of success therefore, is fundamental to the understanding of motivated achievement behavior (Roberts, this volume).

Research in classroom and PE contexts has shown that task and ego goal orientations are differentially correlated with beliefs about the causes of success. For example, in our first study of this area (Duda, Fox, Biddle, & Armstrong, 1992), we found for 10- to 11-year-old boys and girls that a task orientation was strongly correlated with the belief that success in sport is due to motivation/effort but was unrelated to the belief that ability causes success in sport. Conversely, ego orientation was strongly correlated with ability beliefs but rather weakly correlated with motivation/effort. Interestingly, we were able to replicate these results with 12- to 14-year-old children in Zimbabwe (Biddle, Akande, Vlachopoulos, & Fox, 1996), suggesting cross-cultural stability for such findings. Similar results were also reported for 16- to 18-year-olds in voluntary PE classes in England (Spray, Biddle, & Fox, 1999). In that study, the strongest links were between a task orientation and effort beliefs for both males and females.

Beliefs About the Nature of Sport Ability

The approach adopted in this chapter so far suggests that effort and ability beliefs are differentially related to how children define success in PE and sport contexts. However, Nicholls (1989, 1992) and others (e.g., Duda, 1993; Roberts, 1992a, this volume) have written extensively on the fundamental nature of ability and effort perceptions in goals and motivation. For example, children from about the age of 11 or 12 years are able to differentiate ability from effort, and they view ability as "current capacity" (Nicholls, 1992). Here effort is seen to affect performance up to the limits of one's current capacity; that is, ability will limit the effectiveness of effort. However, this begs the question "How is ability actually viewed?" In other words, do all young people in PE view "ability" in the same way?

The results on effort and ability just reviewed support earlier propositions from Nicholls (1989) concerning the perceived causes of performance. However, in those studies we investigated effort and ability beliefs only. Although these constructs are important and highly salient in PE, previous research has suggested that beliefs concerning ability are multidimensional.

For example, Dweck and colleagues have discussed conceptions of ability in terms of beliefs about the nature of intelligence (Dweck, 1999; Dweck & Leggett, 1988). They distinguish between intelligence that is believed to be relatively fixed and intelligence that is thought to be changeable. Children believing in a more fixed notion of intelligence (an "entity theory" of intelligence) were found to be more likely to adopt an ego-oriented achievement goal, whereas children believing that intelligence is changeable (an "incremental theory" of intelligence) were more likely to adopt a task goal.

These notions, although supported by Dweck and Leggett's (1988) data, require further testing in achievement goals research in sport and exercise. Indeed, Nicholls (1992) suggested that there may be parallels between "intellectual" and "athletic" activities in terms of the "nature and growth of skills" (p. 33).

We tested whether beliefs concerning the fixed or incremental nature of sport ability were related to achievement goal orientations in 11- to 12-year-old children in southwest England (Sarrazin et al., 1996). We assessed goals using the Task and Ego Orientation in Sport Questionnaire (TEOSQ), as well as asking the children to choose their preferred goal in the same way that Dweck and Leggett (1988) had; that is, the children simply stated a preference for one of three goals offered.

We found that children choosing a task goal were more likely to be represented in the incremental beliefs group (see table 4.1). This provided support for the propositions of Dweck and Leggett (1988) and showed that such notions could be extended into a new domain—that of sport.

The conception of sport ability is likely to be broader than suggested by either Dweck or Nicholls. Our results, therefore, may have been restricted by an overly narrow view of what constitutes beliefs about sport ability.

Table 4.1   Percentage of Children ($N = 194$) in the "Fixed" and "Incremental" Sport Ability Belief Groups Choosing Either a Task, Ego (Easy), or Ego (Challenging) Goal

Sport ability beliefs	Goal choice		
	Task	Ego (easy)	Ego (challenging)
Fixed	42.0	26.0	32.0
Incremental	55.3	12.8	31.9

Data from Sarrazin et al. 1996.

Consequently, we went back to the views of Fleishman (1964) in the motor behavior literature. Fleishman distinguished between abilities and skills in his "scientific" conception of motor performance factors. He distinguished abilities from skills in relation to their determinants (inheritance/learning), specificity (specific/general), and malleability (stable/changeable). He saw skills as evolving from learning and as being specific to a task or group of tasks. He viewed abilities as quite stable, sometimes genetically determined, and rather general, and saw them as limiting the effect of learning on performance. Fleishman's work preceded that of Dweck and Leggett (1988), but the views are very similar.

Besides Fleishman's scientific view, one can identify a "lay view" of sport ability as expressed by sport spectators, parents, or journalists. Such notions include beliefs that sport ability is a gift ("God-given") or is natural (see also Bandura, 1997b).

Using both scientific and lay conceptions, Sarrazin et al. (1996) developed a questionnaire to assess such beliefs and tested it with over 300 French adolescents aged 11 to 17 years. Labeled the Conception of the Nature of Athletic Ability Questionnaire, the instrument assessed beliefs in the following properties of sport ability: learning (sport ability is the product of learning), incremental (sport ability can change), specific ability (sport ability is specific to certain sports or types of sports), general ability (sport ability generalizes across many sports), stable ability (sport ability is stable across time), and gift induced (sport ability is a "gift," i.e., "God-given"). The results showed correlations in the predicted directions, with a task orientation correlating with beliefs that sport ability is incremental, is the product of learning, and is unstable. Beliefs that sport ability is a gift and that ability is general were associated with an ego goal orientation. Canonical correlation coefficients are illustrated in figure 4.1.

The data discussed so far have been presented as correlations with task and ego goals separately. However, as Nicholls (1989) pointed out, task and ego goal orientations are largely orthogonal. Tackling task and ego goals separately may not yield the true picture, therefore it is important to analyze goal profiles where possible (Fox, Goudas, Biddle, Duda, & Armstrong, 1994). Results may differ when one analyzes goals separately compared to profiles of goals in combination. Most studies in this area have used a mean or median split to create the following four groups: high task and high ego (hi/hi), high task and low ego (hi-T/lo-E), high ego and low task (hi-E/lo-T), and low task and low ego (lo/lo).

In terms of beliefs about sport success, Biddle et al. (1996) found no differences among the four groups concerning ability beliefs, but those in the hi-T/lo-E group were significantly stronger in their effort beliefs than those in the hi-E/lo-T group. Also, hi-T/lo-E scored higher in effort beliefs than

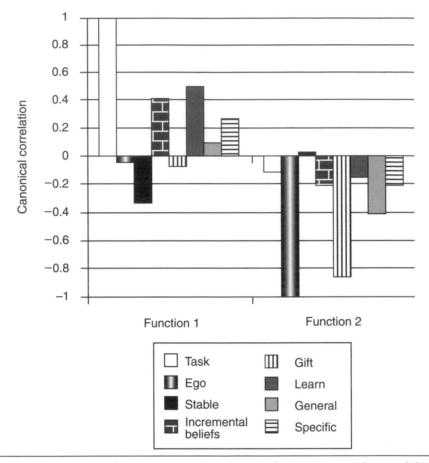

Figure 4.1   Relationships between task and ego goal orientations and sport ability beliefs.

Data from Sarrazin et al. 1996.

the lo/lo group. Sarrazin et al. (1996) also analyzed their data in this way, although they used the upper- and lower-third scores as the cutoff, thus creating more distinct goal groups than are usually found in the literature. Sarrazin et al. found the clearest between-group differences on incremental, learning, and gift beliefs. Specifically, the highest scores on the incremental and learning scales were obtained by those in the hi/hi and hi-T/lo-E groups, whereas the lowest scores for gift beliefs were obtained by those in the hi-T/lo-E group.

The data presented so far suggest that one can detect a pattern concerning a relationship between achievement goal orientations and beliefs about the causes of success and the nature of sport ability. While correlational only, the findings are striking in their consistency and worthy of consideration for practical applications.

Ability and Effort Beliefs

Clearly a task orientation is associated with the belief that effort is a main determinant of success in PE and sport for children. Effort is often believed to be controllable by the individual. The belief that trying hard will bring some success is motivational in that it reflects the "I can!" feeling that teachers so often desire for their pupils. Indeed, effort is considered a virtuous quality and, if displayed, may create a positive rapport between teacher and pupil. In the results of a recent study, both trainee and practicing teachers of primary and secondary PE stated a strong preference for pupils who demonstrated effort independent of ability or outcome (Biddle & Goudas, 1997). These results are shown in figure 4.2. Similarly, as shown in other results from the same study, the preferred grading practices of the teachers reflected a desire to assess pupils through their effort and involvement rather than ability and performance.

The literature on attributions also supports the motivational role of effort, particularly after failure (Weiner, 1986, 1995). For example, it has long

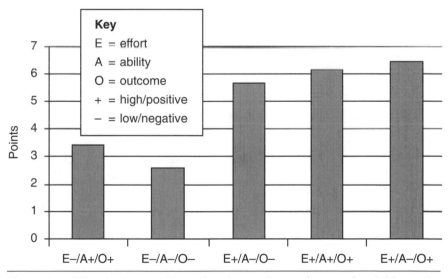

Figure 4.2   Effort is virtuous. Data showing teacher preferences for children who demonstrate combinations of effort and ability in successful and unsuccessful outcomes. *Note:* High scores = stronger, more positive preference.

been known that attributing failure to lack of ability can have negative motivational effects, whereas attributing failure to lack of effort gives participants the possibility of viewing progress in the future. However, as Covington and Omelich (1979) have pointed out, effort can also be a doubled-edged sword insofar as failing after trying hard is likely to lead to perceptions of low ability. On balance, however, effort beliefs allow pupils a greater chance to feel self-determining, whereas "ability," in the relatively stable sense, seems less controllable.

Scientific and Lay Conceptions of Sport Ability

The approach we adopted in assessing the nature of sport ability beliefs (Sarrazin et al., 1996) leads to a more differentiated view of how pupils might think about sport ability and how these beliefs may impact on motivation. According to Nicholls (1992), what is important is the way children view the *meaning* of ability rather than their views of how they have performed or demonstrated ability. However, one could argue that we need to consider both. Although we may have certain views of *what* our abilities are, our motivated behavior will be influenced by whether we think we can change these abilities. Hence, although attributions may not change our view of the *nature* of ability, they may in a motivational sense affect how we view the futility, or usefulness, of trying.

We found that, consistent with the correlations between a task orientation and effort beliefs, a task goal was associated with more controllable aspects of "ability," such as sport ability as an ability that is incremental and developed through learning. The explanation of the motivational benefits of such an approach mirrors the arguments I have made concerning effort over ability. However, such arguments also show that the construct of ability needs to be considered in more than one way. Central to motivational enhancement, therefore, is the controllable and self-determined nature of sport ability. At this stage in our knowledge, it is difficult to say whether this is much different from Nicholls's construct of the more or less differentiated nature of ability. However, by assessing several different types of sport ability beliefs, we may obtain extra information on how children view ability, how this relates to goal orientations, and what the motivational, affective, and behavioral consequences are.

Believing that sport ability can change is correlated with a task goal and seems more motivationally adaptive. Indeed, one could argue that entity beliefs reflect what Fleishman would call "abilities" and that incremental beliefs reflect the nature of "skill." In this sense, one would not necessarily expect entity and incremental beliefs to be bipolar opposites. If so, the same points apply as for studying goal profiles. That is, research should ascertain the consequences of belief profiles, such as being high entity/high incremental or high entity/low incremental.

The data presented on the independent effects of these beliefs suggest that PE teachers need to instill in pupils the belief that "ability" is changeable through learning and trying. Using feedback based on personal rather than normative information is recommended. Teachers seem to prefer this, and in combination with the motivational advantages demonstrated for pupils, the case for such an approach is strong.

Intrinsic Motivational Outcomes

In studies of goal orientations with respect to their relationships with motivational indexes, one popular index has involved the assessment of intrinsic motivation using the Intrinsic Motivation Inventory (McAuley, Duncan, & Tammen, 1989). The link between intrinsic motivation and goals has been made theoretically and empirically (see Deci & Ryan, 1985b; Duda, 1993; Duda, Chi, Newton, Walling, & Catley, 1995; Thill & Brunel, 1995a). For example, with American undergraduate students in PE (activity) classes, Duda et al. (1995) showed through canonical correlation analysis that a high task and low ego goal orientation was associated with enjoyment for one sample, and a high task orientation was associated with effort in another sample.

We studied achievement goals and "intrinsic interest" (effort and enjoyment) of children in three PE classes, specifically boys in football (soccer), girls in netball, and both boys and girls in gymnastics (Goudas, Biddle, & Fox, 1994a). Results showed that a task orientation was directly related to intrinsic interest for the football/netball lessons, whereas the relationship between ego orientation and intrinsic interest was mediated by perceptions of competence. For gymnastics lessons, only a task orientation was related to intrinsic interest. These findings were supported by our study of Romanian children (Dorobantu & Biddle, 1997), confirming cross-cultural validity.

In studies by Goudas et al. (1994a) and Dorobantu and Biddle (1997), children reported generalized perceptions of intrinsic motivation concerning PE. However, it might be better to assess children's actual reactions to PE lessons. Consequently, we (Goudas, Biddle, and Fox, 1994b) assessed adolescents performing an aerobic endurance shuttle-run "test" in normal PE lessons. Before performing the test the students completed the TEOSQ, and immediately after the run they assessed their intrinsic motivation with reference to their current motivational state. Results were analyzed according to the four goal groups specified earlier. In addition, the sample was split into two groups based on their objective running performance.

Results showed that for the less objectively successful runners, enjoyment scores were higher for those in the hi-T/lo-E group in comparison to the lo/lo and hi-E/lo-T groups. Similarly, hi-T/lo-E children had higher effort scores than those classified as hi-E/lo-T. These results suggest that a high task orientation, even for those performing below the group average, preserved some form of intrinsic motivation. This might be an important finding since many physical educators report that they wish to motivate the less able child.

A replication of this study was reported by Vlachopoulos and Biddle (1996) using an 875 yd (800 m) run in a normal PE lesson. For the less successful runners (i.e., those scoring below the median), the hi-T/lo-E group scored higher on enjoyment than the hi-E/lo-T group. Results were similar for runners in the high-performance group; children classified as hi/hi in their goal orientations scored higher on enjoyment than those in the lo-T/hi-E group. In addition, effort scores were higher for hi-T/lo-E and hi/hi groups in comparison to the lo/lo group. Consequently we concluded that "these results reveal the positive motivational consequences of adopting a task orientation singly or in combination with an ego orientation" (Vlachopoulos & Biddle, 1996, p. 162).

Affective Correlates

So far we have seen that goal orientations correlate with beliefs concerning sport success and the nature of sport ability, as well as motivational constructs such as intrinsic interest. These studies have sometimes also assessed the affective correlates of achievement goals, although it is difficult at times to separate out measures of intrinsic motivation (e.g., enjoyment) from affect.

Duda et al. (1992) found that self-reported enjoyment and boredom were associated with task and ego "dimensions." Specifically, a task dimension included a task orientation, as well as beliefs that sport success was due to effort and cooperation. The ego dimension comprised an ego orientation, as well as beliefs in ability and deception as causes of success. Enjoyment was clearly related to scores on the task dimension but not to the ego dimension. Similarly, boredom scores were correlated in a small way with the dimensions of task (negatively) and ego (positively). These results were partially supported by Spray et al. (1999).

Recently we have conducted a meta-analysis of achievement goals and affect to help clarify the literature (Ntoumanis & Biddle, 1999a). We did not restrict ourselves to studies of children, although it is likely that the results will generalize to this group since this population formed an important part of the study. After analyzing 33 studies (N = 6515) and correcting for sampling and measurement errors, we found a large correlation between task orientation and positive affect ($r = .55$). The strength of this correlation is suggested by the fact that 149 missing or yet unknown studies averaging null results would have to exist to bring the corrected correlation down to the small value of .10. The correlation between task orientation and positive affect, however, was not homogeneous, suggesting that moderators of this relationship exist.

Of particular interest to the present chapter was that the relationship between task orientation and positive affect was stronger for PE classes than for recreational settings. One explanation may have to do with the diversity of motivation of participants in PE classes. Such research samples include children representing almost all types of abilities and motivation, whereas recreational settings will comprise biased samples of volunteers. Coupled with the salience of "achievement" in PE classes, high correlations between a task orientation and positive affect may be understandable.

Physical Activity Behaviors

It is surprising that so few studies of goal orientations have addressed behavioral correlates of goals. Although evidence abounds on cognitive and affective factors related to achievement goals, we still know little about how goals may affect behaviors such as choice, persistence, or adherence.

In one application of goal orientations, we studied whether goals predicted voluntary participation in school PE (Spray & Biddle, 1997). Since PE classes are compulsory for children in Britain until the age of 16 years, we sampled students in the 16- to 18-year-old age group in a "sixth-form" college. These students could choose to take PE as part of a wider program of study options. The results, illustrated in figure 4.3, show clearly that participation was higher for those students with a high task orientation, either singly or in combination with a high ego orientation. Viewing achievement goals individually showed a significantly higher task score for participants than for nonparticipants but no difference on ego orientation.

Similar participation differences emerged in our study of 231 children 11 to 12 years old (Fox et al., 1994). We assessed, through self-report, the children's frequency of voluntary participation in sport both in and out of school. The results, illustrated in figure 4.4, reveal a graded relationship; sport involvement was higher for those high in task orientation and for those high in perceived competence. Low sport involvement was clear for those in the lo/lo group, especially when they reported low perceived competence. This group may be particularly vulnerable to amotivation in PE.

The studies by Spray and Biddle (1997) and Fox et al. (1994) reflect correlational evidence that achievement goals are associated with participation in PE and sport. However, there is also a need for experimental evidence on the nature and extent of links between goals and physical activity

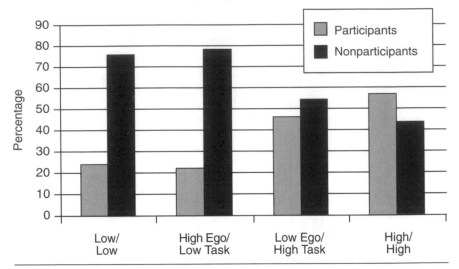

Figure 4.3 Rates of participation in voluntary physical education programs for 16- to 18-year-olds in relation to their goal orientation profiles.

Data from Spray and Biddle 1997.

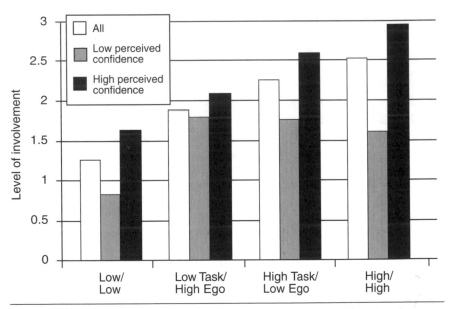

Figure 4.4 Self-reported sport involvement of 11-year-old children in relation to their goal orientation profiles. *Note:* Scores range from 0 (none) to 3 (nearly every day).

Data from Fox et al. 1994.

behaviors. To this effect, Cury, Biddle, Sarrazin, and Famose (1997) conducted two experiments with 12- to 15-year-old French school pupils to see whether goal orientations and perceived competence were predictive of the amount of investment pupils made in learning a sport task. In the first study, Cury, Biddle et al. selected male students on the basis of their goal orientation and perceived competence profiles. Specifically, the following four groups were created: (a) high ego, low task, low perceived competence (PC); (b) high ego, low task, high PC; (c) low ego, high task, low PC; (d) low ego, high task, high PC.

Group sample sizes varied between 13 and 15. The boys took part in a timed attempt at a basketball dribbling task around an obstacle course; they performed the test alone after a period of training and practice. Since the main purpose of the experiment was to test for the amount of investment in practice shown by the boys, the PE teacher (experimenter) left the gymnasium for 5 min (with a suitable excuse for his absence) but having given the boys instructions that they could practice if they wished. During this period the boys were observed unobtrusively, and the time spent practicing was recorded. After 5 min the experimenter returned and continued with the basketball test. As figure 4.5 shows, the amount of time spent practicing the task during the experimenter's absence was significantly less for those boys who were ego oriented with low perceived competence than for the other three groups. This confirms predictions from goal orientations theory.

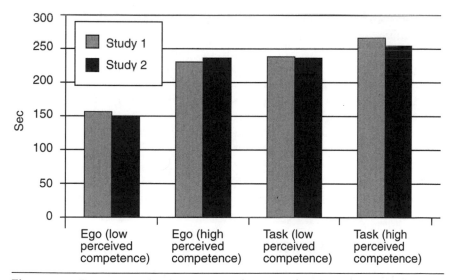

Figure 4.5 Time invested in learning as a function of goal orientations.

Data from Cury, Biddle et al. 1997.

In a second study, Cury, Biddle et al. (1997) used similar methods to examine the investment made in learning the same basketball task but this time after failure. Male French school students, aged 13 to 15 years, were selected from a larger sample on the basis of the same groupings as used in the first study. As shown in figure 4.5, the similarities between the two studies are striking. Again, the boys high in ego orientation with low perceived competence invested much less time in practice than others. They also had significantly lower expectations of success.

Overall, the results of the two experiments conducted by Cury, Biddle et al. (1997) confirm the motivational difficulties experienced by ego-oriented pupils. However, it is important to note that it is not ego orientation per se that is the problem but rather ego orientation when accompanied by low perceived competence. This is wholly consistent with theoretical predictions from goal orientations theory (Nicholls, 1989, 1992). When a child is ego involved in a PE class, the attractiveness of the task is dependent on perceived ability and the normative difficulty of the task. Ability is then often seen to be the cause of performance. The perception of success requires demonstrating superior ability, and the child can do this either by obtaining a better result than others or by achieving an identical result with less effort. On the other hand, failure is perceived when performance confirms inferior ability or when the same result is achieved but only with greater effort. In such a situation, the ego-involved child is quite likely to invest less in the achievement context. The importance of the Cury, Biddle et al. (1997) studies is underscored by their ecological validity.

Once again, the implications for the enhancement of motivation, this time with respect to behavioral outcomes, are that teachers should encourage a high task orientation singly or in combination with an ego orientation. In addition, to be adaptive, an ego orientation needs to be accompanied by high perceptions of competence. These conclusions are consistent with those drawn from the data on beliefs and affective reactions. In addition, teachers should be aware that some pupils, particularly those high in ego orientation and low in perceived competence, may use an attributional bias to minimize the role of effort. Open communication about the reasons for success and failure, as well as an awareness on the part of the teacher of attribution-change principles, is recommended. In this way, teachers can have a proactive role in helping pupils change maladaptive attributions to more adaptive ones.

Motivational Climate

The discussion so far has addressed individual goal orientations. One can argue from the data presented that achievement goal orientations form an important and powerful influence on motivation through cognitive and affective processes. However, individual differences are sometimes difficult to influence directly, and it may not be cost effective to try to do so. As Treasure and Roberts (1995) have argued, "a growing body of literature exists to suggest that the teacher plays an active role in the construction of children's perceptions of the motivational climate and, consequently, the quality of children's motivation" (p. 480). Some researchers, therefore, have emphasized the importance of the achievement environment, or climate.

What Is Motivational Climate?

Much has been written about teaching styles and classroom interaction, yet there has been relatively little research until quite recently on the achievement climate in school PE contexts. Two main climates have been identified according to the work of Ames in school classrooms (see Ames, 1992b; Ames & Archer, 1988; Treasure & Roberts, 1995) and are termed "mastery" and "performance" (see Treasure, this volume). Although the general dimensions of climate have been used satisfactorily in PE research (Biddle et al., 1995; Cury et al., 1996; Dorobantu & Biddle, 1997; Goudas & Biddle, 1994b; Papaioannou, 1994), factors underlying these dimensions are less clear (Ntoumanis & Biddle, 1999b). For example, Papaioannou (1994) identified "teacher-initiated learning orientation" and "students' learning orientation" as mastery-oriented factors, and "students' competitive orientation," "students' worries about mistakes," and "outcome orientation without effort" as performance-oriented climate factors. Similarly, Biddle et al. (1995) found that the mastery dimension was composed of measures of "pursuit of progress by pupils" and "promotion of learning by the teacher" for a sample of French adolescents. However, with British youth they used subdimensions of "class mastery orientation," "teacher's promotion of mastery orientation," "perceptions of choice," and "teacher support." For performance climate, the French data supported the subdimensions of "pursuit of comparison by pupils," "worries about mistakes," and "promotion of comparison by teacher," while the British data supported just two subdimensions—"class performance orientation" and "worries about mistakes."

These results suggest that we have not yet clearly identified the factors underpinning mastery and performance climate. From a measurement perspective, it appears to be satisfactory to use the two higher-order dimensions of mastery and performance. However, we need more information on the subdimensions, as these are likely to be useful in identifying the mechanisms for changing the climate, similar to the TARGET intervention proposed by Epstein (see Ames, 1992b) and discussed in the later section on interventions. Table 4.2 summarizes studies assessing motivational climate in PE contexts.

Table 4.2 Summary of Studies Measuring Motivational Climates in School Physical Education

Study	Sample	Climate measure	Purposes	Results
Papaio-annou (1994)	Studies 1 and 2: 1393 and 394 Greek school students, respectively	LAPOPECQ	Develop a questionnaire to measure percep-tions of learning and performance orientations in physical education (PE) classes	1. Confirmatory factor analysis revealed two high-order factors: a learning-oriented and a performance-oriented factor. 2. Students' intrinsic motivation and positive attitudes toward the lesson were positively related to the learning-oriented scales and unrelated to performance-oriented scales.
Papaio-annou (1995a)	1393 Greek school students	LAPOPECQ	Examine how perceived motiva-tional climate in PE is related to (a) perceptions of teachers' differen-tial treatment toward high and low achievers, (b) reported motiva-tion and anxiety of children with high and low perceived competence during play with high- or low-ability children	Perceived compe-tence had no effect on intrinsic motivation when extremely high learning goals were adopted. When low learning goals were adopted, motiva-tion decreased for children with low perceived ability playing with high achievers and for children with high perceived ability playing with low achievers.

Study	Sample	Climate measure	Purposes	Results
Goudas & Biddle (1994b)	254 English school students	PECCS	Investigate the psychometric properties of PECCS and the relationship of its subscales with intrinsic motivation	1. The construct validity of the PECCS was generally supported through the results of factor analyses. 2. The mastery dimension scores were found to significantly enhance the prediction of intrinsic motivation beyond that accounted for by perceived competence, whereas this was not the case for performance climate scores. 3. A climate profile analysis showed that high performance climate was not detrimental as long as it was accompanied by high mastery climate.
Biddle, Cury, Goudas, Sarrazin, Famose, & Durand (1995)	Studies 1, 2, and 3: 311, 179, and 146 French school students, respectively Studies 4 and 5: 254 and 85 British school students, respectively	1. PECCS 2. EPCM	1. Perform a cross-national research project investigating the measurement of perceived class climate in PE lessons 2. Examine the relationships between motivational climate and related motivational variables	1. Psychometric analysis was more satisfactory for the French than for the English language scale. 2. A shortened version of the PECCS assessing mastery and performance dimensions of climate was shown to predict important motivational measures.

(continued)

Table 4.2 *(continued)*

Study	Sample	Climate measure	Purposes	Results
Cury, Biddle, Famose, Goudas, Sarrazin, & Durand (1996)	700 French female school students	EPCM	Test a model of proposed relationships between motivational climates, dispositional goals, perceived competence, and intrinsic interest	Motivational climates were found to be more important than dispositional goals in influencing pupil interest in PE. Perceived competence was also a significant predictor of intrinsic interest in PE.
Mitchell (1996)	622 American middle school students	PELES	1. Design an instrument (PELES) to measure perceived learning environment in PE 2. Explore relationships between perceived learning environment and intrinsic motivation	1. PELES consisted of three different factors: Perceived Challenge, Perceived Threat, and Perceived Competitiveness. 2. The Perceived Threat and Perceived Challenge predicted intrinsic motivation for males and females.
Treasure (1993)	114 American children	Modified PMCSQ-1	Examine whether participating in a task- or ego-involving climate leads to differences in cognitive and affective responses	Students in the mastery group preferred more challenging tasks, were more satisfied than those in the performance group, and believed that success was caused by motivation and not by external factors.

Study	Sample	Climate measure	Purposes	Results
Solmon (1996)	109 American school students	Modified PMCSQ-1	Examine whether students' persistence and attributions for success differ as a function of motivational climates	1. Students in the mastery climate showed higher persistence at a difficult level than those in a performance climate. 2. Attributions of success to normative ability were more linked to performance than mastery climate.
Treasure (1997)	233 American children	Adapted version of Ames & Archer's (1988) Classroom Achievement Goals Questionnaire	Examine the relationship between perceptions of the motivational climate and children's cognitive and affective responses	Students who perceived a task-involving context reported a positive attitude toward the class, high perceived ability, the belief that effort and ability cause success, and feelings of satisfaction. Students who perceived an ego-involving context focused on ability as a cause of success, reported a negative attitude toward the class, and reported feelings of boredom.
Spray (2000)	$N = 123$ British students with 76 assessed at 5- to 8-month follow-up	PECCS	Test how well goal orientations and motivational climate in compulsory schooling predicted participation in voluntary PE after a move to a tertiary college	Participation in voluntary PE was predicted by a mastery climate but not by goal orientations.

We have calculated effect sizes for physical activity climate studies to indicate the strength of relationships between motivational climate and selected cognitive and affective variables (Ntoumanis & Biddle, 1999b). Although the studies were not restricted to children in PE settings, they indicate the strength of links between climate and associated psychological outcomes.

From this quantitative synthesis of 14 studies with a total sample size of almost 4500, the correlation, corrected for sampling and measurement errors, between mastery climate and positive motivational outcomes (e.g., satisfaction, positive attitudes toward lessons, intrinsic motivation) was .71, indicating a large effect. By contrast, performance climate correlated in a small-to-moderate way and in a negative direction with positive outcomes (effect size [ES] = −.30). Negative outcomes comprised factors such as worry and the emphasis on normative ability. The effect for mastery climate on negative outcomes was small-to-moderate and negative (ES = −.26), and for performance climate on these outcomes it was moderate and positive (ES = .46). These results, overall, indicate the importance of a mastery climate in promoting positive psychological outcomes in physical activity.

Goals or Climate: Which Comes First?

Several of our studies have tested whether individual achievement goal orientations or the situational climate better predicts motivational outcomes in PE. For football and netball lessons in a school in England, we found that task and ego goals predicted either directly, or indirectly through perceived competence, intrinsic interest and intentions to participate. These goals were predicted by their respective climates; that is, a task goal was predicted by mastery climate and ego goal by performance climate (Biddle et al., 1995). However, for gymnastics—an activity reported as less intrinsically interesting to the pupils—mastery climate scores directly predicted intrinsic interest and intention, unlike task or ego goals.

In a similar study of 700 adolescent French girls' perceptions of school PE classes (Cury et al., 1996), again we found that achievement goals were predicted by their respective climate dimension. In addition, intrinsic interest in school PE was best predicted by climate rather than goals. Specifically, mastery climate positively predicted interest, whereas a performance climate was related to interest inversely.

We studied Romanian school students with respect to achievement goals and school PE class climate (Dorobantu & Biddle, 1997). Using hierarchical regression analysis in the prediction of intrinsic motivation in PE, we found that after perceived competence, the best predictor was a mastery climate, accounting for some 25% of the variance in intrinsic motivation beyond that of perceived competence. Similarly, Spray (2000) found that older adolescents in Britain opting to take part in voluntary college PE lessons were those who perceived the PE class climate at their previous school as mastery oriented.

These studies show some cross-cultural stability since they indicate similar results for children in PE in Britain, France, and Romania. Overall, the results suggest that for compulsory PE settings, and particularly when intrinsic interest is not high, the situational climate is more important in determining motivation than individual goals are. There appear to be two possible explanations for this. First, when intrinsic motivation at the individual level is low, the motivational climate can create interest. This is important since the role of the teacher becomes more central, making interventions for increasing motivation viable. Students may also participate in compulsory PE classes for introjected as well as identified and intrinsic reasons (see Chatzisarantis, Biddle, & Meek, 1997; Deci & Ryan, 1985b; Goudas et al., 1994a; Vallerand, 1997). In other words, some children participate because they "have to," thus individual motivation is less self-determined. In such cases, one could suggest that a positive mastery climate can boost intrinsic motivation by making the class ethos self-determining and autonomous, thus overriding initial individual extrinsic or introjected reasons for being in the class.

A second possible explanation is that the studies have assessed goals as *orientations* rather than as measures of goal state involvement in the specific context under study. Situational climate, particularly in contexts in which involvement is compulsory, might be expected to override generalized beliefs or orientations. More work is required, therefore, to ascertain whether the same is true when goals are assessed as situational involvement measures.

Motivational Climate:
Implications for Motivational Enhancement

One could argue that it may be easier to intervene to enhance motivation by manipulating climate than to do so by attempting to change goal orientations or associated correlates of goals already discussed. The best-known intervention possibilities are those outlined by Epstein through his TAR-GET model and discussed by Treasure and Roberts (1995; Treasure, this volume). The key aspects of this model in relation to mastery and performance climates are shown in table 4.3. These involve structuring the environment to take account of the nature of the tasks, the nature and use of authority, how pupils are recognized for their efforts, how groups are formed, how evaluation procedures are structured, and how time is allocated in the lesson.

Table 4.3   Descriptions of Mastery and Performance Climates and TARGET Structures

Mastery	Performance
Tasks	
Challenging and diverse	Absence of variety and challenge
Authority	
Students given choices and leadership roles	No participation by students in decision-making processes
Recognition	
Private and based on individual progress	Public and based on social comparison
Grouping	
Cooperative learning and peer interaction promoted	Groups formed on the basis of ability
Evaluation	
Based on mastery of tasks and on individual improvement	Based on winning or outperforming others
Time	
Time requirements adjusted to personal capabilities	Time allocated for learning uniform for all students

In addition, although the data clearly show the motivational benefits of a mastery climate, two main issues require discussion in relation to motivational enhancement. First, what else, in addition to the TARGET factors, might constitute a mastery climate? Second, do we need to match climate to individual goals to maximize motivation?

Dimensions of Climate

As discussed earlier, it is not clear, at least from a psychometric viewpoint, how mastery and performance climates are constituted. Factors that appear common across studies (e.g., Biddle et al., 1995; Papaioannou, 1995b) for a mastery climate reflect the teachers' promotion of a mastery climate and some form of pupil-oriented mastery orientation. For a performance climate, worries about mistakes and pupils' competitive/performance orientations have been proposed. These may therefore form important aspects for teachers to consider in promoting a motivationally adaptive climate in PE lessons. But until we have more robust and consistent psychometric measures of climate, at least at the first-order level, interventions may be better guided by the TARGET model. However, tests of the TARGET model in PE are scarce (see Treasure and Roberts, 1995; Treasure, this volume).

Compatibility Between Goals and Climate

A persistent difficulty teachers face in PE is how to teach for all children. In the case of goals, in any one class a teacher has children varying in goal profiles, such as high task and high ego, high ego and low task, and so on. If the climate data support the promotion of a mastery climate, where does this leave pupils who are clearly ego oriented? The data on goal orientations do not generally support the view that ego orientation is "bad." Rather they show that ego orientation, when accompanied by low perceived competence and/or by a low task orientation, may produce motivational difficulties. Pupils who are high in ego orientation but who also have a high task orientation are often strongly motivated, sometimes more so than individuals with other goal orientation profiles.

It is unclear how ego-oriented pupils react to PE lessons with a mastery climate. The study by Lloyd and Fox (1992) sheds some light on this issue. In a small-scale teaching intervention, adolescent girls were taught aerobics in two different ways for six weeks. One teaching approach emphasized peer and norm comparison and was externally referenced, so the condition was similar to a performance climate. The second condition promoted a self-referenced class by emphasizing personal improvement and discouraging external comparison, thus being more akin to a mastery climate. Girls were assessed for goal orientation using the TEOSQ. In addition to showing that enjoyment and motivation were higher after learning in the self-referenced condition than in the externally referenced intervention, results indicated that those who were low in ego orientation had significantly raised ego scores after learning in the externally referenced condition. Conversely, those with high ego scores in the self-referenced group had lowered ego scores. This study, though small, highlights the importance of the interaction of class climate and goal orientations, and suggests that goals may not be quite as stable as we sometimes assume. Changing goals through intervention gives hope to teachers that motivational change is possible. However, further research is required on the issue of compatibility between individual achievement goals and the dominant motivational climate.

Intervention Studies

Few studies have manipulated constructs associated with achievement goals or climate to test the efficacy of interventions in PE settings. Clearly, this is an area for development in the future. However, some researchers have manipulated climate; we have already considered the study by Lloyd and Fox (1992) in the context of motivational climate.

Given the close link between teaching styles and perceived climate in PE, and building on Lloyd and Fox's (1992) findings, we sought to investigate whether manipulating teaching styles in line with climate dimensions would result in differential motivational effects (Goudas, Biddle, Fox, & Underwood, 1995). A small, intact class of young adolescent girls attending a private school in England were taught track and field for 10 weeks in their normal PE lessons. An experienced university lecturer, well versed in teaching styles, taught the class and alternated lessons according to two teaching styles:

- Direct style: Most of the decisions were made by the teacher; the type of task, duration of practice, and degree of difficulty were determined by the teacher. This style was chosen to approximate the creation of a climate low in mastery orientation.

- Differentiated style: The teacher gave the children choices; a variety of activities was provided, and degree of difficulty and pace of practice/learning were decided by the child. This style was chosen to approximate the creation of a climate high in mastery orientation.

At the end of each lesson, measures were taken of intrinsic motivation, task and work avoidance goal involvement (in the lesson), and intention to participate in future lessons. Results showed more positive effects for lessons taught in the differentiated style, suggesting an influence for mastery climate. Specifically, after the differentiated-style lessons, the children reported higher intrinsic motivation and task involvement scores than after direct-style lessons.

Marsh and Peart (1988) conducted a 14-session intervention study to compare the effects of "competitive" and "cooperative" aerobic exercise programs on physical fitness and multidimensional self-perceptions of adolescent girls in Australia. Participants in the cooperative program (akin to a mastery climate) reported improvements in perceived physical ability and appearance, whereas those in the competitive program showed a decrease in these constructs. Interestingly, both groups improved their physical fitness, so this could not be a factor in explaining the changes observed.

Theeboom, De Knop, and Weiss (1995) used the TARGET structure to plan an intervention study for children learning new martial arts skills. Children exposed to the mastery climate reported higher levels of enjoyment, perceived competence, and intrinsic motivation, although actual perceptions of the climate were not assessed.

The few intervention studies that exist make it clear that a mastery climate has positive cognitive and affective outcomes. However, most are short term and limited in what they assess. Future research must address the issue of implementing more rigorous controlled trials for longer periods.

Other Motivational Constructs and Likely Mechanisms

A fundamental issue, whether one is dealing with goal orientations and motivational climate from a theoretical or practical perspective, is why a task goal or mastery climate should have such beneficial cognitive, affective, and behavioral effects. Can we identify the likely mechanisms of these relationships? This section deals briefly with two perspectives in this regard: an attributional approach and a self-determination theory approach.

An Attributional Approach

I have already commented on the role of effort and ability in achievement motivation in PE settings. These constructs are also central to an attributional approach. However, despite the popularity of attribution theory research in sport during the 1970s and 1980s, attribution theory has declined as a primary focus in many achievement motivation studies. It has also generated criticism as "less a psychology of motivation than a social psychology of perception" (Roberts, 1992a, p. 11). However, as pointed out by Weiner (1986, 1995), a complex cognitive causal sequence is likely to emanate from an initial perception of success and failure. The full sequence might involve the outcome itself leading to an appraisal of causal information (e.g., past successes), causal ascriptions (e.g., ability, effort), classification into dimensions (e.g., controllability), affective consequences (e.g., guilt), and finally, behavioral consequences. If this sequence is followed, the consequences of making certain attributions may be very important.

For this reason, coupled with the evidence that people make numerous attributional appraisals in achievement events (see Weiner, 1986), attributional approaches may help us understand why a task goal orientation or mastery climate has positive motivational properties. Perhaps the key issue is that a task goal is associated with personal striving—effort, self-determination, and self-referenced criteria to judge success. For this reason, attributions associated with a task goal are likely to involve the factor of effort. We know from attribution research that effort is often seen as internal, controllable, and unstable, thus allowing participants to view success as achievable in the future with the application of effort and—perhaps more importantly—to view failure as redeemable with greater effort. Such an approach has logic and appeal and may help explain the adaptive motivational nature of a task orientation. In short, the key mechanism may be the responsibility that task-oriented persons take for their own actions or that mastery climates create (Weiner, 1995).

A Self-Determination Theory Approach

The impressive theorizing of Deci and Ryan (1985b) provides a complementary view to attributions and goals and helps explain the motivational benefits of a task goal orientation (Ryan & Deci, 2000a, 2000b). These authors propose that humans are driven by three fundamental psychological needs—the needs for competence, autonomy, and relatedness (social needs). Competence is clearly central to achievement motivation and tends to dominate the conceptualization of goals. The need for autonomy or self-determination, however, is also a major driving force for the formation of motives. When autonomy is satisfied, individuals experience choice and freedom, and their behavior is likely to be regulated by intrinsic or "identified" structures. Intentional behavior is then autonomous and conforms to more of a task orientation since this is a self-referenced style of perception. When the need for autonomy is not satisfied, freedom and choice are not evident. Motives are therefore likely to be more extrinsic or "introjected" and will be associated with the external-referencing style of an ego orientation. Such "controlling" regulation of behavior will bring less positive affect and weaker intentions (see Chatzisarantis et al., 1997).

Goal orientations and different motivational climates, therefore, may act according to whether they satisfy the need for autonomy and self-determination. Perceptions of autonomy and control may explain why a task orientation is motivationally adaptive.

Conclusions

There is no doubt that goal orientations, and more recently motivational climate, dominate the literature in sport and exercise when we consider achievement motivation. To understand how to enhance motivation in PE settings, we are fortunate in having a growing literature on achievement goals and climate in this physical activity context. The research is reasonably diverse in terms of samples, though methodologically narrow, and provides conceptually coherent findings on the relationship between individual and situational goals and cognitive, affective, and behavioral factors. There is little doubt that physical educators will increase their chance of enhancing motivation in their classes if they use teaching strategies that promote a mastery climate, as well as attempting to promote a task orientation in children, either singly or in combination with an ego orientation.

Acknowledgments

The contribution of the following people to our research program, much of which is reported here, is greatly appreciated: Ken Fox, Joan Duda, Sue Bock, Monica Dorobantu, Chris Spray, John Wang, Martin Hagger, the "Greek Mafia"—Nikos Chatzisarantis, Manolis Georgiadis, Marios Goudas, Antonis Hatzigeorgiadis, Nikos Ntoumanis, Symeon Vlachopoulos —and the "French connection"—Francois Cury, Marc Durand, Jean Pierre Famose, and Philippe Sarrazin.

Achievement Goal Research in Sport: Pushing the Boundaries and Clarifying Some Misunderstandings

Joan L. Duda

A burgeoning area of inquiry into the nature and determinants of achievement motivation in sport concerns the concept of goal perspectives (see Biddle, Fry, Roberts, Treasure, this volume). Grounded in achievement goal theories of motivated behavior (Ames, 1992a, 1992c; Dweck, 1986; Dweck & Leggett, 1988; Nicholls, 1984a, 1989), this approach presumes that variations in goal perspectives, or ways in which individuals judge their competence and define successful accomplishment, are the critical antecedents to variations in motivational processes. The two central goal perspectives are labeled task and ego

(Nicholls, 1984a, 1989). When task involved, people seek mainly to gain skill or knowledge, exhibit effort, and perform their best and/or experience personal improvement. If the person achieves such purposes, he/she feels competent and successful. When ego involved, people are preoccupied with the adequacy of their ability and with the demonstration of superior competence. Perceptions of competence and subjective achievement entail social comparisons of an individual's performance and exerted effort with those of others. Indicative of the popularity of research on task and ego goals, a recent review of the measures of goal perspectives in the physical domain cited 135 studies[1] published within the past 10 years (Duda & Whitehead, 1998).

A number of reasons for this plethora of investigations are plausible. One is the apparent relevance of achievement goal conceptualizations to sport (Nicholls, 1992; Roberts, 1984, this volume)—an achievement domain where, as in the classroom, perceptions of ability are salient and pertinent to distinctions in motivation.

A second explanation is the seeming simplicity of the concepts of task and ego goals (Duda, 1997b). Achievement goal theories have an intuitive appeal, as everyone believes she/he knows what task and ego goals are and has experienced task and ego involvement in achievement activities. Still another possible explanation stems from the early and rather far-reaching work in sport-related environments on measurement of some central concepts within goal perspective theories (Duda & Whitehead, 1998). The major concepts include task and ego orientations (or individual differences in the tendency to be task and ego involved) and situationally emphasized goal perspectives (or the perceived motivational climate). It is fair to say that assessment has walked hand in hand with the application and extension of achievement goal conceptualizations in the physical domain. Perhaps, as pointed out by Duda and Whitehead (1998), attempts to develop goal perspective questionnaires have occasionally even surpassed current conceptual understanding of the nature of dispositional, environmental, and state task and ego goals.

One benefit of the attractiveness of achievement goal frameworks is that it has brought about ever-increasing examination of concepts and measures across diverse athletic populations, sport contexts, and cultural groups. The literature is marked by sport-related replications of groundbreaking research in the academic domain and by theoretical expansions of this work. Such efforts are important and exciting, as they contribute to a cogent body of knowledge that is evolving over time. Through such extensive scholarly inquiry, we learn where the theory is explanatory with respect to sport motivation, where it falls short, and where it can and should be modified. In this way, sport goal perspective researchers may also advance the larger, mainstream achievement goal frameworks originally formulated to explain differences in the quality and quantity of academic motivation (Ames, 1992a; Dweck, 1986; Nicholls, 1989).

The popularity of goal perspective models of motivation can also prove problematic, however. For example, sometimes in our zeal to conduct research grounded in a promising contemporary theoretical paradigm, central constructs are homogenized or bastardized and theoretical tenets are misinterpreted or "lost in the shuffle." Precision can lose out to productivity as we rush into the next investigation. Existing instruments may be misused or new assessments haphazardly developed. With regard to the most current literature, it is even difficult for goal perspective researchers to keep up! When we are captivated by a theory, we may find ourselves wearing blinders and therefore failing to see how the theoretical framework differs from or accords with other conceptualizations. Finally, theoretical passion can sometimes result in a bad case of confirmation bias.

This chapter presents major directions in and issues arising from contemporary sport achievement goal research. It does not extensively review the literature conducted in the past few years (e.g., since the publication of previous major reviews by Duda [1992, 1993, 1994]; Roberts, Treasure, & Kavussanu [1997]). However, it does highlight recent areas of inquiry that advance past work. My aim is to push the boundaries and help clarify some misunderstandings with regard to the study of goal perspectives in sport settings. In essence, the purpose is to enhance our collective insight into this literature and promote further discovery and discussion. However, as a goal perspective theory enthusiast, I may fall short of this task-involved focus and fail to avoid the pitfalls described. If so, self-referenced, effort-based, and informational feedback is respectfully requested!

Achievement Goal Theory: Major Constructs

The major goal of this section is to elucidate and distinguish the central concepts embedded in achievement goal frameworks. Current limitations in and the challenges facing future assessments of dispositional goals, states of goal involvement, and perceptions of situationally emphasized goals will also be addressed. Finally, I will discuss what is deemed to be the "heart and soul" of achievement goal theory. In other words, what is the purpose and specifics of this model of motivation with respect to the prediction of motivation-related variables?

Goal Perspectives: What They Are

Variations in goal perspectives are manifested at the dispositional (or individual differenece) and psychological state levels. This important point has implications for the assumed association between and presumed stability of task and ego goals at these two levels. Situations also vary with respect to the goal perspectives deemed to be emphasized. In the achievement goal literature, such situational variability is typically examined with respect to the subjective environment, or perceived motivational climate. Although little has been done in this area, the objective motivational climate would be worthwhile to determine as well. Issues relating to the measurement of state, dispositional, and situational goal perspecitves will be reivewed next. Questions about the predictive utility of these three constructs, whether best examined independently or in conjunction, will also be addressed.

Dispositional in Contrast to State Goal Perspectives

According to Nicholls (1989), individuals differ in their proneness to task and ego involvement. In an attempt to move toward consistency in the terminology within the sport literature, Duda (1992, 1996) has drawn from Nicholls's work and suggested that we refer to dispositional goal perspectives, or habitual achievement preoccupations with task and ego goals, as *goal orientations*.

Two major measures of dispositional goal orientations in the sport literature are the Task and Ego Orientation in Sport Questionnaire, or TEOSQ (Duda, 1989), developed by Duda and Nicholls (cited in Duda & Whitehead, 1998), and the Perceptions of Success Questionnaire, or POSQ, by Roberts and Balague (1989; Roberts, Treasure, & Balague, 1998). Many studies have supported the validity and reliability of these instruments (see Duda & Whitehead, 1998; Hanrahan & Biddle, 1997; Marsh, 1994). Consistent with the thinking of Nicholls (1989), both questionnaires tap variation in the proneness to task and ego involvement in sport by assessing individuals' achievement-related concerns or criteria underlying subjective success.

Orthogonality of Goal Orientations

Aligned with the conceptual and empirical contributions of Nicholls (1989) is the proposition that task and ego orientations are orthogonal, not bipolar. In general, this presumed independence has been supported in research using the TEOSQ or POSQ in sport and physical education settings (Duda & Whitehead, 1998). There are some exceptions (e.g., Kim & Gill, 1997; Li, Harmer, Chi, & Vongjaturapat, 1996); but in such studies, correlations between the two dimensions are typically found to be low to moderate, and positive rather than negative (as was the case in Li, Harmer, Acock, Vongjaturapat, & Boonverabut, 1997). To me it seems that whether a significant association between task and ego orientation emerges depends on such factors as competitive level (e.g., as the literature suggests that a larger percentage of elite athletes are high in both task and ego orientation rather than low in both or high in one and low in the other, is it more likely that the two goal orientations will be positively correlated at the higher competitive levels?) and cultural variation (e.g., Kim & Gill, 1997; Li, Harmer, Chi, & Vongjaturapat, 1996; Li et al., 1997). It might be that the motivational climates surrounding the athletes in our studies also impact the observed correlation between task and ego orientation. Future researchers need to carefully sort out the variables influencing the degree of independence between dispositional goal dimensions.

Dweck (Dweck, 1986, 1999; Elliott & Dweck, 1988) holds a different viewpoint from Nicholls (1989) on the assessment of dispositional goal orientations. She distinguishes between two classes of goals: the performance goal, which is aligned with Nicholls's conception of an ego goal, and the learning goal, which is compatible with Nicholls's definition of a task goal. With the former, the aim is to gain favorable judgments or avoid unfavorable judgments of one's competence—that is, to look smart or athletically able/skilled. With the latter, the focus is on increasing one's competence—that is, becoming smarter or increasing one's level of sport ability/skill (Dweck, 1999). Dweck does not operationalize these goals as orthogonal constructs and suggests that assessing the value of each goal separately is not particularly informative (e.g., in predicting whether individuals hold an incremental or an entity theory of intelligence). Rather, for assessing achievement goals she recommends that the goals be pitted against each other. In such a methodological approach it is not possible for someone to be high in both achievement goal emphases. Specifically, Dweck and colleagues (Dweck & Sorich, 1999) suggest the following:

> It is important to understand that both kinds of goals are natural, necessary and pretty much universal. Everyone wants their ability to be esteemed by others and everyone wants to learn new things. The difference among students lies in how much they value each goal, and whether they are willing to sacrifice one goal for the other. (p. 237)

To date, Dweck's conceptualizations of individual differences in achievement goals have not significantly influenced measurement of goal orientations in the sport domain. Dweck and her associates (personal communication, April 27, 1999) have done preliminary work on a measure geared toward children and are currently developing a scale to assess the emphasis on learning versus performance goals for the college-aged population. Perhaps in the future we will see a parallel measure specific to the athletic context. An important question for future research will be whether Dweck's operationalization of achievement goal orientations has greater predictive utility than existing two-dimensional instruments (such as the TEOSQ and POSQ) in the sport environment.

Assessment of Goal States

Task and ego orientations are not equivalent to *task* and *ego involvement* (Nicholls, 1989; see also Roberts, this volume). One current dilemma is the potentially inappropriate use of the TEOSQ or POSQ as measures of goal states or task and ego involvement per se. The TEOSQ and POSQ were developed to assess how individuals *typically* define success in sport[2] with respect to self-referenced (e.g., learning, trying hard) and normatively referenced (i.e., showing that one has more ability than others) criteria. In contrast to the situation with independent dispositional tendencies, it is difficult to imagine how an individual can be in a state of task and ego involvement at the same time,[3] although this individual may experience various degrees of task and ego involvement in the same activity. These two goal states, according to Nicholls in particular (1984a, 1989), entail strikingly different ways of processing an activity that can fluctuate during an event. Thus a suitable assessment of goal states would seem to consist of dependent dimensions that can be measured dynamically throughout a sport event (although one should note that to date, assessments of goal involvement have been administered only before a competition or practice session, not during the activity). Conceptually, it seems a bit problematic (although certainly pragmatic) from the onset to reach for dispositional goal inventories when the purpose is to determine individuals' goal states. By doing so, we are employing a measure of two orthogonal dimensions to assess constructs that possibly are inversely related. Let us turn now to what the literature has told us so far about employment of the TEOSQ or POSQ for such purposes.

To date, there has been limited work on the measurement of goal states in the sport domain, particularly via assessment tools specifically developed for this purpose. A few studies have utilized dispositional measures (such as the TEOSQ or POSQ) to assess task and ego involvement (Hall & Kerr, 1997; Hall, Kerr, & Matthews, 1998; Williams, 1998). In this research, (1) the internal consistency of the adapted scales has been acceptable; (2) the adapted scales have been found to be moderately correlated and not redundant with the original dispositional scales; (3) the "goal state" scales have generally emerged as better predictors of the targeted psychological state-dependent measures than their dispositional counterparts; and (4) the intercorrelation between the task and ego goal state measures has varied, from no appreciable relationship to a low, positive association.

The first three findings are promising with regard to the worthiness of such a modified assessment and are generally consistent with findings on the measurement of and observed interrelationships between trait and state anxiety in the sport setting (Burton, 1998; Smith, Smoll, & Wiechman, 1998). The last finding is somewhat disconcerting if we accept Nicholls's assertions about the incompatibility between task- and ego-involved psychological states at one moment in time. Perhaps we see such results because such modified assessments do not measure an athlete's goal state (or task/ ego involvement), which can fluctuate throughout an activity, but rather provide a composite appraisal of the criteria underlying perceived success in the competitive event that is coming up (rather than in the sport overall, as is presumed to be the case for dispositional measures). That is, there may be three separate but interrelated constructs: one is individual differences in goal perspective or dispositional goal orientations; the second (epitomized in the work of Hall & Kerr [1997], Hall et al. [1998], and Williams [1998]) is a type of "state" goal orientation; and the third is the task and ego involvement processing states.

Researchers in sport have attempted to assess more transitory goal states with measures developed specifically for that purpose. Swain and Harwood (1996) and Harwood and Swain (1998) employed single-item measures that determine athletes' precompetition emphasis on achieving a (high) personal standard of performance (independent of the competitive outcome) and on beating others (regardless of the quality of one's personal performance). The former was equated to a task state goal, the latter to an ego state goal. In an additional item, the participants (junior-level swimmers and tennis players) picked one of these goals over the other. Responses to this item were placed on a continuum with the neutral point presumed to reflect being high in both task and ego involvement.[4] The first two items were moderately correlated with this "goal preference" item. Although this is an interesting approach to measuring task and ego involvement, it appears that the possibility of the orthogonality/interdependence of goal states is confounded in this three-item goal involvement assessment. Moreover, the concepts of task and ego involvement are operationalized in regard to personal performance versus the competitive outcome, respectively, in Swain and Harwood's research (Duda & Whitehead, 1998). The latter, in particular, is not exactly in line with Nicholls's (1989) conceptualization of ego involvement, which is more intimately grounded in a concern for showing superiority (based on a differentiated conception of ability) and focused on the implications of this for how one currently processes an activity.

Duda and Whitehead (1998) provide some suggestions for measuring these seemingly rudimentary but actually quite complex cognitive and affective states of task and ego involvement. They propose that the

> assessment of task and ego involvement per se may very well entail the examination of a pattern of variables that represent task and ego processing and preoccupation . . . [and] the measurement of task- and ego-involved goal states would be dynamic and multifaceted. Variations in attentional focus, concerns about what one is doing and how one is doing, the degree of self-/other awareness and task absorption, level of effort exertion, etc., might constitute the constellation of symptoms reflecting task and ego goal states. (p. 42)

Clearly, the development of such an assessment would be a formidable endeavor. As is the case for any state measure (e.g., cognitive and somatic state anxiety), researchers would also have the practical difficulty of obtaining repeated assessments of goal involvement while athletes are engaged in competition or practice. Remembering the concerns of Csikszentmihalyi (1992) regarding the challenges of measuring flow states, I can't help but wonder whether repetitive assessments of goal states during sport engagement would increase the likelihood that individuals would get out of a state of task involvement (and perhaps increase the probability of their becoming ego involved). To reduce this possibility, it might be worthwhile to have athletes engage in retroactive recall of what they were thinking (and why they were thinking this way) during the event or a previous one.

As I think our current discussion reinforces, measuring task and ego involvement and distinguishing their operational and conceptual definitions from goal orientations have led to some perhaps unavoidable confusion in the sport psychology literature. For example, Harwood and Hardy (1999; see also Harwood, Hardy, & Swain, 2000) contend in a recent article:

> . . . it is important to note that although the origins of dispositional tendencies may have been related to the differentiation process, the fact that goal orientations are orthogonal *(as assessed by the TEOSQ and POSQ)* [italics added] means that they cannot logically be defined by the likelihood of an individual adopting either an undifferentiated or differentiated concept of ability. The construct of ability is either psychologically differentiated from effort, task difficulty, and luck or it remains undifferentiated from these constructs; it cannot be both. In this way, it is argued that differentiation or undifferentiation cannot be the defining characteristics of two independent goal orientations. [In essence] the individual cannot be differentiated and also undifferentiated. (p. 242)

On the basis of my interpretation of the literature, I will try to clear up some of this perplexity. As individuals move into adolescence (see Fry, this volume; Fry & Duda, 1997; Nicholls, 1989; Nicholls & Miller, 1984a), it has been suggested that they are cognitively capable of holding a differentiated *and* an undifferentiated conception of ability. According to Nicholls (1989), the conception of ability we evoke at a particular time impacts how we judge our current performance and how we decide whether high or low ability was demonstrated. When centered on a differentiated conception, ability and effort covary, and ability is viewed as a capacity that "is judged in reference to the performance of others" (Nicholls, 1989, p. 43). This doesn't mean that effort *no longer equals* ability, which has been suggested in the sport literature (Harwood et al., 2000). The covariance between effort and ability means that a person feels especially able if he or she can perform better than others with less effort. (This is also why exerting high effort can be a double-edged sword for those who are ego involved. If they try hard and "fail," the "logical" conclusion is that they are low in ability.) In other words, when a differentiated conception of ability is our concern, exhibiting effort may result in feelings of low competence. The preoccupation here is to show that one is more able than relevant others, and the amount of effort exerted can impact this judgment.

When an undifferentiated conception of ability is operating, ability and effort walk hand in hand. Exerting effort, in this case, is paramount to a sense of demonstrated competence and the ensuing experience of personal success. When people are task involved, only when they are trying and investing can they feel as though their competence has been maximized or improved. Here, achievement without effort would be an "empty" success (i.e., it would occasion little or no sense of subjective success).

Nicholls (1989) holds that the conception of ability being evoked is mirrored in the criteria individuals use to define success. These criteria can be considered "self-referenced" or "other-referenced." If someone tends to focus on an undifferentiated conception of ability, then improvement, mastery of the task, and especially trying hard and learning become the usual standards undergirding subjective success. In contrast, if the person tends to focus on a differentiated conception of ability, then realizing whatever shows her/his superiority occasions a sense of success (e.g., by being the only one who can perform a certain skill, by not making mistakes when others do, by demonstrating that he/she is the best). Goal orientation assessments, such as the TEOSQ or POSQ, were developed to assess people's degree of preoccupation with differentiated and undifferentiated conceptions of ability.[5] It is assumed that these preoccupations or degrees of proneness are captured or implied via the criteria individuals utilize to define success in a sport or in sport in general. The differential criteria compose the item content of the task and ego goal scales of the TEOSQ and POSQ. That is, conceptions of ability per se are not assessed in these dispositional goal orientation measures, whose conceptual foundation is Nicholls's (1984a, 1989) theory of achievement motivation (see also Roberts, this volume).

So, because the conceptual underpinnings of goal orientation measures are far from straightforward, it is understandable that one might ask, "What conception of ability does the individual with a high task/high ego orientation goal profile utilize?" (Harwood and Hardy, 1999, p. 242). I hope that the preceding discussion has suggested an answer. Nicholls, I believe, would respond that such a person is prone to using both conceptions in a given achievement domain and that he/she cares a lot about the demonstration of ability (whether reflected via self-referenced or normatively referenced criteria). Contrary to what a few achievement goal researchers have posited (Harwood et al., 2000), I suspect Nicholls would emphasize that once individuals cognitively understand ability as a capacity (see Fry, this volume), they can focus on a differentiated as well as an undifferentiated conception. I think he also might say that for someone high in both orientations, which conception is evoked at any one moment depends on the climate prevailing in the setting (e.g., the degree to which the prevailing environment is objectively, as well as subjectively, task and ego involving); the characteristics of the current achievement situation (Harwood & Swain, 1998; Swain & Harwood, 1996), and what may be motivationally advantageous to the individual at that moment.

Goal Profiles

Because the dimensions of task and ego orientation (when assessed by instruments grounded in Nicholls's conceptualization of goals, such as the TEOSQ and POSQ) have repeatedly been found to be independent in the sport setting (Chi & Duda, 1995; Duda & Whitehead, 1998; Roberts, Treasure, & Kavussanu, 1996), Biddle and colleagues (Goudas & Biddle, 1994b; Biddle, 1994) and others (e.g., Hardy, 1997) have argued for the utility of "goal profiles" for examining potential effects of goal orientations on variables of interest (see also Roberts, Biddle, this volume). In the formulation of goal profiles, participants in a sample are usually divided by a median or mean split on both the task and ego orientation scales, and then four classifications are formed: participants who are high task and high ego, those who are high task and low ego, those who are low task and high ego, and those who are low task and low ego (e.g., see Duda, 1988; Fox, Goudas, Biddle, Duda, & Armstrong, 1994; White, 1998).

Although the univariate analysis of task and ego orientations (e.g., via simple correlations) with regard to selected dependent variables is not especially revealing, most work on dispositional goal orientations and their motivation-related correlates has examined these interrelationships via analyses that consider task and ego orientations simultaneously (e.g., canonical correlation analysis, second-order factor analysis) and/or in interaction (e.g., moderated hierarchical multiple regression in which the main effects are entered first and the interaction terms are entered subsequently, after the variables are standardized). Moreover, given that we can also employ multifactor analysis of variance designs (in which, for example, we would have two factors such as high/low task and high/low ego orientations), the surrendering to a four-level, one-way analysis at the onset of a study presupposes an interaction between the two goal orientation dimensions. Most critically, goal profiles, if analyzed via the latter strategy exclusively, convey little about potential differential influences of the two dimensions of goal orientations. That is, with respect to the dependent variable(s), does task orientation, ego orientation, and/or the interplay between the two account for the most variance?

I recommend the goal profile approach when (a) the four classifications can be generated on the basis of extreme groups and the researcher has established an interaction effect; and/or (b) the goal profile classification is employed to produce four subsamples from which individuals can be randomly selected for subsequent in-depth qualitative analyses, case studies, and/or interventions (e.g., see Thorne & Duda, 1995).

One alternative to the goal-profiling analytic strategy (in which the four goal categories compose the independent variable) is cluster analysis. Here the researcher determines whether homogeneous groups exist with regard to the sampled individuals' goal orientations and other cognitive, affective, and/or behavioral variables, thereby forming "profile" groups in a way that maximizes between-group variance and minimizes within-group differences.

A second possibility is an ideographic approach using hierarchical class analysis (Vanden Auweele, De Cuyper, Van Mele, & Rzewnicki, 1993; Van Mele & Vanden Auweele, 1995). The aim of this analysis is to discover which emotions and/or actions are most strongly coupled with particular contexts or circumstances. For example, in a study of high-level cricketeers, Georgiadis, Biddle, and Vanden Auweele (1999) interviewed four players who were most representative of the four achievement goal orientation profile groups. When interviewed, the players were asked to identify the situations that were most salient to them in cricket and then describe how they usually felt or reacted in such situations. They then rated the extent to which they felt/carried out the proposed emotions/behaviors in each situation. The results were analyzed via an intra-individual correlation method. The resulting hierarchical model of situations and corresponding affective responses and actions was then tested across and within athletes.

The High/High(s) and the Low/Low(s)

Although one can debate the position on the basis of certain arguments and findings cited later in this chapter, scholars in the field have argued for the adaptive repercussions of being high in task and ego orientation (e.g., Biddle, 1994; Fox et al., 1994; Georgiadis et al., 1999; Hardy, 1997). When I used the goal profile approach in an early study investigating reported persistence and behavioral intensity among recreational sport athletes (Duda, 1988[6]), it became apparent that people who endorse both orientations can exhibit high motivation. I suggested then and later (e.g., Duda, 1997), on the basis of the tenets of achievement goal theories, that what may make high task/high ego individuals "*motivated* 'over the long haul'

. . . is the fact that they have their strong task orientation to fall back on when their sense of normative competence is in jeopardy" (p. 306).

An equally intriguing issue, however, is who are the individuals who are low in both orientations. Sometimes what researchers observe (e.g., Pensgaard & Roberts, 1997; Rethorst, 1997; Walling & Duda, 1995) is that this is the group that significantly differs from the other three goal groups. As is suggested in studies to date, we would expect the low-task- and low-ego-orientation individuals to have motivational deficits, but the mechanisms that bring this about are not clearly stipulated. Given the operational definitions of the two goal orientations, it would seem that such persons do not particularly define sport success with reference to learning/exerted effort or outdoing others. That is, they appear to be less concerned with demonstrating a more or less differentiated conception of sport ability than individuals high in both orientations or high in one orientation (and low in the other).[7] They do not emphasize the demonstration of self-referenced or normatively referenced competence. In terms of predictive utility, are achievement goal theories not as applicable or insightful for this subgroup (as suggested by some, e.g., Wigfield, Eccles, & Pintrich, 1996)? I see this as one potential benefit of a goal profile approach to the study of dispositional achievement goals—the promotion of further, more detailed investigation into the motivational processes (cognitive, affective, and behavioral) among people disinclined to be task and/or ego involved in sport. The Georgiadis et al. study (1999) described earlier was a positive step in this direction. Such a focus in further research might result in intriguing extensions of contemporary achievement goal theories or inform us about the qualifying aspects and limitations of this theoretical framework.

Stability of Goal Orientations

With regard to dispositional goal orientations, another issue arising from the literature is the stability of individual differences in task and ego orientations. Researchers have examined stability in at least two ways. For example, once an individual possesses the cognitive developmental capacity to be task and/or ego oriented (Fry & Duda, 1997; Nicholls & Miller, 1984a; Whitehead & Smith, 1996), how much do these orientations vary across settings? We are referring here to situational stability, or generalizability. Focusing on dispositional orientations specifically, Hardy (1997) has argued that individuals can fluctuate in their emphasis on task and ego goals across situations. He cited a study of professional, county amateur, low-handicap amateur, and high-handicap amateur golfers who completed an assessment of goal orientations preseason, prepractice, and precompetition. The professionals and high-handicap golfers were higher in ego orientation before competition than the other two groups. However, before the competition, the high-handicap group also dropped in their task orientation. The professional golfers did also, but this decline was not significant. Drawing from these findings, Hardy suggested that "it appears that professional, good amateur, and poor golfers may approach competition in radically different ways" (p. 284). He argued that the results provide evidence for the instability of goal orientations in the sport domain.

The limited work on the stability of goal orientation scores across social contexts within sport (such as precompetitive vs. pretraining) is equivocal. For example, Price and Tennant (1998) found goal orientations to be relatively stable regardless of success/failure feedback or whether the participants were involved in a sport competition (i.e., one-on-one basketball contest) or a practice (i.e., basketball drills). Tammen (1998), studying sport participants, observed higher task orientation scores in a training instructional condition. Ego orientation scores, however, did not vary as a function of social context.

In any case, it should not be surprising that the context in which instruments are administered, the instructional set, and so on result in variability in responses to questionnaires—even those assessing dispositional tendencies. This point has been made repeatedly in the test and measurement literature (e.g., Anastasi & Urbina, 1997). In assessment of goal orientations in more neutral settings (e.g., preseason, or perhaps even prepractice), one could reasonably expect athletes to answer differently than they would before an event that is likely to be more intense and salient (i.e., precompetition). One would predict similar variability when administering a measure of sport trait anxiety across diverse environmental conditions (e.g., Smith et al., 1998). Moreover, the type of methodology Hardy (1997) and Price and Tennant (1998) used makes it unclear whether indeed athletes' overall proneness to task and ego involvement in that sport (e.g., with the preseason administration) is being measured or whether perhaps a touch of "state" goal orientations (e.g., with assessments of goal orientations before sport events, such as training or competition) is being tapped. If both constructs are being assessed, this would be another source of "instability" in the task and ego scores.

Although there are no clear-cut answers regarding cross-situational stability in the measure of goal orientations within the athletic experience, task and ego orientations have nevertheless been found to generalize across two rather diverse achievement milieus, the athletic and the academic domains. This pattern of findings has held up among samples of U.S. high school students (Duda & Nicholls, 1992), U.S. college students (Guivernau, Thorne, & Duda, 1994b), and Spanish university-level student-athletes (Guivernau & Duda, 1998a).

All in all, it is not apparent whether or not discrepancies among studies on the situational stability of goal orientations are a function of methodological differences among the investigations (e.g., the instructional set given, the stem provided in the particular goal orientation instrument). More work needs to be done to resolve seeming incongruities. Investigations on the motivation-related implications of the observed cross-contextual generalizability of goal orientations are warranted as well (Guivernau & Duda, 1998a). In such research, however, it is important not to be ambiguous about whether one is determining dispositional goal orientations or a semblance of goal involvement.

A second type of stability is temporal stability. Similar to the situation with goal orientation measures across contexts, the research to date is far from definitive about how stable goal orientations are over repeated assessments. Concerning test-retest reliabilities for the predominant assessments of sport goal orientations in the literature (TEOSQ and POSQ), Duda and Whitehead (1998) report values ranging from .68 to .80 for the task and ego orientation scales, respectively, across time periods ranging from one week to the entire course of a competitive season. Values are lower if the test-retest period extends to one year. In total, these findings suggest that the TEOSQ and POSQ do not tap personality traits but rather dispositional tendencies that are relatively stable, but not fixed, over time.

But the compelling question is, when there is temporal variation in goal orientations, what causes the change? The work of the major achievement goal theorists (Ames, 1992a, 1992c; Dweck, 1986, 1991; Nicholls, 1989) suggests that dispositional goal orientations are malleable and are impacted by situational factors. More specifically, research by Ames (1992a, 1992c) in classroom settings indicates that a task-involving climate promotes a task orientation whereas an ego-involving atmosphere encourages the development of an ego orientation.

The associations between the dispositional goal orientation scales and perceptions of the motivational climate in sport settings, when determined in a cross-sectional design, tend to be low to moderate. This indicates that the constructs are not redundant and that they appear to be capturing different facets of the goal perspectives operating in the athletic domain. Field experiments, in which the environment is modified and the impact of this situational manipulation on individual differences on goal perspectives is examined, would be especially helpful for ascertaining whether dispositional goals can be modified or whether goal orientations influence what individuals attend to and possibly accentuate in a given motivational climate (Lloyd & Fox, 1992; Treasure, 1993). Longitudinal correlational designs examining the interplay between assessments of dispositional goals and situationally emphasized goal perspectives (e.g., Whitehead, Andree, & Lee, 1997; Williams, 1998) also provide insight into these issues.

To determine whether goal orientations would change over a season as a result of the climate operating on female softball teams, Williams (1998) assessed goal orientations both early and late in the season. As the perceived climate was assessed only once (i.e., toward the end of the season), no firm conclusions about the influence of situationally emphasized goal perspectives on dispositional goals (and vice versa) can be drawn.

Ntoumanis and Biddle (1998) studied the interdependencies between the perceived motivational climate and dispositional goals in a crosssectional design via structural equation modeling. Among British university athletes, results showed that a perceived task-involving climate related to task orientation and that perceptions of an ego-involving climate were associated with an ego orientation. The researchers' interpretation was that "athletes prefer to belong to teams with compatible views on the nature and means of achievement" (p. 182), supporting the "matching hypothesis." In the view of Newton and Duda (1999), however, the "matching hypothesis" (or person-environment fit hypothesis) can be adequately tested only if the motivation-related responses of individuals participating in an environment compatible with their goal orientation are contrasted to responses of those participating in a climate discordant with their dispositional goal perspective.

Employing cross-lag analyses and a stronger design, Whitehead et al. (1997) examined the longitudinal interdependencies between perceptions of the motivational climate and goal orientations across one year. They reported a significant increase in task orientation from Year 1 to Year 2 and a decrease in ego orientation. Perceptions of the ego-involving features of the climate were low and did not change over the year. The investigators also found that high perceptions of a mastery climate in Year 1 predicted a drop in ego orientation in Year 2.

More research is warranted on the interconnections between goal orientations and perceptions of the motivational climate at a given point in time and, because a "slice-in-time" design is not particularly informative about potential socialization effects (Duda, 1993), over the course of one or more sport seasons. These relationships are probably dynamic and reciprocal, and thus I agree with the suggestion of Ntoumanis and Biddle (1998) that "goal orientations can influence the selection of cues that an individual will pick up from a sport environment, but also long-term exposure in a certain motivational climate can affect the achievement goal orientation of an individual" (p. 183).

Situationally Emphasized Goal Perspectives

Another central variable in contemporary goal perspective frameworks is contextual and relates to the characteristics of an environment that make us more likely to be task and/or ego involved. Although the literature acknowledges the motivational significance of *objective* facets of the situation (Nicholls, 1989), emphasis on *subjective* appraisal of the environment has been greater, as achievement goal frameworks stress the "meaning" of achievement experiences to individuals (Ames, 1992c; see Biddle, Treasure, this volume). In other words, research has focused on people's perceptions of situational structures that affect the likelihood they will be concerned with demonstrating self-referenced and/or other-referenced conceptions of ability. Ames (1992a, 1992c) uses the term "perceived motivational climate" to refer to individuals' composite views concerning the situationally emphasized goal structures operating in an achievement setting. It is assumed that this perceived atmosphere comprises dimensions such as the ways in which individuals are evaluated, the interactions among group members that are emphasized, and the nature of and basis for the reward structure.

Measurement of the Perceived Motivational Climate

Relevant to the sport domain are assessments of the perceived situationally emphasized goal structure that is stressed by coaches (i.e., the Perceived Motivational Climate in Sport Questionnaire, or PMCSQ; Seifriz, Duda, & Chi, 1992; Walling, Duda, & Chi, 1993) and parents (i.e., the Parent-Initiated Motivational Climate Questionnaire, or PIMCQ; White, 1996; White, Duda, & Hart, 1992). Exploratory and confirmatory factor analysis has supported the factorial validity of PMCSQ; studies have indicated that the task and ego climate dimensions of both questionnaires are internally reliable and that they possess concurrent validity (see Duda & Whitehead, 1998).

More recent work by Newton and colleagues (Newton & Duda, 1993b; Newton, Duda, & Yin, 2000) has focused on modifying the two-dimensional PMCSQ into a hierarchically structured instrument with two predominant scales (i.e., the task- and ego-involving climate dimensions) and six subscales. Conceptually, our efforts are based on the contributions of Ames (1992a, 1992c), who has reinforced the multidimensionality of the motivational climate. The facets of the environment targeted to date also stem from our initial empirical and qualitative inquiry into the nature of the motivational atmospheres that operate on sport teams (and are created by the coach). Presently, the PMCSQ-2 assesses the degree to which the participants perceive that the coach reinforces effort/improvement, makes each player feel that she/he has an important role on the team, and promotes cooperation among team members. These are the task-involving structures of the climate. The PMCSQ-2 also measures athletes' perceptions that mistakes are punished by the coach, that reinforcement and attention are differentially provided as a function of ability level, and that rivalry among players on the same team is fueled. The latter subscale, however, has been plagued with low internal consistency (which might be a function of its limited number of items). We are currently working on further developing and refining the PMCSQ with respect to the hypothesized hierarchical structure.

As there is some confusion on this point in current goal perspective research, I want to emphasize that the two major dimensions of the PMCSQ (and its revised versions) were not designed and have not been found to be orthogonal. In general, the intercorrelation between the two superior dimensions tends to range between −.3 and −.5 (indicating that the task-involving and ego-involving climate scales are not bipolar either). The observed negative association contrasts with observations regarding measures of dispositional goal orientations, as well as the Classroom Goals Achievement Questionnaire (CGAQ)[8] developed by Ames and Archer (1988). Neglect or misunderstanding of this finding seems apparent when researchers move toward creating "motivational climate profiles" in sport. Further confusion is reflected in the suggestion of Hardy (1997), who argued that we shouldn't pit a task-involving experimental condition in comparison to an ego-involving condition because this "ignores an important distinction between task and ego orientations" (p. 283)—namely, their independence. As indicated above, task and ego goal orientations have generally been found to be independent. It is incorrect, however, to assume such an independence for task and ego situational characteristics.

The measurement of situationally emphasized goal perspectives in the physical domain has some limitations. Current questionnaires (including those developed to assess the perceived climate in physical education settings; e.g., Papaioannou's [1994] Learning and Performance Oriented Physical Education Climate Questionnaire [LAPOPECQ]) vary in the social psychological facets of the environment they target. As noted by Duda and Whitehead (1998), some recent assessments of the perceived situationally emphasized goal perspectives appear not to clearly or consistently distinguish the construct from its potential correlates. For example, Walling et al. (1993) utilized degree of performance-related worries as a dependent variable when examining the concurrent validity of the PMCSQ. Reported anxiety that relates to the adequacy of one's performance, however, is tapped via subscales of the ego-involving climate assessment contained in the PIMCQ and the LAPOPECQ. This state of affairs in the measurement of situational goals reflects some "slippage in concept" (Duda & Whitehead, 1998, p. 40).

Another potential problem area concerns employment of dispositional goal items in assessment of the perceived situationally emphasized goal perspectives. Past investigations of the socialization of goal orientations (Duda, 1993, 1994), and thus of perceptions of the goal perspectives emphasized by significant others, have adapted measures of dispositional goals (like the TEOSQ and POSQ; see Duda & Hom, 1993; Ebbeck & Becker, 1994; Kimiecik, Horn, & Shurin, 1996) for such purposes. From both an empirical and conceptual (Ames, 1992a, 1992c) standpoint, though, it would be errant to equate such modified versions of goal orientation assessments to measures of the perceived motivational atmosphere operating in sport. In a study of Spanish adolescents, Peiro, Escarti, and Duda (1997) demonstrated that perceptions of significant others' goal orientations were not highly correlated with perceptions of the motivational climate. It seems, therefore, that the former is another piece of the puzzle in the determination of the goals operating in the social milieu.

Although I concur with Hall, Cawthra, and Kerr's (1997) statement that "the engineering of the achievement climate must extend beyond the immediate competitive context to include all who are influential in creating the climate (such as) . . . parents, teachers, peers, league administrators," the proliferation of climate questionnaires in current sport- and physical education–based work has raised concern (Duda & Whitehead, 1998). Peiro et al. (1997) had this issue in mind in their study of Spanish adolescent sport participants ($N = 141$ females; $N = 136$ males) from a large city in Spain. Acknowledging that a number of instruments had been developed to assess the motivational climate created by coaches, parents, and physical education teachers, we argued for the need to assess potential influences of the goal perspectives emphasized by significant others on young peoples' goal orientations via the same measure. We suggested that if researchers observe differential relationships between dispositional goal orientations and perceptions of the goal structure deemed emphasized by coaches, parents, and others, it is not clear whether this variability is a function of the significant other or of the different instruments used to assess the social situational variables.

As exemplified in the work of Shapiro, Yun, and Ulrich (1998), one could use generalizability theory to distinguish between the sources of variance associated with the questionnaire and the true differences among participants. In the Peiro et al. (1997) investigation, however, significant adults' perceived criteria for judging adolescents' success in sport were tapped via three versions of the same inventory. More specifically, the same set of items was utilized; the only element modified was the initial item stem— "My mother/father/coach thinks I am successful in sport when. . . ."

To reduce the ever increasing number of perceived motivational climate instruments in the sport and physical education literature, Duda and Whitehead (1998) have advocated pulling together a standard set of items that generalize across context and significant others in the physical domain. We emphasized that these items should be based on a theoretical foundation (Ames, 1992a, 1992c). We then proposed that other items might be generated that are conceptually compatible with the initial set but specific to a particular environment and/or one or more socializing agents.

One way to begin to develop such context- and significant-other-specific items is to employ qualitative methods. Harwood and Swain (1998) used interview techniques to ascertain the environmental features that emphasized task and ego goals in young elite tennis players. In particular, they sought to determine how goal perspectives are manifested in the social context surrounding the developing athlete as well as what is situationally induced at the competition per se (i.e., how task and ego involvement are promoted within the match context).

In a qualitative case study of a former elite gymnast, Krane, Greenleaf, and Snow (1997) provided insight into the aspects of the social environment that had influenced this athlete's goal perspective. Three unstructured interviews made it evident that an ego-involving motivational climate had been created and manifested by significant others (in particular, her coaches and parents). This environment stressed winning, being nothing less than perfect in performances, and making normative comparisons with teammates or opponents. Consistent with the surrounding atmosphere, the gymnast's approach to gymnastics appeared to be strongly ego oriented. In total, Krane and colleagues identified important facets of an ego involving motivational climate, the cognitive manifestations of a pronounced ego orientation, and the behavioral implications when such a climate and dispositional orientation coexist.

The Objective Motivational Climate

One intriguing direction for future research on the motivational climate in sport would be to determine the degree of congruence between the objective and subjective environments with regard to their task- and ego-involving features (Duda & Balaguer, 1999). Prior to such investigations, existing assessments of coaches' (or parents') objective behaviors, such as the Coach Behavior Assessment System (Smith, Smoll, & Hunt, 1977; Smoll & Smith, 1989) or the Revised Coaching Behavior Recording Form (Bloom, Crumpton, & Anderson, 1999), would need to be adapted to adequately capture the emphasis placed on task and ego goals in the social environment (Chaumeton & Duda, 1988). Perhaps new observational systems need to be generated. The pioneering work of Ames (1992a, 1992c) on the dimensions of the motivational climate, and the taxonomy of motivationally important structures provided by Epstein (1988) provide an excellent starting point. In the context of physical education, Liukkonen and colleagues (Jaakkola et al., 1999; Sluis, Kiukkonen, Jaakkola, Kokkonen, & Saarelainen, 1999) have begun to tackle this challenging area. Besides being relevant theoretically and methodologically, this research direction is significant from an intervention standpoint. Before we can intervene to modify the climate created by coaches (or physical education teachers, etc.), we need to know that the reality of what coaches (physical education teachers) objectively do is compatible to some extent with what athletes (students) think their coaches/physical education teachers are doing.

Within-Team Variation and Interdependence in Perceptions of the Climate

To date in the sport psychology literature, when we discuss the psychological, affective, and/or behavioral correlates of perceptions of the motivational climate, we tend to interpret these findings as if such perceptions were consistent within the groups sampled. Are such perceptions shared among athletes on a given team? Duda, Newton, and Yin (1999a, 1999b) recently addressed this question among female volleyball players. We found that there was within-team variability in the perceived motivational climate and that the degree of variability varied across teams. Further, we found more within-team inconsistency in terms of the perceived ego-involving features of the environment. When the perceived situationally emphasized goal perspective operating on a team was more pronounced (as indicated via higher mean scores on the PMCSQ-2), the athletes on a team were more consistent in their appraisals of the climate. Also, when the volleyball players were more satisfied with their team as a whole, there was less within-team spread in perceptions of the task-involving aspects of the team environment. The opposite pattern emerged for perceptions of the ego-involving dimensions of the climate. So, not everyone on a team seems to see the same picture with respect to the team's motivational climate. The amount of variance seems to differ from one team to another, even when team size is controlled for. Does this mean that there is no team effect on the perceived motivational climate—that the athletes' perceptions in this regard are independent from each other? If so, we would need to rethink intervention efforts designed to help a coach modify the motivational climate.

To address these latter two questions, we (Duda, Newton, & Yin, 1999a, 1999b) also tested (using an interclass correlation as recommended by Kenny and Lavoie [1985] and Carron, Brawley, and Widmeyer [1998]) for statistical non-independence in perceptions of the motivational climate among this sample of volleyball players. For both the task and ego dimensions of the team environment, evidence for a team effect emerged. These results have important implications for the types of analyses we employ when determining the antecedents or potential consequences of differences in the perceived motivational climate in sport. In particular, it appears to be incorrect to analyze the athletes in our samples (who are members of different sport teams) only as one large group, which is what we have done to date. That is, we need to separate individual and group effects in the analyses (and need large samples of athletes, as well as intact teams, in our studies!). The findings are also significant from an applied perspective. As already mentioned, it would be difficult, and perhaps even questionable, to intervene with coaches in terms of changing the motivational climate if team members showed no agreement on the nature of that climate.

Dispositional and Situational Goal Perspectives

In the hope of maximizing the prediction of motivational patterns in achievement settings, the major achievement goal theorists (Ames, 1992a, 1992c; Dweck, 1986, 1991; Nicholls, 1984a, 1989) have suggested that we need to consider both dispositional and situational goals. It is curious, though, that this has rarely been done in the educational domain (Thorkildsen & Nicholls, 1998).

Best Predictor

In some studies assessing dispositional goal orientations and perceptions of the motivational climate, the investigators have sought to determine which construct better predicts indexes of motivation. Examples of such studies include those of Kavussanu and Roberts (1996b) and Ommundsen, Roberts, and Kavussanu (1997). These investigations typically entail hierarchical multiple regression analyses in which the goal orientations are entered in the first step and the two climate dimensions are entered in the second step (see Seifriz et al., 1992). The researchers examine whether step 2 adds significant variance regarding the dependent variable after the first set of independent variables has been entered. The analysis is then repeated with dimensions of perceived motivational climate included in step 1 and dispositional goal orientations in step 2.

The literature includes a number of propositions about whether and why dispositional versus situationally emphasized goal perspectives should be more salient in the prediction of motivation-related variables. For example, Duda and Nicholls (1992) proposed that with respect to salience, it is important to consider the nature of the variable(s) we are attempting to predict. We suggested that if the dependent variables were more situationally referenced and/or state-like (e.g., related to how much an athlete enjoys his or her sport; state anxiety), the perceived climate should emerge as the primary predictor. In contrast, if the dependent variable was more dispositional (e.g., related to beliefs about the causes of success in that sport in general), then goal orientations (a dispositional construct) would be expected to account for more variance than perceived situationally emphasized goals.

Roberts and Treasure (1992) suggested that in children, because their dispositional goal orientations are not yet fully developed, the motivational climate is more influential and would better predict cognitive, affective, and behavioral responses. Pulling from the arguments of Dweck and Leggett (1988), Treasure and Roberts (1998) hypothesized that if the atmosphere on a team is strongly task or ego involving, perceptions of this climate will override dispositions in predicting affective and cognitive responses in sport. They also suggested that if individuals possess a strong dispositional goal orientation, then the motivational climate should have less influence. Such predictions call for examination of a P × S interaction effect (Treasure, this volume). Finally, Cury and colleagues (Cury et al., 1996) have proposed that situational goal perspectives will be more influential than individual differences in goal perspectives in the case of compulsory physical activities (like mandatory physical education classes). Subsequent studies should clarify which and when particular factors (e.g., the nature/level of the dependent variable, developmental differences, the pervasiveness of the climate, and/ or the voluntary or involuntary nature of the environment) affect the differential predictive utility of goal orientations and perceptions of the motivational climate.

Interaction Approach

More recent research in sport psychology has emphasized the importance of examining the interactive effect of dispositional and situational goals on motivation (see also Roberts, Treasure, this volume). One of the first interactionist studies was conducted by Newton (1994; Newton & Duda, 1999). As part of her dissertation research involving female volleyball players, Newton examined the potential interplay between perceptions of ability, task and ego goal orientations, and perceptions of a task- and ego-involving climate. She found no significant interactions probably because of the high-task-involving features of the team environments and the predominantly high task orientation of the athletes. Consistent with the hypotheses, though, perceptions of task- and ego-involving climates (and their underlying dimensions) predicted pressure/tension, reported effort/importance, enjoyment/interest, and beliefs about the causes of success in a conceptually consistent manner.

Others have also advocated the P × S interactional approach in goal perspective research (see also Swain & Harwood, 1996; Roberts et al., 1997; Treasure, this volume; Treasure & Roberts, 1998; Walker, Roberts, Nyheim, & Treasure, 1998). In general, the research has supported the adoption of an interactionist approach to studying potential consequences of dispositional and perceived situationally emphasized achievement goals. When hypothesized significant interactions did not emerge, a lack of variance in one or both independent variables has been one explanation. The methodological challenge of testing possible interactions between goal orientations and perceptions of the motivational climate is that reasonably large samples of athletes are required. If we also incorporate variation in perceived ability in the factorial design, in accordance with theoretical assumptions (Dweck, 1986; Elliott & Dweck, 1988; Nicholls, 1984a, 1989), then the number of athletes needed increases even more. One should note that although the major goal perspective theorists (e.g., Ames, 1992a, 1992c; Dweck, 1986; Dweck & Leggett, 1988; Nicholls, 1984a, 1989) point to the relevance of person and contextual variables in predicting task and ego involvement in achievement activities, contemporary achievement goal theories are short on specifics of when, how, and how much orientations and the perceived climate might interact. There are more particulars about the expected interplay between task and ego goals and perceptions of ability (e.g., Nicholls, 1989). At best, in terms of person and situational factors exclusively, we have the proposition of Dweck and Leggett (1988, p. 269), who suggest that (1) variations in goal orientations will determine the likelihood of individuals adopting a goal of action and exhibiting a particular behavioral pattern, and (2) situational characteristics, such as the degree to which the environment is task and ego involving, can alter this probability. Clearly, the orthogonality of the goal orientation construct (Nicholls, 1989) greatly complicates the calculation of such probabilities. A more thorough and detailed delineation of hypothesized relationships among goal orientations, perceptions of the motivational climate, and also perceived ability (Newton & Duda, 1999) is needed. This will contribute greatly to achievement goal research in sport psychology and also advance the mainstream goal perspective frameworks.

Achievement Goal Perspectives: What They Are Not

In this section I attempt to distinguish the construct of achievement goals, particularly goal orientations, from some other constructs popular in sport psychology. First, I try to show how task and ego goals are not synonymous with the types of goals we recognize on the basis of goal-setting theory (e.g., process and outcome goals; Locke & Latham, 1990; see also Hall & Kerr, this volume). Second, I outline distinctions between task and ego orientation and other measures of "competitive or sport orientations" in sport.

Goal Perspectives and Goal Setting

As already explained, task and ego goal orientations are dispositional tendencies regarding different ways of processing an activity. They are much more than a particular focus of one's goal-setting efforts (Duda, 1997): it would be suspect and simplistic to equate task and ego orientations (or task and ego involvement, for that matter) with an emphasis on process versus outcome goals, respectively. There should be some correspondence between the two sets of constructs, but they are not the same.

Within athletics specifically, Hardy, Jones, and Gould (1996) distinguish three different type of goals: outcome, performance, and process. Outcome goals are based on competitive outcomes and thus typically entail social comparison (e.g., coming in first in a race). Process goals center on the demonstration of behaviors, skills, and strategies that are part of the performance process per se (e.g., being aggressive at the net in tennis). Performance goals are those specifying absolute or self-referenced standards. These standards are end products of a performance and usually involve a numerical value (e.g., shooting an 85% free-throw percentage in a basketball game).

Each type of goal can be conceived of in a task or ego involved manner. For example, performance *execution*, performance *standards*, and performance *consequences* can render feedback on task mastery/performance improvement for the strongly task oriented and information about the superiority (or inferiority) of one's competence for those with a pronounced ego orientation. That is, one can obtain self-referenced ("my golf swing is feeling smooth," "the rhythm in my swing is much better than earlier in the season") as well as normatively referenced ("I have a much better looking swing than so-and-so") from facets of the sport performance "process." Similarly, "performance" goals can be processed in a task- or ego-involved way. For example, our standards can be self-referenced criteria (such as a personal best or a better golf score than last time on this course) or absolute criteria based on the previous performances of others (e.g., "Today I want to beat the best score that has been shot on this course"). Finally, as has been previously emphasized (Duda, 1992, 1994, 1996), the concept of "outcome goals" is ambiguous from a goal perspective viewpoint. Both the predominantly ego-oriented and the primarily task-oriented individual want to win. Moreover, athletes can look toward recent personal competitive outcomes and focus on the evidence these provide regarding improvement. On the other hand, athletes can tie their perceived competence to competitive outcomes and use these as one important criterion in judging their ability.

Turning first to the two extreme goal orientation groups, the high-task-/low-ego-oriented and the low-task-/high-ego-oriented athletes, it seems that the first group should be more personally referenced when they consider the performance process, performance standards, and performance outcomes in relation to competence information. Moreover, as suggested by Nicholls (1989), they most likely focus more on whether they exerted sufficient effort during the performance process that led to a particular performance standard and outcome. These two attributes, which are more within the person's control and centered on the task, are fundamental to the hypothesized motivational advantages associated with a strong task orientation. In contrast, someone who is largely ego oriented will tend to make social comparisons when evaluating the performance process and level of performance standard and outcome reached. There is a preoccupation with whether superior ability was demonstrated in reference to others as these facets of a total sport "performance" are weighed. If such a person feels that he or she exhibited high effort while performing but that the achieved standard and outcome of the performance were comparatively inferior, low perceived competence will result.

But, once again, what about the high-task- and high-ego-oriented athletes (see also Roberts, this volume)? Perhaps people who strongly endorse both goal orientations differentially (and frequently) utilize the multiple sources of information about ability that come from self- and/or normatively referenced examinations of performance processes, standards, and outcomes. At a particular point in training or competition, which type of goal the high task/high ego athlete focuses on and how he or she processes that goal may be a question of what is deemed conducive to maintaining motivation. Further investigation is recommended to address this very important question.

As Hardy has pointed out (1997, 1998), it is questionable and perhaps naive to conclude from the sport achievement goal literature that outcome goals are "bad" and that athletes should be encouraged to set performance and/or process goals exclusively. I concur with Hardy's argument regarding the benefits or role of the three goal types. I don't agree with his interpretation of the achievement goal literature at large, namely that this literature supports a denigration of outcome goals.

It is recognized that athletes, particularly at the higher levels of competition, tend to set both process and outcome goals and that those who frequently use outcome goals can see themselves as effective goal setters (Burton, Weinberg, Yukelson, & Weigand, 1998). This latter finding on the perceived positive effect of outcome goals may be due to their influence on athletes' initial level of commitment to their sport (Burton et al., 1998). The goal-setting literature (Burton, 1989; Locke & Latham, 1990; Pierce & Burton, 1998), though, also informs us of the positive effects of sound goal setting, which incorporates process goals and performance goals, for sport performance. As reinforced by Kingston and Hardy (1997b), setting of "self-referent" goals may be beneficial because individuals have more control over these aspects of performance. These authors also suggest that process goals may lead particularly to effective allocation of attentional resources, promote effective strategy use, and reduce the occurrence of debilitating anxiety. It seems safe to say that any desirable impact of process, performance, and outcome goals may depend on the desired purpose or meaning of the goal for the athlete (see Hall & Kerr, this volume), when and how the goals are used, and the level of perceived confidence of the athlete.

My fundamental point here is that we should not so quickly equate a task orientation with a focus on process and/or performance-standard goals, or an ego orientation with a focus on outcome goals. The orientations should have some influence on which types of goals are more attractive and, most critically, on how *each type of goal* is processed. That said, it seems reasonable that a greater emphasis on process and (personal) performance-standard goals will tilt individuals toward a state of task involvement. Objective social comparison is not so readily apparent when one concentrates on these components of the sport experience in training or competition. Overt social comparison processes, however, are almost inherent to outcomes in the context of competitive sport. This normative information, particularly if it does not paint a positive picture, can be downplayed or perhaps interpreted in a self-referenced manner if a pronounced task orientation exists. Otherwise, it is possible for a focus on competitive outcomes to pave the way to a state of ego involvement (Nicholls, 1989).

Finally, we should not forget the multidimensionality of environmental messages regarding task and ego goals (Ames, 1992a, 1992c): we cannot be assured of promoting task and/or ego involvement among athletes via goal setting alone (i.e., having them focus on process, performance, and/ or outcome goals). This is only one assumed situational antecedent of goal involvement in achievement activities.

Goal Perspectives and Competitive Orientations

Several years ago I attempted to provide an empirical and conceptual rationale to distinguish between assessments of dispositional goal orientation (such as the TEOSQ and POSQ) that are steeped in achievement goal theories and other measures of "sport achievement orientations" (Duda, 1992). Marsh (1994) later contributed to this discourse. Two popular achievement orientation assessments specific to the sport domain are the Sport Orientation Questionnaire (SOQ) (Gill & Deeter, 1988) and the Competitive Orientation Inventory (COI) (Vealey, 1986).

The SOQ comprises three interrelated subscales labeled Competitiveness, Win Orientation, and Goal Orientation. With respect to the competitiveness subscale, one should note that both strongly task- and strongly ego-oriented individuals can be attracted to competition (i.e., be competitive; Duda, 1992). That is, people can demonstrate both self-referenced and normatively based competence through competitive endeavors. As previously discussed, although one would expect a positive correlation between an ego orientation and a win orientation, even a predominantly task-oriented person looks at the scoreboard at the end of a contest. Finally, the concept of "goal orientation" as captured in the SOQ is obscure when examined through the lens of achievement goal theories (Ames, 1992c; Dweck, 1986; Nicholls, 1984a, 1989). Whether high in both task and ego orientation or strong in one but low in the other, individuals can be "goal oriented" and still have a tendency to subjectively define goal accomplishment (or success) in relation to different criteria.

The COI assesses the degree to which individuals strive for two different types of goals: playing well (which is termed a performance orientation) and winning (which is labeled an outcome orientation). Earlier we considered the ambiguity resulting from efforts to liken an "outcome orientation" to an ego orientation. In terms of "playing well" in a contest, the athlete who is high in both task and ego orientations, as well as the athlete who is high on one dimension and not the other, desires to play well. As suggested in previous work (Duda, 1992, 1994; Duda & Whitehead, 1998), the way in which playing well is construed and the repercussions of not playing well should vary as a function of a person's degree of task and ego orientation (and perceived ability). In alignment with this argument, Hanrahan and Biddle (1997) have also contended that the COI is not an appropriate measure for assessing achievement goal orientations.

In short, if we wish to learn about individual differences in proneness to task and ego involvement in sport, we should turn to established measures of dispositional goal orientations in that context. If we want to know how much competitive athletes focus on winning and setting goals in general, then the SOQ seems to be the instrument of choice. Finally, if we want information about the trade-off between playing well and winning in terms of the criteria underlying satisfaction among athletes, I would recommend the COI.

Achievement Goal Theory: What Are We Trying to Predict?

In this section we consider the "goals" of achievement goal theories as currently conceptualized. Although we in sport psychology might have differing purposes for and wants regarding these theoretical frameworks, Nicholls (1989) is very clear on this issue. For him the aim is to understand inequality in motivation so that we can help people, whatever their capability, to reach their potential. Therefore the focus is on gaining insight into variability in behavioral patterns rather than primarily on predicting performance. We want such theories to allow us to better grasp the mechanisms by which accomplishment is fostered or diminished. The focal point of the achievement goal approach is, therefore, the quality of participation and *not* only the quantity of performance achievement. Let's look at the sport achievement goal literature to see what we are trying to predict and what we have predicted so far, via an examination of achievement goals.

Motivational Patterns Versus Short-Term Performance

Although the study of motivation is juxtaposed with the study of behavioral differences, comparatively less work has been done on the implications of dispositional, situational, and/or state goal perspectives for behavioral indexes, particularly objective ones (Duda & Whitehead, 1998). Achievement goal theories (Ames, 1992a, 1992c; Dweck, 1986; Dweck & Leggett, 1988; Nicholls, 1984a, 1989) presume that a focus on task goals will increase the probability that a person will exhibit maximal performance and high effort, prefer optimally challenging tasks, and demonstrate persistence regardless of whether or not the individual thinks he or she is good at an activity. The same predictions hold for ego involvement as long as the person is confident in his or her level of ability. When an ego goal perspective prevails and perceived ability is low, behaviors that epitomize low achievement (i.e., debilitated performance, rescinded effort, inappropriate choice of task difficulty, and dropping out) will ensue.

Ego Orientation and Perceived Ability

The current sport psychology literature shows occasional signs of a fear that the theoretical tenets just summarized will lead to ego orientation "bashing," or denigration. For example, according to Hardy (1997),

> the notion that high ego orientations are detrimental to performance and predispose one to drop out does not sit very comfortably with the notion that goals motivate and direct behavior. . . . For if goals really do motivate and direct behavior, it is not easy to see how performers could become world champions without having strong ego orientations and setting outcome goals. In fact, there is very little evidence to suggest that ego orientations per se have a detrimental effect upon performance-related variables. Rather, the available evidence suggests that it is the combination of ego orientations with low perceptions of competence that leads to such effects. (p. 283)

The latter point, of course, is consonant with theoretical predictions and the thinking of most achievement goal researchers (this one included). Important to Hardy's argument is the assumption that elite athletes are and should be strongly ego oriented. Besides drawing on the goal perspective literature on the motivation-related characteristics of high task/high ego athletes (see Roberts, this volume), Hardy's position appears to pull from research indicating that more-talented athletes are more highly competitive and place a greater emphasis on winning (e.g., Hellandsig, 1998)—two descriptors that as already argued, are somewhat equivocal with respect to the constructs embedded in achievement goal theory .

First, as to my slant on this issue, I don't fear that we will see strong ego orientations disappearing in our lifetime! Besides all the well-meaning efforts of achievement goal researchers, the societal tide concerning the importance of demonstrating superiority is too strong. Second, I do agree that an ego orientation can be motivating at the higher competitive sport levels, when perceived competence is "rock solid." Perhaps it is this concern with showing superiority that helps propel some elite athletes (although some high-level athletes are high in task orientation and low in ego orientation) to the higher echelons of their sport. Whether a *state of ego involvement* is beneficial *while* an athlete is performing, regardless of ability level, is another question. According to theoretical assumptions, a task-involving goal can provide direction to our actions as well and can be especially motivating over time. Why? One reason, as postulated by achievement goal theorists (Ames, 1992c; Dweck, 1986; Nicholls, 1989), is that a predominant ego orientation puts individuals in jeopardy of feeling incompetent. The psychological and physical rigors of sport training and competition can tend to knock down one's sense of athletic supremacy—even in the elite context, where competitors compare themselves to others and the risk and requirements of the sport are so formidable. Regardless of skill level, it is assumed that individuals who are particularly concerned about their ability become prime candidates for feeling inefficacious. In other words, perceptions of adequate ability are more tenuous when based on ego-involved criteria (Hall, 1990).

Nicholls (1989) has suggested that *ego involvement* sets the stage for performance impairment "more by the expectation of looking incompetent than by the mere expectation of failure to complete a task" (p. 119). The expectation of appearing incompetent can lead to performance debilitation in several ways. First, it can cause a person to form unrealistic aspirations and choose tasks that are too easy or too difficult. Second, it can result in a lack of effort when the possibility of failure looms and with it the prospect of looking incompetent compared to others. Finally, this expectation (especially when it starts to become chronic) can lead to regular doses of high anxiety and, eventually, a devaluing of and loss of interest in the activity. Nicholls also holds that a strong "task orientation might, to some degree, insulate students from negative consequences of low perceived ability" (p. 97).

The possibility that a strong ego orientation coupled with high perceived ability can prove problematic "down the road" is well expressed by Hall, Cawthra, and Kerr (1997). They propose that in the case of

> athletes who adopt an ego goal orientation and who perceive their ability to be high . . . their initial experiences in sport are likely to be positive. They achieve success because of their high ability, and they continue to put forth effort, strive to achieve, and make significant improvements. The adoption of an ego goal at first gives the appearance of being adaptive because normative or comparative success is frequently experienced, and ability is never questioned. On the rare occasions when ability is exposed as being inadequate, these athletes consider that such failure does not fit with their self-perceptions of being able, and so they seek to remedy the situation by applying more effort. However, it is when these athletes continually perceive their ability and their effort levels to be inadequate to meet their achievement goals that the maladaptive nature of their motivational orientation becomes apparent. (p. 307)

As we have touched on already, it may be that persons high in both task and ego orientations are resistant to such problems. Only time will tell whether this is true—the time needed for further research on the topic and the time needed for longitudinal studies of the achievement strivings of such individuals.

Recent work has suggested that the proposed negative, nonadaptive behavioral and cognitive implications of being highly ego oriented and low in perceived ability actually reflect the individual's emphasis on a third type of goal, i.e., a performance (or ego) avoidance goal (Elliot & Church, 1997; Middleton & Midgley, 1997; see Roberts, this volume).[9] This new line of inquiry posits a positive achievement pattern for someone who adopts an ego perspective on achievement that is "approach" oriented. Cury and colleagues have begun to develop an assessment of the approach and avoidance dimensions of an ego orientation and to examine their correlates in the sport context (Cury, De Tonac, & Sot, 1999).

To conclude this section, I believe we need to know much more about the interplay between task and ego goals and perceived ability in terms of when, where, and among whom we are likely to observe debilitation in achievement striving. Understanding the conditions under which people do not try, do not persist, and do not perform up their ability level is a mainstay of this theoretical approach and certainly represents a "hot topic" in sport psychology. We need to examine whether everything is wonderful, now and forever, among those who are strong in both goal orientations. Not everyone is making the same forecast for these individuals. There seems to be more agreement, among theorists and researchers in sport psychology, that persons high in ego orientation and low in task orientation are "at risk" for motivational difficulties. Yet others claim that differential achievement patterns are not particularly a function of task and/or ego orientation but rather a question of whether people are approach motivated (i.e., they strive to succeed and to show that they are capable) or avoidance oriented (i.e., they fear the possibility of failure or fear showing that they are not competent). Let's consider what we do know about the link between achievement goals and sport performance.

Studies of Goal Perspectives and Performance

Although sparse, research to date has revealed a positive relationship between an emphasis on task goals and performance and has provided some evidence for the potentially debilitating influence of ego involvement (Chi, 1993; Hall, 1990). Most of this work in sport psychology has centered on dispositional goal orientations. For example, VanYperen and Duda (1999) studied junior elite male soccer players' (M age = 16.4 +/− 2.0 years) goal orientations and beliefs about the causes of success in soccer. The athletes' coaches rated the performance level of all their players in relation to a number of soccer skills at the onset and end of the season. Controlling for Time 1 performance scores, we found postseason performance ratings to be significantly and positively predicted by the players' degrees of task orientation and the beliefs that effort and positive parental influences were precursors to success.

Kingston and Hardy (1997a) assessed dispositional goal orientations one day before a major golf competition in mixed-ability golfers. With individual differences in ability controlled for, the performance measure was the total gross score minus the golfer's recognized stroke allowance (i.e., the net score above or below par) over 18 holes. Overall, task orientation was associated with better golf scores. In particular, the golfers who were high ego and low task in orientation scored significantly worse than those high in both orientations or high in task and low in ego orientation.

Among a large sample of young adolescent French boys, Sarrazin, Cury, and Roberts (1999) examined variations in exerted effort and performance as a function of goal orientations, perceived ability, and task difficulty. The task was to climb five different climbing courses ranging in difficulty from "very easy" to "very difficult." Effort was operationalized as the maximum heart rate reached in each climb. Performance was equated to successful completion of the climbing course.

Sarrazin and colleagues (1999) reported that the boys who were high task/low ego oriented and had high perceived ability achieved more success (73%) than their high-perceived-ability counterparts who were high ego/low task oriented (60%). In alignment with theoretical assumptions, the boys who were predominantly task oriented with low perceived ability performed better than the boys who were predominantly ego oriented and had low perceived competence (46% and 24%, respectively). The results also indicated that exerted effort varied in relation to goal orientation, perceived ability, and task difficulty in accordance with achievement goal theories (Nicholls, 1989).

As indicated earlier, less has been done on potential associations between perceived situationally emphasized goals and sport performance. In an investigation of 404 intercollegiate-level Korean athletes, Kim and Duda (1998) found a negative relationship between perceptions of a task-involving climate and *reported* degree of performance impairment (for psychological reasons such as heightened anxiety, loss of concentration) experienced by these athletes during important competitions. In contrast, a perceived ego-involving climate corresponded to greater psychological difficulties, resulting in performance problems. A consonant pattern of findings emerged in college athletes from the United States (Kim & Duda, 1999).

In another study, Yoo (1997) assessed the goal orientations, perceptions of the motivational climate, and intrinsic motivation of Korean students enrolled in sport classes. The instructor's evaluation of his students' skill levels at the end of the class, as well as class attendance, was also secured. Students who viewed their sport class as more task involving exhibited better performance and higher levels of adherence. Further, regardless of goal orientation, students in a perceived task-involving environment exhibited significantly higher levels of reported effort than those in a perceived ego-involving atmosphere.

Obviously, much more work is needed on the interdependencies between achievement goals and sport performance. Although the research design and necessary analyses become even more complicated, future investigations are called for that incorporate the myriad variables presumed to impact performance on the basis of Nicholls's theory (1984a, 1989): goals, perceived competence and the individual's certainty of that appraisal, the commitment to demonstrate competence, and a number of task-related factors (e.g., task difficulty, task duration, task clarity, the role of initiative in the task). And let's not forget the possible impact of the perceived motivational climate. With such a complex web of factors to consider, the prediction of performance seems to be a tall order.

Maximizing Motivated and Motivational Involvement

A question that needs to be posed at this juncture is the following: Is the prediction of performance variability the hallmark of a theory of achievement motivation? There are differences of opinion here. If we ground our work primarily in the theoretical contributions (and perhaps philosophical perspective) of John Nicholls, the answer is no—when performance is assessed in the short term. Nicholls (1989) holds that insight into and ways to foster lifetime achievement (for the able and the less so) should be the major focus of research in motivation. This clearly was the focal point of Nicholls's later work. With this multifaceted and longitudinal dependent variable in mind, he stated that "task orientation is more likely to maintain the long-term involvement that . . . significant accomplishments demand" (1989, p. 128). This expectation was rooted primarily in the differential affective and belief-related correlates of task and ego orientation that have consistently emerged in the educational (and sport) domains. Nicholls (1984a, 1989) had repeatedly acknowledged that ego involvement can be coupled with higher performance—particularly when perceived ability is high and the task is moderately challenging.

To a number of current sport psychology researchers (and practitioners), Nicholls's view of the major function of motivation research and resulting interventions is attractive. For example, Treasure (1997) asserted that the determinants of the "quality of involvement in achievement endeavors, [and] the commitment to learning" are important in "their own right" beyond their impact on achievement outcomes.

For the moment, let us restrict the discussion to highly competent sport participants. What do they need in order to move on to athletic excellence? Rather than a "one-shot" demonstration of performance prowess, it would seem that continuous but not necessarily constant (i.e., one after the other) victories leading to the gold-medal performance would be necessary. Most critically, these individuals need to maximize their arduous training and to persist beyond setbacks during the years of their sport careers. They must be willing to exert and maintain high levels of effort, even when facing "failures." In essence, they must be strongly task oriented and/or must be participating in a highly task-involving environment.

Certainly, talented athletes who do not persist in their sport will not move on to high levels of athletic achievement. With respect to the potential impact of the perceived motivational climate on adherence in sport specifically, studies have reported greater persistence among athletes when the atmosphere promoted task involvement and/or de-emphasized ego goals (e.g., Whitehead et al., 1997; Le Bars & Gernigon, 1998).

So, what have we been debating in the recent goal perspective literature? One position is that a strong ego orientation is desirable (and a critical attribute of a champion) as long as perceived ability is high. Another is that there is nothing wrong with keeping ego orientation in check. This stance assumes that the costs of doubts about one's competence are higher and the tendency to have such doubts is greater when ego orientation is strong. We are not sure, at present, how much a strong task orientation will help buffer the possibility of perceptions of low competence in this case. When repeated doses of ego involvement are the modus operandi, a maladaptive pattern is expected to hold for the highly able and accomplished competitor as well as for the equally important, less skilled sport participant we want to keep moving. Besides, the highly ego-involving milieu of competitive sport (e.g., as represented in the perspectives held by some fans, sport/club owners, the mass media) provides enough fuel to keep the fires of ego involvement burning among many athletes in addition to the influence of coaches and parents (Duda, 1997).

I suggest that before we advocate attenuating ego orientation or challenge this strategy, we look at the bigger picture. Certainly, all the answers are not in, and I agree with Hardy (1997) that we shouldn't be so quick and single-minded in our interpretation of the findings from the goal perspective research in sport to date. But what do they tell us so far? In my opinion, it is important that achievement goal researchers look beyond the correlates of task and ego orientations when making conclusions regarding the influence (positive and/or negative) of goal perspectives. First, in this evaluation it is important to also consider what research has found to be the implications of ego-involving, in contrast to task-involving, sport environments. Further, besides potential implications for short-term behavior (such as immediate performance), we should take into account the "story" that unfolds when behavioral patterns (such as persistence, task choice, effort exertion, and also performance) are analyzed over time. As mentioned earlier, beyond performance indicators, the motivational picture becomes more complete when we assess the ramifications of task and ego achievement goals for how people cognitively and emotionally respond to sport activities. Finally, in addition to their potential impact on achievement cognitions, emotions, and behaviors, do differences in goal perspectives provide any insight into whether sport involvement is a quality, moral, and health-conducive experience (Duda, 1996)? I recognize that the significance of a positive response to this last question is a judgment call. Some sport psychology researchers/practitioners find achievement goal theories engaging and consequential because this framework appears to provide such insight, and these researchers place great value on whether sport is a quality, moral, and health-promotive activity. In their view, superior competitive performance is not the "end all" and, although winning is wonderful, it is not "the only thing." Others in the field may hold different opinions, especially with reference to elite competitors (Hardy, 1998). We must respect such differences in priorities and viewpoints.

With the current goal perspective literature in total before us, however, I believe we are secure in recommending that we should do whatever possible to make sure athletes' task orientation is robust. I think there is also ammunition to indicate that ego involvement might best be tempered (perhaps via a manipulation of the motivational climate) and certainly not promoted.

Determinants of Performance Differences

It is one thing to propose that task and/or ego involvement might be linked to superior performance in sport (which is usually defined as outstanding performance outcomes) but quite another to identify the mechanisms by which goals impact performance. In this section I highlight findings on the relationships between (a) achievement goals and skill development, strategy use, and information processing and (b) achievement goals and the occurrence of heightened anxiety. These variables reflect some of the mechanisms by which goal perspectives may lead to an impairment or facilitation of performance.

Skill Development, Strategy Use, and Information Processing

Lochbaum and Roberts (1993) were the first to report that emphasis on the more problem-solving and adaptive learning strategies was tied to a task orientation in a sport setting. Similar findings have emerged in the context of physical education (e.g., Solmon & Boone, 1993).

In three studies, Cury and Sarrazin (1998) examined the effect of goal orientations and perceived ability on the learning of a sport task, task choice, and the type of feedback preferred among young adolescent boys. In the first study, boys had to choose among climbing tasks that varied in difficulty. In the second, the investigators assessed the amount of time (out of 5 min) that boys spent practicing a basketball skill test after having experienced failure at the activity. In the third study, the boys completed the same protocol as in the second study and then were able to obtain the feedback of their choice (i.e., task, normative, or objective information). When compared to high-ego-/low-task-oriented boys who were confident in their abilities, or to high-task-oriented boys regardless of their level of perceived ability, the high-ego-/low-task-oriented boys with low perceived ability were more likely to select extremely easy or difficult tasks, spent less time training for their upcoming basketball skill test, and rejected the type of feedback (i.e., task or objective) that would have facilitated their skill development. Thus, the boys with a pronounced ego orientation who doubted their ability did not display adaptive learning strategies.

In two studies, Cury, Famose, and Sarrazin (1997) examined the link among goal orientations, perceived ability, and the type of performance information desired by boys participating in timed tests of basketball ability. In both studies, the boys received task- versus ego-involving instructions that were aligned with their motivational perspective. In Study 1, after completing the second course, the subjects were told the time they required to complete this targeted trial. The boys could then secure normative information (they could then compare their results to norms for the task) or objective information (they could receive information about their first test performance and calculate the degree of improvement), or they could leave the room without receiving either type of feedback. In the second study, before the start of the last dribbling course, the boys could choose among normative, objective, and task information (which entailed a clarification of the task demands and suggestions regarding strategies to complete the dribbling course effectively) or could refuse the provided information.

Cury, Famose, and Sarrazin (1997) found that the high-ego-oriented and high-perceived-ability boys in Study 1 were significantly more likely to seek out normative information and reject objective information, while their low-perceived-ability peers were more prone toward information refusal and also rejected objective feedback about their performance. The task-oriented boys, regardless of their level of perceived ability, were more likely to select objective information. Study 2 ego-oriented boys with high perceived ability sought out normative feedback and rejected feedback that was more self-referenced, as well as information concerning task execution. Ego-oriented participants who doubted their basketball competence also rejected task information and preferred not to receive objective or normatively based information regarding their performance. Task-oriented boys with high perceived ability actively searched for objective information while avoiding normative feedback. Finally, the task-oriented participants who perceived their ability to be low chose task information while also excluding comparative information regarding their current performance. In discussing these findings, the researchers argued that information selection appears to be impacted by dispositional goal orientations. Cury and colleagues (1997) also proposed the following:

> An ego-involved [participant] is not interested in learning, even if he/she has tools on hand allowing him/her to progress and perform better; he/she tried primarily to situate himself in relation to others. Moreover, if he/she meets difficulties in this situation, he/she rejects all information, and notably task information which will be important to him . . . exhibiting a 'learned helpless psychological state.' (p. 220)

Concerning a potential interdependence between achievement goals and information processing (what information is processed and how it is processed) during sport tasks, Thill and Brunel (1995b) distinguish between deep-processing and surface-level strategies. In deep processing, people manipulate information through elaboration, self-monitoring, and organization, for example. Surface-level strategies entail memorizing the material or simply rehearsing it.

Thill and Brunel (1995b) examined the effect of goal orientations and feedback (i.e., positive, negative, and no feedback) on reported use of deep-processing versus surface-level strategy among varsity soccer players participating in a shooting task. When high in task orientation, the athletes tended to use more spontaneous deep-processing strategies than surface-level strategies, whether they received positive or negative feedback. In contrast, ego-oriented athletes reported use of deeper-processing strategies when they received no feedback; otherwise, they tended to utilize surface-level strategies. In explicating their findings, Thill and Brunel suggest that when ego involvement prevails, the capacity of the working memory is limited by social comparison strategies, resulting in shallow processing of the task at hand.

In sum, the goal orientations that individuals manifest seem to relate to how they interpret and respond to an activity in terms of the strategies they use for increasing performance and for selecting information regarding the quality of that performance. All in all, these findings further explain why a strong task orientation can set the stage for optimal skill development. Subsequent research might also examine how the perceived motivational climate, independently and in interaction with goal orientations, influences these same processes.

Anxiety

Some time ago, Roberts (1986) proposed that variations in achievement goal orientations relate to athletes' levels of precompetition anxiety. He suggested that athletes high in task orientation and low in ego orientation were less likely to be debilitated by excessively high anxiety, assuming, on the other hand, that a predominantly ego-oriented competitor was prone to high state anxiety responses due to her/his concern with social comparisons and propensity for self-focus.

Smith (1996) has proposed a model of performance-related anxiety specific to the sport domain. The model holds that the intensity and direction of precompetitive state anxiety are dependent on the athlete's cognitive appraisal of the environment and the demands placed on the individual, the individual's ability to meet those demands, the perceived personal significance of not meeting the challenge, and the individual's ability to cope with the ensuing stress. Situational factors (such as the perceived motivational climate) and individual differences (such as dispositional goal orientations) are presumed to impact this appraisal process (see Hall et al., 1998).

Some sport studies have revealed a link between ego orientation and higher anxiety (e.g., Boyd et al., 1991; Goudas et al., 1994b). However, equivocal findings exist. For example, Newton and Duda (1995) found no significant associations between goal orientations and cognitive and somatic state anxiety. In a study of young competitive fencers, Hall and Kerr (1997) found that ego orientation coupled with doubts about one's competence significantly predicted pre-match cognitive anxiety. When goal orientations were reassessed at a time closer to the start of the tournament, the athletes who were lower in perceived ability and task orientation reported higher precompetition somatic anxiety. In contrast, perceptions of ability and task orientation emerged as positive predictors of pre-match state confidence.

As part of the same investigation, Hall and Kerr (1997) examined the interdependencies between goal orientations and multidimensional state anxiety among a subsample of the junior fencers who were at least one standard deviation below the sample mean for perceptions of ability. For these fencers, an ego orientation was positively and significantly related to cognitive anxiety two days, one day, and immediately before the tournament. On the other hand, significant negative associations emerged between task orientation and cognitive anxiety one week and one day prior to competition. In total, these findings imply that both goal orientations are relevant to precompetitive state anxiety responses, particularly among athletes with low perceived ability.

In subsequent work, Hall et al. (1998) examined the relationship of goal orientations, perfectionism, and the temporal patterning of precompetitive state anxiety and confidence among 119 British middle school runners. Results indicated that cognitive anxiety was predicted by both pre-meet ego orientation and perfectionism. Perceived ability and the athletes' degrees of pre-meet task orientation emerged as positive predictors of precompetitive state confidence.

With respect to the prediction of trait anxiety, White and Zellner (1996) found that a strong ego orientation and low-to-moderate task orientation corresponded to greater trait cognitive anxiety among male and female high school, intercollegiate, and college-aged recreational athletes. In a study of male and female adolescent-aged athletes, White (1998) reported similar findings.

Consonant with Smith's (1996) model of the stress process, achievement goal research has indicated that the perceived motivational climate also plays a role in the level of anxiety experienced in sport. For example, Walling et al. (1993) found reported tension and pressure associated with adolescents' sport participation to be positively related to a perceived ego-involving climate and negatively associated with a perceived task-involving atmosphere. Pensgaard and Roberts (in press) examined the relationship of the perceived motivational climate and dispositional goals to sources of distress among Norwegian Olympic-level athletes. Perceptions of an ego-involving environment related to greater overall distress and anxiety stemming from one's coach and teammates. In contrast, during the Winter Games, perceptions of a task-involving climate negatively corresponded to the view that the coach was a stressor.

Among a sample of university-level team-sport athletes, Ntoumanis and Biddle (1998) determined the association of goal orientations and the perceived motivational climate with perceptions of the intensity and direction of precompetitive cognitive and somatic state anxiety. Task orientation did not relate to whether state anxiety was perceived as facilitating or debilitating. Ego orientation, however, impacted the intensity and direction of cognitive and somatic state anxiety through its effect on state self-confidence. Perceptions of the climate did not predict the level of state anxiety reported or the way these responses were interpreted in terms of their effect on performance. The researchers proposed that the perceived climate might indirectly affect anxiety responses through its effect on goal orientations. Replications of Ntoumanis and Biddle's important and well-done investigation are called for, perhaps with the inclusion of goal states and consideration of potential interactions between dispositions and the perceived climate.

Whether an individual feels that he or she can adequately cope with heightened anxiety also feeds into the stress process (Smith, 1996). Thill (1993) has found that individuals are more likely to use self-handicapping strategies to cope with the anxiety resulting from ego involvement than is the case for task involvement. Other studies (e.g., Gano-Overway & Duda, in press; Pensgaard & Roberts, 1997) have revealed a positive relationship between dispositional task orientation and reported use of adaptive coping strategies.

With an eye toward integrating achievement goal frameworks and Lazarus's transactional theory of psychological stress and coping, Kim and Duda (1998) examined how dispositional goals and the perceived motivational climate related to athletes' perceived controllability over, and ways of coping with, psychological difficulties during competition. Among a large sample of college-level Korean athletes, reported psychological problems during competition were positively predicted by a perceived ego-involving climate and negatively predicted by perceptions of a task-involving situation. Moreover, athletes who perceived their team environment as more ego involving exhibited a greater reported use of potentially maladaptive coping strategies (e.g., behavioral engagement, venting negative emotion, denial, wishful thinking, and blaming oneself and other people). In contrast, perceptions of a task-involving climate corresponded to a greater utilization of active, problem-focused coping strategies. These findings have been replicated with a sample of intercollegiate athletes from the United States (Kim & Duda, 1999).

Concerning the interdependencies between achievement goals and anxiety, the studies to date suggest some trends. Most often, ego orientation and a perceived ego-involving climate (especially if paired with low perceived ability) are associated with higher state anxiety (especially cognitive state anxiety). When individuals are high in ego orientation and low in task orientation, they are also more likely to be high in sport trait anxiety. Finally, task orientation has been found to correspond to a greater employment of adaptive coping strategies when stressful situations occur in the sport domain. Given these trends, it should not be surprising that recent work has indicated a positive association between the tendency to emphasize ego goals and the occurrence of thoughts about escaping from the competitive situation (Hatzigeorgiadis & Biddle, 1999).

The Quality of Achievement Experiences

Most would not need to be convinced that when people are experiencing debilitating anxiety, they are not having a desirable experience. An abundance of sport studies based on a multitude of conceptual frameworks inform us that when we enjoy and are intrinsically interested in what we are doing, we are motivated and consider the quality of the activity to be high.

As the tendency is to focus on a task for its own sake rather than as a means to an end (Nicholls, 1989), it should not be surprising that task orientation corresponds to greater reported enjoyment and intrinsic motivation in sport (Duda, Chi, Newton, Walling, & Catley, 1995; Duda, Fox, Biddle, & Armstrong, 1992; Hom, Duda, & Miller, 1993), as well as in physical education (Ferrer-Caja & Weiss, 1999; Papaioannou, 1994). A similar pattern has emerged for the task-involving climate (Seifriz et al., 1992), while a perceived ego-involving climate has been coupled with reported negative affect (Biddle & Ntoumanis, 1999). Recent work, representing a remarkable variety of cultural groups, has provided more support for such linkages (e.g., Kim & Gill, 1997; Liukkonen, 1997).

Biddle and Soos (1997) examined the interplay among goal orientations, beliefs about the nature of sport ability, intrinsic/extrinsic motivation, and intentions to engage in sport in the next few months among young adolescent Hungarian school children. The belief that sport ability can be enhanced through learning was associated with a task orientation. These variables predicted the students' perceived competence and degree of relative autonomy or self-regulation (Ryan & Connell, 1989) in a positive direction and related to amotivation negatively. In alignment with the tenets of cognitive evaluation theory (Deci & Ryan, 1985b), students with higher perceived competence, greater self-regulation, and lower levels of amotivation were higher in intrinsic motivation. The intention to engage in sport was predicted by intrinsic motivation and task orientation. Results aligned with the findings of Biddle and Soos have emerged in studies of Finnish (Lintunen, Valkonen, & Biddle, 1997) and Greek (Papaioannou & Diggelidis, 1997) youth.

In sport, Brunel (1996) has found task orientation to be coupled with more self-determining facets of motivation, and ego orientation to be associated with types of motivation (e.g., extrinsic, introjected) that are low in self-determination. Chi (1997), in a study of Taiwanese tennis players, found ego orientation to be positively related to extrinsic motivation.

We have quite consistent results on the interdependencies among enjoyment, intrinsic motivation, and achievement goals. Extrapolating from these findings, if we want athletes to enjoy their sport participation more and exhibit greater intrinsic, self-determined forms of motivation, we need to make sure that their level of task orientation is high.

Achievement Goal Theory: Recent Extensions and Moves Toward Integration

One promising direction in contemporary goal perspective research in the sport domain is reflected in efforts to pull together constructs, assumptions, and proposed relationships from other models of motivated behavior. Previous sport research has centered on consolidating achievement goal theories with other frameworks such as cognitive evaluation theory (Deci & Ryan, 1980; Ryan, 1982), self-determination theory (Deci & Ryan, 1985b, 1992), attribution theory (Weiner, 1986, 1995), self-efficacy theory (Bandura, 1986), and Eccles's Value-Expectancy Model (Eccles & Harold, 1991). Investments in theory building and hopes for practical application are limited when bodies of work stay isolated. I will not review the work of the researchers who have looked for conceptual convergence between the goal perspective concepts and other motivation-related constructs. Suffice it to say I am convinced that such moves toward integration will enhance understanding and prediction of motivational processes in the athletic domain.

Instead I present some examples of extensions of goal perspective research to areas of sport psychology that seem related to motivation but have not typically been directly connected to it. The following sections highlight recent investigations on the potential relationships among goal perspectives and group-related processes (such as effective leadership, group cohesion), moral behaviors and attitudes (such as sportspersonship and judgments concerning aggressive acts), and health-related behaviors and attributes (such as physical activity patterns, the development of eating disorders).

Achievement Goals and Group-Related Processes

Participation and performance in sport often take place within group structures. On teams, formal leaders (such as the coach) are assumed to affect group achievement and the nature and quality of interactions among team members. Although the relationship of leadership behaviors to performance has not been substantiated (Chelladurai, 1993), past work has found variation in leadership style relevant to how players relate to each other.

Effective Leadership

A major component of the sport psychology literature has focused on the conceptualization, measurement, and implications of leadership behaviors. Specifically, two outstanding examples of systematic and practically significant lines of work center on Smith, Smoll, and colleagues' (Smith, Smoll, & Curtis, 1978; Smith et al., 1977) Mediational Model of Leadership and Chelladurai's (1991, 1993) Multidimensional Model of Leadership. Both frameworks concentrate on the antecedents and consequences of the leadership practices of coaches and have important implications for athlete motivation. However, neither model has incorporated variables reflecting motivational processes that stem from contemporary theories of motivation. As pointed out by Duda and Balaguer (1999), these models provide limited insight "into *why* and *how* divergent leader behaviors have differential effects in terms of athletes' self-perceptions, emotional responses to sport, and behavior in the athletic domain" (p. 217).

Balaguer and her associates (Balaguer, Crespo, & Duda, 1996; Balaguer, Duda, & Crespo, 1999; Balaguer, Duda, & Mayo, 1997; Balaguer, Duda, Atienza, & Mayo, 1998) have conducted two studies of the associations among goal perspectives, leadership style, subjective performance, satisfaction, and coach ratings in sport. One purpose was to examine goal orientations and perceptions of the climate in relation to (a) athletes' perceptions of their coaches' leadership style and (b) athletes' preferences for leadership behaviors as exhibited by their coach. A second purpose was to determine the relationship of the perceived situationally emphasized goal structure to athletes' perceptions of improvement, satisfaction, and evaluation of their coach.

The participants in these studies included intermediate- to advanced-level Spanish tennis players (Balaguer et al., 1996, 1999) and elite Spanish female handball players (Balaguer et al., 1997, 1998). The tennis and handball players' perceptions of a task-involving environment positively corresponded to the view that the coach provided high levels of training and instruction and social support. Athletes within a task-involving climate also exhibited a stronger preference for their coaches to engage in such behaviors. In contrast, a perceived ego-involving atmosphere was negatively correlated with the tennis and handball players' view that their coach was concerned with their overall welfare and that their coach engaged in more teaching and instruction. The athletes with a stronger task orientation indicated a greater preference for rigorous training and instructional behaviors from their coach.

The researchers also determined the tennis and handball players' views concerning their season-long improvement in the tactical, technical, physical, and psychological dimensions of their game and concerning their overall competitive results (Balaguer et al., 1996, 1999). They ascertained the athletes' levels of satisfaction with their competitive results, their current levels of play, and the instruction received from their coach. In regard to these variables, the handball players also made such evaluations with respect to their team as a whole. The athletes' preferences for their present coach and ratings of his/her importance in their training were assessed as well.

Perceptions of a task-involving climate positively corresponded to perceived improvement in the tactical, technical, psychological, and competitive facets of tennis and handball performance. For the handball players, this pattern also held for views about progress in their team's performance. If the handball players viewed the atmosphere manifested by the coach as more task involving, they also perceived greater individual and team improvement in the physical aspects of their sport. Overall, the athletes revealed greater satisfaction with their competitive results, level of play, and coach (at the individual and team level) when the motivational climate was deemed more task involving. Less satisfaction was reported when the motivational environment was seen as more pronounced in its ego-involving characteristics.

Drawing from this empirical work, Duda and Balaguer (1999) have proposed an integrated model that includes constructs and suggested interrelationships from the Mediational Model of Leadership (Smith et al., 1978), the Multidimensional Model of Leadership (Chelladurai, 1993), and achievement goal theories (see figure 5.1). Consistent with these two models of leadership behavior, our framework incorporates athletes' perceptions of their coaches' behaviors. It also considers coaches' objective behaviors (Smith et al., 1977) and athletes' preferences concerning these behaviors (Chelladurai, 1993).

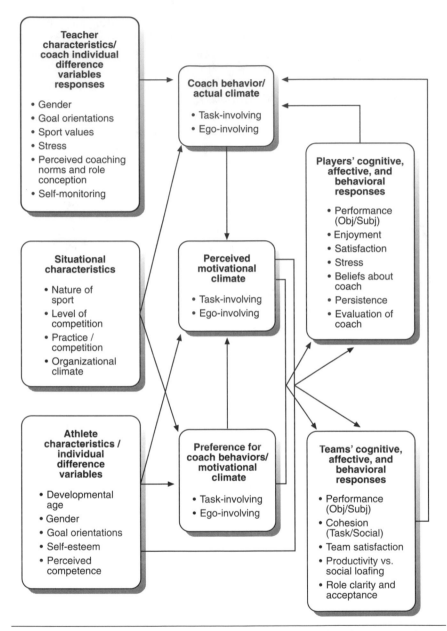

Figure 5.1 Duda and Balaguer's proposed integrated model of the antecedents/consequences of coach leadership.

From "Toward an integration of models of leadership with a contemporary theory of motivation" by J.L. Duda and I. Balaguer. In *Linking theory and practice* (pp. 213-230), by R. Lidor and M. Mar-Eli, 1999, Morgantown, WV: Fitness Information Technology. Copyright 1999 by Fitness Information Technology. Reprinted with permission.

A central feature of the model, however, is that it extends the two existing models of leadership by specifying that coaches' "actual" behaviors, athletes' perceptions of these behaviors, and their preferences concerning the behaviors can be analyzed in terms of their task- and ego-involving characteristics. Constructs fundamental to achievement goal theories (e.g., individual differences in goal orientations) are also assimilated into the model as important antecedent variables—in particular, as attributes of the coach and athlete. Thus hypotheses can be generated about the associations between coach leadership and athletes' responses based on achievement goal models of motivation. We (Duda & Balaguer, 1999) hope that the proposed integrative framework will be systematically tested and more thoroughly explored over time.

Group Cohesion

Another popular area of inquiry in sport psychology concerns the nature, determinants, and effects of team unitedness, or cohesion (Widmeyer, Carron, & Brawley, 1993). According to Carron (1982), cohesion is "a dynamic process which is reflected in the tendency for a group to stick together and remain united in the pursuit of its goals and objectives" (p. 124). Contemporary work distinguishes between the individual and group facets of group life as well as the task and social features of group involvement (Carron et al., 1998). Accordingly, the most widely used assessment of cohesion (i.e., the Group Environment Questionnaire) comprises four subscales. Two of these assess team members' views of the task and social attributes of the team as a whole (i.e., Group Task/Social Integration); the other two determine the degree to which individual team members feel they are attracted to/part of the group with respect to the team's task and social functioning (i.e., Individual's Attractions to the Group Task/Social).

Carron's (1982) model of sport cohesiveness (and more recent extensions; Carron, Widmeyer, & Brawley, 1985; Widmeyer et al., 1993) holds that factors internal to the person, such as personal goals, influence beliefs and perceptions about cohesiveness. The model also postulates that coach-athlete relationships and interactions are fundamental to athletes' sense of their team's cohesion. Consonant with this second proposition, studies have shown interdependencies between perceived leadership behaviors exhibited by coaches and ratings of the cohesiveness exhibited on the team (Gardner, Shields, Bredemeier, & Bostrom, 1996; Westre & Weiss, 1991).

I agree with Roberts and colleagues' (1997) statement that "research on motivation has primarily addressed the role of motivation in individual lives" (p. 413). This emphasis seems particularly limited when we consider the world of sport, in which many participate within team structures.

Achievement goal theories lead to the assumption that there should be inherent conceptual and empirical linkages between dispositional and situationally emphasized goals and group cohesion, and this is a promising aspect of these theories. Earlier investigations of the correlates of goal orientations, for example, revealed strong associations between task and cooperation goals (e.g., Duda & Nicholls, 1992). Further, a task orientation has been found to correspond to the belief that collaborative efforts among team members lead to sport success (e.g., Duda & Nicholls, 1992; Duda & White, 1992). Work on the structural components of the climate created by the coach (Ames, 1992a, 1992c; Newton & Duda, 1993b; Newton et al., 2000) has revealed that emphasizing team member cooperation, as well as fostering a sense that everyone on the team has an important role, is fundamental to a task-involving atmosphere. Perceived coach promotion of rivalry among team members has emerged as a characteristic of a perceived ego-involving environment. On the basis of this work, we would hypothesize that a strong task goal perspective, manifested in the climate and/or goal orientation of the athletes, should relate to greater team cohesion. Preliminary studies have supported this prediction. Among intercollegiate baseball players, Boone and Duda (1999) found that task orientation across the season was positively related to reported attraction to the group and perceived group integration tied to the team's task-related pursuits . Chi and Lu (1995), in their study of intercollegiate men's and women's basketball teams, reported a positive association between a perceived task-involving climate and task cohesion, and a negative relationship between perceptions of an ego-involving climate and task-related and social cohesion.

What are the implications, for group members' appraisals of their groups, of the ways in which they judge their competence and perceive personal success? These implications are important to know, both theoretically and practically. Research on the topic is clearly in its infancy, but this appears to be a fruitful area for further investigation. The research conducted so far (Boone & Duda, 1994; Chi & Lu, 1995) suggests another potential benefit of the adoption of a strong task orientation (or the creation of a highly task-involving environment) in sport: athletes will perceive their team to be more united.

Other Group Processes

In future research involving team-sport athletes, it would be interesting to examine the potential influence of goal perspectives (dispositional, situationally emphasized, and/or as manifested in states of goal involvement) on other group processes. On the basis of the research already presented and the tenets of achievement goal theories (Ames, 1992c;

Dweck, 1986; Nicholls, 1989), one can generate hypotheses regarding the relationships between goal perspectives and group motivation, collective efficacy, group decision making, group attributions, and so on (Carron, 1988).

A nice illustration of an attempted consolidation between the goal perspective framework and other group processes is Swain's (1996) study of the motivational determinants of social loafing. Social loafing is the lowering of individuals' exerted effort when they are part of a group as opposed to working individually. Swain (1996) speculated that social loafing would be more likely to occur in people who are predominantly ego oriented because in this situation an ego-oriented individual is not able to demonstrate his or her individual superiority at the task. Swain assessed the goal orientations of young adolescent British males and then asked them to participate in three 32.8 yd (30 m) dashes. In the first dash, the boys ran as individuals. In the second, they ran as part of a relay, and each participant's relay time was identified at the conclusion of the dash. In the third, they also ran a relay, but their personal contribution to the team performance was not identified. There was no condition effect on the performance times of the high-task-orientation and low-ego-orientation boys. However, congruent with predictions, high-ego- and low-task-oriented participants ran significantly slower when performance times were not going to be identified than in the identifiable condition.

As suggested earlier, we rarely operate in isolation within the athletic domain. More information is needed on how personal achievement goals and the goal perspectives that athletes see as receiving emphasis in sport environments influence the way athletes function in group settings.

Goal Perspectives and Moral Behavior: Sportspersonship

Nicholls (1989) suggested that achievement goals influence people's views about what is acceptable in achievement environments. In other words, variations in goal perspectives should correspond to differences in what is deemed permissible and individuals' moral reasoning about such behaviors. In alignment with Nicholls's proposal, Shields and Bredemeier (1995) incorporated both dispositional and situationally emphasized goals in their 12-component model of moral behavior in sport. In accordance with the thinking of these theorists, sport studies have addressed potential interrelationships between goal perspectives and moral judgments with regard to predicting "sportspersonship" attitudes and perceptions of the legitimacy of intentionally injurious acts in the athletic domain (see Roberts, this volume).

Initial sport studies on the relationships between dispositional goals and athletes' beliefs about the causes of success, as well as their views about the functions of sport, suggest that goals should correspond to variations in sportspersonship. Among samples varying in competitive level, ego orientation has been associated with the belief that "taking an illegal advantage" is an important determinant of success in sport (Duda & White, 1992; White & Zellner, 1996). In an earlier investigation (Duda, 1989), I examined the associations between goal orientations and high school athletes' perceptions of the purposes of sport involvement. The results indicated that a task orientation was coupled with the view that sport participation should function to promote good citizenship (e.g., following the rules). In their study of semiprofessional and amateur British male soccer players, Carpenter and Yates (1997) found a strong task orientation and low negative ego orientation to be negatively associated with the perception that sport should promote aggression and the willingness to do whatever it takes to win (e.g., breaking the rules). This goal perspective combination positively corresponded to the belief that sport should promote sportspersonship (e.g., teach individuals to follow the rules, respect the officials, be a "good sport").

As reviewed in Roberts (this volume), research has established a coherent and conceptually meaningful relationship between goal orientations and sportspersonship (e.g., Duda, Olson, & Templin, 1991; Dunn & Dunn, 1999; Lee & Whitehead, 1999; Papaioannou, 1997; Treasure, Roberts, & Standage, 1998). Studies have also addressed possible linkages between goal perspectives and sportspersonship by examining the interrelationships between goal orientations and competitive personality traits. With respect to the latter, the focus has been on what is termed "hypercompetitiveness" (HC) and "personal development competitive attitude" (PDCA; Ryska, 1998). When people are hypercompetitive, they tend to overemphasize winning and attempt to maintain or enhance their self-esteem through successful competitive outcomes. In contrast, those high in PDCA are more likely to look at competition as a forum for enhancing their personal character.

Among recreational, college, and professional athletes, Ryska (1998) found lower HC and higher PDCA to correspond to higher trait sport confidence, higher task orientation, and lower ego orientation. In their study of netball players from Tasmania, Moodie and colleagues (Moodie, Cooley, & Tammen, 1998) found ego orientation to be a positive predictor of HC. Finally, among youth basketball players, high HC was linked to a low task orientation and high ego orientation as well as to low trait sport confidence and high cognitive trait anxiety (Ryska & Sekerak, 1999). On the other hand, young athletes who were high in PDCA were higher in trait sport confidence and task orientation and lower in cognitive and somatic trait anxiety.

In sum, variations in goal orientations have been found to correspond to differences in sportspersonship attitudes in accordance with Nicholls's (1989) predictions. Athletes higher in ego orientation (and/or lower in task orientation) are more likely to endorse cheating behaviors and to express less respect for their opponents and the rules of the game. They also tend to be hypercompetitive. It also seems that perceptions of the motivational climate operating in sport are aligned with sportspersonship attitudes in a conceptually consistent manner, although less work has been done on this question.

In line with the work on sportspersonship, studies have revealed a logical interdependence between dispositional goals and views about the acceptability of purposely injuring opponents in sport contests. For example, Duda et al. (1991), in research on interscholastic basketball players, reported that a low task and high ego orientation related to higher legitimacy judgments concerning intentionally aggressive acts (e.g., purposely injuring an opponent so that he/she is out for the season). Similar findings have been reported by others (Duda & Huston, 1995; Guivernau & Duda, 1998b, 1998c; Dunn & Dunn, 1999; Kavussanu & Roberts, 1999; Roberts, this volume).

Thus, it seems that examination of individual differences in goal orientations is informative regarding the prediction of aggressive tendencies in sport. More research is necessary, but work so far points to an interdependence between an emphasis on ego goals and the approval of and/or reported likelihood of engaging in aggressive acts. Relatively less work has been done on how the motivational climate influences aggressive tendencies. It would be interesting, in future studies, to determine whether dispositional goals, perceived situationally emphasized goal perspectives, and their interplay are predictive of observed aggressive attitudes and behaviors in the athletic setting.

Achievement Goals and Healthful Sport

As suggested earlier, a comprehensive and meaningful model of human motivation pertinent to the physical domain provides insight not only into differences in achievement striving but also into the potential facilitating or debilitating influence of this realm on people's physical and mental welfare. Only through continued, systematic study will we know whether contemporary achievement goal theories are relevant to such issues.[10] In recent years (Duda, 1996), my intrigue has turned to the question whether variations in goal perspectives help predict the positive and potentially negative health outcomes associated with sport participation and engagement in physical activity. Others, too, have branched out in this direction and focused on possible linkages between dispositional and situationally emphasized goals and health-related attitudes, self-perceptions, and behaviors. Here I briefly review research centered on the prediction of self-reported physical activity via an examination of achievement goals and the etiology of eating disorders among athletes.

Physically Active Lifestyles

Although the work is limited, evidence has pointed to a positive relationship between an emphasis on task goals and engagement in exercise. Dempsey, Kimiecik, and Horn (1993) examined the predictors of moderate-to-vigorous physical activity (MVPA) among a sample of 35 female and 36 male 9- to 12-year-old children and their parents. They found that the children whose parents were strongly task oriented reported greater MVPA and expected to engage in MVPA in the future. Further, the children's task orientation and degree of perceived competence were positively associated with self-reported MVPA. Kimiecik and Horn (1998) found children's MVPA to be linked (albeit weakly) to their mother's degree of task orientation.

Biddle and Goudas (1996) determined the relationship of personal goal orientations and perceived adult encouragement to young British adolescents' self-reported physical activity and intentions to exercise in the future. Findings showed that the youngsters' degrees of task orientation and the amount of encouragement received from adults related to more positive exercise intentions. Exercise intentions were predictors of the present level of physical activity engagement.

The Etiology of Eating Disorders

Colleagues and I (see Duda, 1999, in press) have recently begun to examine not only the motivational implications but also the health-related consequences of an emphasis on task and ego goals in the sport of gymnastics. A central issue is whether variations in goal perspectives (particularly as manifested in the perceived climate created by the coach) are predictive of reported disordered eating behaviors and their psychological and energy-balance correlates. The literature has established that eating disorders are extremely dangerous; and reported prevalence seems to be higher among female athletes who participate in sports, such as gymnastics, that are subjectively evaluated and that require thin and/or small body types. Psychological variables that repeatedly emerge as potential predisposing factors to the etiology of eating disorders include body dissatisfaction, low self-esteem, high anxiety, and less reported enjoyment and intrinsic self-determination in the activity. Athletes also appear to be walking down the road to an eating disorder when their energy intake is insufficient in relation to the amount of energy being expended in training and other daily activities: i.e., they experience a number of energy deficits during the day, and their overall daily energy balance is negative.

In our first investigation on this topic (Duda, Benardot, & Kim, in press), the participants included pre-elite gymnasts who were members of the U.S. Talent Opportunity Program (TOP) National Artistic Gymnastics Team (9-11 years old) and international-caliber gymnasts who were members of the U.S. Women's National Artistic Team (M age = 15.5 years). Perceptions of a task-involving gym environment were positively related and age and a perceived ego-involving climate inversely associated with self-esteem, body image, enjoyment and the frequency of concerns about the competitive outcome. Perceptions of a task-involving atmosphere were negatively related and age was positively related to indicators of an energy deficit among the female gymnasts.

In a large sample of pre-elite female gymnasts, Duda and Kim (1997) examined the climate created by parents, other important psychological factors that predict disordered eating patterns (e.g., the individual's degree of perfectionism), and the reported attitudes toward and behaviors concerning food and eating. The specific purpose was to determine the interrelationships among the perceived motivational climate created by coaches and parents, psychological precursors to the development of eating disorders (i.e., self-esteem, body image, beliefs about success, and perfectionism), and young female gymnasts' preoccupation with food and weight.

Findings indicated that self-esteem and body image were negatively predicted by a perceived ego-involving gym climate. A perceived ego-involving parental climate was a positive predictor of the belief that a low weight and small body were prerequisites to gymnastics achievement. The aspect of perfectionism relating to possessing greater doubts about one's self was exhibited more by those young gymnasts who perceived that their parents emphasized ego-involved goals. On the other hand, a more pronounced fear of making mistakes was positively associated with perceptions of an ego-involving environment created by the coach. Overall, the young gymnasts who saw their home and gym climates as more ego involving were more perfectionistic, and this variable emerged as the best predictor of the gymnasts' preoccupation with eating and weight.

This work on eating disorders has been correlational, but it suggests that the perceived motivational climate in high-level sport relates to indexes of psychological and physical well-being in a theoretically consistent manner. Longitudinal evidence would provide a compelling case for the potential costs of highly ego-involving sport environments. It would be interesting, too, to determine whether examining achievement goals allows a greater awareness of the causes and frequency of other health-related problems in the athletic context (e.g., chronic injuries).

In Conclusion

A major sentiment embraced in this chapter concerns the need for greater clarity and care in measuring and conceptualizing concepts stemming from goal perspective theory. All of us who work in this area are far from finished with such important endeavors. A second theme has been promoting the integration and extension of the construct of achievement goals into other lines of sport psychology research (such as work on group processes and leadership behavior, moral intentions, reasoning and action, health-related behaviors and outcomes) in which motivation processes have not been well articulated.

Although this chapter has highlighted some caveats and some shortcomings in the literature, I hope that the discussion of such challenges and drawbacks has not dimmed the reader's enthusiasm for an achievement goal approach to the study of sport motivation. For this area of inquiry to progress, though, it is necessary that we be more deliberate when referring to goal orientations, the subjective (or objective) motivational climate, and/or task versus ego processing during training or competition. Moreover, subsequent work might center on the potential interdependencies and interactions among these three constructs, in cross-sectional designs as well as via longitudinal study.

With reference to the motivational implications of task and ego goals, I think it is essential to be more comprehensive and to consider short-term as well as long-term achievement patterns. This would surely be in harmony with Nicholls's (1989) thinking. Besides immediate performance, the research reviewed suggests that achievement goal frameworks can foster an understanding of the factors leading to optimal lifetime achievement and quality involvement in sport activities. Indeed, preliminary work indicates that the goal-related choices athletes make in sport and the ensuing interpretations of sport have ramifications for their health, their views on what is morally acceptable, and their attitudes about and ways of interacting with others in this environment. I think this is very important for us in sport psychology to more thoroughly comprehend—from a theoretical standpoint and also as a firm foundation for subsequent, informed practice.

Endnotes

[1] This total includes studies published in refereed journals or conference proceedings/abstracts only.

[2] In numerous investigations, athletes have completed the TEOSQ or POSQ specific to a particular sport. In these cases, the stem "I feel successful in . . ." is modified, and limited changes to the items are required. The psychometric properties of these questionnaires remain strong in such sport-specific administrations.

[3] This is not to suggest that an athlete cannot emphasize both playing as well as possible and winning the contest if queried about his or her goals immediately before a competition. As discussed later, such information is not particularly informative regarding whether the athlete is in a state of task or ego involvement at a particular time.

[4] Thus, the Swain and Harwood assessments of goal states are more in line with Dweck's position on the assessment of individual differences in dispositional achievement goals (i.e., the goals are pitted against each other). However, in contrast, their measures allow for individuals to be high in both goal emphases.

[5] It should be noted that neither the TEOSQ nor the POSQ ego orientation scale taps individuals' emphases on performing better than others *with low effort* (which would be reflective of possessing especially high ability), although other achievement goal inventories consider this aspect of emphasizing a differentiated conception of ability (e.g., Papaioannou, 1994).

[6] The Duda (1988) study was conducted before the development of the TEOSQ or POSQ.

[7] Although other mechanisms might explain the observed low motivation, an examination of goal orientations could be predictive of three groups who are "at risk" for motivational problems: those who are high ego/low task oriented; those who are low ego/low task oriented; and perhaps those with a strong, predominant goal orientation that runs counter to the prevailing motivational atmosphere (Duda, 1997b).

[8] It has been suggested that the two climate dimensions composing Ames and Archer's (1988) CGAQ were found to be orthogonal because the instrument contains a number of items that seemingly assess goal orientations (Duda & Whitehead, 1998).

[9] Only further sport research will tell whether the avoidance goal orientation is truly a distinct dispositional goal perspective or instead reflects chronic manifestations of someone who dwells on the adequacy of his/her ability (i.e., is strongly ego oriented and low in task orientation), still cares very much about "looking good" in terms of competence level, and has doubts about his/her capacity. Determining the antecedents, consequences, and very nature of "approach" and "avoidance" goals is an intriguing direction for future work.

[10] As Roberts (this volume) has pointed out, one can question whether it is appropriate to apply achievement goal theories to the exercise domain. There are myriad reasons for engaging in exercise behavior. I think the examination of achievement goals (whether referring to dispositional goals, situationally emphasized goals, and/or goal involvement) will be particularly informative regarding cognitions, affective responses, and behavior in the exercise setting when perceptions of competence are central to the individuals involved.

Acknowledgments

I would like to thank Dr. Jean Whitehead and Dr. Mi-sook Kim for their critique of and insightful comments on an earlier draft of this chapter.

Goal Setting in Sport and Physical Activity: Tracing Empirical Developments and Establishing Conceptual Direction

Howard K. Hall and Alistair W. Kerr

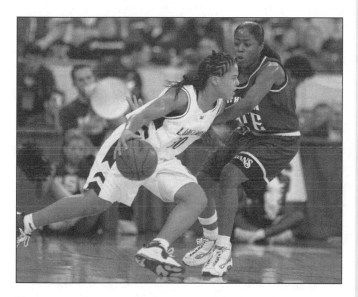

If one examines applied sport psychology texts and recent editions of physical education and sport psychology journals, the popularity of goal setting as a technique to enhance performance becomes abundantly clear. Not only is the efficacy of goal setting assumed; it is also claimed that the technique is a fundamental psychological skill that all athletes must develop if they are to maximize athletic potential (Hardy, Jones, & Gould, 1996). However, a closer inspection of the research literature reveals that until the mid-1980s, much of the evidence concerning the utility of goal setting in sport was anecdotal (Locke & Latham, 1985). The scientific basis for promoting goal setting as an effective motivational tool was gleaned from industrial and organizational psychology. This situation led Locke and Latham to encourage sport psychologists to conduct their own research in order to test theory and establish a reliable knowledge base for the promotion of the technique in sport.

Locke and Latham (1985) maintained that goal-setting effects should be generalizable to sport because of the many contextual similarities between sport and occupational settings. They argued that in both settings performance is concerned with accomplishing some end result. They further suggested that during work and sport performance there is a level of commonality in the cognitive processes utilized and the physical actions involved. Clearly, this line of thought was congruent with the ideas of those practicing in the field, as many coaches, teachers, and physical educators who utilized goal setting in sport appeared to hold similar expectations for the effectiveness of the technique.

Locke and Latham (1985) did not simply advocate that the performance effects of goal setting were generalizable beyond occupational settings. They further proposed that the benefits of goal setting would be more apparent in sport than in organizational contexts. This, they argued, was because it is easier to measure performance in sport than within industry or organizations. Although the idea has an intuitive appeal, because information technology makes it possible to record and maintain vast quantities of performance-related data on elite competitive events, this line of reasoning has never been well developed (Locke, 1991, 1994; Locke & Latham, 1985). To date, there is no empirical evidence to substantiate these claims. In fact, in contrast to Locke and Latham's (1990) assertion, many studies on the goal-setting–performance relationship in sport and physical activity have failed to find overwhelming support for goal-setting theory. Many have concluded that as a technique to enhance performance it is less effective in sport than in organizational settings (Burton, 1992, 1993; Hall & Byrne, 1988; Weinberg & Weigand, 1993).

The purpose of this chapter is to examine the research findings on goal setting in sport and physical activity, as well as to offer some suggestions about why Locke and Latham's original (1985) postulations regarding the generalizability of goal-setting theory have received limited support in this context. The chapter will show that goal-setting research in sport, in attempting to test the predictions of goal-setting theory, has tended to focus solely on performance effects. Consequently, we have had to infer the motivational effects of goal setting. In addition, other sources of motivation that may moderate the goal-setting–performance relationship and that are highly relevant to achievement settings such as sport have largely been ignored. Thus, an aim of the chapter is to demonstrate that if sport psychologists are to better understand the process of goal setting in sport, it will be necessary to consider the technique within the wider context of current motivational theory.

The chapter first presents a brief overview of goal-setting theory (Locke & Latham, 1990), followed by a summary of Locke and Latham's (1985) challenge to sport psychologists to begin testing the specific predictions of goal-setting theory in sport and physical activity. Next is a description of the general findings from research that has sought to provide an empirical test of goal-setting theory in sport. Third, we consider differing explanations of the sport-related findings. These reflect arguments from an ongoing debate that is raging in the literature. This debate emanated from suggestions made by Locke (1991) that the failure to find support for goal-setting theory in sport was due to methodological weaknesses in the research. The final section of the chapter presents recent attempts to integrate goal-setting theory with current social cognitive perspectives on motivation. These efforts suggest that it is not so much a flawed methodology that renders goal-setting research in sport problematic but rather a conceptual narrowness that encourages a preoccupation with performance effects while largely ignoring how athletes who are striving for goals process performance information.

Goal-Setting Theory: An Overview

Goal-setting theory was first developed by Locke (1968) as a motivational approach to enhance productivity in the workplace. Subsequent refinements (Locke & Latham, 1990), based on a detailed and systematic program of empirical testing and theoretical reasoning, made this research area one of the most active in behavioral science (Mento, Steel, & Karren, 1987). The significance of goal-setting theory in the field was noted by Miner in 1980, who suggested at the time that it was one of the few theories in the organizational sciences that could be considered both useful and valid. Pinder (1984) also noted the impact of Locke's original conceptualization, stating that among theories of work motivation, goal-setting theory had demonstrated the greatest scientific validity.

Goal-setting theory is based on the premise that conscious goals and intentions govern an individual's actions (Locke & Latham, 1990). In their attempts to operationalize what is meant by a goal, Locke and Latham (1990) specify that a goal reflects what an individual is trying to accomplish and therefore represents the object or the aim of a specified action. However, their operational definition specifically excludes aims that focus on the process of performing some action and suggests that goals reflect end states or results that are external to the individual rather than the behavioral process itself. Therefore, by definition, the focus of goal-setting theory is limited to how people perform on specified tasks. The central assumption of the theory is that the discrete goals people are seeking to achieve will influence what they will do and how well they will perform. However, while the assumption is that goals are immediate regulators of human action (Locke, Shaw, Saari, & Latham, 1981), the theory does not specify that goals are the sole regulators of action or that there is a perfect correspondence between a goal and subsequent action. Other factors clearly influence this relationship.

Goal-setting theory is thus considered to represent a limited approach to the study of motivation because it makes no attempt to specify the ultimate roots of human action. Its limitations mean that it does not concern the causes underlying the particular goals an individual might adopt. Originally, the study of goal setting focused predominantly on understanding the strength of the functional relationship between established goals and performance on some specified task. As a result, Locke himself (Locke, 1968) considered that his work simply provided the foundations for a theory of task performance rather than a comprehensive theoretical framework. Later, Locke and Latham (1990) integrated the research findings on the topic to present a more thorough conceptual understanding of goal setting and performance. However, they still maintained that theirs was a limited approach because goal-setting theory simply provides a first-level explanation of human action and as such deals with the immediate precursors of behavior. More comprehensive theoretical explanations may be possible if researchers consider human action at a different level. For example, Locke and Latham (1990) suggest that the motives and values that individuals hold and their influence on goal commitment may offer a more comprehensive understanding of behavior but that such explanations should be considered second-level theories. Other perspectives that provide even greater analytical depth and that begin to examine the sources and roots of the individual's motives and values might be considered third-level explanations of human action (Locke & Latham, 1990).

While acknowledging the importance of addressing both motivation and individual needs, Locke and Latham (1990) argue that second- and third-level explanations are considerably distanced from the action itself and therefore offer less specific explanatory power with respect to task performance. They posit that although needs are likely to influence action through their effects on values and values will affect action through their influence on goals, it is the first-level theories such as goal-setting theory (Locke & Latham, 1990), self-efficacy theory (Bandura, 1986), reasoned action theory (Fishbein & Ajzen, 1975), and planned behavior theory (Ajzen, 1991) that seem to offer the greatest potential for explaining immediate action because these approaches focus on antecedents believed to be closest to performance itself.

The Central Postulates of Goal-Setting Theory

Goal-setting theory proposes that two specific characteristics contained within the goals determine the degree to which task performance is influenced. Embedded within any goal is information reflecting both the content of the goal and the intensity with which it should be pursued. The goal content refers to the exact nature of the goal, and it communicates specifically what is to be accomplished if goal attainment is to occur. Goal intensity reflects the degree of difficulty the goal poses, and it communicates how individuals' personal resources must be allocated to attain the level of performance demanded by the goal content. These attributes provide the foundations for the two fundamental premises of goal-setting theory. The first premise states that difficult goals lead to considerably higher levels of performance than easy goals. The second states that specific difficult goals lead to higher levels of performance than do vague goals, do-your-best instructions, or no goals. Support for both premises was gleaned from over 400 studies in industrial and organizational contexts, utilizing 88 different tasks and more than 40 000 subjects from eight different countries (Locke & Latham, 1990). The generalizability of goal-setting effects that verify Locke's (1968) original predictions about goal difficulty and specificity led Mento et al. (1987) to suggest that these effects were deserving of elevation to the lofty status of a scientific law of nature.

The Moderation of the Goal-Setting–Performance Relationship

Although empirical research, narrative and enumerative reviews (Latham & Lee, 1986; Locke et al., 1981; Locke & Latham, 1990), and meta-analyses (Chidester & Grigsby, 1984; Mento et al., 1987; Tubbs, 1986) have all confirmed that performance is a positive function of goal difficulty, evidence also points to the fact that the goal-setting–performance relationship is not simple; rather, it is moderated by a number of critical variables. For example, goal setting will have maximum performance effects when an individual has high ability, when he or she remains committed to the goal, when feedback is provided in relation to goal progress, when the task to be performed remains simple, and when there are no barriers to undermine performance (Locke & Latham, 1990). If there is any fluctuation in the strength of the moderating variables during the pursuit of a goal, the effects will be reflected in performance. In other words, it is the variables moderating the strength of the goal-setting–performance relationship that specify when performance effects will hold.

Locke and Latham (1990) explain how these variables moderate the goal-setting–performance relationship in the following way. First, they argue that individuals cannot perform in accordance with difficult goals if they do not possess the capacity to reach them. Thus, Locke and Latham conclude that ability will have a moderating effect on the goal-setting–performance relationship. In support of this contention they report evidence to suggest that performance tends to plateau as goals become more and more difficult and performance ceilings are reached. Locke and Latham (1990) argue that if set goals are beyond the capabilities of an individual, they will not be met. While this may be true at the point in time when goals are set, any assumption that low ability limits an individual's capacity to respond to a challenge may be incorrect. Low-ability performers are quite capable of responding to challenges posed by extremely difficult goals. Confirmation of this is seen in research by Crawford, White, and Magnusson (1983) and Pritchard, Bigby, Beiting, Coverdale, and Morgan (1981), who found that low-ability subjects demonstrated greater improvements after being assigned difficult goals than did high-ability subjects.

While most research has tended to support Locke and Latham's contention that ability is a key moderating variable, there is a significant body of contradictory evidence. The conclusion, according to Burton (1993), is that although research findings from the organizational literature have confirmed a moderating effect of ability on the goal-setting–performance relationship, the exact nature of these effects is as yet unclear.

The degree of goal commitment shown by the individual also has a moderating influence on the relationship between goals and performance (Locke & Latham, 1990). Numerous studies have shown that with declining commitment, a corresponding deterioration in performance occurs (Erez & Zidon, 1984). Clearly, if a person is not committed to achieving a goal, then it is possible to infer a lack of motivation, and this will be observable in the investment choices that the individual makes. In contrast, by choosing to invest personal resources into goal-directed activity, an individual clearly demonstrates a degree of commitment to goal achievement. Locke et al. (1981) suggested that commitment to a goal can be considered a form of choice, and this is influenced by both expectations for success and the value that the goal achievement holds for the individual. Research has demonstrated that it is possible to maintain or increase commitment through the implementation of various strategies aimed at manipulating either the expectation of success or the value of the task. These include having authority figures assign the goals (Latham, Erez, & Locke, 1988), peer modeling of performance (Earley & Kanfer, 1985), offering incentives or rewards (Oldham, 1975), publicly disclosing the goals (Hollenbeck, Williams, & Klein, 1989), and encouraging active participation in the goal-setting process (Erez & Arad, 1986).

A further moderator of the goal-setting–performance relationship is the provision of adequate feedback about performance or progress toward the goal. Locke et al. (1981) argued that although necessary, feedback itself is not sufficient to lead to improvements in performance. Feedback must be placed in the context of the goals being sought. In other words, neither goals alone nor feedback alone is enough to have a motivational effect on performance. Locke and Latham (1990) explain that when feedback is withheld from an individual who is aiming to achieve a specific goal, the process of setting a goal will have little motivational influence on performance because the individual is unable to monitor progress. Similarly, when an individual has no goal yet receives specific feedback about performance, this information has little motivational effect on future performance because it is not appraised in comparison to any specified target. Thus, the presence of both goals and feedback is necessary. In combination, goals and feedback allow individuals to utilize information about performance and evaluate goal progress effectively. Similarly, their combined effects enable individuals to make suitable adjustments to the allocation of either personal resources or selected strategies.

The complexity of the task being performed has been identified as a critical moderator of the goal-setting–performance relationship. Although evidence indicates that goal setting is effective on complex tasks, meta-analytical findings (Wood, Mento, & Locke, 1987) have shown that the technique has a far greater effect when employed with simple tasks. According to Locke and Latham (1990), this is the case because the immediate exertion of effort usually has a considerable impact on the performance of a simple task, and this will likely result in significantly enhanced performance. This enhanced performance is itself a source of positive feedback. In contrast, on complex tasks, the immediate exertion of effort may not lead to performance effects because effort may easily be misdirected or may not be consonant with the task requirements. The absence of significant performance gains can itself provide failure feedback to the individual, leading to a reduction in goal commitment. To prevent this, it is often necessary for individuals to formulate specific plans outlining just how they will achieve their goal. Complex tasks often require people to engage in detailed strategic planning of resource allocation if goal setting is to lead to enhanced performance effects. Chesney and Locke (1988) argued that on complex tasks, the significance of planning and strategy development is much greater than on simple tasks, where, they suggest, achievement strategies are more limited and appear known to most performers.

A further moderator of the goal-setting–performance relationship is the presence or absence of situational constraints. Locke and Latham (1990) suggested that if situational constraints act to block goal achievement, then the attainment of goals will be less likely. While suggesting that the moderating effects of situational constraints are self-evident, Locke and Latham fail to highlight that it is perceived barriers, rather than any real obstacle to performance, that most often prevent goal attainment.

In summary, Mento et al. (1987) called for the establishment of the central premises of goal-setting theory as the first law of the behavioral sciences. However, it is clear that any prediction about whether difficult goals will lead to higher levels of performance than vague goals or specific, easy goals depends on the strength of these key moderators. Consequently, the performance effects that result from setting specific, difficult goals will be greatest when an individual has high ability, performs on a simple task, is strongly committed to reaching the goal, receives feedback concerning progress toward the goal, and does not perceive any performance barriers (Locke & Latham, 1990).

The Mediation of the Goal-Setting–Performance Relationship

The knowledge that goals regulate action and that the goal-setting–performance relationship is moderated by at least five specific variables does not explain how goals have a regulatory effect. The manner in which goals influence performance is a central part of goal-setting theory. Goals are considered to have both a direct and an indirect influence on performance. Three direct mediational mechanisms are considered to operate at a motivational level, while a further indirect mediational mechanism impacts at both a cognitive and a meta-cognitive level to influence performance (Locke & Latham, 1990). That is, once an individual has a specific difficult goal to which there is some degree of commitment, the direct mechanisms function almost automatically to energize action. A goal directly influences performance by focusing the individual on cues perceived to be relevant to the task. It also signals to the individual the amount of effort necessary to attain the goal and encourages persistence on the task over a protracted time. While these motivational mechanisms operate directly, a goal also has an indirect influence on performance at a cognitive level by encouraging an individual to engage in problem solving and strategic planning in an attempt to discover how he or she might attain the goal. The crucial importance of this indirect mechanism becomes especially evident under circumstances in which the three direct motivational mechanisms are insufficient to facilitate goal attainment. For example, when goals become more complex, strategic planning becomes a requirement for goal attainment, as effort expenditure over time may not be enough to render the individual successful.

If a person is committed to a goal, the act of commitment has the immediate effect of structuring what is necessary to attend to in order to increase the probability of goal attainment. Locke and Latham (1990) argue that it is the specificity of a goal that has the greatest effect in directing an individual's attention toward goal-relevant activity while causing non-goal-relevant information to be ignored. The more detailed attentional focus that results from specific goals, compared to vague goals, is thought to lead to a reduction in performance variability. This is so because the goal conveys clear and explicit information about what is to be achieved. In addition, it is suggested that goals encourage individuals to search long-term memory stores for task-relevant knowledge and existing skills that will be effective in facilitating goal attainment. This may further direct individuals toward the consideration of new strategies for goal achievement.

Once attention has been directed toward the task, an individual who is committed to a difficult goal will begin to exert effort. It is well understood that on most tasks involving some performance objective, effort is a requirement for success. Yet the reason difficult goals increase effort expenditure is that people usually perceive these goals to require performances just beyond the range of current capabilities. Therefore, individuals understand that they cannot rely solely on ability to reach the goal. The perceived demands imposed by the goal are likely to exceed the individual's current perceived capabilities, so he or she must begin to utilize further available resources if goal achievement is to occur. Thus, he or she must allocate increased effort toward goal attainment. Empirical research has confirmed that increased physical effort (Bandura & Cervone, 1983, 1986), enhanced work rate (Bryan & Locke, 1967; Bandura & Schunk, 1981), and greater subjective effort ratings (Brickner & Bukatko, 1987) are all the direct consequence of commitment to attaining difficult goals.

Increased effort combined with goal commitment is likely to result in persistence on a task. However, goals appear to encourage persistence only as long as performance indicates progression toward the goal. If individuals reach their goals, then continued investment on the task is unlikely without the setting of new goals. Bavelas and Lee (1978) confirmed this relationship, finding that performers with easy goals ceased participation once they had reached their targets, whereas those with more difficult goals persisted longer in search of goal achievement.

Locke and Latham (1990) argue that once there is a commitment to a goal, the three direct mechanisms begin to operate automatically. That is, attention is drawn to the task, effort is expended, and persistence is forthcoming until goal attainment occurs. However, as attention is drawn to a task and an ongoing appraisal of the task demands takes place, it is common for individuals to formulate task-achievement strategies as they ask themselves how the goal can be attained. Few goals are ever achieved simply because an individual becomes energized to invest effort over time. Most goals require a great deal of cognitive investment and planning with respect to how personal resources are to be allocated. Thus, the fourth mechanism by which goals influence performance is indirect, through the formation of appropriate strategies. As Locke and Latham (1990) note, strategy development is an indirect mechanism for directing attention, but it is apparent that the action of setting a goal is often enough to initiate strategy development on the part of the individual. In fact, some researchers (Chesney & Locke, 1988; Earley, 1986, 1988; Earley & Perry, 1987) found that when specific, difficult goals were set, subjects engaged in quantitatively more planning activity or in planning that involved greater sophistication and quality.

One can see from the preceding that Locke and Latham (1990) built on the major premises of goal-setting theory by specifying which factors moderate the goal-setting–performance relationship. In addition, they outlined the mediating mechanisms by which goals influence performance. Furthermore, they summarized how and why they believed specific, hard goals lead to greater performance than other goals do. In particular, they state that specific, difficult goals, when associated with high levels of self-efficacy, directly influence an individual's performance. They also state that specific, difficult goals require higher levels of performance to elicit a sense of self-satisfaction and that as individuals seek satisfaction from achievement, hard goals are more likely to facilitate this emotional response. In sum, goals specify exactly what level of performance is required and so reduce task ambiguity. They lead to greater effort and persistence while directing attention to the requirements of the task and facilitating strategy development.

Locke and Latham's Challenge to Sport Scientists

During the development and empirical validation of goal-setting theory, researchers in industrial and organizational psychology and management established that the theoretical premises put forward by Locke (1968) were generalizable outside of a laboratory setting. Support for goal-setting theory was found in the working environment using tasks such as logging, clerical work, truck loading, key punching, assembly work, telephone servicing, and writing (Locke & Latham, 1985). Seeking to expand on the generalizability of these findings, Locke and Latham (1985) identified the area of sport performance as an apparently ideal context for the examination of goal-setting theory. For in sport and physical activity, all participants appear to be striving to reach some measurable end point. Locke and Latham noted that there had been little systematic research to test the efficacy of goal setting as a technique that could be used to develop skill, increase confidence, and enhance performance in the context of sport. However, they discovered a considerable amount of anecdotal evidence to suggest that coaches as well as athletes were using the technique in some form. Consequently they challenged sport researchers to begin a systematic program of research to test the following hypotheses:

1. Specific goals will regulate action more precisely than general goals.
2. For quantitative (specific) goals, the higher the goal the better the performance, assuming sufficient ability and commitment.
3. Specific, difficult goals will lead to better performance than goals of do-your-best or no goals.
4. Using short-term goals plus long-term goals will lead to better performance than using long-term goals alone.
5. Goals will affect performance by directing activity, mobilizing effort, increasing persistence, and motivating the search for appropriate task strategies.
6. Goal setting will be most effective, if not only effective, when there is feedback showing degree of progress in relation to the goal.
7. With goals that are difficult, the higher the degree of commitment the better the performance.
8. Commitment can be affected by asking the individual to accept the goal; showing support; allowing participation in the setting of the goal, training, and team selection, and providing athletes with incentives and rewards for specific levels of achievement.
9. Goal attainment will be facilitated by a suitable plan of action or strategy, especially when the task is complex or long term.
10. Competition will improve performance to the degree that it leads to the setting of higher goals and/or increases in goal commitment.

In formulating these hypotheses, Locke and Latham (1985) made an assumption that performance in sport is identical to performance in an organizational context. However, it may be simplistic to assume that because tasks in both sport and organizational settings focus on performance outcomes, the strength of the goal-setting–performance relationship is the same. Such an assumption ignores the fact that there are contextual factors impacting performance in work and sport that may differentially influence the goal-setting–performance relationship. While there is little doubt that goal setting is an effective performance-enhancing technique, claims for its effectiveness as a motivational technique must also consider the context in which participants are being asked to set goals.

One principal difference between organizational and sporting contexts relates to the issue of choice. Most sport and physical activity participants have chosen to invest their personal resources through their own volition, and although the degree of self-determination remains an empirical question, the choice of whether to work or not is often very different from that surrounding whether to participate in sport. Work tends to be a necessary activity in which the majority of the population must invest if they are to function effectively within society. When a UK Institute of Personnel and Development survey of 100 medium-sized manufacturing companies (*The Times,* London, January 15th, 1998) shows that 53% of managers do not find work intrinsically rewarding, it becomes understandable why techniques such as goal setting appear to be extremely powerful tools for encouraging motivation and performance within the work environment. It is likely that although work and sport contexts have performance in common, they also have many differences, likely to impinge on the utilization of a technique such as goal setting, that may influence its effectiveness.

A fundamental difference between performance in sporting and work environments relates to the overall philosophy underpinning the performance process. As noted by Locke and Latham (1985), "the alleged goal of every competitor is to win" (p. 212). While one might more accurately state that competitors strive to win, this goal is very different from the goal of every employee in business, industry, or commerce, where such a superordinate goal is not a fundamental characteristic of the context. Locke and Latham would perhaps maintain that motivational differences associated with the performance context are not central to goal-setting theory, as they argue for its being a first-level theory that focuses on the functional relationship between goals and performance once they are set. However, as will become clear from a detailed examination of the sport research, we cannot ignore the issue of context impacting motivation.

Goal-Setting Research in the Context of Sport and Physical Activity

Previous reviews of the sport goal-setting literature by Weinberg (1992) and Burton (1993) have suggested that the major premises of goal-setting theory have not stood up to empirical examination in this context. For example, many findings from research comparing difficult and specific goals with vague, do-best, or no goals are equivocal. However, a more recent meta-analysis of 36 sport studies on goal setting by Kyllo and Landers (1995) has provided a more favorable conclusion than previous reviews. The authors reported an overall mean effect size of .34 in favor of goal-setting effects. However, in comparison to findings from other meta-analyses by Chidester and Grigsby (1984), Hunter and Schmidt (1983), Mento et al. (1987), Tubbs (1986), and Wood et al. (1987), which showed effect sizes ranging from .42 to .80, the support that this study generated for goal-setting theory, while clearly evident, remains extremely modest. Unpacking the nature and variability of the goal-setting effects reveals that the sport-focused research still fails to provide convincing support for the central theoretical premises. However, there is some qualified support for the idea that goal setting has generally superior performance-enhancing effects over a directive to do one's best on sporting tasks.

Goal-Specificity Findings

A significant body of research in sport has clearly identified that setting specific goals has superior performance effects over setting no goals, general goals, or vague goals (Bar-Eli, Tenenbaum, Pie, Btesh, & Almog, 1997; Barnett & Stanicek, 1979; Boyce, 1990, 1992a, 1992b; Boyce & Wayda, 1994; Erbaugh & Barnett, 1986; Hall & Byrne, 1988; Hall, Weinberg, & Jackson, 1987; Tenenbaum, Pinchas, Elbaz, Bar-Eli, & Weinberg, 1991). These studies have thus shown support for one of the fundamental premises of Locke and Latham's (1990) theory. In addition, a further body of research has found partial support for the relationship (Burton, 1989a; Johnson, Ostrow, Perna, & Etzel, 1997; Lerner & Locke, 1995; Weinberg, Bruya, & Jackson, 1990; Weinberg, Bruya, Longino, & Jackson, 1988). These studies indicated that subjects in some but not all experimental goal-setting groups performed better than control subjects. They also showed that performance differences occurred on some but not all trials and that on a number of occasions the goal-setting effects approached statistical significance.

Although this evidence appears to confirm that goal-setting effects can generalize to sport in the way that Locke and Latham predicted, a major concern of sport psychologists has been the large proportion of empirical research that has failed to support Locke and Latham's (1990) major premises. Locke et al. (1981), and later Locke and Latham (1990), suggested that 90% of research studies in industrial and organizational settings had shown support for goal-setting theory. In contrast, Burton, Weinberg, Yukelson, and Weigand (1998) report that as many as one-third of all research studies on the goal-setting–performance relationship in sport and physical activity have failed to substantiate that goal setting has greater performance effects than doing one's best (Anshel, Weinberg, & Jackson, 1992; Boyce, 1994; Bar-Eli, Levy-Kolker, Tenenbaum, & Weinberg, 1993; Miller & McAuley, 1987; Weinberg, Bruya, & Jackson, 1985; Weinberg, Bruya, Jackson, & Garland, 1987; Weinberg, Bruya, Garland, & Jackson, 1990; Weinberg, Fowler, Jackson, Bagnall, & Bruya, 1991). The meta-analytic study of Kyllo and Landers (1995) highlights this by providing a statistical summary of the extant literature that fails to offer conclusive support for goal-specificity effects. Kyllo and Landers reported that the effect size (ES) for do-best conditions (.38) was similar to that for specific individualized goals (.27). However, they did report that when all subjects were given specific instructions to work toward the same goal (an absolute goal), the ES was much larger (.93) and was significantly different from those for the other two instructional sets.

Although many of the studies failing to show goal-specificity effects imply that the findings run counter to the predictions of goal-setting theory, such a conclusion may not be warranted. In many studies failing to demonstrate support for goal-setting theory, there were trials main effects but no significant interactions. This suggests that both experimental and control groups improved performance over time (Anshel et al., 1992; Weinberg et al., 1985, 1987; Weinberg, Bruya, Garland, & Jackson, 1990; Weinberg et al., 1991). Goal setting apparently led to improved performance, but the effects were no greater than for subjects performing under do-best conditions. One possible reason is that do-best subjects were setting their own personal goals.

Recent researchers on goal setting in the context of sport and physical activity have attempted to explain why goal-setting findings have not offered consistent support for Locke and Latham's theorizing. According to some (Burton, 1992, 1993; Weinberg & Weigand, 1993), findings may have resulted from possible methodological and experimental design weaknesses. These have included high motivation in control subjects, failure to measure personal goals, spontaneous goal setting of control subjects, lack of commitment to experimenter-set goals, and differences in task characteristics. However, it is possible that some of the findings do not emanate from design weaknesses but instead are a function of certain characteristics of the sport and activity context that encourage participants to specify what do-best performance entails.

Locke's view that goals regulate action implies that when an individual receives do-best instructions, the characteristics reflecting the content and intensity of behavior, which energize and regulate behavioral action, are not clear unless the individual has specific, detailed knowledge of what his/her best performance entails. For many who participate in sport and physical activity, detailed knowledge of their best performance comes from their experience with the activity. Such experience is common to many sport participants because sport tends to be dominated by individuals who participate of their own volition and who choose to engage in sporting and physical activities because they find performance personally meaningful. Furthermore, the socialization of sporting norms that place a high value on effort means that participants often have a detailed knowledge about the limits of their performance capabilities. It perhaps should not be surprising, therefore, that participants instructed to do their best while performing on meaningful activities can specify what their best performance will be. This insight will inevitably lead to performances similar to those of individuals who set specific goals, particularly if these individuals are approaching their current performance capacities. Boyce (1994) obtained evidence to support the notion that sport performers are clearly in touch with the limits of their performance. In an investigation of spontaneous goal setting in pistol shooting, Boyce found that two-thirds of subjects performing under control conditions set specific numeric goals for their performance and that the remaining subjects set generalized improvement goals. When asked to explain why they set goals, some subjects indicated that competition within themselves was a contributory factor. Many also responded that their extensive experience allowed them to determine specific performances that reflected their best.

A similar argument, put forward to account for the enhanced performance of do-best subjects, is that social comparison has often taken place between subjects performing under experimental and control conditions. This social comparison has encouraged do-best subjects to strive for the goals assigned to others (Weinberg et al., 1985). Hall and Byrne (1988) attempted to control for this possibility by assigning groups to conditions and preventing contact between control and experimental subjects. Although this essentially eliminated any possibility of between-group comparison, it did not prevent within-group comparison processes from occurring. One can see this in the responses that do-best subjects gave when asked whether they set goals for performance on a sit-up task: 53% indicated that they were engaged in personal goal setting, and 56% of all performers were engaged in some form of competition with other subjects on the task. Weinberg, Bruya, and Jackson (1990) reported similar findings in their attempts to extend the work of Hall and Byrne.

Locke (1991), while considering the findings from sport and physical activity to be anomalous, did not think they in any way undermined the major premises of goal-setting theory. He argued that the results were an artifact of methodological flaws within the experimental design of the research and that researchers needed to establish greater control over the setting of goals by participants who were not instructed to do so. However, Locke failed to take into account the intrinsic motivation and the extensive performance experience that influence achievement cognitions in a dynamic sporting environment. When participants are able to clearly define the current limits of their best performance and respond to the motivational cues that exist within the social context, they will give their best whether or not they have been set specific goals or given do-best instructions.

Clearly, the use of goal setting as a motivational strategy may not be noticeable when athletes are already motivated to do their best. In other words, the technique may be unlikely to differentially influence athletes' immediate-effort levels or their persistence over time. Athletes who are "doing their best" will usually demonstrate high levels of effort and persistence. Goal-setting effects are likely to occur as a function of attention direction and appropriate strategy development, but longitudinal research is required to test this contention.

Goal Difficulty Findings

Another premise at the center of goal-setting theory, which has found limited support within the realms of sport research, concerns the proposed linear relationship between goal difficulty and performance. Locke and Latham (1990) noted that goal-setting theory is vague with respect to how difficult goals ought to be and how varied the effective range of goals should be. In their meta-analysis, Kyllo and Landers (1995) found that in comparison to easy, difficult, and improbable goals, only moderate goals produced a large ES (.53). This finding, according to Kyllo and Landers, indicates that performers who begin to doubt their ability will experience reduced self-efficacy and commitment to difficult goals. Although this may hold true for some individuals, Weinberg and his colleagues (Weinberg et al., 1987; Weinberg, Bruya, Garland, & Jackson, 1990; Weinberg et al., 1991) obtained contrasting evidence. In a number of studies, the setting of improbable goals failed to undermine performance; and frequently subjects performing in this condition showed performance improvements similar to those of subjects performing in other conditions. In other words, there is no clear evidence that improbable or difficult goals cause subjects to reduce commitment and consequently withhold effort. There is, however, the distinct possibility that these individuals redefine their goals in line with what they believe to be possible.

Because it is problematic to identify what is meant by a difficult goal, one can explain in a post hoc fashion what may have moderated the goal-setting–performance relationship, but one cannot predict why goals may be redefined or why goal commitment may change. Evidence that this is a dynamic process can be gleaned from a study by Hall et al. (1987). Using a hand dynamometer task, the authors predicted that those with a difficult goal, holding a contraction for 70 s, would perform better than those given a less difficult goal, holding a contraction for 40 s. Although both groups performed better than a control group, the 70 s group did not show superior performance. Interview data revealed that those with the 70 s goal continually questioned during their performance whether the goal was achievable; and although they exerted effort toward the goal, only 46% of subjects achieved it. In contrast, as many as 67% of subjects in the 40 s goal group redefined their goal once they had achieved it, and they went on to register performances that were not statistically different from those of subjects assigned a harder goal.

A more recent study by Bar-Eli et al. (1997) showed similar results with a sit-up task. The investigators assigned subjects to either easy (improve by 10%), difficult (improve by 20%), or improbable (improve by 40%) goals over the course of an eight-week training program. After six weeks, the easy- and difficult-goal groups produced the greatest improvements; but after eight weeks, all groups showed significant improvement over do-best subjects. While supporting the goal-specificity hypothesis, the study demonstrates no support for the goal-difficulty hypothesis. Clearly, although it may be accurate to suggest that the goal-setting–performance relationship was moderated by ability, self-efficacy, or commitment, such an explanation is unsatisfactory, as it fails to address the psychological processes that take place as a function of individual differences in other dimensions of motivation. Thus it will not guide sport psychologists who wish to understand how to utilize goal setting as an intervention technique.

Locke (1991) stated that because of the vast quantity of research in industrial and organizational psychology, the conditions under which goal setting works were relatively well known. Research from sport has begun to question this assumption, and work on the central premises of goal-setting theory makes it possible to draw the following conclusions. First, goal setting does have performance effects in sport. Second, goal setting may not always be more effective than asking participants to do their best. Third, setting difficult goals does not always lead to better performance than setting easy goals because the process of goal setting often has the effect of triggering a desire to self-regulate performance. To better understand why the major premises of goal-setting theory have received modest support, at best, requires that researchers begin to understand the motivational implications of setting goals.

The Effectiveness of Short- and Long-Term Goals

A number of studies have tested Locke and Latham's (1985) hypothesis that the use of short-term goals in conjunction with long-term goals would lead to better performance than the use of long-term goals alone. Consistent with other research testing goal-setting theory in sport, these studies have also provided modest empirical support for this hypothesis. For example, Kyllo and Landers's (1995) meta-analysis reported that a combination of long- and short-term goals produced an overall ES of .48, while effect sizes for short-term goals and long-term goals were .38 and .19, respectively.

Investigating whether self-set or experimenter-set short-term goals were the more useful adjuncts to long-term goals, Hall and Byrne (1988) found that both combinations of subgoals produced better performance on a sit-up task than a do-best condition. In contrast, subjects assigned long-term goals did not differ from those asked to do their best. While no performance differences were found among any of the goal-setting groups, there were advantages to be gained from the utilization of proximal goal-setting strategies. The short-term goals were considered a useful feedback device that allowed comparison of performance against intermediate standards on a weekly basis and that enabled participants to feel a sense of relative achievement and positive self-efficacy, as well as to maintain high expectations of future performance in pursuit of long-term goals. For those aiming to achieve long-term goals, a sense of achievement and positive self-efficacy may come about if individuals make a positive comparison with the original baseline performance. However, a comparison of performance with the long-term goal itself also has the potential to indicate failure, and discrepancies may undermine both self-efficacy and future performance.

Weinberg et al. (1988) obtained results similar to those of Hall and Byrne (1988) with children utilizing different goal-setting strategies to enhance sit-up performance. Testing Bandura's (1982) contention that distal goals are necessary to provide purpose and effort to proximal direction, Weinberg et al. found that at the end of a 10-week course, no performance differences existed between those assigned long-term, short-term, or a combination of long- and short-term goals. However, these groups did perform better than a control group assigned do-best goals.

Similar findings were obtained by Boyce (1992b) on a four-week skill acquisition and retention task in riflery. Performance of subjects at the end of a three-week training period and again on a retention task in the fourth week indicated that those assigned long-term, short-term, or a combination of long- and short-term goals performed better than those asked to do their best. These findings confirm that the act of setting goals can trigger the use of self-regulation strategies. In addition, through debriefing the athletes Boyce found that many participants in the short-term goal group were themselves setting long-term goals, while those in the long-term goal group were setting short-term goals for the task.

The only explicit support for Locke and Latham's (1985) hypothesis has come from a study by Tenenbaum et al. (1991). These investigators reported that while short-term and long-term goal groups improved performance on a sit-up task of 10 weeks duration, a group with a combination of long- and short-term goals demonstrated the greatest performance improvements. While it is apparent that clear support for Locke and Latham's (1985) contentions is limited, only one sport study to date has found that long-term goals alone are more effective than a combination of short- and long-term goals. In a field experiment utilizing participants in a beginning bowling course, Frierman, Weinberg, and Jackson (1990) found that those assigned a long-term improvement goal over a five-week period performed better than a group given do-best instructions. The performances of subjects with short-term goals or a combination of short- and long-term goals did not differ from those of the do-best group. However, they also did not differ from the performances of those assigned long-term goals.

In general, goal-setting studies in sport and physical activity that have been conducted over protracted time periods appear to have found some support for Locke and Latham's (1985) contentions that short-term goals are useful adjuncts to the achievement of long-term goals. Similar to many subjects given do-best instructions, participants given long-term goals often engage in spontaneously setting their own short-term goals. It would appear that participants set these goals to give themselves a sense of achievement and satisfaction that might be unlikely if their performance were consistently compared with some long-term goal. Clearly, the point of reference with which an athlete compares performance is an important source of self-efficacy, which means that commitment to long-term goals can be maintained if consistent progress is being made in the form of short-term goal achievement.

Feedback

One of the key moderators of the goal-setting–performance relationship is the availability of feedback. Locke and Latham (1990) argued that for goal setting to be effective, goals must be accompanied by feedback showing the degree of progress in relation to the goal. Few studies have examined the proposed relationships in sport and physical activity, although those that have done so are generally supportive. Bandura and Simon (1977) conducted one of the first studies to demonstrate that goals and feedback were reciprocally dependent. They showed that overweight clients at a weight-loss clinic who were seeking to lose weight reduced their daily food consumption only when they had specific goals and kept daily records of their food consumption. Those who received feedback but did not have goals failed to alter their eating habits and performed similarly to a control group that did not set goals and did not receive feedback. Baron and Watters (1981) obtained similar results in another weight-loss study, reporting that dieters who set goals and monitored their caloric intake were more successful than those who simply monitored their intake.

In a further test to determine the moderating effects of feedback on the goal-setting–performance relationship, Bandura and Cervone (1983) found that aerobic endurance performance was enhanced only under conditions in which subjects were assigned goals and were given performance feedback in relation to those goals. Subjects provided with either goals alone or performance feedback alone showed much lower increases in aerobic endurance performance. Bandura and Cervone suggested that goals influence motivation through self-evaluative and self-efficacy mechanisms. They found that when feedback is combined with goals, the higher the self-dissatisfaction with a substandard performance and the higher the perceived self-efficacy of the individual for future goal attainment, the greater is the intensification of effort.

Only one other study directly examined the effects of feedback in conjunction with goals in a physical activity setting. Hall et al. (1987) attempted to determine whether the form and timing of feedback given to subjects performing an endurance task would have a differential effect on the goal-setting–performance relationship. No performance differences were found among subjects assigned to receive either concurrent or terminal feedback. However, many subjects who received concurrent feedback suggested that they found the feedback disconcerting at the beginning of the performance trial during which they had been assigned goals. Many subjects chose to ignore the feedback until they considered their goal to be in reach. Such a finding supports the views of Bandura and Cervone (1983), who argued that when performances fall markedly short of standards, they can have a demotivating effect because self-efficacy is undermined. In contrast, when discrepancies between goals and performance are small, the individual's self-efficacy with respect to the goal results in satisfaction and a commitment to enhanced performance.

No sport-related study has tested Locke and Latham's (1985) hypothesis that goal setting will be effective only when there is feedback showing progress in relation to the goal. The findings from a limited number of studies addressing this issue clearly indicate that enhanced performance occurs when goals are combined with feedback. The difficulty in testing Locke and Latham's (1985) hypothesis in sport is that it is almost impossible to prevent sport participants from receiving some form of performance-related feedback. More importantly, any attempt to eliminate feedback would bring into question the ecological validity of the manipulation. Similarly, if most behavior is goal directed as Locke and Latham (1990) suggest, it is difficult to imagine participants in sport or physical activity not having a goal of some description—thus, any action undertaken toward a goal will provide feedback.

Commitment

A further moderator of the goal-setting-performance relationship is the degree of commitment that an individual has toward the goal. Locke and Latham (1990) indicated that there are three ways in which goals can be set. A goal can be assigned; it can be set with the participation of the individual concerned; or it can be chosen from a series of alternatives. Support for the suggestion that increased levels of commitment would result from greater levels of choice in the goal-setting process has not materialized, as empirical evidence has indicated few performance differences between subjects assigned goals and those engaged in participatory goal setting (Latham & Lee, 1986; Mento et al., 1987). According to Locke and Latham, the reason may be that assigning goals to individuals establishes the performance level of which they are capable and thus indirectly influences self-efficacy. In contrast, providing individuals with a choice of goals may not always be beneficial, especially if the array of goals appears ambiguous to the individual or if the selection of a difficult goal is not matched by a high level of self-efficacy (Bandura, 1986).

A number of sport-related studies have examined whether participation in the goal-setting process produces greater levels of commitment and performance. Although Locke and Latham (1990) suggested that further research on this issue was unnecessary, sport researchers have remained less than convinced about an argument implying that simply assigning goals to sport participants is as effective as involving them in the process. A clear preference for involvement by athletes has been highlighted by the work of Burton, Weinberg, Yukelson, and Weigand (in press) and Weinberg, Burton, Yukelson, and Weigand (1993). Furthermore, sport researchers (e.g., Vallerand & Fortier, 1998) have found that greater levels of autonomy tend to increase athletes' intrinsic motivation to participate in sport and physical activity. Thus, it seems plausible that these effects should generalize to sport performance. However, the results from sport research have been similar to those from industrial and organizational settings; in the latter, performance differences between those assigned goals and those participating in the goal-setting process have been found to be negligible (Boyce, 1992a; Hall & Byrne, 1988; Lee & Edwards, 1984). Fairall and Rodgers (1997) recently extended work in this area beyond the performance domain, finding that the similarities among assigned goals, self-set goals, and participative goal setting extended to the goal-setting attributes of commitment, certainty over attainability, clarity, influence on behavior, and satisfaction. No differences were reported in any of these constructs despite manipulation checks suggesting that athletes perceived clear differences in the degree of perceived participation in the goal-setting process.

A study by Boyce and Wayda (1994) has demonstrated that under certain circumstances, assigned goals are more effective than self-set goals. Investigating the effects of goal setting on weight-training performance in female university students, the authors found that assigned goals produced superior performance compared to self-set goals in the later stages of a 12-week program. In agreement with Bandura (1986), Boyce and Wayda concluded that the assignment of goals by the instructor had an indirect influence on the athletes' confidence levels. That is, the act of assigning the goal conveyed to the participants that others believed them capable of goal attainment, thereby raising self-efficacy. However, as the self-set and the assigned-goal groups had the same long-term goal, it remains possible that the findings simply reflect that the self-set goal group failed to set appropriately challenging short-term goals.

Although most published studies in the sport literature have shown that participative and assigned goals have similar performance effects, it is notable that Kyllo and Landers's (1995) meta-analysis showed greater effect sizes for cooperative (.62) and participative (.49) goals than for assigned goals (.30). Perhaps the most logical explanation for this finding is that the inclusion in the meta-analysis of nonpublished studies may well have resulted in conclusions deviating from those in the narrative summaries of published research. Within these studies, the critical issue is the degree to which the participant has ownership of the goals. Participants always have part ownership of cooperative and participatively set goals, but this is not always the case when goals are set by others. Lack of ownership is likely to be reflected in a lack of personal commitment, subsequent investment, and performance.

There has been little research on methods of enhancing commitment to specific, difficult goals. Kyllo and Landers (1995) reported that commitment and performance could be enhanced through the setting of public goals. The results of their meta-analysis indicated that publicly set goals (.79) led to greater levels of performance than did privately set goals (.18). However, in the only published study to date that has directly examined this issue in sport and physical activity, Smith and Lee (1992) found no differences in the performance of individuals who publicly set goals and those who set goals privately. Nevertheless, participants who expressed their goals publicly did practice significantly longer than those with private goals.

A further attempt to determine whether the type of goal setting would induce differential levels of commitment to goals was that of Johnson et al. (1997). Comparing group and individual goal setting on a bowling task, they found that over the course of a five-week program, subjects assigned group goals performed significantly better than subjects with individual goals or do-best goals. In addition, those in the group goal-setting condition set more difficult personal goals, suggesting that the comparative nature of the goal-setting format effectively induced commitment to difficult goals.

To summarize, some evidence from Kyllo and Landers's (1995) meta-analysis supports Locke and Latham's (1985) hypothesis that higher levels of commitment lead to better performance. Kyllo and Landers found that in studies in which over 51% of subjects in the treatment group accepted their goals, an ES of .26 was obtained. In those studies reporting less than 50% acceptance, an ES of –.15 was obtained. Although greater commitment clearly leads to enhanced performance, sport studies aimed at determining the most effective strategies for enhancing commitment to difficult goals have produced inconclusive findings.

Strategic Planning

In attempts to determine how to prevent commitment to difficult goals from waning, some sport researchers have examined the effectiveness of goal-setting training programs that encourage athletes to engage in strategic planning. Locke and Latham (1990) suggest that strategic planning is necessary if there are to be performance effects. As noted by Burton (1993), many sport goal-setting studies have utilized experimental methodologies that tend to facilitate direct mediational effects on performance. That is, the goals direct attention toward the task and encourage increased effort and persistence. However, most designs have failed to encourage strategy development in participants, and even fewer studies have taught athletes skills for developing effective strategies. Consequently, most performance gains in sport goal setting appear to have resulted from increased effort and persistence alone. Clearly, when athletes begin to perform close to their current optimum level, effort alone is unlikely to result in noticeable performance gains. Such gains will result only from appropriate reflection on the areas of skilled performance that require improvement, as well as the development of strategies addressing areas of weakness that will ultimately result in performance gains.

One study involving an effort to train athletes in all aspects of goal setting was conducted by Burton (1989b). Burton trained collegiate swimmers through an educational program that focused on setting personal performance goals rather than goals related solely to the outcome of competition. He also trained the swimmers over the course of a season to keep a daily log of their goals, their practice performance, and the psychological skills that they used to enhance goal-setting effectiveness. The results indicated that when athletes were trained in setting specific individual and short-term goals focused on personal performance, they experienced more positive cognitions and affective responses to performance. In addition, female athletes who were trained in the skills of goal setting demonstrated better performances than their nontrained counterparts. Burton also compared athletes who were deemed more accurate in their goal-setting ability (goals and performance showed little discrepancy) with athletes who were considered less accurate (subsequent performances showed great discrepancy from their goals). He found that the athletes considered to be accurate goal setters experienced significantly more performance improvements, perceptions of success, satisfaction, and higher levels of perceived ability. Burton concluded that goal-setting skill mediated goal-setting effectiveness and that athletes could be trained to set goals and develop strategies that would enhance performance.

One can glean further evidence that goal-setting skills can be taught from a novel study by Swain and Jones (1995) that used a single-subject multiple-baseline design to investigate the effectiveness of goal setting with collegiate basketball players. Swain and Jones reported that performance improvements in targeted behaviors occurred in three of the four participants in an eight-week intervention. On the basis of data obtained from competitive matches during the first eight weeks of the season, subjects selected target skills to develop and also set performance goals for the remaining competitive matches with respect to these skills. Improvements in the targeted skills in three of the participants were attributed to directing attention and effort to specific skills that could help the team. Improvements were also attributed to the development of strategies that included soliciting advice from the coach and senior players on the team and implementing additional practice sessions to work on the skills.

In another study, Kingston and Hardy (1997b) trained golfers to set either process goals that focused on specific aspects of their golf game or performance goals that focused on personal performance on each round. Both types of training resulted in improved skill levels over the course of a year, whereas a control group given no training showed no such improvements. However, only those golfers in the process-goal training group appeared to experience positive changes in self-efficacy, cognitive anxiety control, and concentration.

Not all training studies have demonstrated performance effects. A study by Weinberg, Stitcher, and Richardson (1994) assessing the effects of goal setting on four specific lacrosse skills, using competition statistics as the basis for setting goals, failed to find goal-setting effects. Weinberg et al. suggest that although nonsignificant, the improvements demonstrate the efficacy of the intervention. They argue that with a larger sample, performance differences would be statistically significant. However, a factor that may have contributed to the reported nonsignificant effects was the insistence by the experimenter that the individuals not discuss assigned goals with anyone else. Such an approach makes it difficult for an athlete to solicit information to develop strategies to assist in goal achievement. Clearly, if strategy development fails to occur on complex sporting tasks, then one cannot assume that effort and persistence will be sufficient to facilitate performance improvements.

Effective strategic planning is clearly necessary when athletes are setting goals for complex tasks. This point is consistent with propositions advanced by Wood et al. (1987) and Locke and Latham (1990) suggesting that on simple tasks, goals affect performance by directing attention, increasing effort, and encouraging persistence, and also that the use of any task-specific plans tends to be highly automated. On simple tasks participants usually have a clear idea about how to enhance performance, and often this requires nothing more than the exertion of greater levels of physical or mental effort over a longer period. As tasks become more complex, it becomes less obvious how to make performance gains, and the exertion of effort and increased persistence are insufficient to produce gains unless the person also develops strategies that clearly identify how to enhance future performance. Indeed, effort and persistence in this case may even have negative effects. It has been suggested that stating highly specific end goals on complex tasks may generate pressures for immediate performance and lead to the selection of unsuitable and/or simple strategies, when the need may be for more complex strategies requiring creative problem-solving skills (Earley, Connolly, & Ekegren, 1989). For example, on sporting tasks, it is counterproductive to focus attention on an end goal when a broader consideration of appropriate strategies to enhance component skills may be necessary (Janis & Mann, 1977), as the athlete's attention is directed toward the wrong component of performance.

Only one sport-related study has directly examined the effectiveness of goal setting on tasks of differing complexity. Burton (1989a) had members of a basketball class aim to improve their performance of skills of varying complexity during an eight-week course. The participants were assigned either specific goals or do-best goals for each skill. Seven skills were chosen based on a model of task complexity put forward by Landers and Boutcher (1986). Shooting skills were classified as highly complex; ball handling, dribbling, and passing were classified as moderately complex; and footwork and agility skills were classified as low in complexity. The assignment of specific goals resulted in performance improvements on one low-complexity skill and one moderate-complexity skill, offering partial support for the hypothesis that specific goals would be more effective in enhancing performance on simple than on complex skills. Although this study did not demonstrate clear support for Locke and Latham's (1985) contention that goal attainment on complex tasks would be facilitated by a suitable plan of action, the failure to find that goal setting was effective on complex tasks offered indirect support for this perspective.

Some studies in industrial and organizational settings have confirmed that on complex tasks, improvements tend to occur on later trials. This may also be true when participants are initially performing close to their potential on relatively simple tasks, such as sit-ups. Under these conditions, performance improvements are more likely to occur over time if subjects reflect upon how they might improve specific aspects of performance, such as strength, endurance, or technique. This may account for the improved performance that Weinberg et al. (1988) found in children on the later trials of a 10-week study measuring sit-up performance. Other studies using sit-ups as a dependent measure have run for much shorter durations and have failed to show convincing performance effects. It has been noted in research using this experimental paradigm (Hall & Byrne, 1988) that while subjects expend high levels of effort during class testing, they are often unwilling to practice the sit-up task outside of the class. The significant strength and endurance gains required to produce improvement are unlikely to occur over short periods without engaging in physical practice outside of class. This means that the use of any alternative strategy must be given sufficient time to take effect.

What this body of research demonstrates is that with increasing task complexity, or when athletes are performing close to their maximum potential, strategic plans must be implemented if goal setting is to be effective. Furthermore, it appears that it is possible to facilitate this process through a process of training in goal setting.

Competition

Another factor that Locke and Latham believe will lead to greater levels of commitment and the setting of higher goals is competition. Although Hall and Byrne (1988) noted that social comparison and competition frequently led to goal setting by participants given do-best instructions, few researchers have tested Locke and Latham's (1985) contentions. Some support for their views comes from a study by Giannini, Weinberg, and Jackson (1988). Here, participants in a one-on-one basketball task who were first asked to compete and then given information about their own and a competitor's performance performed better than subjects who set only personal goals or who set goals cooperatively. However, these findings were not replicated with a 3 min basketball shooting task. Giannini et al. explained the superior performance of the competitive-goal group in the one-on-one task as a function of competition instructions that encouraged extra effort.

The aim in a more recent study by Lerner and Locke (1995) was to determine whether competition would influence the level of goals set by participants, their commitment to the goals, and their self-efficacy. Participants were assigned to either a moderate- or high-goal condition and required to perform a 1 min sit-up task alone or in competition against a confederate. The results indicated that competition did not lead to enhanced performance, the setting of higher goals, or increased self-efficacy. According to Lerner and Locke's conclusion, these findings verify that competition is simply another form of goal setting. Kyllo & Landers's (1995) meta-analysis fails to confirm this, however. The results of the meta-analysis indicate that competitive goals (ES = .65) and cooperatively set goals (ES = .57) result in greater performance improvements than goals that involve seeking personal mastery (ES = .37), suggesting that goal setting and competition have differential effects. A further analysis confirmed this point, indicating that when competition was not controlled (ES = .58), goal-setting effects were inflated and were much greater than when competition was controlled (ES = .25) or when individual performance was being tested. Thus, it may be more accurate to consider competition a completely separate facet of sport that may or may not have motivational or performance effects. It is clearly different from goal setting, as a commitment to compete does not specify the requisite performance level until an opponent's score is known or, in the case of a simultaneous competition, until the end of the contest.

Goals As Mediators
of the Self-Efficacy–Performance Relationship

In an attempt to assess some of the psychological mechanisms through which goals are thought to have motivational and performance effects, a number of studies have examined the models put forward by Locke and Latham (1990) and by Earley and Lituchy (1989). These models outline how personal goals have a mediating effect on the relationship between self-efficacy and performance. Locke and Latham suggested that assigned goals are positively related to personal goals and self-efficacy. Furthermore, they claim that self-efficacy has a direct effect on personal goals and performance, while personal goals have a direct influence on performance (see figure 6.1). Thus, personal goals are considered to mediate the relationship between self-efficacy and performance.

Earley and Lituchy (1989) put forth a similar mediational model suggesting that an individual's previous performance experiences have a direct effect on self-efficacy, personal goals, and performance. Moreover, self-efficacy affects goals and performance, while goals have a direct influence on performance (see figure 6.2). This again points to goals as mediators between self-efficacy and performance.

One of the first to test the mediational effects of goals on the relationship between self-efficacy and performance was Lee (1988). After measuring the goal attributes and self-efficacy of athletes from nine different sports, Lee regressed these constructs on the winning percentage of the team. She found that regardless of the order of entry into the equation, goal-setting attributes had the strongest direct influence on winning percentage, thus providing support for the mediating role of goal setting.

A further test of the mediational effects of goals was performed by Theodorakis (1995). Swimmers completed four trials of a swimming task that required them to swim sprints over a specified time. After performing

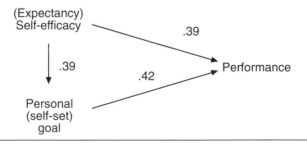

Figure 6.1   Relationships among self-efficacy, self-set goals, and performance.

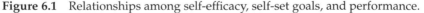

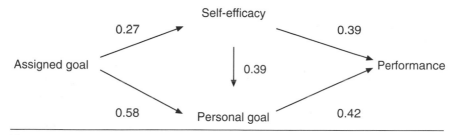

Figure 6.2 Relationships among assigned goals, personal goals, self-efficacy, and performance.

A theory of goal setting and task performance by Locke/Latham, © 1990. Reprinted by permission of Prentice-Hall, Inc., Upper Saddle River, NJ.

the first two trials under do-best instructions, participants were asked to set goals and strive to achieve them in trials 3 and 4. A path model outlining the predicted relationships included measures of each swimmer's past performance, self-efficacy, self-satisfaction, goals for trials 3 and 4, and performance on trials 3 and 4. Using structural equation modeling (see figure 6.3), Theodorakis found that while past performance influenced self-efficacy and personal goals on trial 3, neither goals nor self-efficacy had a direct influence on performance. Past performance was the only significant predictor. These findings were replicated for trial 4. The results provide some indirect support for the argument presented earlier. That is, when

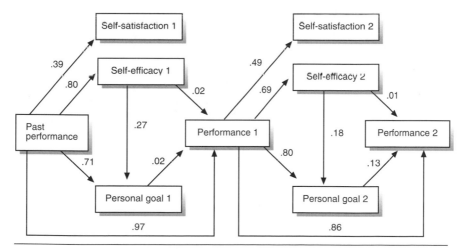

Figure 6.3 Path diagram of the estimated structural models. Path coefficients greater than .16 are significant at $p < .01$.

Reprinted, by permission, from Y. Theodorakis, 1995, "Effects of self-efficacy, satisfaction, and personal goals on swimming performance," *The Sport Psychologist* 9, 250.

athletes are knowledgeable about their sporting performance on a familiar task and they appear to be performing close to performance ceilings, the degree to which goals and self-efficacy may influence performance is largely superseded by the level at which participants have performed in the past. Such suggestions are congruent with previous work by Feltz (1988) demonstrating that when athletes have little specific experience of past performance, then self-efficacy tends to predict performance. With greater experience of the task being performed, past performance seems to override the performance effects that self-efficacy may have.

In a reformulation of Theodorakis's model with past performance eliminated as a predictor, self-satisfaction and self-efficacy were both found to predict goals. However, only the athletes' goals showed a direct relationship with performance, suggesting that the self-efficacy–performance relationship was mediated by the goals of the athlete (see figure 6.4).

Kane, Marks, Zaccaro, and Blair (1996) tested a similar self-regulatory model using 216 high school wrestlers enrolled in a summer wrestling camp. The athletes participated in five days of competition; and measures of previous performance, personal goals, self-efficacy, wrestling performance, and satisfaction were taken. Kane et al. found that the personal goals set by athletes for wrestling camp performance mediated the relationship between self-efficacy and performance. Similar to the findings of Theodorakis, results showed that previous performance had the strongest direct effect on

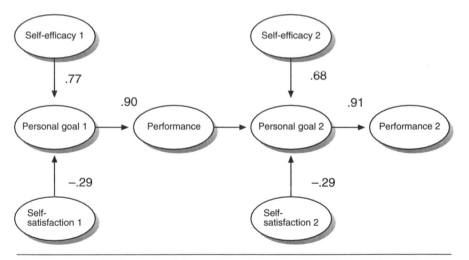

Figure 6.4   Path diagram of the estimated structural models. Path coefficients greater than .16 are significant at $p < .01$.

Reprinted, by permission, from Y. Theodorakis, 1995, "Effects of self-efficacy, satisfaction, and personal goals on swimming performance," *The Sport Psychologist* 9, 250.

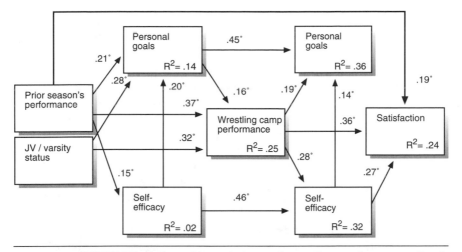

Figure 6.5   LISREL VI results: self-regulation and wrestling performance. Goodness of fit = .98. Goodness of fit (adjusted) = .94 χ^2 (12, N = 195) = 15.23, p = .23.

Reprinted, by permission, from T.D. Kane, M.A. Marks, S.J. Zaccaro, and V. Blair, 1996, "Self-efficacy, personal goals, and wrestlers' self-regulation," *Journal of Sport and Exercise Psychology* 18, 39.

performance. Previous performance also had a significant influence on personal goals and self-efficacy (see figure 6.5).

Although these studies provided some support for Locke and Latham's (1990) model, confirming that goals mediate the relationship between self-efficacy and performance, neither study employing structural relational models showed complete support for the direct performance effects of both goals and self-efficacy as suggested in Locke and Latham's model. What these studies point to is the need to go beyond a first-level theory of task performance as outlined by Locke and Latham (1990). Researchers must explore a wider motivational framework that considers why athletes are most likely to feel efficacious, remain committed to goal achievement, and thus experience enhanced personal performance when striving to reach discrete goals.

Anomalies in Sport Goal-Setting Research: A Methodological or a Conceptual Problem?

Many of the findings from goal-setting studies in sport have been reported by Locke (1991, 1994) as anomalous, and this is clearly evident when one considers the overwhelming support for the technique's effectiveness in improving performance on industrial and management tasks.

Locke (1991, 1994) has argued that much of the sport research is seriously flawed. He suggests that if sport research were methodologically more rigorous, sport scientists would be producing findings consistent with those in the industrial and organizational literature. Explicit in Locke's argument is the notion that the psychological processes central to goal-setting theory are robust enough to transcend any contextual boundaries. Clearly, sport researchers would be unlikely to claim that the contexts they are investigating have "special, unique properties that absolve experimenters of the responsibility of conducting methodologically sound research" (Locke, 1994, p. 214). However, it is clear that aspects of the sporting context may influence the effectiveness of goal setting as a motivational technique and may require researchers to modify existing conceptual views on the subject.

Although some published studies on goal setting in sport contain serious methodological difficulties, Weinberg and Weigand (1993) have rightly highlighted that not all the results contradictory to findings in the industrial and organizational literature can be dismissed as a product of fundamental inadequacies in research design. The challenge facing researchers working in the context of sport is to determine which findings might be anomalous because of erroneous scientific inquiry and which sport-related findings present a challenge to a conceptual model developed in quite separate contexts. Whatever the outcome, researchers need to be mindful that one of the beauties of scientific inquiry is that it appeals to self-correction—so if the ongoing debate on this issue promotes enhanced understanding in the future, then the field of sport psychology will benefit immensely.

The work of Locke (1991, 1994) and his colleagues (Locke & Latham, 1985) focuses almost exclusively on the outcome of task performance as the dependent measure of interest. In adopting such a focus, these researchers ignore the fact that sport motivation and performance involve considerably more than event outcomes, or objective indexes of productivity. To truly understand whether goal setting has either motivational or performance effects, one must begin to understand the complexities of the context in which individuals are being asked to set goals.

The importance of context is highlighted by evidence suggesting that when goal-setting research is removed from the well-controlled environment of the laboratory and examined in ecologically valid contexts, the strength of the goal-setting effects is reduced (Hall & Byrne, 1988; Tubbs, 1986). Specifically, in a review of the literature addressing whether goal setting was effective in sport, Hall and Byrne (1988) indicated that the contexts least likely to produce goal-setting effects were field experiments, where tight control of experimental manipulations was not possible. Interestingly, while not reporting the same equivocal findings that had been observed in sport contexts, Tubbs (1986) found a similar pattern of results in organizational settings. That is, the strength of goal-setting findings obtained from laboratory-based research was not replicated in the field when task performance on more meaningful work-related activities was measured. These findings suggest that all goal-setting research ought to be sensitive to the context in which it is being conducted. Moreover, they emphasize the need to begin examining the complex psychological processes that are operating to influence motivation and performance in specific contexts.

Methodological Inadequacies Identified by Locke and His Solutions

Locke's (1991, 1994) criticism of goal-setting research in sport has focused on what he believes to be a number of crucial methodological flaws. These are (1) the manipulation failure of "do-best" conditions, (2) failure to measure personal goals, (3) failure to make specific goals difficult, (4) failure to adequately measure goal commitment, (5) failure to equate baseline levels of performance, (6) failure to control for competition among participants, and (7) measuring subjective difficulty or effort rather than self-efficacy. The significance of Locke's (1991, 1994) criticisms is that they raise questions about the internal validity of a considerable body of literature concerned with goal setting in sport. However, in providing solutions to increase the internal validity of research in this area, Locke seems to ignore the fact that their implementation in future research may undermine the external validity of the findings because the experimental constraints suggested bear little resemblance to realistic sporting contexts. If goal setting is to be an important motivational technique in sporting contexts then researchers can ill afford to ignore the environment and what gives it meaning in a quest to establish internal validity. Having said this, we would agree with two of Locke's suggestions for improved goal-setting research in sport. First, that sport researchers must seek to equate baseline levels of performance in experimental research if meaningful findings are to accrue. Second, that it may be more appropraite for researchers to measure self-efficacy instead of assessing the subjective difficulty of a task. This is because a more detailed appraisal of the task must be undertaken, and furthermore, the possibility of any confound between the probability of goal achievement and the objective difficulty of the task is reduced. We do not agree with five of the methodological solutions put forth by Locke (1991, 1994), and the following section provides a more detailed commentary.

Lack of Experimental Control in Do-Best Conditions

In Locke's view, much of the research that has failed to find performance effects has also failed to prevent subjects in control groups from engaging in spontaneous goal setting. This lack of experimental control has often compromised experimental manipulations and has led to the reporting of equivocal findings. Locke (1991) suggested that the best way to overcome this problem is either to withhold feedback from the subjects in control conditions or to provide feedback in a varied manner that prevents subjects from being able to monitor and regulate their performance. In a study by Lerner and Locke (1995), subjects performing sit-ups in a control condition were asked to do their best on the task while audibly counting backward from 100 in increments of three. Although enhanced control of this kind may solve one problem, it creates further difficulties with respect to methodological adequacy. Specifically, forming exacting controls raises an important issue about whether researchers can truly say that they are examining goal setting in the context of sport. Lerner and Locke's methodology also highlights a concern about whether the additional instructions given to the control group themselves constituted a confound. Specifically, requesting that subjects count backward leads to cognitive interference that undermines the performance of the do-best group.

Weinberg and Weigand (1993) noted this point in their response to Locke's criticisms of sport research on goal setting. They argued that denying feedback to control subjects while providing it to subjects in other experimental conditions does not constitute an appropriate design. Either all subjects must receive feedback or none should receive feedback. Alternatively, the number of groups could be doubled through the addition of another experimental condition in which one group receives feedback and the other receives no feedback. Weinberg and Weigand (1993) point out that if you eliminate feedback from the experimental procedure, you defeat the purpose of conducting research in an ecologically valid context. Furthermore, if researchers were to heed Locke's suggestions, it is unclear what type of feedback they should withhold from the sport participants performing in control conditions in order to allow observation of goal effects. As feedback can come from many diverse sources in sport, and not simply from objective outcomes, withholding feedback about the outcome of performance may not be an appropriate strategy for maintaining control.

Unfortunately, the extreme measures to establish experimental control that Locke (1991) suggested will not allow investigators to understand many important psychological mechanisms underlying goal setting in sport. Self-regulation of performance is an important element of the achievement process in sport, even for participants attempting to do their best. Therefore, rather than seeking to prevent self-regulation, researchers must begin to examine why subjects in sporting contexts appear more likely to set goals when asked to do their best than subjects in other achievement settings. Clearly, researchers need to begin investigating the motivational process rather than focusing solely on the mechanistic performance effects of goal setting. Similar calls for increased conceptual clarity are not new, as Hall (1990), Tubbs (1986), and Weinberg and Weigand (1993) all noted. It is well known that goal setting can be effective (even in sport); however, we need much greater insight into the processes underlying its effectiveness in sporting contexts if we are to achieve an adequate level of clarity.

Failure to Assess Personal Goals

A second methodological criticism that Locke (1991) aimed at sport research on goal setting was that sport researchers failed to assess the personal goals of subjects participating in different goal-setting conditions. This weakness led to compromising of the experimental manipulation of goals because subjects were aiming for something other than the set goal. Locke (1991) suggested that if researchers obtained information on personal goals, they could classify subjects into appropriate goal-setting conditions, and consequently the research would confirm his predictions regarding goal difficulty and specificity. Although one can achieve greater insight into the goal setting process by assessing personal goals or the personal meaning an individual gives to a goal, Locke (1991, 1994) does not elaborate on when this information should be gleaned. If one were to obtain the information before the subjects performed (which would be the most appropriate time), one would be in danger of compromising the integrity of the design by focusing the individual on something other than the specific manipulation. If one solicited this information after individuals had performed, subjects would be likely to provide information confounded with attributional responses for performance. Whereas the assessment of performance-related cognitions will provide further insight into the goal-setting process, and might help explain some of the sport-related findings, there is no adequate solution to the dilemma facing researchers as to the best time to accurately determine an individual's personal goals.

This problem is compounded by the fact that the goal-setting process is dynamic and that it must be viewed as conceptually similar to more general perspectives on motivation. According to current perspectives on achievement motivation in sport and education (Duda, this volume; Duda & Hall, 2000; Roberts, this volume; Ames, 1992c), it is the achievement goals of the individual that energize the motivational process. Moreover,

Roberts (1992a; this volume) and Dweck and Leggett (1988) have suggested that multiple goals exist and that the endorsement of specific achievement goals provides a clear framework for understanding how achievement information is processed. Dweck and Elliott (1983) reported that when individuals engaged in achievement activities, the achievement goal adopted reflected the subjective meaning of success and failure, created a specific cognitive set for processing information, and highlighted the means by which the goal could be achieved. Although individuals may hold dispositional achievement goals that have a relatively consistent influence on achievement behavior, the meaning of achievement and the resultant cognitive set are subject to change by environmentally salient cues (Ames, 1992c). This means that people may alter their perspective on achievement, as well as their interpretation of information regarding assigned or self-set goals, at any time during the performance process, dependent on their cognitive processing of information. Consequently, attempts to assess subjects' personal goals need to take into account the complexity of the cognitive motivational process involved in goal setting. One cannot simply assume that assessing these goals at a single point in time will provide an accurate picture of the personal meaning of achievement or identify what an individual is aiming to achieve over a protracted time.

Failure to Make Specific Goals Difficult

Locke's (1991) third major criticism of goal-setting research in sport focuses on whether subjects in experimental conditions have actually been assigned difficult goals. He implies that because more than 10% of subjects typically achieve the goals assigned to them, the goals cannot really be considered difficult. However, one must question the logic of a line of thought that assumes objective success and failure to be the central determinants of goal difficulty and investment potential. Determining goal difficulty through some objective measure of success ignores the fact that it is the subjective difficulty of the goal, along with the value of the activity, that is central to investment. In a further criticism of the sport research, Locke (1991) rightly suggested that measuring self-efficacy would allow researchers to better understand the perceived difficulty of a goal. Clearly, athletes' perceptions of whether they possess the skills deemed necessary to reach specified goals are more likely to predict personal investment than some level of goal difficulty imposed by a researcher. However, as Hall (1990) has suggested, without a clear understanding of the achievement goals of the individual, it may not be possible to make an accurate prediction of the motivational qualities of assigned goals. The assessment of self-efficacy alone may be inadequate to predict whether a goal will be motivating. For example, an individual with high self-efficacy may choose not to invest energy toward a specified goal if he/she believes that the investment will not reflect positively on the self. Equally, an individual with low self-efficacy may choose to invest a great deal of energy in attempting to reach a goal if he/she believes that the goal provides an opportunity for development. Only when individuals' achievement goals are taken into account can such behavior be adequately explained.

Although Locke does not explicitly state that an examination of achievement goals is central to a conceptual understanding of the effects of goal setting, the need for such an understanding is implicit in his work. For example, an early article by Latham and Locke (1979) is entitled "Goal Setting: A Motivational Technique That Works." The phrasing implies that goal setting enhances performance through its motivational qualities. This would seem to suggest that if researchers wish to understand more than just the performance effects of goal setting, they cannot ignore important process variables that impact personal meaning.

Failure to Adequately Measure Goal Commitment

A suggestion by Weinberg and Weigand (1993), though not confirmed by empirical investigation, is that subjects in sport research on goal setting may be more committed than those who perform experimental tasks in industrial or organizational settings. The reason, Weinberg and Weigand argue, is that the activities are inherently more meaningful and have greater personal value. Locke (1994) disagrees, claiming that most subjects in industrial/organizational experiments were motivated to perform for class credit. While it may be true that extrinsic factors induced motivation in these subjects, Locke does not consider that a subject's motivation to invest in a task is likely to be influenced by the meaning that the activity holds for him or her. However, as stated earlier, it is not unreasonable to assume that performing sporting tasks will have greater relevance and more meaning for individuals already enrolled in physical activity classes than will performing some obscure task for class credit. Similarly, one could assume that because most sport participants are engaging in activities out of choice, the personal meaning of achievement in the activity will be more salient than for individuals in industrial and environmental settings, where the degree of choice about whether to invest may be more limited. This may encourage enhanced performance on meaningful sporting tasks when individuals are given do-best instructions. In industrial and organizational settings, where the meaning of achievement on work-related activities may not be as salient, other motivational incentives may be necessary to increase performance under do-best conditions. If, as Locke (1991, 1994) has suggested, researchers undertook to measure commitment adequately, it would be possible to determine whether those seeking to achieve discrete goals were committed to goal achievement or to the receipt of some external incentive.

Spontaneous Goal Setting and Competition Among Participants

One must also consider that if sport is a meaningful activity, it is likely that an individual will possess some knowledge of what is acceptable performance in that activity. Therefore, because of a familiarity with the task requirements and the general standards for performance, it is more likely that participants will engage in spontaneous goal setting on sporting tasks than on occupational activities or on mundane laboratory tasks. In laboratory settings, the task is often novel and may have little value, and subjects may be oblivious to an appropriate standard of achievement other than performance on an initial trial. Achieving a specific standard without having learned what that level of performance indicates will do little for the individual's motivation. Therefore, instructing people to do their best on an obscure task is unlikely to encourage spontaneous goal setting, especially if the task carries little meaning and the context is contrived. In sport, however, cognizance of the meaning of performing at a specific level may well encourage spontaneous goal setting even though instructions are limited to doing one's best. When a task has some value and personal meaning, it is more likely to promote self-regulation and careful monitoring of performance. Consequently, asking people to do their best on a meaningful activity is likely to result in their performing close to their optimal capability because performance is regulated against specific knowledge about personal limits of performance.

Unfortunately, some sporting tasks are not always inherently meaningful. If indeed they were, coaches, teachers, and trainers would have few problems motivating athletes. It is quite clear that some sport research has utilized tasks that may have had little meaning or value to the participants outside the immediate testing environment. For example, Burton (1993) points out that studies by Weinberg and his colleagues using sit-ups as a dependent measure may not have offered much personal incentive for subjects to utilize goal setting in other situations because of the limited appeal of the task. Indeed, Hall & Byrne (1986) found evidence that supports this notion, reporting that the amount of time subjects spent practicing sit-ups outside of the test setting was negligible in all groups. If goal setting is to be effective over an extended time (such as in a five-week sit-up program), then the task needs to be meaningful to encourage strategy development that will help individuals achieve their goals. Alternatively, if the task has little meaning or value, then strategy development occurring as a result of goal setting will be negligible. Goal-setting effects will simply be the result of increased effort put forth by subjects during the testing session or, more likely, will not be observed at all because task constraints impose a ceiling on performance.

Some investigators have attempted to utilize more meaningful and more complex sporting tasks such as basketball free throws (Miller & McAuley, 1987), basketball field goals (Giannini et al., 1988), and ball throwing (Wraith & Biddle, 1989). However, these studies encountered methodological problems and failed to find that goal setting was more effective than doing one's best. It is distinctly possible that in these studies the ceiling effects associated with the measurement of performance prohibited any goal-setting effects. It is also possible that these investigations experienced some of the design inadequacies outlined by Locke (1991, 1994). That is, confounds may have been a function of variability in the baseline performances of the experimental groups, or competition between subjects may have been a more salient motivator than the assigned goals.

However, other explanations should also be considered. Because of the complexity of these tasks, it is likely that the interventions were not of sufficient duration to allow subjects to develop appropriate strategies to enable the successful achievement of set goals. Evidence to support this idea was generated by Wood et al. (1987), who found through meta-analytic procedures that the effect of goal setting on performance was greater for simple tasks than for complex tasks. Wood et al. also argued that differences in goal effects between complex and simple tasks may diminish over time due to the adoption of appropriate performance strategies. It therefore remains possible that much of the equivocal evidence concerning the effects of goal setting in sport stems from the failure to consider strategy development as an important mediating variable. Perhaps if goal-setting interventions were conducted over a long enough time to encourage strategy development, there would be fewer anomalous findings.

Goal-Setting Anomalies: Moving Beyond First-Level Theories to Examine Motivational Processes

It seems clear from his reaction papers that Locke remained unconvinced that factors other than methodological inadequacy could explain the anomalies in sport research on goal setting (Locke, 1991, 1994). Although many of Locke's suggestions will help sport researchers develop tightly controlled experimental designs, it is clear that the anomalous findings cannot be a function solely of research design weaknesses. Sport researchers must depart from a singular mechanistic focus that attempts to demonstrate how goal setting influences performance when exacting controls are maintained. They must begin to conceptually investigate why goal setting influences performance. If the technique is supposed to enhance motivation as well as performance, it ought to be influenced and informed by current conceptual approaches to understanding the motivational process. A growing number of researchers investigating motivation and achievement in sport and physical activity are utilizing an achievement goal perspective as a guiding conceptual framework (see Biddle, Duda, Fry, Roberts, Treasure, this volume). According to this approach, personal meaning is the critical determinant of achievement behavior, and that meaning is reflected in the athlete's achievement goals. We contend that when researchers begin to examine goal setting from a perspective that considers personal meaning to be the critical variable underpinning the goal-setting process, a better understanding of motivational and performance effects will be possible. Furthermore, such a strategy will enable us to understand why goal-setting effects may not be constant across contexts. An integration of goal-setting theory with current social cognitive perspectives on motivation in sport would seem to be a suitable approach for further examining the anomalous findings related to goal setting in sport.

Integrating Goal-Setting Theory With Achievement Goal Theory

Burton and others have begun to explore the relationship between goal setting and achievement goals but because the two literatures address such different constructs while utilizing similar terms, many challenges remain. Perhaps the greatest of the challenges is for researchers to move beyond first-level explanations and further explore the important psychological processes that moderate the goal-setting–performance relationship. A further challenge is for researchers to address the nomenclature associated with goal setting and achievement motivation that appears to underpin some of the confusion in the current sport psychology literature.

Burton's Proposed Integration

Burton (1993) suggested that a principal reason for the apparent ineffectiveness of goal setting in sport was the failure of researchers to consider the potential for important individual differences, other than self-efficacy, to moderate the goal-setting–performance relationship. His response was to propose a competitive goal-setting model (see Burton 1992, 1993, for a

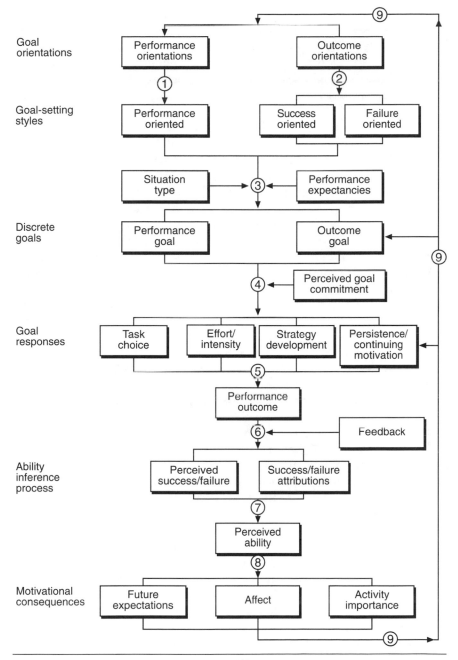

Figure 6.6 Competitive goal-setting model.

Reprinted, by permission, from D. Burton, 1992, The Jekyll/Hyde nature of goals: Reconceptualizing goal setting in sport. In T. Horn (Ed.) *Advances in sport psychology* (Champaign, IL: Human Kinetics) 267–297.

review) (figure 6.6) that integrates the social cognitive perspectives on achievement motivation espoused by Dweck (1980), Maehr (1984), and Nicholls (1984b) with the goal-setting theory outlined by Locke and Latham (1990). Burton argues that the dispositional achievement goals (see Roberts, Duda, this volume) endorsed by athletes interact with their perceived ability to produce three distinct goal-setting styles. Identified as performance-oriented, success-oriented, and failure-oriented styles, these are considered to reflect athletes' preferences for particular goal-setting attributes during either practice or competition.

A performance-oriented goal-setting style is considered to reflect a strong dispositional task orientation, and it is argued that athletes adopting this style will show a preference for discrete goals that are specific, difficult, and focused on individual performance. In addition, this goal-setting style is seen as leading to the setting of long- and short-term goals directed toward the production of positive (desirable) behaviors and focused on self-referenced aspects of performance. In contrast, a success-oriented goal-setting style is thought to correspond with a strong dispositional ego orientation and the perception that one is competent. Athletes possessing this goal-setting style also prefer goals that are specific, moderately difficult, and focused on individual performance. However, they also prefer long- and short-term goals directed toward the production of positive (desirable) behaviors and/or the elimination of negative (undesirable) behaviors. Furthermore, these athletes prefer that their goals be focused on aspects of performance that are either socially or normatively comparable.

A dispositional ego orientation is also considered to underlie a failure-oriented goal-setting style, although those adopting this style have a tendency to perceive their ability to be low. Consequently, their preferences are said to be for goals that are general rather than specific, moderately easy rather than difficult, and focused on team rather than individual performance. In addition, they display a preference for goals that are long term and are directed toward the production of positive (desirable) behaviors. However, it is their preference for goals focused on comparative or normative aspects of performance that renders them vulnerable to experiencing maladaptive performance-related cognitions, affective responses, and behavior. This is because athletes who endorse strong dispositional ego orientations, while constantly perceiving their ability to be low, will rarely encounter outcomes that can be interpreted as favorable.

Burton (1992, 1993) claims that in practice and competitive contexts, the three goal-setting styles lead to the setting of discrete goals that demonstrate the preferred characteristics. Once set, these discrete goals become subject to the same moderating and mediating influences as outlined by Locke and Latham (1990). However, Burton's model (1992, 1993) implies that although athletes have a choice over the goals they set, the motivational impact of the goal-setting–performance relationship will be a consequence of the specific goal-setting style adopted. The reason is that the goal-setting style determines the nature of the specific attributes embedded in the goal the athlete is seeking to achieve.

In Burton's (1992, 1993) view, the competitive goal-setting model permits a more comprehensive explanation of the goal-setting process in sport. To date, however, there is still no direct empirical evidence to support the existence of goal-setting styles in sport or any other context. The evidence Burton uses to support the competitive goal-setting model was generated from contemporary perspectives on achievement motivation (Elliott & Dweck, 1988; Maehr, 1984; Nicholls, 1989); and although intuitively appealing, a direct correspondence between dispositional goal orientations and goal-setting styles is difficult to substantiate at either a conceptual or an empirical level.

In addition, the implication that a dispositional task orientation equates with a performance-oriented goal-setting style, whereas a dispositional ego orientation corresponds with either a success-oriented or a failure-oriented style, appears to have generated some confusion in the literature. Rather than being a heuristic tool as Burton intended, the model has obscured important issues because it does not specify precise relationships among the central components. Key constructs, such as goal-setting styles, have not been adequately defined, and the proposed relationships between achievement goals and goal-setting styles are unclear. It is thus difficult to make accurate predictions about the antecedents of achievement behavior or to discern the motivational and performance consequences of setting discrete goals. In fact, the competitive goal-setting model is not consistent with the view held by achievement goal theorists that athletes may endorse multiple achievement goals. Nor is it consistent with the view that the salience of situational cues may override any dispositional goal and influence the immediate meaning of success and failure in either practice or competitive contexts. Moreover, the model does not appear to account for the idea of achievement goal theorists that task and ego goals are orthogonal—in other words, that an athlete's endorsement of both goal orientations may vary on separate continuums from low to high. Consequently, identifying discrete goal preferences that are considered to reflect *either* task *or* ego orientations becomes somewhat challenging.

Problems With Integrating the Two Perspectives

Burton's attempt to integrate the goal-setting literature with social cognitive perspectives on motivation has encouraged others to explore the relationship between goal setting and achievement goals (Hardy, 1997; Jones

& Hanton, 1996). However, rather than advancing our conceptual understanding, these approaches appear to have further contributed to confusion in the field. The principal factor that appears to be impeding satisfactory integration of the two approaches is the lack of clarity in the terminology used to describe key constructs. Following Burton's initial attempts to associate achievement goals with specific goal-setting styles, there has been a tendency to equate achievement goals with specific types of discrete goals. This was demonstrated by Hardy (1997) in a paper emanating from his 1996 Coleman Griffith Address to the Association for the Advancement of Applied Sport Psychology Conference. In this paper Hardy implied that a strong ego orientation seems to be responsible for an athlete's setting outcome goals, whereas a task orientation is responsible for the setting of performance and process goals. He also proposed that sport psychologists begin to question the myth that outcome goals and ego orientations have a detrimental impact on performance-related cognition, affect, and behavior, and therefore that athletes should be encouraged to set performance goals rather than outcome goals. Although Hardy does not explicitly state that ego orientations have a direct correspondence with a focus on outcome goals, or that task orientations frequently equate with setting performance goals, such a link is implied. Specifically, Hardy (1997) attempts to explain that outcome goals usually focus on the end point of some event and tend to involve interpersonal comparison of performance, whereas performance goals focus on some end product for which the comparative standard is self-referenced. Hardy argues that in addition to setting outcome and performance goals, athletes also set process goals that identify the strategic actions required to perform satisfactorily. He suggests that this is the intersection where achievement goal theory and goal-setting theory becomes confusing. This is because current conceptualizations of a task orientation often confound the notions of personal improvement with seeking to achieve process goals. Hardy feels that athletes who set outcome goals may also hold process goals.

Hardy (1997) also implies that there is a correspondence between a task orientation and performance goals, and an association between an ego orientation and outcome goals. Yet he presents evidence, citing work by Jones and Hanton (1996), that effectively dismisses the likelihood of a direct association between an athlete's dispositional goal orientation and the type of discrete goals set. In the study by Jones and Hanton, exploring goal setting in a sample of competitive swimmers, 50% of the participants set all three types of discrete goals. That is, they set outcome, process, and performance goals. Such a finding corresponds with the argument put forward by Duda (1997b) that predominantly task-oriented athletes are just as likely to set outcome goals, such as winning in competition, as those who endorse a dispositional ego orientation. Similarly, athletes endorsing a strong ego orientation may also set performance goals that focus on personal improvement. The critical process influencing achievement cognition, affect, and behavior is the athlete's interpretation of information concerning performance toward these goals. It is within this process that the athlete's goal orientation can be considered crucial to understanding motivation and achievement in sport and physical activity.

Clearly, confusion will result from any attempt to merge two distinct literatures without attending to important conceptual details that give rise to distinct differences in the resultant psychological processes. Although they adopt similar terminology, the goal-setting and achievement goal literatures address qualitatively different constructs. However, a clear understanding of these constructs is critical for a more comprehensive understanding of sport motivation. In his attempts to merge the two literatures, Hardy (1997) claims that a view of a high ego orientation as detrimental to performance—and thus an orientation that may predispose an athlete to drop out—is not congruent with the view that goals motivate and direct behavior. The underlying source of the conceptual confusion lies within such an argument. Hardy appears to consider achievement goals and discrete goals as having the same motivational function—a view that achievement goal theorists (Duda, 1992, 1996, 1997b; Hall, 1990, 1995; Nicholls, 1989; Roberts, 1992a) have been at pains to dispel. As stated earlier, Locke and Latham (1990) proposed that goal-setting theory is a first-order theory of motivation that focuses on how people perform specific tasks. Goals are thus considered end states that regulate human action by specifying an aim or an objective standard for a specific task. In contrast, using Locke and Latham's (1990) classification system, achievement goal theory might be identified as a second- or third-level theory. It attempts to go beyond explaining the functional relationship between discrete goals and performance by addressing the sources, or roots, of an individual's achievement behavior. The achievement behavior of an athlete frequently incorporates the setting of discrete goals. Consequently, the meaning of achievement cannot be ignored once goals are set, for performance feedback will be processed within the context of what it means to achieve at that point in time.

In response to Hardy (1997), Duda (1997b) commented that achievement goals provide much more than an indication of whether an athlete will attend to self-referenced or comparative outcomes from performance. She argued that they give meaning to personal investment and thus provide a framework for understanding the performance-related cognitions, affective responses, and achievement behaviors exhibited by the athlete. Consequently, achievement goals not only play a significant role in an athlete's decision to invest in an activity, they also give meaning to the pursuit of discrete goals. Maehr and Nicholls (1980) were among the first to note this. They suggested that people do not pursue discrete goals or seek goal attainment simply because the goal exists but because successful accomplishment carries a specific meaning that can be understood only within the context of achievement goals. Achievement goals reflect two different conceptualizations of success and failure and thus might be considered dispositional tendencies to process information and interpret achievement-related activity in a particular manner. They should not, however, be confused with performance and outcome goals, which simply represent two different goal standards (Duda, 1997b). Discrete goals may indeed direct attention, mobilize effort, encourage persistence, and stimulate increased strategy development. However, it is an athlete's dispositional achievement goals that give meaning to the investment of personal resources aimed at accomplishing some discrete goal. Thus, achievement goals provide the framework within which an athlete can interpret performance-related information. Outcomes resulting from the goal-setting–performance relationship are interpreted differently when athletes endorse strong task or ego orientations, and this information has implications for an individual's concept of self (Hall & Kerr, 1997, 1998; Hall, Kerr, & Matthews, 1998).

Empirical Support

In only one study to date has there been any attempt to examine how the meaning of achievement on a specific task influences the goal-setting–performance relationship and its associated cognitions. Hall (1990) proposed that the endorsement of an ego orientation in combination with low perceived ability would lead to poorer performance toward discrete goals, and less adaptive patterns of cognitions than either the endorsement of a task orientation or high perceived ability. Hall had subjects perform a series of trials on a novel balance task while striving to reach discrete goals. To facilitate the testing of specific comparisons, the experimental design manipulated perceived ability and the meaning of achievement through the provision of fictitious performance feedback.

To encourage the endorsement of different achievement goals, false feedback was employed to emphasize different goal structures (see Ames, 1984a; Ames & Ames, 1981). The aim of manipulating the goal structure was to evoke either an ego or a task goal on the part of the subjects. Ames and her colleagues (Ames, 1984a; Ames & Ames, 1981) had demonstrated that performances under the two different goal structures elicit very different performance cognitions. Specifically, performance under an individualistic goal structure tends to evoke a task orientation, in which the individual is concerned with self-referenced improvement or developing ability. In contrast, performance under a normative goal structure tends to evoke an ego orientation; here the aim is to demonstrate ability compared to others and avoid any negative inferences regarding this capacity.

In Hall's (1990) study, participants assigned to perform under an individualistic goal structure received information about how performance on each trial compared to their own previous performance. In addition, they received information about how performance compared with the discrete goal they were aiming to achieve. Participants assigned to the normative goal structure received the same information as subjects in the individualistic conditions. However, they also received information suggesting that their performance was normatively poor. In addition, participants performing under each goal structure were informed either that they had successfully achieved their discrete goal or that their performance was discrepant from their goal. Under both of these conditions, false feedback was also given to indicate gradual improvement over previous performance.

Hall (1990) found that participants who performed under a normative goal structure and perceived their ability to be low experienced significantly smaller performance gains over trials than those who performed under an individualistic goal structure. Performance differences were similar when the former group was compared with all those who perceived their ability to be high. These differences were matched by corresponding differences in performance-related cognitions and affective responses. Specifically, low-perceived-ability participants who performed under a normative goal structure reported lower performance expectancies, lower levels of satisfaction, diminishing levels of confidence, and reductions in the perceived importance of the task when compared with their low-ability counterparts who performed under an individualistic goal structure. Furthermore, those performing under an individualistic goal structure attributed their performance more to their effort than did subjects performing under a normative goal structure. It is likely that these differences in attributional responses contributed to the finding that low-ability participants who performed in an individualistic goal structure showed an increase in perceived ability over time. Comparable perceptions of ability did not occur for low-ability participants who performed in a normative goal structure.

Clearly, under a normative goal structure, the achievement of discrete goals or the improvement of personal performance becomes much less salient than maintaining a sense of comparative success. Moreover, for those who doubt their ability, the likelihood of perceiving comparative success will frequently appear low. Striving to reach discrete goals appeared to be of secondary importance to these participants in Hall's (1990) study. For although they perceived a degree of personal improvement, it was the recurrent impact of perceiving others to be performing better that led low-ability subjects under the normative goal structure to experience disaffection with achievement striving and subsequently demonstrate poorer performances.

The conclusions to be drawn from Hall's (1990) work suggest that performing under a normative goal structure or endorsing a dispositional ego orientation may not be conducive to beneficial motivational effects of goal setting when one's perception is of normative or comparative failure. The resultant threat to an individual's self-worth clearly impacts any decision about the investment of personal resources toward discrete goals. High levels of perceived ability may initially serve to moderate the threat of comparative failure. However, when comparative failure is experienced, Hall suggests that this information conflicts with initial perceptions of high ability. Thus, individuals increase their efforts to redress the imbalance between their perception of high ability and the information signifying comparative failure. If this increased effort leads to future normative or comparative failure, these individuals may begin to further question their ability, experience threats to self-worth, and suffer the same debilitating performance cognitions and affective responses as those perceiving low ability. This will occur whether or not they show improvement toward, or attainment of, their discrete goals.

Hall's (1990) study suggests that in contrast to performing under a normative goal structure, performing under an individualistic goal structure or endorsing a task orientation is likely to foster striving for even the most challenging discrete goals. This is so because failure to reach the discrete goal does not impact negatively on an individual's self-worth. Negative affective responses may occur as a result of a perceived failure to achieve discrete goals. However, it is likely that the individual will interpret performance information in a self-referenced manner, resulting in detailed strategy development, future effort, sustained achievement striving, improved performance, and ultimately more positive achievement-related cognitions. Although there is evidence that such a task-oriented focus will lead to adaptive achievement striving for the vast majority of individuals, such a focus is clearly most beneficial for those who perceive their ability to be low.

The Advantages of Understanding Goal-Setting Effects Within a Broader Motivational Context

Clearly, research on the motivational impact of goal setting would benefit from further systematic examination of its effects within an achievement goal framework. This would enable motivational researchers and practitioners to understand considerably more about the direction of behavior and about why athletes make particular motivational choices than is possible from considering Locke and Latham's (1990) goal-setting theory alone (Danish, Kleiber, & Hall, 1987). Locke and Latham's (1990) approach limits us to understanding changes in intensity and persistence once discrete goals are set; it tells us little about the motivational choices an athlete makes or the motivational consequences of those choices that take place during the goal-setting process. Moreover, understanding goal setting within the context of achievement goal theory will enable us to go beyond noting that an athlete is energized to achieve discrete goals, to explain why the athlete is energized and what the accompanying cognitions might be.

Utilizing achievement goal theory will also enable researchers to understand some of the empirical findings that Locke (1991, 1994) suggests are idiosyncratic to the sporting context and that appear to be a function of flawed methodology. For example, achievement goal theory may offer further insight into why athletes asked to do their best often perform as well as those assigned discrete goals. It may also help explain why some individuals who perceive their ability to be low and who experience repeated failures will continue to strive to achieve extremely challenging goals, while others will not even consider attempting them or will reduce commitment at the first sign of failure. Similarly, achievement goal theory may help explain some of the empirical findings that Weinberg and his colleagues (Weinberg et al., 1987; Weinberg, Bruya, Garland, & Jackson, 1990) have reported. Weinberg et al. found, for example, that some athletes show high levels of commitment and will pursue seemingly impossible goals over protracted periods, with no apparent decrease in effort and persistence, despite having an awareness that the goals are clearly beyond their current capacities. These observations question the goal attainability assumption put forward by Locke and Latham (1990).

Achievement goal theory will also help explain an apparent motivational paradox. That is, the setting of discrete goals is considered by the majority of sport psychologists to be an adaptive motivational and performance strategy, and it is often thought to be the cornerstone of psychological skills training programs for athletes (Hardy et al., 1996). However, although setting discrete goals may frequently encourage adaptive achievement behavior and lead to enhanced effort, increased persistence, and improved performance, the technique may not always have a positive motivational impact on athletes. Indeed, engaging in the goal-setting process may, over time, precipitate maladaptive or even dysfunctional achievement behavior (Beggs, 1990; Burton, 1992; Hall, 1990). This may occur when the discrete goals toward which the athlete is striving are interpreted as performance standards that directly reflect on the athlete's self-worth. Under these conditions, any possibility of failure to achieve the discrete goals that have been set becomes a potential threat to self.

Thus, although an athlete might appear motivated to strive for a challenging goal because of the anticipated esteem that success will bring, the risk of failing to achieve the goal will also remain a powerful energizing force because of the anticipated threat to self-worth. If goal-setting researchers remain preoccupied with performance and fail to consider how the athlete's achievement goals give meaning to performance feedback, a more comprehensive understanding of the adaptive and potentially dysfunctional nature of goals will continue to elude us. Similarly, if sport psychologists focus solely on the performance impact of goals, there is the possibility of misinterpreting critical empirical findings. For example, the literature suggests that setting outcome goals results in better performances than setting performance goals (Kyllo & Landers, 1995). Furthermore, it suggests that if goals are public rather than private, then performance improvements will be greater (Hollenbeck et al., 1989; Kyllo & Landers, 1995). However, if enhanced performance resulting from goal striving is accompanied by perceived threats to self-worth, then the ultimate impact of these two goal-setting strategies will be to undermine long-term motivation. Only when goal-setting strategies are considered within the context of what success and failure mean to the athlete will it be possible to clearly establish whether their long-term effects on achievement behavior will be adaptive or maladaptive.

It is clear that for goal setting to be an effective motivational and performance strategy in sport and physical activity, practitioners must also be able to place the technique within the wider context of motivation. A failure to do this is likely to result in further claims that goal setting does not work as well in sporting contexts as in occupational settings. It is suggested that goal setting is most likely to encourage adaptive achievement striving when athletes endorse a strong dispositional task orientation. Similarly, it is argued that goals will facilitate adaptive achievement striving when the performance or practice context has been engineered so that athletes perceive a mastery climate. Furthermore, if goal-setting strategies are to be effective, practitioners must also understand how to facilitate high levels of self-efficacy and encourage a high degree of intrinsic motivation. Enabling athletes to maintain a high degree of self-determination will avoid the potentially maladaptive achievement cognitions that can result in indifference toward discrete goals (Vallerand & Fortier, 1998) or even dysfunctional achievement behavior.

In sum, to ensure the effectiveness of goal setting as a technique to enhance motivation and performance, it is essential to move beyond simply training athletes to set discrete goals, as Burton has suggested (1989a, 1989b, 1992, 1993). Practitioners must also develop a detailed conceptual understanding of the factors impinging on the cognitions and affective responses of athletes when they engage in the goal-setting process. In an applied sense, this means that practitioners should be cognizant of how an athlete gives meaning to achievement through the endorsement of dispositional achievement goals. They should also be aware of the nature, as well as the level, of an athlete's commitment to discrete goals. Finally, they should understand the impact that changes in the perceived motivational climate may have on the meaning of achievement when an athlete is striving to attain discrete goals.

For without a detailed knowledge of the athlete's achievement goals, the practitioner cannot be aware of the motivational and affective consequences that different performance outcomes may have for this individual. Similarly, without some knowledge about the nature of the athlete's commitment to a discrete goal, the practitioner cannot help the athlete maximize the goal-setting–performance relationship. This is because fluctuations in the level of athlete commitment will be difficult to explain, and consequently the implementation of strategies to alleviate waning commitment may not always be effective. Finally, without taking into account the motivational climate perceived by the athlete at the point of performance, the practitioner cannot be aware of the extent to which the achievement context will either support or undermine the athlete's striving to attain discrete goals. Taken together, these considerations mean that in contrast to Locke's proclamation, one cannot simply assume that if the demands are challenging, if the facilitating moderators are present, and if the mediators of performance are operative, then goals will lead to enhanced motivation and performance. One can understand the motivational and performance effects of goal setting only when taking into account the meaning of achievement.

Author's Note

Some of the information in this chapter was previously reported in the *International Society of Sport Psychology Newsletter*, October 1995.

Self-Efficacy As a Determinant and an Outcome of Exercise

Edward McAuley, Melissa M. Peña, and Gerald J. Jerome

It has been reliably demonstrated that habitual physical activity positively influences a broad range of health conditions, both physiological and psychological. Physical activity and fitness have been linked to risk or symptom reduction in coronary heart disease, cancer, and osteoporosis (Bouchard, Shephard, & Stephens, 1994); all-cause mortality (Blair et al., 1989); and depression (Camacho, Roberts, Lazarus, Kaplan, & Cohen, 1991). Links to enhanced cognitive (Dustman, Emmerson, & Shearer, 1994; Kramer et al., 1999) and psychosocial function (McAuley & Rudolph, 1995; Gauvin & Spence, 1996) have been found as well.

Best epidemiological estimates indicate that less than 20% of the 18- to 65-year-old population exercise at sufficient levels of intensity, frequency, and duration to accrue positive health and fitness benefits (Centers for Disease Control, 1992, 1994). Furthermore, it is estimated that between 30% and 59% of the adult population lead a sedentary lifestyle (Casperson, Christenson, & Pollard, 1986). More importantly, many individuals who engage in organized fitness or exercise programs withdraw before any health benefits have been realized. Indeed, the statistics are well documented regarding the alarming attrition rate in exercise programs, which approximates 50% within the first six months for those initiating a program (Dishman, 1982).

One of the most frequently identified psychosocial determinants of adherence to physical activity is the individual's perceptions of personal capabilities, or self-efficacy (Bandura, 1986, 1995b, 1997b). Efficacy expectations, or the individual's beliefs in his or her capabilities to execute necessary courses of action to satisfy situational demands, are theorized to influence the activities that individuals choose to approach, the effort they expend on such activities, and the degree of persistence they demonstrate in the face of failure or aversive stimuli (Bandura, 1986). Recently, Bandura (1995b, 1997b) has refined the definition of self-efficacy to encompass beliefs regarding individuals' capabilities to produce performances that will lead to anticipated outcomes. The term *self-regulatory efficacy* is now employed, and both the term and definition encompass a social cognitive stance that represents the role cognitive skills play in behavioral performance. Maddux (1995) suggests that this definitional development has led to the distinction between task self-efficacy, which involves assessment of simple motor skills or capabilities (e.g., walking a certain distance), and self-regulatory or coping efficacy, which involves assessing efficacy relative to impediments or challenges to successful behavioral performance (e.g., carrying out one's walking regimen when tired or stressed or during foul weather).

Research in the exercise domain has demonstrated self-efficacy to be implicated in exercise adherence in diseased (Ewart, Stewart, Gillilan, Kelemen, Valenti et al., 1986; Toshima, Kaplan, & Ries, 1990; Ries, Kaplan, Limberg, & Prewitt, 1995) and asymptomatic populations (Dzewaltowski, 1989), in large-scale community studies (Sallis et al., 1986), and in training studies (McAuley, 1992b; McAuley, Courneya, Rudolph, & Lox, 1994). Moreover, it appears that the role of efficacy cognitions in exercise participation is more potent under those circumstances in which physical activity presents the greatest challenge, such as the initial stages of adoption (McAuley, 1992b) and long-term maintenance of activity (McAuley, Lox, & Duncan, 1993), as well as exercise prescribed for secondary prevention of disease (Ewart, Taylor, Reese, & DeBusk, 1983).

In addition to being a determinant of physical activity, self-efficacy expectations are also influenced by the exercise experience. Exercise effects on self-efficacy cognitions would appear particularly important given the broad constellation of physiological, behavioral, cognitive, and biochemical outcomes that self-efficacy is theorized to influence (Bandura, 1986, 1997b). For example, McAuley and his colleagues (McAuley, Courneya, & Lettunich, 1991; McAuley et al., 1993; McAuley, Katula et al., 1999) demonstrated in a series of studies that long-term exercise participation and acute bouts of exercise could enhance perceptions of physical self-efficacy in middle-aged males and females. Additionally, Bandura and Cervone (1983, 1986) present evidence to suggest that self-efficacy operates as a motivator during acute exercise, with greater efficacy leading to enhanced effort regardless of whether exercise performance exceeds or fails to meet set goals. Moreover, ample evidence suggests that self-efficacy plays an important role in determining exercise behaviors, is influenced by exercise participation, and is also linked to affective responses associated with acute and chronic exercise behavior (e.g., McAuley, 1991; McAuley, Bane, & Mihalko, 1995; McAuley, Blissmer, Katula, & Duncan, 2000).

In this chapter, we begin by providing a brief theoretical backdrop to the role played by self-efficacy in social cognitive theory (Bandura, 1986, 1997b) and argue the case for self-efficacy as a particularly relevant theoretical construct in the study of exercise behavior. We also discuss a number of other self-related constructs and how they are effectively distinguished from self-efficacy. Next is a brief discussion of issues pertaining to the measurement of self-efficacy in the exercise domain. The primary sections of the review concern self-efficacy as a determinant of exercise behavior and as a behavioral outcome resulting from exercise participation. In discussing self-efficacy as a determinant of behavior, we consider efficacy influences on adherence to exercise in community and clinical samples and also the extent to which efficacy is implicated in exercise performance. In the section on exercise as a determinant of self-efficacy, we focus not only on acute exercise bouts and their impact on perceptions of personal capabilities but also on exercise interventions that have documented changes in efficacy over time. We provide a brief summary of work previously reviewed but concentrate more fully on more contemporary articles that have been published since an earlier review (McAuley, 1992a). Finally, we conclude with some summary remarks and recommendations for further empirical study in this area.

Theoretical Backdrop and Relevance of Self-Efficacy to Exercise Behavior

Self-efficacy refers to the individual's beliefs in his or her capabilities to successfully carry out a course of action to meet particularized task demands; as such, self-efficacy is the primary construct of interest within

Bandura's (1986) more comprehensive social cognitive theory. As already noted, it is possible to differentiate between task and self-regulatory efficacy, and the reader is directed to Maddux (1995) for a fuller discussion of this differentiation. These judgments of personal efficacy are by definition situation specific, and efficacy measures are therefore specific to domains of functioning rather than generalized. Efficacy expectations influence human behavior through a variety of processes. Individuals with a strong sense of personal efficacy approach more challenging tasks, expend greater efforts in these tasks, and persist longer in the face of aversive stimuli. Efficacy beliefs also act as motivational regulators in that they contribute to the formulation of desires and aspirations, as well as to one's degree of commitment to these aspirations (Bandura, 1995b). In short, self-efficacy beliefs are theorized to influence motivation, affect, and behavior (Bandura, 1986, 1997b).

The decision to embark on an exercise program and the subsequent maintenance of this health behavior are fraught with challenges, especially when individuals are sedentary, older, or recovering from a life-threatening disease. Inherent in any successful attempt at changing exercise behavior is the ability to exert appropriate amounts of effort to accrue the requisite physiological and health benefits and to persist in the face of the naturally occurring aversive stimuli associated with initial exercise exposure. Contrary to the images presented in the fitness media, exercise is not always fun and enjoyable. Early exposures are associated with muscle stiffness and soreness, early onset of fatigue, possible injury, and potential embarrassing moments as sedentary bodies are exposed in exercise attire for perhaps the first time in many years. Individuals with a robust sense of physical/exercise efficacy are likely to address such challenges and to be more successful in maintaining this exercise behavior than are their less efficacious counterparts (McAuley, 1992b, 1993). More efficacious individuals are likely to expend greater amounts of effort in attaining health-promoting levels of physical activity (Ewart et al., 1983); and when faced with setbacks, these individuals are likely to persist in their pursuits and redouble their efforts (McAuley et al., 1993). Exercise has for many years been linked to various aspects of positive mental health such as reduced anxiety (Landers & Petruzzello, 1994) and depression (Camacho et al., 1991). Although the underlying mechanisms that may be operating to bring about these positive emotional changes are unclear, greater self-efficacy has consistently been linked to lower levels of anxiety and depression (Bandura, 1986, 1992). Additionally, several recent studies have shown that self-efficacy mediates exercise's effects on affective responses (e.g., McAuley & Courneya, 1992; McAuley, Blissmer, Katula, & Duncan, 2000). Given the importance of choice, effort, persistence, and emotional dimensions of exercise behavior, it appears clear that self-efficacy expectations represent a crucial social cognitive element of this behavioral domain.

Self-Efficacy and Related Constructs

Lest there be any confusion in differentiating self-efficacy from other self-related constructs, we take a brief opportunity to outline how self-efficacy should be considered conceptually distinct from self-esteem/worth, general self-confidence (efficacy), intentions, perceived behavioral control, and outcome expectations.

• **Self-esteem/Self-worth.** Self-esteem, or self-worth, can broadly be defined as encompassing the favorable view that one holds regarding oneself. It is considered a focal aspect of psychological health and well-being and is relatively stable (Rosenberg, 1979). Self-efficacy, on the other hand, concerns individuals' beliefs in their capabilities in varying behavioral domains and is a dynamic construct that can be influenced by cognitive, physiological, behavioral, and social information. Several recent studies have examined the underlying role that self-efficacy may play in the development of self-esteem (McAuley, Mihalko, & Bane, 1997; McAuley, Blissmer, Katula, Duncan, & Mihalko, 2000; Sonstroem, Harlow, & Josephs, 1994).

• **Self-confidence (efficacy).** A generalized sense of self-confidence, or efficacy, can be conceptualized as a dispositional quality to be optimistic about one's abilities to be successful across a broad array of unrelated domains. This is clearly distinct from self-efficacy, which concerns beliefs about capabilities in specific domains or situations. When omnibus measures of confidence have been compared to more specific efficacy measures, the latter have uniformly been more predictive of behavioral outcomes. Efficacy cognitions are composed of several dimensions. *Level* of efficacy concerns individuals' beliefs in their capability to accomplish a specific task or element of a task. *Strength* of efficacy concerns the degree of conviction that one can successfully carry out a task. Thus I may indicate that I can walk a block in 3 min (level) but be only 50% confident about successfully carrying out this task (strength). The final dimension of efficacy is *generality*, which concerns the facility of efficacy expectations to predict behavior in related tasks or domains that require parallel skills. Whether or not some authors are confusing general efficacy/confidence with the generality dimension of self-efficacy is unclear. Efficacy measures that tap individuals' capabilities to engage in strenuous aerobic activity, although developed specifically to predict walking or jogging, may also be useful in the prediction of aerobic dance or exercise cycling.

- **Intentions and perceived control.** Intentions and perceived behavioral control are two other constructs sometimes unwittingly confused with self-efficacy. The belief that one can successfully execute behaviors that bring about certain outcomes (i.e., self-efficacy) is clearly differentiated from what one plans or intends to do (i.e., intention). Unfortunately, if efficacy is measured as the degree to which one believes that one *will* carry out a course of action, as opposed to the degree to which one believes one *can* carry out those actions, then the two constructs become conceptually blurred; and intention, rather than efficacy, is measured. The case for differentiating perceived behavioral control and self-efficacy is less clear-cut. Perceived behavioral control is a pivotal construct in Ajzen's (1985) theory of planned behavior. Ajzen conceptualizes perceived behavioral control as the perceived ease or difficulty of performing a behavior (Ajzen, 1991). Although often measured differently from self-efficacy, perceived behavioral control has frequently been treated as synonymous with self-efficacy. However, this view is not universally held (see Terry & O'Leary, 1995). In this chapter, several studies of planned-behavior approaches to exercise behavior are considered because of the fact that perceived behavioral control is typically assessed as efficacy.

- **Outcome expectations versus efficacy expectations.** There is an important distinction between outcome expectations and efficacy expectations. The former concern beliefs regarding the outcomes that behavioral repertoires will bring about. The latter, however, concern one's belief in one's capabilities to successfully carry out a particular behavior. Thus, belief that a regular regimen of exercise for a prolonged time will bring about decreases in one's weight is an outcome expectation, whereas the belief that one can actually exercise at the prescribed frequency, duration, and intensity over time is an efficacy expectation. For example, Bandura (1995b) has argued that losing weight is not an outcome but a marker of performance. However, Maddux (1995) takes the perspective that it is quite logical and practical to view weight loss as an outcome of weight-loss strategies such as exercising. Although looking healthier and appearing attractive are also important outcomes of losing pounds, this does not relegate weight loss to the level of simply a performance marker. It merely suggests that outcomes do lead to other outcomes and, as Maddux argues, that outcomes evolve at differing levels.

Measuring Exercise-Related Self-Efficacy

An extensive review of the measurement of exercise-related self-efficacy has recently been published by McAuley and Mihalko (1998), and we therefore direct the reader to this work for a more thorough discussion. Several categories of self-efficacy measures exist. *Exercise efficacy* refers to measures directed at the assessment of beliefs regarding subjects' capabilities to successfully engage in incremental bouts of physical activity. Such measures capture the traditional behavioral or task efficacy construct and typically assess beliefs in capabilities relative to frequency and duration at some level of intensity (e.g., Courneya & McAuley, 1994; McAuley et al., 1999), exercising over time (e.g., Biddle, Goudas, & Page, 1994), and particularized activities, such as walking successive numbers of blocks in incremental periods (e.g., Ewart et al., 1983). *Barriers efficacy* is employed to determine beliefs in capabilities to overcome social, personal, and environmental barriers to exercising. Barriers efficacy clearly represents what has been more recently referred to by Bandura (1995b, 1997b) as *self-regulatory efficacy*. Such barriers typically encompass time management, fatigue, weather, family and social demands, and inaccessibility of facilities (e.g., Marcus, Eaton, Rossi, & Harlow, 1994; McAuley, 1992b). Because it is argued that self-efficacy is particularly useful in predicting behavior in challenging situations, McAuley and Mihalko (1998) identify a category of measures as *disease-specific/health behavior efficacy*. These are efficacy measures that have been used in populations engaged in exercise rehabilitation for secondary prevention of disease (e.g., arthritis [Buckelew, Murray, Hewett, Johnson, & Huyser, 1995], diabetes [Kavanagh, Gooley, & Wilson, 1993], and chronic obstructive pulmonary disease [Toshima et al., 1990]) or measures that have an exercise component incorporated with subjects' beliefs in their capabilities to engage in health-promoting behaviors (e.g., Grembowski et al., 1993).

In spite of the strong emphasis that Bandura (1986) placed on the relevance of efficacy measurement to the behavioral domain of interest, and the consistent superiority of specific measures over omnibus assessments of global confidence, the use of these latter measures persists in the exercise literature. Measures of *general efficacy* vary in their content, assessing such beliefs as generalized efficacy (Tipton & Worthington, 1984), trait self-efficacy (Long, 1985), and physical self-efficacy (Kavussanu & McAuley, 1995). The latter is typically assessed by the Physical Self-Efficacy Scale (PSE; Ryckman, Robbins, Thornton, & Cantrell, 1982). Of the more general measures of the efficacy construct, the PSE would appear more relevant to the exercise domain than the more general measures of overall confidence in the self because of its generalizing to physical activity. This may be particularly true if the PSE subscale of Perceived Physical Ability is employed to predict physical activity behavior. However, such measures are less likely to be predictive of more specific behaviors (e.g., exercise adherence) or to be changed as a function of exposure to acute bouts of exercise, as more specific measures of efficacy are (e.g., McAuley et al., 1993; Taylor, Bandura, Ewart, Miller, & DeBusk, 1985).

Self-Efficacy As a Determinant
of Exercise Behavior

An earlier review (McAuley, 1992a) presented considerable evidence to suggest that efficacy played an important role in the adoption of and adherence to exercise regimens. We now review some contemporary research that includes several prospective studies, embraces an array of theoretical models, and offers further compelling evidence for the contribution of efficacy expectations to the prediction of physical activity behavior.

We begin by reviewing a group of studies on self-efficacy and the behavioral epidemiology of exercise conducted by Sallis and his colleagues (Sallis, Hovell, Hofstetter, & Barrington, 1992; Hovell et al., 1991; Sallis et al., 1986, 1989). This group has conducted two major community studies of social learning correlates of physical activity in the general population that provide evidence that self-efficacy plays an important role in the etiology of exercise behavior. Presenting data from the Stanford Community Health Survey, Sallis et al. (1986) reported self-efficacy to be significantly related to exercise behavior at different stages of the natural history of the exercise process. That is, efficacy cognitions predicted adoption but not maintenance of *vigorous* activity and the maintenance but not adoption of *moderate* activity. Moreover, self-efficacy with respect to vigorous physical activity predicted change in such activity, whereas moderate-activity efficacy led to reported changes in moderate activity. Of particular note is that this study was one of the first to adopt the perspective that exercise is a dynamic and complex process with different determinants being more salient at distinct stages of the process.

A further study of the correlates of physical activity in a large ($N = 2053$) California community (San Diego) sample showed self-efficacy to be the strongest predictor of exercise behavior among a host of social learning variables (Sallis et al., 1989). Moreover, in examining a subset of the sample, Hovell et al. (1991) demonstrate similar findings in 127 adult Latino subjects. Given that Latinos, as an ethnic minority, are reported to be at greater risk of hypercholesterolemia (Kautz, 1982) and obesity and diabetes (Castro, Balzconde-Garbanati, & Betra, 1985) and that exercise participation is a preventive health behavior for reducing these and other risk factors, the role of efficacy as a potential intervention target is underscored. The Sallis et al. (1989) study was followed up two years later (Sallis et al., 1992), this time using sets of social, cognitive, and environmental variables (considered to be dynamic or susceptible to change) to predict changes in activity over the two-year period. In fairly conservative analyses, changes in self-efficacy were the most consistent predictors of changes in exercise behavior, although the variation accounted for was not large ($\beta = .20$ to $.22$). As noted, however, the authors conducted stringent analyses whereby variation in baseline efficacy was controlled, as well as variation due to demographic characteristics known to be associated with self-efficacy. Additionally, the efficacy measure was somewhat restrictive, assessing only beliefs in capabilities to exercise when sad, under stress, or in the face of family or social demands.

In our own work, we have been able to demonstrate that exercise-related self-efficacy plays different roles at different stages of the exercise process (McAuley, 1992b, 1993; McAuley et al., 1993) and that employing efficacy-based strategies in training studies serves to enhance adherence (McAuley et al., 1994). This work has been conducted largely in the context of initially sedentary older adults. In the first report (McAuley, 1992b), self-efficacy and body fat were predictive of exercise frequency and intensity at the midpoint of a five-month program, but exercise participation up to that point was the only predictor of adherence over the remaining period of the program. Such findings are consistent with the perspective that cognitive control systems play their most important role in the acquisition of behavioral proficiencies (Bandura, 1989b). When behaviors are less demanding and more easily engaged in (in this case, beyond adoption and adaptation), cognitive control systems give way to lower control systems (Bandura & Wood, 1989). Clearly, different mechanisms take on differing degrees of importance at various stages of the exercise process. In a follow-up study (McAuley, 1993), the relationship between self-efficacy and exercise participation was examined in a more demanding context: continued exercise maintenance following termination of the program. Participants were contacted four months after program completion and interviewed by telephone and surveyed by mail as to their exercise participation patterns since program termination. Hierarchical regression analyses indicated that self-efficacy predicted 12.5% unique variance in continued exercise participation and shared a further 14% of the variance with physiological (VO_2max) and behavioral (past exercise frequency and intensity) parameters. However, only efficacy was a significant individual predictor of exercise behavior.

Further follow-up data were collected at nine months postprogram when participants returned for further physiological testing. Physiological, behavioral, and cognitive variables were employed to predict adherence to activity since program end (frequency of activity), as well as compliance to the specific exercise prescription given to each participant at program end. Aerobic power at the end of the program and self-efficacy accounted for approximately 24% of the variance in exercise maintenance, with efficacy being a significant unique contributor. In the case of compliance, efficacy, aerobic power, and attendance during the program significantly discriminated between compliers and noncompliers. Although it appears that when situations or behaviors become more demanding, efficacy cognitions assume a more important role, the pattern of relationships was slightly different for compliance and adherence. Such findings may have important implications for how exercise programs are structured. For example, if one is interested in having participants continue to be active without necessarily mirroring the content of the formal structured exercise program, then establishing conditions that maximize perceived capabilities appears crucial. What does appear clear, however, is that diverse parameters take on varying degrees of influence at different stages of the exercise process (McAuley, 1992b; Oman & King, 1998; Sallis & Hovell, 1990).

In an attempt to go beyond the efficacy-adherence relationship, McAuley et al. (1994) conducted a randomized controlled trial contrasting an efficacy information-based exercise program with an attentional control exercise program. The efficacy-based group monitored progress in activity and physiological adaptation, viewed videotape of formerly sedentary adults becoming fitter through physical activity, exercised together in buddy systems, and received appropriate information for interpretation of physiological responses to activity. Clear differences in activity patterns appeared over time, with the intervention group adhering at a significantly greater rate than the control group over the five-month period. Efficacy was also significantly related to patterns of adherence but not to the degree expected. It may well be that in the situation created, in which individuals are committed to each other in activity, collective efficacy plays a more crucial role than individual efficacy (Bandura, 1997b). The assessment of collective exercise efficacy has received little attention and should be considered in subsequent research examining determinants of exercise in group settings.

Self-efficacy has frequently been identified as an important determinant of physical activity behavior in symptomatic populations. We have previously reviewed the work of Ewart and his associates (Ewart, Stewart, Gillilan, & Kelemen, 1986; Ewart, Stewart, Gillilan, Kelemen, Valenti, et al., 1986; Ewart et al., 1983; Taylor et al., 1985), which has yielded some compelling data underscoring the role played by psychosocial variables in the adoption of, adherence to, and performance of exercise-related activities in this population. More recent studies are supportive of these early findings, although in large part the methodological rigor and measurement of key constructs have been less impressive. Oka, Gortner, Shotts, and Haskell (1996) examined the determinants of physical activity levels in 43 chronic heart failure patients. $\dot{V}O_2$peak, ratings of perceived exertion, social support, and self-efficacy were employed as predictors of activity level, a metabolic equivalent calculated using the Duke Activity Status Index (Hlatky et al., 1989). Oka et al. reported self-efficacy to be the strongest predictor of activity levels; however, they provided no data relative to the extent of this relationship. Although correlational, this study does support the premise that efficacy expectations are important correlates of physical activity and may be most important in diseased populations. Such a perspective is dramatically supported by the work of Kaplan and his colleagues (Kaplan, Ries, Prewitt, & Eakin, 1994) comparing standard physiological predictors of remaining life expectancy with a simple measure of exercise self-efficacy. In a series of analyses examining univariate and multivariate models, self-efficacy was a significant predictor of survival ($p < .01$) when compared to all physiological indicators; but when compared to the strongest predictor alone (forced expiratory volume), efficacy was borderline significant.

In a careful study of 62 males and females, Bock et al. (1997) examined the roles of decisional balance (perceived costs and benefits of participation), self-efficacy, and processes of change in the prediction of exercise behavior during a 12-week cardiac rehabilitation program and at three-month follow-up. As one would expect in a sample entering a program based on supervised physical conditioning, exercise behavior increased over the course of the program, as did self-efficacy. As one would also expect, at follow-up a regression in activity had occurred. More negative decisional balance, lower levels of self-efficacy, and a reduced likelihood of endorsing behavioral change processes at program end resulted in reductions in activity at follow-up. Unfortunately, the degree of physical activity during rehabilitation was not controlled in these latter analyses, thereby reducing confidence in the extent of the contributions of these other predictor variables.

Self-Efficacy and Other Theoretical Models

A growing trend in exercise efficacy research has been to incorporate the self-efficacy construct in other theoretical models (e.g., theory of planned behavior) or to use it as a variable to discriminate individuals at various stages of the exercise process (e.g., employing models such as the transtheoretical model of behavior change). There are both merits and problems associated with the manner in which this has been done, and we now review this body of research.

Self-Efficacy and the Theory of Planned Behavior

As an extension of the theory of reasoned action (TRA; Fishbein & Ajzen, 1975), the theory of planned behavior (TPB; Ajzen, 1985) has been warmly embraced by scientists interested in identifying determinants of physical activity participation. The TRA and TPB assume that people behave in a sensible and rational manner by taking account of available information and considering the potential implications of their behavior. The basis of the reasoned action model is an expectancy-by-value summation of beliefs about performing a particular behavior. Intention is hypothesized as the immediate determinant of behavior and is in turn determined by attitude toward performing the behavior and perceived social pressure to perform the behavior (subjective norm). These latter determinants of intention are undergirded by behavioral beliefs and normative beliefs, respectively, which form the expectancy-value base. The TRA proposes a hierarchical model in which the path from cognition to behavior travels through beliefs, attitude and subjective norm, intention, and behavior.

The TPB (Ajzen, 1985) extends the TRA by adding the concept of perceived behavioral control for those behaviors not fully under volitional control. Perceived behavioral control is conceptualized as the perceived ease or difficulty of performing a behavior (Ajzen, 1988). For nonvolitional behaviors, perceived behavioral control is theorized as an additional determinant of intention, as well as actual performance. The indirect measurement of perceived behavioral control involves assessment of a set of control beliefs in the form of perceived barriers. The summary proposition of the TPB is that people will intend to perform a behavior when they evaluate it positively, believe that important others think they should perform it, and perceive it to be under their own control (Ajzen, 1988).

Important to this chapter, of course, is the construct of perceived behavioral control. Many of the studies reviewed have treated perceived behavioral control as synonymous with self-efficacy, a course of action precipitated by Ajzen's (1987, 1991) claim that perceived behavioral control was similar to self-efficacy. However, closer examination of the measurement of perceived behavioral control (see Ajzen & Madden, 1986; Madden, Ellen, & Ajzen, 1992) suggests that items being measured reflect both control over whether the behavior is performed and ease or difficulty associated with performing the behavior. We will return to the problems associated with this issue later in this section. First, we briefly overview the extent to which perceived behavioral control/self-efficacy plays a role in predicting exercise intentions and behaviors in the TPB model.

Godin and Kok (1996) note that in approximately 50% of the studies of health behavior (including exercise) that they reviewed, perceived behavioral control contributed significant variation to behavior beyond that explained by intention. Hausenblas, Carron, and Mack (1997) have recently published a meta-analytic review of 31 studies in this area and conclude that perceived behavioral control has a strong influence on both exercise behavior and intention (effect sizes for both relationships approximately 1.0). Brawley and his colleagues (DuCharme & Brawley, 1995; Rodgers &

Brawley, 1996) have reported studies of novice exercisers in which self-efficacy/perceived behavioral constructs are predictive of exercise intentions (Rodgers & Brawley, 1996) and exercise behavior (DuCharme & Brawley, 1995). Similarly, in a large sample of Canadian female homemakers ($N = 630$), Horne (1994) used a planned-behavior approach to predict exercise intentions of active and inactive participants. In already active individuals, all three belief components contributed significantly to intentions. However, the intentions of the inactive participants were predicted only by social support (a proxy for subjective norm) and self-efficacy.

Biddle et al. (1994) employed a cross-sectional design to examine the contribution of planned-behavior components to self-reported exercise behavior in a university work site. Addressing the problems of conceptual clarity associated with perceived behavioral control, Biddle et al. assessed perceived control, self-efficacy, and benefits and barriers to exercise as separate constructs. In separate analyses for males and females, intention was best predicted by attitude in the case of males and by efficacy, control, benefits, and attitude in the case of females. Intention was the primary predictor of an index of exercise behavior in both samples, with attitude playing a role for males and self-efficacy, for women. Clearly, these findings are somewhat at odds with other findings in the literature and need to be replicated, preferably in a prospective manner. One additional finding of interest, however, was the correlation between perceived behavioral control and self-efficacy ($r = .40$), which does not suggest a great deal of equivalence between constructs in this study. However, no measure of efficacy related to barriers was used, a tactic that may have served to decrease the convergence between measures.

Because the intention-behavior relationship appears to hold up best over shorter periods, it is instructive to examine studies that are prospective and that attempt to predict short-term exercise behavior. Yordy and Lent (1993) and Courneya and McAuley (1994) conducted such studies using self-reported exercise behavior over one week (Yordy & Lent, 1993) and two and four weeks (Courneya & McAuley, 1994). In the Yordy and Lent study, perceived behavioral control and self-efficacy were distinguished from each other. Interestingly, whereas self-efficacy (as measured by barriers efficacy) contributed significant variance to intention to exercise, perceived behavioral control (measured in the original Ajzen fashion tapping control over exercise, exercising if one wanted to, and exercise being mostly up to the individual) was of no predictive value whatsoever. Additionally, in a discriminant function analysis, intention, self-efficacy, and outcome expectations were significant predictors of those who did or did not exercise. Although it might appear from these results that perceived behavioral control is of little value, one should note that the control measure was skewed, indicating that most participants considered exercise to be under their control. Recall that the planned-behavior model is designed to predict behaviors not under one's volitional control. Under the circumstances of the Yordy and Lent study, perceived behavioral control would not be expected to predict intention or behavior. However, the findings do question the degree to which perceived behavioral control and self-efficacy are synonymous.

Courneya and McAuley (1994) treated self-efficacy and perceived behavioral control synonymously in their effort to determine whether different elements of the planned-behavior model acted as differential determinants of intensity, frequency, and duration of activity. Their results suggested that intention was a better predictor of duration than of intensity and frequency of activity but that self-efficacy (perceived behavioral control) contributed significant variance to these latter two elements of exercise behavior beyond that explained by intention. Additionally, self-efficacy was the most consistent predictor of intention relative to all three exercise components. That different parameters of this model are instrumental in predicting different aspects of exercise behavior is quite provocative but can be explained in the context of volitional control. Courneya and McAuley (1994) argue that duration is perhaps the most personally controllable aspect of exercise behavior. Intensity and frequency, on the other hand, are less controllable: frequency is subject to multiple external factors, and intensity is subject to the limitations of ability and physical capacity. Such results and interpretation are certainly worthy of replication.

Thus far, we have reviewed the work of researchers who have elected to equate perceived behavioral control and self-efficacy to varying degrees. Lechner and De Vries (1995) confound the similarity still further in a study of 236 Dutch police personnel involved in an employee fitness program. These authors embrace perceived behavioral control and self-efficacy as conceptual equals but measured efficacy in a "direct" and an "indirect" manner. They assessed "indirect self-efficacy" by asking respondents whether they would be able to exercise under six problem circumstances. A seven-point scale ranging from +3 (certainly) to –3 (certainly not) was employed to assess this construct. In essence, this is a measure of barriers efficacy, although the scoring method is unlike that typically used in efficacy assessment. The "direct self-efficacy" measure required participants to complete one item assessing the frequency with which they were placed in situations likely to prevent exercising. This is simply not a measure of efficacy. It assesses frequency of external constraints or the likelihood of encountering barriers, a topic we will return to subsequently. These two measures of "efficacy" were weakly correlated, $r = .22$. Stepwise regression analyses suggested that the "indirect" measure of efficacy (barriers efficacy) was the best predictor of exercise frequency. However, given that intention was not measured, that the measures are conceptually suspect, and that the analytical strategy is questionable, it is difficult to put any faith in the findings. The results do, however, identify the continued problem of conceptual clarification associated with the perceived behavioral control construct.

This issue is addressed in a thought-provoking study by Terry and O'Leary (1995). These authors assert that perceived behavioral control and self-efficacy are not the same constructs and that the former deals with external constraints, whereas the latter concerns internal constraints to action. They further conceptualize perceived behavioral control in the same vein as outcome expectancies yet measure this construct relative to control over exercise behavior, while measuring efficacy relative to ease or difficulty of carrying out a two-week exercise regimen. At issue here is the conceptualization of self-efficacy. When one assesses self-efficacy as perceived ease or difficulty, there is the suggestion that perceiving a behavior as difficult is indicative of low efficacy and that perceiving it as easy indicates high efficacy. Beginning an exercise program, particularly for people who are sedentary, elderly, or impaired, is clearly difficult; but this does not mean one cannot be efficacious about carrying out the behavior. If it did, even fewer than 50% of initial exercisers would be likely to adhere. Simply put, perceived ease or difficulty is not self-efficacy. It is a related concept, but it is not self-efficacy.

Interestingly, Terry and O'Leary (1995) elected not to consider the work of Dzewaltowski (1989; Dzewaltowski, Noble, & Shaw, 1990) comparing the relative merits of social cognitive theory and the theories of reasoned action and planned behavior, suggesting that the findings were difficult to interpret. They base this assertion on the fact that Dzewaltowski and his colleagues measured efficacy to overcome barriers, the conceptual equivalent of perceived behavioral control in the view of Terry and O'Leary. Yet Bandura (1997b) clearly sees this as an accurate assessment of self-efficacy:

> For example, consider the measurement of perceived self-efficacy to stick to a health-promoting exercise routine. Individuals judge how well they can get themselves to exercise regularly under various impediments, such as when they are under pressure from work, are tired, or are depressed; in foul weather; or when they have other commitments or more interesting things to do. (p. 43)

Clearly, in this instance, efficacy is measured as beliefs in capabilities to overcome those barriers that might prevent exercise participation (see McAuley & Mihalko, 1998). Thus, we would agree with Terry and O'Leary (1995) that self-efficacy should be an integral part of the planned-behavior model but disagree with their conceptualization of the construct. Bandura (1997b) has further argued that all components of the reasoned action and planned-behavior models are redundant with constructs already present in his social cognitive model of behavior change. However, the full social cognitive model remains to be tested in the exercise domain.

Self-Efficacy and the Transtheoretical Model

One of the most popular contemporary topics in exercise and health psychology is the behavioral determinants at various stages of health behaviors. In examining this topic, researchers in exercise psychology have whole-heartedly embraced Prochaska and DiClemente's (1983, 1985) transtheoretical model. At its base, the transtheoretical model concerns the intentional changing of behavior and suggests that individuals pass through the stages of precontemplation, contemplation, preparation, action, and maintenance. The model attempts to place individuals in a stage of behavior change using a host of process variables (including self-efficacy) to explain, predict, and bring about change at each stage (Prochaska & Velicer, 1997). Whether the transtheoretical model is or is not a true stage theory has been the subject of debate (see Bandura, 1997a, for an opposing stance and Prochaska & Velicer, 1997, for a rejoinder), and there do remain some problems with the translation of this model from a huge body of work in smoking cessation to more positive health behaviors such as exercise. Additionally, the measurement of stages and key constructs such as efficacy in the exercise domain is sometimes questionable. However, in this chapter, our concern is largely with the extent to which self-efficacy has been identified as a determinant of exercise behavior in studies embracing the transtheoretical model. In addition, we review the similarities between this model and the TPB.

The bulk of this work has emanated from Marcus and her colleagues (Marcus & Owen, 1992; Marcus, Selby, Niaura, & Rossi, 1992; Marcus, Pinto, Simkin, Audrain, & Taylor, 1994; Marcus, Eaton et al., 1994). This work and other applications of the stage model typically show a linear increase of self-efficacy across stages (e.g., Cardinal, 1997; Gorley & Gordon, 1995; Lechner & De Vries, 1995; Wyse, Mercer, Ashford, Buxton, & Gleeson, 1995). Lechner and De Vries employed a quasi-planned-behavior approach to predict stage of exercise behavior, noting that self-efficacy accounted for the bulk of variation in stage, over attitude and social influence. However, the statistical analyses were questionable and failed to demonstrate the unique contributions of these variables. Much of this work has involved large work-site populations and employed definitions and measures that have as their template the work by Prochaska and his colleagues in smoking cessation (Prochaska & DiClemente, 1983). From an efficacy perspective, the key construct is measured as confidence to participate in exercise in the face of five difficult situations. The first two stages of exercise change (precontemplation, contemplation) are often reflected by gradations in intention to exercise; the third stage (preparation) represents an overlap of stronger intention and some preparatory behavior; the action and maintenance phases reflect having begun to exercise regularly within the last six months and having been exercising for longer than the last six months, respectively. Setting aside the issue of arbitrary categorization, we draw attention to the obvious intention-behavior distinction inherent in the definition of these stages of readiness. The first three stages clearly represent intention, whereas the last two stages are behavior—two key components of the TPB.

Courneya (1995) has noted these conceptual similarities in a study applying the TPB to the stages of change. It is, of course, necessary to note that these two models typically have different objectives. The TPB attempts to predict participation or engagement in some behavioral criterion, whereas the transtheoretical model strives to explain behavioral, cognitive, and motivational elements of stages of readiness. Stage of change is, in essence, a variable, not a theory (Prochaska & Velicer, 1997). Courneya (1995) and his colleagues (Courneya, Nigg, & Estabrooks, 1998; Courneya, Estabrooks, & Nigg, 1997) reported cross-sectional and longitudinal data on a sample of older adults showing that control beliefs (barriers efficacy) are predictive of perceived behavioral control (perceived ease or difficulty of engagement); both variables demonstrated a linear increase across the stages of change. Courneya is one of the few researchers using the planned-behavior model to assess perceived behavioral control along with the broader construct of control beliefs, as laid out in the theory (Ajzen, 1985). In their three-year follow-up of the original study, Courneya et al. (1998) reported a strong correlation between intention and stage ($r = .78$) and noted that in path analyses, intention predicted stage of behavior. This is hardly surprising when the two constructs share over 60% of common variance. One wonders how strong the correlation might be if intention were used to predict only the first three stages.

To their credit, Courneya et al. (1997) confront the issue but argue that to break the stage definition into an intention and behavior component is insufficient. They base this assertion on the fact that the definition and operationalization of the first stage (precontemplation) are often assessed by the individuals "considering" or "thinking about" change rather than "intending to change." They further argue that considering and intention are not isomorphous constructs. We would agree. However, in the majority of the studies reviewed, intention is employed in the definition of stages.

It should be noted, however, that "thinking about" exercising is often encompassed in the contemplation stage of these studies, and one could argue that "not intending to exercise" (precontemplation) has now progressed to some loosely defined form of intention. In a large community study, Armstrong, Sallis, Hovell, and Hofstetter (1993) contribute further to the confusion of the intention-behavior distinction in relation to stages by classifying stages of readiness relative to degree of interest. This issue of overlap of one construct with another needs to be addressed if we are to more completely understand how the process of exercise behavior is determined. Whether intention and behavior should be considered separately or combined into one variable and whether all of these constructs are currently operative in a grander social cognitive model (cf. Bandura, 1997b), are crucial issues yet to be resolved.

Physical Activity Influences on Self-Efficacy

In this section we review more contemporary published reports that provide evidence of exercise participation as a potent source of efficacy information. In the past, this relationship has typically been addressed through documentation of the acute effects of activity on efficacy (e.g., McAuley, Courneya, & Lettunich, 1991; McAuley & Courneya, 1992). However, the literature now includes an increasing number of studies that document physical activity intervention effects on self-efficacy expectations.

Acute Exercise and Self-Efficacy

Perhaps one of the most consistent applications of self-efficacy theory to the exercise domain appears in studies that employ the exercise stimulus as a source of efficacy information. In most cases, exposure to a bout of activity serves as a mastery experience, and self-efficacy expectations are enhanced. In our own work, primarily with older adults, this course of events has been well replicated. In an early study, McAuley et al. (1991) assessed self-efficacy relative to various activity modes (walking/jogging, stationary cycling, sit-ups) prior to and following graded maximal exercise testing at baseline and following a five-month program of walking for middle-aged adults. The acute exposure to exercise served to increase self-efficacy significantly—an effect that was unsurprisingly demonstrated more dramatically over the course of the program. In a nine-month follow-up, McAuley et al. (1993) reported significant declines in efficacy from postprogram testing, but exposure to an acute bout of graded exercise testing (cycle ergometry) and assessment of abdominal strength served to increase cycling and sit-up efficacy to levels that were not statistically different from those at the end of the exercise program. Walking efficacy was, however, unchanged as a function of the exercise bout. Clearly such findings speak to the specificity of the stimulus, underscore the dynamic qualities of efficacy cognitions, and suggest that self-monitoring of physical progress and conditioning may provide sufficient information to maintain efficacy at optimal levels.

In a more recent study, McAuley, Katula et al. (1999) compared the effects of two exercise modes (walking and stretching/toning) on efficacy responses of older adults in a six-month exercise program with six-month follow-up. Latent growth curve models revealed that both activities significantly influenced growth of efficacy, with a growth pattern that was curvilinear. That is, there were gains in efficacy over the exercise intervention and declines six months later. Further structural analyses indicated that frequency of exercise participation, rather than fitness change, was the primary predictor of change in efficacy over time. Such findings may have important implications for exercise interventions that focus on lifestyle activity (Coleman et al., 1999).

McAuley et al. (1991) detailed some intriguing gender differences in efficacy responses, reporting males to be significantly more efficacious than females prior to the onset of the exercise program. However, these differences were eradicated by the end of the program. This latter pattern of relationships was maintained at follow-up. No significant gender effects for efficacy were revealed, suggesting that even though efficacy declined over the course of follow-up, it did not do so differentially for males and females. It appears that the increased efficacy brought about by the exercise program served to provide the female participants with a robust sense of efficacy that although showing a decline at follow-up, was not any more adversely affected than that of the male participants. In a replication of this study, McAuley, Bane, and Mihalko (1995) reported similar increases in cycling, walking, and physical efficacy as a function of exposure to acute exercise at baseline and after the exercise program in middle-aged males and females. They also reported that males were more efficacious than females in cycling and walking efficacy and that this difference was maintained over time. Gender differences with respect to exercise and health self-efficacy, and the extent to which age, physical, social, and cultural experiences influence such cognitions, have largely gone ignored in the literature. For example, Wilcox and Storandt (1996) reported that age was negatively correlated with self-efficacy in a large cross-sectional sample of females but that exercisers had significantly higher self-efficacy than nonexercisers. Clearly, further examination of these potential moderators of the exercise-efficacy relationship is necessary.

In an earlier publication examining efficacy change as a function of acute exercise and affective responses to exercise, McAuley and Courneya (1992) suggested that the efficacy-affect relationship may grow stronger as the situation (exercise stimulus) becomes more demanding. In testing this hypothesis, Tate, Petruzzello, and Lox (1995) contrasted efficacy and affective responses under two different exercise intensities and in a no-exercise control. Contrasting low- and high-efficacy groups based upon a median split, Tate et al. (1995) reported significant increases in affect from pre- to postexercise at 55% and 70% of $\dot{V}O_2$max. These increases were more marked, as one would expect, in the low-efficacy condition. Similarly, McAuley, Shaffer, and Rudolph (1995) found that older impaired males (M age = 66.93 years) were less efficacious than their younger counterparts (M age = 49.18 years) prior to exercise testing but showed a significant increase postexercise, while the efficacy of the younger adults remained unchanged. Finally, in contrasting active and less active young adults exercising at 60% $\dot{V}O_2$max, Rudolph and McAuley (1995) reported increases in efficacy from pre- to postexercise, with the less active group being less efficacious at both time points but demonstrating proportionally greater increases over time.

The findings from the studies just reviewed combined with those from earlier research (e.g., Ewart et al., 1983; Taylor et al., 1985) offer consistent evidence to support the position that acute exercise bouts can serve as mastery experiences and therefore as important sources of efficacy information. However, little is known about the extent to which this relationship holds under varying intensity conditions. For example, under maximal exercise intensity in which individuals exercise to volitional exhaustion, are efficacy expectations undermined as the physiological cues overpower cognitions? Some have argued, and a number of studies have demonstrated, that changes in efficacy as a function of acute exercise contribute to affective change associated with exercise (e.g., Mihalko, McAuley, & Bane, 1996; Tate et al., 1995). However, whether such changes and associations remain positive under maximally taxing situations has yet to be established. In all likelihood, the efficacy-affect relationship and the acute exercise effect on efficacy may be curvilinear rather than following the linear pattern tentatively suggested by McAuley and Courneya (1992). That is, under conditions in which cognitive appraisal is not overridden by physiological stimuli, the relationship is likely to hold, with the exercise bout perceived as a mastery experience and efficacy likely to be enhanced. In contrast, conditions under which one exercises at maximal intensity or to exhaustion are unlikely to be perceived in a favorable light; negative affect is maximized, and efficacy is minimally enhanced or possibly attenuated. Clearly, the dose-response question in relation to acute exercise and efficacy responses remains an important one for the future.

Chronic Exercise and Self-Efficacy

In the previous section we reviewed the effects of acute exercise on self-efficacy responses. We now turn to the literature examining how exercise interventions of varying duration bring about changes in efficacy. A number of such studies were reviewed earlier in this chapter in connection with the TPB or the transtheoretical model, or within the context of acute exercise bouts.

In several clinical samples, older individuals suffering from coronary artery disease (e.g., Ewart et al., 1983; Gulanick, 1991; Oldridge & Rogowski, 1990) or chronic obstructive pulmonary disease (e.g., Kaplan, Atkins, & Reinsch, 1984; Toshima et al., 1990) were exposed to an acute bout of exercise, generally a physician-supervised, symptom-limited, graded exercise test, followed by an exercise-based intervention. Measures of physical efficacy were taken prior to and following activity and in some rare cases, during the program and at follow-up. Ewart, Stewart, Gillilan, and Kelemen (1986) examined the relative merits of adding different components (either weight training or volleyball) to an exercise program (walk/jog) for elderly coronary artery disease patients; the aim was to examine the specificity effects of information on efficacy. Analyses revealed that arm- and leg-strength beliefs (lifting, climbing, push-ups) were enhanced in the weight-training group, but neither group reported increases in walking/jogging capabilities. As the authors pointed out, patients had been involved in walking/jogging for 35 months, and the additional 10 weeks of jogging in the treatment program would have been unlikely to provide new information from which to bolster efficacy cognitions. The importance of such findings should be obvious. With the use of exercise and physical activity interventions to enhance aging individuals' sense of efficacy, it is important to provide the necessary information specific to the domain of function that one wishes to enhance.

Kaplan and his colleagues (Kaplan et al., 1984; Toshima et al., 1990; Ries et al., 1995; Kaplan et al., 1994) have pursued an active research agenda focusing on physical and psychosocial responses to physical activity in older adults with chronic obstructive pulmonary disease (COPD). In an earlier study, Kaplan et al. (1984) reported effects of various behavioral programs for exercise compliance on specific and generalized efficacy cognitions, as well as the relation of efficacy to exercise compliance and performance, in 60 older COPD patients (M age = 65 years). Experimental groups that received training specific to compliance reported significantly greater exercise behavior (walking) at three months compared to an attention control group. Greater changes in efficacy specific to walking, as opposed to other behaviors, also occurred, and these changes in turn mediated walking compliance.

Kaplan's research group has since embarked on the longitudinal assessment of exercise-efficacy relations in a single group of older adults (initial N = 119, M age = 62 years) over a period of several years. Subjects completed self-efficacy measures and graded maximal exercise testing at baseline, after a 2-month intervention, and at 6-month intervals for six years. In the initial study, Toshima et al. (1990) compared an 8-week COPD rehabilitation intervention (including education and exercise training) with an education-only control condition on exercise tolerance and self-efficacy. As expected, there were large and significant differences in treadmill endurance at program end and at 6-month follow-up, with the rehabilitation group demonstrating superior physical performance. Additionally, significant increases in efficacy occurred in the experimental group at the end of the intervention, and, although these expectations declined at 6-month follow-up, the experimental subjects were still more efficacious than the control group. Further follow-up studies showed that efficacy differences between the two groups declined but were still significant at 18-month follow-up, whereas maximal treadmill workload and endurance difference still existed at 12 months but not thereafter. The combination of a relatively short intervention period and monthly reinforcements for 12 months appears to have had a significant influence on efficacy and physical function. However, we suspect that these differences in efficacy may vary as a function of the time point at which efficacy is measured relative to exercise testing. In our own work (McAuley et al., 1991, 1993; McAuley et al., 1999), we typically assess efficacy cognitions twice in association with exercise testing, once before and once following testing. Invariably, we find that the exercise session serves as a mastery experience and that efficacy expectations increase following testing. As noted earlier, McAuley et al. (1993) showed that exercise efficacy declined at 9-month follow-up to a 20-week exercise program but increased after exercise testing to the point that efficacy at follow-up was not significantly different from efficacy at the end of the program. In essence, depending on when efficacy is measured relative to exercise, people may use different or more sources of information to form these expectations.

In further analyses of their COPD sample, Ries et al. (1995) compared survival curves for the exercise and control groups but found no significant differences, although the proportions of survival were in the correct direction (67%, exercise vs. 56%, control). However, using a different approach to examine survival curves, Kaplan et al. (1994) compared standard physiological predictors of remaining life expectancy with a simple measure of exercise self-efficacy. In a series of analyses using univariate and multivariate models, self-efficacy was a significant predictor of survival (p < .01) when compared to all physiological indicators. However, when compared to the strongest predictor alone (forced expiratory volume), efficacy was only marginally significant. The longitudinal nature of this work, the comprehensive approach to measurement, and the strong theoretical approach make this series of studies compelling testimony to the ability of exercise interventions to influence self-efficacy not only as an independent element of psychological function but also as an important correlate of physical health and survival.

Scherer and Schmieder (1997) conducted a simple pretest-posttest single-group-design study to examine the relative merits of attendance at a 12-week outpatient pulmonary rehabilitation program, consisting of education and exercise training, on exercise endurance, dyspnea, and self-efficacy in 60 COPD patients (M age = 65 years). Findings showed a significant increase in exercise self-efficacy and exercise endurance as measured by a 12 min walk. Correlational evidence suggested that increases in self-efficacy were associated with greater endurance and reduced perceptions of dyspnea. These latter findings are of particular interest because few researchers have reported any analyses designed to examine the efficacy-fitness change relationship. Two other studies have also shown relationships among physical fitness indexes and efficacy expectations (Ewart, Stewart, Gillilan, Kelemen, Valenti et al., 1986; McAuley et al., 1991). In both cases there was a significant positive association between these variables. However, weaknesses in the Scherer and Schmieder (1997) study override any enthusiasm regarding the findings, given the lack of a control group, an acknowledged potential learning effect of the 12 min walk, and virtually no information about the efficacy measure used.

Summary

In summary, the evidence from a growing body of physical activity intervention studies suggests that the effects of exercise on perceptions of personal efficacy are consistent and fairly robust. Such a conclusion appears to hold for studies of clinical and asymptomatic populations. Most of the studies employ acceptable measures of physical fitness change and self-efficacy (see McAuley & Mihalko, 1998, for a detailed discussion of the measurement of exercise-related self-efficacy), but rarely do they include analyses of the relationship between these constructs. Such examination is warranted, as it is not yet clear whether physical activity participation or physical fitness change has a more powerful effect on self-efficacy. For example, as adults age, the attendant declines in physical function (flexibility, stamina, mobility, and so forth) are typically characterized as the natural outcomes of biological aging. The evidence is clear that participation in a physically active lifestyle does much to attenuate these declines. Given that such deficits in physical function are partially a product of reduced physical efficacy (Bandura, 1997b), the further exploration of physical activity's role in enhancing perceptions of control is well warranted.

Future Directions in Exercise and Self-Efficacy Research

We have restricted our review to discussion of how exercise can influence and be influenced by perceptions of personal efficacy relevant to the exercise and physical activity domain. This literature has been quite consistent in demonstrating that self-efficacy is a consistent determinant of physical activity behavior but may vary in its influence depending upon the individual's current stage of exercise development. Additionally, acute participation and long-term exercise participation appear to serve as effective sources of efficacy-based information. In this section, we consider a few of the possible research avenues that might be explored in the future with respect to exercise and self-efficacy.

Efficacy and Exercise Behavior

Earlier in the chapter we made several recommendations for research examining the extent to which efficacy may operate in various competing models of exercise behavior. We will not repeat them here. We do, however, further recommend that future researchers (a) adopt longitudinal models to examine changing relationships between efficacy and exercise; and (b) attempt to enhance self-efficacy in experimental designs to determine what key factors in the exercise environment, prescription, and social milieu might be most effective in enhancing efficacy in the early stages of exercise adoption and adaptation (McAuley et al., 1994). This section presents further discussion of the issue of effectively manipulating efficacy.

Efficacy-Affect Relationships

Social cognitive theory (Bandura, 1986) predicts that enhanced perceptions of capabilities lead to increases in positive affect, and mastery, or competence, has long been identified as one of the potential underlying mechanisms that might explain the exercise-psychological health relationship.

Although a number of studies have explored this relationship, they have been largely cross-sectional (e.g., McAuley & Courneya, 1992; Lox, McAuley, & Tucker, 1995; Mihalko et al., 1996); and the exact nature of the exercise efficacy-affect relationship has yet to be effectively delineated. Typically, more efficacious individuals report more positive affective experiences associated with exercise (e.g., McAuley & Courneya, 1992), and changes in self-efficacy are related to changes in affect (Lox et al., 1995; Mihalko et al., 1996). In addition, research has shown that exercising in social as compared to solitary conditions results in greater affective responsivity, and again, self-efficacy plays a role in these affective responses (McAuley, Blissmer, Katula, & Duncan, 2000). An important question for subsequent studies is whether there is some threshold relative to exercise intensity in the efficacy-affect relationship (McAuley, Blissmer, Katula, & Duncan, 2000). That is, at what point do physiological cues override cognitive processing and its influence on affect responses to exercise?

Experimental Manipulation of Self-Efficacy

One approach to isolating self-efficacy's role in exercise-generated affect would be to experimentally manipulate self-efficacy in the exercise domain and examine its impact on subsequent affect. Theoretically, if one can successfully manipulate high and low efficacy, one ought to see a commensurate difference in affective responsivity. Turner, Rejeski, and Brawley (1997) argued that the social environment in which one is active can enhance perceptions of capabilities and affective responses (see Dawson, Gyurcsik, Culos-Reed, & Brawley, this volume). To test this proposal, they contrasted the responses of females randomly assigned to either a socially enriched or a bland leadership style. The activity involved a single session of ballet for beginners, and efficacy and affective responses were assessed at baseline and approximately 10 min following the activity. In this novel experiment, Turner et al. (1997) found significant increases in self-efficacy, revitalization, and positive engagement across conditions, but in the case of efficacy and revitalization, these increases were significantly greater in the socially enriched condition. However, the investigators were unable to demonstrate a significant relationship between efficacy at baseline or changes in efficacy and changes in feeling states. Thus, their results offer some support for the importance of the nature of the environment in influencing efficacy and feeling-state responses. However, the findings fail to substantiate other work that has linked efficacy to exercise-induced feeling states (e.g., McAuley & Courneya, 1992; McAuley, Blissmer, Katula, & Duncan, 2000).

There are several potential reasons for this latter failure. First, as Turner et al. (1997) point out, the activity, ballet, differs markedly in its composition from the typical bout of aerobic activity associated with affective change. Second, the affect-efficacy relationship may be more salient in activities that are less novel and that the participants have some experience with as a frame of reference (Turner et al., 1997). Additionally, it may well be that the content of the intervention was too diverse in its focus to impact the relationship of interest. That is, although the social environment represents an important source of efficacy information, there is an argument that other sources of efficacy information specific to individual performance accomplishments may be more potent.

McAuley, Talbot, and Martinez (1999) offer some convincing evidence for the mediational role of self-efficacy in the generation of exercise-related affect. In this study they successfully manipulated high and low self-efficacy using a bogus-feedback protocol. Participants in the high-efficacy condition reported more positive and less negative affect than did the low-efficacy group, even though participants exercised at equivalent objective and subjective workloads. Furthermore, efficacy was significantly related to feeling-state responses during and after activity but only in the high-efficacy condition.

Although these findings are encouraging, it would be remiss to give the impression that self-efficacy is the only mediator of the exercise-psychological health relationship. A sense of control appears to be very important for physical and psychological health, but it will be important for future studies to determine the extent to which efficacy expectations interact with and are independent of physiological, biochemical, social, demographic, and neurocognitive influences on the emotional responses associated with acute bouts of physical activity. Future studies are encouraged that draw upon the major sources of efficacy information—performance accomplishments, social modeling, social performance, and interpretation of physiological symptoms (Bandura, 1986, 1997b)—to manipulate these cognitions. Additionally, it would be informative to examine how other social cognitive processes, such as causal attributions, are implicated in differential affective responses arising from efficacy manipulation. Finally, incorporating such manipulations into longitudinal designs would be highly informative in relation to the developmental sequence of efficacy-affect relationships in the exercise environment.

Efficacy and Psychobiologic Function

Although a number of reports have suggested a link between perceived efficacy and endocrine, catecholamine, and endogenous opioid systems (Bandura, Cioffi, Taylor, & Brouillard, 1988; Bandura, Taylor, Williams, Mefford, & Barchas, 1985; Weidenfeld et al., 1990), there is little work examining efficacy with respect to the responses these systems might generate as a result of exercise. In terms of adrenocortical responses, self-efficacy would be hypothesized to be inversely related to biological stress responses. In a recent test of such a position, Rudolph and McAuley (1995) employed Dienstbier's (1989) psychological toughness model to demonstrate that preexisting self-efficacy was a significant predictor of cortisol responses during an acute bout of exercise after pre-exercise cortisol levels, aerobic capacity, anaerobic threshold levels, and activity history were controlled for. Additionally, postexercise efficacy was inversely related to cortisol levels at 30 min postexercise. These findings were interpreted as support for other evidence of psychological toughening effects of mastery over stressors (Dienstbier, 1989).

Adrenocortical responses are but one physiological system known to be linked to exercise behavior. Exercise participation also influences neuroendocrine responses, which have been shown to be related to self-efficacy as well (Bandura, 1997b). It remains to be determined whether preexisting levels of exercise self-efficacy and/or changes in efficacy brought about by exercise serve to buffer the biological stress response associated with acute and chronic exercise.

Concluding Remarks

The construct of self-efficacy has been widely employed in an effort to understand how aspects of personal control are related to, are influenced by, and act as mediators of the effects of a broad array of health behaviors, in particular exercise and physical activity. Self-efficacy has consistently been identified as a determinant of exercise behavior; is influenced by acute and chronic exercise participation; and has been implicated in affective, cognitive, and biological responses to exercise behavior. The extent to which this variable interacts with other social cognitive, physiological, and cultural variables in influencing and being influenced by exercise is less well established and warrants attention. For example, some evidence suggests that information garnered from changes in physical performance or function influences self-esteem changes attributed to exercise via effects on physical self-efficacy (Sonstroem & Morgan, 1989; Baldwin & Courneya, 1997; McAuley et al., 1997; McAuley, Blissmer, Katula, Duncan, & Mihalko, 2000). Examination of models that combine physical, psychological, and social functioning will be vital for understanding how control-related constructs (see Skinner, 1996), physical activity, and quality of life are interrelated.

Acknowledgment

This chapter was completed while the authors were supported by a grant from the National Institute on Aging (#AG12113).

A Hierarchical Model
of Intrinsic and Extrinsic
Motivation
in Sport and Exercise

Robert J. Vallerand

For the past 30 years, psychologists have researched two types of motivated behavior. The first, intrinsic motivation, is behavior engaged in for itself and for the pleasure and satisfaction derived from participation. The athlete who plays soccer for the mere pleasure of learning new moves displays this type of motivation. The second type, extrinsic motivation, is behavior carried out to attain contingent outcomes outside the activity (Deci, 1971). The athlete who plays baseball to be popular at school acts out of extrinsic motivation. To these two types of motivation, theorists and researchers have recently added a third concept that captures the relative absence of motivation. This construct has been called amotivation

(Deci & Ryan, 1985a). The individual who feels that it's not worth it anymore to exercise shows some form of amotivation.

Since the first intrinsic motivation experiment (Deci, 1971), over 800 publications have explored the concepts of intrinsic and extrinsic motivation and amotivation. Such research can be grouped into three major categories (Vallerand, 1997). The first type of research has focused on the immediate effects of situational variables (e.g., feedback, rewards) on one's current level of intrinsic motivation. An example is the Orlick and Mosher (1978) study on the effects of awards (trophies) on intrinsic motivation toward a motor task (stabilometer). Research in the second category has focused on the determinants and outcomes of more or less generalized levels of intrinsic motivation, extrinsic motivation, and amotivation toward specific life contexts, such as education, interpersonal relationships, and sport. For instance, Thompson and Wankel (1980) studied the impact of active participation in the decision-making process in a fitness class on participants' general levels of intrinsic motivation toward fitness activities. The third group of studies has researched the link between intrinsic and extrinsic motivation as a global motivational orientation (akin to a personality trait), unrelated to specific contexts, and some psychological correlates. For instance, Guay, Blais, Vallerand, and Pelletier (1996) have assessed the relations between global intrinsic motivation and overall life satisfaction.

Several theoretical positions have been proposed over the past 30 years (e.g., Csikszentmihalyi & Nakamura, 1989; Deci & Ryan, 1985a, 1991; Harter, 1978; Lepper & Greene, 1978) to make sense of this rich and diverse literature. While these theories have made several advances in our understanding of motivation, none has specified a formal integrated model of the relations among the three levels of motivation researched so far. Recently, I (Vallerand, 1997; Vallerand & Perreault, 1999; Vallerand & Ratelle, in press) offered a theoretical model that proposes such an integration. The model takes into consideration the variety of ways motivation is represented in the individual, how these various representations are related among themselves, and the determinants and consequences of these motivational representations.

The purpose of this chapter is to outline this model, called the Hierarchical Model of Intrinsic and Extrinsic Motivation (Vallerand, 1997), and to show that it provides a framework for organizing and understanding the basic mechanisms underlying intrinsic and extrinsic motivational processes found in sport and exercise settings. Much research has already shown the intrinsic and extrinsic motivation paradigm to be very useful in leading to an understanding of motivated behavior in the realm of sport and exercise (e.g., Frederick & Ryan, 1995; Ryan, Vallerand, & Deci, 1984; Vallerand, Deci, & Ryan, 1987; Vallerand & Reid, 1990; Whitehead & Corbin, 1997). I intend to show that the present model goes one step further not only by providing an integrative framework (see Vallerand & Rousseau, in press) but also by leading to new perspectives on the study of intrinsic and extrinsic motivation in sport and exercise settings. The present chapter consists of seven sections. The first section presents an overview of the model, and the second deals with the importance of intrinsic and extrinsic motivation for the study of sport and exercise behavior. We then consider conceptual, definitional, and measurement issues. The following two sections focus on the determinants and consequences of motivation, respectively. A section on integrative research that tests several postulates and corollaries of the model then follows. Finally, after a discussion of future research directions, I offer some concluding thoughts on the model.

The Hierarchical Model in a Nutshell

Several elements of the Hierarchical Model of Intrinsic and Extrinsic Motivation need to be underlined. The whole model is depicted in figure 8.1. One element is the three constructs of motivation already mentioned: intrinsic motivation, extrinsic motivation, and amotivation. Years of research in psychology in general (e.g., Deci & Ryan, 1985a, 1991; Vallerand, 1997), and in sport and exercise psychology in particular (e.g., Frederick & Ryan, 1995; Ryan et al., 1984; Vallerand et al., 1987; Vallerand & Reid, 1990; Whitehead & Corbin, 1997), have shown that these constructs are crucial for understanding the psychological processes underlying behavior. A second important element to consider is that intrinsic and extrinsic motivation and amotivation exist within the individual at three hierarchical levels of generality. From the lower to higher levels, these are the situational (or state), the contextual (or life domain), and the global (or personality) levels. These different levels of generality should allow us to study motivation with considerable precision and refinement.

A third element of the model deals with the determinants of motivation (see the left side of figure 8.1). Several aspects related to determinants deserve attention. First, motivation results from social factors at each of the three levels of generality. Second, the impact of social factors on motivation is mediated by perceptions of competence (interacting effectively with the environment), autonomy (feeling free to choose one's course of action), and relatedness (feeling connected to significant others) at each of the three levels. A third aspect related to the determinants of motivation is that there is a top-down effect from motivation at a given level in the hierarchy on motivation at the next lower level (see the arrow between the motivation concepts in the center of the figure). Thus, for instance, global motivation will affect contextual motivation, and contextual motivation

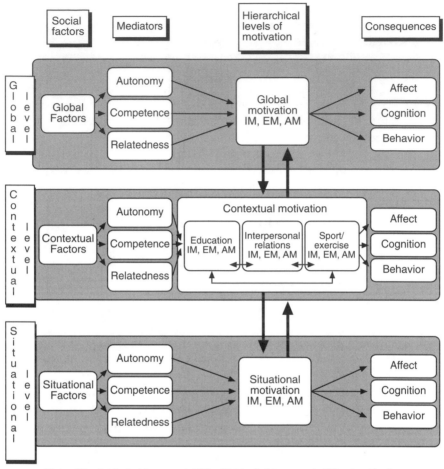

Note: IM = Intrinsic Movement, EM = Extrinsic Movement, AM = Amotivation

Figure 8.1   The Hierarchical Model of Intrinsic and Extrinsic Motivation.

will affect situational motivation. A final aspect related to the motivational determinants is the postulate that motivation at lower levels (e.g., situational motivation) can affect motivation at higher levels (e.g., contextual motivation toward sport) through recursive effects (thus the double arrows in the center of figure 8.1) that may occur on a temporal basis.

A last element of the model is the idea that motivation produces important consequences. This part of the model can be subdivided into four aspects. First, these motivational outcomes can be cognitive, affective, and behavioral (see the right side of figure 8.1). Second, different motivations affect outcomes differently: the more positive consequences are typically produced by intrinsic motivation, whereas the most negative ones are engendered by amotivation and certain types of extrinsic motivation (to be detailed later). The third point on consequences made explicit by the model (see figure 8.1) is that consequences exist at the three levels of generality (the situational, contextual, and global levels) because they are at the same level of generality as the motivation producing them. Finally, contextual consequences should be mainly determined by relevant contextual motivations. For instance, sport-related outcomes (e.g., sport enjoyment) should be the result of motivation toward sport much more than that toward educational activities.

Let's use an example to illustrate some of the issues that the model deals with. Joan is an adolescent, 12 years old. She is the type of person who does things generally because she likes them. Thus, she goes to school and interacts with other people out of a sense of fun. Consequently, such activities generally lead her to experience pleasure and satisfaction. However, contrary to the situation with school and interpersonal relationships, Joan plays tennis because she feels she has to. In the sport context, Joan feels that other people (including her dad), especially her coach (a former professional tennis player), force her to do things she would not choose to do. She feels controlled and experiences very little sense of autonomy in tennis. Consequently, her performance is not very good, and she generally derives little satisfaction from her sport involvement. However, in the last three weeks, things have started to change. Her former coach has been replaced by a new coach who is much less controlling. The new coach allows players to express themselves and try new things. For instance, players are encouraged to try different strokes in various situations, and Joan likes that. More and more Joan feels that she is going to practices and matches out of choice and, at times, pleasure. Consequently, her performance has started to improve and she generally feels happier on the court. This afternoon, before her match, the new coach asked Joan if she wanted to try to go to the net or wanted to stay behind on the baseline against her opponent. Joan indicated that she wanted to go to the net, especially on her serve. Joan experiences feelings of autonomy throughout the match because the coach shows confidence in her by letting her decide what to do. She focuses on her serve, fully concentrates on her rhythm, and follows to the net with much success. Although her opponent manages to hit a few passing shots, Joan feels good and is very satisfied with herself. After the match, she also experiences an inclination to play tennis some more. So she goes over to the practice wall and works on her volley for a few more minutes.

This example makes a number of points with respect to motivation. First, humans are motivationally complex. It is therefore not sufficient to talk about motivation in general to describe a person. It seems more appropriate to refer to a collection of motivations that vary in types and levels of generality. In the example, Joan appeared to be intrinsically motivated toward school and interpersonal relationships but extrinsically motivated toward tennis. Each of these types of motivation represents a part of Joan, and if we are to understand this particular person we need to consider the different motivations that describe her (and not simply those related to sport). In line with the Hierarchical Model, different types of motivation are posited to exist within the individual at three levels of generality. For instance, in the example we noted that Joan generally does things because she enjoys them. At the global level, Joan would therefore appear to have an intrinsic motivation personality that would generally predispose her to be intrinsically motivated toward various contexts. Thus, Joan was depicted as being generally intrinsically motivated toward school and interpersonal relationships. Finally, at the situational level, on that specific day on the court, Joan was intrinsically motivated to play tennis.

A second point of interest is that motivation is not only an intrapersonal but also a social phenomenon. Indeed, other people can have a powerful impact on our motivation, as Joan's former coach had on her contextual motivation toward tennis. Although Joan has an intrinsic motivation personality, she was nevertheless extrinsically motivated toward tennis in general. Thus, intrapersonal factors (global motivation) are not the sole influence on motivation. Social factors, and in this case contextual factors, can play an important role as determinants of her (contextual) motivation toward tennis. The same applies at the situational level. For instance, the new coach's supportive approach in letting Joan decide which strategy to use in her match seems to have had a positive effect on Joan's immediate (or situational) motivation at that specific time on the court. It thus appears that intra- and interpersonal forces can influence global, contextual, and situational motivation at their respective levels of generality.

Third, motivation leads to important consequences, and these also occur at the three levels of generality. At the contextual level, these consequences may vary from context to context as a function of the relevant contextual motivation. For instance, Joan generally experiences positive benefits from her engagement in school and interpersonal activities. Such was not the case in tennis, however, because there her motivation was extrinsic; she felt unsatisfied with the game, and her performance was low. However, with the change of coach (a change in contextual factors), her motivation shifted from extrinsic to intrinsic. Consequently, her performance started to improve and she felt much happier playing tennis. At the situational level, we see that Joan's intrinsic motivation allowed her to remain focused on her serve during the match, to feel good about herself, and to want to keep practicing later that day. Therefore, motivation is crucial because it can lead to important outcomes that vary in terms of their level of generality.

Finally, I propose that repeated instances of situational intrinsic motivation and associated positive benefits, such as those Joan experienced while playing tennis that afternoon, served to facilitate contextual intrinsic motivation toward tennis in general. It is thus not surprising that Joan is now more intrinsically motivated toward tennis in general: repeated instances of situational intrinsic motivation like the one described have had recursive effects on her contextual motivation toward tennis in general.

Thus the model posits that motivation results from an ongoing transaction between the person and the environment. Indeed, the model integrates the personality and social psychological traditions of motivation. The personality tradition (e.g., McClelland, 1985) basically claims that motivation results from traits and stable orientations. On the other hand, the social psychological tradition (e.g., Lepper & Greene, 1978) proposes that motivation results from social factors. The present perspective posits that these positions are complementary. Thus, a coherent model of motivation should incorporate both positions. The model makes some statements with respect to the nature of motivation, its determinants, and its consequences. In so doing, it proposes five postulates. These appear in the sections that follow.

On the Importance of Intrinsic and Extrinsic Motivation and Amotivation

It is proposed that a complete analysis of motivation must deal with three important concepts, namely, intrinsic motivation, extrinsic motivation, and amotivation. As this chapter makes explicit, these concepts are important because they (1) explain a large part of human behavior, (2) represent an important aspect of human experience, and (3) lead to important and varied consequences. This leads to the first postulate.

Postulate 1: A complete analysis of motivation must include intrinsic and extrinsic motivation and amotivation.

In this section, we address conceptual issues related to motivation. In this respect, four issues appear particularly important. First, we need to delineate the very nature of intrinsic and extrinsic motivation and amotivation and show how they can be distinguished from one another. Second, it is important to determine whether we should consider motivation a unidimensional or a multidimensional entity. Third, we need to address the levels of generality of motivation. Should we focus on a broad description of motivation akin to a personality orientation, or should we deal with immediate or state motivation? Finally, it is crucial that we discuss assessment issues.

The Nature of Intrinsic and Extrinsic Motivation and Amotivation

Intrinsic motivation generally refers to performing an activity for itself, as well as for the pleasure and satisfaction derived from participation (e.g., Deci, 1975; Deci & Ryan, 1985a; Lepper, Greene, and Nisbett, 1973). Athletes who engage in their sport because of the pleasure they derive from their engagement exemplify individuals who act out of intrinsic motivation. In contrast, extrinsic motivation refers to engaging in an activity as a means to an end and not for its own sake (Deci, 1975). Athletes who participate in sport simply to please their parents or friends are examples of individuals who act out of extrinsic motivation.

A conceptual analysis of intrinsic and extrinsic motivation suggests that it is possible to distinguish intrinsic and extrinsic motivation on at least three counts (Vallerand & Fortier, 1998). First, these two forms of motivation differ fundamentally from a teleological (or purposive) perspective (Bolles, 1967). Whereas for intrinsic motivation the purpose of participation lies within the process itself, that of extrinsic motivation focuses on benefits that may accrue following participation. This distinction allows us to better understand the motivation underlying the participation of individuals engaged in various activities, such as exercise. For instance, if we asked such individuals if they would pursue their engagement in exercise if they could take a magic pill that would allow them to lose weight and to be in great shape without exercising, those who are intrinsically motivated would probably say that they would still continue, whereas those who are extrinsically motivated would probably say that they would likely stop. This is because when intrinsically motivated, people are not involved in the activity for some external benefit, such as losing weight, but rather to enjoy themselves. They focus on the process not on the outcome. Conversely, when extrinsically motivated, individuals engage in the activity to reach some end, such as losing weight and looking good. If they can achieve these ends more easily, they will gladly do so (see Vallerand, 1997, for a discussion on this issue).

Second, intrinsic and extrinsic motivation can be distinguished from a phenomenological perspective. That is, the experiences of being intrinsically and extrinsically motivated are different. Being intrinsically motivated leads individuals to experience pleasant emotions, such as enjoyment, freedom, and relaxation. They then experience little pressure or tension, and they are focused on the task. Conversely, being extrinsically motivated leads individuals to feel tense and pressured. Social approval (an important extrinsic motive), for instance, depends on others and therefore to a large extent is outside of one's control. It is easy to understand the pressure that people can experience when extrinsically motivated in such a fashion. However, as we will see, different types of extrinsic motivation exist, some of which are self-determined and thus minimize the experience of tension and pressure.

A third and final useful distinction between intrinsic and extrinsic motivation pertains to the type of rewards that individuals seek when in these two motivational modes. When intrinsically motivated, individuals try to derive affective rewards (e.g., enjoyment, pleasure) from their participation (Berlyne, 1971a, 1971b). When extrinsically motivated, individuals seek to obtain social and material rewards from participation (Deci & Ryan, 1985a; Harter, 1978). Approval from others (e.g., fame, recognition, popularity) would appear to loom large in the world of sport and physical activity (Vallerand et al., 1987). Thus, it would seem that when intrinsically motivated, individuals seek different goals than when extrinsically motivated (Ryan, Sheldon, Kasser, & Deci, 1996).

Finally, amotivation refers to the lack of intentionality and thus the relative absence of motivation (Deci & Ryan, 1985a; Koestner, Losier, Vallerand, & Carducci, 1996; Vallerand & O'Connor, 1989, 1991). This concept is somewhat similar to learned helplessness (Abramson, Seligman, & Teasdale, 1978) in that the amotivated individual experiences feelings of incompetence and expectancies of uncontrollability. With respect to the three dimensions identified earlier, athletes who are amotivated play their sport without purpose, typically experience negative affect (e.g., apathy, helplessness, depression), and do not seek any goals—either affective, social, or material. When amotivated, athletes are neither intrinsically nor extrinsically motivated; they are not motivated.

Intrinsic and Extrinsic Motivation and Amotivation: A Multidimensional Perspective

Although most researchers have posited the presence of a unidimensional intrinsic motivation construct, certain theorists such as White (1959) and Deci (1975) have proposed that intrinsic motivation might be differentiated into more specific motives. More recently, Vallerand and his colleagues (Vallerand, Blais, Brière, & Pelletier, 1989; Vallerand et al., 1992, 1993) posited the existence of three types of intrinsic motivation: intrinsic motivation to know, intrinsic motivation toward accomplishments, and intrinsic motivation to experience stimulation. Because this differentiation has been used to explore motivation in several life contexts, including sport, we will elaborate on this tridimensional conceptualization.

Being intrinsically motivated to know can be defined as engaging in an activity for the pleasure and satisfaction that one experiences while learning, exploring, or trying to understand something new. It relates to constructs such as exploration (Berlyne, 1971a, 1971b), intrinsic intellectuality (Lloyd & Barenblatt, 1984), intrinsic motivation to learn (Brophy, 1987), and intrinsic curiosity (Harter, 1981b). For instance, baseball players who practice because they enjoy learning new ways to complete a double play exhibit intrinsic motivation to know.

Intrinsic motivation toward accomplishments focuses on engaging in an activity for the pleasure and satisfaction experienced while one is *attempting* to accomplish or create something or to surpass oneself. The focus is on the process of accomplishing something and not on the end result. This type of motivation relates to constructs such as mastery motivation (Kagan, 1972), effectance motivation (White, 1959), and intrinsic challenge (Harter, 1981b). For example, tennis players who work on their serve for the pleasure they experience while trying to hit an ace display this type of intrinsic motivation.

The third type of intrinsic motivation, intrinsic motivation to experience stimulation, is operative when one engages in an activity to experience pleasant sensations associated mainly with one's senses (e.g., sensory and aesthetic pleasure). This type of intrinsic motivation would appear to be related to constructs such as aesthetic experiences (Berlyne, 1971a), flow (Csikszentmihalyi, 1975, 1978), sensation seeking (Zuckerman, 1979), and peak experiences (Maslow, 1970). Individuals who swim because they enjoy the pleasant sensations they experience while their bodies glide through water display this type of intrinsic motivation. The proposed taxonomy should prove useful because, among other things, it leads to the prediction of engagement in specific sport activities related to the three types of intrinsic motivation (Vallerand & Brière, 1990).

Extrinsic motivation has also been considered from a multidimensional perspective. Theory and research by Deci, Ryan, and their colleagues (e.g., Chandler & Connell, 1987; Deci & Ryan, 1985a; Ryan & Connell, 1989; Ryan, Connell, & Deci, 1985; Ryan, Connell, & Grolnick, 1992) have shown that different types of extrinsic motivation exist, some of which are self-determined. That is, some behaviors, although not necessarily pleasurable, may still be engaged in as a matter of choice. Deci and Ryan (1985a, 1991) have proposed the existence of four types of extrinsic motivation: external regulation, introjected regulation, identified regulation, and integrated regulation.

The first type, *external regulation,* refers to extrinsic motivation as it is generally construed in the literature. That is, behavior is regulated through external means such as rewards and constraints. For instance, an athlete might say, "I'm going to today's practice because I want the coach to let me play tomorrow." With *introjected regulation,* the individual begins to internalize the reasons for his or her actions. However, such internalization is not truly self-determined because it merely replaces the external source of control with an internal one (such as self-imposed guilt and anxiety). For instance, the athlete who says that she's going to the practice because she would feel guilty if she did not go displays introjected regulation. Motivation is internal, but it is not self-determined, because self-imposed pressure is its source. It is only with the third type of extrinsic motivation, *identified regulation,* that behavior arises out of choice. When the behavior is identified, it is highly valued and judged as important by the individual. It will thus be performed freely even if the activity is not pleasant in itself. For instance, an athlete might say, "I want to improve my stamina. This is important to me. Thus, I've decided to come to today's practice." Finally, an *integrated regulation* also involves emitting an activity choicefully. However, in this case, such choice represents a harmonious part of the self of the individual. One's choices are made as a function of their coherence with other aspects of the self. For instance, the integrated athlete may decide to stay home on Saturday night (rather than go out with his friends) to be ready for tomorrow's football game.

Researchers have also considered amotivation from a multidimensional perspective. Pelletier and his colleagues (e.g., Pelletier, Dion, Tuson, & Green-Demers, 1998) have proposed four major types of amotivation. The first is amotivation due to capacity/ability beliefs. This is in line with the usual definition of Deci and Ryan (1985a), according to which amotivation results from a lack of ability to perform the behavior. The second type is amotivation resulting from the individual's conviction that the proposed strategy will not bring forth the desired outcomes (strategy-beliefs amotivation). The third type of amotivation deals with capacity-effort beliefs. This type of amotivation results from the belief that the behavior is too demanding, and the person does not want to expend the necessary effort to engage in it. Finally, the fourth type of amotivation, termed *helplessness beliefs,* refers to a general perception that one's efforts are inconsequential considering the enormity of the task to be accomplished. Pelletier et al. have obtained support for a model predicting that amotivation due to lack of effort influences amotivation due to a lack of ability beliefs and amotivation due to lack of strategy beliefs, which in turn leads to amotivation due to helplessness beliefs. No research to date has focused on these types of amotivation in sport and exercise. This is unfortunate in light of the high dropout rate in youth sports (e.g., Roberts, 1984a; Seefeldt, Blievernicht, Bruce, & Gilliam, 1978; Weiss & Chaumeton, 1993) and the fact that research reveals amotivation to be an important predictor of dropping out (see Pelletier, Fortier, Vallerand, & Brière, 2001; Vallerand & Bissonnette, 1992; Vallerand, Fortier, & Guay, 1997).

Deci and Ryan (1985a) have also proposed that the different types of motivation vary in terms of their inherent level of self-determination. Thus, they can be ordered along a self-determination continuum. From lower to higher levels of self-determination, the types are amotivation; external, introjected, identified, and integrated regulation; and intrinsic motivation. Much research now supports the self-determination continuum in psychology in general (e.g., Blais, Sabourin, Boucher, & Vallerand, 1990; Ryan & Connell, 1989; Vallerand & Bissonnette, 1992) and in sport and exercise (e.g., Brière, Vallerand, Blais, & Pelletier, 1995; Li & Harmer, 1996; Pelletier, Fortier et al., 1995). As we will later see, the self-determination continuum is useful with respect to measurement and consequence issues.

Motivation at Different Levels of Generality

Although personality and social psychologists have typically focused on different aspects of motivation, they agree that self-representations can be integrated within hierarchical models of the self (e.g., Carver & Scheier, 1981; Harter, 1985; Kihlstrom & Cantor, 1984; McAdams, 1994; Shavelson, Hubner, & Stanton, 1976). For instance, Shavelson et al. posit the existence of the self-concept at three levels of a hierarchy—namely, the general self-concept, the academic and non-academic self-concept, and self-concepts relating to specific activities. The latter are of limited generality, are quite specific, and are closely related to actual behavior. In the same vein, a hierarchy of motivation is proposed here:

> **Postulate 2:** Intrinsic and extrinsic motivation and amotivation exist at three levels of generality: the global, contextual, and situational levels.

In line with past motivation research, the second postulate states that intrinsic and extrinsic motivation and amotivation are represented within the individual at three hierarchical levels of generality. As figure 8.1 shows, these are the situational, contextual, and global levels. In the following sections we consider each of these levels.

Motivation at the Situational Level

The situational level represents the lowest level in the hierarchy (see figure 8.1). Situational motivation refers to the motivation that individuals experience when they are currently engaging in an activity. It refers to the here and now of motivation. It is a motivational state rather than a trait. An example is seen in the baseball player who engages in batting practice at 1:45 P.M., right before the game, out of the sheer pleasure of feeling the bat connect with the ball. Maybe yesterday her situational motivation toward the batting practice was not intrinsic (maybe she wanted to impress her friends). But today it is. As we will later see, if we are to predict situational consequences, for instance this player's performance in today's batting practice, we need to focus on the motivation underlying her current behavior (and not that of yesterday). We feel that the situational level represents a central part of the motivational hierarchy because it focuses on people's motivation when and where they experience it. The situational level is thus essential to a better understanding of people's engagement in sport and related activities.

Much research in sport has taken place at the situational level in laboratory and field settings. Typically, at this level, the experimenter introduces an independent variable and assesses its impact on the subject's motivation at that specific moment. The study of McAuley and Tammen (1989) on the positive effects of winning and performing well on immediate levels of intrinsic motivation toward a basketball task represents motivation research at the situational level.

Motivation at the Contextual Level

Motivation at the second level, that is, the contextual level, is one's usual motivational orientation toward a specific context. By context, we refer to "a distinct sphere of human activity" (Emmons, 1995). Examples of social contexts are education, work, interpersonal relationships, and sport. It is important to incorporate the contextual level into the present model for at least two reasons. First, it reflects a basic fact: people's motivational orientation may vary drastically from one context to another (Graef, Csikszentmihalyi, & Gianinno, 1983). For instance, in our introductory example, Joan was generally intrinsically motivated toward school and interpersonal activities but extrinsically motivated toward tennis. Second, it is important to consider motivation at the contextual level because contextual motivation is more subject to variations than is global motivation, as we will see. Therefore, it is more likely to be useful in explaining and predicting changes in outcomes that may take place in specific contexts.

Over the past 20 years, there has been a surge of scientific interest in motivation at the contextual level. This research has been conducted in contexts as diverse as education (e.g., Deci, Nezlek, & Sheinman, 1981; Vallerand & Bissonnette, 1992), politics (Koestner et al., 1996), work (Blais, Brière, Lachance, Riddle, & Vallerand, 1993), leisure (Pelletier, Vallerand,

Blais, Brière, & Green-Demers, 1996), and interpersonal and couple relationships (Blais, Sabourin et al., 1990; Blais, Vallerand, Pelletier, & Brière, 1994) (for reviews of motivation research in various contexts see Deci & Ryan, 1991; Ryan, 1995; Vallerand, 1993, 1997).

There has been much research in sport and exercise settings at the contextual level, with some studies examining the determinants (e.g., Thompson & Wankel, 1980) and others the consequences (e.g., Biddle & Brooke, 1992) of contextual motivation. Other research has considered the determinants and consequences of motivation using longitudinal designs. For example, Beauchamp, Halliwell, Fournier, and Koestner (1996) showed that over a 14-week period, beginning golfers who were coached in an autonomy-supportive manner eventually developed high levels of intrinsic motivation and identified regulation for playing golf. In turn, they showed greater evidence of having internalized the strategies that were taught, and they displayed better performance than golfers coached in a controlling manner.

Motivation at the Global Level

Motivation at the global level is a general motivational orientation to interact with the environment in an intrinsic, extrinsic, or amotivated way. Global motivation refers to relatively enduring individual differences with respect to people's motivations. This global level can be taken to represent the personality tradition in intrinsic and extrinsic motivation research. In the introductory example, Joan was described as an individual with a global intrinsic motivation orientation since she's the type of person who generally participates in activities because she enjoys them. This global type of motivation would typically orient Joan to interact with the environment for intrinsic reasons.

Research at the global level has generally related global assessments of intrinsic and extrinsic motivation and amotivation to adaptive versus maladaptive adjustment outcomes (Deci & Ryan, 1985b; Guay et al., 1996). For instance, Guay et al. reported that all three types of global intrinsic motivation and identified regulation were positively associated with life satisfaction, whereas external regulation and amotivation were negatively related to it.

To the best of my knowledge, no research conducted at the global level in sport and exercise has been published. However, one recent study of ours (Blanchard & Vallerand, 1998a) in an exercise setting has revealed that global motivation is positively related to contextual motivation toward exercise. More specifically, this study showed that the more self-determined the global motivation, the more self-determined the contextual motivation to exercise. In other words, people who have a disposition to behave out of choice and pleasure will typically engage in exercise activities out of choice and pleasure. Obviously in light of the absence of research involving global motivation, much research remains to be done at this level of the hierarchy.

Summary

This quick review reveals that motivation research in sport has been conducted at each of the three levels of generality, although only one study (Blanchard & Vallerand, 1998a) has involved the global level. However, within each study, researchers have typically focused on motivation at only one level of generality. Thus, although research on self-processes (e.g., Schell, Klein, & Babey, 1996; Shavelson et al., 1976) supports the validity of hierarchies similar to the one proposed here, very little direct support exists for such a structure with respect to intrinsic and extrinsic motivation and amotivation. However, in a recent study to be detailed later, Vallerand, Guay, Blanchard, and Codorette (2000, Study 3) had adults in an exercise program complete motivation scales at the three levels of generality. Results from a structural equation modeling analysis provided support for a model involving motivation at the three levels of generality as proposed by the Hierarchical Model. It would thus appear that these levels of motivation can be empirically distinguished from one another in sport and exercise settings and that they do form a three-level hierarchy as posited.

On Measuring Intrinsic and Extrinsic Motivation and Amotivation

To test the Hierarchical Model, an important first step was to construct and validate scales assessing intrinsic and extrinsic motivation and amotivation at each of the three levels of generality. We started at the contextual level. Our work at this level has focused mostly on young adults' motivation, and we sought to identify the most relevant contexts for this population. We thus conducted a study in which we asked male and female college students to rate the importance of 21 life contexts (Blais, Vallerand, Gagnon, Brière, & Pelletier, 1990). The results showed that the three most important contexts (besides biological needs, such as eating, sleeping, etc.) for both males and females were education, interpersonal relationships, and leisure. For athletes, sport of course represents a significant life context in itself that can substitute for leisure. In addition, sport and exercise represent an important form of leisure for a substantial portion of the population, especially those who are not "elite athletes." Thus, as figure 8.1 shows, the three life contexts hypothesized to have significant importance for athletes and sport and exercise participants are education, interpersonal relationships, and sport/exercise (not necessarily in that order). There are other life contexts, of course (spirituality, part-time work, health, etc.), but it would appear that these three are the ones we need to focus on.

There were no scales to assess intrinsic and extrinsic motivation in interpersonal relationships, and although there were some in education (e.g., Gottfried, 1985; Harter, 1981b) and sport (e.g., McAuley, Duncan, & Tammen, 1989; Weiss, Bredemeier, & Shewchuk, 1985), these did not assess the entire spectrum of motivations we were interested in (see Vallerand, 1997; Vallerand & Fortier, 1998, on this issue). Thus we developed and validated the Academic Motivation Scale (Vallerand et al., 1989, 1992, 1993) and the Interpersonal Motivation Inventory (Blais et al., 1994) to measure motivation toward education and interpersonal relationships, respectively. To assess contextual motivation toward sport, we developed the Sport Motivation Scale in French first (Brière et al., 1995) and then in English (Pelletier, Fortier et al., 1995).

The development of these questionnaires involved several steps. For instance, with respect to the French form of the Sport Motivation Scale (Brière et al., 1995), we first conducted interviews with junior-college athletes to obtain ecologically valid reasons that participants had for engaging in sport that were also theoretically meaningful. Second, these reasons were translated into items. Third, we conducted a pretest with athletes to ensure that the items were clear and relevant for these participants. Fourth, we conducted an initial study to verify the scale factor structure using exploratory factor analysis. Fifth, we gave a second version of the scale to a second sample of athletes and conducted a confirmatory factor analysis on the data. Sixth, correlations were computed between the Sport Motivation Scale and other scales assessing contextual determinants and consequences to test for the scale's construct validity. Finally, test-retest correlations were computed. These steps were also taken to validate scales toward the life contexts of education and interpersonal relationships. High levels of validity and reliability have been demonstrated for all scales (see Vallerand, 1997).

Table 8.1 shows some of the items of the Sport Motivation Scale. This scale consists of seven subscales of four items each, assessing the three types of intrinsic motivation (intrinsic motivation to know, to accomplish things, and to experience stimulation), three types of extrinsic motivation (external, introjected, and identified regulation), and amotivation.[1] The scale contains the question, "Why do you practice your sport?"; items represent possible answers to that question, thus reflecting the different types of motivation.

Mullan, Markland, and Ingledew (1997) developed a scale that measures contextual motivation toward exercise. This scale, the Behavioural Regulation in Exercise Questionnaire, contains five subscales (intrinsic

Table 8.1   Sample Items From Each of the Seven Subscales of the Sport Motivation Scale (SMS)

Subscales	Why do you practice your sport?
Intrinsic motivation—knowledge	*For the pleasure it gives me to know more about the sport that I practice.*
Intrinsic motivation—accomplishment	*For the pleasure I feel while improving some of my weak points.*
Intrinsic motivation—stimulation	*For the excitement I feel when I am really involved in the activity.*
Identified regulation	*Because it is one of the best ways I have chosen to develop other aspects of myself.*
Introjected regulation	*Because I would feel bad if I was not taking time to do it.*
External regulation	*For the prestige of being an athlete.*
Amotivation	*I often ask myself; I can't seem to achieve the goals that I set for myself.*

motivation, external regulation, introjected regulation, identified regulation, and amotivation). Because low mean values were obtained with the amotivation subscale, the validity studies were conducted only on the other four subscales. Results provided support for the factor structure (through confirmatory factor analysis), the internal consistency, and the invariance of the scale across gender. This scale thus appears to be well suited for investigations on motivation in the exercise context. More recently, Li (1999) has developed an even more complete instrument that assesses the three types of intrinsic motivation; integrated, identified, introjected, and external regulation; and amotivation. Preliminary findings support the validity of the Exercise Motivation Scale.

Some researchers have developed scales to assess the motivation of other types of sport and physical activity participants. For instance, Losier, Gaudette, and Vallerand (1997) developed a scale to assess motivation toward coaching, the Coaching Motivation Scale. This scale, adapted from the Sport Motivation Scale, assesses seven different types of motivation for coaching (the same types of motivation as discussed previously with respect to the Sport Motivation Scale). The scale has been found to have adequate psychometric properties, such as appropriate factor structure and internal consistency, and also to lead to various outcomes as theoretically predicted (see Losier et al., 1997). Although still in the validation phase, this scale could be useful for research on coaches' motivation.

In a similar fashion, Reid and colleagues developed the Pictorial Motivation Scale to assess the motivation of intellectually challenged children, specifically in four types of contextual motivation toward sport and exercise (intrinsic motivation, identified regulation, external regulation, and amotivation). Each item is read to participants, and a picture is presented to complement the item. The original French version of the scale (Reid, Poulin, & Vallerand, 1994) had 5 items per subscale. In the more recent English version (Reid, Vallerand, & Poulin, 2001), there are 4 items per subscale for a total of 16 items. This lower number of items is deemed more appropriate in light of the cognitive demands of this type of scale on this population. The scale has shown excellent psychometric properties (four-factor solution, high internal consistency, and high temporal stability). The scale may encourage further research on the motivation of special populations.

In line with the Hierarchical Model, we have also developed scales to assess motivation at the global (Guay et al., 1996) and situational levels (Guay & Vallerand, 1995; Guay, Vallerand, & Blanchard, in press). Whereas the Global Motivation Scale assesses the seven types of motivation discussed previously, the Situational Motivation Scale assesses only four types: intrinsic motivation, identified and external regulation, and amotivation. The use of only four subscales was dictated by the need for the scale to be as short as possible to assess situational motivation in a variety of settings. Research on the Global Motivation Scale (Guay et al., 1996) and the Situational Motivation Scale (Guay & Vallerand, 1995; Guay et al., in press) has followed the same sequence of development as for the Sport Motivation Scale and has yielded impressive support for the reliability and validity of these scales. Both scales have a sound factor structure, independently assessing the various types of motivation described earlier (intrinsic and extrinsic motivation and amotivation). In addition, they have adequate levels of internal consistency and temporal stability (except, of course, for the situational motivation measure, which should show variability). In addition, the scales are unrelated to social desirability (see Blais, Sabourin et al., 1990; Pelletier et al., 1996). Finally, as we will see in later sections, the construct validity of the scales is supported by the fact that they predictably relate to various determinants and consequences.

A final point related to the assessment of intrinsic and extrinsic motivation and amotivation is that sometimes researchers combine the various subscales into a self-determination index (e.g., Fortier, Vallerand, & Guay, 1995; Grolnick & Ryan, 1987; Vallerand & Bissonnette, 1992; Vallerand et al., 1997). This is done by specifically weighting and adding the scores of the subscales so as to derive a single score. Because it is theoretically posited that the various types of motivation lie on a continuum of self-determination from intrinsic motivation to identified, introjected, and external regulation and to amotivation (Deci & Ryan, 1985b, 1991), weights are given to the motivational items according to their placement on this continuum.[2] Research reveals that this index, which has been used in some of the studies reviewed in this chapter, displays high levels of reliability and validity (e.g., Blais, Sabourin et al., 1990; Fortier, Vallerand, & Guay, 1995; Grolnick & Ryan, 1987; Ryan & Connell, 1989; Vallerand & Bissonnette, 1992; Vallerand et al., 1997). Individuals with a high positive score are described as having a self-determined motivational profile, while those who have a low (or even negative) score are portrayed as having a non-self-determined motivational profile.

In summary, the concepts of intrinsic and extrinsic motivation and amotivation do seem important to a better understanding of human behavior. In addition, conceptual developments now allow us to consider these concepts from a multidimensional perspective. Finally, recent methodological advances give us the means to assess these various types of motivation at the three levels of generality.

On the Determinants of Intrinsic and Extrinsic Motivation and Amotivation

This section deals with the effects of determinants or antecedents on intrinsic and extrinsic motivation and amotivation in sport and exercise. Thus, in this section the aim is to integrate current knowledge on the causal forces acting on sport and exercise motivation. I do not attempt to review all research that has been conducted in sport and exercise settings. Rather, the intent is to show the heuristic value of the model as an integrative framework for sport and exercise research. Thus, the third postulate reads as follows:

> **Postulate 3:** Motivation at a given level results from two potential sources: (1) social factors and (2) top-down effects from motivation at the proximal level.

In addition, I propose psychological processes through which such forces act upon motivation. Thus, this third postulate is subdivided into three corollaries as explained in the next section.

On Social Factors and Their Impact on Motivation

As the left side of figure 8.1 shows, it is proposed that social factors influence motivation. Corollary 3.1 deals specifically with this issue.

Corollary 3.1: Motivation at a given level can result from social factors that can be global, contextual, or situational, depending on the level in the hierarchy.

By social factors, we refer to human and nonhuman factors in our social environment. We distinguish among situational, contextual, and global determinants in the following manner. Situational factors refer to variables that are present at a given time but not permanently. Receiving positive feedback from the coach at 4:29 in the second half of a basketball game is an example of a situational factor. Contextual factors refer to variables that are present on a general or recurrent basis in one specific life context (e.g., a controlling tennis coach) but not in another (e.g., the coach is part of the sport context but not of the educational context). Finally, global factors are social factors whose presence is so pervasive that they are part of most aspects of the person's life. A good example of such a global factor is living year-round in houses for elite athletes, as in countries of the Eastern Bloc some years ago (see Riordan, 1977). Being confined to such an environment for an extended time may have important consequences on an athlete's global motivation. We feel that it is important to distinguish among the three types of social factors because doing so enables us to make more precise hypotheses about which types of factors should influence motivation at the various levels of the hierarchy. Specifically, it is hypothesized that social factors should mostly influence motivation at their own level of the hierarchy.

Situational Factors

Much research in psychology in general reveals that situational factors do influence motivation (see Deci & Ryan, 1985a, 1987; Vallerand, 1997). Findings in the realm of sport and exercise have been similar. The Whitehead and Corbin (1991) study is a good example of such research. In that study, 105 seventh- and eighth-grade students performed the Illinois Agility Run, which involves running a certain distance in the fastest time possible. In the first phase, participants performed the test without any feedback. The athletes' intrinsic motivation on the activity was assessed through the Intrinsic Motivation Inventory (McAuley et al., 1989). Two weeks later, participants performed the activity again, but this time they had been randomly assigned to receive bogus positive or negative performance feedback or no feedback. Participants then completed the intrinsic motivation measure again. As predicted, positive feedback led to increases in intrinsic motivation, while negative feedback produced decreases in intrinsic motivation. The no-feedback group did not experience any change in intrinsic motivation. These findings reveal that verbal feedback that is perceived as a true representation of participants' competence has a positive impact on their situational intrinsic motivation.

Other research in sport and physical activity has shown that variables such as rewards (Orlick & Mosher, 1978; Thomas & Tennant, 1978), competition (Vallerand, Gauvin, & Halliwell, 1986a, 1986b; Weinberg & Ragan, 1979), negative performance feedback (Thill & Mouanda, 1990; Vallerand & Reid, 1984, 1988; Vallerand & Rousseau, 2001; Whitehead & Corbin, 1991), and negative outcomes such as losing (McAuley & Tammen, 1989; Weinberg & Jackson, 1979) can all have negative effects on intrinsic motivation toward a variety of sports, motor tasks, and physical activities at a specific time (at the situational level). On the other hand, receiving positive verbal feedback (Thill & Mouanda, 1990; Vallerand, 1983; Vallerand & Reid, 1984, 1988), experiencing positive outcomes (McAuley & Tammen, 1989; Weinberg & Jackson, 1979), and even receiving factual performance information (Rutherford, Corbin, & Chase, 1992) can all have positive effects on situational intrinsic motivation toward motor tasks and sport and physical activities (see Frederick & Ryan, 1995; Vallerand et al., 1987; Vallerand & Reid, 1990; Weiss & Chaumeton, 1993, for reviews of studies dealing with the effect of situational factors on intrinsic motivation in sport).

It should be noted that the impact of a given situational factor on situational motivation may not be long lasting, especially if the factor is presented only once (see Loveland & Olley, 1979, to that effect). Thus, although situational factors may impact situational motivation at the time they are present, their impact may be limited to that very moment. To have long-lasting effect, they may need to be presented on a more regular basis and in the same context. At that point they become contextual factors.

Contextual Factors

As indicated earlier, contextual factors represent variables that are present on a general basis in one specific life context or that are present regularly in that particular domain. Such variables are hypothesized to affect motivation toward that specific context only. For instance, the behavior of coaches should influence the motivation of athletes toward their sport but not toward school. Many studies have examined the effects of contextual factors on contextual motivation in the education context. For instance, in education, variables that students perceive as controlling undermine their contextual intrinsic motivation toward education; some of these variables are the type of school (e.g., Harter, 1981b; Matthews, 1991), curriculum (e.g., Senécal, Vallerand, & Pelletier, 1992), classroom structure (e.g., Garibaldi, 1979; Johnson, Johnson, Johnson, & Anderson, 1976), and the teacher's and parents' interactive styles (e.g., Deci , Nezlek, & Sheinman, 1981; Deci, Schwartz, Sheinman, & Ryan, 1981; Grolnick & Ryan, 1989). However, when students perceive these variables as supporting their autonomy, their intrinsic motivation toward education in general is preserved or even enhanced (see Deci & Ryan, 1987; Vallerand, 1997). There is much less research on the contextual determinants of motivation toward interpersonal relationships, in part because most studies have focused on motivational consequences in this life context (e.g., Blais, Sabourin et al., 1990; Rempel, Holmes, & Zanna, 1985; Seligman, Fazio, & Zanna, 1980). However, initial research has reproduced the effects obtained in the educational context at least with respect to the interpersonal climate (Blais et al., 1994; see also Pittman, Boggiano, & Main, 1992, for a review).

An increasing number of sport studies have been conducted at the contextual level. For instance, a series of studies (e.g., Brière et al., 1995; Pelletier et al., 2001; Pelletier, Fortier et al., 1995) has shown that coaching behavior perceived as controlling is negatively related to intrinsic motivation and identified regulation but positively related to amotivation and external regulation. Other studies in sport and exercise settings have shown that sport scholarships (Ryan, 1977, 1980), highly competitive structures (e.g., Fortier, Vallerand, Brière, & Provencher, 1995), and a controlling teaching style in fitness (Cadorette, Blanchard, & Vallerand, 1996; Thompson & Wankel, 1980) and physical education settings (Goudas, Underwood, & Biddle, 1993, cited in Goudas & Biddle, 1994a), as well as a climate in which performance is emphasized at the expense of task enjoyment and learning (Lloyd & Fox, 1992; Papaioannou, 1995a; Seifriz, Duda, & Chi, 1992; Theeboom, De Knop, & Weiss, 1995), all undermine contextual motivation toward sport and exercise. On the other hand, autonomy-supportive behavior from coaches (Brière et al., 1995; Pelletier et al., 2001; Pelletier, Brière, Blais, & Vallerand, 1988; Pelletier, Fortier et al., 1995) is positively associated with intrinsic motivation and identified regulation but negatively associated with amotivation and external regulation.

In sum, research in the three contexts of interest (education, interpersonal relationships, and sport/exercise) reveals that contextual factors are numerous and varied. Typically, research in the context of sport and exercise reveals that contextual factors (structures; motivational climate; the interactive style of physical education teachers, parents, coaches, fitness instructors, etc.) that are controlling—that direct a person to behave in a particular way—will lead to an undermining of intrinsic motivation and identified regulation toward sport and exercise. On the other hand, factors that encourage personal initiatives and autonomy will facilitate intrinsic motivation and identified regulation (see Deci & Ryan, 1985a, 1991; Ryan et al., 1984; Vallerand & Reid, 1990; Vallerand, 1997).

Global Factors

Finally, global factors are social factors that are present in most contexts of the person's life. Such factors can affect the individual's usually stable global motivation. As indicated earlier, living on a prolonged basis in houses for elite athletes, as was the case in Communist countries and is still the case for future professional soccer players in France and other countries, is an example of a global factor. Unfortunately, no research to date has assessed the impact of such an environment on global motivation. Available research with elderly nursing home residents suggests that confinement to a single social environment for all (or most) of one's life activities can have a profound impact on most of one's contextual motivations (O'Connor & Vallerand, 1994; Vallerand & O'Connor, 1991). It is therefore likely that global motivation is also affected by the nursing home. If changes in global motivation can be obtained with individuals who are elderly, who should have rather stable levels of global motivation, imagine what can happen with adolescents and young adults.

The Mediational Role of Perceptions of Competence, Autonomy, and Relatedness

Over the past 25 years or so, several theoretical frameworks have been proposed to explain how social factors may affect motivation (e.g., Bandura, 1986; Csikszentmihalyi & Nakamura, 1989; Deci & Ryan, 1985a; Dweck & Leggett, 1988; Lepper & Greene, 1978). One theoretical perspective that appears to provide a rather complete account of such processes is cognitive evaluation theory (Deci, 1975; Deci & Ryan, 1985a, 1991), a subtheory of self-determination theory. According to this theory, social factors (more precisely, situational factors as proposed by cognitive evaluation theory) affect motivation through their impact on people's perceptions of competence, autonomy, and relatedness. As we will see, much research now supports this perspective of cognitive evaluation theory, which leads to Corollary 3.2.

> **Corollary 3.2:** The impact of social factors on motivation is mediated by perceptions of competence, autonomy, and relatedness.

The mediational role is attributable to the fact that these perceptions relate to fundamental human needs that individuals seek to satisfy. The need for competence implies that individuals have a desire to interact effectively with the environment to experience a sense of competence in producing desired outcomes and preventing undesired events (Connell &

Wellborn, 1991; Deci, 1975; Deci & Ryan, 1985a; Harter, 1978; White, 1959). On the other hand, the need for autonomy reflects a desire to engage in activities of one's own choosing, to be the origin of one's own behavior (deCharms, 1968; Deci, 1975, 1980; Deci & Ryan, 1985a). Finally, the need for relatedness (Bowlby, 1988; Harlow, 1958; Richer & Vallerand, 1998; Ryan, 1993) involves feeling connected (or feeling that one belongs in a given social milieu; see Baumeister & Leary, 1995; Ryan, 1993, for recent reviews on belongingness and/or relatedness). As Deci and Ryan (1994) have suggested, "People are inherently motivated to feel connected to others within a social milieu, to function effectively in that milieu, and to feel a sense of personal initiative while doing so" (p. 7).

Situational factors that facilitate feelings of competence, autonomy, or relatedness will lead individuals to freely re-engage in the activities in which these perceptions were experienced because such activities allow individuals to satisfy their needs. Thus, according to cognitive evaluation theory (Deci, 1975; Deci & Ryan, 1985a, 1991), situational factors that facilitate perceptions of competence, autonomy, and relatedness will increase situational intrinsic motivation and self-determined forms of extrinsic motivation (integrated and identified regulation), whereas those that impair such perceptions will have a negative effect on intrinsic motivation and self-determined forms of motivation and will lead to non-self-determined forms of extrinsic motivation (external and introjected regulation) and amotivation. Expanding from cognitive evaluation theory, it is proposed here that the mediational role of perceptions of competence, autonomy, and relatedness is not limited to the situational level but applies to all three levels of the hierarchy. In other words, global, contextual, and situational factors will have an impact on motivation to the extent that they influence people's perceptions of competence, autonomy, and relatedness at their respective levels of the hierarchy.

Much support exists for Corollary 3.2 at the situational level in psychology in general (see Vallerand, 1997), especially with respect to the mediational role of perceptions of competence. A similar situation prevails in the context of sport and physical activity. For instance, in the first study to test the mediational effects of perceptions of competence on intrinsic motivation, Vallerand and Reid (1984) had male participants engage in a balancing task (the stabilometer) during a pretest and a posttest. During the posttest, participants received either positive, negative, or no performance feedback. Following both the pretest and the posttest, participants completed questionnaires assessing situational perceptions of competence and intrinsic motivation (the Mayo Task Reaction Questionnaire; Mayo, 1977). A path analysis was conducted using the change scores from pretest to posttest in perceptions of competence and intrinsic motivation and dummy coding for the feedback conditions. As hypothesized, results revealed that the more positive the feedback, the more participants felt competent. In turn, the more participants felt competent, the more they were intrinsically motivated. Perceptions of competence explained 40% of 48% of the variance in situational intrinsic motivation. Thus, results from the Vallerand and Reid (1984) laboratory study reveal that the effects of performance feedback on intrinsic motivation are mediated by perceptions of competence. These findings have been replicated with women (e.g., Vallerand & Reid, 1988) and in exercise settings (Whitehead & Corbin, 1991). Finally, the mediating effects of perceptions of competence should be particularly strong when the main goal of the individual is to achieve competence (Sansone, 1986) and when the individual's feelings of autonomy are supported (Goudas & Biddle, 1994b; Ryan, 1982; Thill & Mouanda, 1990).

These studies examined the mediating role of perceived competence only. The study of the impact of perceived autonomy and relatedness has been sorely neglected. In addition, much of the research has focused on tasks that participants engage in individually. The team or group dimension has not been addressed. Thus, in a recent study, Blanchard and Vallerand (1996a) attempted to ascertain the mediating role of all three psychological mediators (perceived autonomy, competence, and relatedness) at the situational level in a team setting. Basketball players completed scales measuring situational perceptions of personal and team performance (as well as objective indicators of team performance); situational perceptions of competence, autonomy, and relatedness; and situational motivation during a game. In line with the Hierarchical Model, it was hypothesized that both individual and team performance would influence the psychological mediators that then would determine self-determined motivation (as assessed by the self-determination index). A path analysis was conducted on the data. Results, presented in figure 8.2, supported the hypothesized model. Subjective and objective indexes of personal and team success positively influenced perceptions of competence, autonomy, and relatedness, which in turn facilitated self-determined situational motivation. Hence, perceptions of autonomy, competence, and relatedness do play a mediational role between performance and self-determined motivation at the situational level within a team sport setting.

Other sport and exercise research has assessed the mediating role of perceptions of competence, autonomy, and relatedness at the contextual level. For instance, Cadorette et al. (1996) asked adult exercisers ($N = 208$) to complete scales assessing perceptions of the fitness leader's style (autonomy support) and the ambiance of the fitness center (i.e., autonomy support from the center); contextual perceptions of competence (based on Losier, Vallerand, & Blais, 1993), autonomy (adapted from Blais & Vallerand,

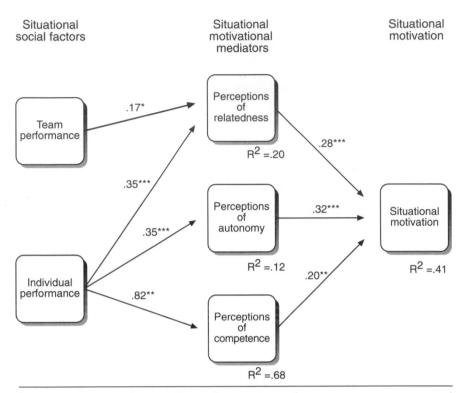

Figure 8.2 The mediating effects of perceptions of competence, autonomy, and relatedness on the relationship between social factors and self-determined situational motivation. Numbers on the arrows are the Beta weights, and R^2 is the percentage of explained variance (*$p < .10$, **$p < .01$, ***$p < .001$).

Reprinted, by permission, from C. Blanchard and R.J. Vallerand, 1996, "The mediating effects of perceptions of competence, autonomy, and relatedness on the social factors–self-determined situational motivation relationship," Unpublished manuscript, Université du Québec à Montréal.

1992), and relatedness (adapted from Richer & Vallerand, 1998); and contextual motivation toward exercising (adapted from the Sport Motivation Scale, Brière et al., 1995). Cadorette et al. (1996) then conducted a path analysis on the data. The results provided support for the mediating hypothesis. Autonomy-supportive behavior from the fitness monitor facilitated participants' perceptions of competence, autonomy, and relatedness toward exercise. In addition, perceptions of the ambiance in the center led to perceptions of relatedness and autonomy. In turn, participants' perceptions of competence, autonomy, and relatedness had positive effects on their self-determined motivation toward exercising. These findings have also been replicated in basketball (Blanchard & Vallerand, 1996c). In sum, the findings on the mediating role of perceived autonomy, competence, and relatedness at the situational level by Blanchard and Vallerand (1996a) were replicated at the contextual level both in sport (Blanchard & Vallerand, 1996c) and in exercise settings (Cadorette et al., 1996).

Finally, no study to date has tested the mediating role of perceptions of competence, autonomy, and relatedness at the global level. As indicated earlier, it is hypothesized that living on a prolonged basis in residences for elite athletes has some effects on athletes' global motivation. In addition, parents who coach their children for several years and thus whose presence is very salient in several of the children's life contexts may also have potent effects on their children's global motivation. By influencing their children's motivation in several life contexts, such parents may eventually produce important effects on their children's global motivation.

In sum, extensive evidence exists for the mediating role of perceived autonomy, competence, and relatedness on the impact of social factors on motivation. However, such evidence comes mainly from the situational and contextual levels. No research so far has dealt with the mediational effects at the global level.

Motivation at Higher Levels in the Hierarchy Can Affect Motivation at Lower Levels in the Hierarchy

In line with the personality tradition in motivation, the Hierarchical Model posits that motivation at a given level in the hierarchy also represents an important determinant of motivation at lower levels in the hierarchy. This leads to Corollary 3.3.

> **Corollary 3.3:** Motivation at a given level also results from top-down effects of motivation at the proximal level higher up in the hierarchy.

The third corollary recognizes the potential top-down impact of motivation at higher levels in the hierarchy on motivation at the next lower level. More specifically, it is proposed that motivation at the proximal level should have stronger top-down effects on motivation at the next lower level than on motivation at a distal level. Thus, contextual motivation should have a stronger impact on situational motivation than on global motivation. Similarly, global motivation should have a strong impact on contextual motivation. For instance, one would expect someone with a global intrinsic motivation orientation to display an intrinsic motivational orientation in different contexts such as education and sport. It is then proposed that self-determined motivation at the higher level will facilitate self-determined levels of motivation at the next level down in the hierarchy. Thus, ice hockey players who display a self-determined contextual motivational profile (i.e., high levels of intrinsic motivation and identified regulation but low levels of external regulation and amotivation) toward their sport are likely to display a similar motivational profile at the situational level while playing their sport.

Corollary 3.3 is in line with recent conceptual work on self-regulatory processes indicating that global properties of the self influence more specific aspects of the self (Brown, 1993; Brown & Dutton, 1997; Sansone & Harackiewicz, 1996). Although there is some evidence for the corollary in settings other than those related to sport or exercise (e.g., Williams, Grow, Freedman, Ryan, & Deci, 1996), much of the support comes from research in sport and exercise settings. Three studies have tested Corollary 3.3 in such settings. In a first study, Blanchard and Vallerand (1998a) were able to show that global motivation assessed at Time 1 was an important predictor of contextual motivation toward an exercise program as measured four weeks later. As predicted, the more self-determined the global motivation, the more self-determined the contextual motivation toward exercising one month later. Two studies have assessed the link between contextual motivation and situational motivation in sport settings. Thus, Blanchard, Vallerand, and Provencher (1998) were able to show that contextual motivation toward basketball in general, as assessed either just before (Study 1) or several weeks before (Study 2) a game, predicted situational motivation experienced during the basketball game. Here again, the more self-determined the athletes' contextual motivation toward basketball, the more self-determined their situational motivation. Overall, the findings from these three studies indicate that motivation can produce top-down effects on motivation at the next lower level in the hierarchy. Although the results are encouraging, all these studies involved correlational designs. Thus, additional research is needed to test the hypothesis experimentally.

The Specificity Hypothesis

We suggest that the influence of social determinants on motivation is specific in at least three ways. First, the effects of the three types of social factors on motivation are largely specific to the corresponding level in the hierarchy (see figure 8.1). Thus, situational factors should mainly influence situational motivation and less so contextual and global motivation; contextual factors should influence contextual motivation much more than global motivation; and global factors should primarily influence global motivation. Although there is no support for this hypothesis in sport and exercise, some support comes from the leisure context. In a recent study (Vallerand, 1996), we assessed the effect of a commonly used situational variable (success/failure) on motivation at the situational, contextual (leisure), and global levels. College students performed a hidden-word task (the NINAs) and were led to experience either success or failure. They then completed the Situational Motivation Scale (Guay et al., in press), the Leisure Motivation Scale (Pelletier et al., 1996), and the Global Motivation Scale (Guay et al., 1996). In line with our reasoning, the impact of success/failure on the task affected situational motivation only, not contextual or global motivation. These findings provide some support for the specificity effect of at least situational determinants.

The second type of specificity effect refers to the fact that situational motivation toward a specific activity (e.g., playing soccer) should be mainly influenced by contextual motivation directly related to this activity (e.g., soccer) and not so much by nonrelevant contextual motivations (e.g., motivation toward school or interpersonal relationships). Research by Vallerand, Chantal, Guay, and Brunel (2000) supports this prediction. In a first study the authors showed that when individuals performed an educational task, their situational motivation was largely determined by their contextual motivation toward education. On the other hand, when these same individuals engaged in a leisure task, their situational motivation was determined by their contextual leisure motivation. In both cases, nonpertinent contextual motivations had very little effect on situational motivation. In a second study, Vallerand, Chantal et al. (2000, Study 2) also showed that when a word-association task was presented to participants as pertinent to the realm of education, situational motivation toward the task was predicted by the contextual motivation toward education. Conversely, when the same task was presented to other participants as a leisure task, situational motivation was predicted by the leisure contextual motivation. In both cases, nonrelevant contextual motivations did not relate to situational motivation. In addition, in both studies, the more self-determined the relevant contextual motivation, the more self-determined the situational motivation. Finally, these findings were replicated in a third study (Vallerand, Chantal et al., 2000, Study 3) in sport settings.

Finally, it is hypothesized that the same reasoning applies to situational events. That is, there should be a specificity effect such that situational events related to the realm of activities being engaged in at a given moment should have stronger effects on situational intrinsic and extrinsic motivation than nonrelevant situational factors. For instance, a swimmer's situational intrinsic motivation toward practice on a Friday afternoon should be mainly influenced by situational events related to swimming, such as having done badly at a swim meet, and not so much by having failed an exam or having argued with a close friend.

We tested this hypothesis in a study with university swimmers (Provencher & Vallerand, 1995). Participants ($n = 23$) were asked to report their usual level of intrinsic and extrinsic motivation (external regulation) during a typical swimming practice. They then were asked to indicate their level of intrinsic and extrinsic motivation immediately following each of the following hypothetical situations: (1) they had had an argument with a close friend; (2) they had failed an important exam; (3) they had performed badly at a swim meet. These are significant events dealing with the three most important life contexts in student-athletes' lives. In line with the specificity hypothesis, it was predicted that the event related to swimming would have strongest effects on situational motivation toward the swimming. Social factors from nonrelevant contexts should have less important effects on intrinsic motivation. Results, which appear in figure 8.3, supported this prediction. While intrinsic motivation was typically higher than extrinsic motivation (external regulation) in practice (in the absence of situational factors), only one situational event reversed this trend: the bad swimming performance.

To summarize, there is support for the specificity hypothesis. Although this hypothesis may appear obvious, it is nevertheless important because it forces us to consider individuals in a multidimensional fashion in order to better predict and explain their motivation. It is posited that social factors at a given level in the hierarchy influence motivation at that same level in the hierarchy. Further, situational events will affect situational motivation to the extent that they are relevant to the activity being performed. Situational events do not only happen to people; they are also experienced

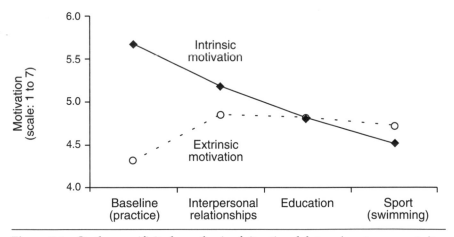

Figure 8.3   On the specificity hypothesis of situational determinants on sport situational motivation.

Reprinted, by permission, from P. Provencher and R.J. Vallerand, 1995, "Situational factors and situational motivation: A test of the specificity effect," Paper presented at the annual conference of the Société Québécoise de la Recherche en Psychologie, Ottawa, Ontario, Canada.

as more or less related to the activity of the moment. When they are relevant, situational factors should influence situational motivation. When they are not, such effect will be minimal. Similarly, contextual motivational orientations may not always affect people's current (situational) motivation. Their effect depends on their relevance to the activity being performed. A woman may be highly intrinsically motivated toward playing the piano in general, but this is not likely to help her enjoy her softball practice on a given Saturday afternoon. If we want to predict this athlete's situational motivation for softball practice on a Saturday afternoon, we need to know about her relevant motivational orientation and the situational factors that are in effect in that situation at that time. In this case this amounts to being able to assess contextual motivation toward the sport (softball) and the factors present on the field at that moment (the drill being performed, the coach's and the other players' behavior, the weather conditions). It is important to note that this is not to negate the potential influence that other contextual motivations and irrelevant situational factors may have on motivation. However, as demonstrated in the studies cited, such forces should have a lower impact on motivation than those directly relevant to the activity being performed.

Recursive Effects: When Motivation at Lower Levels in the Hierarchy Influences Motivation at Higher Levels

A final determinant of motivation proposed by the Hierarchical Model relates to the effects that motivation at lower levels in the hierarchy can have over time on motivation at the next higher level. For instance, one would expect that repeated experiences of intrinsic motivation at the situational level with respect to sport activities (perhaps due to repeated success experiences) should eventually lead to the development of a contextual intrinsic motivation toward the sport. This may explain why Joan's contextual motivation toward tennis, in our introductory example, was becoming more self-determined. Repeated experiences of situational intrinsic motivation, like the one she had on the tennis court when the coach let her determine her own strategy, may have produced recursive positive effects on Joan's contextual motivation toward tennis. In a similar fashion, nurturing self-determined motivation in several life contexts, or at least in a few meaningful ones, should have recursive positive effects on global motivation. This leads to the fourth postulate:

> **Postulate 4:** There is a recursive bottom-up relationship between motivation at the proximal level and motivation at the next level up in the hierarchy.

The fourth postulate underscores that the effects among the motivations at the three levels of generality are not only top-down (see Corollary 3.3) but also bottom-up. This reasoning on the recursive or bottom-up effects is in line with much theorizing in the developmental literature (e.g., Harter, 1985) indicating that more specific elements of the self contribute on a temporal basis to more global self-conceptions. For instance, it is expected that behavior emitted in various situations are contextualized and are eventually perceived by children as describing them in specific areas. Thus, positive experiences in specific settings might lead children to eventually say, "I'm good in sports." Over time, such specific self-conceptions will contribute to general self-esteem (Harter, 1985). We believe that the same reasoning applies to motivation. Bottom-up effects from situational to contextualized to global motivations occur, and they are most likely to take place when individuals start to question their motivation toward a given context. In such instances, when individuals start feeling uncertain (e.g., Swann, 1983) about their motivation, they may be ripe to undergo an unfreezing of their beliefs about their motivation (Kruglanski, 1989). The outcome may be a change in contextualized, or even global, motivation.

Postulate 4, in conjunction with Corollaries 3.1 and 3.3, also allows us to explain how the interplay among the different levels of motivation can account for motivational changes that occur over time. For instance, an athlete who experiences success (Corollary 3.1) and who has an intrinsic contextual motivation toward sport (Corollary 3.3) will be predisposed to be intrinsically motivated at the situational level toward sport activities. In turn, being intrinsically motivated at the situational level should lead the athlete to become even more intrinsically motivated at the contextual level toward sport over time (Postulate 4).

We have tested these hypotheses with respect to basketball. In a first study, Blanchard et al. (1998, Study 1) had basketball players complete the Sport Motivation Scale (Brière et al., 1995) before a basketball tournament, as well as the Situational Motivation Scale (Guay et al., in press) and the Sport Motivation Scale after each of two games of the tournament. Finally, 10 days after the tournament, subjects again completed the Sport Motivation Scale. It was predicted that contextual motivation toward sport (here basketball) and situational factors (individual and team performance) would jointly influence situational motivation right after the first game, which in turn would influence athletes' subsequent contextual motivation. This cycle was expected to be repeated for the second game. Finally, it was hypothesized that situational motivation would influence subsequent contextual motivation after the tournament. Path analytic techniques were conducted on the data, and self-determination indexes were used to assess motivation. As figure 8.4 illustrates, the results supported all hypotheses. First, there was a top-down effect from contextual motivation to situational self-determined motivation. Second, both situational factors (team and individual performance) affected situational motivation. Third, there was a recursive relation between situational motivation and contextual motivation. More specifically, contextual motivation toward basketball influenced situational motivation for game 1, which in turn influenced subsequent contextual motivation. This effect was also obtained after game 2 and at 10 days following the tournament. Finally, as predicted by the model, the more self-determined the athletes' situational motivation in the tournament, the more

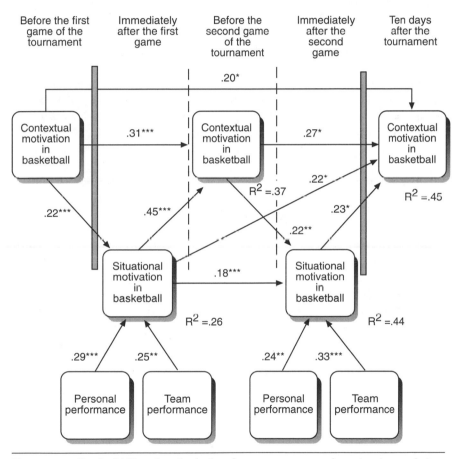

Figure 8.4 On the bidirectional relations between contextual motivation and situational motivation during a basketball tournament: results from the path analysis. Numbers are the Beta weights, and R^2 is the percentage of explained variance (*$p <$ .10, ** $p <$ .01, ***$p <$ .001).

Reprinted, by permission, from C. Blanchard, R.J. Vallerand, and P. Provencher, 1998, "An analysis of the bi-directional effects between contextual and situational motivation in a natural setting." Unpublished manuscript.

self-determined their contextual motivation after the tournament. These findings have been replicated over a season (Blanchard et al., 1998, Study 2).

The same reasoning can be applied to the next level. For example, if for various reasons an individual displays repeated high levels of contextual intrinsic motivation toward exercise, eventually on a repeated basis such changes could bring about changes in intrinsic motivation at the global level. Blanchard and Vallerand (1998a) tested this hypothesis with individuals engaged in an exercise program. Participants completed the Global Motivation Scale at Time 1 (Guay et al., 1996). Four weeks later, at Time 2, participants completed a scale to assess their contextual motivation toward exercise (based on the Sport Motivation Scale of Brière et al., 1995). Finally, four weeks later at Time 3, they again completed the Global Motivation Scale. Using the self-determination index, the authors conducted a structural equation modeling analysis (using EQS) on the data. The results supported Postulate 4. Global motivation at Time 1 was found to predict contextual exercise motivation at Time 2 (Beta = .29), which in turn predicted global motivation at Time 3 (Beta = .23). While global motivation at Time 1 also significantly predicted global motivation at Time 3 (Beta = .50), the Beta weight from contextual motivation at Time 2 to global motivation at Time 3, four weeks later, was still significant. The fit indexes for this model were excellent. These findings replicate those of Blanchard et al. (1998) involving motivation at the contextual and situational levels. It would thus appear that bidirectional relations exist between adjacent motivations at all three levels of the hierarchy.

To summarize, research reviewed in this section provides strong support for Postulates 3 and 4 and their corollaries on the determinants of motivation. One sees that it is quite heuristic to distinguish among global, contextual, and situational factors. In addition, the role of perceptions of competence, autonomy, and relatedness as psychological mediators of the social factors–motivation relationship was strongly supported, especially at the situational and contextual levels. It was also shown that motivation at a higher level in the hierarchy can influence motivation at the next lower level. Finally, the existence of a bottom-up effect from motivation at lower levels (e.g., situational motivation) to the next-adjacent higher level (e.g., contextual motivation) was demonstrated. Postulates 3 and 4 allow us to integrate much of what we know about the determinants of intrinsic and extrinsic motivation and amotivation.

On the Consequences of Intrinsic and Extrinsic Motivation and Amotivation

So far in this chapter, I have devoted attention to the factors that instigate changes in intrinsic and extrinsic motivation and amotivation, as well as the psychological processes responsible for such changes—the determinants of motivation. One may rightfully ask, "Why is it so important to understand how motivation is changed?" One answer is that motivation produces important outcomes. Thus, by understanding the nature and processes of motivational determinants, we can induce positive changes in motivation that will translate into positive outcomes for athletes and individuals in sport and exercise settings. This leads to the fifth postulate of the Hierarchical Model:

Postulate 5: Motivation leads to important consequences.

Some readers may object to the term "consequences," preferring "correlates" instead. However, we feel that it is more appropriate to use the term "consequences" for at least three reasons. First, from an intuitive perspective, it seems appropriate to see variables as diverse as attention, satisfaction, and behavioral persistence as influenced by motivation. For instance, an intrinsically motivated athlete should concentrate more fully during a practice than one who is amotivated. Second, from an empirical perspective, there is extensive evidence that motivation "causes" consequences to be found in sport (i.e., cognitions, affect, and behavior). For instance, Amabile (1985) has shown that inducing extrinsic motivation in writers leads to lower-quality poems than inducing intrinsic motivation or a control condition. Lepper and his colleagues (e.g., Lepper & Cordova, 1992; Parker & Lepper, 1992) have shown that augmenting (or embellishing) intrinsic motivation enhances learning. Moreover, other research provides support for the causal effects of motivation on consequences (e.g., Curry, Wagner, & Grothaus, 1991; Harackiewicz, Sansone, Blair, Epstein, & Manderlink, 1987). Finally, "correlates" presupposes that motivation and outcomes are merely correlated and that there is no causal link between the two. There is then a vague inference that both are the product of some unknown third entity. As the research reviewed reveals, motivation does cause a host of outcomes. Therefore, "consequences" is deemed more appropriate than "correlates."

On Differentiating Outcomes

It would also appear useful to conceive of consequences as cognitive, affective, and behavioral. Concentration, attention, and memory are examples of cognitive consequences that intrinsic/extrinsic motivation researchers have studied. Affective consequences that have been particularly popular include enjoyment, positive emotions, and satisfaction. Finally, choice of behavior, persistence at the task, intensity, task complexity, behavioral intentions, and performance are examples of behavioral consequences that have been studied in the area (see Vallerand, 1997, for a review on motivational consequences).

One important reason for using this tripartite division of consequences, or outcomes, is that distinguishing among the three types of consequences may eventually make it possible to determine the motivation-consequences relations more precisely. Such an enterprise should take into consideration the situation or the context in which individuals interact because it is possible that certain types of motivation lead to different consequences depending on the particular situation or context in which they are operating. Thus, it may be that situational external regulation will not lead to behavior in a free-choice situation. For instance, an athlete may not engage in an uninteresting activity (e.g., weight training) if he or she does not have to. However, external regulation might lead to adaptive behavior (i.e., behavioral engagement) in a highly pressured situation (e.g., if the coach forces the athlete to engage in weight training). But being externally regulated may also produce negative cognitive (e.g., poor concentration) and affective (e.g., feelings of frustration) consequences during performance of the behavior. Thus, the three types of consequences may be negatively correlated depending on the situation or context (see Ryan, Koestner, & Deci, 1991). It would thus appear useful to distinguish among them.

Consequences As a Function of the Types of Motivation

Not only does motivation produce consequences, it is also posited that different types of motivation lead to different outcomes. The self-determination continuum proposed by Deci and Ryan (1985a) is especially useful in making predictions about motivational consequences. Because it is hypothesized that intrinsic motivation, regulation (integrated, identified, introjected, and external), and amotivation lie on a continuum from high to low self-determination (Deci & Ryan, 1985a), and because self-determination is associated with enhanced psychological functioning (Deci, 1980; Ryan, Deci, & Grolnick, 1995), one would expect a corresponding pattern of consequences. Thus, one would expect intrinsic motivation to have the most positive consequences, followed by identification. On the other hand, one might also expect external regulation and especially amotivation to be associated with negative consequences. Finally, introjection should lead to consequences between those produced by identification and external regulation. This leads to Corollary 5.1:

> **Corollary 5.1:** Consequences are decreasingly positive from intrinsic motivation to amotivation.

Testing Corollary 5.1 entails correlating scales assessing the different types of motivation (such as the ones we've developed) with various consequences. For instance, in a series of studies using the Situational Motivation Scale, Guay et al. (in press) reported that situational motivation toward either an educational or a leisure task was related as expected to variables assessing situational consequences, such as concentration, emotions, and intentions to engage in a future interpersonal exchange. Thus, the most positive correlations were obtained with intrinsic motivation, followed by identified regulation. Correlations with external regulation were either negative or close to zero. Finally, correlations involving amotivation were strongly negative. Other research at the situational level has contrasted intrinsic motivation and extrinsic motivation (external regulation) but not the other types of motivation. Such research reveals that intrinsic motivation leads to the most positive consequences (see Deci & Ryan, 1987; Vallerand, 1997).

Consequences at the Situational Level

There has been a recent surge of interest in assessing the link between motivation and consequences at the situational level in sport and exercise. In one study involving basketball players during a game, Blanchard and Vallerand (1996b) found that the four subscales of the Situational Motivation Scale (Guay et al., in press) were correlated as expected with variables assessing situational consequences (i.e., concentration and positive emotions). Results from this study were replicated in a second study (Blanchard & Vallerand, 1998b) with individuals (n = 274) engaged in a weight-loss program based on exercise and dietary changes. The findings of these two studies are shown in table 8.2. As can be seen, overall the most positive correlations were obtained with intrinsic motivation, followed by identified regulation. Correlations with external regulation were either negative or close to zero. Finally, correlations with amotivation were strongly negative.

Also of interest is the recent work by Kowal and Fortier (1999) on the relationship between situational motivation and a different type of consequence—flow. Flow refers to the feeling that one experiences while being totally immersed in the activity (Csikszentmihalyi, 1975). Kowal and Fortier hypothesized (1) that flow is a consequence of motivation and (2) in line with Corollary 5.1, that the more self-determined the motivation, the more positive the levels of flow experienced. In their study, Kowal and Fortier had swimmers complete the Situational Motivation Scale (Guay et al., in press) and the Flow Scale (Jackson & Marsh, 1996) after a swim practice. Results supported the hypotheses. More specifically, swimmers who were swimming out of intrinsic motivation experienced the highest levels of flow

Table 8.2 Correlations Between the Subscales of the Situational Motivation Scale (SIMS) and Scales Assessing Concentration, Affect, and Enjoyment in Sport (Basketball) and Exercise

	Sport (Basketball)[a]		Exercise[b]		
	Positive emotions	Concentration	Positive emotions	Concentration	Enjoyment
Intrinsic motivation (IM)	.74	.37	.79	.51	.81
Identified regulation (IR)	.45	.45	.25	.13	.22
External regulation (ER)	.07	−.04	.03[c]	−.01[c]	.02[c]
Amotivation (AMO)	−.24	−.51	−.11[c]	−.22	−.11[c]

[a] Reprinted, by permission, from C. Blanchard and R.J. Vallerand, 1996, "Perceptions of competence, autonomy, and relatedness as psychological mediators of the social factors-contextual motivation relationship," Université du Québec à Montréal.

[b] Reprinted, by permission, from C. Blanchard and R.J. Vallerand, 1998, "Relations between situational motivation and situational consequences toward exercise," Université du Québec à Montréal.

[c] Nonsignificant, $p > .05$.

during practice, followed by those performing out of identified regulation, external regulation, and amotivation. These results are important at least for two reasons. First, they provide support for Corollary 5.1, as outcomes varied as a function of the inherent level of self-determination of the different motivations. Second, results revealed that flow should be seen as a motivational consequence rather than as intrinsic motivation per se. Most theorists, including Csikszentmihalyi (1975; Csikszentmihalyi & Nakamura, 1989), have never clearly pointed out the relationship that exists between the two constructs. What the Kowal and Fortier (1999) findings suggest is that it would appear more appropriate to consider flow a motivational consequence than to infer that intrinsic motivation and flow are synonymous.

Consequences at the Contextual Level

The adaptive consequences of various types of motivation have also been examined at the contextual level in a variety of life contexts, including education, the workplace, interpersonal relationships, leisure activities, religion, and health (see Ryan, 1995; Vallerand, 1993, 1997, for reviews). The findings of such research show, as predicted, that the most positive consequences are typically obtained with intrinsic motivation, followed by integrated (when assessed), identified, introjected, and external regulation, and finally amotivation. Such results have been obtained with a variety of consequences such as concentration; cognitive flexibility; positive affect; educational, relational, and leisure satisfaction; persistence; performance; conceptual learning; and meaningful relationships (see Ryan, 1995; Vallerand, 1993, 1997, for reviews). Finally, these results have been obtained with diverse populations including children (e.g., Ryan & Connell, 1989), teenagers (e.g., Vallerand et al., 1997), young adults (e.g., Vallerand et al., 1993), mature adults (e.g., Blais, Sabourin et al., 1990), and persons who are elderly (e.g., Vallerand & O'Connor, 1989; Vallerand, O'Connor, & Hamel, 1995). Thus these findings appear to be very robust.

Similar findings have been obtained in the context of sport and exercise. For instance, research involving athletes in different sports (Pelletier, Fortier et al., 1995; Pelletier et al., 2001), as well as participants in exercise programs (Fortier & Grenier, 1999), has shown that behavioral consequences such as effort, intentions to continue in sport, and actual persistence are positively correlated with the most self-determined forms of contextual motivation (intrinsic motivation and identified regulation) but negatively with amotivation (the least-self-determined form of motivation). Similarly, Biddle and Brooke (1992) have found that intrinsic motivation (relative to extrinsic motivation) leads to higher levels of performance by children on a physical education task. Others have also found support for the self-determination continuum (and Corollary 5.1) by demonstrating that a negative cognitive consequence (distraction) was negatively correlated with intrinsic motivation and identified regulation but positively correlated with amotivation (Pelletier, Fortier et al., 1995). Finally, other studies have assessed Corollary 5.1 with respect to affective consequences. Thus, Brière et al. (1995) have related the Sport Motivation Scale to various affective outcomes, including positive emotions, interest, satisfaction, and anxiety. Results from correlations provided support for the corollary.

Recent research has looked at the relations between sport motivation and outcomes with other populations. For instance, Perreault and Vallerand (1998) studied the link between the sport motivation of wheelchair basketball players and their coping abilities. The authors found that the more self-determined athletes' motivation, the more efficacious their coping abilities. Of additional interest is a series of studies involving intellectually challenged children conducted by Reid and his colleagues (Reid et al., 1994; Reid et al., 2001).

Reid and colleagues related children's motivation toward physical activity to various outcomes to test Corollary 5.1. Thus, in the Reid et al.

(1994) study, children's contextual sport motivations as assessed by the Pictorial Motivation Scale (Reid et al., 2001) were related to physical education teachers' perceptions of children's interest, concentration, and positive affect during involvement in sport activities. As predicted, the most positive correlations were obtained with either intrinsic motivation or identified regulation. On the other hand, amotivation yielded the most negative correlations. External regulation typically led to nonsignificant correlations. In the study involving the English version of the scale (Reid et al., 2001), children's motivations were related to teachers' evaluation of the children's effort in sport activities. Again, results provided support for Corollary 5.1. Results of both of these studies are summarized in table 8.3.

Losier et al. (1997) recently adopted a different perspective and have started to study the motivational consequences of other sport participants, namely coaches, at the contextual level. Losier et al. related coaching motivation to various outcomes, including quality of interpersonal relationships

Table 8.3   Correlations Between the Subscales of the Pictorial Motivation Scale (PMS) and Scales Assessing Consequences of Interest, Concentration, Affect, and Effort in Physical Education Classes

	Consequences			
	Interest[a]	Concentration[a]	Positive affect[a]	Effort[b]
Intrinsic motivation (IM)	.21	.15	.22	.38
Identified regulation (IR)	.29	.15	.24	.26
External regulation (ER)	.18	.01[c]	.11[c]	−.05[c]
Amotivation (AMO)	−.53	−.31	−.57	−.17[c]

Note: The consequence scales were completed by the teacher.

[a] Reprinted, by permission, from G. Reid, C. Poulin, and R.J. Vallerand, 1994, "A pictorial motivational scale in physical activity for people with a mental disability: Development and initial validation," Paper presented at the annual conference of the NASPSPA, Clearwater Beach, Florida.

[b] Data from G. Reid and R.J. Vallerand, 1998, "The development and validation of the Pictorial Motivation Scale in physical activity," unpublished manuscript, McGill University.

[c] Nonsignificant, $p > .05$.

with athletes, coaches' sportspersonship orientations, satisfaction with coaching, and intentions to pursue coaching. In this particular study, participants were 472 certified coaches from the Province of New Brunswick (Canada) who were involved in various sports. Coaches completed the Coaching Motivation Scale as well as scales assessing the outcomes just mentioned. Results provided support for Corollary 5.1: the more positive correlations were obtained with intrinsic motivation, and the most negative correlations were obtained with amotivation, followed by external regulation. These findings are important because they reveal that motivation matters not only for athletes but also for other types of participants.

Consequences at the Global Level

Very little research has assessed the link between global motivation and outcomes. In one study involving college students, Guay et al. (1996) found that all three types of global intrinsic motivation on the Global Motivation Scale were positively related to life satisfaction, whereas external regulation and especially amotivation were negatively related. In a similar fashion, Vallerand and Blanchard (1998) found that participants in an exercise program who displayed a self-determined global motivational profile experienced lower levels of negative affect (as measured by the Positive and Negative Affect Scales [PANAS]; Watson, Clark, & Tellegen, 1988) than those with a less self-determined global motivational profile.

Exceptions to Corollary 5.1

Finally, although the bulk of research on the effects of motivation on consequences reveals that intrinsic motivation leads to the most positive outcomes, there have been exceptions. Identified regulation at times has been found to lead to more positive consequences than intrinsic motivation (e.g., Koestner et al., 1996; Pelletier et al., 1996). Although it is too early to make a definitive statement about the reason for this, one potential explanation may have to do with the task. It appears that when the task is typically perceived as not interesting, identified regulation may become a more important determinant of positive consequences than intrinsic motivation. It could be that the most positive motivational force for less interesting activities such as working out with weights in order to better play football, for instance, is identified regulation, while intrinsic motivation is the ultimate motivational force for interesting activities (like playing a football game). Further, it is plausible that certain types of less self-determined motivation (i.e., introjected regulation) may at times lead to some positive effects. For instance, Chantal, Guay, Dobreva-Martinova, and Vallerand (1996) found that non-self-determined types of motivation (external and introjected regulation) were conducive to performance in high-elite adult athletes in a highly controlling culture (the former Communist regime in

Bulgaria). Similarly, in a study on exercise, Rovniak, Blanchard, and Koestner (1998) found that introjection positively predicted the number of days adults went to the exercise center. Thus, although one expects the self-determined forms of motivation to generally yield positive benefits for the individual, non-self-determined forms of motivation may at times also produce some positive outcomes. This latter effect may be likely to take place under controlling conditions (Chantal et al., 1996) and over the short term (Rovniak et al., 1998).

In summary, research reviewed in this section provides support for Corollary 5.1, positing the presence of a continuum of consequences as a function of the different types of motivation. It appears that the most positive consequences are engendered by self-determined forms of motivation (intrinsic motivation, integrated and identified regulation), whereas the most negative types of consequences are induced especially by amotivation and external regulation. Much of this research has been conducted at the contextual and situational level, however.

Motivational Consequences at the Three Levels of Generality

Postulate 2 states that motivation exists at three levels of generality. In line with Postulate 5, we have also seen that important consequences derive from motivation. It thus follows that such consequences should occur at the three levels of generality. This leads to the second corollary:

> **Corollary 5.2:** Motivational consequences exist at the three levels of the hierarchy, and the level of generality of the consequences depends on the level of the motivation that has produced them.

This second corollary proposes basically that the degree of generality of the various consequences depends on the level of motivation that engenders them. Thus, Corollary 5.2 leads to the prediction that consequences at the global level will have the greatest degree of generality (e.g., life satisfaction) and will vary as a function of global motivation. Similarly, consequences at the contextual level will be of moderate generality, will relate to the various life contexts (e.g., education, interpersonal relationships, and sport), and will be specific to the context. Finally, consequences of situational motivation should be experienced at the situational level—for instance, positive affect, levels of concentration, and persistence for a particular task at a specific time.

Corollary 5.2 is important because it encourages researchers to pay attention to conceptual and methodological issues in conducting their research.

Thus, from a conceptual perspective, researchers need to determine the level of generality of the outcomes they seek to predict. Then, methodologically, they need to choose outcome and motivational measures at the appropriate (and same) level of generality. Failing to do so may lead to motivational effects that are weaker than they should be. Similar analyses (Ajzen & Fishbein, 1977) in the attitude literature, for instance, have shown that to predict behavior well, attitude must be measured at the same level of generality as behavior. The same logic is applied here to motivation and its consequences.

Much research provides *indirect* support for Corollary 5.2 by providing strong within-level relations. For instance, as we saw in the previous section, research at the contextual level has shown that self-determined forms of motivation toward sport and exercise are positively related to several contextual outcomes such as attention, positive affect, enjoyment, and satisfaction (e.g., Brière et al., 1995; Pelletier, Fortier et al., 1995). There have been parallel findings at the situational level; studies have shown that self-determined forms of sport and exercise motivation are positively related to situational measures of attention, positive affect, and intentions of behavioral persistence (Blanchard & Vallerand, 1996b; Fortier & Grenier, 1999). Much research in psychology in general leads to the same conclusion (see Guay et al., in press; Vallerand, 1997).

It is important, however, to underscore that these findings provide only indirect support for Corollary 5.2 because each of these studies assessed motivation and outcomes at only one level of generality. To provide more direct support for Corollary 5.2, researchers need to assess motivation and outcomes at multiple levels of generality. It would then be possible to conduct comparative analyses to determine the validity of Corollary 5.2. A recent study by Vallerand and Blanchard (1998) meets these criteria.

In this study, exercise participants completed motivation and consequences scales at various points in time. At Time 1, they completed the Global Motivation Scale (Guay et al., 1996) and the contextual motivation scale toward exercise (an adaptation of the Sport Motivation Scale; Brière et al., 1995). Four weeks later (Time 2), they completed the Situational Motivation Scale (Guay et al., in press) and scales assessing situational consequences dealing with concentration and positive emotions. Finally, another four weeks later (Time 3), participants completed scales dealing with global consequences of general negative affect (from the PANAS scales; Watson et al., 1988) and contextual consequences related to exercise, such as levels of satisfaction with exercise, positive attitudes toward exercise, and actually enrolling in another exercise program in a fitness center. Thus, motivation and outcomes were assessed at the three levels of the hierarchy. Further, for global and contextual motivation, the study used a prospective design (because situational consequences derive from situational motivation, which fluctuates from moment to moment, it is essential to assess consequences as closely as possible to situational motivation—thereby precluding the use of prospective designs at the situational level). Regression analyses were conducted on the data. Results provided support for Corollary 5.2. Global motivation was found to be the most important predictor of global consequences; contextual motivation toward exercise yielded the strongest Beta weights with contextual consequences (related to exercise); and situational motivation was the most important predictor of situational consequences. Further, in line with Corollary 5.1, the more self-determined the motivation, the more positive the outcomes at all three levels. In sum, these findings provide important support for Corollary 5.2, as well as Corollary 5.1.

Finally, we also propose a specificity hypothesis with respect to consequences. Thus, outcomes experienced in one specific context should generally result from motivation in that particular context and not another context. A recent study (Chantal, Guay, & Vallerand, 1998) provides support for this hypothesis. Chantal et al. (1998) showed that contextual motivation toward education (as assessed by the Academic Motivation Scale; Vallerand et al., 1989) prospectively predicted educational consequences (i.e., cognitive strategy utilization and academic satisfaction), while contextual interpersonal motivation (as assessed by the Interpersonal Motivation Inventory; Blais et al., 1994) predicted relational consequences (loneliness and quality of relationships) five weeks later. In addition, global motivation predicted both contextual motivations but did not predict either type of consequence. No study so far has tested the specificity hypothesis of consequences at the contextual level in the realm of sport and exercise.

To summarize, Postulate 5 and its associated corollaries reveal that motivation is particularly important in the lives of individuals, in large part because it produces significant consequences. Such consequences can be cognitive, affective, and behavioral, and take place at three levels of generality in line with the motivation that produces them. In addition, consequences are in general decreasingly positive as we move from intrinsic motivation to amotivation. Finally, a specificity effect, according to which motivation in one context leads to consequences mostly in that specific context, was proposed and obtained.

Integrative Studies

Up to this point I have reviewed evidence dealing with each of the postulates and corollaries of the model. Other research has provided an integrative analysis of motivational determinants and consequences by addressing more than one postulate or corollary in a given study. In this section, I survey some of these studies. We will not review all available evidence; rather we will focus on research germane to the realm of sport and exercise. The reader is referred to Vallerand (1997) for a more complete analysis of integrative studies.

One type of integrative study has looked at how social factors, motivation, and consequences relate in the specific context of sport. In a recent investigation, Pelletier et al. (2001) provided support for the Hierarchical Model in supporting the motivational sequence involving determinants, motivation, and one important consequence at the contextual level, namely, dropping out of sport. In this study, 368 competitive swimmers completed various questionnaires, including one on perceptions of the coach's interactive style dealing with autonomy support and control, as well as the Sport Motivation Scale. During the next two years the authors determined which swimmers persisted and which ones dropped out of swimming. Results from the structural equation modeling analysis (using LISREL) revealed that perceptions of the coach's autonomy-supportive behavior were positively related to intrinsic motivation and identified regulation but negatively to external regulation and amotivation. On the other hand, the coach's controlling behavior was negatively related to intrinsic motivation and identified regulation but positively related to external regulation and amotivation (perceptions of the coach's autonomy-supportive and controlling behavior were unrelated to introjection). In turn, amotivation and intrinsic motivation had, respectively, the most negative and positive impact on persistence over the two years. Similar findings also have been obtained with respect to persistence in handball (Sarrazin, Vallerand, Guillet, Pelletier, & Cury, 2001). Finally, it is important to underscore the fact that in the Pelletier, Fortier et al. (1995) study, the impact of some types of motivation varied over time. Thus, the impact of external regulation on persistence was negligible in the first year but negative in the second, while that of introjected regulation was positive in the first year but negligible in the second.

These findings underscore at least four important points. First, in line with Corollary 3.1, a contextual factor in the form of the coach's behavior was found to influence athletes' motivation. Second, in accord with Postulate 5, motivation affected an important consequence, namely, persistence in sport. Third, the study obtained support for Corollary 5.1 in that persistence was decreasingly positive from intrinsic motivation to amotivation. It should be underscored that similar models have been supported with respect to dropping out of high school (Vallerand et al., 1997) and graduate school (Losier et al., 1996), and in relation to high school performance (Fortier, Vallerand, & Guay, 1995; Guay & Vallerand, 1997). Finally, although this finding was not predicted by the Hierarchical Model, results of the

Pelletier et al. (2001) study showed that the impact of external regulation may become increasingly negative over time. It may be, for instance, that athletes who are externally regulated pursue their engagement in sport as long as their participation is externally rewarded. However, when material or social rewards are no longer forthcoming, they may cease participation. Intrinsic motivation, on the other hand, may become even more important over time. Indeed, sport and exercise participants are likely to stick with something that is enjoyable. A recent study by Ingledew, Markland, and Medley (1998) lends credence to this analysis in an exercise setting. These authors assessed British government employees' contextual motivation toward exercise and stage of change in exercise over a three-month period. They found that extrinsic motivation dominated the early stages of exercise adoption, whereas intrinsic motivation played a major role in the progression and maintenance of exercise behavior. These findings were replicated in a subsequent study (Mullan & Markland, in press) with a broad sample from the general population. It would thus appear that extrinsic motivation (in the form of external regulation) can take you only so far. If a person is to pursue engagement in a sport or exercise activity on a long-term basis, such engagement must eventually become intrinsically motivated.

A second type of integrative study has examined motivation at two levels of generality within the same experiment. For instance, as we saw in figure 8.4, Blanchard et al. (1998) assessed the combined impact of motivation at the contextual level and situational social factors on motivation at the situational level (the top-down effect) and how the resultant situational motivation leads to consequences at the situational level. The investigators (Blanchard et al., 1998, Study 1) found that self-determined motivation toward basketball at the contextual level, coupled with positive personal and team performance (two situational factors), led to higher levels of self-determined situational motivation. Additional analyses not presented in figure 8.4 showed that situational motivation, in turn, led to higher levels of positive affect and concentration. Thus, the integration of motivation at two levels of generality leads to an increased understanding of the psychological processes through which motivation is related to determinants and consequences in sport.

The integrative studies reviewed so far have provided important support for the Hierarchical Model. However, these studies are limited in scope because they involve two levels of generality at best. It would appear important to test elements of the Hierarchical Model by incorporating all three of the model's levels of generality. Vallerand, Guay, Blanchard, and Cadorette (2000, Study 1) performed such a study in the realm of education. Going into classrooms where students were involved in a given educational activity, they assessed students' situational motivation and consequences, as well as their situational perceptions of competence, autonomy, and relatedness. In addition, the authors measured contextual perceptions of competence, autonomy, and relatedness and motivation with respect to the contexts of education, leisure, and interpersonal relationships. Finally, they assessed global perceptions of competence, autonomy, and relatedness and global motivation. Vallerand et al. were then in a position to test the Hierarchical Model tenets that perceptions of competence, autonomy, and relatedness influence motivation at the appropriate level in the hierarchy global motivation influences the three contextual motivations; contextual motivation toward education (but not toward leisure and interpersonal relationships) influences situational motivation toward the educational task being performed in the classroom; and situational motivation determines the three types of consequences. Thus, Vallerand et al. tested all postulates and corollaries of the model except Postulate 1 (on the importance of intrinsic and extrinsic motivation for a complete analysis of motivation), Corollary 3.1 (on the effects of social factors on motivation), and Postulate 4 (on the recursive effects of motivation). Results from a structural equation modeling (EQS) supported the hypothesized model.

Although the findings of the Vallerand, Guay et al. (2000, Study 1) study are important, we should notice that all constructs were measured at the same time. Thus, although competing models were tested and found to be less adequate than the one in line with the Hierarchical Model, the issue of causality remains problematic. In addition, the model was not tested within the realm of sport and exercise. Therefore, in a subsequent study, Vallerand, Guay et al. (2000, Study 3) tested the following model. They hypothesized that fitness participants' (n = 203) global motivation at the beginning of an exercise program would influence their contextual motivation toward exercise at Time 2 (one month later). Contextual motivation toward exercise then would determine situational motivation (toward exercise) that very day, which in turn would produce situational consequences, namely, levels of concentration and enjoyment during exercise. A structural equation modeling analysis (with EQS) was conducted, and results provided support for the model. More specifically, as figure 8.5 shows, global motivation influenced contextual motivation toward exercise (Beta = .31), which in turn had an important impact on situational motivation (Beta = .76). Finally, situational motivation led to high levels of concentration (Beta = .67) and enjoyment (.81). Fit indexes for this model were quite satisfactory.

Results from this study are important for at least three reasons. First, they provide important support for several of the model's postulates and corollaries, including Postulate 2 (on the existence of motivation at three levels of generality) and Corollaries 3.3 (on the top-down effects), 5.1 (on

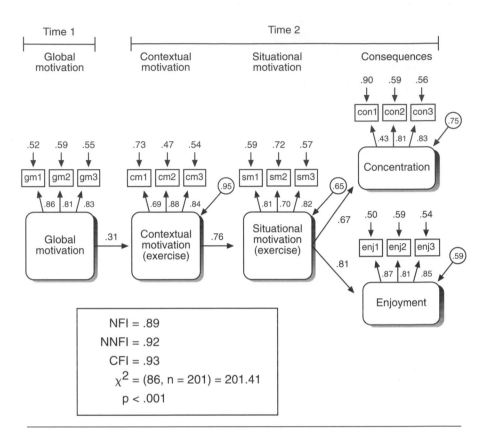

Figure 8.5 A prospective test of the Hierarchical Model of Intrinsic and Extrinsic Motivation in an exercise setting. Numbers on the arrows leading to the shadowed boxes are the fully standardized Betas from the LISREL analyses (all values are significant).

the positive effect of self-determined motivation on consequences), and 5.2 (on the specificity between motivation and outcomes). Second, the findings show that in spite of the complexities of the model, it is possible to test aspects of the model with respect to sport and exercise while involving all three levels of generality. Finally, such research sheds light on the processes that may influence one's thoughts, affect, and behavior at a given time in exercise settings. It would seem that such experiences result from a complex chain of influences that involve motivation at the global (personality), contextual, and situational levels. It would thus appear that future research on the model within the arena of sport and exercise settings is promising. Let us now turn to this aspect.

Directions for Future Research

The research reviewed in this chapter has yielded an impressive amount of scientific support for the postulates and corollaries of the Hierarchical Model of Intrinsic and Extrinsic Motivation. Accordingly, it appears that the Hierarchical Model offers a sound theoretical framework that serves to integrate current knowledge on motivation in sport and exercise settings. In addition, the model leads to novel and unique hypotheses for future research in the area. In the following pages I present a few suggestions for future research based on the model.

On the Interaction Between Personal and Social Determinants of Motivation

A first avenue for future research involves the study of the interaction between social and personal forces in the model. We have seen that at a given level, such as the contextual level, motivation results from social factors at that level (e.g., contextual factors) and personal forces at the next higher level (e.g., global motivation). We know very little about the interactional effects of these two types of determinants on motivation. We need to know whether situational factors (e.g., coaches' behavior) influence athletes' situational motivation differently as a function of their level of contextual sport motivation. A recent study by Richer and Vallerand (1995, Study 2) suggests that this might be the case. In that study, 40 male and female swimmers were asked to complete the Sport Motivation Scale (Brière et al., 1995) as well as scales assessing their perceptions of autonomy, after reading hypothetical scenarios that depicted different coaching behaviors. The scenarios presented the coach as acting in a controlling or an autonomy-supportive manner. Results with the perceived autonomy measure revealed an interaction between athletes' contextual sport motivation and the coach's behavior. When the coach was presented as autonomy-supportive, athletes with a self-determined contextual motivational profile reported higher levels of perceived autonomy than those with a non-self-determined motivational profile. Conversely, when the coach was depicted as controlling, athletes with a non-self-determined motivational profile reported higher levels of perceived autonomy than those with a self-determined motivational profile.

Richer and Vallerand (1995) reasoned that individuals with a self-determined motivational profile are more attuned to social factors that may affect their sense of autonomy than are those with a non-self-determined motivational profile. Thus, when autonomy-supportive social factors are present in the environment, these individuals experience greater feelings of autonomy than those who have a non-self-determined motivational profile. On the other hand, athletes with a self-determined motivational profile would appear to be very quick to pick up on social factors that tend to undermine their autonomy. Consequently, under controlling conditions their perceived autonomy will decrease much more than that of athletes with a non-self-determined contextual motivational profile. However, two comments are in order. First, the findings were obtained with hypothetical scenarios. Thus, the external validity of the findings to real-life settings is uncertain. And second, the results were obtained not with intrinsic motivation but with perceptions of autonomy. Nevertheless, the findings would appear to be in line with past research on interactional effects of contextual motivation and situational factors in laboratory settings (e.g., Boggiano & Barrett, 1985; Loveland & Olley, 1979). Thus, future research on this issue would appear fruitful.

On Motivational Conflict

A second direction for future research involves the dynamic interplay between motivational processes occurring in different life contexts. Of interest is how the different motivations toward two or more life contexts may conflict in influencing situational motivation, thus leading to situational consequences related to one specific context. For instance, if motivation toward school is primed while someone is engaged in a sport-related activity, situational motivation toward the sport activity may be influenced by the contextual motivations toward education and sport. Which contextual motivation will have the most prevalent effects on situational motivation should depend on the relative strength of each contextual motivation and on situational factors in the current situation. Motivational conflict can then arise. Without considering all the conflict possibilities, let us focus on two that result from an approach-avoidance conflict (e.g., Lewin, 1951) in pressured and non-pressured situations. An approach-avoidance conflict occurs when an individual has motivations to both approach and avoid a task. Most research on this phenomenon (e.g., Lewin, 1951; Miller, 1944) has shown that the relative strength of the competing motivations will determine the resultant behavior.

However, the current situation may interact with the contextual motivation in determining the resulting situational motivation. One key situational element to be considered is whether the situation is pressuring behavior in one direction or is pressure free. In line with classic research on conflict, we would predict that in pressure-free situations, the relative strength of the competing motivations will determine situational motivation and ensuing consequences. Thus, if Matt is studying for a dull history exam scheduled for next week and is asked by his friends to play basketball, his favorite sport, chances are that he will go play basketball because (1) his contextual motivation toward playing basketball is more self-determined than that toward school and (2) the situation is rather pressure free (the exam is not scheduled until next week). On the other hand, if Matt's exam were scheduled for tomorrow, then chances are that he would keep on studying. However, during studying, his contextual motivations toward school and basketball might clash. Matt's situational motivation toward studying would then be undermined (i.e., highly externally regulated); and although he would still perform the behavior (i.e., studying) because of the situational pressure of the exam deadline, he would nevertheless experience some negative consequences (e.g., lack of concentration, anxiety, frustration, poor recall, etc.). In other words, priming another context in which intrinsic motivation is high should increase extrinsic motivation (i.e., external regulation) toward the activity to be performed in a pressured situation, leading to some negative consequences, especially if the latter activity is deemed less interesting. As this example suggests, a complete understanding and prediction of situational motivation and ensuing consequences may require knowledge of the motivational strength of more than one life context as well as of situational factors. Future research on this issue would appear particularly exciting.

On Motivational Compensation

The dynamic interplay between motivational processes in different life contexts may also lead to what may be called the compensation effect. The structure of the model, especially at the contextual level, permits the possibility that losses of self-determined motivation in one life context may be compensated for by motivational gains in a second life context. There is some indirect support for this hypothesis. For instance, the work of Taylor (see Taylor, 1989; Taylor, Kemeny, Reed, & Aspinwall, 1991) has consistently shown that most victims of various misfortunes that attack the self seem to react with renewed interest and a sense of meaning in life. There does seem to be a homeostasis mechanism within the self that attempts to regulate and protect it (O'Connor & Rosenblood, 1996). Losses in one life context are countered by gains in other life contexts, presumably to restore a general equilibrium in the self. Perceptions of competence, autonomy, and relatedness may be at the very heart of this psychological compensation mechanism. Because needs for competence, autonomy, and relatedness are fundamental needs that human organisms seek to fulfill (Deci & Ryan, 1985a), one could postulate a compensation mechanism in the self that may serve to regulate losses in any of these perceptions. Furthermore, because changes in one's perceptions of competence, autonomy, and relatedness translate into motivational changes (e.g., Blanchard & Vallerand, 1996a, 1996c; Reeve & Deci, 1996; Vallerand & Reid, 1984, 1988), it can be predicted that a loss of perceived competence, autonomy, or relatedness—and the consequential motivational loss in one life context—should trigger a compensation effect that should lead to the enhancement of perceptions of competence, autonomy, or relatedness and therefore increased self-determined motivation in a second life context.

Blanchard, Vallerand, and Provencher (1996) tested the compensation effect with respect to contextual motivation toward basketball. Basketball players (who were also college students) completed two series of questionnaires: one near the end of the fall term and the second at the beginning of the winter term. Questionnaires assessed participants' contextual motivation and perceptions of competence toward education and basketball at both points in time. In addition, participants were asked in January to evaluate their school performance for the previous term. Blanchard et al. were interested in seeing whether individuals who perceived their school performance as a failure would experience a loss in contextual perceptions of competence and self-determined motivation toward school and whether such a motivational loss would translate into motivational gains toward the basketball context. However, such a compensation effect was expected to occur only for participants who perceived themselves as competent toward basketball (as assessed during the fall term) because it was unlikely that they should compensate in an activity in which they felt incompetent.

To test for the compensation effect, participants were divided into four groups according to whether they perceived their school performance as positive or negative and whether they perceived themselves as competent or not at basketball during the fall term. Results basically supported the hypothesis. Most participants experienced a drop in self-determined motivation toward basketball from the first to the second term. The sharpest decrease in motivation took place for individuals who had experienced a school failure and who perceived themselves as incompetent in basketball. Only one group experienced a small (but nonsignificant) increase in self-determined motivation toward basketball. In line with the compensation hypothesis, these participants were the ones who experienced a negative school performance but who perceived themselves as competent at basketball. This makes sense because only participants who experienced a loss of competence and motivation in education should have been motivated to restore their sense of self and consequently experience an increase in motivation toward a second life context, in this case basketball. These findings are encouraging, and it appears that future research along these lines should prove worthwhile.

On Motivational Consequences

A final direction for future research relates to motivational consequences. Three issues deserve attention. The first is the importance of considering motivation in a multidimensional fashion to better predict consequences. Thus, clearly it is insufficient, for instance, to describe an athlete as extrinsically motivated, because different types of extrinsic motivation exist, some leading to negative consequences and others to positive outcomes. In the same vein, it is now evident that we should not pit intrinsic against extrinsic motivation, because both motivations are present within the individual to different degrees. It may be more useful to uncover which configurations involving the different types of motivation lead to the most desirable outcomes. We have already shown that a self-determined motivational profile, in which intrinsic motivation and identified regulation are high but amotivation and external regulation are low, leads to positive outcomes (e.g., Brière et al., 1995; Pelletier, Fortier et al., 1995; Pelletier et al., 2001; Vallerand & Losier, 1994, 1999). Future research is needed to determine whether other types of profiles (e.g., high intrinsic motivation and high identified, introjected, and external regulation but low amotivation) may also lead to positive adjustment—and if so, for whom and under what types of circumstances.

Second, we need to deal with outcomes other than those studied to date. Past research has typically looked at outcomes such as concentration, affect, and persistence. One outcome sorely neglected by researchers is sport performance. In line with the IIierarchical Model, we suggest that it is important to distinguish between two types of sport performance, namely situational and contextual performance. Situational performance refers to one instance of performance that is currently occurring or has just occurred. Contextual performance refers to a "collection" of performances that may have taken place over time (e.g., over a given stretch or even a complete season). With ability differences controlled for, situational performance should be in large part the product of situational motivation, whereas contextual performance should reflect contextual motivation. In general, it would be predicted that the more self-determined the motivation, the more positive the performance. However, as indicated earlier, it might be that in certain circumstances, under which there is tight control, for instance, less-self-determined forms of motivation (introjected regulation or external regulation) may lead to high levels of performance (Chantal et al., 1996). Clearly, future research is needed on this issue.

In addition to doing research on sport performance, it is also time to redirect at least part of our attention toward interpersonal consequences. One such consequence is the quality of relationships that athletes develop in sport. As is the case with performance, quality of relationships in sport and exercise can be assessed at the situational and contextual levels. In line with research in the field of couple relationships (e.g., Blais, Sabourin et al., 1990), it is hypothesized that the more self-determined athletes' motivation toward sport, the more positive their interpersonal relationships. Research by Losier and Vallerand (1995) provides initial support for this hypothesis. Using the self-determination index of the Sport Motivation Scale with male hockey players, these authors showed that the more self-determined the contextual sport motivation, the more positive athletes' interpersonal relationships with their coach and their teammates in general (at the contextual level). These findings have also been obtained with coaches (Losier et al., 1997). Future research is needed to replicate and extend these findings, especially through prospective designs with male and female athletes and participants in various types of sport and exercise.

The third and final issue with respect to future research on consequences concerns the integrative value of the "social factors → motivation → consequences" sequence for intervention. We have seen that this sequence, inherent in the Hierarchical Model, is useful in predicting the consequences experienced by sport participants. For instance, a controlling coach is likely to undermine athletes' intrinsic motivation and consequently to jeopardize their chances of persisting in their sport (Pelletier et al., 2001). We believe that this sequence has the potential for providing a solid base for the design of adaptation-promoting interventions. More specifically, by intervening on specific social factors, one can nurture (or re-establish) self-determined forms of motivation that will then lead to positive outcomes. For example, Pelletier et al. (1988) developed an intervention program with respect to swimmers' motivation and persistence. The intervention mainly focused on helping the coach become more autonomy-supportive toward his athletes. In line with the motivational sequence, the authors believed that through helping the coach become a more autonomy-supportive individual, the athletes' perceived competence and intrinsic motivation would be enhanced and in turn their persistence would be preserved. Results supported the hypothesis. Thus, the motivational sequence captured by the model merits attention as a catalyst to applied research and useful interventions.

Summary and Conclusion

The purpose of this chapter was to outline the Hierarchical Model of Intrinsic and Extrinsic Motivation (Vallerand, 1997) and to show its applicability to the realm of sport and exercise settings. The Hierarchical Model serves two major purposes. First, it provides a framework for organizing and understanding the basic mechanisms underlying intrinsic and extrinsic motivational processes to be found in sport and exercise settings. Thus, we have seen that the various postulates and corollaries of the model provide a comprehensive picture of the determinants and consequences of motivation. More important, all postulates and corollaries have been empirically supported (see figure 8.6 for a survey of postulates and corollaries).

The second purpose of the model is to lead to novel and testable hypotheses. This is made possible through conceptual and methodological advances. From a methodological perspective, we now have the tools to study postulates and corollaries of the Hierarchical Model in sport and exercise settings. More specifically, we have scales to assess motivation at all levels of the hierarchy. Furthermore, scales now exist to assess contextual motivation toward sport (Brière et al., 1995; Pelletier, Fortier et al., 1995) and exercise (Mullan et al., 1997). From a conceptual standpoint, the Hierarchical Model provides a comprehensive framework for studying

Postulate 1:	A complete analysis of motivation must include intrinsic and extrinsic motivation and amotivation.
Postulate 2:	Intrinsic and extrinsic motivation and amotivation exist at three levels of generality: the global, contextual, and situational levels.
Postulate 3:	Motivation at a given level results from two potential sources: (1) social factors and (2) top-down effects from motivation at the proximal level.
Corollary 3.1:	Motivation at a given level can result from social factors that can be global, contextual, or situational, depending on the level in the hierarchy.
Corollary 3.2:	The impact of social factors on motivation is mediated by perceptions of competence, autonomy, and relatedness.
Corollary 3.3:	Motivation at a given level also results from top-down effects of motivation at the proximal level higher up in the hierarchy.
Postulate 4:	There is a recursive bottom-up relationship between motivation at the proximal level and motivation at the next level up in the hierarchy.
Postulate 5:	Motivation leads to important consequences.
Corollary 5.1:	Consequences are decreasingly positive from intrinsic motivation to amotivation.
Corollary 5.2:	Motivational consequences exist at the three levels of the hierarchy, and the level of generality of the consequences depends on the level of the motivation that has produced them.

Figure 8.6   Postulates and corollaries of the Hierarchical Model of Intrinsic and Extrinsic Motivation.

motivation from a multidimensional perspective. The model makes it clear that sport and exercise participants are not simply intrinsically or extrinsically motivated, or even amotivated, but rather have all three types of motivation to various degrees. Further, we also need to pay attention to motivation at multiple levels of generality (the situational, contextual, and global levels). The model also suggests that we must move from the mere study of athletes (or exercise participants) to the study of whole individuals—who in addition to being athletes or exercise participants are students (or workers) and are part of a social matrix. This means that if we are to better understand their sport (or exercise) motivation, we need to know more about their motivations in other life contexts, such as education and interpersonal relationships. Thus, in line with Rogers (1961), we suggest that only through the careful multidimensional study of motivation at all three levels will we be able to develop a complete picture of the fully functioning individual in sport and exercise settings.

In sum, the Hierarchical Model of Intrinsic and Extrinsic Motivation represents an organizing and integrating theoretical framework to study motivation in sport and exercise settings. It is our belief that this model, and the research we hope it generates, will allow us to better understand the psychological processes underlying motivational phenomena experienced by sport and exercise participants.

Acknowledgments

Preparation of this paper was facilitated through grants from the Social Sciences and Humanities Research Council of Canada (SSHRC), Le Fonds Pour la Formation des Chercheurs et l'Aide à la Recherche (FCAR Québec), and the Université du Québec à Montréal. I would like to thank Céline Blanchard, Stéphane Perreault, and Julie Michaud for their constructive feedback on an earlier version of this manuscript.

Endnotes

[1] Integrated regulation was not included in the Sport Motivation Scale because pilot data based on the interviews conducted by Brière et al. (1995) revealed that integrated regulation did not come out as a perceived reason for participating in sport activities. These findings may have been due to a host of potential factors, including the fact that young adults may be too young to have achieved a sense of integration within the self. Similar findings have been obtained with the Academic Motivation Scale and the Interpersonal Motivation Inventory. Thus, scales assessing motivation at the contextual levels typically do not assess integrated regulation.

[2] The self-determination index is calculated in the following manner. Intrinsic motivation, integrated regulation, and identified regulation items are assigned the weights of +3, +2, and +1, respectively. On the other hand, amotivation, external regulation, and introjected regulation items, because they are conceptualized as less self-determined forms of motivation, are respectively assigned the weights of –3, –2, and –1. It should be noted that all three types of intrinsic motivation are given the same weight (+3) and that the total for the three types of intrinsic motivation is divided by 3 to make it comparable to that of the other scales. When integrated regulation is not used in the index, intrinsic motivation and identified regulation are respectively given the weights of +2 and +1, while amotivation is given the weight of –2. Introjected and external regulation are then added up, divided by 2, and given the weight of –1. In both indexes, the total score reflects the person's relative level of self-determined motivation.

Perceived Control: A Construct That Bridges Theories of Motivated Behavior

Kimberley A. Dawson, Nancy C. Gyurcsik,
S. Nicole Culos-Reed, and Lawrence R. Brawley

Control, conceptualized and measured in many ways, has been shown to be an effective predictor of mental and physical health (Bandura, 1986, 1997b; Rodin, 1986; Skinner, 1996). In sport and exercise, researchers have used a number of theories to examine motivated behavior. Among these theories, several have the notion of perceived control as one of their central constructs.

For example, perceived control has been directly examined as a part of the Lazarus and Folkman model (1984) to study anxiety and stress in sport (e.g., primary and secondary control) and as part of Deci and Ryan's (1985b) theory of intrinsic motivation (i.e., self-determination, self-competence). It has also been viewed as part of expectancy-value models frequently used to examine exercise and sport motivation, as in the case of exercise adherence (cf. theory of planned behavior, self-efficacy theory, or persistence toward a goal [self-efficacy theory and goal theory]). Beliefs about personal control and its outcomes are strongly represented in two of these three theories (theory of planned behavior and self-efficacy theory) and are linked to the other (goal theory). Sport scientists' considerations of these theories within the field's general understanding of perceived control are also represented (i.e., implicitly through the adoption of various approaches to behavior change for the purposes of self-regulating sport and exercise behavior).

However, the area of control in psychology is fraught with confusion because of the multiplicity of concepts, terms, and types of control (cf. Skinner, 1996). Indeed, Skinner's recent guide to constructs of control contains an appendix of approximately 100 control-related constructs. For this reason, we believe it is necessary for sport psychology to recognize perceived control as a bridging concept between specific theories of motivated behavior. We believe that illustrating the bridge between theories is important because of the centrality of control to theories of motivated behavior. We also believe that it is important for the discipline of sport psychology to avoid continued use of independent theories of motivated behavior with little attention to the overlap among them. Failure to understand the overlap would continue to promote a state of theoretical confusion on which we all rely.

The purpose of this chapter is to deal with three theories of motivated behavior in which perceived control is central for (a) the prediction of behavior and (b) behavior-change interventions. These theories have frequently been used to examine sport and, in particular, exercise-related actions. The theories are (1) the theory of planned behavior (Ajzen, 1985); (2) self-efficacy theory—the outcome expectancy aspect (Bandura, 1986, 1997b); and (3) goal theory (Locke & Latham, 1990). Other authors in this volume examine two of these in more depth (e.g., self-efficacy: McAuley, Peña, & Jerome, this volume; goal theory: Hall & Kerr, this volume). However, our purposes are, first, to briefly present each theory as it relates to the bridging concept of control and, second, to discuss research trends and issues in the exercise/sport literature that are related to the theory or to the specific aspect of the theory that concerns perceived control. In addition, we intend to show overlaps as well as distinctions and similarities among the constructs of control.

The research offered in support of each theory is represented by conclusions reported in reviews and by research exemplars; our intention is not to present all-encompassing independent reviews. Such reviews are cited as references.

In the sections of this chapter that relate to each theory, we explain concerns about the conceptualization and measurement of control and offer research suggestions. As well, we clearly identify the issues surrounding control in the theory. To have a frame of reference for these discussions, however, it is important to understand the distinctions Skinner (1996) has offered in her "Guide to Constructs of Control."

Skinner's Framework for Considering Control Constructs: Sets of Distinctions

Two sets of distinctions form the basis of Skinner's framework for examining control concepts. The first distinction is among three aspects of control—objective control, subjective control, and experiences of control. Objective control reflects the actual control a person has within him- or herself and in the social context. By contrast, perceived control is the individual's *beliefs* about how much control is available. Perceived control (subjective) is sufficient to motivate action even under conditions in which no objective control is evident (cf. Skinner, 1996). Competence and contingency are necessary conditions for objective and subjective control. The third aspect of control—experiences of control—refers to a person's feelings during interaction with the social environment while the individual is trying to either achieve a desired outcome or avoid a negative outcome. Individuals are consciously being effortful to obtain a goal. They feel or "experience" the effort as it is expended in the environment to reach the goal or outcome.

The second set of distinctions that Skinner (1996) emphasizes is among *agents* of control, *means* of control, and *ends* of control. In this typology, *agents* of control are individuals (including the self) or groups who exert control; *means* are the routes through which control is applied (i.e., the response in an individual's repertoire of skills). Thus agent-means relationships are characterized by beliefs about the response one can make (e.g., self-efficacy beliefs). *Ends* of control refer to either wanted or unwanted outcomes over which control is applied. Means-ends relationships refer to the link between a cause (e.g., behavior or efforts) and an outcome. For example, causal attributions could represent this link. Agent-ends relationships characterize the degree to which an agent can produce or prevent desired or undesired outcomes.

The most central representation of control is personal control, which involves the self as the agent of control, the individual's actions as the means of control, and the resultant change in the physical and social context as the outcome of control. In this conceptualization, a sense of control requires the self to be viewed as competent/efficacious and the world to be viewed as responsive (cf. Bandura, 1997b).

Importance of the Framework for Sport and Exercise Research

Skinner's clarification is useful in providing a perspective about the conceptualization of control relative to the theories of motivated behavior that we discuss—the theory of planned behavior (TPB), self-efficacy theory (SET), and goal theory (GT). In exercise and sport research, an important question is whether we are understanding, measuring, and interpreting the same aspects of control as conceptualized in these theories.

Understanding the phenomena associated with control is critical if we are to address the issue of adherence/compliance to physical activity (i.e., sport and exercise). Increased physical activity participation, elite sport performance, and health promotion through physical activity are all heavily influenced by adherence/compliance behavior. Thus, practical behavior-change interventions to increase adherence are badly needed. Bandura (1995a) has emphasized the need in relation to health promotion, but his statement applies equally well to sport and physical activity: "This calls for a more ambitious social-oriented agenda of research and practice" (p. 12). As well, if the intention is to use any of the theories we discuss as the foundation for interventions that motivate behavior, it would be important to be certain about *which aspects of control* will be altered, controlled, or measured.

Assuming that there is no difference among constructs of control could lead to oversights that prevent the success of an intervention. For example, failing to diagnose the objective control conditions in a sport context and focusing on intervention solely around subjective control ignores the influence of the objective conditions and relies on the person's beliefs about his/her own control as being accurate. Although it is true that individuals are motivated by their personal beliefs, these same individuals do not ignore their external surroundings. Thus, interventions focused on changing perceived-control beliefs such as self-efficacy will not necessarily succeed if the recipients of the intervention do not believe their skills will yield a desired outcome (i.e., they recognize that there is no objective control or that for reasons beyond their control, the outcome is unattainable). If objective control conditions do not lead to experiences of control (e.g., individuals would not act based on their assessment of actual control), then having actual control may not result in desired outcomes (e.g., the personal aspiration of successful adherence, winning a competition, the social recognition of losing weight).

Overlapping Theoretical Concepts

Some have argued that the models have elements in common (Bandura, 1997b; Maddux, Brawley, & Boykin, 1995; Barone, Maddux, & Snyder, 1997), and these common elements are part of the focus of this chapter. Perceived control is a central aspect of each model in that each assumes that people are capable of forethought, planning, and rational decision making. Each model also assumes that people are goal directed and capable of self-regulating their actions. However, there is still uniqueness among the constructs in that each theory does not account for every aspect of control as described by Skinner (1996). Also, there is still debate about whether self-efficacy can totally reflect all the aspects of the perceived behavioral control construct advanced by Ajzen (1988). Ajzen has acknowledged that self-efficacy does represent a major component of what he conceptualized as perceived behavioral control. The SET has the additional construct of valued outcome expectancies. Outcome expectancy provides another overlapping concept with the theory of planned behavior (Ajzen, 1985). We see this additional overlap in the valued outcomes thought to be a reflection of attitudes toward an action.

The "intention" construct in the theories of reasoned action and planned behavior has overlap with aspects of social cognitive theory (Bandura, 1995b). Bandura argues that cognized goals may be either (a) distal (i.e., broad or global) and serve an orienting function or (b) proximal (i.e., specific and immediate) and serve to regulate effort and guide action. Intentions, according to Bandura, are equivalent to proximal goals. From this perspective, intentions and goals are overlapping. Self-efficacy beliefs (i.e., perceived-control beliefs) influence people's choices of goals and goal-directed activities (Bandura, 1997b; McAuley, Peña, & Jerome, this volume; Maddux, 1995; Locke & Latham, 1990).

The physical activity research evidence would support the notion that efficacy predicts intentions toward an activity (cf. Maddux et al., 1995). In other situations in which positive outcomes are desired and anticipated, the evidence suggests that efficacy and intentions are psychologically distinct, as both efficacy and intent serve to predict exercise behavior (cf. examples later in this chapter; Maddux et al., 1995; McAuley & Mihalko, 1998).

The models we discuss in this chapter are more complementary than different and should be understood as such. Inasmuch as perceived control is a central conceptual bridge between models, there is opportunity to (a) recognize this and enrich our conceptual understanding, (b) consider the exercise and sport research based on these theories as broadly compatible, and (c) consider interventions based on these theories and designed to increase control from a common behavior-change perspective (i.e., common strategies to promote self-regulation).

The Theories of Reasoned Action and Planned Behavior

The goal of social cognitive models, and more specifically attitude-behavior models, is to understand and predict social actions. In recent years, researchers have utilized this theoretical approach in an attempt to understand physical activity behaviors such as adherence to exercise programs. Two related theories that have been frequently applied to the investigation of health behaviors and specifically to exercise behavior are the TRA (Ajzen & Fishbein, 1980; Fishbein & Ajzen, 1975;) and the TPB (Ajzen, 1985, 1988). Although both theories concern attitude-behavior relationships and assume that individuals are capable of forethought and that they make rational decisions about their behavior and its consequences, the focus of behavioral control differs.

The Theory of Reasoned Action

The TRA (Ajzen & Fishbein, 1980; Fishbein & Ajzen, 1975) was developed to explain volitional, or freely chosen, behavior. Thus for exercise, behavior is determined by one's intentions to perform, or not perform, the exercise-related behavior. Intentions are the immediate and sole determinant of behavior in the TRA. In turn, the determinants of intentions are one's attitude about performing the exercise actions and the influence of normative social forces (i.e., subjective norms) on the individual performing the physical activity. These two factors are weighted because their impact on behavioral intention is a function of factors such as the individual's experience and the situational constraints. For example, it is proposed that the specific social context, the proximity of the action in time (e.g., immediate or in the future), and the particular aspect of the activity (e.g., the specific exercise, sport, or behavior) all vary the weighted influence of attitude and subjective norms on the individual's intention to attempt an activity (e.g., exercise).

As the first determinant of intentions, attitudes (i.e., the individual's affective feelings) are a function of beliefs concerning the perceived consequences of performing a behavior and a personal evaluation of these consequences. For example, an individual who regularly engages in physical activity may believe that exercise is important for staying healthy and may highly value this healthy lifestyle. As the second determinant of intentions, subjective norms (i.e., the social pressures to behave in a specific manner) are a function of the perceived expectations of salient others (referred to as normative beliefs) and the motivation to comply with these expectations. In essence, this is an outcome expectation (cf. Maddux et al., 1995). For example, if an individual believes his spouse wants him to remain active and he values this opinion, subjective norm for exercising will be high and thus will positively influence intentions. Figure 9.1 outlines the relationships between the factors in the TRA and the TPB.

As this theory concerns freely chosen behavior, objective control and subjective control are assumed to be high. In examining behaviors with this model, one must therefore assume that control is high (rather than measuring it). Indeed, Ajzen (1985) notes that when control is high, the TPB operates like the TRA. A brief explanation of the TPB will help clarify this idea.

The Theory of Planned Behavior

The TPB (Ajzen, 1985, 1988) is an extension of the TRA with the addition of a single factor, perceived behavioral control (see figure 9.1). This factor was added to take into account real and perceived limitations to performing the behavior. According to Ajzen (1991), perceived behavioral control is thus conceptualized as one's belief regarding how easy or difficult performance of the behavior is likely to be. Underlying this conceptualization are individuals' beliefs about their resources and capabilities. Perceived behavioral control is viewed not only as an indirect predictor of behavior via intentions but also as a direct predictor of behavior. A direct link is hypothesized between perceived behavioral control and behavior for nonvolitional behaviors, such as exercise behavior, in cases in which there

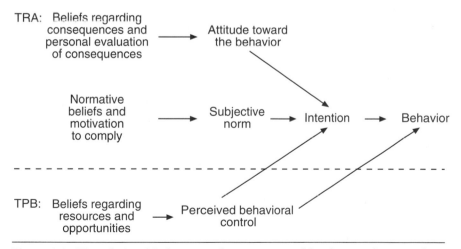

Figure 9.1   The relationship between the constructs of the theory of reasoned action and the theory of planned behavior.

are real or perceived limitations to carrying out the behavior. Thus, if the individual's perceived behavioral control is high, the exercise behavior is more likely to be performed. In contrast, when perceived control is low, the exercise behavior is not likely to occur. Perceived behavioral control is in turn influenced by control beliefs and by the perceived power of a particular control factor to facilitate or inhibit performance of the behavior. Similar to the influence of attitude and subjective norm on intentions, the precursors of perceived behavioral control are weighted and thus have an indirect weighted influence on behavioral intention and behavior.

Physical Activity Research Findings

Research in the physical activity domain has been examined extensively within the framework of either the TRA or the TPB. A number of reviews have elaborated on and critiqued these studies, and thus they will not be re-examined here (see Godin, 1993; Godin & Kok, 1996; Hausenblas, Carron, & Mack, 1997). Rather, we highlight some of the major findings from the reviews and also address some more conceptual issues regarding the research. It is important to obtain some perspective about the findings for the variables within these theories to appreciate the "added value" of the perceived behavioral control construct.

The TRA and the TPB have been successfully applied to the physical activity/exercise setting. Although many of these studies have a number of limitations, recent investigation has supported the relationships within the TRA. In general, attitude and subjective norm explain 30% of the variance in intentions to exercise (Godin, 1993). However, attitude is far more consistently associated with intentions than is subjective norm. The small associations between subjective norm and exercise intentions may be related to one of two factors: (a) the nature of the behavior under study and (b) the measurement and conceptualization of the subjective norm construct.

In regard to the first factor, in many cases the views of significant others may not play a crucial role in an individual's intentions to exercise. However, if we were to study exercise intentions in a different setting, such as cardiac rehabilitation, the relationship between subjective norms and intentions might be stronger. Indeed, social support, or the views of significant others, is an important factor in adherence to the rehabilitation process (Ewart, 1995).

The second factor, the measurement and conceptualization of subjective norms, remains inconsistent among studies. The operationalization of the subjective norm construct may limit its relationship with behavioral intentions, especially for exercise contexts (cf. Godin & Kok, 1996). A stronger relationship between those constructs may be observed if the effects of social influences are measured in terms of the perceived behaviors of others and social pressure received from significant others.

Recent investigations applying the TPB to exercise behavior have generated inconsistent results (Godin, 1993; Godin & Kok, 1996). Of the approximately 18 reviewed studies that have examined exercise behavior, there remains greater evidence for the indirect pathway from perceived behavioral control via intentions to behavior than for the direct pathway from perceived behavioral control to behavior. Some have suggested that this supports the idea of exercise as a volitional behavior. However, whether the direct or the indirect pathway between perceived behavioral control and behavior is supported may be a function of the conceptualization and measurement of perceived behavioral control. We will address this measurement issue later (see also the discussion by McAuley, Peña, & Jerome, this volume). In any case, the addition of the perceived behavioral control construct does explain between 4% and 20% of the variance in exercise intentions, with an average of 8% across studies (Godin, 1993).

It is important to note that very few studies have directly compared the TRA and the TPB (see Bagozzi & Kimmel, 1995; Sutton, 1998). However, the results reported by Bagozzi and Kimmel indicated that the addition of the perceived behavioral control construct increased the explained variance in intentions from an R^2 of .10 to .35 and that in behavior from an R^2 of .04 to .14. These results would seem to suggest that the TPB is a useful extension of the original TRA. Indeed, a meta-analysis revealed that the TPB is superior to the TRA in accounting for exercise behavior (Hausenblas et al., 1997). However, there remains a significantly large portion of unexplained variance in exercise intentions and in actual exercise behavior.

The TRA and the TPB maintain that variables not included in the theory only indirectly affect intentions and behavior through their impact on attitudes, subjective norms, or perceived behavioral control. For example, Ajzen (1988) holds that perceived behavioral control should mediate past behavior's impact on either intentions or behavior because people who have performed the behavior in the past should have developed a feeling of control over performing it. However, research (Valois, Desharnais, & Godin, 1988) and theory (Triandis, 1980) support the notion that past behavior may directly influence intentions as well as behavior. This is not to say that the inclusion of perceived behavioral control is not important. Rather, the point highlights the need to understand how the relationships among the theoretical constructs may change with one's experience with performing the behavior.

Exercise Research:
Issues About Measures, Design, and Analysis

Research on exercise behavior conducted within the framework of either the TRA or the TPB must respect the basic measurement assumptions that underlie the theory. Perhaps the single most important consideration in research within the framework of either the TRA or the TPB is the operationalization and measurement of the theoretical constructs (see reviews and descriptions by Brawley & Rodgers, 1993; Godin, 1993; Godin & Kok, 1996; Hausenblas et al., 1997; Sutton, 1998). Although this consideration is important for all the variables within each theory, it becomes central to selecting the measure that might best represent each construct and the first principles of measurement that are used in a test of theory. As outlined in this section, these points are critical in the choice of a measure to best reflect perceived behavioral control.

The aforementioned reviews of the literature highlight two potential problems that occur with improper operationalization and measurement. First, the researcher may not be measuring what the theoretical construct proposes to measure. For example, a perceived-barriers measure such as "I do not like the way I feel when I exercise" may really be an indicator of the affective component of attitude and not of perceived behavioral control. A second problem that can arise from improper operationalization is that two different variables may be measuring the same thing. For example, if perceived behavioral control is operationalized as "I am determined to exercise three times per week for the next four weeks" and intention is operationalized as "I intend to try to exercise three times per week for the next four weeks" or "I will exercise three times per week for the next four weeks," one can raise a legitimate question with respect to the similarity of measurement. In fact, Ajzen and Madden (1986) used these operational definitions in predicting intention from perceived behavioral control. In such cases, given that the measures are slight variations of the same construct, it is hardly surprising that findings show a strong relationship.

An important issue related to the operationalization of theoretical constructs is consistency across studies. This becomes consequential when one is compiling studies to assess the usefulness of various theories. One must be careful to note the use of different measures of the same variable when comparing study results. The best way to highlight this issue is to consider the conceptualization and measurement of perceived behavioral control. Specifically, the theoretical construct of perceived behavioral control has been operationalized most often in one of two ways. One way is to conceptualize perceived behavioral control using a measure of self-efficacy (cf.

Conner & Armitage, 1998). Thus, if a person's confidence in his/her ability to perform a behavior is high, this is taken as an indicant of greater perceived control.

In a second conceptualization, control has been operationally defined using a measurement of perceived barriers. This measure was used in early investigations based on the TPB. Thus, if the influence of perceived barriers to exercise was high, control was deemed low. Likewise, if the influence of perceived barriers was not limiting, perceived control for exercise behavior was considered high. Reviews of the literature suggest that with proper measurement, either method for assessing perceived behavioral control has received some support (Brawley & Rodgers, 1993; Godin, 1993). However, once again, the method of measurement may have influenced the interpretation of the results (cf. measurement of barriers: Brawley, Martin, & Gyurcsik, 1998).

Although we have advocated the importance of operationalizing a theory's measures as originally conceived, it is equally important to recognize empirical/mathematical problems with the construction of measures that will be used in a test of theory through multiple regression procedures (commonly used to examine the TRA and TPB). Briefly, the calculation of a product measure like the indirect measures of the constructs in these attitude-behavior models may be problematic. For example, the indirect measures are weighted composites of expectancies or beliefs about an action weighted by the value or importance or likelihood of that action (i.e., depending on the nature of each variable). Thus, a belief about the outcome of an action (e.g., physical activity provides cardiovascular fitness) is multiplied (weighted) by the importance of a specific type of physical activity to the individual. Attitude, or perceived behavioral control, is therefore the end result of these weighted beliefs.

The mathematical problem arises because the amount of variance accounted for in a dependent variable by a multiplicative composite varies depending on the numerical scale used to measure each component variable of the composite (Evans, 1991). Thus, the unique variance accounted for by composite predictor variables, such as the indirect measures of attitude, subjective norm, and perceived behavioral control, might well be inaccurate if the scales of the composite are different. Exercise investigators considering the use of Ajzen's (1985) formulation should read the Evans paper carefully before constructing their measures and conducting their analyses. We discuss the multiplicative composite issue and proposed solution in more depth later in the outcome expectancy section of this chapter (see "An Analysis Caveat"); these are obviously important when one is considering how to operationalize and test the construct of perceived behavioral control.

The relationship between intentions and exercise behavior is central to the TRA and the TPB (Courneya & McAuley, 1993). In the TPB, perceived behavioral control can be linked indirectly through intention to behavior in a mediational relationship, as well as being linked directly to behavior. For prediction of behavior within the context of the TPB, intention should be an excellent predictor if (a) enough variability is available in the intention and behavior measures; (b) the instability of intentions is minimized; (c) a high degree of correspondence is maintained between intention and behavior with respect to the action, target, time, and context; and (d) the behavior does not need to be under volitional control (cf. Conner & Armitage, 1998).

Courneya and McAuley (1993) highlight two issues relevant to understanding this intention-exercise behavior relationship. The first is the need to conceptually distinguish between intentions and expectations, which have been confounded in past research. Behavioral intent is the degree to which an individual has formulated conscious plans (i.e., has a goal in mind); expectations are an estimation of the likelihood that the future behavior will occur. Researchers must be careful to assess intentions appropriately, in line with the conceptual definition, to successfully examine the intention-behavior relationship.

A second intention-behavior issue that Courneya and McAuley (1993) emphasize is scale correspondence (cf. Fishbein & Ajzen, 1975). For there to be correspondence, the two constructs must be measured similarly with respect to the action, target, context, and time elements. A lack of scale correspondence results when different frequencies, magnitudes, or response formats are used for the assessment of intentions toward behavior. Courneya and McAuley suggest the use of a scale format, called dichotomous-graded, to provide the most suitable test of the intention-behavior relationship. Thus, intention could be measured with a statement such as "I intend to engage in physical activity at least ___ times during the next four weeks." A corresponding self-report measure of actual behavior would be "I engaged in physical activity at least ___ times during the past four weeks."

A different intention-behavior issue was raised by Fishbein and Stasson (1990), who suggested that the relationship among perceived behavioral control, behavioral intention, and actual behavior may vary depending on the type of behavioral intention measured. In particular, they specify a difference between a self-prediction form of behavioral intention (indicated by "I will" statements) and a motivational form of behavioral intention (indicated by "I want to" statements). They propose that a stronger relationship between perceived behavioral control (e.g., self-efficacy) and behavioral self-prediction exists because the notion of what one "will do" is part of the perceived behavioral control concept.

A final issue has to do with testing behavioral intention as a mediator in the TPB framework. Inasmuch as it is proposed that intention is a mediator of perceived behavioral control via the indirect path to the prediction of behavior, exercise investigators who examine this path should apply correct statistical tests of mediation instead of assuming that intention is a mediator of control. Baron and Kenny (1986) offer methods of doing this with hierarchical multiple regression procedures (a common method of examining the TPB) that allow investigators to draw empirical conclusions about mediation hypotheses involving perceived control.

Finally, application of the TPB to the exercise setting should involve two other methodological considerations. First, to determine the impact of each factor on exercise intention, it is helpful to use a prospective design in which theoretical variables are measured at more than one time. This allows for an ongoing comparison of change in relationships in the theory and comparisons of differences between times for the same variable (e.g., perceived control at Time 1 compared to perceived control at Time 2). Unfortunately, research utilizing this design is scant. Studies tend to focus on self-reported behavior for a single period (e.g., 3-4 weeks, without repeating the assessment process and examining a second period). It is important to measure actual exercise behavior rather than relying solely on self-reported behavior, as many TPB studies have done (cf. Godin, 1993; Godin & Kok, 1996). A more objective measure of activity, although more challenging to obtain, will increase the validity of an observed relationship between intentions and/or perceived behavioral control and the actual behavior.

Concluding Comment

Perceived behavioral control is a concept still under construction in the TPB, but it appears to be most validly and reliably assessed (given the wealth of literature on the topic) through at least one indicant of control—self-efficacy. Indeed, investigators stress that the measurement protocol for self-efficacy must take into account a specificity similar to that recommended for measures in the TPB. Applying target, context, and time elements to the action assessment of self-efficacy is in keeping with the methodological specificity recommended by Bandura (1986), McAuley and Mihalko (1998), and Skinner (1996). Until Ajzen's (1985) concept of perceived behavioral control is assessed in a consistent manner, the use of an efficacy measure as a means of examining one indicant of control may be a "best-practice" recommendation in exercise settings. In this volume, the reader should also refer to the McAuley, Peña, and Jerome discussion of efficacy as perceived behavioral control to gain additional perspective on this recommendation and on the critique we have offered.

The use of efficacy as one indicant of perceived behavioral control is not inconsistent with the recommendations of Maddux et al. (1995), who argued that self-efficacy could function as a bridge between several expectancy-value-type theories. Their argument was that theories do not necessarily have to be pitted against one another if they examine many of the same concepts. In fact, these authors proposed a "revised TPB model" that linked the planned-behavior model with efficacy theory (SET). In this proposal, efficacy and outcome expectancy (i.e., the incentive aspect of SET) were examined, as both constructs were conceptualized in the TPB and in SET. Rodgers and Brawley (1993) presented data from nutrition/exercise/weight-loss clinic participants, suggesting that information from both theories was more useful in providing a clear explanation of the intentions and behavior of participants than information from either theory alone.

Self-Efficacy and Outcome Expectancy

Self-efficacy theory (cf. Bandura, 1986, 1997b) is another social cognitive theory with a direct link to perceived control (see McAuley, Peña, & Jerome, this volume). Recall that perceptions of control revolve around the belief that one can achieve a specific goal. As a result, these perceptions incorporate beliefs about the contingency between a behavior and an outcome (i.e., outcome expectation) and beliefs in one's ability to perform the specific behavior (i.e., self-efficacy expectation: cf. Maddux, 1995).

In the health, exercise, and sport psychology domains, a plethora of research studies involving SET have examined the impact of self-efficacy beliefs on such behaviors as wrestling performance, adherence to exercise programs for the aged and for healthy and diseased populations, and on perceptions such as pain tolerance (e.g., Buckelew, Murray, Hewett, Johnson, & Huyser, 1995; DuCharme & Brawley, 1995; Kane, Marks, Zaccaro, & Blair, 1996; Kaplan, Atkins, & Reinsch, 1984; McAuley & Katula, 1998). For a thoughtful and more detailed discussion of research involving self-efficacy beliefs about behavior, refer to the chapter by McAuley, Peña, and Jerome in this volume, as well as a review by McAuley and Mihalko (1998).

In contrast to the research on efficacy beliefs, relatively minimal sport and exercise research has examined the impact of outcome expectations (independent of and in conjunction with self-efficacy beliefs) on the dependent variable of interest. Bandura (1986, 1997b) defined outcome expectations as beliefs concerning the likely consequences of a behavior. Thus, outcomes are not the behavioral performance itself; rather they result from the behavior. For example, jogging for 45 min each day is the behavior (in which one is confident), whereas the resultant weight loss and muscle gain, and the social compliments that arise from these changes in physical appearance, are the outcomes. In general, Bandura (1997b) suggested that outcome expectations can take three major forms: (1) the physical outcomes of the behavior, (2) the social outcomes of the behavior, and (3) self-evaluative reactions to the behavior. Within each type of outcome, positive and negative expectations can exist and can serve as either incentives or disincentives of behavioral performance.

Self-efficacy theory conceptually distinguishes between outcome expectations and self-efficacy beliefs and suggests that incentives (i.e., outcome expectancies) are necessary for self-efficacy to impact behavior (cf. Bandura, 1986, 1997b). However, it has been suggested that outcome expectations do not explain significant variation, beyond that explained by self-efficacy when one is predicting behaviors in which outcomes are highly contingent on the quality of performance (Bandura, 1986, 1997b). In these situations, how well an individual expects to perform (i.e., self-efficacy) also determines the outcomes the individual expects. For example, someone who is highly confident that she can run faster than any other competitor in the 100 m dash at the Olympics will also expect to receive, if she is successful, social outcomes (e.g., recognition) and monetary rewards (e.g., product-endorsement packages, sponsorship). These outcome expectations occur directly as a result of the runner's performance and thus would not significantly contribute beyond self-efficacy beliefs to the prediction of running performance.

In contrast, many outcomes in the health, exercise, and sport areas are not directly determined by the quality of performance. The lack of contingency between performance and outcomes can occur in one of two ways. First, a lack of contingency can exist when extraneous factors, in addition to performance quality, impact sought-after outcomes. For example, an individual may exercise 40 min each day to lose weight (and gain the outcome of social approval) but not shed any pounds because he has maintained a high-fat, high-calorie diet (i.e., extraneous factor). Second, a lack of contingency can occur when there is no behavior that can produce the desired outcomes. For example, in the sport setting, a 35th-ranked basketball team may play the best game of their season and still lose to their top-ranked opponent. Thus, when there is a direct lack of contingency between performance quality and outcomes, outcome expectations may be an important predictor of behavior accounting for explained variance in addition to that predicted by self-efficacy (cf. Bandura, 1986, 1997b).

Bandura (1995b) also distinguishes "attainment markers" from outcome expectations. An attainment marker is a level of attainment such as losing x pounds, running x seconds faster in a race, smoking x fewer cigarettes than last week, or exercising x more times than last week. An outcome expectation is what arises as a function of reaching that "marker"—for example, an outcome expectation of *positive self-evaluation* after losing x pounds, or *social approval* after running faster, or *feeling more fit and invigorated* or *tired and fatigued* after completing consecutive days of difficult exercise bouts. For additional distinctions, readers may also refer to Maddux (1995).

To place this discussion into the context of perceived control, a reminder about Skinner's (1996) taxonomy of concepts may be useful. Specifically, in her review Skinner suggested that perceptions of control involve (a) agent-means relations and (b) means-ends relations. Agent-means relations concern the perception that a particular mean (e.g., behavior, cognition, effort) is available to a particular agent. Within SET, the agent-means aspect of perceived control can be assessed through efficacy beliefs (i.e., belief that a particular behavior, cognition, or the like is available to an individual). In contrast, means-ends relations concern the perception that a particular mean produces one or more particular outcomes. Clearly, in SET, means-ends relations can be assessed through outcome expectations.

Although it has been generally accepted that perceived control involves perceptions of competence (i.e., agent-means) and contingency (i.e., means-ends), one shortcoming in many perceived-control studies is that both of these control aspects are not always assessed (cf. Skinner, 1996). If either competency or contingency perceptions are excluded, an overall measure of perceived control is not obtained. Consequently, it does not become entirely clear how perceptions of high or low control influence motivation and actual behavior.

Physical Activity Research on Outcome Expectations

The few studies that have examined outcome expectancy in conjunction with self-efficacy without confounding the two constructs have shown both variables to independently predict various types of behavioral intentions (e.g., weight training: Rodgers & Brawley, 1996; structured exercise class: Rodgers, 1992; interpersonal assertiveness techniques: Maddux, Norton, & Stoltenberg, 1986). At the same time, in the health, exercise, and sport domains, relatively few studies with proper operational definitions of self-efficacy and outcome expectancy have addressed the independent predictiveness of these constructs on *actual* behavior (cf. Maddux, 1995; McAuley & Mihalko, 1998). However, results from these studies measuring both constructs are promising. For example, Rodgers and Poag-DuCharme (1993) found that self-efficacy and outcome expectations were independent predictors of attendance at structured exercise classes. Thus, in the health, exercise, and sport domains, there is limited evidence indicating that self-efficacy and outcome expectations have independent motivational influences on behavioral intentions and actual behavior. Consequently more research is needed to determine the reliability of these findings in all three domains.

As well, more research is needed to identify (a) when it is that outcome expectations exert a stronger influence on behavioral intention and actual behavior than self-efficacy and (b) what specific type(s) of outcome expectations is (are) most influential (cf. Rodgers & Brawley, 1996; Sexton & Tuckman, 1991; Sexton, Tuckman, & Crehan, 1992). For example, social cognitive theory suggests (cf. Bandura, 1986) that when individuals are beginning a new behavior, for example, starting exercise or enrolling in a cardiac rehabilitation program that uses exercise as a treatment prescription, outcome expectations should play a larger role than efficacy beliefs in helping to motivate the behavior. On the other hand, as an individual gains mastery experience, efficacy beliefs should be more influential.

Understanding when the relationships among efficacy, outcome expectations, and behavior occur is important especially for the design of intervention programs aimed at increasing adherence to various health and exercise programs. If immediately achievable outcome expectations are important early in the exercise and behavior-change component of a cardiac rehabilitation program (e.g., feeling less tired, having more energy), one may implement an intervention that helps people identify their progression toward these outcomes as well as more distant, salient health outcomes. However, as individuals progress through the program and efficacy beliefs become more influential, interventions aimed at providing mastery, vicarious, verbal, affective, and physiological experiences may encourage self-efficacy for adherence. Clearly, it is necessary to assess multiple measures of outcome expectations and self-efficacy beliefs over time to understand the dynamic relationship between these cognitions and motivated behavior (cf. Poag-DuCharme, 1993; Rodgers & Brawley, 1993; Sexton & Tuckman, 1991; Sexton et al., 1992).

Concerning outcome type, it may be important to focus on which specific types have the most influence on motivation and behavior at various times. Recall that Bandura (1997b) classified outcomes into three major forms—(a) pleasant or aversive physical outcomes, (b) the positive/negative social reactions of other individuals, and (c) one's positive and negative self-evaluative reactions to personal behavior. For example, an individual may engage in a regular program of exercise because he expects that the exercise will help him lose 10 lb (4.5 kg), which in turn may encourage social reinforcement about his improved appearance. However, once he has lost the weight, it would be erroneous to assume that this particular outcome alone would continue to contribute to his motivation and behavior. It may be that other outcomes, such as feelings of less tiredness and less stress after exercise, contribute to his continued behavior.

As for determining what types of outcome expectations are influential, the specific types that fall within Bandura's (1997b) classification in the exercise literature have been identified as (a) physical (e.g., weight control, increased muscle strength), (b) social (e.g., meeting new people, socializing with friends), and (c) psychological (e.g., feeling energized, having more self-confidence), which may be considered as part of either physical, social, or self-evaluative outcomes, respectively. However, continued research is needed to determine whether these three types of outcomes are consistent within and across various exercise populations (e.g., structured exercise, unstructured exercise). As well, research is needed to identify salient outcomes for other health-related and sport behaviors (e.g., cardiac rehabilitation, basketball).

Another issue linked to outcome type is the directness of the relationship between outcome and performance. Primary outcomes have been defined as those that occur as a direct result of the behavior (cf. Poag-DuCharme, 1993; Rodgers & Brawley, 1993, 1996). Primary outcomes can be (a) acute, occurring immediately after the behavior (e.g., feeling less tense, more relaxed) or (b) distal, occurring as a result of adherence over a lengthier time (e.g., loss of 5 lb [2.3 kg], increased muscle mass). In contrast to these primary outcomes, secondary outcomes result from the achievement of a primary outcome (cf. Poag-DuCharme, 1993; Rodgers & Brawley, 1993, 1996). For example, an individual may expect to obtain more social compliments as a result of achieving her primary outcome of weight loss. None of these categorizations are inconsistent with the three forms outlined by Bandura (1997b). They are simply labels that refer to when outcomes occur relative to the behavior.

Although only a few studies in the exercise, health, and sport domains have examined the outcome expectancy aspect of SET (Bandura, 1997b), evidence suggests that the type of the outcome (i.e., physical, social, self-evaluative) and its classification as primary or secondary influence intention and behavior (e.g., Gyurcsik, Brawley, & Martin, 1997; Poag-DuCharme, 1993; Rodgers & Brawley, 1996). For example, Rodgers and Brawley found that beginners' intention to weight train was predicted by (a) primary physical outcomes and (b) secondary physical, psychological, and appearance outcomes. In addition, Gyurcsik et al. (1997) found that primary *acute* outcomes significantly predicted attendance to structured exercise classes at two times for a group of experienced exercisers.

The Value of Outcomes

One reason outcome expectations have not always been assessed in the exercise, health, and sport literature is an assumption on the part of researchers that most of this behavior is highly motivated and thus incentives are always operating. However, the importance of an outcome and the degree of its influence may have a great deal of variability among individuals, particularly when they are beginning new activities. Thus, it is important not to make the assumption that outcomes always act as incentives for motivated behavior (cf. Maddux, 1995; Poag-DuCharme, 1993; Rodgers & Brawley, 1996). One needs to measure the incentive aspects (i.e., value) of behavioral outcomes to examine their differential influence on behavior, because some outcomes may not be as highly valued as others. Indeed, social cognitive theory (cf. Bandura, 1986) suggests that individuals—even highly efficacious individuals—will not carry out a specific behavior if the associated incentive is low. For example, individuals who more highly value the outcomes associated with smoking (e.g., appetite suppression, socializing with other smokers) than the outcomes associated with smoking cessation (e.g., lower blood pressure, decreased risk of specific types of cancer) would not be motivated to stop smoking even though they may be highly efficacious in their abilities to do so. Not measuring outcome value might lead to the erroneous conclusion that efficacy and outcome expectations (assessed without the value component) are not predictive of behavior when in fact individuals do not value the behavior and thus are very unlikely to perform it even when confident that they can.

Several studies have addressed this issue through the measurement of the value or importance of outcomes to individuals (e.g., Blalock, Bunker, & DeVillis, 1994; Maddux et al., 1986; Poag-DuCharme, 1993; Rodgers & Brawley, 1991, 1996). As a result, outcome value has been proposed as a component of SET (cf. Maddux et al., 1986; Manning & Wright, 1983; Rodgers & Brawley, 1996); this is in keeping with the theoretical foundation, which highlights the importance of incentive in influencing motivated behavior (cf. Bandura, 1986, 1997b). In addition, this notion is similar to that in other expectancy-value theories (e.g., protection motivation: Maddux & Rogers, 1983; TRA: Fishbein & Ajzen, 1975; TPB: Ajzen, 1985) that assess (a) the expectations that a behavior will produce certain outcomes and (b) the value of these outcomes.

Measuring Valued Outcomes

In the social psychological and exercise science research, outcome value has been operationally defined in one of two ways. First, it has been measured as an independent variable within the SET framework (e.g., Blalock et al., 1994; Maddux et al., 1986; Sexton et al., 1992). When assessed as such, outcome value has been found to be a significant independent predictor of behavioral intentions (e.g., use of assertiveness training technique: Maddux et al., 1986) and to be significantly and positively associated with psychological distress in burn victims (Blalock et al., 1994).

Second, outcome value has been combined in a multiplicative fashion with the likelihood that a behavior will produce specific outcomes to provide an overall indicant of outcome expectancy (e.g., Desharnais, Bouillon, & Godin, 1986; Poag-DuCharme, 1993; Rodgers, 1992; Rodgers & Brawley, 1991, 1993, 1996; Sexton & Tuckman, 1991). As outlined by Rodgers and Brawley (1996), there are several reasons for this operationalization. First, in the health and exercise domain, it would be remiss to expect outcome expectations to predict behaviors among those who do not value the associated outcomes (cf. Lau, Hartman, & Ware, 1986). Second, this weighted measure better captures the joint influence of value and likelihood. And third, this operationalization is consistent with other expectancy-value approaches when individuals are dealing with uncertain outcomes. For example, in the theories of reasoned action/planned behavior (cf. Ajzen, 1985; Fishbein & Ajzen, 1975), a measure of attitudes is derived by a weighted influence of the expected consequences of a behavior and the importance of these consequences.

In the exercise setting, Rodgers and Brawley (1991) assessed outcome expectations for female beginner weight trainers as a weighted influence of likelihood and value. They found that the likelihood and value constructs were not isomorphic, which indicated that two independent aspects of outcome expectations were being assessed. They also found that the weighted measure better captured the motivating potential of various outcomes than an unweighted measure of expectancy (i.e., likelihood alone). For example, although the subjects rated the likelihood of strength gains as quite high (i.e., 73% on a 0-100% scale), they ranked the associated value lower than other outcomes. This implies that if only likelihood had been used as an indicant of outcome expectancy, the motivating aspect of strength gains would have been misrepresented in this sample (i.e., too high). In addition, other research has found the weighted measure of outcome expectations to be predictive of exercise intention and behavior (e.g., Poag-DuCharme, 1993; Rodgers, 1992; Rodgers & Brawley, 1996).

An Analysis Caveat

Although this evidence indicates that outcome expectancy may be assessed through the multiplicative composition of outcome likelihood and outcome value, a statistical flag must be waved. Specifically, past researchers have calculated the overall outcome expectancy value as a sum of all of the multiplicative outcome expectancy composites. This calculation is problematic because the size of the correlation and thus the amount of variance accounted for in a criterion variable by a multiplicative composite vary depending on the numerical scale used to measure each component variable (cf. Evans, 1991). Specifically, the standard deviation of each composite (i.e., outcome likelihood × outcome value) varies depending on the means and standard deviations of its component variables.

As a solution, Evans (1991) suggested a three-step multiple regression analysis. In the first step, the criterion is regressed on each of the items of the first component variable (e.g., 10 outcome likelihood items). Second, the criterion is regressed on each item of the second component variable (e.g., 10 outcome value items). In the last step, the criterion is regressed on each of the multiplicative composite items (e.g., 10 outcome likelihood items × 10 outcome value items). If the amount of variance accounted for in the criterion going from step two to step three is significant (i.e., R^2 change), then the multiplicative composite model is better than the additive model (see Evans, 1991). However, one limitation with this method of analysis is the sample-size requirements needed to maintain power. For example, to detect a medium effect size at an alpha of .05 in a regression involving 10 outcome expectations and therefore 30 variables, a sample size of 187 is needed (cf. Green, 1991). This number escalates to 1247 for detection of a small effect size.

However, another approach to the use of multiple regression analysis may be appropriate. This type of analysis involves first calculating three predictor variables: (a) the sum of the first component variable (e.g., sum of 10 outcome likelihoods), (b) the sum of the second component variable (e.g., sum of 10 outcome values), and (c) an interaction term derived from multiplying the sum of the first component variable (i.e., outcome likelihood scale) by the sum of the second component variable (i.e., outcome value scale). Then, the criterion is regressed on each of these three variables, with the interaction term always being entered last. This analysis is the same as testing for moderation (cf. Baron & Kenny, 1986), which suggests that if the interaction term is significant, then the interaction of the two summed variables adds unique variance to the prediction of the criterion variable.

When measured and also analyzed correctly, the weighted measure of likelihood and value or its independent components may be an interesting approach to examining (a) when "incentive" makes a difference in the prediction of behavior, (b) what type of incentive makes a difference, and (c) which target samples exhibit this difference. Obviously, more of this type of research is required in the exercise and sport domains.

Summary: Outcome Expectations

When examining individuals' perceived control over their health, exercise, and/or sport behaviors, it is important to consider the influence that self-efficacy and outcome expectations have on behavioral intention and actual behavior. Indeed, the majority of outcomes in these domains are not directly contingent on the quality of behavioral performance. Rather, many extraneous factors have the potential to impact outcomes in addition to performance quality. For example, in the health domain, an individual may adhere to his physiotherapy program for treatment of shinsplints, but if he continues with his daily regimen of high-intensity activities (e.g., running), his shinsplints will not heal. In other cases, no matter how well the person performs the behavior, the outcomes may not occur. In a sport setting, for example, an individual may train as hard as she can for a marathon but not achieve the outcome of a first-place performance because her competitors are faster. According to SET (cf. Bandura, 1986, 1997b), in both these cases, outcome expectations may explain further variation in motivation and behavior in addition to efficacy beliefs.

When conducting this research, one must remain cognizant of not only the conceptual but also the operational distinction between self-efficacy expectations and outcome expectations. Consequently the independent influence of both variables may be illuminated. In addition, it is important to continue to build on recent research showing that there are specific forms of efficacy and outcome expectancies that are important predictors of motivated behavior. A final issue that has yet to be clearly resolved involves the measurement of outcome expectations. As previously suggested (cf. Maddux et al., 1995; Weinstein, 1993), we may be at the point at which it would be beneficial to examine how various social cognitive theories/models have measured common variables. Existing studies that have used various theories or models to measure outcome expectations have taken into account outcome likelihood and value (e.g., theory of reasoned action/planned behavior: Fishbein & Ajzen, 1975; Ajzen, 1985; protection motivation: Rogers, 1975; health belief model: Janz & Becker, 1984). Thus, it may be useful to continue with the same measurement of outcome expectations within the SET framework so that it is possible to compare the influence of outcome expectations on motivated behavior across theoretical frameworks. In so doing, one must keep in mind the appropriate statistical method for analyzing multiplicative composites such as outcome expectations (see Evans, 1991).

Cognitive Efficacy

It is important to understand that efficacy beliefs and outcome expectations for behaviors do not constitute all factors that contribute to perceptions of control over motivated behavior. Indeed, myriad other factors, such as thoughts (e.g., about barriers, benefits), affective states, physiological states, and powerful others, may contribute to perceptions of control (cf. Bandura, 1997b; Skinner, 1996). For example, when attempting to control stress, individuals employ cognitive and behavioral coping strategies (Lazarus & Folkman, 1984). These strategies can be problem focused (i.e., coping directed at the problem causing the stress) or emotion focused (i.e., controlling emotional responses to the stress). In the sport setting, Gould, Eklund, and Jackson (1993) found that the most prevalent strategy among high-level wrestlers for controlling stressful situations was thought control.

In relation to this latter finding, social cognitive theory (cf. Bandura, 1986) suggests that thoughts are one tool of self-influence for motivated behavior. Specifically, since future behavior is guided by forethought and anticipation of consequences, having control over one's thoughts may have important impacts on motivated behavior in various domains (cf. Bandura, 1997b; Maddux, 1995). This implies that thoughts may influence *cognitive self-efficacy* beliefs that in turn have an impact on motivation and actual behavior. Although researchers have paid much attention to various forms of behavioral self-efficacy as it influences sport performance and health- and exercise-related behavior, few investigations in exercise science have examined cognitive self-efficacy and thus this aspect of perceived control.

Cognitive self-efficacy is defined as confidence in one's ability to exercise control over one's thoughts (Maddux, 1995; Ozer & Bandura, 1990). Research on individuals' abilities to control their thoughts has taken place mainly in populations experiencing anxiety or depression (e.g., Kent, 1987; Kent & Gibbons, 1987), as well as in populations with more chronic psychological disorders (e.g., obsessive intrusions: Purdon & Clark, 1994; obsessive-compulsive disorders: Amir, Cashman, & Foa, 1997; phobias: Muris, Merckelbach, Horselenberg, Sijsenaar, & Leeuw, 1997). The majority of this research has focused on (a) identifying the thought content of individuals and/or (b) the use of various interventions (e.g., thought suppression) that prevent negative ruminations and therefore encourage behavioral (e.g., for phobias) or psychological (e.g., for depression) change. In general, findings indicate that populations with these disorders experience a high frequency of negative thoughts and have a difficult time controlling these thoughts. In addition, evidence suggests that it is not the frequency of negative thoughts but efficacy in controlling them that influences behavior and the incidence of other variables such as anxiety (e.g., Kent, 1987; Kent & Gibbons, 1987; Ozer & Bandura, 1990).

Controlling Thoughts About Sport, Health, and Exercise Behavior

The importance of thought control has been alluded to in the sport literature through research on the use of cognitive techniques (e.g., self-talk, thought stoppage, countering) for improving athletes' performances (cf. Bunker, Williams, & Zinsser, 1993). Thought stoppage involves the elimination of negative thoughts through the use of a trigger (e.g., a word, a physical action) to stop or interrupt them. Countering thoughts involves recognizing that one is experiencing a negative thought and immediately countering it with a positive thought. In recent studies, Gould and his colleagues (e.g., Gould, Eklund, & Jackson, 1993; Gould, Finch, & Jackson, 1993) found that thought control was one technique prevalent among high-level athletes for controlling stress. For these athletes, thought control entailed such techniques as positive thinking, thought stoppage, focusing on what can be controlled, and rational self-talk. Future research should focus on efficacy beliefs in studies that examine (a) whether thought-control strategies increase cognitive self-efficacy that in turn has positive impacts on performance; and (b) which specific thought-control strategies have the greatest positive impacts on cognitive self-efficacy.

In the health domain, recent investigations have highlighted the influence that thoughts have on health-related variables. For example, Aydin (1997) found that negative automatic thoughts were positively correlated with physical illness (e.g., coughs, dizziness, headaches). Others have found that an increase in negative thoughts predicts increased pain levels as well as differences in psychosocial and functional adjustment in adults with sickle cell disease (Gil, Abrams, Phillips, & Keefe, 1989; Gil, Abrams, Phillips, & Williams, 1992; Gil et al., 1995). Although preliminary, these results have not only begun to illuminate the role of thoughts with respect to certain health-related variables, they also point to the potential health-related benefits of thought control. For example, people in a cardiac rehabilitation program who are able to control their negative thoughts (e.g., my heart can't handle the exercise; I feel too tired to exercise) about the prescribed exercise may be more motivated to adhere than those who have little confidence in their ability to control such anxiety-producing thoughts.

In the exercise domain, research has addressed the acute thoughts that individuals have when deciding whether to exercise as planned. For these people, exercise behavior is not habitual; therefore, they may experience myriad thoughts when contemplating exercise (see Maddux et al., 1995) that may operate to encourage (i.e., a high frequency of positive thoughts) or discourage (i.e., a high frequency of negative thoughts) exercise intention and behavior. As a first step in examining acute exercise-related thoughts, Kendzierski and Johnson (1993) developed the 25-item Exercise Thoughts Questionnaire to identify the frequency with which individuals experienced negative thoughts when deciding whether to exercise as planned. Results showed that the frequency of negative exercise thoughts experienced by healthy college students in the past week was negatively correlated with their exercise intention and self-reported behavior during that week. In addition, thought frequency was negatively correlated with self-reported exercise behavior three months later.

Although these correlational findings suggest that acute negative thoughts have a role in influencing exercise behavior, it is important to understand (a) how acute thoughts influence motivated behavior and (b) what aspect of control it is that thoughts impact. First, according to Bandura (1997b), self-efficacy may be one social cognition that is influenced by acute thoughts. Specifically, the myriad positive and negative thoughts or cognitive simulations that one experiences when deciding whether to perform a behavior may influence self-efficacy beliefs. That is, since individuals are able to think about and visualize possible scenarios when considering whether to perform a behavior, the content (i.e., successful or unsuccessful) and tone (i.e., positive or negative) may impact on efficacy beliefs that in turn influence intention and behavior. Second, thoughts may impact subjective assessments of control. Subjective control may influence motivated behavior independent of the actual, objective control conditions that exist in a situation (cf. Skinner, 1996). As a result, if individuals are unable to control or cope with their acute negative thoughts about exercising, regardless of whether the thoughts reflect legitimate reasons or excuses for not exercising, perceptions of control over the behavior could be affected (i.e., reduced). This in turn should influence actual behavior (i.e., decreased motivation leading to nonadherence).

To provide some insight on these issues, Gyurcsik and Brawley (1998) tested two different hypotheses in an exercise setting. They hypothesized (a) whether salient, acute thoughts acted as a source variable for an indicant of perceived control (i.e., efficacy to attend exercise after considering retrospective or prospective thoughts) and (b) whether self-efficacy influenced exercise intention and behavior. They judged it important to examine both positive and negative thoughts because individuals may use both when making a decision regarding their exercise actions (e.g., TPB: cf. Ajzen, 1985). Specifically, expectancy-value theories suggest that positive and negative beliefs play a role in the system of relationships that leads to behavior. Such beliefs originate not only in direct behavioral experience but also in the experience of acute ruminations or simulations about the behavior over time. For example, a person may think she is too tired (negative thought) to attend her fitness class on a particular day but also think she will feel more energetic (positive thought) if she does go to her class.

Findings from the Gyurcsik and Brawley (1998) study indicated that exercisers in a fitness program experienced acute positive and acute negative retrospective and prospective thoughts when deciding whether to exercise as planned. These thoughts tended to be negative for the sample mean, indicating a small tendency for negative thoughts to dominate positive thoughts. As well, regression analyses indicated that retrospective and prospective thoughts were predictive of related efficacy. This efficacy predicted exercise intention and behavior. Taken together, these results support the proposition offered by SET (Bandura, 1997b) that acute thoughts influence efficacy beliefs.

This study also indicated that individuals who were mainly positive in their acute exercise thinking (i.e., had a higher frequency of positive than negative thoughts) had significantly higher self-efficacy and exercise attendance than those who were mainly negative in their acute thinking. However, it is important to note that the negative thinkers still managed to attend their fitness classes at a fairly high rate and were somewhat successful at controlling their dysfunctional negative thoughts. In a follow-up study, Gyurcsik and Brawley (1999) sought to examine this control ability.

To do so, they examined (a) the strategies that adherent exercisers used to control/cope with their acute negative exercise-related thoughts, (b) whether confidence in these strategies reduced the detrimental impact of their negative thoughts (i.e., coping efficacy), and (c) whether coping efficacy predicted a perceived change in the strength of exercise intention pre- to post-coping. Results showed that for adherent exercisers, the most frequently employed coping strategies were (a) behavioral (e.g., making plans to exercise with a partner, scheduling the exercise session into a day planner) and (b) cognitive (e.g., thinking about how much more energy one will feel after exercising, about being less tired, about weight loss). Overall, the exercisers were fairly confident that these strategies worked to reduce the impact of their negative thoughts (i.e., $M_{coping efficacy}$ = 77%). Coping efficacy significantly predicted a perceived change in exercise intention. This finding suggested that even for adherent exercisers, efficacy to control their acute negative thoughts appeared to influence their intention. If this is the case for adherent exercisers, then future investigation with less adherent individuals, who may experience a greater struggle with their negative thoughts, may reveal more pronounced effects.

Goals and Control

Barone et al. (1997) note that goals and self-efficacy have an interactive effect on the self-regulation of action. Goal setting is intuitively connected to perceived control, and this is one of the intertwined aspects of a larger motivational engine. Goals spur human action in order to achieve task performance that approaches the target (goal). They are the foundation for self-regulation because they are the reason for taking action (cf. Barone et al., 1997). They are not beliefs about the availability of control. Self-efficacy beliefs concern progress toward a goal. As suggested by Bandura (1997b), self-efficacy beliefs influence goal setting, which in turn encourages actions—called *behavioral mechanisms* by Locke and Latham (1990). These actions are what Skinner (1996) refers to as "experiences of control."

Although Bandura has not advanced a specific goal theory, much of his writing (1986, 1988, 1989a, 1991, 1995a, 1997b) details the role that cognized goals play in regulating human action in his social cognitive theory. More specifically, the capability for goal intentions to influence action is rooted in symbolic activity. Cognitive representations of desirable future events serve to motivate individuals and guide their actions anticipatorily (Bandura, 1989a).

Bandura (1997b) argues that goals operate via self-reactive influences (i.e., self-efficacy for goal attainment, self-dissatisfaction with goal performance, adoption of challenging goals), in which personal standards create motivational effects. Although it is Bandura's social cognitive approach that may best complement theories about control, others have theorized that goal setting operates somewhat differently (cf. Garland, 1985).

The model that has been adopted in the physical activity domain (Weinberg, 1992) involves viewing goals as determinants or predictors of motivated behavior, including the choice of behaviors and the effort and persistence that follow in behavioral actions. The motivational approach to studying goals can be both mechanistic (Locke, 1968), with goals influencing behavior through specific actions, and cognitive (Bandura, 1986, 1988, 1989a, 1991, 1997b; Burton, 1989b; Garland, 1985), with goals influencing one's performance through one's cognitive, or thought, processes. In this volume, Hall and Kerr provide extensive description, review, and thoughtful discussion of various goal-related theories in the sport psychological research. By contrast, the focus in this chapter is on the link between goals and control and goals and efficacy in physical activity. The notion of self-regulation as a process is important, with goals and self-efficacy as parts of that interactive process.

Goals specify the conditions for either positive or negative self-evaluation. Therefore, people come to recognize a level of personal satisfaction that depends on achieving a specific performance level (i.e., goal attainment, in Bandura's terms). As individuals, people create their own "social incentives" (Bandura, 1986; Locke & Latham, 1990). Comparison of feedback about performance to their goals, combined with the resultant self-satisfaction, helps individuals maintain goal-directed actions over time without observable outcomes that are recognized by others (Bandura, 1986; Barone et al., 1997).

Exercise-Related Research Focused on Goals

Only a few studies document the exclusive role played by goals in participants' successful control of their adherence to exercise programs. Most exercise-related intervention studies use goal setting as part of a self-regulatory behavior-change regimen that participants learn, but it is not possible from these studies to isolate the effects of goal setting from the context of the intervention.

Poag and McAuley (1992) suggested that goals have their greatest effect on individuals who require additional motivational strategies (i.e., help to increase their control) but may not be as helpful for people who have already habitualized their exercise behavior. For habitual or regular exercisers, Maddux (1993) suggested that when people maintain exercise there is less conscious decision making and behavior is under less conscious control. Indeed, Locke and Latham (1990) also proposed this point. Goals do not have to be in complete consciousness at all times. In fact, according to Locke and Latham, once individuals are experienced with a task, they attend to their goals only when something goes wrong. Bandura (1986) strengthened this argument by stating that goals are used anticipatorily to guide individuals in the beginning stage of an activity rather than in the maintenance phase. Finally, Locke and Latham suggested that if goals are to influence behavior they must be clear to the individual, and the person must be committed to their fulfillment. Two hypotheses that emerge from these suggestions are that (a) the relationships between clarity and commitment, and exercise behavior are *mediated* by the way individuals perceive their goals as influencing their behavior (the four mechanisms described earlier), and (b) these effects should be more pronounced for beginner exercisers.

Poag-DuCharme and Brawley (1994) attempted to evaluate Locke and Latham's (1990) contentions within an exercise context. Exercise behavior was assessed through self-reported measures of the frequency of exercise (bouts per week) and the intensity of exercise (9-point Likert scale) required to reach the participants' goals. Mediator relationships were evaluated using the statistical techniques suggested by Baron and Kenny (1986). Results indicated that goal influence mediated the relationship between goal clarity and exercise intensity, as well as the relationship between goal commitment and exercise intensity, early in participants' exercise programs (R^2 = .37, $p < .003$ and R^2 = .28, $p < .04$, respectively). The findings suggest that perceived goal influence is the route by which clarity and commitment affect exercise intensity.

This exploratory investigation represented a first attempt to understand some of the relationships between perceptions of goal-related variables and exercise behavior. Individuals set clear, personal activity goals to which they are committed, and participants perceive these goals as being able to influence self-reported exercise behavior.

Using a group of beginning exercisers to determine whether the observed effects would be more pronounced for this sample, DuCharme and Brawley (1995) attempted once again to investigate the clarity, commitment, and influence hypotheses of Locke and Latham (1990). Even though beginning exercisers were selected as the target group and more than one aspect of overt exercise behavior was examined (i.e., intensity and frequency), the predictions of Locke and Latham were only partly supported. That is, with respect to actual exercise behavior, no goal perceptions at all (clarity, commitment, or influence) were significantly related to exercise attendance. Perceptions of goal commitment did, however, predict self-reported exercise intensity at the end of the program ($R^2 - .19$, $p < .03$).

Relationships Between Efficacy and Goals

We turn now to a similar social cognitive approach to goal setting and personal control that was developed by Bandura (1986, 1988, 1989a, 1991, 1997b). Bandura (1995b) identified goals as an important part of a personal control system:

> Goals are an interlinked facet of a motivational mechanism, not simply a discrete predictor to be tucked on a conceptual model. Goals operate through self-monitoring of habit patterns, aspirational standards, and positive and negative self-reactions to one's behavior. Efficacy beliefs affect goal setting, and whether substandard performances spark greater effort, or are demoralizing. But goals make independent contribution to performance. (p. 3)

Unlike Locke and Latham, Bandura (1989a) views goals as operating largely through self-referent processes rather than regulating motivation and action directly. According to Bandura (1988, 1989a, 1997b), cognitive motivation based on goal intentions is mediated by three types of self-influences: (a) perceptions of self-efficacy for goal attainment, (b) affective self-evaluation, and (c) ongoing readjustment of personal standards.

In Bandura's view (1988, 1997b), self-efficacy is the first self-referent factor that influences the self-regulation of motivation through goal systems. It is partly on the basis of self-efficacy that people choose what challenges to undertake, how much effort to expend in the endeavor, and how long to persevere in the face of difficulties (Bandura, 1986, 1997b). Whether negative discrepancies between personal standards and attainments are motivating or discouraging is partly determined by people's beliefs that they can attain the goals they have set for themselves. When faced with goal-attainment discrepancies, individuals high in self-efficacy increase their effort and persistence, whereas those less efficacious about their capabilities are easily dissuaded by failure (Bandura, 1989a, 1997b). As efficacy beliefs develop, goals are affected, thereby enacting relationships of reciprocal causation (Bandura, 1997b).

Affective self-evaluation is the second aspect of self-influence whereby individuals seek self-satisfactions from fulfilling valued goals. Discontent with substandard goal performances prompts people to intensify their efforts (Bandura, 1988, 1997b). The goals people set for themselves at the beginning of an endeavor are subject to change depending on the pattern and level of progress they are making (Campion & Lord, 1982). They may keep their original goal, increase it slightly, or adopt a less challenging goal.

The third self-influence factor concerns the readjustment of internal standards in light of one's attainments. A dual control system of self-regulation, combining proactive guidance with reactive adjustments, is in operation (Bandura 1989a, 1997b).

Goals and Efficacy: Fitness-Related Research

Limited physical activity research has evaluated the self-regulatory influence of goals as suggested by Bandura. Bandura and Cervone (1983) tested the hypothesis that self-evaluative and self-efficacy mechanisms mediate the effects of goals on performance motivation. These self-reactive influences are activated through cognitive comparison requiring personal standards and knowledge of performance. Subjects performed a bicycle ergometer task with either goals and performance feedback, goals alone, feedback alone, or without either factor. The condition combining performance information and a goal had a strong motivational impact, whereas neither goals alone nor feedback alone affected changes in motivational level. When both comparative factors (goals and feedback) were present, the evaluative and the efficacy influences predicted the magnitude of motivation enhancement. The higher the self-dissatisfaction with a substandard performance and the stronger the perceived self-efficacy for goal attainment, the greater was the subsequent intensification of effort.

Bandura and Cervone (1986) also tested the hypothesis that self-reactive influences exert differential impact on motivation as a function of the level and direction of discrepancy between a comparative standard and attainments. Subjects again pursued a challenging standard on a bicycle ergometer task and received preselected feedback that their effort fell either markedly, moderately, or minimally short of the standard or that it exceeded the standard. In accord with the prediction, self-efficacy contributed to motivation across a wide range of discrepancy conditions. Bandura and Cervone suggested that self-evaluation operated as an influential motivator only when attainments fell markedly or moderately short of a comparative standard. The authors concluded that the relevant self-influences operating at particular discrepancy levels explained a substantial amount of the variance in the motivated exercise behavior observed.

One of the few studies that has looked at the various social cognitive and behavioral influences related to the goals of fitness class participants was conducted by Poag and McAuley (1992). The authors considered the relationships among exercise importance, goal efficacy, self-efficacy, perceived goal achievement, and the frequency and intensity of exercise behavior. Results demonstrated that goal efficacy accounted for approximately 15.8% of the variation in fitness class goal achievements. More efficacious participants perceived themselves as more successful in achieving their goals at the end of the exercise program than their less efficacious counterparts did. Exercise self-efficacy was significantly related to the intensity but not the frequency of subsequent exercise participation.

Although the goal-related results of the Poag and McAuley (1992) study are interesting, specific limitations of that investigation required attention. First, it may have been premature to assume that various goal-related variables (e.g., efficacy) would mediate between goal processes and behavior. Although goal efficacy predicted perceptions of goal achievement, this cognition was not related to exercise behavior. The reason may have been the lack of correspondence between the predictor (goal efficacy) and the criterion variables (exercise frequency and intensity). Goal efficacy was measured as an individual's confidence in his/her ability to attain the fitness goal rather than as a specific estimation of ability to complete each behavior necessary to accomplish the goals. A compatible linking between cognition and behavior was not established. Second, mediational influences were discussed but never analyzed in relation to goal efficacy-behavior relationships. As emphasized by Baron and Kenny (1986), assuming that a variable is a mediator without testing for such effects can serve to confuse rather than add to the literature and should be remedied.

Poag and McAuley (1992) also suggested that attending exercise classes was not a problem for this group of exercisers. The sample consisted of experienced participants, and adherent exercise behavior was observed. As noted earlier in this chapter, it is proposed that goals are most influential when behavior requires conscious planning, as in the cases of starting an activity, setting a new level of attainment (e.g., perfect adherence), or setting off in a new direction (e.g., trying a different exercise activity for variety or cross-training purposes). Therefore, it is less-experienced exercisers who may benefit from or require additional motivational strategies such as goal setting.

DuCharme and Brawley (1994) addressed the Poag and McAuley (1992) study limitations and prospectively evaluated the conceptual mediational relationships among goals, self-efficacy, and exercise behavior among less experienced participants (cf. Bandura, 1986, 1997b). More specifically, they hypothesized that goal cognitions would influence exercise behavior (frequency and intensity) through the mediating variable of self-efficacy. A second purpose of the study was to assess cognitive and behavioral changes of adherent exercisers over time, and a third was to discriminate potential program dropouts and adherers at program onset based on goal cognitions.

Results demonstrated that during the first four weeks of the program, there were modest independent relationships between (a) goal influence and exercise frequency and (b) self-efficacy and exercise frequency. However, there was no evidence that self-efficacy functioned as a mediator between goal cognitions and exercise behavior. In contrast, participants' self-efficacy beliefs later in the program clearly mediated the relationship between goal influence and exercise frequency. What could have accounted for the changing nature of the relationship?

One can readily argue that as a result of their adherence and in-class experience between the onset and the middle of the program, the strength of participants' social cognitions and behaviors could change (cf. Bandura 1986, 1997b). Temporal changes supported this argument, as there were significant increases from program onset to midprogram in the self-efficacy and perceived exertion (exercise intensity) of adherers.

Interestingly, however, there was also a decline in participants' mean weekly attendance over the eight-week period (i.e., 85% during the first half of the program to 52% during the second half). However, adherers continued to view their goals as influencing their exercise behavior. Thus, it may be that these exercisers believed they were balancing their fitness levels through their upward adjustment of exercise intensity to compensate for their decrease in weekly-attendance frequency. These findings clearly demonstrate that goals are an integral part of individual self-regulation within the exercise context. Strengthening this conclusion was the finding that onset goal influence and self-efficacy perceptions significantly discriminated adherers from dropouts. Adherers had higher onset values for efficacy and goal influence than nonadherers. This finding offers preliminary evidence that social cognitive control-related variables are linked to nonadherence as well as adherence behavior. Few exercise investigations have evaluated control-related antecedents of nonadherent behavior.

Comment: Physical Activity Goals and Perceived Control

One of the main limitations to understanding goal-related sport and exercise research relative to perceived control is the small amount of empirical research evaluating theoretical explanations of goal influences in true field settings. Preliminary investigations (e.g., DuCharme & Brawley, 1994; Poag & McAuley, 1992) appear to support the contention that cognized goals operate as anticipatory cognitive motivators capable of influencing future behavior through forethought (Bandura, 1997b). However, more research is required to strengthen this assertion about self-regulation/control, at least with respect to exercise and other health behaviors.

As Barone et al. (1997) point out, it may be best to view goal and self-efficacy beliefs as part of a self-regulatory process that is interactive. Beliefs about efficacy and goal attainment are thought to influence persistence in the face of obstacles and challenges. The stronger these beliefs, the greater the striving of individuals; the greater striving in turn increases the probability of success in sport and in adherence-related behaviors. Accordingly, these mastery experiences strengthen efficacy (i.e., control) beliefs, which then motivate us to reset goals of greater challenge. Thus it would be possible to examine a reciprocal, interactive influence of the relationships among these aspects of control given the appropriate research design (e.g., prospective for reciprocal tests of hypotheses).

From Theory to Intervention

In this chapter we have attempted to make a case for an understanding of perceived control as a bridge across theories. It should be clear that the theoretical propositions and the data for the three theories suggest a compatibility among specific constructs. However, these statements serve only as a perspective on the literature, without consideration of the advantages for research on motivated behavior.

Advantages for Research

The clarity that comes through considering the compatibility of constructs among theories goes beyond classifying constructs into one of the relationship categories described by Skinner (1996: e.g., agent-means relationships). Understanding the similarities among constructs provides the opportunity to clarify the measurement of indexes of perceived control. All three theories examined in this chapter stress the necessity of explicit links from the concept to the measure to prediction. Skinner noted that the explicitness of perceived-control measures was essential for the successful operationalization of perceived-control constructs. Her point is that people have sophisticated, complex perceptions of perceived control. Accurate measurement of these perceptions requires greater specificity and precision than has been demonstrated in previous studies. Underestimating the complexity/specificity of peoples' estimates of perceived control has led to the development of different measures for the same construct and the use of similar measures to assess different constructs.

Given that the measurement guidelines suggested for SET (Bandura, 1997b), social cognitive theory (Bandura, 1986), the TPB (Ajzen, 1985), and GT (Locke & Latham, 1990) stress specificity, explicitness, and precision, these theories offer compatible approaches to the measurement of perceived control. A key question for future research is whether self-efficacy, for example, could be used as a representative indicant of control for each of the theories we have examined without compromising tests of theory. On the basis of the compatibility issues we have raised in this chapter and the issues of measurement just discussed, we believe the answer is yes. These suggestions would raise the probability that perceived-control findings could be compared across theories and studies.

Implications for Intervention

It is presumed that behavioral interventions cause changes in behavioral outcomes through mediating variables. Perceived control is a mediator of behavior as reflected in the theories we have discussed. Essential knowledge for interventions is knowledge about effective means to reliably change perceived control. However, as Baranowski, Lin, Wetter, Resnicow, and Davis Hearn (1997) point out, most interventions that have attempted to change a mediator with a resultant change in an outcome have demonstrated only modest results. Although Baranowski et al. were referring to community-based health interventions, their comments and suggestions apply equally well to interventions in sport and exercise contexts. Their point is that we fail to account for very much of the explained variance in the behavior change that is predicted by the mediator variable. Their conclusion does not appear to bode well for future interventions whose purposes are to change behavior and thus encourage desired health outcomes by altering perceived control (a mediator variable).

However, Baranowski et al. (1997) offer an explanation for their criticism, as well as ideas for a solution. Theories of motivated behavior, they note, were constructed to offer hypothesized relationships that lead to the prediction of behavior. These theories were not advanced with behavior-change strategies in mind and are therefore not explicit about cognitive-behavioral change procedures that alter the strength of a mediator. To direct criticism at those theories for an apparent deficiency would be inappropriate given the original purpose for their development. However, the solution proposed encourages the use of well-supported theory. The authors propose that using such theories as a foundation we expand their content to include probable means for changing mediators and linking mediators to outcome-promoting behavior (i.e., first and second steps in the solution). What is encouraging is the fact that the theories we have discussed offer the kind of foundation required. They offer (a) determinants that researchers can address to change the mediator of perceived behavioral control and (b) evidence that speaks to at least partial success in altering these determinants such that change is observed and is related to behavior.

Recognizing the theories that have this potential is a first step in linking theory and intervention. As their second step, Baranowski et al. (1997) propose expansion of the theory as just described. The third step they suggest is conducting the research to determine whether the mediators directly impact on the performance-causing behaviors leading to desired outcomes. Although the authors discuss other steps that are specific to community-based interventions, pursuing the first three steps would seem to be wise if we wish to produce stronger theory-to-intervention links for motivated behavior than we currently have.

From the discussion in this chapter, we hope that identifying compatible constructs and theories concerning perceived behavioral control allows for the future integration of findings across theories. The goal is to develop a broad base of common understanding and research support in order to pursue Baranowski et al.'s (1997) ideas systematically. Their suggestions provide opportunity for investigators in sport and exercise to gain "control" in motivating people to change. It is a challenging research agenda that we must have the motivation to pursue.

Acknowledgments

Although Dr. Brawley was the invited author for this chapter, the work of colleagues and doctoral students was equal to his, and all authors are considered equal contributors to this publication. Drs. Nancy Gyurcsik and

Nicole Culos-Reed were funded by doctoral fellowships from the Social Sciences and Humanities Research Council of Canada while writing this chapter, and we gratefully acknowledge their support. Dr. Nancy Gyurcsik is now an assistant professor at Kansas State University, Manhattan, Kansas. Dr. Nicole Culos-Reed completed postdoctoral research with the Center for Behavioral Research and Program Evaluation, a Canadian Cancer Society-funded center, Lyle Hallman Institute for Health Promotion, University of Waterloo, during chapter editing and is now an assistant professor at the University of Calgary, Calgary, Alberta.

Author Note

Correspondence regarding this chapter should be addressed to Dr. L.R. Brawley, Department of Kinesiology, University of Waterloo, Waterloo, Ontario, Canada, N2L-3G1. Electronic mail correspondence may be sent to Dr. Brawley at the following e-mail address: **lrbrawle@healthy.uwaterloo.ca**.

REFERENCES

Abramson, L.Y., Seligman, M.E.P., & Teasdale, J.D. (1978). Learned helplessness in humans: Critique and reformulation. *Journal of Abnormal Psychology, 87*, 49–74.

Aguinis, H., & Stone-Romero, E.F. (1997). Methodological artifacts in moderated multiple regression and their effects on statistical power. *Journal of Applied Psychology, 82*, 192–206.

Ajzen, I. (1985). From intentions to actions: A theory of planned behavior. In J. Kuhl & J. Beckmann (Eds.), *Action-control: From cognition to behavior* (pp. 11–39). Heidelberg: Springer-Verlag.

Ajzen, I. (1987). Attitudes, traits, and actions: Dispositional prediction of behavior in personality and social psychology. In L. Berkowitz (Ed.), *Advances in experimental social psychology* (pp. 1–63). San Diego, CA: Academic Press.

Ajzen, I. (1988). *Attitudes, personality, and behavior.* Chicago: Dorsey Press.

Ajzen, I. (1991). The theory of planned behavior. Special Issue: Theories of cognitive self-regulation. *Organizational Behavior and Human Decision Processes, 50*, 179–211.

Ajzen, I., & Fishbein, M. (1977). Attitude-behavior relations: A theoretical analysis and review of empirical research. *Psychological Bulletin, 84*, 888–918.

Ajzen, I., & Fishbein, M. (1980). *Understanding attitudes and predicting behavior.* Englewoods Cliffs, NJ: Prentice Hall.

Ajzen, I., & Madden, T.J. (1986). Prediction of goal-directed behavior: Attitudes, intentions, and perceived behavioral control. *Journal of Experimental Social Psychology, 22*, 453–474.

Amabile, T.M. (1985). Motivation and creativity: Effects of motivational orientation on creative writers. *Journal of Personality and Social Psychology, 48*, 393–399.

Ames, C. (1981). Competitive versus cooperative rewards structures: The influence of individual and group performance factors on achievement attributions and affect. *American Educational Research Journal, 18*, 273–287.

Ames, C. (1984a). Achievement attributions and self-instructions under competitive and individualistic goal structures. *Journal of Educational Psychology, 76*, 478–487.

Ames, C. (1984b). Competitive, cooperative, and individualistic goal structures: A motivational analysis. In R. Ames & C. Ames (Eds.), *Research on motivation in education: Student motivation* (Vol. 1, pp. 177–207). New York: Academic Press.

Ames, C. (1984c). Conceptions of motivation within competitive and noncompetitive goal structures. In R. Schwarzer (Ed.), *Self-related cognitions in anxiety and motivation*. Hillsdale, NJ: Erlbaum.

Ames, C. (1987). The enhancement of student motivation. In M.L. Maehr & D.A. Kleiber (Eds.), *Advances in motivation and achievement* (pp. 123–148). Greenwich, CT: JAI Press.

Ames, C. (1992a). Achievement goals and the classroom motivational climate. In J. Meece & D. Schunk (Eds.), *Students' perceptions in the classroom: Causes and consequences* (pp. 327–348). Hillsdale, NJ: Erlbaum.

Ames, C. (1992b). Achievement goals, motivational climate, and motivational processes. In G.C. Roberts (Ed.), *Motivation in sport and exercise* (pp. 161–176). Champaign, IL: Human Kinetics.

Ames, C. (1992c). Classrooms, goals, structures, and student motivation. *Journal of Educational Psychology, 84,* 261–271.

Ames, C., & Ames, R. (1981). Competitive versus individualistic goal structures: The salience of past performance information for causal attributions and affect. *Journal of Educational Psychology, 73,* 451–418.

Ames, C., & Archer, J. (1987). Mothers' beliefs about the role of ability and effort in school learning. *Journal of Educational Psychology, 18,* 409–414.

Ames, C., & Archer, J. (1988). Achievement goals in the classroom: Students' learning strategies and motivation processes. *Journal of Educational Psychology, 80*(3), 260–267.

Ames, C., & Archer, J. (1990). *Longitudinal effects of mastery goal structure on students' learning strategies and motivation.* Unpublished manuscript, University of Illinois at Urbana-Champaign.

Ames, C., & Machr, M.L. (1989). [Home and school cooperation in social and motivational development]. Unpublished raw data. Project funded by U.S. Office of Education, Office of Special Education and Rehabilitative Services, Contract No. DE-HO23T80023.

Ames, R. (1983). Help-seeking and achievement orientation: Perspectives from attribution theory. In B. DePaulo, A. Nadler, & J. Fisher (Eds.), *New directions in helping* (pp. 165–180). New York: Academic Press.

Amir, N., Cashman, L., & Foa, E.B. (1997). Strategies of thought control in obsessive-compulsive disorder. *Behavior Research and Therapy, 35,* 775–777.

Anastasi, A., & Urbina, S. (1997). *Psychological testing* (7th ed.) Upper Saddle River, NJ: Simon & Schuster.

Andree, K.V., & Whitehead, J. (1995, June). *The interactive effect of perceived ability and dispositional or situational achievement goals on intrinsic motivation in young athletes.* Paper presented at the annual meetings of the North American Society for the Psychology of Sport and Physical Activity, Asilomar, CA.

Anshel, M.H., Weinberg, R.S., & Jackson, A.W. (1992). The effect of goal difficulty and task complexity on intrinsic motivation and motor performance. *Journal of Sport Behavior, 15,* 159–178.

Armstrong, C.A., Sallis, J.F., Hovell, M.F., & Hofstetter, C.R. (1993). Stages of change, self-efficacy, and the adoption of vigorous exercise: A prospective analysis. *Journal of Sport and Exercise Psychology, 15,* 390–402.

Atkinson, J.W. (1957). Motivational determinants of risk-taking behavior. *Psychological Review, 6,* 359–372.

Aydin, G. (1997). The relationship between negative automatic thoughts and illness. *International Journal of Mental Health, 25,* 69–74.

Bagozzi, R.P., & Kimmel, S.K. (1995). A comparison of leading theories for the prediction of goal-directed behaviors. *British Journal of Social Psychology, 34,* 437–461.

Bailey, T., Jr. (1994, November 20). An open letter to Debbie Tucker, 2. *The Commercial Appeal,* p. A-13.

Balaguer, I., Crespo, M., and Duda, J.L. (1996). The relationship of motivational climate and athletes' goal orientations to perceived/preferred leadership style. *Journal of Sport and Exercise Psychology, 18,* S13.

Balaguer, I., Duda, J.L., Atienza, F.L., & Mayo, C. (1998, August). *Motivational climate as a predictor of individual and team improvement ratings and satisfaction among elite female handball players.* Presentation given at the International Congress of Applied Psychology, San Francisco.

Balaguer, I., Duda, J.L., & Crespo, M. (1999). Motivational climate and goal orientations as predictors of perceptions of improvement, satisfaction and coach ratings among tennis players. *Scandinavian Journal of Medicine and Science in Sports, 9,* 381–388.

Balaguer, I., Duda, J.L., & Mayo, C. (1997). The relationship of goal orientations and the perceived motivational climate to coaches' leadership style in competitive handball. In R. Lidor & M. Bar-Eli (Eds.), *Innovations in sport psychology: Linking theory and practice. Proceedings of the IX World Congress in Sport Psychology: Part I* (pp. 94–96). Netanya, Israel: Ministry of Education, Culture and Sport.

Baldwin, M.K., & Courneya, K.S. (1997). Exercise and self-esteem in breast cancer survivors: An application of the exercise and self-esteem model. *Journal of Sport and Exercise Psychology, 19,* 347–358.

Bandura, A. (1977). Self-efficacy: Toward a unifying theory of behavioral change. *Psychological Review, 84,* 191–215.

Bandura, A. (1982). Self-efficacy mechanisms in human agency. *American Psychologist, 37,* 122–147.

Bandura, A. (1983). Self-evaluative and self-efficacy mechanisms governing the motivational effects of goal systems. *Journal of Personality and Social Development, 45,* 1017–1028.

Bandura, A. (1986). *Social foundations of thought and action: A social cognitive view.* Englewood Cliffs, NJ: Prentice Hall.

Bandura, A. (1988). Self-regulation of motivation and action through goal systems. In V. Hamilton, G.H. Bower, & N.Y. Frijda (Eds.), *Cognitive perspectives on emotion and motivation* (pp. 37–61). Dordrecht, The Netherlands: Kluwer Academic.

Bandura, A. (1989a). Human agency in social cognitive theory. *American Psychologist, 44,* 1175–1184.

Bandura, A. (1989b). Regulation of cognitive processes through perceived self-efficacy. *Developmental Psychology, 25,* 729–735.

Bandura, A. (1990). Foreword. In E.A. Locke & G.P. Latham (Eds.), *A theory of goal setting and task performance* (pp. xi–xii). Englewood Cliffs, NJ: Prentice Hall.

Bandura, A. (1991). Social cognitive theory of self-regulation. *Organizational Behavior and Human Decision Processes, 50,* 248–287.

Bandura, A. (1992). Exercise of personal agency through the self-efficacy mechanism. In R. Schwarzer (Ed.), *Self-efficacy: Thought control and action* (pp. 3–38). Washington, DC: Hemisphere.

Bandura, A. (1995a). *Moving into forward gear in health promotion and disease prevention.* Keynote address presented at the Annual Meeting of the Society of Behavioral Medicine, San Diego.

Bandura, A. (1995b). On rectifying conceptual ecumenism. In J.E. Maddux (Ed.), *Self-efficacy, adaptation, and adjustment: Theory, research, and application* (pp. 347–375). New York: Plenum Press.

Bandura, A. (1997a). The anatomy of stages of change. *American Journal of Health Promotion, 12,* 8–10.

Bandura, A. (1997b). *Self-efficacy: The exercise of control.* New York: Freeman.

Bandura, A., & Cervone, D. (1983). Self-evaluative and self-efficacy mechanisms governing the motivational effects of goal systems. *Journal of Personality and Social Psychology, 45,* 1017–1028.

Bandura, A., & Cervone, D. (1986). Differential engagement of self-reactive influences in cognitive motivation. *Organizational Behavior and Human Decision Processes, 38,* 92–113.

Bandura, A., Cioffi, D., Taylor, C.B., & Brouillard, M.E. (1988). Perceived self-efficacy in coping with cognitive stressors and opioid activation. *Journal of Personality and Social Psychology, 55,* 479–488.

Bandura, A., & Schunk, D.H. (1981). Cultivating competence, self efficacy, and intrinsic interest through proximal self-motivation. *Journal of Personality and Social Psychology, 41,* 586–598.

Bandura, A., & Simon, K.M. (1977). The role of proximal intentions in self-regulation of refractory behavior. *Cognitive Therapy and Research, 1,* 177–193.

Bandura, A., Taylor, C.B., Williams, S.L., Mefford, I.N., & Barchas, J.D. (1985). Catecholamine secretion as a function of perceived coping self-efficacy. *Journal of Consulting and Clinical Psychology, 53,* 406–414.

Bandura, A., & Wood, R. (1989). Effect of perceived controllability and performance standards on self-regulation of complex decision making. *Journal of Personality and Social Psychology, 56,* 805–814.

Baranowski, T., Lin, L.S., Wetter, D.W., Resnicow, K., & Davis Hearn, M. (1997). Theory as mediating variables: Why aren't community interventions working as desired? *American Journal of Epidemiology, 7(S7),* S89–S95.

Bar-Eli, M., Levy-Kolker, N., Tenenbaum, G., & Weinberg, R.S. (1993). Effect of goal difficulty on performance of aerobic, anaerobic and power tasks in laboratory and field settings. *Journal of Sport Behavior, 16,* 17–32.

Bar-Eli, M., Tenenbaum, G., Pie, J.S., Btesh, Y., & Almog, A. (1997). Effect of goal difficulty, goal specificity and duration of practice time intervals on muscular endurance performance. *Journal of Sports Sciences, 15,* 125–135.

Barnett, M.L., & Stanicek, J.A. (1979). Effects of goal setting on achievement in archery. *Research Quarterly, 50,* 328–332.

Baron, P., & Watters, R.G. (1981). Effects of goal setting on weight loss induced by self-monitoring of caloric intake. *Canadian Journal of Behavioral Science, 13,* 161–170.

Baron, R.M., & Kenny, D.A. (1986). The moderator-mediator variable distinction in social psychological research: Conceptual, strategic, and statistical considerations. *Journal of Personality and Social Psychology, 51,* 1173–1182.

Barone, D.F., Maddux, J.E., & Snyder, C.R. (1997). *Social cognitive psychology: History and current domains.* New York: Plenum Press.

Bar-Or, O. (1996). *The child and adolescent athlete.* London: Blackwell Science.

Baumeister, R.F., & Leary, M.R. (1995). The need to belong: Desire for interpersonal attachments as a fundamental human motivation. *Psychological Bulletin, 117,* 497–529.

Bavelas, J., & Lee, E.S. (1978). Effect of goal level on performance: A trade-off of quantity and quality. *Canadian Journal of Psychology, 32,* 219–240.

Beauchamp, P.H., Halliwell, W.R., Fournier, J.F., & Koestner, R. (1996). Effects of cognitive-behavioral psychological skills training on the motivation, preparation, and putting performance of novice golfers. *The Sport Psychologist, 10,* 157–170.

Becker, S.L. (1995). *An examination of the relationship among TARGET structures, team motivational climate, and achievement goal orientation.* Unpublished doctoral dissertation, Oregon State University.

Beggs, W.D.A. (1990). Goal setting in sport. In J.G. Jones & L. Hardy (Eds.), *Stress and performance in sport* (pp. 171–201). Chichester, UK: Wiley.

Bentler, P.M. (1995). *EQS structural equations program manual.* Encino, CA: Multivariate Software.

Berlyne, D.E. (1971a). *Aesthetics and psychobiology.* New York: Appleton-Century-Crofts.

Berlyne, D.E. (1971b). What next? Concluding summary. In H.I. Day, D.E. Berlyne, & D.E. Hunt (Eds.), *Intrinsic motivation: A new direction in education* (pp. 186–196). Toronto: Holt, Rinehart & Winston.

Biddle, S.J.H. (1994). Motivation and participation in exercise and sport. In S. Serpa, J. Alves, & V. Pataco (Eds.), *International perspectives on sport and exercise psychology* (pp. 103-126). Morgantown, WV: Fitness Information Technology.

Biddle, S., Akande, A., Vlachopoulos, S., & Fox, K. (1996). Towards an understanding of children's motivation for physical activity: Achievement goal orientations, beliefs about sport success, and sport emotion in Zimbabwean children. *Psychology and Health, 12*(1), 49–55.

Biddle, S., & Brooke, R. (1992). Intrinsic versus extrinsic motivational orientation in physical education and sport. *British Journal of Educational Psychology, 62,* 247–256.

Biddle, S., Cury, F., Goudas, M., Sarrazin, P., Famose, J-P., & Durand, M. (1995). Development of scales to measure perceived physical education class climate: A cross-national project. *British Journal of Educational Psychology, 65,* 341–358.

Biddle, S., & Goudas, M. (1996). Analysis of children's physical activity and its association with adult encouragement and social cognitive variables. *Journal of School Health, 66,* 75–78.

Biddle, S., & Goudas, M. (1997). Effort is virtuous: Teacher preferences of pupil effort, ability and grading in physical education. *Educational Research, 39,* 350–355.

Biddle, S., Goudas, M., & Page, A. (1994). Social-psychological predictors of self-reported actual and intended physical activity in a university workforce sample. *British Journal of Sports Medicine, 28,* 160–163.

Biddle, S., & Ntoumanis, N. (1999). Motivational climate in physical activity: A meta-analysis of cognitive and affective outcomes. In V. Hosek, P. Tilinger, & L. Bilek (Eds.), *Psychology of sport and exercise: Enhancing the quality of life. Proceedings of the 10th European Congress on Sport Psychology—FEPSAC* (pp. 99–101). Prague: Charles University of Prague Press.

Biddle, S., & Soos, I. (1997). Social-cognitive predictors of motivation and intention in Hungarian children. In R. Lidor & M. Bar-Eli (Eds.), *Innovations in sport psychology: Linking theory and practice. Proceedings of the IX World Congress in Sport Psychology: Part I* (pp. 121–123). Netanya, Israel: Ministry of Education, Culture and Sport.

Blair, S.N., Kohl, H.W. III, Paffenbarger, R.S., Jr., Clark, D.G., Cooper, K.H., & Gibbons, L.W. (1989). Physical fitness and all-cause mortality: A prospective study of healthy men and women. *Journal of the American Medical Association, 262,* 2395–2401.

Blais, M.R., Brière, N.M., Lachance, L., Riddle, A.S., & Vallerand, R.J. (1993). L'Inventaire des motivations au travail de Blais [The Blais Work Motivation Inventory]. *Revue Québécoise de Psychologie, 14,* 185–215.

Blais, M.R., Sabourin, S., Boucher, C., & Vallerand, R.J. (1990). Toward a motivational model of couple happiness. *Journal of Personality and Social Psychology, 59,* 1021–1031.

Blais, M.R., & Vallerand, R.J. (1992). *Construction et validation de l'Echelle des Perceptions d'Autonomie dans les Domaines de Vie* [Development and validation of the Autonomy Perceptions in Life Contexts Scale]. Unpublished manuscript, Université du Québec à Montréal.

Blais, M.R., Vallerand, R.J., Gagnon, A., Brière, N.M., & Pelletier, L.G. (1990). Significance, structure, and gender differences in life domains of college students. *Sex Roles, 22,* 199–212.

Blais, M.R., Vallerand, R.J., Pelletier, L.G., & Brière, N.M. (1994). *Construction et validation de l'Inventaire des Motivations Interpersonnelles* [Construction and validation of the Inventory of Interpersonal Motivations]. Unpublished manuscript, Université du Québec à Montréal.

Blalock, S.J., Bunker, B.J., & DeVillis, R.F. (1994). Psychological distress among survivors of burn injury: The role of outcome expectations and perceptions of importance. *Journal of Burn Care and Rehabilitation, 15,* 421–427.

Blanchard, C., & Vallerand, R.J. (1996a). *The mediating effects of perceptions of competence, autonomy, and relatedness on the social factors–self-determined situational motivation relationship.* Unpublished manuscript, Université du Québec à Montréal.

Blanchard, C., & Vallerand, R.J. (1996b). [On the relations between situational motivation and situational consequences in basketball]. Unpublished raw data, Université du Québec à Montréal.

Blanchard, C., & Vallerand, R.J. (1996c). *Perceptions of competence, autonomy, and relatedness as psychological mediators of the social factors–contextual motivation relationship.* Unpublished manuscript, Université du Québec à Montréal.

Blanchard, C., & Vallerand, R.J. (1998a). [On the recursive relations between global motivation and contextual exercise motivation]. Unpublished raw data, Université du Québec à Montréal.

Blanchard, C., & Vallerand, R.J. (1998b). [On the relations between situational motivation and situational consequences toward exercise]. Unpublished raw data, Université du Québec à Montréal.

Blanchard, C., Vallerand, R.J., & Provencher, P. (1996, August 24). *Une analyse motivationnelle des mécanismes de compensation et de contagion du soi* [A motivational analysis of the compensation and contagion mechanisms of the self]. Paper presented at the first annual conference on social psychology in the French language, Montreal, Canada.

Blanchard, C., Vallerand, R.J., & Provencher, P. (1998). *Une analyse des effets bidirectionnels entre la motivation contextuelle et la motivation situationnelle en milieu naturel* [An analysis of the bi-directional effects between contextual and situational motivation in a natural setting]. Unpublished manuscript.

Bloom, G.A., Crumpton, R., & Anderson, J.E. (1999). A systematic study of teaching behaviors of an expert basketball coach. *Journal of Sport and Exercise Psychology, 13,* 157–170.

Blumenfeld, P.C. (1992). Classroom learning and motivation: Clarifying and expanding goal theory. *Journal of Educational Psychology, 84,* 272–281.

Bock, B.C., Albrecht, A.E., Traficante, R.M., Clark, M.M., Pinto, B.M., Tilkemeier, P., & Marcus, B.H. (1997). Predictors of exercise adherence following participation in a cardiac rehabilitation program. *International Journal of Behavioral Medicine, 4,* 60–75.

Boggiano, A.K., & Barrett, M. (1985). Performance and motivational deficits of helplessness: The role of motivational orientations. *Journal of Personality and Social Psychology, 49,* 1753–1761.

Boggiano, A.K., & Ruble, D.N. (1986). Children's responses to evaluative feedback. In R. Schwartzer (Ed.), *Self related cognitions in anxiety and motivation* (pp. 195–228). Hillsdale, NJ: Erlbaum.

Bolles, R.C. (1967). *Theory of motivation.* New York: Harper & Row.

Boone, K., & Duda, J.L. (1999). *The relationship of goal orientations to multidimensional cohesion across a baseball season.* Unpublished manuscript.

Bouchard, C., Shephard, R.J., Stephens, T. (Eds.) (1994). *Physical activity, fitness, and health: International proceedings and consensus statement.* Champaign, IL: Human Kinetics.

Bowlby, J. (1988). *A secure base: Parent-child attachment and healthy human development.* New York: Basic Books.

Boyce, B.A. (1990). The effect of instructor-set goals upon skill acquisition and retention of a selected shooting task. *Journal of Teaching in Physical Education, 9,* 115–122.

Boyce, B.A. (1992a). Effects of assigned versus participant-set goals on skill acquisition and retention of a selected shooting task. *Journal of Teaching in Physical Education, 11,* 220–234.

Boyce, B.A. (1992b). The effects of goal proximity on skill acquisition and retention of a shooting task in a field-based setting. *Journal of Sport and Exercise Psychology, 14,* 298–308.

Boyce, B.A. (1994). The effects of goal setting on performance and spontaneous goal-setting behavior of experienced pistol shooters. *Journal of Sport and Exercise Psychology, 16,* 87–93.

Boyce, B.A., & Wayda, V.K. (1994). The effects of assigned and self-set goals on task performance. *Journal of Sport and Exercise Psychology, 16,* 258–269.

Boyd, M.P. (1990). *The effects of participation orientation and success-failure on post-competitive affect in young adults.* Unpublished dissertation, University of Southern California, Los Angeles.

Boyd, M.P., Callaghan, J., & Yin, Z. (1991). *Competitive involvement and low competence in sport as a source of competitive trait anxiety.* Paper presented at the annual meeting of the North American Society for the Psychology of Sport and Physical Activity, Asilomar, CA.

Boyd, M., & Yin, Z. (1996). Cognitive-affective sources of sport enjoyment in adolescent sport participants. *Adolescence, 31,* 283–295.

Brawley, L.R., Martin, K.A., & Gyurcsik, N.C. (1998). Problems in assessing perceived barriers to exercise: Confusing obstacles with attributions and excuses. In J.L. Duda (Ed.), *Advances in sport and exercise psychology measurement* (pp. 337–350). Morgantown, WV: Fitness Information Technology.

Brawley, L.R., & Rodgers, W.M. (1993). Social-psychological aspects of fitness promotion: In P. Seraganian (Ed.), *Exercise psychology: The influence of physical exercise on psychological processes* (pp. 254–298). New York: Wiley.

Bredemeier, B.L. (1999). Character in action: Promoting moral behavior in sport. In R. Lidor & M. Bar-Eli (Eds.), *Innovations in sport psychology: Linking theory and practice* (pp. 247–260). Morgantown, WV: Fitness Information Technology.

Brickner, M.A., & Bukatko, P.A. (1987). *Locked into performance: Goal setting as a moderator of the social loafing effect.* Unpublished manuscript, University of Akron.

Brière, N.M., Vallerand, R.J., Blais, M.R., & Pelletier, L.G. (1995). Développement et validation d'une mesure de motivation intrinsèque, extrinsèque et d'amotivation en contexte sportif: l'Échelle de motivation dans les sports (EMS) [On the development and validation of the French form of the Sport Motivation Scale]. *International Journal of Sport Psychology, 26,* 465–489.

Brophy, J. (1983). Conceptualizing student motivation. *Educational Psychologist, 18,* 200–214.

Brophy, J. (1987). Socializing students' motivation to learn. In M.L. Maehr & D.A. Kleiber (Eds.), *Advances in motivation and achievement. Vol. 5. Enhancing motivation* (pp. 181–210). Greenwich, CT: JAI Press.

Brown, J.D. (1993). Self-esteem and self-evaluation: Feeling is believing. In J. Suls (Ed.), *Psychological perspectives on the self* (Vol. 4, pp. 27–58). Hillsdale, NJ: Erlbaum.

Brown, J.D., & Dutton, K.A. (1997). Global self-esteem and specific self-views as determinants of people's reactions to success and failure. *Journal of Personality and Social Psychology, 73,* 139–148.

Brunel, P. (1996). The relationship of task and ego orientation to intrinsic and extrinsic motivation. *Journal of Sport and Exercise Psychology, 18* (Suppl.), S59.

Brunel, P. (1997). Toward an integrative approach to sport motivation. In R. Lidor & M. Bar-Eli (Eds.), *Innovations in sport psychology: Linking theory and practice. Proceedings of the IX World Congress in Sport Psychology: Part I* (pp. 160–162). Netanya, Israel: Ministry of Education, Culture and Sport.

Brunel, P. (1999a). Predicting cognitions and strategies to cope with the situation: Influence of motivational climate and goal orientation. *Journal of Sport and Exercise Psychology, 21* (Suppl.), S22.

Brunel, P. (2000). *Achievement motivation: Toward interactive effects of dispositional and situational variables on motivation and social cognition.* Habilitation a diriger les researches, University of Limoges, France.

Brunel, P.C. (1999b). Relationship between achievement goal orientations and perceived motivational climate on intrinsic motivation. *Scandinavian Journal of Medicine and Science in Sports, 9,* 365–374.

Brustad, R.J. (1993). Youth sport: Psychological considerations. In R.N. Singer, L.K. Tenant, & M. Murphy (Eds.), *The handbook on research in sport psychology* (pp. 695-717). New York: Mcmillan.

Bryan, J.F., & Locke, E.A. (1967). Goal setting as a means of increasing motivation. *Journal of Applied Psychology, 51,* 274–277.

Buckelew, S.P., Murray, S.E., Hewett, J.E., Johnson, J., & Huyser, B. (1995). Self-efficacy, pain, and physical activity among fibromyalgia subjects. *American College of Rheumatology, 8,* 43–50.

Bunker, L., Williams, J.M., & Zinsser, N. (1993). Cognitive techniques for improving performance and building confidence. In J.M. Williams (Ed.), *Applied sport psychology. Personal growth to peak performance* (pp. 225–242). Mountain View, CA: Mayfield.

Burton, D. (1989a). The impact of goal specificity and task complexity on basketball skill development. *The Sport Psychologist, 3,* 34–47.

Burton, D. (1989b). Winning isn't everything: Examining the impact of performance goals on collegiate swimmers' cognitions and performance. *The Sport Psychologist, 3,* 105–132.

Burton, D. (1992). The Jekyll/Hyde nature of goals: Reconceptualizing goal setting in sport. In T. Horn (Ed.), *Advances in sport psychology* (pp. 267–297). Champaign, IL: Human Kinetics.

Burton, D. (1993). Goal setting in sport. In R.N. Singer, M. Murphey, & L. Tennant (Eds.), *Handbook of research on sport psychology* (pp. 467–491). New York: Macmillan.

Burton, D. (1998). Measuring competitive state anxiety. In J.L. Duda (Ed.), *Advances in sport and exercise psychology measurement* (pp. 129–148). Morgantown, WV: Fitness Information Technology.

Burton, D., Weinberg, R., Yukelson, D., & Weigand, D. (1998). The goal effectiveness paradox in sport: Examining the goal profiles of collegiate athletes. *The Sport Psychologist, 12,* 404–418.

Burton, D., Weinberg, R., Yukelson, D., & Weigand, D. (in press). Back to basics: Identifying effective goal setting practices of collegiate athletes. *The Sport Psychologist.*

Butler, R. (1987). Task-involving and ego-involving properties of evaluation: Effects of different feedback conditions on motivational perceptions, interest, and performance. *Journal of Educational Psychology, 79,* 474–482.

Butler, R. (1988). Enhancing and undermining intrinsic motivation: The effects of task-involving and ego-involving evaluation on interest and performance. *British Journal of Educational Psychology, 58,* 1–14.

Cadorette, I., Blanchard, C., & Vallerand, R.J. (1996, October). *Programme d'amaigrissement: Influence du centre de conditionnement physique et du style de l'entraîneur sur la motivation des participants* [On the influence of fitness centers and monitors' interactional style on participants' motivation toward a weight-loss program]. Paper presented at the annual conference of the Québec Society for Research on Psychology, Trois-Rivières, Québec, Canada.

Camacho, T.C., Roberts, R.E., Lazarus, N.B., Kaplan, G.A., & Cohen, R.D. (1991). Physical activity and depression: Evidence from the Alameda County Study. *American Journal of Epidemiology, 134,* 220–230.

Campion, M.A., & Lord, R.G. (1982). A control system conceptualization of the goal-setting and changing process. *Organizational Behavior and Human Decision Process, 30,* 265–287.

Cardinal, B.J. (1997). Construct validity of stages of change for exercise behavior. *American Journal of Health Promotion, 12,* 68–74.

Carpenter, P., & Yates, B. (1997). Relationship between achievement goals and the perceived purposes of soccer for semiprofessional and amateur players. *Journal of Sport and Exercise Psychology, 19,* 302–312.

Carpenter, P.J., & Morgan, K. (1999). Motivational climate, personal goal perspectives, and cognitive and affective responses in physical education classes. *European Journal of Physical Education, 4,* 31–44.

Carron, A.V. (1982). Cohesiveness in sport groups: Interpretations and considerations. *Journal of Sport Psychology, 4,* 123–138.

Carron, A.V. (1988). *Group dynamics in sport: Theoretical and practical issues.* London, Ontario: Spodym.

Carron, A.V., Brawley, L., & Widmeyer, N. (1998). The measurement of cohesiveness in sport groups. In J.L. Duda (Ed.), *Advances in sport and exercise psychology measurement* (pp. 213–226). Morgantown, WV: Fitness Information Technology.

Carron, A.V., Widmeyer, N., & Brawley, L. (1985). The development of an instrument to assess cohesion in sport teams: The Group Environment Questionnaire. *Journal of Sport Psychology, 7,* 244–266.

Carver, C.S., & Scheier, M.F. (1981). *Attention and self-regulation.* New York: Springer-Verlag.

Casperson, C.J., Christenson, G.M., & Pollard, R.A. (1986). Status of the 1990 physical fitness and exercise objectives. Evidence from NHIS 1985. *Public Health Report, 101,* 587–592.

Castro, F., Balzconde-Garbanati, L., & Betra, H. (1985). Risk factors for coronary heart disease in Hispanic populations: A review. *Hispanic Journal of Behavioral Science, 7,* 153–175.

Centers for Disease Control. (1992). *1992 BRFSS summary prevalence report.* Atlanta: U.S. Department of Health and Human Services.

Centers for Disease Control and Prevention. (1994). *1994 BRFSS summary prevalence report.* Atlanta: U.S. Department of Health and Human Services.

Chandler, C.L., & Connell, J.P. (1987). Children's intrinsic, extrinsic, and internalization motivation: A developmental study of children's reasons for liked and disliked behaviors. *British Journal of Developmental Psychology, 5,* 357–365.

Chantal, Y., Guay, F., Dobreva-Martinova, T., & Vallerand, R.J. (1996). Motivation and elite performance: An exploratory investigation with Bulgarian athletes. *International Journal of Sport Psychology, 27,* 173–182.

Chantal, Y., Guay, F., & Vallerand, R.J. (1998). *A structural analysis of motivational consequences: A test of the specificity hypothesis.* Manuscript in preparation.

Chatzisarantis, N.L.D., Biddle, S.J.H., & Meek, G.A. (1997). A self-determination theory approach to the study of intentions and the intention-behaviour relationship in children's physical activity. *British Journal of Health Psychology, 2,* 343–360.

Chaumeton, N., & Duda, J.L. (1988). Is it how you play the game or whether you win or lose? The effect of competitive level and situation on coaching behaviors. *Journal of Sport Behavior, 11,* 157–174.

Chelladurai, P. (1991). Management. In B.L. Parkhouse (Ed.), *The management of sport: Its foundation and application* (pp. 135–148). St. Louis: Mosby.

Chelladurai, P. (1993). Leadership. In R. Singer, M. Murphey, & L.K. Tennant (Eds.), *Handbook of research on sport psychology* (pp. 647–671). New York: Macmillan.

Chelladurai, P., & Saleh, S.D. (1980). Dimensions of leader behavior in sports: Development of a leadership scale. *Journal of Sport Psychology, 2,* 34–45.

Chesney, A.A., & Locke, E.A. (1988). *An examination of the relationship among goals, strategies and performance on a complex management simulation task.* Unpublished manuscript, College of Management, Georgia Institute of Technology.

Chi, L. (1993). *Prediction of achievement-related cognitions and behaviors in the physical domain: A test of the theories of goal perspectives and self-efficacy.* Unpublished doctoral dissertation, Purdue University.

Chi, L. (1997). The relationships of task and ego orientation to intrinsic motivation, extrinsic motivation and amotivation among tennis players. In R. Lidor & M. Bar-Eli (Eds.), *Innovations in sport psychology: Linking theory and practice. Proceedings of the IX World Congress in Sport Psychology: Part I* (pp. 200–202). Netanya, Israel: Ministry of Education, Culture and Sport.

Chi, L., & Duda, J.L. (1995). Multi-group confirmatory factor analysis of the Task and Ego Orientation in Sport Questionnaire. *Research Quarterly for Exercise and Sport, 66,* 91–98.

Chi, L., & Lu, S-E. (1995, June). *The relationships between perceived motivational climates and group cohesiveness in basketball.* Paper presented at the annual meetings of the North American Society for the Psychology of Sport and Physical Activity, Clearwater, FL.

Chidester, T.R., & Grigsby, W.C. (1984). A meta-analysis of the goal setting performance literature. *Academy of Management Proceedings, 202–206.*

Chung, C-H., Sim, Y-S., Kim, J-S., & Choi, E-K. (1997). The effect of achievement goal orientations on perceived psychological momentum and self-efficacy. In R. Lidor & M. Bar-Eli (Eds.), *Innovations in sport psychology: Linking theory and practice. Proceedings of the IX World Congress in Sport Psychology: Part I* (pp. 209–211). Netanya, Israel: Ministry of Education, Culture and Sport.

Coleman, J.S. (1961). Athletics in high school. *Annals of the American Academy of Political and Social Science, 338,* 33–43.

Coleman, K.J., Raynor, H.R., Mueller, D.M., Cerny, F.J., Dorn, J.M., & Epstein, L.H. (1999). Providing sedentary adults with choices for meeting their walking goals. *Preventive Medicine, 28,* 510–519.

Connell, J.P., & Wellborn, J.G. (1991). Competence, autonomy, and relatedness: A motivational analysis of self-esteem processes. In M.R. Gunnar & L.A. Sroufe (Eds.), *The Minnesota symposium on child psychology. Vol. 22. Self-processes in development* (pp. 43–77). Hillsdale, NJ: Erlbaum.

Conner, M., & Armitage, C.J. (1998). Extending the theory of planned behavior: A review and avenues for further research. *Journal of Applied Social Psychology, 28,* 1429–1464.

Cooley, C.H. (1902). *Human nature and the social order.* New York: Scribner's.

Courneya, K.S. (1995). Understanding readiness for regular physical activity in older individuals: An application of the theory of planned behavior. *Health Psychology, 14,* 80–87.

Courneya, K.S., Estabrooks, P.A., & Nigg, C.R. (1997). Predicting change in exercise stage over a three-year period: An application of the theory of planned behavior. *Avante, 3,* 1–13.

Courneya, K.S., & McAuley, E. (1993). Predicting physical activity from intention: Conceptual and methodological issues. *Journal of Sport and Exercise Psychology, 15,* 50–62.

Courneya, K.S., & McAuley, E. (1994). Are there different determinants of the frequency, intensity, and duration of physical activity? *Behavioral Medicine, 20,* 84–90.

Courneya, K.S., Nigg, C.R., & Estabrooks, P.A. (1998). Relationships among the theory of planned behavior, stages of change, and exercise behavior in older persons over a three year period. *Psychology and Health, 13,* 355–367.

Covington, M.V. (1984). The motive for self worth. In R. Ames & C. Ames (Eds.), *Research on motivation in education: Student motivation* (Vol. 1, pp. 77–113). New York: Academic Press.

Covington, M.V. (1992). *Making the grade: A self-worth perspective on motivation and school reform.* New York: Cambridge University Press.

Covington, M.V., & Omelich, C.L. (1979). Effort: The double-edged sword in school achievement. *Journal of Educational Psychology, 71,* 169–182.

Covington, M.V., & Omelich, C.L. (1984). It's best to be able and virtuous too: Student and teacher evaluation response to successful effort. *Journal of Educational Psychology, 71,* 688–700.

Covington, M.V., & Omelich, C.L. (1991). Need achievement revisited: Verification of Atkinson's original 2 × 2 model. In C. Spielberger & I. Sarason (Eds.), *Stress and emotion: Anxiety, anger, and curiosity. Vol. 14. The series in clinical psychology and the series in stress and emotion: Anxiety, anger, and curiosity* (pp. 85–105). New York: Hemisphere.

Crawford, K.S., White, M.A., & Magnusson, P.A. (1983). *The impact of goal setting and feedback on the productivity of navy industrial workers.* No. NPRDC TR 83-4. Navy Personnel Research and Development Center, San Diego.

Csikszentmihalyi, M. (1975). *Beyond boredom and anxiety.* San Francisco: Jossey-Bass.

Csikszentmihalyi, M. (1978). Intrinsic rewards and emergent motivation. In M.R. Lepper & D. Greene (Eds.), *The hidden costs of reward* (pp. 205–216). Hillsdale, NJ: Erlbaum.

Csikszentmihalyi, M. (1992). A response to the Kimiecik & Stein and Jackson papers. *Journal of Applied Sport Psychology, 4,* 181–183.

Csikszentmihalyi, M., & Nakamura, J. (1989). The dynamics of intrinsic motivation: A study of adolescents. In C. Ames & R. Ames (Eds.), *Motivation in education. Vol. 3. Goals and cognitions* (pp. 45–71). New York: Academic Press.

Curry, S.J., Wagner, E.H., & Grothaus (1991). Evaluation of intrinsic and extrinsic motivation interventions with a self-help smoking cessation program. *Journal of Consulting and Clinical Psychology, 59,* 318–324.

Cury, F., Biddle, S.H., Famose, J.P., Goudas, M., Sarrazin, P., & Durand, M. (1996). Personal and situational factors influencing intrinsic interest of adolescent girls in physical education: A structural equation modeling analysis. *Educational Psychology, 16*(3), 305–314.

Cury, F., Biddle, S.H., Sarrazin, P., & Famose, J.P. (1997). Achievement goals and perceived ability predict investment in learning a sport task. *British Journal of Educational Psychology, 67*(3), 293–309.

Cury, F., De Tonac, A., & Sot, V. (1999). An unexplored aspect of achievement goal theory in sport: Development and predictive validity of the Approach and Avoidance Achievement in Sport Questionnaire (AAASQ). In V. Hosek, P. Tilinger, & L. Bilek (Eds.), *Psychology of sport and exercise: Enhancing the quality of life. Proceedings of the 10th European Congress on Sport Psychology—FEPSAC* (pp. 153–155). Prague: Charles University of Prague Press.

Cury, F., Famose, J.P., & Sarrazin, P. (1997). Achievement goal theory and active search for information in a sport task. In R. Lidor & M. Bar-Eli (Eds.), *Innovations in sport psychology: Linking theory and practice. Proceedings of the IX World Congress in Sport Psychology: Part I* (pp. 218–220). Netanya, Israel: Ministry of Education, Culture and Sport.

Cury, F., & Sarrazin, P. (1998). Achievement motivation and learning behaviors in sport tasks. *Journal of Sport and Exercise Psychology, 20* (Suppl.), S11.

Cury, F., Sarrazin, P. & Famose, J. P. (1997). Achievement goals, perceived ability and active search for information. *European Yearbook of Sport Psychology, 1,* 167–183.

Danish, S.J., Kleiber, D.A., & Hall, H.K. (1987). Developmental intervention and motivation enhancement in the context of sport. In M.L. Maehr & D.A. Kleiber (Eds.), *Advances in motivation and achievement. Vol. 5*, (pages 211–238).

deCharms, R. (1976). *Enhancing motivation: Change in the classroom.* New York: Irvington.

deCharms, R. (1984). Motivation enhancement in educational settings. In R. Ames & C. Ames (Eds.), *Research on motivation in education* (Vol. 2, pp. 275–310). New York: Academic Press.

deCharms, R.C. (1968). *Personal causation: The internal affective determinants of behavior.* New York: Academic Press.

Deci, E.L. (1971). Effects of externally mediated rewards on intrinsic motivation. *Journal of Personality and Social Psychology, 18*, 105–115.

Deci, E.L. (1975). *Intrinsic motivation.* New York: Plenum Press.

Deci, E.L. (1980). *The psychology of self-determination.* Lexington, MA: Heath.

Deci, E.L. (1992). The relation of interest to the motivation of behavior: A self-determination theory perspective. In K. Ann and S. Hidi et al. (Eds.), *The role of interest in learning and development* (pp. 43–70). Hillsdale, NJ: Erlbaum.

Deci, E.L., Nezlek, J., & Sheinman, L. (1981). Characteristics of the rewarder and intrinsic motivation of the rewardee. *Journal of Personality and Social Psychology, 40*, 1–10.

Deci, E.L., & Ryan, R.M. (1980). The empirical exploration of intrinsic motivation processes. In L. Berkowitz (Ed.), *Advances in experimental social psychology*, (Vol. 13, pp. 39–80). New York: Academic Press.

Deci, E.L., & Ryan, R.M. (1985a). The General Causality Orientations Scale: Self-determination in personality. *Journal of Research in Personality, 19*, 109–134.

Deci, E.L., & Ryan, R.M. (1985b). *Intrinsic motivation and self-determination in human behavior.* New York: Plenum Press.

Deci, E.L., & Ryan, R.M. (1987). The support of autonomy and the control of behavior. *Journal of Personality and Social Psychology, 53*, 1024–1037.

Deci, E.L., & Ryan, R.M. (1991). A motivational approach to self: Integration in personality. In R. Dienstbier (Ed.), *Nebraska symposium on motivation. Vol. 38. Perspectives on motivation* (pp. 237–288). Lincoln, NE: University of Nebraska Press.

Deci, E.L., & Ryan, R.M. (1992). The initiation and regulation of intrinsically motivated learning and achievement. In A.K. Boggiano & T.S. Pittman (Eds.), *Achievement and motivation: A social-developmental perspective* (pp. 9–36). New York: Cambridge University Press.

Deci, E.L., & Ryan, R.M. (1994). Promoting self-determined education. *Scandinavian Journal of Educational Research, 38*, 3–14.

Deci, E.L., Schwartz, A.J., Sheinman, L., & Ryan, R.M. (1981). An instrument to assess adults' orientations toward control versus autonomy with children: Reflections on intrinsic motivation and competence. *Journal of Educational Psychology, 73*, 642–650.

Dempsey, J.M., Kimiecik, J.C., & Horn, T.S. (1993). Parental influence on children's moderate to vigorous physical activity participation: An expectancy-value approach. *Pediatric Exercise Science, 5*, 151–167.

Dennett, D.C. (1978). *Brainstorms: Philosophical essays on mind and psychology*. Montgomery, VT: Bradford.

Derryberry, D., & Reed, M. (1994). Temperament and attention: Orientating toward and away from positive and negative signals. *Journal of Personality and Social Psychology, 66*, 1128–1139.

Desharnais, R., Bouillon, J., & Godin, G. (1986). Self-efficacy and outcome expectations as determinants of exercise adherence. *Psychological Reports, 59*, 1155–1159.

Dienstbier, R.A. (1989). Arousal and physiological toughness: Implications for mental and physical health. *Psychological Review, 96*, 84–100.

Dishman, R.K. (1982). Compliance/adherence in health-related exercise. *Health Psychology, 1*, 237–267.

Dorobantu, M., & Biddle, S. (1997). The influence of situational and individual goals on the intrinsic motivation of Romanian adolescents towards physical education. *European Yearbook of Sport Psychology, 1*, 148–165.

DuCharme, K.A., & Brawley, L.R. (1994, June). *Examining the relationship between goals and overt behavior with beginning exercisers: A mediational analysis*. Paper presented at the annual meeting of the North American Society for the Psychology of Sport and Physical Activity, Clearwater, FL.

DuCharme, K.A., & Brawley, L.R. (1995). Predicting the intentions and behavior of exercise initiates using two forms of self-efficacy. *Journal of Behavioral Medicine, 18*, 479–497.

Duda, J. L. (1981). A cross cultural analysis of achievement motivation in sport and the classroom. Unpublished doctoral dissertation, University of Illinois, Urbana.

Duda, J.L. (1987). Toward a developmental theory of children's motivation in sport. *Journal of Sport Psychology, 9*, 130–145.

Duda, J.L. (1988). The relationship between goal perspectives, persistence and behavioral intensity among male and female recreational sport participants. *Leisure Sciences, 10*(2), 95–106.

Duda, J.L. (1989). The relationship between task and ego orientation and the perceived purpose of sport among male and female high school athletes. *Journal of Sport and Exercise Psychology, 11*, 318–335.

Duda, J.L. (1992). Motivation in sport settings: A goal perspective approach. In G.C. Roberts (Ed.), *Motivation in sport and exercise* (pp. 57–91). Champaign, IL: Human Kinetics.

Duda, J.L. (1993). Goals: A social-cognitive approach to the study of achievement motivation in sport. In R.N. Singer, M. Murphey, & L.K. Tennant (Eds.). *Handbook of research on sport psychology* (pp. 421–436). New York: Macmillan.

Duda, J.L. (1994). A goal perspective theory of meaning and motivation in sport. In S. Serpa (Ed.), *International perspectives on sport and exercise psychology* (pp. 127–148). Indianapolis: Benchmark Press.

Duda, J.L. (1996). Maximizing motivation in sport and physical education among children and adolescents: The case for greater task involvement. *Quest, 48*, 290–302.

Duda, J.L. (1997a). Goal perspectives and their implications for an active and healthy life style among girls and women. *Women in Sport and Physical Activity Journal, 6,* 239–253.

Duda, J.L. (1997b). Perpetuating myths: A response to Hardy's 1996 Coleman Griffith Address. *Journal of Applied Sport Psychology, 9,* 307–313.

Duda, J.L. (1999). The motivational climate and its implications for motivation, health, and the development of eating disorders in gymnastics. *Revista de Psicologia Social Aplicada, 9* (1), 7–25.

Duda, J.L. (in press). Goal perspectives and their implications for health-related outcomes in the physical domain. In F. Cury, P. Sarrazin, & F.P. Famose, (Eds.), *Advances in motivation theories in the sport domain.* Paris: Presses Universitaires de France.

Duda, J.L., & Balaguer, I. (1999). Toward an integration of models of leadership with a contemporary theory of motivation. In R. Lidor & M. Bar-Eli (Eds.), *Sport psychology: Linking theory and practice* (pp. 213–230). Morgantown, WV: Fitness Information Technology.

Duda, J.L., Benardot, D., & Kim, M-S. (in press). The relationship of the motivational climate to psychological and energy balance correlates of eating disorders in female gymnasts. *The Sport Psychologist.*

Duda, J.L., Chi, L., Newton, M.L., Walling, M.D., & Catley, D. (1995). Task and ego orientation and intrinsic motivation in sport. *International Journal of Sport Psychology, 26,* 40–63.

Duda, J.L., Fox, K.R., Biddle, S.J.H., & Armstrong, N. (1992). Children's achievement goals and beliefs about success in sport. *British Journal of Educational Psychology, 62,* 313–323.

Duda, J.L., & Hall, H.K. (2000). Achievement goal theory in sport: Recent extensions and future directions. In R.N. Singer, H.A. Hausenblas, & C.M. Janelle (Eds.), *Handbook of sport psychology* (2nd ed., pp. 417–443). New York: Wiley.

Duda, J.L., & Hom, H.L. (1993). Interdependencies between the perceived and self-reported goal orientations of young athletes and their parents. *Pediatric Exercise Science, 5*(3), 234–241.

Duda, J.L., & Huston, L. (1995). The relationship of goal orientation and degree of competitive sport participation to the endorsement of aggressive acts in American football. In R. Vanfraechem-Raway & Y. Vanden Auweele (Eds.), *Proceedings of the IX European Congress on Sport Psychology* (pp. 655–662). Brussels: Belgian Federation of Sport Psychology.

Duda, J.L., & Kim, M-S. (1997). Perceptions of the motivational climate, psychological characteristics, and attitudes toward eating among young female gymnasts. *Journal of Sport and Exercise Psychology, 19,* (Suppl.), S48.

Duda, J.L., Newton, M.L., & Yin, Z. (1999a). *The perceived motivational climate in sport: Within-team member variability/interdependence and the correspondence to perceptions held by the coach.* Manuscript under review.

Duda, J.L., Newton, M.L., & Yin, Z. (1999b). Within-team variation in perceptions of the motivational climate and its predictors. In V. Hosek, P. Tilinger, & L. Bilek (Eds.), *Psychology of sport and exercise: Enhancing the quality of life. Proceedings of the 10th European Congress on Sport Psychology—FEPSAC* (pp. 167–169). Prague: Charles University of Prague Press.

Duda, J.L., & Nicholls, J.G. (1992). Dimensions of achievement motivation in schoolwork and sport. *Journal of Educational Psychology, 84*(3), 290–299.

Duda, J.L., Olson, L., & Templin, T. (1991). The relationship of task and ego orientation to sportsmanship attitudes and the perceived legitimacy of injurious acts. *Research Quarterly for Exercise and Sport, 62,* 79–87.

Duda, J.L., & White, S.A. (1992). Goal orientations and beliefs about the causes of sport success among elite skiers. *The Sport Psychologist, 6*(4), 334–343.

Duda, J.L., & Whitehead, J. (1998). Measurement of goal perspectives in the physical domain. In J. Duda (Ed.), *Advances in sport and exercise psychology measurement* (pp. 21–48). Morgantown, WV: Fitness Information Technology.

Duncan, T., & Stoolmiller, M. (1993). Modeling social and psychological determinants of exercise behaviors via structural equation systems. *Research Quarterly for Exercise and Sport, 64,* 1–16.

Dunn, J.C. (2000). Goal orientations, perceptions of the motivational climate, and perceived competence of children with movement difficulties. *Adapted Physical Activity Quarterly, 17,* 1–19.

Dunn, J.G.H., & Dunn, J.C. (1999). Goal orientations, perceptions of aggression, and sportspersonship in elite youth male ice hockey players. *The Sport Psychologist, 13,* 183–200.

Dustman, R.E., Emmerson, R., & Shearer, D.E. (1994). Physical activity, age, and cognitive-neuropsychological function. *Journal of Aging and Physical Activity, 2,* 143–181.

Dweck, C.S. (1980). Learned helplessness in sport. In C.H. Nadeau, W.R. Halliwell, K.M. Newell, & G.C. Roberts (Eds.), *Psychology of motor behavior and sport, 1979* (pp. 139–149). Champaign, IL: Human Kinetics.

Dweck, C.S. (1986). Motivational processes affecting learning. *American Psychologist, 41,* 1040–1048.

Dweck, C.S. (1991). Self-theories and goals: Their role in motivation, personality, and development. In R.A. Dienstbier (Ed.), *Nebraska symposium on motivation— 1990* (pp. 199–235). Lincoln, NE: University of Nebraska Press.

Dweck, C.S. (1999). *Self-theories: Their role in motivation, personality, and development.* Philadelphia: Psychology Press.

Dweck, C.S., & Elliott, E.L. (1983). Achievement motivation. In E.M. Hetherington (Ed.), *Handbook of child psychology. Vol. 4. Socialization, personality and social development* (pp. 643–691). New York: Wiley.

Dweck, C.S., & Leggett, E. (1988). A social-cognitive approach to motivation and personality. *Psychological Review, 95,* 256–273.

Dweck, C.S., & Sorich, L.A. (1999). Mastery-oriented thinking. In C.R. Snyder (Ed.), *Coping: The psychology of what works.* New York: Oxford University Press.

Dzewaltowski, D.A. (1989). Toward a model of exercise motivation. *Journal of Sport and Exercise Psychology, 11,* 251–269.

Dzewaltowski, D.A., Noble, J.M., & Shaw, J.M. (1990). Physical activity participation: Social cognitive theory versus the theories of reasoned action and planned behavior. *Journal of Sport and Exercise Psychology, 12,* 388–405.

Earley, P.C. (1986). Trust, perceived importance of praise and criticism and work performance: An examination of feedback in the U.S. and England. *Journal of Management, 12,* 457–473.

Earley, P.C. (1988). Computer generated performance feedback in the magazine subscription industry. *Organizational Behavior and Human Decision Processes, 41,* 50–64.

Earley, P.C., Connolly, T., & Ekegren, G. (1989). Goals, strategy development and task performance: Some limits on the efficacy of goal setting. *Journal of Applied Psychology, 74,* 24–33.

Earley, P.C., & Kanfer, R. (1985). The influence of component participation and role models on goal acceptance, goal satisfaction and performance. *Organizational Behavior and Human Decision Processes, 36,* 378–390.

Earley, P.C., & Lituchy, T.R. (1989). *Delineating goals and efficacy effects: A test of three models.* Unpublished manuscript, Department of Management and Policy, University of Arizona.

Earley, P.C., & Perry, B.C. (1987). Work plan availability and performance: An assessment of task strategy priming on subsequent task completion. *Organizational Behavior and Human Decision Processes, 39,* 279–302.

Ebbeck, V., & Becker, S.L. (1994). Psychosocial predictors of goal orientations in youth soccer. *Research Quarterly for Exercise and Sport, 65,* 355–362.

Eccles, J., & Harold, R.D. (1991). Gender differences in sport involvement: Applying the Eccles' expectancy-value model. *Journal of Applied Sport Psychology, 3,* 7–35.

Eccles, J., Midgley, C., & Adler, T. (1984). Grade-related changes in the school environment: Effects on achievement motivation. In J. Nicholls (Ed.), *The development of achievement motivation* (pp. 283–332). Greenwich, CT: JAI Press.

Elliot, A.J. (1997). Integrating the "classic" and "contemporary" approaches to achievement motivation: A hierarchical model of avoidance achievement motivation. In P. Pintrich & M. Maehr (Eds.), *Advances in motivation and achievement* (Vol. 10, pp. 143–179). Stamford, CT: JAI Press.

Elliot, A.J., & Church, M.A. (1997). A hierarchical model of approach and avoidance achievement motivation. *Journal of Personality and Social Psychology, 72*(1), 218–232.

Elliot, A.J., & Harackiewicz, J.M. (1996). Approach and avoidance achievement goals and intrinsic motivation: A mediational analysis. *Journal of Personality and Social Psychology, 70*(3), 461–475.

Elliot, A.J., & Sheldon, K.M. (1997). Avoidance achievement motivation: A personal goals analysis. *Journal of Personality and Social Psychology, 73*(1), 171–185.

Elliot, A.J., Sheldon, K.M., & Church, M.A. (1997). Avoidance personal goals and subjective well-being. *Personality and Social Psychology Bulletin, 23*(9), 915–927.

Elliott, E.S., & Dweck, C.S. (1988). Goals: An approach to motivation and achievement. *Journal of Personality and Social Psychology, 54,* 5–12.

Emmons, R.A. (1995). Levels and domains in personality: An introduction. *Journal of Personality, 63,* 341–364.

Epstein, J. (1988). Effective schools or effective students? Dealing with diversity. In R. Haskins & B. MacRae (Eds.), *Policies for America's public schools* (pp. 89–126). Norwood, NJ: Ablex.

Epstein, J. (1989). Family structures and student motivation: A developmental perspective. In C. Ames & R. Ames (Eds.), *Research on motivation in education* (Vol. 3, pp. 259–295). New York: Academic Press.

Erbaugh, S.J., & Barnett, M.L. (1986). Effects of modeling and goal-setting on the jumping performance of primary-grade children. *Perceptual and Motor Skills, 63,* 1287–1293.

Erez, M., & Arad, R. (1986). Participative goal setting: Social, motivational and cognitive factors. *Journal of Applied Psychology, 71,* 591–597.

Erez, M., & Zidon, I. (1984). Effect of goal acceptance on the relationship of goal difficulty to task performance. *Journal of Applied Psychology, 69,* 69–78.

Escarti, A., Peiro, C., & Duda, J.L. (1996). The assessment of significant others' perceived goal perspectives in sport settings. *Journal of Applied Sport Psychology, 8,* S138.

Evans, J., & Roberts, G.C. (1987). Physical competence and the development of children's peer relations. *Quest, 38,* 23–35.

Evans, M.G. (1991). The problem of analyzing multiplicative composites. Interactions revisited. *American Psychologist, 46,* 6–15.

Ewart, C.K. (1995). Self-efficacy and recovery from heart attack: Implications for a social cognitive analysis of exercise and emotion. In J.E. Maddux (Ed.), *Self-efficacy, adaptation, and adjustment: Theory, research, and application* (pp. 203–227). New York: Plenum Press.

Ewart, C.K., Stewart, K.J., Gillilan, R.E., & Kelemen, M.H. (1986). Self-efficacy mediates strength gains during circuit weight training in men with coronary artery disease. *Medicine and Science in Sports and Exercise, 18,* 531–540.

Ewart, C.K., Stewart, K.J., Gillilan, R.E., Kelemen, M.H., Valenti, S.A., Manley, J.D., & Kelemen, M.D. (1986). Usefulness of self-efficacy in predicting overexertion during programmed exercise in coronary artery disease. *American Journal of Cardiology, 57,* 557–561.

Ewart, C.K., Taylor, C.B., Reese, L.B., & DeBusk, R.F. (1983). Effects of early postmyocardial infarction exercise testing on self-perception and subsequent physical activity. *American Journal of Cardiology, 51,* 1076–1080.

Ewing, M. (1981). *Achievement orientations and sport behaviors of males and females.* Unpublished doctoral dissertation, University of Illinois.

Ewing, M.E., & Seefeldt, V. (1989). *Teenagers motivations for sport participation help predict lifelong habits.* North Palm Beach, FL: Athletic Footwear Association.

Fairall, D.G., & Rodgers, W.M. (1997). The effects of goal-setting method on goal attributes in athletes: A field experiment. *Journal of Sport and Exercise Psychology, 19,* 1–16.

Feltz, D. (1988). Self confidence and sports performance. In K.B. Pandolf (Ed.), *Exercise and Sport Science Reviews* (pp. 423–457). New York: Macmillan.

Feltz, D. (1992). Understanding motivation in sport: A self-efficacy perspective. In G.C. Roberts (Ed.), *Motivation in sport and exercise* (pp. 93–106). Champaign, IL: Human Kinetics.

Ferrer-Caja, E., & Weiss, M.R. (1999). Determinants of intrinsic motivation in physical education: Cross-validation with high school students in elective courses. *Journal of Sport and Exercise Psychology, 21* (Suppl.), S42.

Finney, J.W., Mitchell, R.E., Cronkite, R.C., & Moos, R.H. (1984). Methodological issues emanating in estimating main and interactive effects: Examples from coping/social support and stress field. *Journal of Health and Social Behavior, 25,* 85–98.

Fishbein, M., & Ajzen, I. (1975). *Belief, attitude, intention and behavior: An introduction to theory and research.* Reading, MA: Addison-Wesley.

Fishbein, M., & Stasson, M. (1990). The role of desires, self-predictions, and perceived control in the prediction of training session attendance. *Journal of Applied Social Psychology, 20,* 173–199.

Fleishman, E.A. (1964). *Structure and measurement of physical fitness.* Englewood Cliffs, NJ: Prentice Hall.

Ford, M. (1992). *Motivating humans: Goals, emotions, and personal agency beliefs.* Boston: Sage.

Fortier, M.S., & Grenier, M. (1999). Déterminants personnels et situationnels de l'adhérence à l'exercice: Une étude prospective [Personal and structural determinants of exercise: A prospective study]. *Revue STAPS, 48,* 25–37.

Fortier, M.S., Vallerand, R.J., Brière, N.M., & Provencher, P. (1995). Competitive and recreational sport structures and gender: A test of their relationship with sport motivation. *International Journal of Sport Psychology, 26,* 24–39.

Fortier, M.S., Vallerand, R.J., & Guay, F. (1995). Academic motivation and school performance: Toward a structural model. *Contemporary Educational Psychology, 20,* 257–274.

Fox, K.R. (1988). The self-esteem complex and youth fitness. *Quest, 40,* 230–246.

Fox, K.R., Goudas, M., Biddle, S., Duda, J., & Armstrong, N. (1994). Children's task and ego goal profiles in sport. *British Journal of Educational Psychology, 64,* 253–261.

Frederick, C.M., & Ryan, R.M. (1995). Self-determination in sport: A review using cognitive evaluation theory. *International Journal of Sport Psychology, 26,* 5–23.

Frierman, S.H., Weinberg, R.S., & Jackson, A.W. (1990). The relationship between goal proximity and specificity in bowling: A field experiment. *The Sport Psychologist, 4,* 145–154.

Frost, R.O., & Marten, P.A. (1990). Perfectionism and evaluative threat. *Cognitive Therapy and Research, 14,* 559–572.

Frost, R.O., Marten, P.A., Lahart, C., & Rosenblate, R. (1990). The dimensions of perfectionism. *Cognitive Therapy and Research, 14,* 449–468.

Fry, M.D. (2000a). A developmental analysis of children's and adolescents' understanding of luck and ability in the physical domain. *Journal of Sport and Exercise Psychology, 22,* 145–166.

Fry, M.D. (2000b). A developmental examination of children's understanding of task difficulty in the physical domain. *Journal of Applied Sport Psychology, 12,* 180–202.

Fry, M.D., & Duda, J.L. (1997). Children's understanding of effort and ability in the physical and academic domains. *Research Quarterly for Exercise and Sport, 68,* 331–334.

Gano-Overway, L., & Duda, J.L. (1996). Goal perspectives and their relationship to beliefs and affective responses among African and Anglo American athletes. *Journal of Applied Sport Psychology, 8* (Suppl.), S138.

Gano-Overway, L., & Duda, J.L. (in press). Goal perspectives and their relationship to beliefs and affective responses among African and Anglo American athletes. *International Journal of Sport Psychology.*

Gardner, D.E., Shields, D.L.L., Bredemeier, B.J.L., & Bostrom, A. (1996). The relationship between perceived coaching behaviors and team cohesion among baseball and softball players. *The Sport Psychologist, 10,* 367–381.

Garibaldi, A.M. (1979). Affective contributions of cooperative and group goal structures. *Journal of Educational Psychology, 71,* 788–794.

Garland, H. (1985). A cognitive mediation theory of task goals and human performance. *Motivation and Emotion, 9,* 345–367.

Gauvin, L., & Spence, J. (1996). Physical activity and psychological well-being: Knowledge base, current issues, and caveats. *Nutrition Reviews, 54,* 53–65.

Georgiadis, M., Biddle, S., & Vanden Auweele, Y. (1999). *Cognitive, emotional, and behavioural connotations of task and ego orientation profiles: An ideographic approach using hierarchical class analysis.* Manuscript under review.

Giannini, J., Weinberg, R.S., & Jackson, A. (1988). The effects of mastery, competitive and cooperative goals on the performance of simple and complex basketball skills. *Journal of Sport and Exercise Psychology, 10,* 408–417.

Gil, K.M., Abrams, M.R., Phillips, G., & Keefe, F.J. (1989). Sickle cell disease pain: Relation of coping strategies to adjustment. *Journal of Consulting and Clinical Psychology, 57,* 725–731.

Gil, K.M., Abrams, M.R., Phillips, G., & Williams, D.A. (1992). Sickle cell disease pain. II: Predicting health care use and activity level at nine month follow-up. *Journal of Consulting and Clinical Psychology, 60,* 267–273.

Gil, K.M., Phillips, G., Webster, D.A., Martin, N.J., Abrams, M., Grant, M., Clark, W.C., & Janal, M.N. (1995). Experimental pain sensitivity and reports of negative thoughts in adults with sickle cell disease. *Behavior Therapy, 26,* 273–293.

Gill, D.S., & Deeter, T. (1988). Development of the Sport Orientation Questionnaire. *Research Quarterly for Exercise and Sport, 59,* 191–202.

Godin, G. (1993). The theories of reasoned action and planned behavior: Overview of findings, emerging research problems and usefulness for exercise promotion. *Journal of Applied Sport Psychology, 5,* 141–157.

Godin, G., & Kok, G. (1996). The theory of planned behavior: A review of its applications to health-related behaviors. *American Journal of Health Promotion, 11,* 87–98.

Gorley, T., & Gordon, S. (1995). An examination of the transtheoretical model and exercise behavior in older adults. *Journal of Sport and Exercise Psychology, 17,* 312–324.

Gottfried, A.E. (1985). Academic intrinsic motivation in elementary and junior high school students. *Journal of Educational Psychology, 77,* 631–645.

Goudas, M., & Biddle, S. (1994a). Intrinsic motivation in physical education: Theoretical foundations and contemporary research. *Educational and Child Psychology, 11,* 68–76.

Goudas, M., & Biddle, S.J.H. (1994b). Perceived motivational climate and intrinsic motivation in school physical education classes. *European Journal of Psychology of Education, 9,* 241–250.

Goudas, M., Biddle, S., & Fox, K. (1994a). Perceived locus of causality, goal orientations, and perceived competence in school physical education classes. *British Journal of Educational Psychology, 64*(3), 453–463.

Goudas, M., Biddle, S.J.H., & Fox, K.R. (1994b). Achievement goal orientations and intrinsic motivation in physical fitness testing with children. *Pediatric Exercise Science, 6,* 159–167.

Goudas, M., Biddle, S.J.H., Fox, K.R., & Underwood, M. (1995). It ain't what you do, it's the way that you do it! Teaching style affects children's motivation in track and field lessons. *The Sport Psychologist, 9,* 254–264.

Goudas, M., Fox, K., Biddle, S., & Armstrong, N. (1992) Children's task and ego goal profiles in sport: Relationship with perceived competence, enjoyment, and participation. *Journal of Sports Sciences, 10,* 606–607.

Goudas, M., Underwood, A.M., & Biddle, S. (1993). [The effect of two teaching styles on students' intrinsic motivation in school physical education classes]. Unpublished raw data, University of Exeter.

Gould, D., Eklund, R.C., & Jackson, S.A. (1993). Coping strategies used by more versus less successful U.S. Olympic wrestlers. *Research Quarterly for Exercise and Sport, 64,* 83–93.

Gould, D., Finch, L.M., & Jackson, S.A. (1993). Coping strategies used by national champion figure skaters. *Research Quarterly for Exercise and Sport, 64,* 453–468.

Gould, D., Tuffey, S., Udry, E., & Loehr, J. (1996). Burnout in competitive junior tennis players: I. A quantitative psychological assessment. *The Sport Psychologist, 10,* 332–340.

Gould, D., Wilson, C.G., Tuffey, S., & Lochbaum, M. (1993). Stress and the young athlete: The child's perspective. *Pediatric Exercise Science, 5,* 286–297.

Graef, R., Csikszentmihalyi, M., & Gianinno, S.M. (1983). Measuring intrinsic motivation in everyday life. *Leisure Studies, 2,* 155–168.

Green, S.B. (1991). How many subjects does it take to do a regression analysis? *Multivariate Behavioral Research, 26,* 499–510.

Grembowski, D., Patrick, D., Diehr, P., Durham, M., Beresford, S., Kay, E., & Hecht, J. (1993). Self-efficacy and health behavior among older adults. *Journal of Health and Social Behavior, 34,* 89–104.

Grolnick, W.S., & Ryan, R.M. (1987). Autonomy in children's learning: An experimental and individual difference investigation. *Journal of Personality and Social Psychology, 52,* 890–898.

Grolnick, W.S., & Ryan, R.M. (1989). Parent styles associated with children's self-regulation and competence in school. *Journal of Educational Psychology, 81,* 143–154.

Guay, F., Blais, M.R., Vallerand, R.J., & Pelletier, L.G. (1996). *The Global Motivation Scale.* Unpublished manuscript, Université du Québec à Montréal.

Guay, F., & Vallerand, R.J. (1995, June 30). *The Situational Motivation Scale.* Paper presented at the annual convention of the American Psychological Society, New York.

Guay, F., & Vallerand, R.J. (1997). Social context, student's motivation and academic achievement: Toward a process model. *Social Psychology of Education, 1*, 211–233.

Guay, F., Vallerand, R.J., & Blanchard, C.M. (in press). On the assessment of situational intrinsic and extrinsic motivation: The Situational Motivation Scale. *Motivation and Emotion.*

Guivernau, M., & Duda, J.L. (1995). Psychometric properties of a Spanish version of the Task and Ego Orientation in Sport Questionnaire (TEOSQ) and Beliefs about the Causes of Success Inventory. *Revista de Psicologia del Deporte, 5*, 31–51.

Guivernau, M., & Duda, J.L. (1998a). Domain generality of goal orientations, beliefs about success, perceived ability and interest among Spanish student-athletes. *European Yearbook of Sport Psychology, 2*, 56–72.

Guivernau, M., & Duda, J.L. (1998b). Integrating concepts of motivation and morality: The contribution of norms regarding aggressive and rule-violating behaviors. *Journal of Sport and Exercise Psychology, 20*, S13.

Guivernau, M., & Duda, J.L. (1998c). Norms for aggression/cheating, goal orientations, beliefs, perceived motivational climate, and athletic aggression: Potential gender differences. *Journal of Applied Sport Psychology, 10*, S132.

Guivernau, M., Thorne, K., & Duda, J.L. (1994a). *Cross domain generality of goals, beliefs, perceived ability, and interest: A replication.* Paper presented at the 4th Annual Midwest Sport and Exercise Psychology Symposium, Michigan State University, East Lansing.

Guivernau, M., Thorne, K., & Duda, J.L. (1994b, June). *Cross-situational generality of dimensions of achievement motivation: A replication.* Presentation made at the meetings of the North American Society for the Psychology of Sport and Physical Activity, Clearwater, FL.

Gulanick, M. (1991). Is phase 2 cardiac rehabilitation necessary for early recovery of patients with cardiac disease? A randomized, controlled study. *Heart and Lung, 20*, 9–15.

Gyurcsik, N.C., & Brawley, L.R. (1998, March). *Mindful deliberation about exercise: Influence of positive and negative thinking.* Paper presented at the annual meeting of the Society of Behavioral Medicine, New Orleans, LA.

Gyurcsik, N.C., & Brawley, L.R. (1999). Coping with negative exercise thoughts: Strategies, efficacy, and intention. *Annals of Behavioral Medicine, 21* (Suppl.), S057.

Gyurcsik, N.C., Brawley, L.R., & Martin, K.A. (1997, September). *Efficacy and the value of acute outcomes in predicting exercise adherence.* Paper presented at the annual meeting of the Association for the Advancement of Applied Sport Psychology (AAASP), San Diego, CA.

Hall, H.K. (1990). *A social-cognitive approach to goal setting: The mediating effects of achievement goals and perceived ability.* Unpublished doctoral dissertation, University of Illinois at Urbana-Champaign.

Hall, H.K. (1995, October). Expanding the debate on goal setting: A motivational technique that *sometimes* works. *International Society of Sport Psychology Newsletter,* 13–17.

Hall, H. K., & Byrne, A. T. J. (1986) Goals, subgoals, their effects on the performance of an endurance task. Paper presented at the North American Society for the Psychology of Sport and Physical Activity Conference in Scottsdale, Arizona, June 1986.

Hall, H.K., & Byrne, A.T.J. (1988). Goal setting in sport: Clarifying recent anomalies. *Journal of Sport and Exercise Psychology, 10,* 184–198.

Hall, H.K., Cawthra, I.W., & Kerr, A.W. (1997). Burnout: "Motivation gone awry or a disaster waiting to happen"? In R. Lidor & M. Bar-Eli (Eds.), *Innovations in sport psychology: Linking theory and practice. Proceedings of the IX World Congress in Sport Psychology: Part I* (pp. 306–308). Netanya, Israel: Ministry of Education, Culture and Sport.

Hall, H.K., Humphrey, E., & Kerr, A. (1997). Understanding and enhancing children's intrinsic motivation in sport: Adopting the tenets of Eccles' Expectancy-Value Model. In R. Lidor & M. Bar-Eli (Eds.), *Innovations in sport psychology: Linking theory and practice. Proceedings of the IX World Congress in Sport Psychology: Part I* (pp. 309–311). Netanya, Israel: Ministry of Education, Culture and Sport.

Hall, H.K., & Kerr, A.W. (1997). Motivational antecedents of precompetitive anxiety in youth sport. *The Sport Psychologist, 11*(1), 24–42.

Hall, H.K., & Kerr, A.W. (1998). Predicting achievement anxiety: A social cognitive perspective. *Journal of Sport and Exercise Psychology, 20,* 100–113.

Hall, H.K., Kerr, A.W., & Matthews, J. (1998). Precompetitive anxiety in sport: The contribution of achievement goals and perfectionism. *Journal of Sport and Exercise Psychology, 20,* 194–217.

Hall, H.K., Weinberg, R.S., & Jackson, A.W. (1987). Effects of goal specificity, goal difficulty, and information feedback on endurance performance. *Journal of Sport Psychology, 9,* 43–54.

Hanrahan, S.J., & Biddle, S. (1997). Questionnaire measures of achievement goal orientations. In R. Lidor & M. Bar-Eli (Eds.), *Innovations in sport psychology: Linking theory and practice. Proceedings of the IX World Congress in Sport Psychology: Part I* (pp. 315–316). Netanya, Israel: Ministry of Education, Culture and Sport.

Harackiewicz, J.M., Sansone, C., Blair, L.W., Epstein, J.A., & Manderlink, G. (1987). Attributional processes in behavior change and maintenance: Smoking cessation and continued abstinence. *Journal of Consulting and Clinical Psychology, 55,* 372–378.

Hardy, L. (1997). The Coleman Roberts Griffith Address: Three myths about applied consultancy work. *Journal of Applied Sport Psychology, 9,* 277–294.

Hardy, L. (1998). Responses to the reactants on three myths in applied consultancy work. *Journal of Applied Sport Psychology, 10,* 212–219.

Hardy, L., Jones, G., & Gould, D. (1996). *Understanding psychological preparation for sport: Theory and practice for elite performers.* Chichester, UK: Wiley.

Harlow, H.F. (1958). The nature of love. *American Psychologist, 13,* 673–685.

Harter, S. (1978). Effectance motivation reconsidered: Toward a developmental model. *Human Development, 1,* 34–64.

Harter, S. (1981a). The development of competence motivation in the mastery of cognitive and physical skills: Is there still a place for joy? In G.C. Roberts and D.M. Landers (Eds), *Psychology of motor behavior and sport* (pp. 3–29). Champaign, IL: Human Kinetics.

Harter, S. (1981b). A new self-report scale on intrinsic versus extrinsic orientation in the classroom: Motivational and informational components. *Developmental Psychology, 17,* 300–312.

Harter, S. (1985). Competence as a dimension of self-evaluation: Toward a comprehensive model of self-worth. In R.L. Leahy (Ed.), *The development of the self* (pp. 55–121). Orlando, FL: Academic Press.

Harter, S. (1987). The determinants and mediational role of global self-worth in children. In N. Eisenberg (Ed.), *Contemporary topics in developmental psychology* (pp. 219–242). New York: Wiley-Interscience.

Harter, S. (1990). Self and identity development. In S.S. Feldman & G.R. Elliot (Eds.), *At the threshold: The developing adolescent* (pp. 352–387). Cambridge, MA: Harvard University Press.

Harter, S. (1993). Causes, consequences of low self-esteem in children and adolescents. In R.F. Baumeister (Ed.), *Self-esteem: The puzzle of low self-regard* (pp. 87–116). New York: Plenum Press.

Harter, S. (1999). *The construction of the self: A developmental perspective.* New York: Guilford Press.

Harter, S., & Connell, J.P. (1984). A model of achievement and related self-perceptions of competence, control, and motivational orientation. In J.G. Nicholls (Ed.), *Advances in motivation* (Vol. 3, pp. 219–250). Greenwich, CT: JAI Press.

Harter, S., & Marold, D.B. (1991). A model of the determinants and mediational role of self-worth: Implications for adolescent depression and suicidal ideation. In J. Strauss and G.R. Goethals (Eds.), *The self: Interdisciplinary approaches* (pp. 66–92). New York: Springer-Verlag.

Harter, S., Marold, D.B., Whitesell, N.R., & Cobbs, G. (1996). A model of the effects of perceived parent and peer support on adolescent false self behavior. *Child Development, 67,* 360–374.

Harter, S., Waters, P., & Whitesell, N.R. (1998). Relational self-worth: Differences in perceived worth as a person across interpersonal contexts among adolescents. *Child Development, 69,* 756–766.

Harter, S., Waters, P.L., Whitesell, N.R., & Kastelic, D. (1998). Level of voice among female and male high school students: Relational context, support, and gender orientation. *Developmental Psychology, 34,* 892–901.

Harter, S., & Whitesell, N.R. (1989). Developmental changes in children's understanding of single, multiple and blended emotion concepts. In C. Saarni & P.L. Harris (Eds.), *Children's understanding of emotion* (pp. 81–116). Cambridge, UK: Cambridge University Press.

Harter, S., Whitesell, N.R., & Junkin, L.J. (1998). Similarities and differences in domain-specific and global self-evaluations of learning-disabled, behaviorially disordered, and normally achieving adolescents. *American Educational Research Journal, 35,* 653–680.

Harwood, C.G. (2000). Measuring achievement goals in competitive sport: Could our research better inform our practice? Under review, *Journal of Applied Sport Psychology*.

Harwood, C., & Hardy, L. (1999). Achievement goals in competitive sport: A critique of conceptual and measurement issues. *Proceedings of the 10th European Congress of Sport Psychology* (pp. 241-243). Prague, Czech Republic: Charles University Press.

Harwood, C., Hardy, A., & Swain A. (2000). Achievement goals in sport: A critique of conceptual and measurement issues. *Journal of Sport and Exercise Psychology, 22*, 235–255.

Harwood, C.G., & Swain, A.B.J. (1998). Antecedents of pre-competition achievement goals in elite junior tennis players. *Journal of Sports Sciences, 16*, 357–371.

Hatzigeorgiadis, A., & Biddle, S. (1999). Relationships between goal orientation, self consciousness and thoughts of escape athletes experience during competition. In V. Hosek, P. Tilinger, & L. Bilek (Eds.), *Psychology of sport and exercise: Enhancing the quality of life. Proceedings of the 10th European Congress on Sport Psychology—FEPSAC* (pp. 247–249). Prague: Charles University of Prague Press.

Hausenblas, H.A., Carron, A.V., & Mack, D.E. (1997). Application of the theories of reasoned action and planned behavior to exercise behavior: A meta-analysis. *Journal of Sport and Exercise Psychology, 19*, 36–51.

Hellandsig, E.T. (1998). Motivational predictors of high performance and discontinuation in different types of sports among talented teenage athletes. *International Journal of Sport Psychology, 29*, 27–44.

Hewitt, P.L., & Flett, G.L. (1991). Perfectionism in the self and social contexts: Conceptualization, assessment, and association with psychopathology. *Journal of Personality and Social Psychology, 60*, 456–470.

Higgins, E.T., & Tykocinski, O. (1992). Self-discrepancies and biographical memory: Personality and cognition at the level of psychological situation. *Personality and Social Psychology Bulletin, 18*, 527–535.

Hilgard, E.R. (1987). *Psychology in America: A historical survey.* Orlando, FL: Harcourt Brace Jovanovich.

Hlatky, M.A., Boineau, R.E., Higginbotham, M.B., Lee, K.L., Mark, D.B., Califf, R.M., Cobb, F.R., & Pryor, D.B. (1989). A brief self-administered questionnaire to determine functional capacity (the Duke Activity Status Index). *American Journal of Cardiology, 64*, 651–654.

Hollenbeck, J.R., Williams, C.R., & Klein, H.J. (1989). An empirical examination of the antecedents of commitment to difficult goals. *Journal of Applied Psychology, 74*, 18–23.

Hom, H.L., Duda, J.L., & Miller, A. (1993). Correlates of goal orientations among young athletes. *Pediatric Exercise Science, 5*(2), 168–176.

Horn, T.S., Glen, S.D., & Wentzell, A.B. (1993). Sources of information underlying personal ability judgments in high school athletes. *Pediatric Exercise Science, 5*, 263–274.

Horn, T.S., & Hasbrook, C. (1986). Informational components influencing children's perceptions of their physical competence. In M. Weiss & D. Gould (Eds.), *Sport for children and youth: Proceedings of the 1984 Olympic Scientific Congress* (pp. 81–88). Champaign, IL: Human Kinetics.

Horn, T.S., & Hasbrook, C.A. (1987). Psychological characteristics and the criteria children use for self-evaluation. *Journal of Sport Psychology, 9,* 208–221.

Horn, T.S., & Weiss, M.R. (1991). A developmental analysis of children's self-ability judgments in the physical domain. *Pediatric Exercise Science, 3,* 310–326.

Horne, T.E. (1994). Predictors of physical activity intentions and behaviour for rural homemakers. *Canadian Journal of Public Health, 85,* 132–135.

Hosek, V., Tilinger, P., & Bilek, L. (Eds.), *Psychology of sport and exercise: Enhancing the quality of life. Proceedings of the 10th European Congress on Sport Psychology—FEPSAC* (pp. 247–249). Prague: Charles University of Prague Press.

Hovell, M., Sallis, J., Hofstetter, R., Barrington, E., Hackley, M., Elder, J., Castro, F., & Kilbourne, K. (1991). Identification of correlates of physical activity among Latino adults. *Journal of Community Health, 16,* 23–36.

Hunter, J.E., & Schmidt, F.L. (1983). Quantifying the effect of psychological interventions on employee job performance and work force productivity. *American Psychologist, 38,* 473–478.

Ingledew, D.K., Markland, D., & Medley, A.R. (1998). Exercise motives and stages of change. *Journal of Health Psychology, 3,* 477–489.

Jaakkola, T., Kokkonen, J., Liukkonen, J., Telama, R., Pakkala, P., & Piirainen, U. (1999). The reliability and validity of the observation scale of the motivational climate in physical education. In V. Hosek, P. Tilinger, & L. Bilek (Eds.), *Psychology of sport and exercise: Enhancing the quality of life. Proceedings of the 10th European Congress on Sport Psychology—FEPSAC* (pp. 271–273). Prague: Charles University of Prague Press.

Jaccard, J., Turrisi, R., & Wan, C.K. (1990). *Interaction effects in multiple regression.* Sage Series: Quantitative Applications in the Social Sciences. Newbury Park, CA: Sage.

Jackson, S.A., & Marsh, H.W. (1996). Development and validation of a scale to measure optimal experience: The flow state scale. *Journal of Sport and Exercise Psychology, 18,* 17–35.

Jackson, S., & Roberts, G.C. (1992). Positive performance states of athletes: Toward a conceptual understanding of peak performance. *The Sport Psychologist, 6,* 156–171.

Jagacinski, C., & Nicholls, J. (1984). Conceptions of effort and ability and related affects in task involvement and ego involvement. *Journal of Educational Psychology, 76,* 909–919.

Jagacinski, C., & Nicholls, J. (1987). Competence and affect in task involvement and ego involvement: The impact of social comparison information. *Journal of Educational Psychology, 79,* 107–114.

James, W. (1892). *Psychology: The briefer course.* New York: Holt.

Janis, I.L., & Mann, L. (1977). *Decision making: A psychological analysis of conflict, choice and commitment.* New York: Free Press.

Janz, N.K., & Becker, M.H. (1984). The health belief model: A decade later. *Health Education Quarterly, 11,* 1–47.

Johnson, D.W., Johnson, R.T., Johnson, J., & Anderson, D. (1976). Effects of cooperative versus individualized instruction on student prosocial behavior, attitudes toward learning, and achievement. *Journal of Educational Psychology, 68,* 446–452.

Johnson, S.R., Ostrow, A.C., Perna, F.M., & Etzel, E.F. (1997). The effects of group versus individual goal setting on bowling performance. *Journal of Sport and Exercise Psychology, 19,* 190–200.

Jones, J.G., & Hanton, S. (1996). Interpretation of competitive anxiety symptoms and goal attainment expectancies. *Journal of Sport and Exercise Psychology, 18,* 144–157.

Joreskog, K.G., & Sorbom, D. (1993). *LISREL 8: Structural equation modeling with the SIMPLIS command language.* Chicago: Scientific Software International.

Jourden, F. J., Bandura, A., & Banfield, J. (1991). The impact of conceptions of ability on self-regulatory factors and motor skill acquisition. *Journal of Sport and Exercise Psychology, 8,* 213–226.

Kagan, J. (1972). Motives and development. *Journal of Personality and Social Psychology, 22,* 51–66.

Kane, T.D., Marks, M.A., Zaccaro, S.J., & Blair, V. (1996). Self-efficacy, personal goals, and wrestlers' self-regulation. *Journal of Sport and Exercise Psychology, 18,* 36–48.

Kaplan, R.M., Atkins, C.J., & Reinsch, S. (1984). Specific efficacy expectations mediate exercise compliance in patients with COPD. *Health Psychology, 3,* 223–242.

Kaplan, R.M., Ries, A.L., Prewitt, L.M., & Eakin, E. (1994). Self-efficacy expectations predict survival for patients with chronic obstructive pulmonary disease. *Health Psychology, 13,* 366–368.

Kautz, J. (1982). Ethnic diversity in cardiovascular mortality. *Atherosclerosis Review, 9,* 85–108.

Kavanagh, D.J., Gooley, S., & Wilson, P.H. (1993). Prediction of adherence and control in diabetes. *Journal of Behavioral Medicine, 16,* 509–522.

Kavussanu, M. (1997). *Moral functioning in sport: An achievement goal perspective.* Unpublished dissertation, University of Illinois.

Kavussanu, M., & McAuley, E. (1995). Exercise and optimism: Are highly active individuals more optimistic? *Journal of Sport and Exercise Psychology, 17,* 246–258.

Kavussanu, M., & Roberts, G.C. (1995, June). Motivation and physical activity: The role of motivatoinal climate, intrinsic interest, and self-efficacy. Paper presented at the North American Society of Sport and Physical Activity. Asilomar, CA.

Kavussanu, M., & Roberts, G.C. (1996a). Motivation in physical activity contexts: The relationship of perceived motivational climate to intrinsic motivation and self-efficacy. *Journal of Sport and Exercise Psychology, 18*(3), 264–280.

Kavussanu, M., & Roberts, G.C. (1996b). The utility of dispositional versus situational factors in predicting intrinsic motivation, beliefs about the causes of success, and task choice in physical activity classes. *Journal of Sport and Exercise Psychology, 18* (Suppl.), S46.

Kavussanu, M., & Roberts, G.C. (1998, June). *Team norms and moral functioning in college athletes.* Paper presented to the North American Society of Sport Psychology and Physical Activity, Chicago.

Kavussanu, M., & Roberts, G.C. (1999). Predicting moral functioning in college athletes: The contribution of goal orientations, perceived motivational climate, and team norms. In V. Hosek, P. Tilinger, & L. Bilek (Eds.), *Psychology of sport and exercise: Enhancing quality of life*. Proceedings of the 10th European Congress of Sport Psychology–FEPSAC. Part I. (pp. 298–300). Prague, CZ: Charles University Press.

Kavussanu, M., & Roberts, G.C. (in press). Moral functioning in sport: An achievement goal perspective. *Journal of Sport and Exercise Psychology*.

Kendzierski, D., & Johnson, W. (1993). Excuses, excuses, excuses: A cognitive behavioral approach to exercise implementation. *Journal of Sport and Exercise Psychology, 15*, 207–219.

Kenny, D.A., & Lavoie, L. (1985). Separating individual and group effects. *Journal of Personality and Social Psychology, 48*, 339–348.

Kent, G. (1987). Self-efficacious control over reported physiological, cognitive, and behavioral symptoms of dental anxiety. *Behavior Research and Therapy, 25*, 341–347.

Kent, G., & Gibbons, R. (1987). Self-efficacy and the control of anxious cognitions. *Journal of Behavior Therapy and Experimental Psychiatry, 18*, 33–40.

Kihlstrom, J.K., & Cantor, N. (1984). The self as a knowledge structure. In L. Berkowitz (Ed.), *Advances in experimental social psychology* (Vol. 17, pp. 1–48). New York: Academic Press.

Kim, B.J., & Gill, D.L. (1997). A cross-cultural extension of goal perspective theory to Korean sport youth. *Journal of Sport and Exercise Psychology, 19*, 142–155.

Kim, M.S., & Duda, J.L. (1998). Achievement goals, motivational climates, and occurrence of and responses to psychological difficulties and performance debilitation among Korean athletes. *Journal of Sport and Exercise Psychology, 20* (Suppl.), S124.

Kim, M.S., & Duda, J.L. (1999). *Predicting coping responses: An integration of Lazarus' transactional theory of psychological stress and coping and goal perspective theory*. Manuscript under review.

Kimiecik, J.C., & Horn, T.S. (1998). Parental beliefs and children's moderate-to-vigorous physical activity. *Research Quarterly for Exercise and Sport, 69*, 163–175.

Kimiecik, J.C., Horn, T.S., & Shurin, C.S. (1996). Relationships among children's beliefs, perceptions of their parents' beliefs and their moderate-to-vigorous physical activity. *Research Quarterly for Exercise and Sport, 67*, 324–336.

Kingston, K.M., & Hardy, L. (1997a). *Do goal orientation profiles impact upon competition performance?* Unpublished manuscript.

Kingston, K.M., & Hardy, L. (1997b). Effects of different types of goals on processes that support performance. *The Sport Psychologist, 11*, 277–293.

Kleiber, D. A., & Roberts, G. C. (1981). The effects of sport experience in the development of social character: A preliminary investigation. *Journal of Sport and Exercise Psychology, 3*, 114–122.

Koestner, R., Losier, G.F., Vallerand, R.J., & Carducci, D. (1996). Identified and introjected forms of political internalization: Extending self-determination theory. *Journal of Personality and Social Psychology, 70*, 1025–1036.

Kohn, A. (1986). *No contest: The case against competition.* Boston: Houghton Mifflin.

Kowal, J., & Fortier, M.S. (1999). Motivational determinants of flow: Contributions from self-determination theory. *Journal of Social Psychology, 139,* 355–368.

Kramer, A.F., Hahn, S., Cohen, N.J., Banich, M.T., McAuley, E., Harrison, C.R., Chason, J., Vakil, E., Bardell, L., Boileau, R.A., & Colcombe, A. (1999). Ageing, fitness and neurocognitive function. *Nature, 400,* 418–419.

Krane, V., Greenleaf, C.A., & Snow, J. (1997). Reaching for gold and the price of glory: A motivational case study of an elite gymnast. *The Sport Psychologist, 11,* 53–71.

Krug, S.E. (1989). Leadership and learning: A measurement-based approach for analyzing school effectiveness and developing effective school leaders. In M.L. Maehr & C. Ames (Eds.), *Advances in motivation and achievement* (Vol. 3, pp. 73–105). New York: Academic Press.

Kruglanski, A.W. (1989). *Lay epistemics and human knowledge: Cognitive and motivational bases.* New York: Plenum Press.

Kuhl, J. (1986). Motivation and information processing: A new look at decision making, dynamic change, and action control. In R.M. Sorrentino & E. Higgins (Eds.), *Handbook of motivation and cognition: Foundations of social behavior* (pp. 403–434). New York: Guilford Press.

Kuhl, J., & Koch, B. (1984). Motivational determinants of motor performance: The hidden second task. *Psychological Research, 46*(1–2), 143–153.

Kyllo, L.B., & Landers, D.M. (1995). Goal setting in sport and exercise: A research synthesis to resolve the controversy. *Journal of Sport and Exercise Psychology, 17,* 117–137.

Landers, D.M., & Boutcher, S. (1986). Arousal-performance relationships. In J.M. Williams (Ed.), *Applied sport psychology: Personal growth to peak experience* (pp. 163–184). Palo Alto, CA: Mayfield.

Landers, D.M., & Petruzzello, S.J. (1994). Physical activity, fitness, and anxiety. In C. Bouchard, R.J. Shepard, & T. Stephens (Eds.), *Physical activity, fitness, and health—International Proceedings and Consensus Statement* (pp. 868–882). Champaign, IL: Human Kinetics.

Latham, G.P., Erez, M., & Locke, E.A. (1988). Resolving scientific disputes by the joint design of crucial experiments by the antagonists: Application to the Erez-Latham dispute regarding participation in goal setting. *Journal of Applied Psychology, 73,* 753–772.

Latham, G.P., & Lee, T.W. (1986). Goal setting. In E.A. Locke (Ed.), *Generalizing from laboratory to field settings.* Lexington, MA: Lexington Books.

Latham, G.P., & Locke, E.A. (1979). Goal-setting: A motivational technique that works. *Organizational Dynamics, 8,* 68–80.

Lau, R.R., Hartman, K.A., & Ware, J.E., Jr. (1986). Health as a value: Methodological and theoretical considerations. *Health Psychology, 5,* 25–43.

Lazarus, R.S., & Folkman, S. (1984). *Stress, appraisal, and coping.* New York: Springer.

Le Bars, H., & Gernigon, C. (1998). Perceived motivational climate, dispositional goals, and participation withdrawal in judo. *Journal of Sport and Exercise Psychology, 20* (Suppl.), S58.

Lechner, L., & De Vries, H. (1995). Starting participation in an employee fitness program: Attitudes, social influence, and self-efficacy. *Preventive Medicine, 24,* 627–633.

Lee, A.M., & Edwards, R.V. (1984). Assigned and self-selected goals as determinants of motor skill performance. *Education, 105,* 87–91.

Lee, C. (1988). The relationship between goal setting, self-efficacy, and female field hockey team performance. *International Journal of Sport Psychology, 20,* 147–161.

Lee, M., & Whitehead, J. (1999). *The effect of values, achievement goals, and perceived ability on moral attitudes in youth sport.* Report provided to the Economic and Social Research Council, Swindon, England.

Lemyre, P.N., Ommundsen,Y. & Roberts, C.C. (2000). Moral functioning in sport: The role of dispositional goals and perceived ability. *International Journal of Psychology, 35* (3-4), 23.

Lepper, M.R., & Cordova, D.I. (1992). A desire to be taught: Instructional consequences of intrinsic motivation. *Motivation and Emotion, 16,* 187–208.

Lepper, M.R., & Greene, D. (1978). Overjustification research and beyond: Toward a means-ends analysis of intrinsic and extrinsic motivation. In M.R. Lepper & D. Greene (Eds), *The hidden costs of reward* (pp. 109–148). Hillsdale, NJ: Erlbaum.

Lepper, M.R., Greene, D., & Nisbett, R.E. (1973). Undermining children's interest with extrinsic rewards: A test of the "overjustification effect." *Journal of Personality and Social Psychology, 28,* 129–137.

Lepper, M.R., & Hodell, M. (1989). Intrinsic motivation in the classroom. In C. Ames & R. Ames (Eds.), *Research on motivation in education* (Vol. 3, pp. 73–105). New York: Academic Press.

Lerner, B.S., & Locke, E.A. (1995). The effects of goal setting, self-efficacy, competition, and personal traits on the performance of an endurance task. *Journal of Sport and Exercise Psychology, 17,* 138–152.

Lewin, K. (1951). *Field theory in social science.* New York: Harper & Row.

Li, F. (1999). The Exercise Motivation Scale: Its multifaceted structure and construct validity. *Journal of Applied Sport Psychology, 11,* 97–115.

Li, F., & Harmer, P. (1996). Testing the simple assumption underlying the Sport Motivation Scale: A structural equation modeling analysis. *Research Quarterly for Exercise and Sport, 67,* 396–405.

Li, F., Harmer, P., & Acock, A. (1996). The Task and Ego Orientation in Sport Questionnaire: Construct equivalence and mean differences across gender. *Research Quarterly for Exercise and Sport, 67,* 228–238.

Li, F., Harmer, P., Acock, A., Vongjaturapat, N., & Boonverabut, S. (1997). Testing the cross-cultural validity of TEOSQ and its factor covariance and mean structures across gender. *International Journal of Sport Psychology, 28,* 271–286.

Li, F., Harmer, P., Chi, L., & Vongjaturapat, S. (1996). Cross-cultural validation of the Task and Ego Orientation Questionnaire. *Journal of Sport and Exercise Psychology, 18,* 392–407.

Lintunen, T., Valkonen, A., & Biddle, S. (1997). Social-cognitive predictors of motivation and intention to participate in sports in Finnish children. In R. Lidor &

M. Bar-Eli (Eds.), *Innovations in sport psychology: Linking theory and practice. Proceedings of the IX World Congress in Sport Psychology: Part II* (pp. 437–439). Netanya, Israel: Ministry of Education, Culture and Sport.

Liukkonen, J. (1997). Motivational climate and enjoyment in male youth soccer players. In R. Lidor & M. Bar-Eli (Eds.), *Innovations in sport psychology: Linking theory and practice. Proceedings of the IX World Congress in Sport Psychology: Part II* (pp. 440–442). Netanya, Israel: Ministry of Education, Culture and Sport.

Lloyd, J., & Barenblatt, L. (1984). Intrinsic intellectuality: Its relations to social class, intelligence, and achievement. *Journal of Personality and Social Psychology, 46,* 646–654.

Lloyd, J., & Fox, K. (1992). Achievement goals and motivation to exercise in adolescent girls: A preliminary intervention study. *British Journal of Physical Education Research Supplement, 11,* 12–16.

Lochbaum, M., & Roberts, G.C. (1993). Goal orientations and perceptions of the sport experience. *Journal of Sport and Exercise Psychology, 15,* 160–171.

Locke, E.A. (1968). Toward a theory of task motivation and incentives. *Organizational Behaviour and Human Performance, 3,* 157–189.

Locke, E.A. (1991). Problems with goal setting research in sports—and their solution. *Journal of Sport and Exercise Psychology, 13,* 311–316.

Locke, E.A. (1994). Comments on Weinberg and Weigand. *Journal of Sport and Exercise Psychology, 16,* 212–215.

Locke, E.A., & Latham, G.P. (1979, Autumn). Goal setting: A motivational technique that works. *Organizational Dynamics,* 68–80.

Locke, E.A., & Latham, G.P. (1985). The application of goal setting to sports. *Journal of Sport Psychology, 7,* 205–222.

Locke, E.A., & Latham, G.P. (1990). *A theory of goal setting and task performance.* Englewood Cliffs, NJ: Prentice Hall.

Locke, E.A., Shaw, K.M., Saari, L.M., & Latham, G.P. (1981). Goal setting and task performance; 1969–1980. *Psychological Bulletin, 90,* 125–152.

Locke, L.F., Spirduso, W.W., & Silverman, S.J. (1993). *Proposals that work: A guide for planning dissertations and grant proposals* (3rd ed.). Newbury Park, CA: Sage.

Long, B.C. (1985). Stress-management interventions: A 15-month follow-up of aerobic conditioning and stress inoculation training. *Cognitive Therapy and Research, 9,* 471–478.

Losier, G.F., Gaudette, G.M., & Vallerand, R.J. (1997). *Une analyse motivationnelle des orientations à l'esprit sportif auprès d'entraineurs certifiés du Nouveau-Brunswick* [A motivational analysis of the sportspersonship orientations of certified coaches from New Brunswick]. Paper presented at the annual conference of the Quebec Society for Research in Psychology, Sherbrooke, Quebec, Canada.

Losier, G.F., & Vallerand, R.J. (1995). Développement et validation de l'Échelle des relations interpersonnelles dans le sport (ERIS) [Development and validation of the Interpersonal Relationships in Sport Scale]. *International Journal of Sport Psychology, 26,* 307–326.

Losier, G.F., Vallerand, R.J., & Blais, M.R. (1993). Construction et validation de l'Échelle des perceptions de compétence dans les domaines de vie (EPCDV)

[Construction and validation of the Perceived Competence in Life Contexts Scale]. *Science et comportement, 23,* 1–16.

Losier, G.F., Vallerand, R.J., Provencher, P., Fortier, M.S., Senécal, C.B., & Rinfret, N. (1996). *Persistence in graduate school: A motivational analysis.* Manuscript in preparation.

Loveland, K.K., & Olley, J.G. (1979). The effect of external reward on interest and quality of task performance in children of high and low intrinsic motivation. *Child Development, 50,* 1207–1210.

Lox, C.L., McAuley, E., & Tucker, R.S. (1995). Exercise as an intervention for enhancing subjective well-being in an HIV-1 population. *Journal of Sport and Exercise Psychology, 17,* 345–362.

Madden, T.J., Ellen, P.S., & Ajzen, I. (1992). A comparison of the theory of planned behavior and the theory of reasoned action. *Personality and Social Psychology Bulletin, 18,* 3–9.

Maddux, J.E. (1993). Social cognitive models of health and exercise behavior: An introduction and review of conceptual issues. *Journal of Applied Sport Psychology, 5,* 116–140.

Maddux, J.E. (1995). Looking for common ground: A comment on Kirsch and Bandura. In J. Maddux (Ed.), *Self-efficacy, adaptation, and adjustment: Theory, research, and application* (pp. 377–385). New York: Plenum Press.

Maddux, J.E., Brawley, L., & Boykin, A. (1995). Self-efficacy and healthy behavior. Prevention, promotion, and detection. In J.E. Maddux (Ed.), *Self-efficacy, adaptation, and adjustment. Theory, research, and application* (pp. 173–202). New York: Plenum Press.

Maddux, J.E., Norton, L.W., & Stoltenberg, C.D. (1986). Self-efficacy expectancy, outcome expectancy, and outcome value: Relative effects on behavioral intentions. *Journal of Personality and Social Psychology, 51,* 783–789.

Maddux, J.E., & Rogers, R.W. (1983). Protection motivation and self-efficacy: A revised theory of fear appeals and attitude change. *Journal of Experimental Social Psychology, 19,* 469–479.

Maehr, M.L. (1983). On doing well in science. Why Johnny no longer excels; Why Sarah never did. In S.G. Paris, G.M. Olsen, & H.W. Stevenson (Eds.), *Learning and motivation in the classroom* (pp. 179–210). Hillsdale, NJ: Erlbaum.

Maehr, M.L. (1984). Meaning and motivation: Toward a theory of personal investment. In R. Ames & C. Ames (Eds.), *Research motivation in education: Student motivation* (Vol. 1, pp. 115–144). New York: Academic Press.

Maehr, M.L. (1991). The "psychological environment" of the school: A focus for school leadership. In P. Thurston & P. Zodhiates (Eds.), *Advances in educational administration. Vol. 2. School leadership* (pp. 51–81). Greenwich, CT: JAI Press.

Maehr, M.L., & Braskamp, L.A. (1986). *The motivation factor: A theory of personal investment.* Lexington, MA: Lexington Books/Heath.

Maehr, M.L., & Midgley, C. (1991). Enhancing student motivation: A schoolwide approach. *Educational Psychologist, 26,* 399–427.

Maehr, M.L., & Nicholls, J.G. (1980). Culture and achievement motivation: A second look. In N. Warren (Ed.), *Studies in cross-cultural psychology* (Vol. 2, pp. 221–267). New York: Academic Press.

Manning, M.M., & Wright, T.L. (1983). Self-efficacy expectancies, outcome expectancies, and the persistence of pain control in childbirth. *Journal of Personality and Social Psychology, 45,* 421–431.

Marcus, B.H., Eaton, C.A., Rossi, J.S., & Harlow, L.L. (1994). Self-efficacy, decision-making, and stages of change: An integrative model of physical exercise. *Journal of Applied Social Psychology, 24,* 489–508.

Marcus, B.H., & Owen, N. (1992). Motivational readiness, self-efficacy and decision-making for exercise. *Journal of Applied Social Psychology, 22,* 3–16.

Marcus, B.H., Pinto, B.M., Simkin, L.R., Audrain, J.E., & Taylor, E.R. (1994). Application of theoretical models to exercise behavior among employed women. *American Journal of Health Promotion, 9,* 49–55.

Marcus, B.H., Selby, V.C., Niaura, R.S., & Rossi, J.S. (1992). Self-efficacy and the stages of exercise behavior change. *Research Quarterly for Exercise and Sport, 63,* 60–66.

Marsh, H. (1994). Sport motivation orientations: Beware of jingle-jangle fallacies. *Journal of Sport and Exercise Psychology, 16,* 365–380.

Marsh, H.W., & Peart, N.D. (1988). Competitive and cooperative physical fitness training programs for girls: Effects on physical fitness and multidimensional self-concepts. *Journal of Sport and Exercise Psychology, 10,* 390–407.

Marshall, H.H., & Weinstein, R.S. (1984). Classroom factors affecting students' self evaluations: An interactional model. *Review of Educational Research, 54,* 301–325.

Martens, R. (1975). *Social psychology of physical activity.* New York: Harper & Row.

Martinek, T. (1989). The psycho-social dynamics of the pygmalion phenomenon in physical education and sport. In T. Templin & P. Schemp (Eds.), *Socialization into physical education: Learning to teach* (pp. 199–217). Indianapolis: Benchmark Press.

Maslow, A. (1968). *Toward the psychology of being* (2nd ed.). New York: D. Van Nostrand.

Maslow, A. (1970). *Motivation and personality.* New York: Harper & Row.

Matthews, D.B. (1991). The effects of school environment of intrinsic motivation of middle-school children. *Journal of Humanistic Education and Development, 30,* 30–36.

Mayo, R.J. (1977). The development and construct validation of a measure of intrinsic motivation (Doctoral dissertation, Purdue University, 1976). *Dissertation Abstracts International, 37,* 5417B. (University Microfilms No. 77-7491)

McAdams, D.P. (1994). Can personality change? Levels of stability and growth in personality across the life span. In T.F. Heatherton & J.L. Weinberger (Eds.), *Can personality change?* (pp. 299–314). Washington, DC: American Psychological Association.

McArthur, L.Z., & Baron, R.M. (1983). Toward an ecological theory of social perception. *Psychological Review, 90,* 215–283.

McAuley, E. (1991). Efficacy, attributional, and affective responses to exercise participation. *Journal of Sport and Exercise Psychology, 13,* 382–393.

McAuley, E. (1992a). Exercise and motivation: A self-efficacy perspective. In G.C. Roberts (Ed.), *Motivation in sport and exercise.* Champaign, IL: Human Kinetics.

McAuley, E. (1992b). The role of efficacy cognitions in the prediction of exercise behavior in middle-aged adults. *Journal of Behavioral Medicine, 15,* 65–88.

McAuley, E. (1993). Self-efficacy and the maintenance of exercise participation in older adults. *Journal of Behavioral Medicine, 16,* 103–113.

McAuley, E., Bane, S.M., & Mihalko, S.L. (1995). Exercise in middle-aged adults: Self efficacy and self-presentational outcomes. *Preventive Medicine, 24,* 319–328.

McAuley, E., Blissmer, B., Katula, J.A., & Duncan, T.E. (2000). Exercise environment, self-efficacy, and affective responses to acute exercise in older adults. *Psychology and Health, 15,* 341–355.

McAuley, E., Blissmer, B., Katula, J., Duncan, T.E., & Mihalko, S.L. (2000). Physical activity, self-esteem, and self-efficacy relationships in older adults: A randomized controlled trial. *Annals of Behavioral Medicine, 22,* 131–139.

McAuley, E., & Courneya, K.S. (1992). Self-efficacy relationships with affective and exertion responses to exercise. *Journal of Applied Social Psychology, 22,* 312–326.

McAuley, E., Courneya, K.S., & Lettunich, J. (1991). Effects of acute and long-term exercise on self-efficacy responses in sedentary, middle-aged males and females. *Gerontologist, 31,* 534–542.

McAuley, E., Courneya, K.S., Rudolph, D.L., & Lox, C.L. (1994). Enhancing exercise adherence in middle-aged males and females. *Preventive Medicine, 23,* 498–506.

McAuley, E., Duncan, T., & Tammen, V. (1989). Psychometric properties of the Intrinsic Motivation Inventory in a competitive sport setting: A confirmatory factor analysis. *Research Quarterly for Exercise and Sport, 60,* 48–58.

McAuley, E., & Katula, J. (1998). Physical activity interventions in the elderly: Influence on physical health and psychological function. In R. Schulz, G. Maddox, & M. Lawton (Eds.), *Annual review of gerontology and geriatrics* (Vol. 18, pp. 111–153). New York: Springer.

McAuley, E., Katula, J., Mihalko, S., Blissmer, B., Duncan, T., Pena, M., & Dunn, E. (1999). Mode of physical activity differentially influences self-efficacy in older adults: A latent growth curve analysis. *Journal of Gerontology: Psychological Sciences, 54B,* P283–P292.

McAuley, E., Lox, D.L., & Duncan, T. (1993). Long-term maintenance of exercise, self-efficacy, and physiological change in older adults. *Journal of Gerontology, 48,* P218–P223.

McAuley, E., & Mihalko, S.L. (1998). Measuring exercise-related self-efficacy. In J.L. Duda (Ed.), *Advances in sport and exercise psychology measurement* (pp. 371–390). Morgantown, WV: Fitness Information Technology.

McAuley, E., Mihalko, S.L., & Bane, S.M. (1997). Exercise and self-esteem in middle-aged adults: Multidimensional relationships and physical fitness and self-efficacy influences. *Journal of Behavioral Medicine, 20,* 67–83.

McAuley, E., & Rudolph, D. (1995). Physical activity, aging, and psychological well-being. *Journal of Aging and Physical Activity, 3,* 67–96.

McAuley, E., Shaffer, S.M., & Rudolph, D. (1995). Affective responses to acute exercise in elderly impaired males: The moderating effects of self-efficacy and age. *International Journal of Aging and Human Development, 41,* 13–27.

McAuley, E., Talbot, H.M., & Martinez, S. (1999). Manipulating self-efficacy in the exercise environment in women: Influences on affective responses. *Health Psychology, 18*(3), 288–294.

McAuley, E., & Tammen, V.V. (1989). The effects of subjective and objective competitive outcomes on intrinsic motivation. *Journal of Sport and Exercise Psychology, 11,* 84–93.

McCarthy, K., Kavussanu, M., & White, S. (1996). *Achievement goals and perceived purposes of sport.* Unpublished manuscript.

McClelland, D.C. (1985). *Human motivation.* London: Scott, Foresman.

McCullum, R.C. (1995). Model specification: Procedures, strategies, and related issues. In R.H. Hoyle (Ed.), *Structural equation modeling: Concepts, issues, and applications* (pp. 16–36). London: Sage.

McKiddie, B., & Maynard, I.W. (1997). Perceived competence of schoolchildren in physical education. *Journal of Teaching in Physical Education, 16,* 324–339.

Mento, A.J., Steel, R.P., & Karren, R.J. (1987). A meta-analytic study of the effects of goal setting on task performance: 1966-1984. *Organizational Behavior and Human Decision Processes, 39,* 52–83.

Middleton, M.J., & Midgley, C. (1997). Avoiding the demonstration of lack of ability: An underexplored aspect of goal theory. *Journal of Educational Psychology, 89,* 710–718.

Mihalko, S.L., McAuley, E., & Bane, S.M. (1996). Self-efficacy and affective responses to acute exercise in middle-aged adults. *Journal of Social Behavior and Personality, 11,* 375–385.

Miller, A. (1986). Performance impairment after failure: Mechanism and sex differences. *Journal of Educational Psychology, 78,* 486–491.

Miller, J.T., & McAuley, E. (1987). Effects of a goal setting training program on basketball free throw self efficacy and performance. *The Sport Psychologist, 1,* 103–113.

Miller, N.E. (1944). Experimental studies of conflict. In J. McV. Hunt (Ed.), *Personality and the behavioral disorders* (Vol. 1, pp. 431–465). New York: Ronald Press.

Miner, J.B. (1980). *Theories of organizational behavior.* Hinsdale, IL: Dryden.

Mitchell, S.A. (1996). Relationships between perceived learning environment and intrinsic motivation in middle school physical education. *Journal of Teaching in Physical Education, 15,* 369–383.

Moodie, A., Cooley, D., & Tammen, V. (1998). Hypercompetitiveness in Australian netball players. *Journal of Sport and Exercise Psychology, 21* (Suppl.), S89.

Mosston, M., & Ashworth, S. (1986). *Teaching physical education* (3rd ed.). Columbus, OH: Merrill.

Mullan, E., & Markland, D. (in press). Variations in self-determination across the stage of change for exercise in adults. *Motivation and Emotion.*

Mullan, E., Markland, D., & Ingledew, D.K. (1997). Motivation for exercise: Development of a measure of behavioral regulation. *Journal of Sports Sciences, 15,* 98–99.

Muris, P., Merckelbach, H., Horselenberg, R., Sijsenaar, M., & Leeuw, I. (1997). Thought suppression in spider phobia. *Behavior Research and Therapy, 35,* 769–774.

Newton, M., & Duda, J.L. (1993a). The relationship of task and ego orientation to performance-cognitive content, affect, and attributions in bowling. *Journal of Sport Behavior, 16*(4), 209–220.

Newton, M., & Duda, J.L. (1999). The interaction of motivational climate, dispositional goal orientations, and perceived ability in predicting indices of motivation. *International Journal of Sport Psychology, 30,* 63-82.

Newton, M., Duda, J.L., & Yin, Z. (2000). Examination of the psychometric properties of the Perceived Motivational Climate in Sport Questionnaire-2 in a sample of female athletes. *Journal of Sports Sciences, 18,* 275–290.

Newton, M.L. (1994). *The effect of differences in perceived motivational climate and goal orientations on motivational responses of female volleyball players.* Ann Arbor, MI: University Microfilms International.

Newton, M.L., & Duda, J.L. (1993b). The Perceived Motivational Climate in Sport Questionnaire-2: Construct and predictive validity. *Journal of Sport and Exercise Psychology, 15* (Suppl.), S59.

Newton, M.L., & Duda, J.L. (1995). The relationship of goal orientations and expectations on multi-dimensional state anxiety. *Perceptual and Motor Skills, 81,* 1107–1112.

Nicholls, J.G. (1976). Effort is virtuous, but it's better to have ability: Evaluative responses to perceptions of effort and ability. *Journal of Research in Personality, 10*(3), 306–315.

Nicholls, J.G. (1978). The development of the concepts of effort and ability, perception of academic attainment, and the understanding that difficult tasks require more ability. *Child Development, 49*(3), 800–814.

Nicholls, J.G. (1979). Quality and equality in intellectual development. *American Psychologist, 34,* 1071–1084.

Nicholls, J.G. (1980a, August). An intentional theory of achievement motivation. In W.U. Meyer & B. Weiner (Chairpersons), *Attributional approaches to human behavior.* Symposium presented at the Center for Interdisciplinary Studies, University of Bielfield, Germany.

Nicholls, J.G. (1980b). The development of the concept of difficulty. *Merrill-Palmer Quarterly, 26*(3), 271–281.

Nicholls, J.G. (1984a). Conceptions of ability and achievement motivation. In R. Ames & C. Ames (Eds.), *Research on motivation in education: Student motivation* (Vol. 1, pp. 39–73). New York: Academic Press.

Nicholls, J.G. (1984b). Achievement motivation: Conceptions of ability, subjective experience, task choice, and performance. *Psychological Review, 91,* 328–346.

Nicholls, J.G. (1989). *The competitive ethos and democratic education.* Cambridge, MA: Harvard University Press.

Nicholls, J.G. (1992). The general and the specific in the development and expression of achievement motivation. In G.C. Roberts (Ed.), *Motivation in sport and exercise* (pp. 31–57). Champaign, IL: Human Kinetics.

Nicholls, J.G., Cobb, P., Wood, T., Yackel, E., & Patashnick, M. (1990). Assessing students' theories of success in mathematics: Individual classroom differences. *Journal for Research in Mathematics Education, 21,* 109–122.

Nicholls, J.G., Cheung, P.C., Lauer, J., & Patashnick, M. (1989). Individual differences in academic motivation: Perceived ability, goals, beliefs, and values. *Learning and Individual Differences, 1*(1), 63–84.

Nicholls, J.G., & Hazzard, S.P. (1993). *Education as an adventure: Lessons from the second grade.* New York: Teachers College Press.

Nicholls, J.G., & Miller, A.T. (1983). The differentiation of the concepts of difficulty and ability. *Child Development, 54,* 951–959.

Nicholls, J.G., & Miller, A. (1984a). Development and its discontents: The differentiation of the concept of ability. In J. Nicholls (Ed.), *Advances in motivation and achievement. Vol. 3. The development of achievement motivation* (pp. 185–218). Greenwich, CT: JAI Press.

Nicholls, J.G., & Miller, A.T. (1984b). Reasoning about the ability of self and others: A developmental study. *Child Development, 55,* 1990–1999.

Nicholls, J.G., & Miller, A.T. (1985). Differentiation of the concepts of luck and skill. *Developmental Psychology, 21,* 76–82.

Nicholls, J.G., Patashnick, M., & Nolen, S.B. (1985). Adolescents' theories of education. *Journal of Educational Psychology, 77,* 683–692.

Nicholls, J.G., Patashnick, M., & Nolen, S.B. (1986). Conceptions of ability and intelligence. *Child Development, 57,* 636–645.

Nicholls, J.G., & Thorkildsen, T.A. (1995). *Reasons for learning: Expanding the conversation on student-teacher collaboration.* New York: Teachers College Press.

Ntoumanis, N., & Biddle, S. (1998). The relationship between competitive anxiety, achievement goals, and motivational climates. *Research Quarterly for Exercise and Sport, 69,* 176–187.

Ntoumanis, N., & Biddle, S.J.H. (1999a). Affect and achievement goals in physical activity: A meta-analysis. *Scandinavian Journal of Medicine and Science in Sports, 9,* 315–332.

Ntoumanis, N., & Biddle, S.J.H. (1999b). A review of motivational climate in physical activity. *Journal of Sports Sciences, 17,* 643–665.

Nyheim, M., Kavussanu, M., Roberts, G.C., & Treasure, D.C. (1996, June). *Goal orientations, beliefs about success, and satisfaction in summer sports camp participation.* Paper presented at the annual conference of the North American Society for the Psychology of Sport and Physical Activity, Ontario, Canada.

O'Connor, B.P., & Vallerand, R.J. (1994). Motivation, self-determination, and person-environment fit as predictors of psychological adjustment among nursing home residents. *Psychology and Aging, 9,* 189–194.

O'Connor, S.C., & Rosenblood, L.K. (1996). Affiliation motivation in everyday experience: A theoretical comparison. *Journal of Personality and Social Psychology, 70,* 513–522.

Oka, R.K., Gortner, S.R., Stotts, N.A., & Haskell, W.L. (1996). Predictors of physical activity in patients with chronic heart failure secondary to either ischemic or idiopathic dilated cardiomyopathy. *American Journal of Cardiology, 77,* 159–163.

Oldham, G.R. (1975). The impact of supervisory characteristics on goal acceptance. *Academy of Management Journal, 18*, 461–475.

Oldridge, N.B., & Rogowski, B.L. (1990). Self-efficacy and in-patient cardiac rehabilitation. *American Journal of Cardiology, 66*, 362–365.

Oman, R., & King, A. (1998). Predicting the adoption and maintenance of exercise participation using self-efficacy and previous exercise participation rates. *American Journal of Health Promotion, 12*, 154–161.

Ommundsen, Y., & Pedersen, B.H. (1999). The role of achievement goal orientations and perceived ability upon somatic and cognitive indices of sport competition trait anxiety. *Scandinavian Journal of Medicine and Science in Sports, 9*, 333–343.

Ommundsen, Y., & Roberts, G.C. (1999). Effect of motivational climate profiles on motivational indices in team sport. *Scandinavian Journal of Medicine and Science in Sports, 9*, 389–397.

Ommundsen, Y., Roberts, G.C., & Kavussanu, M. (1997). Perceived motivational climate and cognitive and affective correlates among Norwegian athletes. In R. Lidor & M. Bar-Eli (Eds.), *Innovations in sport psychology: Linking theory and practice. Proceedings of the IX World Congress in Sport Psychology: Part II* (pp. 522–524). Netanya, Israel: Ministry of Education, Culture and Sport.

Ommundsen, Y., Roberts, G.C., & Kavussanu, M. (1998). Perceived motivational climate and cognitive and affective correlates among Norwegian athletes. *Journal of Sports Sciences, 16*(2), 153–164.

Ommundsen, Y., Roberts, G.C., & Lemyre, N. (2000). Motivational climate and social-moral reasoning and behavior. *International Journal of Psychology, 35* (3 4), 23.

Orlick, T. (1978). *Winning through cooperation: Competitive insanity, cooperative alternatives.* Washington DC: Acropolis Press.

Orlick, T. (1990). *In pursuit of excellence.* Champaign, IL: Human Kinetics.

Orlick, T.D., & Mosher, R. (1978). Extrinsic awards and participant motivation in a sport related task. *International Journal of Sport Psychology, 9*, 27–39.

Ozer, E.M., & Bandura, A. (1990). Mechanisms governing empowerment effects: A self-efficacy analysis. *Journal of Personality and Social Psychology, 58*, 472–486.

Papaioannou, A. (1990). *Goal perspectives, motives for participation, and purposes of P.E. lessons in Greece as perceived by 14 and 17 year old pupils.* Manchester, England: University of Manchester.

Papaioannou, A. (1994). Development of a questionnaire to measure achievement orientations in physical education. *Research Quarterly for Exercise and Sport, 65*, 11–20.

Papaioannou, A. (1995a). Differential perceptual and motivational patterns when different goals are adopted. *Journal of Sport and Exercise Psychology, 17*(1), 18–34.

Papaioannou, A. (1995b). Motivation and goal perspectives in children's physical education. In S.J.H. Biddle (Ed.), *European perspectives on exercise and sport psychology* (pp. 245–269). Champaign, IL: Human Kinetics.

Papaioannou, A. (1997). Perception of the motivational climate, beliefs about the causes of success, and sportsmanship behaviors of elite Greek basketball players. In R. Lidor & M. Bar-Eli (Eds.), *Innovations in sport psychology: Linking theory and practice. Proceedings of the IX World Congress in Sport Psychology: Part II* (pp. 534–536). Netanya, Israel: Ministry of Education, Culture and Sport.

Papaioannou, A. (1998). Goal perspectives, reasons for being disciplined, and self-reported discipline in physical education lessons. *Journal of Teaching in Physical Education, 17,* 421–441.

Papaioannou, A., & Diggelidis, N. (1997). Social cognitive correlates of motivation and intention in Greek children and the social desirability scale. In R. Lidor & M. Bar-Eli (Eds.), *Innovations in sport psychology: Linking theory and practice. Proceedings of the IX World Congress in Sport Psychology: Part II* (pp. 537–539). Netanya, Israel: Ministry of Education, Culture and Sport.

Papaioannou, A., & Kouli, O. (1999). The effect of task structure, perceived motivational climate, and goal orientations on students' task involvement and anxiety. *Journal of Applied Sport Psychology, 11,* 51–71.

Papaioannou, A., & McDonald, A.I. (1993). Goal perspectives and purposes of physical education as perceived by Greek adolescents. *Physical Education Review, 16,* 41–48.

Parker, L.E., & Lepper, M.R. (1992). Effects of fantasy contexts on children's learning and motivation: Making learning more fun. *Journal of Personality and Social Psychology, 62,* 625–633.

Pascuzzi, D. (1981). *Young children's perceptions of success and failure.* Unpublished doctoral dissertation, University of Illinois.

Passer, M.W. (1996). At what age are children ready to compete?: Some psychological considerations. In F.L. Smoll & R.E. Smith (Eds.), *Children and youth in sport: A biopsychosocial perspective* (pp. 73–88). Chicago: Brown & Benchmark.

Peiro, C., Escarti, A., & Duda, J.L. (1997). Significant others' socializing influences on Spanish adolescent athletes' goal orientations. In R. Lidor & M. Bar-Eli (Eds.), *Innovations in sport psychology: Linking theory and practice. Proceedings of the IX World Congress in Sport Psychology: Part II* (pp. 549–551). Netanya, Israel: Ministry of Education, Culture and Sport.

Pelletier, L.G., Brière, N.M., Blais, M.R., & Vallerand, R.J. (1988, June 11). *Persisting vs dropping out: A test of Deci and Ryan's theory.* Paper presented at the annual conference of the Canadian Society of Psychology, Montréal, Canada.

Pelletier, L.G., Dion, S., Tuson, K., & Green-Demers, I. (1998). *Why do people fail to adopt environmental behaviors? Towards a taxonomy of environmental amotivation.* Unpublished manuscript, University of Ottawa.

Pelletier, L.G., Fortier, M.S., Vallerand, R.J., & Brière, N.M. (2001). *Perceived autonomy support, motivation, and persistence in physical activity: A longitudinal investigation.* Manuscript submitted for publication.

Pelletier, L.G., Fortier, M.S., Vallerand, R.J., Tuson, K.M., Brière, N.M., & Blais, M.R. (1995). Toward a new measure of intrinsic motivation, extrinsic motivation, and amotivation in sports: The Sport Motivation Scale (SMS). *Journal of Sport and Exercise Psychology, 17,* 35–53.

Pelletier, L.G., Vallerand, R.J., Blais, M.R., Brière, N.M., & Green-Demers, I. (1996). Vers une conceptualisation motivationnelle multidimensionnelle du loisir: Construction et validation de l'Échelle de motivation vis-à-vis des loisirs (EML)

[Construction and validation of the Leisure Motivation Scale]. *Loisir et Société, 19*, 559–585.

Pelletier, L.G., Vallerand, R.J., Green-Demers, I., Brière, N.M., & Blais, M.R. (1995). Loisirs et santé mentale: Les relations entre la motivation pour la pratique des loisirs et le bien-être psychologique [Leisure and mental health: Relationships between leisure involvement and psychological well-being]. *Canadian Journal of Behavioural Science, 27*, 214–225.

Pensgaard, A.M. (1999). The dynamics of motivation and perceptions of control when competing in the Olympic Games. *Perceptual and Motor Skills, 89*, 116–125.

Pensgaard, A.M., & Roberts, G.C. (1997). The interaction between goal orientations and use of coping strategies among elite sport participants. In R. Lidor & M. Bar-Eli (Eds.), *Innovations in sport psychology: Linking theory and practice. Proceedings of the IX World Congress of Sport Psychology* (pp. 552–554). Netanya, Israel: Ministry of Education, Culture and Sport.

Pensgaard, A.M., & Roberts, G.C. (1995). Competing at the Olympics: Achievement goal orientations and coping with stress. IXth European Congress on Sport Psychology Proceedings: Integrating Laboratory and Field Studies. FEPSAC Brussels, part II: 701–708.

Pensgaard, A.M., & Roberts, G.C. (in press). The relationship between motivational climate, perceived ability, and sources of distress among elite athletes. *Journal of Sports Sciences.*

Pensgaard, A.M., Roberts, G.C., & Ursin, H. (1999). Motivational factors and coping strategies of Norwegian paralympic and Olympic winter sport athletes. *Adapted Physical Activity Quarterly, 16*, 238–250.

Perreault, S., & Vallerand, R.J. (1998). *On the relationship between sport motivation and coping abilities of wheelchair basketball players.* Manuscript in preparation.

Piaget, J. (1952). *The origins of intelligence in children.* New York: Norton.

Piaget, J., & Inhelder, B. (1975). *The origin of the idea of chance in children.* London: Routledge & Kegan Paul.

Pierce, B.E., & Burton, D. (1998). Scoring a perfect 10: Investigating the impact of goal setting styles on a goal-setting program for female gymnasts. *Sport Psychologist, 12*, 156–168.

Pinder, C.C. (1984). *Work motivation.* Glenview, IL: Scott, Foresman.

Pintrich, P., & Schunk, D. (1995). *Motivation in education. Theory, research and applications.* Englewood Cliffs, NJ: Prentice Hall.

Pittman, T.S., Boggiano, A.K., & Main, D.S. (1992). Intrinsic and extrinsic motivational orientations in peer interactions. In A.K. Boggiano & T.S. Pittman (Eds.), *Achievement and motivation: A social-developmental perspective* (pp. 37–53). Cambridge: Cambridge University Press.

Poag, K.A., & McAuley, E. (1992). Goal setting, self-efficacy and exercise behavior. *Journal of Sport and Exercise Psychology, 14*, 352–360.

Poag-DuCharme, K.A. (1993). *Goal-related perceptions of social-cognitive predictors of exercise behavior.* Unpublished doctoral dissertation, University of Waterloo, Waterloo, Ontario, Canada.

Poag-DuCharme, K.A., & Brawley, L.R. (1994). Perceptions of the behavioral influence of goals: A mediational relationship to exercise. *Journal of Applied Sport Psychology, 6*, 32–50.

Price, S.L., & Tennant, L.K. (1998). Task and ego orientation changes produced with success/failure feedback during practice and competitive settings. *Journal of Sport and Exercise Psychology, 20* (Suppl.), S12.

Pringle, R. (2000). Physical education, positivism, and optimistic claims from achievement goal theorists. *Quest, 52*, 18–31.

Pritchard, R.D., Bigby, D.G., Beiting, M., Coverdale, S., & Morgan, C. (1981). *Enhancing productivity through feedback and goal setting*. No. AFHRL-TR-81-7. Air Force Human Resources Laboratory, Brooks Air Force Base, TX.

Prochaska, J.O., & DiClemente, C.C. (1983). Stages and processes of self-change of smoking: Toward an integrative model of change. *Journal of Consulting and Clinical Psychology, 51*, 390–395.

Prochaska, J.O., & DiClemente, C.C. (1985). Common processes of self-change in smoking, weight control, and psychological distress. In S. Shiffman & T. Willis (Eds.), *Coping and substance use* (pp. 345–363). New York: Academic Press.

Prochaska, J.O., & Velicer, W.F. (1997). Misinterpretations and misapplications of the transtheoretical model. *American Journal of Health Promotion, 12*, 11–12.

Provencher, P., & Vallerand, R.J. (1995, October 28). *Facteurs situationnels et motivation situationnelle: Un test de l'effet de spécificité* [Situational factors and situational motivation: A test of the specificity effect]. Paper presented at the annual conference of the Société Québécoise de la Recherche en Psychologie, Ottawa, Ontario, Canada.

Purdon, C., & Clark, D.A. (1994). Obsessive intrusive thoughts in nonclinical subjects. Part II. Cognitive appraisal, emotional response and thought control strategies. *Behavior Research and Therapy, 32*, 403–410.

Rascle, O., Coulomb, G., & Pfister, R. (1998). Aggression and goal orientations in handball: Influence of institutional sport context. *Perceptual and Motor Skills, 86*(3, Pt. 2), 1347–1360.

Reeve, J., & Deci, E.L. (1996). Elements of the competitive situation that affect intrinsic motivation. *Personality and Social Psychology Bulletin, 22*, 24–33.

Reid, G., Poulin, C., & Vallerand, R.J. (1994, June 10). *A pictorial motivational scale in physical activity for people with a mental disability: Development and initial validation*. Paper presented at the annual conference of the NASPSPA, Clearwater Beach, Florida.

Reid, G., Vallerand, R.J., & Poulin, C. (2001). *The development and validation of the Pictorial Motivation Scale in physical activity*. Manuscript submitted for publication.

Rempel, J.K., Holmes, J.G., & Zanna, M.P. (1985). Trust in close relationships. *Journal of Personality and Social Psychology, 49*, 95–112.

Rethorst, S. (1997). The relationship of goal orientations to cognitions and emotions following success in a ski slalom contest. In R. Lidor & M. Bar-Eli (Eds.), *Innovations in sport psychology: Linking theory and practice. Proceedings of the IX World*

Congress of Sport Psychology (pp. 564–566). Netanya, Israel: Ministry of Education, Culture and Sport.

Richer, S., & Vallerand, R.J. (1995). Supervisors' interactional styles and subordinates' intrinsic and extrinsic motivation. *Journal of Social Psychology, 135,* 707–722.

Richer, S., & Vallerand, R.J. (1998). Construction et validation de l'Échelle du sentiment d'appartenance sociale [Construction and validation of the Relatedness Feeling Scale]. *Revue européenne de psychologie appliquée, 48,* 129–137.

Ries, A.L., Kaplan, R.M., Limberg, T.M., & Prewitt, L.M. (1995). Effects of pulmonary rehabilitation on physiologic and psychosocial outcomes in patients with chronic obstructive pulmonary disease. *Annals of Internal Medicine, 122,* 823–832.

Riordan, J. (1977). *Sport in soviet society.* Cambridge: Cambridge University Press.

Roberts, G.C. (1982). Achievement and motivation in sport. In R. Terjung (Ed). *Exercise and Sport Science Reviews:* (Vol. 10.) Philadelphia, Franklin Institute Press.

Roberts, G.C. (1984a). Achievement motivation in children's sports. In J.G. Nicholls (Ed.), *Advances in motivation and achievement. Vol. 3. The development of achievement motivation* (pp. 251–281). Greenwich, CT: JAI Press.

Roberts, G.C. (1984b). Toward a new theory of motivation in sport: The role of perceived ability. In J. Silva & R. Weinberg (Eds.), *Psychological foundations of sport* (pp. 214–228). Champaign, IL: Human Kinetics.

Roberts, G.C. (1986). The perception of stress: A potential source and its development. In M.R. Weiss & D.R. Gould (Eds.), *Sport for children and youths* (pp. 119–126). Champaign, IL: Human Kinetics.

Roberts, G.C. (1992a). Motivation in sport and exercise: Conceptual constraints and convergence. In G.C. Roberts (Ed.), *Motivation in sport and exercise* (pp. 3–29). Champaign, IL: Human Kinetics.

Roberts, G.C. (Ed.). (1992b). *Motivation in sport and exercise.* Champaign, IL: Human Kinetics.

Roberts, G.C. (1993). Motivation in sport: Understanding and enhancing the motivation and achievement of children. In R. Singer, M. Murphey, & K. Tennant (Eds.), *Handbook of research on sport psychology* (pp. 405–420). New York: Macmillan.

Roberts, G.C. (1997). Future research directions in understanding the motivation of children in sport: A goal orientation perspective. In R. Lidor & M. Bar-Eli (Eds.), *Innovations in sport psychology: Linking theory and practice. Proceedings of the IX World Congress in Sport Psychology: Part II* (pp. 576–580). Netanya, Israel: Ministry of Education, Culture and Sport.

Roberts, G.C., & Balague, G. (1989, August). *The development of a social cognitive scale of motivation.* Paper presented at the Seventh World Congress of Sport Psychology, Singapore.

Roberts, G.C., & Balague, G. (1991, September). *The development and validation of the Perception of Success Questionnaire.* Paper presented in the FEPSAC Congress, Cologne, Germany.

Roberts, G.C., Hall, H.K., Jackson, S.A., Kimiecik, J.C., & Tonymon, P. (1995). Implicit theories of achievement and the sport experience: Effect of goal orientations on achievement strategies and perspectives. *Perceptual and Motor Skills, 81*(1), 219–224.

Roberts, G.C., & Ommundsen, Y. (1996). Effect of goal orientations on achievement beliefs, cognitions, and strategies in team sport. *Scandinavian Journal of Medicine and Science in Sport, 6,* 46–56.

Roberts, G.C., & Ommundsen, Y. (2000). Moral functioning in sport: Children's responses to moral dilemmas. *International Journal of Psychology, 35*(3-4), 23.

Roberts, G.C., & Treasure, D.C. (1992). Children in sport. *Sport Science Review, 1*(2), 46–64.

Roberts, G.C., & Treasure, D.C. (1995). Achievement goals, motivational climate and achievement strategies and behaviors in sport. *International Journal of Sport Psychology, 26*(1), 64–80.

Roberts, G.C., Treasure, D.C., & Balague, G. (1998). Achievement goals in sport: The development and validation of the Perception of Success Questionnaire. *Journal of Sports Sciences, 16,* 337–347.

Roberts, G.C., Treasure, D.C., & Hall, H.K. (1994). Parental goal orientation and beliefs about the competitive-sport experience of their child. *Journal of Applied Social Psychology, 24*(7), 631–645.

Roberts, G.C., Treasure, D.C., & Kavussanu, M. (1996). Orthogonality of achievement goals and its relationship to beliefs about success and satisfaction in sport. *The Sport Psychologist, 10*(4), 398–408.

Roberts, G.C., Treasure, D.C., & Kavussanu, M. (1997). Motivation in physical activity contexts: An achievement goal perspective. In P. Pintrich & M. Maehr (Eds.), *Advances in motivation and achievement* (Vol. 10, pp. 413–447). Stamford, CT: JAI Press.

Roberts, G.C., & Walker, B. (in press). Achievement goal theory in sport and exercise. In F. Cury, P. Sarrazin, & J. Famose (Eds.), *Advances in motivation theories in the sport domain.* Paris: Presses Universitaires de France.

Robertson, D., & Keller, C. (1992). Relationships among health beliefs, self-efficacy, and exercise adherence in patients with coronary artery disease. *Heart and Lung, 21,* 56–63.

Rodgers, W.M. (1992). *Examining the motivational potential of outcome expectations and self-efficacy in exercise.* Unpublished doctoral dissertation, University of Waterloo, Waterloo, Ontario, Canada.

Rodgers, W.M., & Brawley, L.R. (1991). The role of outcome expectancies in participation motivation. *Journal of Sport and Exercise Psychology, 13,* 411–427.

Rodgers, W.M., & Brawley, L.R. (1993). Using both self-efficacy theory and the theory of planned behavior to discriminate adherers and dropouts from structured programs. *Journal of Applied Sport Psychology, 5,* 195–206.

Rodgers, W.M., & Brawley, L.R. (1996). The influence of outcome expectancy and self-efficacy on the behavioral intentions of novice exercisers. *Journal of Applied Social Psychology, 26,* 618–634.

Rodin, J. (1986). Health, control, and aging. In M.M. Baltes & P.B. Baltes (Eds.), *The psychology of control and aging* (pp. 139–165). Hillsdale, NJ: Erlbaum.

Rogers, C.R. (1961). *On becoming a person: A therapist's view of psychotherapy.* Boston: Houghton Mifflin.

Rogers, R.W. (1975). A protection motivation theory of fear appeals and attitude change. *Journal of Psychology, 91,* 93–114.

Rosenberg, M. (1979). *Conceiving the self.* New York: Basic Books.

Rosenholtz, S.J., & Simpson, C. (1984). Classroom organization and student stratification. *Elementary School Journal, 85,* 21–37.

Rovniak, L., Blanchard, C., & Koestner, R. (1998). *The emotional consequences of introjected and integrated regulation in an exercise setting.* Manuscript submitted for publication.

Rudolph, D.L., & McAuley, E. (1995). Self-efficacy and salivary cortisol responses to acute exercise in physically active and less active adults. *Journal of Sport and Exercise Psychology, 17,* 206–213.

Rutherford, W.J., Corbin, C.B., & Chase, L.A. (1992). Factors influencing intrinsic motivation towards physical activity. *Health Values, 16,* 19–24.

Ryan, E.D. (1977). Attribution, intrinsic motivation, and athletics. In L.I. Gedvilas & M.E. Kneer (Eds.), *Proceedings of the National College of Physical Education Association for Men/National Association for Physical Education of College Women, National Conference* (pp. 346–353). Chicago: Office of Publications Services, University of Illinois at Chicago Circle.

Ryan, E.D. (1980). Attribution, intrinsic motivation, and athletics: A replication and extension. In C.H. Nadeau, W.R. Halliwell, K.M. Newell, & G.C. Roberts (Eds.), *Psychology of motor behavior and sport—1979* (pp. 19–26). Champaign, IL: Human Kinetics.

Ryan, R., & Connell, J. (1989). Perceived locus of causality and internalization: Examining reasons for acting in two domains. *Journal of Personality and Social Psychology, 57,* 749–761.

Ryan, R.M. (1982). Control and information in the intrapersonal sphere: An extension of cognitive evaluation theory. *Journal of Personality and Social Psychology, 43,* 450–461.

Ryan, R.M. (1993). Agency and organization: Intrinsic motivation, autonomy and the self in psychological development. In R. Dientsbier (Ed.), *Nebraska symposium on motivation* (Vol. 40, pp. 1–56). Lincoln, NE: University of Nebraska Press.

Ryan, R.M. (1995). The integration of behavioral regulation within life domains. *Journal of Personality, 63,* 397–429.

Ryan, R.M., & Connell, J.P. (1989). Perceived locus of causality and internalization: Examining reasons for acting in two domains. *Journal of Personality and Social Psychology, 57,* 749–761.

Ryan, R.M., Connell, J.P., & Deci, E.L. (1985). A motivational analysis of self-determination and self-regulation in education. In C. Ames & R.E. Ames (Eds.), *Research on motivation in education: The classroom milieu* (pp. 13–51). New York: Academic Press.

Ryan, R.M., Connell, J.P., & Grolnick, W.S. (1992). When achievement is not intrinsically motivated: A theory and assessment of self-regulation in school. In A.K.

Boggiano & T.S. Pittman (Eds.), *Achievement and motivation: A social-developmental perspective* (pp. 167–188). Cambridge: Cambridge University Press.

Ryan, R.M., & Deci, E.L. (2000a). Intrinsic and extrinsic motivations: Classic definitions and new directions. *Contemporary Educational Psychology, 25*, 54–67.

Ryan, R.M., & Deci, E.L. (2000b). Self-determination theory and the facilitation of intrinsic motivation, social development, and well-being. *American Psychologist, 55*, 68–78.

Ryan, R.M., Deci, E.L., & Grolnick, W.S. (1995). Autonomy, relatedness, and the self: Their relation to development and psychopathology. In D. Cicchetti & D.J. Cohen (Eds.), *Developmental psychology. Vol. 1. Theory and methods* (pp. 618–655). New York: Wiley.

Ryan, R.M., & Grolnick, W.S. (1986). Origins and pawns in the classroom: Self report and protective assessments of individual differences in children's perceptions. *Journal of Personality and Social Psychology, 50*, 550–558.

Ryan, R.M., Koestner, R., & Deci, E.L. (1991). Ego-involved persistence: When free-choice behavior is not intrinsically motivated. *Motivation and Emotion, 15*, 185–205.

Ryan, R.M., Sheldon, K.M., Kasser, T., & Deci, E.L. (1996). All goals are not created equal: An organismic perspective on the nature of goals and their regulation. In P.M. Gollwitzer & J.A. Bargh (Eds.), *The psychology of action* (pp. 7–26). New York: Guilford Press.

Ryan, R.M., Vallerand, R.J., & Deci, E.L. (1984). Intrinsic motivation in sport: A cognitive evaluation theory interpretation. In W. Straub & J. Williams (Eds.), *Cognitive sport psychology*. Lansing, NY: Sport Science Associates.

Ryckman, R.M., Robbins, M.A., Thornton, B., & Cantrell, P. (1982). Development and validation of a physical self-efficacy scale. *Journal of Personality and Social Psychology, 42*, 891–900.

Ryska, T.A. (1998). The role of hypercompetitiveness on self-confidence and goal orientation in sport. *Journal of Sport and Exercise Psychology, 20* (Suppl.), S123.

Ryska, T.A., & Richey, V. (1999). The role of achievement goals, competitiveness, and perceived purposes of sport in sportspersonship among Hispanic female athletes. *Journal of Sport and Exercise Psychology, 21* (Suppl.), S94.

Ryska, T.A., & Sekerak, H. (1999). The relationship of competitive trait anxiety, goal perspectives, and trait sport confidence to competitive dispositions. *Journal of Sport and Exercise Psychology, 21* (Suppl.), S94.

Sakamoto, B., & Parsons, C. (1993, November 25). Libertyville coach quits after motivational skit backfires. *The Chicago Tribune*, Sports, p. 1.

Sallis, J.F., Haskell, W.L., Fortmann, S.T., Vranizan, K.M., Taylor, C.B., & Solomon, D.S. (1986). Predictors of adoption and maintenance of physical activity in a community sample. *Preventive Medicine, 15*, 331–341.

Sallis, J.F., & Hovell, M.F. (1990). Determinants of exercise behavior. *Exercise and Sport Science Review, 18*, 307–330.

Sallis, J.F., Hovell, M.F., Hofstetter, C.R., & Barrington, E. (1992). Explanation of vigorous physical activity during two years using social learning variables. *Social Science and Medicine, 34*, 25–32.

Sallis, J.F., Hovell, M.F., Hofstetter, C.R., Faucher, P., Elder, J.P., Blanchard, J., Casperson, C.J., Powell, K.E., & Christenson, G.M. (1989). A multivariate study of determinants of vigorous exercise in a community sample. *Preventive Medicine, 18,* 20–34.

Sallis, J.F., Simons-Morton, B., Stone, E., Corbin, C., Epstein, L.H., Faucette, N., Iannotti, R., Killen, J., Klesges, R., Petray, C., Rowland, T., & Taylor, W. (1992). Determinants of physical activity and interventions in youth. *Medicine and Science in Sports and Exercise, 24* (Suppl.), S248–257.

Sansone, C. (1986). A question of competence: The effects of competence and task feedback on intrinsic interest. *Journal of Personality and Social Psychology, 51,* 918–931.

Sansone, C., & Harackiewicz, J.M. (1996). "I don't feel like it": The function of interest in self-regulation. In L. Martin & A. Tesser (Eds.), *Striving and feeling: Interactions between goals and affect.* Hillsdale, NJ: Erlbaum.

Sarrazin, P., Biddle, S., Famose, J.P., Cury, F., Fox, K., & Durand, M. (1996). Goal orientations and conceptions of the nature of sport ability in children: A social cognitive approach. *British Journal of Social Psychology, 35,* 399–414.

Sarrazin, P., Cury, F., & Roberts, G. (1999). Exerted effort in climbing as a function of achievement goals, perceived ability, and task difficulty. In V. Hosek, P. Tilinger, & L. Bilek (Eds.), *Psychology of sport and exercise: Enhancing the quality of life. Proceedings of the 10th European Congress on Sport Psychology—FEPSAC* (pp. 138–140). Prague: Charles University of Prague Press.

Sarrazin, P., Cury, F., Roberts, G., Biddle, S., & Famose, J. (1999). *Effort exerted in climbing: The influence of task and ego goals, perceived ability, and task difficulty.* In V. Hosek, P. Tilinger, & L. Bilek (Eds.), *Psychology of sport and exercise: Enhancing the quality of life. Proceedings of the 10th European Congress on Sport Psychology—FEPSAC* (pp. 138–140). Prague: Charles University of Prague Press.

Sarrazin, P., Vallerand, R.J., Guillet, E., Pelletier, L.G., & Cury, F. (2001). *Motivation and dropout in female handballers: A 21-month prospective study.* Manuscript submitted for publication.

Schell, T.L., Klein, S.B., & Babey, S.H. (1996). Testing a hierarchical model of self-knowledge. *Psychological Science, 7,* 170–173.

Scherer, Y.K., & Schmieder, L.E. (1997). The effect of a pulmonary rehabilitation program on self-efficacy, perception of dyspnea, and physical endurance. *Heart and Lung, 26,* 15–22.

Seefeldt, V., Blievernicht, D., Bruce, R., & Gilliam, T. (1978). *Joint legislative study on youth sport programs, Phase II: Agency-sponsored sports.* State of Michigan.

Seifriz, J., Duda, J.L., & Chi, L. (1992). The relationship of perceived motivational climate to intrinsic motivation and beliefs about success in basketball. *Journal of Sport and Exercise Psychology, 14,* 375–391.

Seligman, C., Fazio, R.H., & Zanna, M.P. (1980). Effects of salience of extrinsic rewards on liking and loving. *Journal of Personality and Social Psychology, 38,* 453–460.

Senécal, C.B., Vallerand, R.J., & Pelletier, L.G. (1992). Les effets du type de programme universitaire et du sexe de l'étudiant sur la motivation académique [Effects of type of curriculum and student gender on academic motivation]. *Revue des sciences de l'éducation, 18,* 375–388.

Sexton, T.L., & Tuckman, B.W. (1991). Self-beliefs and behavior: The role of self-efficacy and outcome expectation over time. *Personality and Individual Differences, 12,* 725–736.

Sexton, T.L., Tuckman, B.W., & Crehan, K. (1992). An investigation of the patterns of self-efficacy, outcome expectation, outcome value, and performance across trials. *Cognitive Therapy and Research, 16,* 329–348.

Shapiro, D.R., Yun, J., & Ulrich, D. (1998). Evaluation of perceived physical competence: A generalizability study. *Journal of Sport and Exercise Psychology, 20* (Suppl.), S96.

Shavelson, R.J., Hubner, J.J., & Stanton, G.C. (1976). Self-concept: Validation of construct interpretations. *Review of Educational Research, 46,* 407–441.

Shavelson, R.J., & Marsh, H.W. (1986). On the structure of self-concept. In R. Schwarzer (Ed.), *Anxiety and cognitions* (pp. 305–330). Hillsdale, NJ: Erlbaum.

Sherif, C.W. (1976). The social context of competition. In D.M. Landers (Ed.), *Social Problems in Athletics.* (pp. 18–36). Urbana, IL: University of Illinois Press.

Sherif, M., & Sherif, C.W. (1969). *Social psychology.* New York: Harper & Row.

Sherman, E. (1992, September 15). Sherrill unable to steer clear of controversy. *The Chicago Tribune,* Sports, p. 3.

Shields, D., & Bredemeier, B.J. (1995). *Character development and physical activity.* Champaign, IL: Human Kinetics.

Skaalvik, E.M. (1997). Self-enhancing and self-defeating ego orientation: Relations with task and avoidance orientation, achievement, self-protections, anxiety. *Journal of Educational Psychology, 89*(1), 71–81.

Skaalvik, E.M., & Valas, H. (1994). Task involvement and ego involvement: Relations with academic achievement, academic self-concept, and self-esteem. *Scandinavian Journal of Educational Research, 38,* 231–243.

Skaalvik, S. (1993). Ego-involvement and self-protection among slow learners: Four case studies. *Scandinavian Journal of Educational Research, 37,* 305–315.

Skinner, B.F. (1953). *Science and human behavior.* New York: Macmillan.

Skinner, E.A. (1996). A guide to constructs of control. *Journal of Personality and Social Psychology, 71,* 549–570.

Sluis, M., Kiukkonen, J., Jaakola, T., Kokkonan, J., Saarelainen, S., Piirainen, U., & Pakkala, P. (1999). Obsevation of physical education teacher feedback from the motivational climate perspective. In V. Hosek, P. Tilinger, & L. Bilek (Eds.) *Psychology of sport and exercise: Enhancing quality of life. Proceedings of the 10th European Congress of Sport Psychology–FEPSAC.* Part II. (pp. 166–168). Prague, CA: Charles University Press.

Smith, M., & Lee, C. (1992). Goal setting and performance in a novel coordination task: Mediating mechanisms. *Journal of Sport and Exercise Psychology, 14,* 169–176.

Smith, R.E. (1996). Performance anxiety, cognitive interference, and concentration strategies in sports. In I.G. Sarason, G.R. Pierce, & B.R. Sarason (Eds.), *Cognitive interference: Theories, methods, and findings* (pp. 261–283). Mahwah, NJ: Erlbaum.

Smith, R.E. (1998). A positive approach to sport performance enhancement: Principles of reinforcement and performance feedback. In J.M. Williams (Ed.), *Applied sport psychology: Personal growth to peak performance* (pp. 28–40). Mountain View, CA: Mayfield.

Smith, R.E., & Smoll, F.L. (1990). Self-esteem and children's reactions to youth sport coaching behaviors: A field study on the self enhancement processes. *Developmental Psychology, 26,* 987–993.

Smith, R.E., Smoll, F., & Curtis, B. (1978). Coaching behaviors in Little League baseball. In F.L. Smoll & R.E. Smith (Eds.), *Psychological perspectives on youth sports* (pp. 173–201). Washington, DC: Hemisphere.

Smith, R.E., Smoll, F.L., & Curtis, B. (1979). Coach effectiveness training: A cognitive behavioral approach to enhancing relationship skills in youth sport coaches. *Journal of Sport Psychology, 1,* 59–75.

Smith, R.E., Smoll, F., & Hunt, E.B. (1977). A system for the behavioral assessment of athletic coaches. *Research Quarterly, 48,* 401–407.

Smith, R.E., Smoll, F., & Schutz, R. (1990). Measurement and correlates of sport-specific cognitive and somatic trait anxiety: The Sport Anxiety Scale. *Anxiety Research, 2,* 263–280.

Smith, R.E., Smoll, F.L., & Wiechman, S.A. (1998). In J.L. Duda (Ed.), *Advances in sport and exercise psychology measurement* (pp. 105-128). Morgantown, WV: Fitness Information Technology.

Smoll, F.L., & Smith, R.E. (1989). Leadership behaviors in sport: A theoretical model and research paradigm. *Journal of Applied Social Psychology, 19,* 1522–1551.

Smoll, F.L., & Smith, R.E. (1998). Conducting psychologically oriented coach-training programs: Cognitive-behavioral principles and techniques. In J.M. Williams (Ed.), *Applied sport psychology: Personal growth to peak performance* (pp. 41–62). Mountain View, CA: Mayfield.

Solmon, M., & Boone, J. (1993). The impact of student goal orientation in physical education classes. *Research Quarterly for Exercise and Sport, 64,* 418–424.

Solmon, M.A. (1996). Impact of motivational climate on students' behaviors and perceptions in a physical education setting. *Journal of Educational Psychology, 88,* 731–738.

Sonstroem, R.J., Harlow, L.L., & Josephs, L. (1994). Exercise and self-esteem: Validity of model expansion and exercise associations. *Journal of Sport and Exercise Psychology, 16,* 29–42.

Sonstroem, R.J., & Morgan, W.P. (1989). Exercise and self-esteem: Rationale and model. *Medicine and Science in Sports and Exercise, 21,* 329–337.

Spink, K.S., & Roberts, G.C. (1980). Ambiguity of outcome and causal attributions. *Journal of Sport Psychology, 2*(3), 237–244.

Spray, C.M. (2000). Predicting participation in noncompulsory physical education: Do goal perspectives matter? *Perceptual and Motor Skills, 90,* 1207–1215.

Spray, C.M., & Biddle, S.J.H. (1997). Achievement goals, beliefs about the causes of success and reported emotion among male and female sixth form students. *European Physical Education Review, 3*(1), 83–90.

Spray, C.M., Biddle, S.J.H., & Fox, K.R. (1999). Achievement goals, beliefs about the causes of success, and reported emotion in post-16 physical education. *Journal of Sports Sciences, 17*, 213–219.

Steinberg, G. (1996). *The effect of different goal strategies on achievement-related cognitions, affect, and behavior during the learning of a golf-putt.* Unpublished doctoral dissertation, University of Florida, Gainesville.

Stephens, D. (1993). *Goal orientation and moral atmosphere in youth sport: An examination of lying, hurting, and cheating behaviors in girls' soccer.* Unpublished doctoral dissertation, University of California at Berkeley.

Stephens, D., & Bredemeier, B.J. (1996). Moral atmosphere and judgments about aggression in girls' soccer: Relationships among moral and motivational variables. *Journal of Sport and Exercise Psychology, 18*, 174–193.

Sutton, S. (1998) Predicting and explaining intentions and behavior: How are we doing? *Journal of Applied Social Psychology, 28*, 1317–1338.

Swain, A., & Jones, J.G. (1995). Effects of goal-setting interventions on selected basketball skills: A single subject design. *Research Quarterly for Exercise and Sport, 66*, 51–63.

Swain, A.B.J. (1996). Social loafing and identifiability: The mediating role of achievement goal orientations. *Research Quarterly for Exercise and Sport, 67*, 337–344.

Swain, A.B.J., & Harwood, C.G. (1996). Antecedents of state goals in age group swimmers: An interactionist perspective. *Journal of Sports Sciences, 14*, 111–124.

Swann, W.B., Jr. (1983). Self-verification: Bringing social reality into harmony with the self. In J. Suls & A.G. Greenwald (Eds.), *Psychological perspectives on the self* (Vol. 2, pp. 3–66). Hillsdale, NJ: Erlbaum.

Tammen, V.V. (1998). Changes in task and ego orientations in relation to training in competitive situations. *Journal of Sport and Exercise Psychology, 20* (Suppl.), S120.

Tate, A.K., Petruzzello, S.J., & Lox, C.L. (1995). Examination of the relationship between self-efficacy and affect at varying levels of aerobic exercise intensity. *Journal of Applied Social Psychology, 25*, 1922–1936.

Taylor, C.B., Bandura, A., Ewart, C.K., Miller, N.H., & DeBusk, R.F. (1985). Exercise testing to enhance wives' confidence in their husbands' cardiac capability soon after clinically uncomplicated acute myocardial infarction. *American Journal of Cardiology, 55*, 635–638.

Taylor, S.E. (1989). *Positive illusions: Creative self-deception and the healthy mind.* New York: Basic Books.

Taylor, S.E., Kemeny, M.E., Reed, G.M., & Aspinwall, L.G. (1991). Assault on the self: Positive illusions and adjustment to threatening events. In J. Strauss & G. Goethals (Eds.), *The self: Interdisciplinary approaches.* New York: Springer-Verlag.

Taylor, S.L. (1997). *Physical education teachers' views on motivation: Bridging theory and practice.* Unpublished master's thesis, University of Memphis, Memphis, TN.

Tenenbaum, G., Pinchas, S., Elbaz, G., Bar-Eli, M., & Weinberg, R.S. (1991). Effect of goal proximity and goal specificity on muscular endurance performance: A replication and extension. *Journal of Sport and Exercise Psychology, 13*, 174–187.

Tenenbaum, G. (1999). *An integrated model of motivation: Examination under physical and emotionally demanding conditions.* Manuscript under review.

Terry, D.J., & O'Leary, J.E. (1995). The theory of planned behaviour: The effects of perceived behavioural control and self-efficacy. *British Journal of Social Psychology, 34,* 199–220.

Theeboom, M., De Knop, P., & Weiss, M.R. (1995). Motivational climate, psychological responses, and motor skill development in children's sport: A field-based intervention study. *Journal of Sport and Exercise Psychology, 17,* 294–311.

Theodorakis, Y. (1995). Effects of self-efficacy, satisfaction, and personal goals on swimming performance. *Sport Psychologist, 9,* 245–253.

Thill, E., & Brunel, P. (1995). Ego involvement and task involvement: Related conceptions of ability, effort, and learning strategies among soccer players. *International Journal of Sport Psychology, 26,* 81–97.

Thill, E., & Mouanda, J. (1990). Autonomy or control in the sports context: Validity of cognitive evaluation theory. *International Journal of Sport Psychology, 21,* 1–20.

Thill, E.E. (1993). Conceptions differenciees et non differenciees de l'effort et de la competence en fonction de l'age: Consequences sur les affects et les strategies d'auto-handicap. *International Journal of Sport Psychology, 26,* 81–97.

Thill, E.E., & Brunel, P. (1995a). Cognitive theories of motivation in sport. In S.J.H. Biddle (Ed.), *European perspectives on exercise and sport psychology* (pp. 195–217). Champaign, IL: Human Kinetics.

Thill, E.E., & Brunel, P. (1995b). Ego-involvement and task-involvement: Related conceptions of ability, effort, and learning strategies among soccer players. *International Journal of Sport Psychology, 26,* 81–97.

Thill, E.E., & Cury, F. (2000). Learning to play golf under different goal conditions: Their effects on irrelevant thoughts and on subsequent control strategies. *European Journal of Social Psychology, 30,* 101–122.

Thomas, J.R., & Tennant, L.K. (1978). Effects of rewards on children's motivation for an athletic task. In F.L. Smoll & R.E. Smith, *Psychological perspectives in youth sports.* Washington, DC: Hemisphere.

Thompson, C.E., & Wankel, L.M. (1980). The effect of perceived activity choice upon frequency of exercise behavior. *Journal of Applied Social Psychology, 10,* 436–443.

Thorkildsen, T.A. (1988). Theories of education among academically precocious adolescents. *Contemporary Educational Psychology, 13,* 323–330.

Thorkildsen, T.A., & Nicholls, J.G. (1998). Fifth graders' achievement orientations and beliefs: Individual and classroom differences. *Journal of Educational Psychology, 90,* 179–201.

Thorne, K., & Duda, J.L. (1995, June). *The motivation related correlates of goal orientation in sport: An idiographic analysis.* Paper presented at the 1995 meetings of the North American Society for the Psychology of Sport and Physical Activity, Asilomar, CA.

Tipton, R.M., & Worthington, E.L. (1984). The measurement of generalized self-efficacy: A study of construct validity. *Journal of Personality Assessment, 48,* 545–548.

Toshima, M.T., Kaplan, R.M., & Ries, A.L. (1990). Experimental evaluation of rehabilitation in chronic obstructive pulmonary disease: Short-term effects on exercise endurance and health status. *Health Psychology, 9*(3), 237–252.

Treasure, D.C. (1993). *A social-cognitive approach to understanding children's achievement behavior, cognitions, and affect in competitive sport.* Unpublished doctoral dissertation, University of Illinois.

Treasure, D.C. (1997). Perceptions of the motivational climate and elementary school children's cognitive and affective response. *Journal of Sport and Exercise Psychology, 19*(3), 278–290.

Treasure, D.C., & Biddle, S.J.H. (1998). *Antecedents of physical self-worth and global self-esteem: Influence of achievement goal orientations and perceived ability.* Manuscript under review.

Treasure, D.C., & Roberts, G.C. (1994a). Cognitive and affective concomitants of task and ego goal orientations during the middle school years. *Journal of Sport and Exercise Psychology, 16*(1), 15–28.

Treasure, D.C., & Roberts, G.C. (1994b). Perception of Success Questionnaire: Preliminary validation in an adolescent population. *Perceptual and Motor Skills, 79,* 607–610.

Treasure, D.C., & Roberts, G.C. (1995). Applications of achievement goal theory to physical education: Implications for enhancing motivation. *Quest, 47,* 475–489.

Treasure, D.C., & Roberts, G.C. (1998). Relationship between female adolescents' achievement goal orientations, perceptions of the motivational climate, belief about success and sources of satisfaction in basketball. *International Journal of Sport Psychology, 29,* 211–230.

Treasure, D.C., & Roberts, G.C. (2000). *Predicting sportspersonship orientations: Interaction of achievement goal orientations and perceptions of the motivational climate.* Manuscript submitted for publication.

Treasure, D.C., & Roberts, G.C. (in press). Students' perceptions of the motivational climate, achievement beliefs and satisfaction in physical education. *Research Quarterly for Exercise and Sport.*

Treasure, D.C., Duda, J.L., Hall, H.H., Roberts, G.C., Ames, C., & Maehr, M. (in press). Clarifying misconceptions and misrepresentations in achievement goal research: A response to Harwood, Hardy, and Swain (2000). *Journal of Sport and Exercise Psychology.*

Treasure, D.C., Roberts, G.C., & Standage, M. (1998). Predicting sportspersonship: Interaction of achievement goal orientations and perceptions of the motivational climate. *Journal of Sport and Exercise Psychology, 20* (Suppl.), S12.

Triandis, H.C. (1977). *Interpersonal behavior.* Monterey, CA: Brooke/Cole.

Triandis, H.C. (1980). Values, attitudes, and interpersonal behavior. In *Nebraska symposium on motivation—1979* (Vol. 27, pp. 195–259). Lincoln, NE: University of Nebraska Press.

Tubbs, M.E. (1986). Goal setting: A meta-analytic examination of the empirical evidence. *Journal of Applied Psychology, 71,* 474–483.

Turner, E.E., Rejeski, W.J., & Brawley, L.R. (1997). Psychological benefits of physical activity are influenced by the social environment. *Journal of Sport and Exercise Psychology, 19,* 119–130.

Vallerand, R.J. (1983). Effect of differential amounts of positive verbal feedback on the intrinsic motivation of male hockey players. *Journal of Sport Psychology, 5,* 100–107.

Vallerand, R.J. (1993). La motivation intrinsèque et extrinsèque en contexte naturel: Implications pour les contextes de l'éducation, du travail, des relations interpersonnelles et des loisirs [Intrinsic and extrinsic motivation in natural contexts: Implications for the education, work, interpersonal relationships, and leisure contexts]. In R.J. Vallerand & E.E. Thill (Eds.), *Introduction à la psychologie de la motivation* [Introduction to the psychology of motivation] (pp. 533–582). Laval, Quebec: Etudes Vivantes.

Vallerand, R.J. (1996). [On the effects of success/failure on motivation at three levels of generality]. Unpublished raw data, Université du Québec à Montréal.

Vallerand, R.J. (1997). Toward a Hierarchical Model of Intrinsic and Extrinsic Motivation. In M.P. Zanna (Ed.), *Advances in experimental social psychology* (Vol. 29, pp. 271–360). New York, San Diego: Academic Press.

Vallerand, R.J., & Bissonnette, R. (1992). Intrinsic, extrinsic, and amotivational styles as predictors of behavior: A prospective study. *Journal of Personality, 60,* 599–620.

Vallerand, R.J., Blais, M.R., Brière, N.M., & Pelletier, L.G. (1989). Construction et validation de l'Echelle de motivation en éducation (EME) [On the construction and validation of the French form of the Academic Motivation Scale]. *Canadian Journal of Behavioural Science, 21,* 323–349.

Vallerand, R.J., & Blanchard, C. (1998). [A test of the motivation-consequences relationship at three levels of generality]. Unpublished raw data, Université du Québec à Montréal.

Vallerand, R.J., & Brière, N.M. (1990). *Développement et validation d'un instrument de mesure par questionnaire de motivation intrinsèque, extrinsèque, d'amotivation pour le domaine des sports* [Validation of the French form of the Sport Motivation Scale]. Final report presented to the Canadian Fitness and Lifestyle Research Institute.

Vallerand, R.J. Brière, N.M., Blanchard, C., & Provencher, P. (1997). Development and validation of the multidimensional sportspersonship orientation scale. *Journal of Sport and Exercise Psychology, 8,* 89–101.

Vallerand, R.J., Chantal, Y., Guay, F., & Brunel, P. (2000). *From contextual motivation to situational motivation: A top-down analysis.* Manuscript submitted for publication.

Vallerand, R.J., Deci, E.L., & Ryan, R.M. (1987). Intrinsic motivation in sport. In K. Pandolf (Ed.), *Exercise and Sport Science Reviews* (Vol. 15, pp. 389–425). New York: Macmillan.

Vallerand, R.J., Deshaies, P., Cuerrier, J.P., Brière, N.M., & Pelletier, L.G. (1996). Toward a multidimensional definition of sportsmanship. *Journal of Applied Sport Psychology, 8,* 89–101.

Vallerand, R.J., & Fortier, M.S. (1998). Measures of intrinsic and extrinsic motivation in sport and physical activity: A review and critique. In J.L. Duda (Ed.), *Advancements in sport and exercise psychology measurement.* Morgantown, WV: Fitness Information Technology.

Vallerand, R.J., Fortier, M., & Guay, F. (1997). Self-determination and persistence in a real-life setting: Toward a motivational model of high school dropout. *Journal of Personality and Social Psychology, 72,* 1161–1176.

Vallerand, R.J., Gauvin, L., & Halliwell, W.R. (1986a). Effects of zero-sum competition on children's intrinsic motivation and perceived competence. *Journal of Social Psychology, 126,* 465–472.

Vallerand, R.J., Gauvin, L., & Halliwell, W.R. (1986b). Negative effects of competition on children's intrinsic motivation. *Journal of Social Psychology, 126,* 649–657.

Vallerand, R.J., Guay, F., Blanchard, C.M., & Codorette, I. (2000). *Self-regulatory processes in human behavior: A confirmatory test of some elements of the Hierarchical Model of Intrinsic and Extrinsic Motivation.* Manuscript submitted for publication.

Vallerand, R.J., & Losier, G.F. (1994). Self-determined motivation and sportsmanship orientations: An assessment of their temporal relationship. *Journal of Sport and Exercise Psychology, 16,* 229–245.

Vallerand, R.J., & Losier G.F. (1999). An integrative analysis of intrinsic and extrinsic motivation in sport. *Journal of Applied Sport Psychology, 11,* 142–169.

Vallerand, R.J., & O'Connor, B.P. (1989). Motivation in the elderly: A theoretical framework and some promising findings. *Canadian Psychology, 30,* 538–550.

Vallerand, R.J., & O'Connor, B.P. (1991). Construction et validation de l'Échelle de Motivation pour les personnes âgées (EMPA) [Construction and validation of the French form of the Elderly Motivation Scale]. *International Journal of Psychology, 26,* 219–240.

Vallerand, R.J., O'Connor, B.P., & Hamel, M. (1995). Motivation in later life: Theory and assessment. *International Journal of Aging and Human Development, 41,* 221–238.

Vallerand, R.J., Pelletier, L.G., Blais, M.R., Brière, N.M., Senécal, C., & Vallières, E.F. (1992). The Academic Motivation Scale: A measure of intrinsic, extrinsic, and amotivation in education. *Educational and Psychological Measurement, 52,* 1003–1019.

Vallerand, R.J., Pelletier, L.G., Blais, M.R., Brière, N.M., Senécal, C., & Vallières, E.F. (1993). On the assessment of intrinsic, extrinsic, and amotivation in education: Evidence on the concurrent and construct validity of the Academic Motivation Scale. *Educational and Psychological Measurement, 53,* 159–172.

Vallerand, R.J., & Perreault, S. (1999). Intrinsic and extrinsic motivation in sport: Toward a hierarchical model. In R. Lidor & M. Bar-Eli (Eds.), *Sport psychology: Linking theory and practice* (pp. 191-212). Morgantown, WV: Fitness Information Technology.

Vallerand, R.J., & Ratelle, C.F. (in press). Intrinsic and extrinsic motivation: A hierarchical model. In E.L. Deci and R.M. Ryan (Eds.), *The motivation and self-determination of behavior: Theoretical and applied issues.* Rochester, NY: University of Rochester Press.

Vallerand, R.J., & Reid, G. (1984). On the causal effects of perceived competence on intrinsic motivation: A test of cognitive evaluation theory. *Journal of Sport Psychology, 6,* 94–102.

Vallerand, R.J., & Reid, G. (1988). On the relative effects of positive and negative verbal feedback on males' and females' intrinsic motivation. *Canadian Journal of Behavioural Sciences, 20,* 239–250.

Vallerand, R.J., & Reid, G. (1990). Motivation and special populations: Theory, research and implications regarding motor behavior. In G. Reid (Ed.), *Problems in motor control* (pp. 159–197). New York: North Holland.

Vallerand, R.J., & Rousseau, F.R. (2001). Intrinsic and extrinsic motivation in sport and exercise: A review using the Hierarchical Model of Intrinsic and Extrinsic Motivation. In R. Singer, H. Hausenblas, and C. Janelle (Eds.), *Handbook of Sport Psychology (2nd ed.).* New York: John Wiley & Sons.

Valois, P., Desharnais, R., & Godin, G. (1988). A comparison of the Fishbein and Ajzen and the Triandis attitudinal models for the prediction of exercise intention and behavior. *Journal of Behavioral Medicine, 11,* 459–472.

Vanden Auweele, Y., De Cuyper, B., Van Mele, V., & Rzewnicki, R. (1993). Elite performance and personality: From description and prediction to diagnosis and intervention. In R.N. Singer, M. Murphey, & L.K. Tennant (Eds.), *Handbook of research on sport psychology* (pp. 257–289). New York: Macmillan.

Van Mele, V., & Vanden Auweele, Y. (1995). The use of intra-individual grids and hierarchical class analysis in a sports context. In R. Vanfraechem & Y. Vanden Auweele (Eds.), *Proceedings of the IX European Congress on Sport Psychology* (pp. 294–301). Brussels: Belgian Federation of Sport Psychology.

VanYperen, N.W., & Duda, J.L. (1999). Goal orientations, beliefs about success, and performance improvement among young elite Dutch soccer players. *Scandinavian Journal of Medicine and Science in Sports, 9,* 358–364.

Vealey, R.S. (1986). Conceptualization of sport-confidence and competitive orientation: Preliminary investigation and instrument development. *Journal of Sport Psychology, 8,* 221–246.

Vealey, R.S., & Campbell, J.L. (1988). Achievement goals of adolescent figure skaters: Impact on self-confidence, anxiety and performance. *Journal of Adolescent Research, 3*(2), 227–243.

Vlachopoulos, S., & Biddle, S. (1996). Achievement goal orientations and intrinsic motivation in a track and field event in school physical education. *European Physical Education Review, 2,* 158–164.

Vlachopoulos, S., & Biddle, S.J.H. (1997). Modeling the relation of goal orientations to achievement-related affect in physical education: Does perceived ability matter? *Journal of Sport and Exercise Psychology, 19,* 169–187.

Vlachopoulos, S., Biddle, S.J.H., & Fox, K.R. (1997). Determinants of emotion in children's physical activity: A test of goal perspectives and attribution theories. *Pediatric Exercise Science, 9,* 65–79.

Walker, B. (2000). *Reconceptualizing achievement goal theory: A test of the relationship between approach and avoidance goals and intrinsic interest.* Doctoral dissertation, University of Illinois at Urbana-Champaign.

Walker, B.W., Roberts, G.C., & Harnisch, D. (1998). Predicting self-esteem in a national sample of disadvantaged youth. *Journal of Sport and Exercise Psychology, 20* (Suppl.), S20.

Walker, B.W., Roberts, G.C., & Nyheim, M., & Treasure, D.C. (1998). Predicting enjoyment and beliefs about success in sport: An interactional perspective. *Journal of Sport and Exercise Psychology, 20* (Suppl.), S59.

Walling, M.D., & Duda, J.L. (1995). Goals and their associations with beliefs about success in and perceptions of the purposes of physical education. *Journal of Teaching in Physical Education, 14*(2), 140–156.

Walling, M.D., Duda, J.L., & Chi, L. (1993). The Perceived Motivational Climate in Sport Questionnaire: Construct and predictive validity. *Journal of Sport and Exercise Psychology, 15*(2), 172–183.

Watkins, B., & Montgomery, A. (1989). Conceptions of excellence among children and adolescents. *Child Development, 60,* 1362–1372.

Watson, D., Clark, L.A., & Tellegen, A. (1988). Development and validation of brief measures of positive and negative affect; The PANAS scales. *Journal of Personality and Social Psychology, 54,* 1063–1070.

Wegner, D. (1994). Ironic process of mental control. *Psychological Review, 101,* 34–52.

Weidenfeld, S.A., Bandura, A., Levine, S., O'Leary, A., Brown, S., & Raska, K. (1990). Impact of perceived self-efficacy in coping with stressors on components of the immune system. *Journal of Personality and Social Psychology, 59,* 1082–1094.

Weinberg, R.S. (1992). Goal setting and motor performance: A review and critique. In G.C. Roberts (Ed.), *Motivation in sport and exercise* (pp. 177–197). Champaign, IL: Human Kinetics.

Weinberg, R.S., Bruya, L., Garland, H., & Jackson, A.W. (1990). Effect of goal difficulty and positive reinforcement on endurance performance. *Journal of Sport and Exercise Psychology, 12,* 144–156.

Weinberg, R.S., Bruya, L., & Jackson, A.W. (1985). The effects of goal proximity and goal specificity on endurance performance. *Journal of Sport Psychology, 7,* 296–305.

Weinberg, R.S., Bruya, L., & Jackson, A.W. (1990). Goal setting and competition: A reaction to Hall and Byrne. *Journal of Sport and Exercise Psychology, 12,* 92–97.

Weinberg, R.S., Bruya, L., Jackson, A.W., & Garland, H. (1987). Goal difficulty and endurance performance: A challenge to the goal attainability assumption. *Journal of Sport Behavior, 10,* 82–92.

Weinberg, R.S., Bruya, L., Longino, J., & Jackson, A.W. (1988). Effect of goal proximity and specificity on endurance performance of primary-grade children. *Journal of Sport and Exercise Psychology, 10,* 81–91.

Weinberg, R.S., Burton, D., Yukelson, D., & Weigand, D.A. (1993). Goal setting in competitive sport: An exploratory investigation of practices of collegiate athletes. *The Sport Psychologist, 7,* 275–289.

Weinberg, R.S., Fowler, C., Jackson, A.W., Bagnall, J., & Bruya, L. (1991). Effect of goal difficulty on motor performance: A replication across tasks and subjects. *Journal of Sport and Exercise Psychology, 13,* 160–173.

Weinberg, R.S., & Gould, D. (1999). *Foundations of sport and exercise psychology.* Champaign, IL: Human Kinetics.

Weinberg, R.S., & Jackson, A. (1979). Competition and extrinsic rewards: Effect on intrinsic motivation and attribution. *Research Quarterly, 50,* 494–502.

Weinberg, R.S., & Ragan, J. (1979). Effects of competition, success/failure, and sex on intrinsic motivation. *Research Quarterly, 50,* 503–510.

Weinberg, R.S., Stitcher, T., & Richardson, P. (1994). Effects of a seasonal goal-setting program on lacrosse performance. *The Sport Psychologist, 8,* 166–175.

Weinberg, R.S., & Weigand, D. (1993). Goal setting in sport and exercise: A reaction to Locke. *Journal of Sport and Exercise Psychology, 15,* 88–96.

Weiner, B. (1972). *Theories of motivation: From mechanism to cognition.* Chicago: Markham.

Weiner, B. (1986). *An attributional theory of motivation and emotion.* New York: Springer-Verlag.

Weiner, B. (1995). *Judgments of responsibility: A foundation for a theory of social conduct.* New York: Guilford Press.

Weinstein, N.D. (1993). Testing four competing theories of health-protective behavior. *Health Psychology, 12,* 324–333.

Weinstein, R.S. (1989). Perceptions of classroom processes and student motivation: Children's views of self-fulfilling prophecies. In: C. Ames & R. Ames (Eds.), *Research on motivation in education* (Vol. 3, pp. 187-221). San Diego: Academic Press.

Weiss, M.R., & Bredemeier, B.J. (1990). Moral functioning in sport. In K.B. Pandolf & J.O. Holloszy (Eds.), *Exercise and Sport Science Reviews, 18,* 331–378.

Weiss, M.R., Bredemeier, B.J., & Shewchuk, R.M. (1985). An intrinsic/extrinsic motivation scale for the youth sport setting: A confirmatory factor analysis. *Journal of Sport Psychology, 7,* 75–91.

Weiss, M.R., & Chaumeton, N. (1993). Motivational orientations in sport. In T.S. Horn (Ed.), *Advances in sport psychology* (pp. 61–99). Champaign, IL: Human Kinetics.

Weiss, M.R., Ebbeck, V., & Horn, T.S. (1997). Children's self-perceptions and sources of physical competence information: A cluster analysis. *Journal of Sport and Exercise Psychology, 19,* 52–70.

Weiss, M.R., & Horn, T.S. (1990). The relation between children's accuracy estimates of their physical competence and achievement-related characteristics. *Research Quarterly for Exercise and Sport, 61,* 250–258.

Weiss, M.R., & Smith, A. (1999). Quality of youth sport friendships: Measurement development and validation. *Journal of Sport and Exercise Psychology, 21,* 145–166.

Weiss, M.R., Smith, A.L., & Theeboom, M. (1997). "That's what friends are for": Children's and teenagers' perceptions of peer relationships in the sport domain. *Journal of Sport and Exercise Psychology, 18,* 347–379.

Weitzer, J.E. (1989). Childhood socialization into physical activity: Parental roles in perceptions of competence and goal orientation. Unpublished master's thesis, University of Wisconsin, Milwaukee.

Westre, K.R., & Weiss, M.R. (1991). The relationship between perceived coaching behavior and group cohesion in high school football teams. *The Sport Psychologist, 5*, 41–54.

White, R.W. (1959). Motivation reconsidered: The concept of competence. *Psychological Review, 66*, 297–333.

White, R.W. (1963). Ego and reality in psychoanalytic theory [Monograph]. *Psychological Issues, 3.*

White, S.A. (1996). Goal orientation and perceptions of the motivational climate initiated by parents. *Pediatric Exercise Science, 8*(2), 122–129.

White, S.A. (1998). Adolescent goal profiles, perceptions of the parent-initiated motivational climate, and competitive trait anxiety. *The Sport Psychologist, 12*, 16–28.

White, S.A., & Duda, J.L. (1993). Dimensions of goals and beliefs among adolescent athletes with physical disabilities. *Adapted Physical Activity Quarterly, 10*(2), 125–136.

White, S.A., & Duda, J.L. (1994). The relationship of gender, level of sport involvement, and participation motivation to task and ego orientation. *International Journal of Sport Psychology, 25*(1), 4–18.

White, S.A., Duda, J.L., & Hart, S. (1992). An exploratory examination of the Parent-Initiated Motivational Climate Questionnaire. *Perceptual and Motor Skills, 75*(3, Pt. 1), 875–880.

White, S.A., Duda, J.L., & Keller, M.R. (1998). The relationship between goal orientation and perceived purposes of sport among youth sport participants. *Journal of Sport Behavior, 21*(4), 474–483.

White, S.A., & Zellner, S.R. (1996). The relationship between goal orientation, beliefs about the causes of sport success, and trait anxiety among high school, intercollegiate, and recreational sport participants. *The Sport Psychologist, 10*(1), 58–72.

Whitehead, J., & Smith, A.G. (1996). Issues in development of a protocol to evaluate children's reasoning about ability and effort in sport. *Perceptual and Motor Skills, 83*, 355–364.

Whitehead, J., Andree, K.V., & Lee, M.J. (1997). Longitudinal interactions between dispositional and situational goals, perceived ability, and intrinsic motivation. In R. Lidor & M. Bar-Eli (Eds.), *Innovations in sport psychology: Linking theory and practice. Proceedings of the IX World Congress in Sport Psychology: Part II* (pp. 750–752). Netanya, Israel: Ministry of Education, Culture and Sport.

Whitehead, J.R., & Corbin, C.B. (1991). Youth fitness testing: The effect of percentile-based evaluative feedback on intrinsic motivation. *Research Quarterly for Exercise and Sport, 62*, 225–231.

Whitehead, J.R., & Corbin, C.B. (1997). Self-esteem in children and youth: The role of sport and physical education. In K.R. Fox (Ed.), *The physical self* (pp. 175–203). Champaign, IL: Human Kinetics.

Widmeyer, N., Carron, A.V., & Brawley, L.R. (1993). Group cohesion in sport and exercise. In R. Singer, M. Murphey, & L.K. Tennant (Eds.), *Handbook of research on sport psychology* (pp. 572–592). New York: Macmillan.

Wigfield, A., Eccles, J.S., & Pintrich, P.R. (1996). Development between the ages of 11 and 25. In D. Berliner & R.C. Calfee (Eds.), *Handbook of educational psychology* (pp. 148–185). New York: Macmillan.

Wilcox, S., & Storandt, M. (1996). Relations among age, exercise, and psychological variables in a community sample of women. *Health Psychology, 15,* 110–113.

Williams, G.C., Grow, V.M., Freedman, Z.R., Ryan, R.M., & Deci, E.L. (1996). Motivational predictors of weight loss and weight-loss maintenance. *Journal of Personality and Social Psychology, 70,* 115–126.

Williams, L. (1994). Goal orientations and athletes preferences for competence information sources. *Journal of Sport and Exercise Psychology, 16(4),* 416–430.

Williams, L. (1998). Contextual influences and goal perspectives among female youth sport participants. *Research Quarterly for Exercise and Sport, 69,* 47–57.

Wood, R.E., & Bandura, A. (1989). Impact of conceptions of ability on self-regulatory mechanisms and complex decision making. *Journal of Personality and Social Psychology, 56,* 407–415.

Wood, R.E., Mento, A.J., & Locke, E.A. (1987). Task complexity as a moderator of goal effects: A meta-analysis. *Journal of Applied Psychology, 72,* 416–425.

Wraith, S., & Biddle, S. (1989). Goal setting in children's sport: An exploratory analysis of goal participation, ability and effort instructions, and post event cognitions. *International Journal of Sport Psychology, 20,* 79–92.

Wyse, J., Mercer, T., Ashford, B., Buxton, K., & Gleeson, N. (1995). Evidence for the validity and utility of the stages of exercise behaviour change scale in young adults. *Health Education Research, 10,* 365–377.

Xiang, P., & Lee, A. (1998). The development of self-perceptions of ability and achievement goals and their relations in physical education. *Research Quarterly for Exercise and Sport, 69,* 231–241.

Yin, Z., Boyd, M.P., & Callaghan, J. (1991). *Patterns between mastery/competitive goal orientations and their cognitive/affective correlates in high school athletes.* Paper presented at the annual meeting of the North American Society for the Psychology of Sport and Physical Activity, Asilomar, CA.

Yoo, J. (1997). Motivational and behavioral concomitants of goal orientation and motivational climate in the physical education context. In R. Lidor & M. Bar-Eli (Eds.), *Innovations in sport psychology: Linking theory and practice. Proceedings of the IX World Congress in Sport Psychology: Part II* (pp. 773–775). Netanya, Israel: Ministry of Education, Culture and Sport.

Yordy, G.A., & Lent, R.W. (1993). Predicting aerobic exercise participation: Social cognitive, reasoned action, and planned behavior models. *Journal of Sport and Exercise Psychology, 15,* 363–374.

Zuckerman, M. (1979). *Sensation-seeking: Beyond the optimal level of arousal.* Hillsdale, NJ: Erlbaum.

INDEX

Note: Tables are indicated by an italicized *t* following the page number; figures by an italicized *f;* notes by "n." followed by the note number.

ABOUT THE EDITOR

Glyn C. Roberts, PhD, is a professor of psychology at the Norwegian University of Sport Science. He earned his bachelor's degree at Loughborough University in England, his master's degree from the University of Massachusetts, and his PhD from the University of Illinois.

Dr. Roberts is a former president of the North American Society for the Psychology of Sport and Physical Activity, a former president of the Division of Sport Psychology and current member of the executive committee of the International Association of Applied Psychology, a former secretary-general of the International Society of Sport Psychology, a member of the board of the Norwegian Sport Psychology Association, and the current president of the European Federation of Sport Psychology. He is a fellow in the American Academy of Kinesiology and Physical Education and the Association for the Advancement of Applied Sport Psychology.

Dr. Roberts has published extensively on motivation in sport, especially as it affects children. He resides in Oslo, Norway, and enjoys cross-country skiing, cycling, and playing golf.

ABOUT THE CONTRIBUTORS

Stuart J.H. Biddle, PhD, is a professor of exercise and sport psychology in the Department of Physical Education, Sports Science, and Recreation Management, Loughborough University, United Kingdom. He is also associated with the Institute of Youth Sport and the British Heart Foundation National Centre for Physical Activity and Health in the same department. Stuart graduated from Loughborough University and The Pennsylvania State University. In 1988, he was awarded a PhD in psychology from Keele University in the United Kingdom. He is a chartered psychologist and health psychologist of the British Psychological Society. In 1999, he completed eight years as president of the European Federation of Sport Psychology and, in 1998, was the Distinguished International Scholar of the Association for the Advancement of Applied Sport Psychology. Currently he is the inaugural editor-in-chief of *Psychology of Sport & Exercise.* His main research interests focus on motivational influences on health-related physical activity as well as emotion and other psychological outcomes of physical activity. He has published nine edited books in sport, exercise, and psychology and has authored two, including *The Psychology of Physical Activity: Determinants, Well-Being and Interventions*, published by Routledge in 2001 and coauthored with Nanette Mutrie. Stuart is a motivated(!) "active commuter," cycling to work for a 10-mile round trip. He is married to Fiona and has two boys, Jack and Greg.

Lawrence R. Brawley, PhD, is a professor in the Department of Kinesiology and the Department of Health Studies and Gerontology, University of Waterloo. He has been a scientific adviser to the development of Canada's Guide to Healthy Physical Activity and to the companion guide on children and youth. He is an affiliated scientist with the Center for Behavioral Research and Program Evaluation, a Canadian Cancer Society/National Cancer Institute of Canada–funded center. His physical activity–related research concerns the use of social psychological theories and behavior-change models in predicting and changing adherence behavior. The self-regulation of physical function for normal and chronic disease populations, as well as for older adult physical independence, are major interests. Dr. Brawley collaborates with his coauthors Drs. Dawson, Culos-Reed, and Gyurcsik in regard to a variety of topics that concern perceived control, physical activity, and health-related quality of life in asymptomatic and diseased populations. His research has been published in journals such as the *Journal of Applied Social Psychology, Journal of Applied Biobehavioral Research, Journal of Behavioral Medicine, Arthritis Care and Research, Medicine and Science in Exercise and Sport, Personality and Individual Differences,* and *Controlled Clinical Trials.*

S. Nicole Culos-Reed, PhD, completed her PhD in kinesiology at the University of Waterloo, with a focus in health and exercise psychology. Her research examines the physical and psychological benefits that physical activity provides for individuals with chronic disease and the resulting improved quality of life that these individuals may attain. A postdoctoral fellowship with the Canadian Cancer Society/National Cancer Institute of Canada (CCS/NCIC) has allowed her to examine these physical activity issues in cancer populations. As a doctoral fellow, Dr. Culos-Reed worked with the Centre for Behavioural Research and Program Evaluation, a CCS/NCIC–funded center, in the Lyle Hallman Institute for Health Promotion at the University of Waterloo while concluding the writing of this chapter. Dr. Culos-Reed is currently an assistant professor in the faculty of kinesiology at the University of Calgary, in Alberta, Canada. She has published recently in the *Journal of Applied Social Psychology, Arthritis Care and Research,* and *Controlled Clinical Trials* as well as in a chapter on theories of motivated behavior in exercise in the forthcoming volume of the *International Handbook of Research on Sport Psychology.*

Kimberley A. Dawson, PhD, is an associate professor in the Department of Kinesiology and Physical Education at Wilfrid Laurier University. She also holds adjunct status in the Department of Kinesiology at the University of Waterloo. Her research addresses how individual perceptions of control influence various health behaviors, including exercise adherence. Dr. Dawson recently completed a collaborative project examining how participation in a community-based exercise program geared toward individuals with fibromyalgia influenced psychological well-being, physiological work capacity, and gait patterns. She has also completed multidisciplinary research studies in alternative health practices such as massage therapy and chiropractic care. Her future research will focus on perceptions of control in the rehabilitation of athletic injuries and examine the effectiveness of an adapted physical activity camp on children with exercise-induced asthma. Dr. Dawson has published her work on perceptions of control, goals, and self-efficacy in the *Journal of Behavioral Medicine, Journal of Applied Social Psychology, Journal of Sport and Exercise Psychology,* and in the edited volume *The Handbook of Health Behavior Research.*

 **Joan L. Duda, PhD,** is a professor of sports psychology in the School of Sport and Exercise Sciences at The University of Birmingham in the United Kingdom and an adjunct professor in the Department of Psychological Sciences at Purdue University in the United States. She completed her BA (1977) in psychology at Rutgers University, her MS degree (1978) at Purdue University, and her PhD (1981) at the University of Illinois at Urbana-Champaign. Dr. Duda is currently president of the Association for the Advancement of Applied Sport Psychology and has also been a member of the executive boards of the North American Society for the Psychology of Sport and Physical Activity, the Sport Psychology Academy, and the International Society for Sport Psychology. She was editor of the *Journal of Applied Sport Psychology* and is on the Editorial Board of the *Journal of Sport and Exercise Psychology*, the *International Journal of Sport Psychology*, and the *Sport and Exercise Psychology Journal*. Dr. Duda has over 130 scientific publications focused on the topic of sport motivation and the psychological dimensions of sport and exercise behavior and has presented over 150 papers at professional meetings. She is the editor of *Advances in Sport and Exercise Psychology Measurement* (1998). Dr. Duda has been an invited speaker in over 15 countries around the world and, in 1997, she was named the Visiting International Scholar by the Australian Sport Psychology Society. She is certified as a sport psychology consultant by the Association for the Advancement of Applied Sport Psychology and is listed on the U.S. Olympic Registry. Between 1992 and 1996, she was the sport psychology consultant for the U.S.A. Gymnastics Women's Artistic Program and National Team and has also worked with coaches and athletes from a variety of sports and competitive levels. Dr. Duda was an intercollegiate athlete at Rutgers University, participating in the sports of basketball, softball, and tennis. Her hobbies include music, playing tennis, and traveling.

Mary D. Fry, PhD, is an associate professor of sport and exercise psychology in the Department of Human Movement Sciences and Education at the University of Memphis. This Texas native received her BS degree from Texas Wesleyan University, her MD from the University of North Carolina-Greensboro, and her PhD from Purdue University. Her research interests focus on the cognitive developmental processes impacting children's motivation in physical activity settings. Her children, Jared and Lindsey, provide a fun and exciting avenue for observing these processes in action on a daily basis.

Nancy C. Gyurcsik, PhD, came to Kansas State University after graduating from the University of Waterloo, Ontario, Canada. Dr. Gyurcsik has a joint appointment in the Research and Extension Office of Community Health and in the Department of Kinesiology. Her research focus is on the social-cognitive processes that impact on the motivation for and adherence to physical activity and health behaviors. Typical social cognitions that she examines include various indicants of perceived control such as reasons provided for adherence or nonadherence, outcomes expected as a result of performing a behavior, and the confidence in specific behavioral and cognitive abilities (i.e., self-efficacy) important for adherence. Dr. Gyurcsik also examines the impact that acute thoughts have on motivated health behavior and how individuals cope with acute, demotivating thoughts. Her research is being conducted with healthy young adults, older adults, and clinical (e.g., arthritic) populations. Dr. Gyurcsik has been successful in obtaining national-level funding for her research. Her perceived control research has appeared in the *Journal of Applied Social Psychology* and the *Weight Control Digest,* as well as in a chapter on theories of motivated behavior in exercise in the forthcoming volume of the *International Handbook of Research on Sport Psychology.*

Howard K. Hall, PhD, is currently a professor of sport and exercise psychology within the faculty of Education and Sport Science at De Montfort University Bedford. He earned an MS from the University of North Texas in 1984, earned a PhD from the University of Illinois at Urbana-Champaign in 1990, and taught at the University of Colorado and Syracuse University prior to returning to England in 1991. Howard's research and teaching focus broadly on the psychological processes underpinning both motivation and stress. In recent years Howard has been active in a number of scholarly societies. He has held an elected position on the managing council of the International Society of Sport Psychology since 1993 and was re-elected as a vice-president of the same organization for the period of 1997-2001. He is also secretary-treasurer of the International Association of Applied Psychology-Division 12, a position he will hold until 2002. Howard also serves as a section editor of the *International Journal of Sport Psychology.*

Gerald J. Jerome, MD, received his BA in psychology from Oglethorpe University in Atlanta, Georgia. He has worked in the community mental health field as a counselor with at-risk youth and at a suicide prevention clinic. Jerry received his MS from the University of Arizona with an emphasis in sport psychology. Currently he is a PhD candidate at the University of Illinois at Urbana-Champaign, where he is studying exercise psychology.

Alistair W. Kerr, MSc, is a principal lecturer in the faculty of Education and Sport Science at De Montfort University, England. He received his undergraduate degree in psychology from the City University London and two masters degrees from the University of London. The first of these was in modern social and cultural studies at Chelsea College, and the second, in occupational psychology, from Birkbeck College. His primary research interest is in the area of social cognitive antecedents of stress, an area in which he has published jointly with Howard Hall with whom he is engaged in a number of ongoing research projects. In addition, he has contributed to the statistical well being of the faculty at De Montfort University and as a consequence, has published an introductory text in univariate statistics and is currently working on a multivariate graduate text.

Edward McAuley, PhD, is a professor in the Department of Kinesiology at the University of Illinois at Urbana-Champaign, where he also holds appointments in the Department of Psychology and the Beckman Institute for Advanced Science and Technology. He received his doctoral degree from the University of Iowa. His research interests are focused in exercise, aging, and psychological function. He has published widely in the fields of kinesiology, psychology, behavioral medicine, and gerontology.

Melissa M. Peña, MD, has a master's degree in wellness program management from Colorado State University and a master's degree in kinesiology specializing in exercise psychology from the University of Illinois at Urbana-Champaign. She is currently employed in a physical therapy clinic treating individuals with chronic neck and back pain. Her work includes the use of strength and cardiovascular exercise with behavior modification to restore functional mobility to her clients.

Darren C. Treasure, PhD, is an associate professor in sport and exercise psychology in the Department of Exercise Science and Physical Education at Arizona State University. He earned a BA honors degree (1987) at Brunel University in England and an MS (1990) and PhD (1993) at the University of Illinois at Urbana-Champaign. His research interests focus on motivational aspects of physical activity. Ongoing research includes the examination of the effects of achievement goals and self-determination in sport and exercise settings and the effect of self-presentation issues (for example, social physique anxiety and body image) on physical activity, self-esteem, and eating behaviors of children and adolescents. A second line of research focuses on the effects of acute and chronic bouts of exercise on psychological functioning. Treasure has recently assumed the position of associate editor for the *Journal of Sport and Exercise Psychology* and is an editorial board member of *The Sport Psychologist*. Treasure is also an active sport psychology consultant working with Olympic and professional athletes from a wide range of sports. He enjoys traveling and spending as much time as possible with his family.

Robert J. Vallerand, PhD, obtained his PhD from the Université de Montréal and pursued postdoctoral studies in experimental social psychology at the University of Waterloo. He is presently a full professor of psychology and director of the Laboratoire de Recherche sur le Comportement Social at the Université du Québec à Montréal. Professor Vallerand has been involved in several professional functions. He has served as chair of the Psychology Department, president of the Quebec Society for Research in Psychology, chair of the Social Psychology section of the Canadian Psychological Association, and associate editor of the *Canadian Journal of Behavioural Sciences*. He is currently an editorial board member of several journals, including the *Journal of Personality and Social Psychology* and *Psychology of Sport and Exercise*. Dr. Vallerand has received several honors, including being elected fellow of the Canadian Psychological Association, being elected a member of the Society of Experimental Social Psychology, and receiving the President Award from the International Olympic Committee. Professor Vallerand has published 4 books and more than 125 articles and book chapters, mainly in the area of human motivation. His more recent work has focused on the development of a hierarchical model of intrinsic and extrinsic motivation, as well as a model on passion.

Advances in motivation in sport and exercise